Vo4 X a ZEY r G

Oz Clarke's
POCKET
WINE
BOOK
2000

WEBSTERS

LITTLE, BROWN AND COMPANY
BOSTON   NEW YORK   LONDON

A LITTLE, BROWN/WEBSTERS BOOK

This edition first published in 1999 by
Little, Brown and Company (UK)
Brettenham House
Lancaster Place
LONDON WC2E 7EN

Created and designed by
Websters International Publishers Limited
Axe and Bottle Court
70 Newcomen Street
London SE1 1YT
www.websters.co.uk
www.ozclarke.com

A CIP catalogue for this book is available from the
British Library.

ISBN 0-316-85086-1

Printed and bound in China

Thanks are due to the following people for their invaluable help with
the 2000 edition and the generous spirit in which they have shared
their knowledge: Stephen Brook, Bob Campbell MW, Huon Hooke,
James Lawther MW, Angela Lloyd, Maggie McNie MW, David Moore,
Stuart Pigott, Norm Roby, Victor de la Serna, Phillip Williamson.

CONTENTS

INTRODUCTION

The 1990s saw a mighty struggle for the very soul of wine, and the first decade of the new century will see the struggle intensify. The fiery debate has been between those who wish to allow nature free rein and those who believe that nature is there to be tamed and exploited. It has been between those who see tradition as sacrosanct and those who regard progress and innovation as the ultimate aim. It has been between those for whom a hallowed sense of place is the purest expression of character in a wine, and those for whom geographical limits hold no thrills, but for whom the most intense and memorable expression of a particular grape variety's flavours is their burning ambition.

But far from being a bruising, attritional struggle, this conflict of wills has been of enormous benefit to the world of wine, because it has meant that both sides – the traditionalists and the modernists – have had to start listening to each other's point of view – and, like it or not, they have realized they both have much to learn from each other.

Can you remember as far back as 1990? In wine terms, that is? Was there such a thing as thrillingly pungent Hungarian Sauvignon Blanc? Had you ever experienced the juicy, crunchy delights of Chilean Merlot? What about heady Primitivo from Southern Italy or scented, lip-staining Malbec from Argentina? You can't remember? Well, I can. I'd never tried them, because they didn't exist. Oh sure, there was Merlot in Chile, Malbec in Argentina and so on – but it didn't taste any good, because the old and the new hadn't started to settle their differences and see how they could each give each other a few tips.

There was so much waste in the world of wine. Now, every year, there's less and less. Ten years ago there were so many vineyards in excellent traditional sites where no one had learnt how to make a modern-tasting wine by care, cleanliness and attention to detail. So many potentially fine vineyards dying through neglect and ignorance. At the same time, so many new vineyards and wineries charged like bulls into a bottle shop, neither growing the quality of grapes they could nor producing the quality of wine, because they thought they had nothing to learn from those who'd done it all before.

As we march into the new century, the potential for good, fine and great wine is almost unlimited as old tempers new and new revitalizes old. In this guide we cover this whole new dawning world of wine with new profiles, total revision of all vintages and assessments of taste, plus new features on millennium fizz, hopes for the future, and a glossary of wine terms.

I'm excited. I'm ready for the new century. But I'm also grateful for the last one. After all, it taught me a lot about tradition, as well as a lot about the great new things to come. And as I'm sitting here, I'm looking at this wine list. There's no postal address, just a website! In ten years time we'll be buying half our wine off the web. Am I *really* ready?

HOW TO USE THE A–Z

The A–Z section starts on page 46 and covers over 1600 entries on wines, producers, grapes and wine regions from all over the world. There are also entries on some of the more common winemaking terms that are often seen on labels.

Detailed Vintage Charts with information on which of the world's top wines are ready for drinking in 2000 can be found on pages 22–5; pages 22–3 feature vintages back to 1989; pages 24–5 cover a selection of older vintages for premium wines.

Glass Symbols   These indicate the wines produced.

🍷 Red wine   🍷 Rosé wine   🍷 White wine

The order of the glasses reflects the importance of the wines in terms of volume produced. For example:

🍷 White followed by rosé wine

🍷 Red followed by white wine

🍷 Red followed by rosé, then white wine

Grape Symbols   These identify entries on grape varieties.

🍇 Red grape   🍇 White grape

Star Symbols   These indicate wines and producers that are highly rated by the author.

★   A particularly good wine or producer in its category

★★   An excellent wine or producer in its category – one especially worth seeking out

★★★   An exceptional, world-class wine or producer

Best Years   Recommended vintages are listed for many producer and appellation entries. Those listed in bold, e.g. **1998**, **97**, indicate wines that are ready for drinking now, although they may not necessarily be at their best; those appearing in brackets, e.g. (1998) (97), are preliminary assessments of wines that are not yet ready for drinking.

Cross References   To help you find your way round the A–Z, wine names, producers and regions that have their own entries elsewhere in the A–Z are indicated by SMALL CAPITALS.

Special Features   The A–Z section includes special 2-page features on the world's most important wine styles and grape varieties. These features include recommended vintages and producers, as well as lists of related entries elsewhere in the A–Z.

Index   The Index on page 299 will help you find over 3250 recommended producers, including all of those that don't have their own entry in the A–Z.

PICK OF MY LIFE

How can I make a 'Pick of My Life' and not miss out as much as I include? How can I be sure I don't only remember as many as I've forgotten? But these I *do* remember. For many reasons – of friendship, time and place as much as sheer quality of wine. Some of these wines are amongst the greatest ever made. Some are important to me, and me alone. But it's my list. Share it with me.

HOW I STARTED

My brother was drowning in the river. My father dived in to save him. My mother was having hysterics. So I drank the damson wine. The whole bottle. That's how I started. I was three.

My brother survived, you'll be pleased to hear. But I nearly didn't. Even so, I can still remember the piercing fruit taste of the damsons, and, ever since, I've loved wine with a damson perfume. I didn't drink wine again for a fairly long time, and through my teens my father reckoned that the only suitable drink for a young chap was a half pint of Frank Pardoe's draught bitter down at the George and Dragon. So, until I was about 20, these were the only drinks of any importance in my life.

But then I went up to Oxford. Life was never the same again. I discovered wine, and devoured wine and all the mystery and magic of wine with an enthusiasm verging on the obsessive, and these following wines all mark an important early step down the primrose path of indulgence and understanding. Here's the list of how I started:

- **My mother's damson wine**
- **Frank Pardoe's draught bitter**
- **Graacher Himmelreich 1964** Bottled by some long ago English shipper but the thrilling summer meadow mix of acidity and blossom-scented fruit is still one of my favourite wine sensations.
- **Pommery 1961** Half bottles of this taught me that good Champagne is transformed into a dazzling golden haze by a few years extra age.
- **Gallo's Hearty Burgundy** On a theatre trip to the US, I discovered that cheap wine could be packed with fruit and sunshine ripeness. Why did it take Europe so long to discover this blindingly obvious fact?
- **Dow's 20-year-old tawny port** I got that theatre job after a night spent drinking this lovely nutty tawny out of half bottles. Don't ask me why they cast such an evident reprobate. I wouldn't have.
- **Vieux-Chateau-Certan 1952** My first ever wine-tasting prize. Actually, I'd thought it was Latour 1955. If it had been – well, Latour 55 would be on my list instead!
- **La Lagune 1961** Not a great 61 they tell me. Let them carp. It's the first Bordeaux I ever bought, and I've drunk it on every general election night since with sublime pleasure.
- **Nuits-St-Georges 1966, Vienot** Bottled in a brewery in the Midlands this was the first Burgundy I bought. It was wonderful savoury yet sweet red wine then. Amazingly, it still is.
- **Montecillo Rioja 1971** The first sign I had that France was not the only country that could make sumptuous red wine. And is it still good? You're going to hate me, but yes. Yes it is.

6

THE CLASSICS

I got my first taste of the classics at university. They made me catch my breath at their solemn, haughty beauty. Classics are a little friendlier now, but no more memorable, even if they are a little more fun.

WHITE BURGUNDY

• **Puligny Montrachet Clos de la Mouchère 1961** I bought a case of half bottles from a tiny ramshackle merchant next to a Chinese takeaway. For the first time I fell under the spell of the luscious yet dry, sensuous yet restrained marriage of opposites that is great Burgundy.

• **Chevalier-Montrachet 1966, Domaine Leflaive** On a sunny summer's lunchtime in a garden in Hampshire, the awesome beauty of great white Burgundy was revealed to me. And I was surrounded by my dearest friends. Bliss.

• **Unlabelled, declassified Meursault 1970** Don't laugh till you've tasted it. Subtle, soothing, irresistible. and it cost me £1.80/$3.00 a dozen at a bankrupt sale. The producer was in jail. So I always kept a bottle in the fridge for when the vicar called. Which wasn't often. But I drank it anyway. And, yes, I still have a bottle.

• **Corton-Charlemagne 1992, Coche-Dury** Into the modern era with a bang. One of Burgundy's greatest artists and my favourite white Burgundy vintage of the 90s.

• **Bâtard-Montrachet 1996, Jean-Noël Gagnard** Will this fabulous mouthful of power and succulence turn out as well as my 1966 Chevalier? Oh yes. Even better if I can gather my friends.

RED BURGUNDY

• **Grands Échézeaux 1966, Domaine de la Romanée-Conti** Have I ever had such a stunning bottle of red Burgundy as this gorgeous sweethearted brute? I must have done. But this was my first and...

• **Échézeaux 1985, Henri Jayer** From a vintage that made me want to dance in the streets with delight every time I tasted it – and from the old master to whom the young Burgundy tyros owe so much.

• **Clos de Vougeot 1990, Anne and François Gros** From so many wonderful 1990s, I pick this because Clos de Vougeot, when it is good, has a sultry silk and syrup sensuality unlike any other.

• **Nuits-St-Georges, Les St-Georges 1996, Chevillon** Nuits-St-Georges has always been one of my favourite wine villages (see above). To find such thrilling wine being made, suave and modern yet burnished with the smoky moods of Nuits shows that red Burgundy is in good hands at the moment.

• **Au Bon Climat Isabelle Pinot Noir 1995** Burgundy? Yes, supreme, sensuous perfumed Burgundy in all but name; evidence that California justifiably claims to be the world's other great Pinot Noir producer.

RED BORDEAUX

• **Léoville-Barton 1962** My first taste of great Bordeaux. At my first ever wine tasting. That's what I call luck. I can still remember every nuance of its wonderful aroma of dry blackcurrant and cigar box cedarwood scent. I took as my guest a girl with green hair covered in green sequins. I can still remember every ... nuance of her too.

• **Mouton Rothschild 1959** In a tiny office above the shipping quays in Bordeaux, this memorable exotic wine moved me and Bordeaux on to another plane. I just smelled it for half an hour before even taking a sip.

• **Lynch-Bages 1955** Over an old-fashioned ramble of a lunch in Bristol, an old friend of mine showed me the perfection of scent and restrained, almost intellectual, indulgence that a Bordeaux can achieve at a quarter of a century old.

• **Pichon-Lalande 1978** This wine ushered in the modern, more approachable, more perfumed, more sensuous ideal of Bordeaux, and Pichon-Lalande has stood for a plump and juicy beauty ever since.

• **Lafite-Rothschild 1990** Vying with Chateau Margaux for the honours, this wine is the epitome of class in the greatest of modern vintages – 1990.

• **Pétrus 1982** I've never tasted more thrilling wine from the barrel, a wine viscous in its richness and intoxicating in its scent. As a bottled wine its sultry power has never failed to transport me to another level of utterly non-critical bliss.

MY JERICHO LIST
When Joshua and his boys blew their horns full on, the walls of Jericho tumbled. These are my wines that challenged the old order, swept away the barriers of complacency and preconception and changed for ever the way we look at wine.

• **Cloudy Bay Sauvignon Blanc 1985** The whole world held its breath when this astonishing snap, crackle, popinjay thriller of a wine hit the scene. A new star born in the southern seas.

• **Sassicaia 1968** One of the greatest Cabernets made in Europe in the last 50 years. And it sprang from nothing on an anonymous hillside above Tuscany's marshy western flank. This world-class red led the renaissance in Tuscany which in turn has transformed the whole of Italy.

• **Schramsberg Blanc de Blancs 1966** Fabulous fizz that I came across in a Chinese restaurant on the wrong side of Hollywood and, as I downed draught after draught of the soft, foaming nectar, I knew Champagne's citadel had finally been breached.

• **Tyrell's Vat 47 Chardonnay 1971** This didn't attempt to copy Burgundy, it merely showed that Australia was ready to enter the big time and would do so with magnificent, brash, upfront flavours – and devil take the hindmost.

• **Ridge Zinfandel Geyserville 1978** California needed Ridge to remind her that she had an identity all her own which owed nothing to Bordeaux and Burgundy. And Ridge has never stopped reminding us in the best possible way – wines of power and personality which blow away mere comparison.

• **Saint Helena Pinot Noir 1982** Startling, scented Pinot Noir from New Zealand's South Island which set a standard for perfume and gentle, doe-eyed fruit and which insolently challenged Burgundy's sole bragging rights for Pinot Noir.

- **Errázuriz Chilean Merlot 1990** Wow! When this crunchy, juicy, dark-staining red sashayed across the equator, splurging fruit and juice and hardly any tannin down our throats, a new generation of wine drinkers finally had the talisman they needed to give them the courage to switch from white to red.
- **Gyöngyös Hungarian Sauvignon Blanc 1991** Thrilling tangy white to lead the march towards modernity in the former Eastern Bloc. Hungary now leads Europe in providing great flavoured whites at sensible prices.
- **Mission Hill Canadian Chardonnay 1995** Are there no frontiers left? If chilly, snow-capped Canada can produce this beautifully balanced Burgundy look-alike, who's next?
- **Nyetimber Blanc de Blancs 1992** Well, not Burgundian Chardonnay, but magnificent Champagne look-alike fizz from the Sussex Downs of southern England showing that even rainy old England's winemakers can be world-class at something.

THE KEATS' COLLECTION
If you've never read Keats' 'Ode to a Nightingale' – you must. Wine writing doesn't come much better than this. Keats cries out 'O for a beaker full of the warm south', and ever since I first discovered wine, the call of the warm, scented south has tugged at my heart.
- **Domaine de Trévallon 1981** There's no wine that speaks more powerfully of its place of birth than this dark, herb-strewn red from the sun-bleached slopes of Baux-en-Provence.
- **Domaine Beaurenard Chateauneuf-du-Pape 1978** The perfect southern Rhône red, made sweet and supple by the blazing sun, yet that same sun gives it the power and giddy strength to make my head spin.
- **Hermitage La Chapelle 1978** Has there ever been a greater Hermitage than this? This stunning marriage of beauty and brawn alerted the world to the greatness of the mighty Rhône reds.
- **Mas de Daumas Gassac 1990 (white)** Out of nowhere sprang this scented, heady, voluptuous white. Well, not out of nowhere, out of the fertile imagination of Aimé Guibert contemplating his virgin forest acres a mile or two from the Mediterranean.
- **Aldo Conterno Gran Bussia 1982** Barolo isn't an easy wine to embrace. You need a grand master like Conterno, yet one whose blood was warm enough to create this rich yet bitter-sweet aristocrat.
- **Chateau Musar 1970** The early red wines from the war-torn vineyards of the Lebanon combined the classical structure of Bordeaux with the irresistible rank odours of the souk, like a gastronomic faultline between the cultures.
- **Grange 1953** I could choose so many Australian Shirazes, and indeed so many great Granges, but I choose the 1953 as the first I ever tasted of that raucous, dionysian, careening, carousing band of revellers who now comprise the genius of Australian Shiraz.
- **Stanton and Killeen Liqueur Muscat** While I'm down under, I can't resist the ultra sweet, intensely perfumed Muscats of Rutherglen. My mother and I used to drink these by the bottle in a marvellous

subterranean dive under Leicester Square. There's the two of us, not just under the table, but under the Square itself, and happy as jam jars.

• **Valdespino Coliseo** Ancient oloroso sherry, nut brown and sombre, aid to contemplation, to reminiscence, to quiet satisfaction with goals attained, confidence in goals to come and a greater appreciation of leather armchairs, cigar smoke and Harris Tweed.

• **Antonopoulos Peloponnese Chardonnay 1997** Brilliant Burgundian Chardonnay from the parched terrain at the very cradle of our ancient culture of wine? And so the warm south reaches through the ages and twines fingers with the modern classicism of the chilly north.

PICK OF MY AFTERLIFE

At the beginning of the new millennium, cheap wine will be better than ever, but the downside of this will be that the large international companies will attempt to grasp market share all around the globe and so, while basic wine will certainly be at its best, it will also be far more homogenous. Thankfully the wine world is also full of individualists determined to make the most original wine that's ever been and we'll be seeing more of these. And equally importantly, there are countries old and new with no wine culture, or with cultures almost forgotten, that one by one will lurch or tiptoe onto the world wine stage, bringing diversity and personality. Below, I list a few of very future favourites:

• **Spice Route Pinotage 2004** To celebrate ten years since the end of Apartheid in South Africa, Spice Route will produce a thrilling Pinotage to confirm its position as the leader of a growing band of wineries with genuine black involvement.

• **Chilean Carmenère 2005** Chile will stop pretending the fabulous Carmenère is Merlot and start producing red wines from it that ooze with fruit and personality – and owe nothing to European styles.

• **Rio Negro Malbec 2006** Rio Negro, almost in Patagonia in the far south of Argentina, will prove the perfect site for violet-scented, damson-ravished reds from the mighty Malbec.

• **Paso Robles Syrah/Shiraz 2010** The greatest vintage yet of Rhône varieties from the high wild Paso Robles vineyards south of San Francisco will finally break the stranglehold of Cabernet and Merlot in California's red wine psyche.

• **Chinese Shandong Chardonnay 2015** At last, China produces some world-class wines as the palate preference of the world, and of China in particular, switches once more back to white.

• **Georgian Saperavi 2020** And, as European palates swing back to red, Georgia celebrates a decade of political and financial stability with this deep, scented, thrillingly powerful red from the ancient Saperavi grape.

• **Bordeaux Chardonnay and Burgundy Syrah 2025** With the relentless progress of global warming in France's vineyards, the Appellation Contrôlée system implodes as growers take the law into their own hands and grow whatever they want. Pessac-Léognan proves excellent for Chardonnay, and Gevrey-Chambertin adopts a new identity as the centre for Burgundy's Shiraz. Sorry, Syrah.

MILLENNIUM BUBBLES

So what kind of party are you going to have on millennium night? You'd better think about it, because it will make a massive difference to the kind of wine you want to drink. Will you be dancing the night away in some vast aircraft hangar of a ballroom? Cosily carousing with a few close friends as the clock hands teeter irrevocably past the midnight hour. Or are you going to be standing with your loved one on the very edge of the world, waiting for the first pale gleamings of light that will usher our new millennium in? Each one demands quite different kinds of wine, so here's my fairly broad shopping list to cover pretty well all eventualities. If you dashed out and bought every wine I recommend you'd have a happy stash to keep your head in the air and your feet off the ground from Christmas Eve till New Year's Day – not a bad idea, come to think of it. But these should all do the business, and I'll start right at the top.

I am not going to be downing great gulps of Dom Perignon, Roederer Cristal or Krug – a) because the price has become insane; b) because it follows naturally that I don't have any. No, I'm going to rely on my favourite Champagne houses, the ones that always offer up gentle foaming nectar that dances playfully over my palate and makes me think I'm the wittiest man in the world. I've actually already put aside some 1985 – gorgeous vintage, and for once I did plan ahead – but both 1989 and 1990 are ripe, soft vintages that will happily take more age, but are lovely now.

Billecart-Salmon Cuvée Nicolas-François 1990 and **Charles Heidsieck 1990** – these are the two most consistently classy Champagne producers at work today. But there are quite a few other goodies too: **Deutz Blanc de Blancs 1989; Henriot 1989; Gratien 1989; Gosset 1989** – and just in case I feel naughty enough – **Veuve Clicquot Rosé 1989**. These houses all do lovely non-vintage wine too – an important consideration in this millennium year, because there's a lot of cheap sharp muck on the market trying to capitalize on the party season. In particular Charles Heidsieck do a superior non-vintage with a 'Mise en Cave' date. Always good, you can get 1992, 93, 94 or 95.

But I'll have a few non-Champagne bottles nearby too – in case the mood takes me. My favourite 'almost' Champagne is the fabulously nutty **Pelorus** from Cloudy Bay in New Zealand, and Australia follows with the thrilling **Cope-Williams** from near Melbourne.

The US has been teaching the Champenois a few quiet lessons for some years now – even if many of the top estates are actually owned by the Champagne companies. My top three sparkling delights are: **Roederer Estate L'Ermitage**; **Domaine Carneros Blanc de Blancs**; and **Schramsberg Reserve Brut**.

There are gems in Britain too. Indeed in the new millennium Britain will eventually take its place among Europe's classiest producers of fizz. **Nyetimber** is heavenly wine from Sussex. **Heritage Brut** is delicious stuff from **Thames Valley**, and for a burst of hedgerow fragrance nothing beats Bedfordshire's **Warden Vineyard Brut**.

MODERN WINE STYLES

Not so long ago, if I were to outline the basic wine styles, the list would have been strongly biased towards the classics – Bordeaux, Burgundy, Sancerre, Mosel Riesling, Champagne. These flavours were the models against which would-be imitators had to be judged and, in any case, there weren't many imitators.

This just isn't so any more. The great old classic names have, over time, become expensive and unreliable – thus opening the door to other, perhaps less established wine-producing regions, and giving them the chance to offer us wines that may or may not owe anything to the old originals. *These* are the flavours to which ambitious winemakers now aspire.

WHITE WINES

Ripe, up-front, spicy Chardonnay Fruit is the key here: round, ripe, apricot and peach fruit, sweetened and spiced up by some new oak – probably American oak – to make a delicious, approachable, easy-to-drink fruit cocktail of taste. Australia created this style and still effortlessly leads the field.

Green tangy Sauvignon New Zealand is the master of this style – all tangy, grassy, nettles and asparagus and then green apples and peach. Chile has the potential to produce something similar and there are hopeful signs in southern France. Bordeaux and the Loire are the original sources of dry Sauvignon wines, but only the most committed modern producers manage to match green tang with fruit.

Bone-dry neutral whites This doesn't sound very appetizing, but it is the limit of what most white wine aspires to. Many Italian whites fit this bill. Southern French wines, where no grape variety is specified, will be like this; so will many wines from Bordeaux, the South-West, Muscadet and Anjou. Modern young Spanish whites and Portuguese Vinho Verdes are good examples, as are Swiss Fendant and southern German Trocken wines. Most Eastern European whites could actually *use* more neutrality.

White Burgundy By this I mean the nutty, oatmealy-ripe but dry, subtly oaked styles of villages like Meursault at their best. It's a difficult style to emulate and few people do it well, even in Burgundy itself. California makes the most effort. Washington, Oregon and New York State each have occasional successes.

Perfumy, off-dry whites Gewurztraminer, Muscat and Pinot Gris from Alsace will give you this style and in southern Germany Gewürztraminer, Scheurebe, Kerner, Grauburgunder and occasionally Riesling may also do it. Riesling in Australia is often aromatic and mildly fruity. In New Zealand Riesling and Müller-Thurgau can produce excellent results.

Mouthfuls of luscious gold Good sweet wines are difficult to make. Sauternes is the world's most famous sweetie, but the Loire, too, and sometimes Alsace, is in the running. Germany made wonderful examples in 1990 and since then Australia and New Zealand have produced some beauts.

RED WINES

Spicy warm-hearted reds Australia is out in front at the moment through the ebullient resurgence of her Shiraz reds – ripe, almost sweet, sinfully easy to enjoy. France's Rhône Valley is also on the up and Syrahs from the far south of France are looking good. In Italy Piedmont is producing delicious beefy Barbera and juicy exotic Dolcetto. Spain's Ribera del Duero and Portugal's south also deliver the goods.

Juicy fruity reds This used to be the Beaujolais spot, but there hasn't been much exciting Beaujolais recently. Gamay Vins de Pays are better bets, as are grassy, sharp Loire reds. Modern Spanish reds from Navarra, Valdepeñas and La Mancha do the trick, while in Italy young Chianti and Teroldego hit home.

Blackcurranty Cabernet Australia leads the field here, but New Zealand also strikes the blackcurrant bell in a much greener, sharper way. California only sometimes hits the sweet spot, and often with Merlot rather than Cabernet. Chilean Cabernets get there less often than they used to. Eastern Europe, in particular Hungary, is doing well, as is southern France. And what about Bordeaux? Only a few of the top wines reach the target; for the price Tuscan Cabernet often does it better.

Tough, tannic long-haul boys Bordeaux does lead this field, and the best wines are really good after 10 years or so – but don't expect wines from minor properties to age in the same way. It's the same in Tuscany and Piedmont – only the top wines will get there – especially Chianti Classico, Barolo and Barbaresco. In Portugal there's plenty of tannin to be found and some increasingly good long-lasting reds from the Douro.

Soft, strawberryish charmers Good Burgundy definitely tops this group. Rioja in Spain can sometimes get there too, but Navarra and Valdepeñas do so more often. Pinot Noir in California is frequently delicious, as it is in New Zealand. Germany gets there with Spätburgunder now and then. Italy's Lago di Caldaro often smooches in; and over in Bordeaux, of all places, both St-Émilion and Pomerol can do the business.

SPARKLING AND FORTIFIED WINES

Fizz This can be white or pink or red, dry or sweet, and I sometimes think it doesn't matter what it tastes like as long as it's cold enough and there's enough of it. Champagne can be best, but frequently isn't – and there are lots of new-wave winemakers who produce good-value lookalikes. Australia is tops for super-tasty bargain fizz, followed by California and New Zealand.

Fortified wines For once in my life I find myself saying that the old ways are definitely the best. There's still nothing to beat the top ports and sherries in the deep, rich old-fashioned stickies stakes – though for the glimmerings of a new angle look to Australia and South Africa.

MATCHING FOOD AND WINE

Give me a rule, I'll break it – well, bend it anyway. So when I see the proliferation of publications laying down rules as to what wine to drink with what food, I get very uneasy and have to quell a burning desire to slosh back a Grand Cru Burgundy with my Chilli con Carne.

The pleasures of eating and drinking operate on so many levels that hard and fast rules simply make no sense. What about mood? If I'm in the mood for Champagne, Champagne it shall be, whatever I'm eating. What about place? If I'm sitting gazing out from the Amalfi cliffs across the glimmering waters of the bay, hand me anything, just anything local – it'll be perfect.

Even so, there are some things that simply don't go well with wine. Artichokes, asparagus, spinach, kippers and mackerel, chilli, salsas and vinegars, chocolate, all flatten the flavours of wines. The general rule here is avoid tannic red wines and go for juicy young reds, New World styles or whites with plenty of fruit and fresh acidity. And for chocolate, liqueur Muscats are just about the only thing. Tomatoes are both sweet and acidic and can ruin most red wines; and, contrary to expectation, salty cheeses go best with sweet white wines (Roquefort and Sauternes is classic). So, with these factors in mind, the following pairings are not quite rules – just my recommendations.

FISH

Plain grilled or baked white fish White Burgundy, fine Chardonnay, Pessac-Léognan, Viognier, Australia and New Zealand Riesling.

Plain grilled or baked more strongly flavoured fish (e.g. salmon, salmon trout) Alsace aromatics, fruity New World Chardonnay or Semillon, Chinon/Bourgueil (unoaked), New World Pinot Noir.

Fried/battered fish Simple, fresh whites, e.g. Soave, Mâcon Blanc, Pinot Gris, white Rheingau or Pfalz.

Shellfish Soft dry whites, e.g. Pinot Blanc or unoaked Chardonnay; *clams and oysters*: Aligoté, Vinho Verde, Seyval Blanc.

Smoked fish Ice-cold basic fizz, manzanilla or fino sherry, Pinot Gris from Alsace or southern Germany, Mosel Kabinett, New World Riesling or Gewürztraminer.

MEAT

Beef/steak *Plain roasted or grilled*: tannic reds, e.g. top Bordeaux, New World Cabernet or Merlot, South African Pinotage, Chianti Classico Riserva, Ribera del Duero.

Lamb *Plain roasted or grilled*: top red Burgundy, soft top Bordeaux, e.g. St-Émilion, Rioja Reserva, fine New World Pinot Noir or Merlot.

Pork *Plain roasted or grilled*: full, soft dry whites, e.g. Alsace Pinot Gris, soft oaky Chardonnays, Rioja, Alentejo; *ham and bacon*: young, fruity reds, preferably unoaked, e.g. Beaujolais, Teroldego, unoaked Tempranillo or Malbec, Lambrusco Secco; *prepared pork products*: forthright, uncomplicated young reds, Beaujolais, Italian Merlot, Zinfandel, Pinotage.

Veal *Plain roasted or grilled*: (reds) old Rioja, mature Côte de Beaune or Pessac-Léognan/Margaux; (whites) Alsace/German/Austrian Pinot Gris, Vouvray, Châteauneuf-du-Pape; *with cream-based sauce*: full, ripe whites, e.g. Alsace Pinot Blanc or Pinot Gris, Vouvray, white Châteauneuf-du-Pape, oaked New World Chardonnay; *with rich red-wine sauce* (e.g. osso buco):

young Italian reds, New World Zinfandel, Gamay or Grenache.

Venison *Plain roasted or grilled*: Barolo, St-Estèphe, Pomerol, Côte de Nuits, Hermitage, big Zin, Alsace or German Pinot Gris; *with red-wine-based sauce*: Piedmont reds, Pomerol, St-Émilion, New World Syrah/Shiraz or Pinotage, Portuguese Garrafeira, Priorat.

Chicken and Turkey *Plain roasted or grilled*: fine red or white Burgundy, red Rioja Reserva, New World Chardonnay or Semillon.

Duck *Plain roasted*: gutsy reds, e.g. Pomerol, St-Émilion, Côte de Nuits, Rhône reds, New World Syrah/Shiraz or Merlot; also full, soft whites such as Austrian Riesling; *with orange*: off-dry weighty whites, or Barsac.

Game birds *Plain roasted or grilled*: top reds, e.g. Rhône, Burgundy, Tuscan and Piedmont, Ribera del Duero, New World Cabernet; also whites, e.g. Pinot Gris or New World Semillon.

All meat casseroles, stews and mince dishes Match the dominant ingredient, e.g. red wine for *boeuf bourguignon*, robust reds for *coq au vin*, dry whites for a fricassee. The weight of the wine should match the richness of the sauce, e.g. not too heavy for *navarin* of lamb. For strong tomato flavours see under Pasta.

EGGS

Light, fresh reds from Gamay or Grenache, full, dry unoaked whites, New World rosé or fizz.

PASTA

With tomato sauce: Soave, Verdicchio, New World Sauvignon Blanc; *with meat-based sauce*: basic north/central Italian reds, French/New World Syrah/Shiraz, Zinfandel; *with cream- or cheese-based sauce*: soft, full, dry unoaked whites from northern Italy, light Austrian reds, New World Gamay; *with seafood/fish sauce*: basic dry, tangy whites, e.g. Verdicchio, Vermentino, Austrian Grüner Veltliner, Muscadet; *with pesto*: New World Sauvignon Blanc, Dolcetto, Minervois.

SALADS

Sharp-edged whites, e.g. New World Sauvignon, dry Riesling, Vinho Verde.

ETHNIC CUISINES

Chinese Riesling or Gewürztraminer, unoaked New World Chardonnay; mild German and Austrian reds.

Indian/Tex-Mex Spicy whites, e.g. Gewürztraminer, Mosel Kabinett, Spätlese, New World Sauvignon, Viognier; soft reds, e.g. Rioja, Valpolicella, New World Cinsaut, Grenache, Syrah/Shiraz.

Thai Riesling, Gewürztraminer, New World Sauvignon.

CHEESES

Hard (mild and mature) Full reds from southern Italy, France or Spain, New World Merlot or Zinfandel, Alsace Pinot Gris, dry oloroso sherry, tawny port.

Soft (mild and mature) LBV port, rich, fruity reds, e.g. Rhône, Shiraz, Zinfandel, Alsace Pinot Gris, Gewürztraminer.

Blue Botrytized sweet whites, e.g. Sauternes, vintage port, Malmsey Madeira, old oloroso sherry.

Goats' Sancerre, New World Sauvignon Blanc, cool-climate reds, e.g. Chinon, Saumur-Champigny, Teroldego.

DESSERTS

Chocolate Liqueur Muscat, Asti Spumante.

Fruit-based Botrytized sweet whites, e.g. Sauternes.

MATCHING WINE AND FOOD

With very special bottles, when you have found an irresistible bargain or when you are casting around for culinary inspiration, it can be a good idea to let the wine dictate the choice of food.

Although I said earlier that rules in this area are made to be bent if not broken, there are certain points to remember when matching wine and food. Before you make specific choices, think about some basic characteristics and see how thinking in terms of grape varieties and wine styles can point you in the right direction.

In many cases, the local food and wine combinations that have evolved over the years simply cannot be bettered (think of ripe Burgundy with *coq au vin* or *boeuf bourguignon*; Chianti Riserva with *bistecca alla Fiorentina*; Muscadet and Breton oysters). Yet the world of food and wine is moving so fast that it would be madness to be restricted by the old tenets. Californian cuisine, fusion food, the infiltration of innumerable ethnic influences coupled with the re-invigoration of traditional wines, continuous experiment with new methods and blends and the opening up of completely new wine areas mean that the search for perfect food and wine partners is, and will remain, very much an on-going process.

Here are some of the characteristics you need to consider, plus a summary of the main grape varieties and their best food matches.

Body As well as matching the taste of the wine to the flavour of the food you need to match the weight or body of the wine to the intensity of that flavour. A heavy alcoholic wine will not suit a delicate dish; and *vice versa*.

Acidity The acidity of a dish should balance the acidity of a wine. High-acid flavours, such as tomato, lemon or vinegar, need matching acidity in their accompanying wines. Use acidity in wine to cut through the richness of a dish but for this to work, make sure the wine is full in flavour.

Sweetness Sweet food makes dry wine taste unpleasantly lean and acidic. With desserts and puddings your task is very clear: find a wine that is at least as sweet as the food (sweeter than the food is fine). However, many savoury foods, such as carrots, onions and parsnips, taste slightly sweet and dishes in which they feature prominently will go best with wines that also have a touch of sweetness.

Age/Maturity Pay the wine the compliment of rewarding it for aging well. The bouquet of a wine is only acquired over time and should be savoured and appreciated: with age many red wines acquire complex flavours and perfumes and a similar degree of complexity in the flavour of the food is often a good idea.

Wine in the food If you want to use wine in cooking it is best to use the same style of wine as the one you are going to drink with the meal (it can be an inferior version though).

Oak Oak flavours in wine vary from the satisfyingly subtle to positively strident. This latter end of the scale can conflict with food, although it may be suitable for smoked fish (white wines only) or full-flavoured meat or game.

16

RED GRAPES

Barbera Wines made to be drunk young have high acidity that you need to match with rich Piemontese food. Rich, complex older wines from the top growers can hold their own with rich beef casseroles, jugged hare or the robust Italian *bollito misto.*

Cabernet Franc Best drunk with plain rather than sauced meat dishes, or, slightly chilled, with grilled or baked salmon or salmon trout. Try it with Indian food.

Cabernet Sauvignon All over the world the Cabernet Sauvignon makes full-flavoured reliable red wine: the ideal food wine. Classic combinations include Cru Classé Pauillac with roast, milk-fed lamb; Super-Tuscan *vini da tavola* with *bistecca alla Fiorentina;* softer, riper New World Cabernet Sauvignons with roast turkey or goose. Cabernet Sauvignon seems to have a particular affinity for lamb but it partners all plain roast or grilled meats and game well and would be an excellent choice for many sauced meat dishes such as *boeuf bourguignon*, steak and kidney pie or rabbit stew and any substantial dishes made with mushrooms.

Dolcetto Dolcetto produces fruity purple wines that go beautifully with hearty local North Italian meat dishes such as calves' liver and onions or casseroled game with polenta.

Gamay The grape of red Beaujolais, Gamay, makes wine you can drink whenever, wherever, however and with whatever you want. It goes particularly well with meat dishes, especially charcuterie products (because its acidity provides a satisfying foil to all that richness). It would be a good choice for many vegetarian dishes. If in doubt you are unlikely to go far wrong with Gamay.

Grenache Generally blended with other grapes, Grenache nonetheless dominates, with its high alcoholic strength and rich, spicy flavours. These are wines readily matched with food: casseroles, charcuterie and grills for concentrated older wines; almost anything from light vegetarian dishes to *soupe de poisson* for lighter reds and rosés.

Merlot The Bordeaux grape that has come into its own all over the world, Merlot makes soft, rounded, fruity wines that are some of the easiest red wines to enjoy without food. All the same, these qualities make them a good choice with many kinds of food. Spicier game dishes, herby terrines and pâtés, pheasant, pigeon, duck or goose all blend well with Merlot; substantial casseroles made with wine are excellent with top Pomerol châteaux; and the soft fruitiness of the wines is perfect for savoury foods with a hint of sweetness such as Bayonne ham.

Nebbiolo Fruity, fragrant, early-drinking styles of Nebbiolo wine are best with local salami, pâtés, *bresaola* and lighter meat dishes. The best Barolos and Barbarescos need substantial food: *bollito misto*, jugged hare, spiced beef casseroles and *brasato al Barolo* (a large piece of beef marinated then braised slowly in Barolo) are just the job in Piedmont, or anywhere else for that matter.

Pinot Noir The great grape of Burgundy has taken its food-friendly complexity all over the wine world. However, nothing can beat the marriage of great wine with sublime local food that is Burgundy's heritage, and it is Burgundian dishes that spring to mind as perfect partners for the Pinot Noir: *coq au vin*, *boeuf bourguignon*, rabbit with mustard, braised ham, chicken with tarragon, steaks from prized Charolais cattle with a rich red-wine sauce ... the list is endless.

Pinot Noir's subtle flavours make it a natural choice for complex meat dishes but it is also excellent with plain grills and roasts and, in its lighter manifestations from, say, the Loire or Oregon, a good match for salmon or salmon trout.

In spite of the prevalence of superb cheese in Burgundy, the best Pinot Noir red wines are wasted on cheese.

Sangiovese Tuscany is where Sangiovese best expresses the qualities that can lead it, in the right circumstances, to be numbered among the great grapes of the world. And Tuscany is very much food with wine territory. Sangiovese wines such as Chianti, Chianti Riservas, Rosso di Montalcino or Montepulciano, Vino Nobile and the biggest of them all, Brunello, positively demand to be drunk with food. Drink them with *bistecca alla Fiorentina*, roast meats and game, calves' liver, casseroles, hearty pasta sauces, *porcini* mushrooms and Pecorino cheese.

Syrah/Shiraz Whether from France (in the Northern Rhône), Australia, California or South Africa, this grape always makes powerful, rich, full-bodied wines that are superb with equally full-flavoured food: roasts, game, hearty casseroles or intensely flavoured charcuterie. It can also be good with tangy cheeses.

Tempranillo Spain's best native red grape makes aromatic wines for drinking young, and matures well to a rich (usually) oaky flavour. Tempranillo is good with game, local cured hams and sausages, casseroles and meat grilled with herbs; it is particularly good with lamb. It can partner some Indian dishes and goes well with strong soft cheeses such as ripe Brie.

Zinfandel California's much-planted, most versatile grape is used for a bewildering variety of wine styles from bland, slightly sweet pinks to rich, elegant, fruity reds. And the good red Zinfandels themselves may vary greatly in style. If they aren't too oaky they are good with barbecued meats, venison and roast chicken. The hefty old-style wines are a great match with the spicy, mouthfilling San Francisco cuisine. The pale blush style of Zin goes well with tomato sauce.

WHITE GRAPES

Aligoté This Burgundian grape can, at its best, make very nice, versatile food wine. It goes well with many fish and seafood dishes, smoked fish, salads and snails in garlic and butter.

Chardonnay More than almost any other grape Chardonnay responds to different climatic conditions and to the winemaker's art. This, plus the relative ease with which it can be grown, accounts for the marked gradation of flavours and styles: from steely, cool-climate austerity to almost tropical lusciousness. The relatively sharp end of the spectrum is one of the best choices for simple fish dishes; most Chardonnays are superb with roast chicken or other white meat; the really full, rich, New World blockbusters need rich fish and seafood dishes. Oaky Chardonnays are a good choice for smoked fish.

Chenin Blanc One of the most versatile of grapes, Chenin Blanc makes wines ranging from averagely quaffable dry whites to the great sweet whites of the Loire. The lighter wines can be good as apéritifs or with light fish dishes or salads. The sweet wines are good with most puddings and superb with those made with slightly tart fruit.

Gewürztraminer Spicy and perfumed, Gewürztraminer has the weight and flavour to go with such hard-to-match dishes as *choucroute* and smoked fish. It is also a good choice for Chinese or indeed any oriental food.

Marsanne These rich, fat wines are a bit short of acid so match them with simply prepared chicken, pork, fish or vegetables.

Muscadet The dry, light Muscadet grape (best wines are *sur lie*) is perfect with seafood.

Muscat Fragrant, grapy wines ranging from delicate to downright syrupy. The drier ones are more difficult to pair with food; the sweeties come into their own with most desserts. Sweet Moscato d'Asti, delicious by itself, goes well with rich Christmas pudding or mince pies.

Pinot Blanc Clean, bright and appley, Pinot Blanc is very food-friendly. Classic white wine dishes, modern vegetarian dishes, pastas and pizzas all match up well.

Pinot Gris Rich, fat wines that need rich, fat food. Go (in Alsace) for *choucroute*, *confit de canard*, rich pork dishes. The Italian Pinot Gris (Grigio) wines are lighter and more suited to pizza or pasta.

Riesling Good dry Rieslings are really best appreciated without food. Luscious sweet ones on the other hand are very pudding-friendly. In between, those with a slight acid bite can counteract the richness of, say, goose or duck, and the fuller examples can be good with oriental food and otherwise hard-to-match salads.

Sauvignon Blanc This grape makes wines with enough bite and sharpness to accompany quite rich fish dishes as well as being an obvious choice for seafood. The characteristic acid intensity makes a brilliant match with dishes made with tomato but the best match of all is Sancerre and local Loire goats' cheese.

Sémillon/Semillon Dry Bordeaux Blancs are excellent with fish and shellfish; fuller, riper New World Semillons are equal to spicy food and rich fish sauces, often going even better with meat than with fish; sweet Sémillons can partner many puddings, especially rich, creamy ones. Sémillon also goes well with many cheeses, and Sauternes with Roquefort is a classic combination.

Viognier A subtle and characterful grape, Viognier is at its best as an apéritif. It can also go well with spicy Indian dishes.

MAKING THE MOST OF WINE

Most wine is pretty hardy stuff and can put up with a fair amount of rough handling. Young red wines can knock about in the back of a car for a day or two and be lugged from garage to kitchen to dinner table without coming to too much harm. Serving young white wines when well chilled can cover up all kinds of ill-treatment – a couple of hours in the fridge should do the trick. Even so, there are some conditions that are better than others for storing your wine – especially if they are on the mature side. And there are certain ways of serving wines which will emphasize any flavours or perfumes they have.

STORING

Most wines are sold for drinking soon, and it will be hard to ruin them in the next few months before you pull the cork. Don't stand them next to the central heating or the cooker, though, or on a sunny windowsill.

Light and extremes of temperature are also the things to worry about if you are storing wine long-term. Some wines, Chardonnay for instance, are particularly sensitive to exposure to light over several months, and the damage will be worse if the bottle is made of pale-coloured glass. The warmer the wine, the quicker it will age, and really high temperatures can spoil wine quite quickly. Beware in the winter of garages and outhouses, too: a very cold snap – say -4°C (25°F) or below – will freeze your wine, push out the corks and crack the bottles. An underground cellar is ideal, with a fairly constant temperature of 10°–12°C (50°–53°F). And bottles really do need to lie on their sides, so that the cork stays damp and swollen, and keeps out the air.

TEMPERATURE

The person who thought up the rule that red wine should be served at room temperature certainly didn't live in an efficient, modern, centrally-heated flat. It's no great sin to serve a big beefy red at the temperature of your central heating, but I prefer most reds just a touch cooler. Over-heated wine tastes flabby, and may lose some of its more volatile aromas. In general, the lighter the red, the cooler it can be. Really light, refreshing reds, such as Beaujolais, are nice lightly chilled. Ideally, I'd serve Burgundy at larder temperature, Bordeaux a bit warmer, Australian Cabernet at the temperature of a draughty room.

Chilling white wines makes them taste fresher, emphasizing their acidity. White wines with low acidity especially benefit from chilling, and it's vital for sparkling wines if you want to avoid exploding corks and a tableful of froth. Drastic chilling also subdues flavours, however – a useful ruse if you're serving basic wine, but a shame if the wine is very good.

A good guide for whites is to give the cheapest and lightest a spell in the fridge, but serve bigger and better wines – Australian

Chardonnays or top white Burgundies – perhaps half-way between fridge and central-heating temperature. If you're undecided, err on the cooler side, for whites or reds.

OPENING THE BOTTLE

There's no corkscrew to beat the Screwpull and the Spinhandle Screwpull is especially easy to use. Don't worry if bits of cork crumble into the wine – just fish them out of your glass. Tight corks that refuse to budge might be loosened if you run hot water over the bottle neck to expand the glass. If the cork is loose and falls in, push it right in and don't worry about it.

Opening sparkling wines is a serious business – point the cork away from people! Once you've started, never take your hand off the cork until it's safely out. Remove the foil, loosen the wire, hold the wire and cork firmly and twist the bottle. If the wine froths, hold the bottle at 45 degrees, and have a glass at hand.

AIRING AND DECANTING

Scientists have proved that opening young to middle-aged red wines an hour before serving makes no difference whatsoever. The surface area of wine in contact with air in the bottle neck is too tiny to be significant. Decanting is a different matter, because sloshing the wine from bottle to jug or decanter mixes it up quite thoroughly with the air. The only wines that really need to be decanted are those that have a sediment which would cloud the wine if they were poured directly – mature red Bordeaux, Burgundy and vintage port are the commonest examples. Ideally, if you are able to plan that far in advance, you need to stand the bottle upright for a day or two to let the sediment settle in the bottom. Draw the cork extremely gently. As you tip the bottle, shine a bright light through from underneath as you pour in one, steady movement. Stop pouring when you see the sediment approaching the bottle neck.

Contrary to many wine buffs' practice, I would decant a mature wine only just before serving; elderly wines often fade rapidly once they meet with air, and an hour in the decanter could kill off what little fruit they had left. By contrast, a good-quality young white wine can benefit from decanting.

KEEPING LEFTOVERS

Leftover white wine keeps better than red, since the tannin and colouring matter in red wine is easily attacked by the air. Any wine, red or white, keeps better in the fridge than in a warm kitchen. And most wines, if well made in the first place, will be perfectly acceptable if not pristine after 2 or 3 days re-corked in the fridge. But for better results it's best to use one of the gadgets sold for this purpose. The ones that work by blanketing the wine with heavier-than-air inert gas are much better than those that create a vacuum in the air space in the bottle.

VINTAGE CHARTS

FRANCE	98	97	96	95	94	93	92	91	90	89
Alsace	80	100	70	80	50	60	70	50	100	90
Champagne (vintage)	80	70	90	70	50	50	50	60	90	80
Bordeaux										
Margaux	70	60	80	80	70	60	40	40	100	80
St.-Jul., Pauillac, St-Est.	70	60	90	80	70	60	40	40	100	90
Graves/Pessac-L. (R)	80	60	80	70	60	60	40	40	80	80
Graves/Pessac-L. (W)	90	50	80	80	80	60	40	40	90	80
St-Émilion, Pomerol	80	70	70	90	80	60	40	20	100	90
Sauternes	70	90	90	70	50	40	30	30	100	90
Burgundy										
Chablis	70	100	90	80	60	70	70	60	90	80
Côte de Beaune (W)	80	90	90	90	60	70	90	60	90	80
Côte de Nuits (R)	70	80	90	80	50	80	60	60	100	80
Beaujolais Cru	80	70	80	80	50	70	50	90	60	80
Loire										
Bourgueil, Chinon	80	90	100	80	40	60	50	40	90	100
Sancerre (W)	80	90	90	80	60	60	50	70	90	80
Loire Sweet	70	90	90	90	70	70	40	50	90	100
Rhône										
Hermitage (W)	80	60	80	90	70	60	60	70	100	90
Hermitage (R)	70	60	80	90	60	30	60	80	100	90
Côte-Rôtie	70	60	80	90	60	40	60	90	80	90
Châteauneuf (R)	90	70	60	90	70	70	50	50	100	90
GERMANY										
Mosel Riesling	80	80	70	90	70	90	60	50	100	80
Rheingau Riesling	80	80	80	80	70	80	80	50	90	70
Pfalz Riesling	80	80	90	50	70	80	80	50	100	90

ITALY	98	97	96	95	94	93	92	91	90	89
Barolo, Barbaresco	9	10	9	8	6	7	4	5	10	10
Chianti Classico Ris.	7	10	8	9	7	8	5	6	10	5
Brunello, Vino Nobile	9	10	8	9	8	8	5	7	10	6
Amarone	7	10	7	10	7	8	5	5	10	6
SPAIN										
Ribera del Duero	7	6	9	8	9	4	6	8	9	6
Rioja (R)	6	7	8	8	9	5	6	7	7	8
PORTUGAL										
Alentejo	7	8	6	8	7	5	6	7	9	8
Dão	7	8	8	7	7	4	7	7	6	6
Port (vintage)	6	9	7	8	10	2	9	8	6	6
USA										
California Cabernet	8	8	7	8	9	7	8	9	8	5
California Chardonnay	7	7	6	8	8	7	7	9	8	7
Oregon Pinot Noir	6	6	7	5	10	6	9	8	9	8
Wash. State Cabernet	9	8	9	8	9	7	9	8	7	9
AUSTRALIA										
Coonawarra Cabernet	9	7	8	5	8	7	7	9	10	5
Hunter Chardonnay	9	6	8	7	7	7	8	10	5	8
Barossa Shiraz	10	8	9	8	9	7	6	8	8	5
Marg. River Cabernet	6	8	8	7	8	7	6	9	8	8
NEW ZEALAND										
M'lborough Sauvignon	7	9	9	4	10	7	6	10	6	9
Hawkes Bay Cabernet	10	8	8	7	8	5	5	9	7	9
SOUTH AFRICA										
Cape Cabernet	8	9	5	9	8	6	8	8	7	8

Numerals (1–10) represent an overall rating for each year. ◗ Not ready
● *Just ready* ● *At peak* ◖ *Past best* ○ *Not generally declared*

23

OLDER VINTAGE CHARTS *(top wines only)* ___

FRANCE									
Alsace	88	85	83	81	76	71	69	64	61
	8◆	8◆	9◊	7◆	10◆	9◆	8◊	8◊	9◊
Champagne (vintage)	88	86	85	83	82	81	79	76	75
	8◊	7◆	9◆	8◊	10◆	8◊	7◊	9◊	9◆
Bordeaux	88	86	85	83	82	81	79	78	75
Margaux	7◊	9◆	8◆	9◆	8◆	7◆	6◆	7◆	6◆
St.-Jul., Pauillac, St-Est.	8◊	9◊	8◆	8◆	10◊	7◆	7◆	7◆	8◊
Graves/Pessac-L. (R)	8◊	6◆	8◆	9◆	9◆	7◆	7◆	8◊	6◆
St-Émilion, Pomerol	8◊	7◆	9◆	7◆	10◆	7◆	7◆	7◆	8◆
Bordeaux (cont.)	70	66	62	61	59	55	52	49	47
Margaux (cont.)	8◆	7◊	8◊	10◆	8◊	6◊	6◊	9◆	8◊
St.-Jul. etc. (cont.)	8◆	8◆	9◊	10◆	9◊	8◊	7◊	10◊	9◆
Graves etc. (R) (cont.)	8◆	8◊	8◊	10◆	9◊	8◊	7◊	10◊	9◊
St-Émilion etc. (cont.)	8◆	6◊	8◊	10◊	7◊	7◊	8◊	9◊	10◊
Sauternes	88	86	83	82	81	80	76	75	71
	9◊	9◊	9◊	6◆	5◊	7◆	8◆	8◆	8◆
Sauternes (cont.)	62	59	55	53	50	49	47	45	37
	8◊	9◊	8◊	8◊	8◊	10◊	10◊	9◊	10◊
Burgundy									
Chablis	88	87	86	85	83	81	78	75	71
	7◊	6◊	9◊	9◆	7◊	8◊	9◊	8◊	9◊
Côte de Beaune (W)	88	86	85	83	81	78	75	71	69
	7◊	8◆	9◆	7◊	8◊	8◊	2◊	9◊	7◊
Côte de Nuits (R)	88	86	85	83	80	78	76	71	69
	8◆	5◊	8◆	6◊	6◊	9◆	7◊	9◊	8◊

Loire	88	86	85	83	76	71	62	59	49
Sweet wines	8◊	4/5◆	8◆	9◆	9◆	9◆	9◆	9◆	9◆
Rhône									
Côte-Rôtie/ Hermitage (R)	88	85	83	79	78	76	71	69	64
	8◊	9◆	9◆	8◊	10◆	9◊	9◊	9◊	9◊
GERMANY									
Mosel Riesling	88	85	83	76	75	71	69	64	59
	9◆	8◊	9◆	9◆	8◊	10◆	9◆	8◊	10◊
ITALY									
Barolo, Barbaresco	88	86	85	82	78	74	71	70	61
	8◆	7◊	9◊	9◆	8◆	7◊	9◆	8◊	10◊
Brunello, Chianti Riserva	88	87	86	85	83	82	75	71	70
	9◆	6◊	8◊	10◆	8◊	8◊	8◊	10◊	9◊
PORTUGAL									
Port (vintage)	87	85	83	82	80	77	75	70	66
	7◊	9◊	8◊	5◊	8◆	9◆	5◊	8◆	9◆
	63	55	48	47	45	35	34	31	27
	10◆	9◊	9◆	9◆	10◆	8◊	8◊	9◊	10◊
USA									
Napa Cabernet	88	87	86	85	84	81	79	78	74
	7◊	8◆	9◊	10◆	8◊	7◊	8◊	9◊	9◊
AUSTRALIA									
Barossa/Clare Shiraz	88	87	86	85	84	83	82	81	79
	7◆	8◆	10◊	8◆	7◊	9◆	9◆	8◆	7◊

Numerals (1–10) represent an overall rating for each year.

◊ *Could be drunk, but should be kept* ◆ *Drink now, but will age further* ◊ *Fading, drink up now*

FRANCE _____

I've visited most of the wine-producing countries of the world by now, but the one I come back to again and again, with my enthusiasm undimmed by time, is France. The sheer range of its wine flavours, the number of wine styles produced, and indeed the quality differences, from very best to very nearly worst, continue to enthral me, and as each year's vintage nears, I find myself itching to leap into the car and head for the vineyards of Champagne, of Burgundy, of Bordeaux and the Loire.

CLIMATE AND SOIL

France lies between the 40th and 50th parallels north, and the climate runs from the distinctly chilly and almost too cool to ripen grapes in the far north near the English Channel, right through to the swelteringly hot and almost too torrid to avoid grapes overripening in the far south on the Mediterranean shores. In the far north the most refined and delicate sparkling wine is made in Champagne. In the far south rich, luscious dessert Muscats and fortified wines dominate. In between is just about every sort of wine you could wish for.

The factors that influence a wine's flavour are the grape variety, the soil and climate, and the winemaker's techniques. Most of the great wine grapes, like the red Cabernet Sauvignon, Merlot, Pinot Noir and Syrah, and the white Chardonnay, Sauvignon Blanc, Sémillon and Viognier, find conditions in France where they can ripen slowly but reliably – and slow, even ripening always gives better flavours to a wine. Since grapes have been grown for over 2000 years in France, the most suitable varieties for the different soils and meso-climates have naturally evolved. And since winemaking was brought to France by the Romans, generation upon generation of winemakers have refined their techniques to produce the best possible results from their different grape types. The great wines of areas like Bordeaux and Burgundy are the results of centuries of experience and of trial and error, which winemakers from other countries of the world now use and are the role models for their attempts to create good wine.

WINE REGIONS

White grapes generally ripen more easily than red grapes and they dominate the northern regions. Even so, the chilly Champagne region barely manages to ripen its red or white grapes on its chalky soil. But the resultant acid wine is the ideal base for sparkling wine, and the acidity of the young still wine can, with good winemaking and a few years' maturing, transform into a golden honeyed sparkling wine of incomparable finesse.

Alsace, on the German border, is warmer and drier than Champagne but still produces mainly white wines. The German influence is evident in the fragrant but dry wine styles from grapes like Riesling, Pinot Gris and Gewurztraminer.

Just south-east of Paris, Chablis marks the northernmost tip of the Burgundy region, and the Chardonnay grape here produces very dry wines usually with a streak of green acidity, but nowadays with a fuller softer texture to subdue any harshness.

It's a good 2 hours' drive further south to the heart of Burgundy – the Côte d'Or which runs between Dijon and Chagny. World-famous villages such as Gevrey-Chambertin and Vosne-Romanée (where the red Pinot Noir dominates) and Meursault and Puligny-Montrachet (where Chardonnay reigns) here produce the great Burgundies that have given the region renown over the centuries. Lesser Burgundies – but they're still good – are produced further south in the Côte Chalonnaise, while between Mâcon and Lyon are the white Mâconnais wine villages and the villages of Beaujolais, famous for bright, easy-going red wine from the Gamay grape.

South of Lyon in the Rhône Valley red wines begin to dominate. The Syrah grape makes great wine at Hermitage and Côte-Rôtie in the north, while in the south the Grenache and a host of supporting grapes make full, satisfying reds of which Châteauneuf-du-Pape is the most famous. The white Viognier makes lovely wine at Condrieu and Château-Grillet in the north.

27

The whole of the south of France is now changing and improving at a bewildering rate. Provence and the scorched Midi vineyards are learning how to produce exciting wines from unpromising land and many of France's tastiest and most affordable wines now come under a Vin de Pays label from the south. In the Languedoc the red wines can now be exceptional, and in the Roussillion the sweet Muscats and Grenache-based fortifieds are equally fine.

The south-west of France is dominated by wines of Bordeaux, but has many other gems benefiting from the cooling influence of the Atlantic. Dry whites from Gascony and Bergerac can be exciting. Jurançon down in the Basque country produces some remarkable dry and sweet wines, while Madiran, Cahors and Bergerac produce good to excellent reds.

But Bordeaux is the king here. The Cabernet Sauvignon and Merlot are the chief grapes, the Cabernet dominating the production of deep reds from the Médoc peninsula and its famous villages of Margaux, St-Julien, Pauillac and St-Estèphe. Round the city of Bordeaux are Pessac-Léognan and Graves, where Cabernet and Merlot blend to produce fragrant refined reds. On the right bank of the Gironde estuary, the Merlot is most important in the plump rich reds of St-Émilion and Pomerol. Sweet whites from Sémillon and Sauvignon Blanc are made in Sauternes, with increasingly good dry whites produced in the Entre-Deux-Mers, and especially in Graves and Pessac-Léognan.

The Loire Valley is the most northerly of France's Atlantic wine regions but, since the river rises in the heart of France not far from the Rhône, styles vary widely. Sancerre and Pouilly in the east produce tangy Sauvignon whites, the centre of the river produces fizzy wine at Vouvray and Saumur, sweet wine at Vouvray and the Layon Valley, red wines at Chinon and Bourgueil, and dry whites virtually everywhere, while down at the mouth of the river, as it slips past Nantes into the Atlantic swell, the vineyards of Muscadet produce one of the world's most famous and often least memorable dry white wines.

CLASSIFICATIONS

France has an intricate, but eminently logical system for controlling the quality and authenticity of its wines. The system is divided into 4 broad classifications (in ascending order): Vin de Table, Vin de Pays, VDQS (Vin Délimité de Qualité Supérieure) and AC (Appellation Contrôlée). Within the laws there are numerous variations, with certain vineyards or producers singled out for special mention. The 1855 classification in Bordeaux or the Grands Crus of Alsace or Burgundy are good examples. The intention is a system which rewards quality. VDQS and Vin de Pays wines can be promoted to AC, for example, after a few years' good behaviour. The AC system is now under increasing attack from critics, both inside and outside France, who feel that it is outmoded and ineffectual and that too many poor wines are passed as of Appellation Contrôlée standard.

1998 VINTAGE REPORT

Twice the normal amount of rain in September put paid to any thoughts of a 'vintage of the century' in Bordeaux. The extraordinary thing, though, is that some good to excellent wines have been made. The key month was August when hot, dry, sunny weather (temperatures around 30°C) helped compensate for an indifferent June and July. The earlier ripening varieties, Sauvignon Blanc and Merlot in particular, benefited from the clement conditions, achieving satisfactory levels of ripeness. Dry whites, largely harvested before the diluvial rains arrived, will be aromatic and good to excellent. Producers were more than happy with the Merlot which resulted in some deeply coloured, concentrated, well-structured wines from the Right Bank (St-Émilion, Pomerol, Fronsac). Maturity in the Cabernet Sauvignons was more suspect leading to varied levels of quality in the Médoc and Graves. The first and last *tris* in Sauternes yielded the most botrytized grapes. Quality will be good rather than exceptional.

A warm, dry summer in Burgundy encouraged hopes of a great vintage, but rain in early September dashed them. Ten days of fine weather from 16th September, however, allowed the grapes to ripen fully, and patient growers were rewarded with excellent grapes. Rot was rampant though so careful selection was essential.

In the northern Rhône a long, warm summer has resulted in potentially very good and ageworthy wines although some early frost damage will result in a crop reduction. The south enjoyed exceptional weather and wines are deeply coloured with excellent fruit depth. It's been similar in Provence, Languedoc and Roussillon, although there's likely to be a significantly reduced yield in Corbières due to frost damage.

The Loire had an uneven growth cycle with damp and cold late spring and early summer weather followed by a very hot August. Early September rain with high humidity was followed by sunny weather resulting in good Muscadet, Sancerre and Pouilly as well as decent reds from Anjou and Touraine. Chenin Blanc fared less well. There will be good dry and demi-sec whites but this is not a great year for sweet whites. A high incidence of malevolent rot has seen to that.

In Alsace early hopes of a follow on to the exceptional 1997 vintage were dashed by intermittent rain throughout the harvest. Those growers who maintained a tight control on yields will be more successful. There was no frost damage this year in Champagne. Producers are pleased with the size of the crop and the harvest took place in good conditions. A vintage year is widely predicted.

In most areas of the country volume is down due to a combination of frost, a cool late spring and a hot summer. Generally the south appears to have fared better and some excellent wines are likely.

See also ALSACE, BORDEAUX RED WINES, BORDEAUX WHITE WINES, BURGUNDY RED WINES, BURGUNDY WHITE WINES, CHAMPAGNE, CORSICA, JURA, LANGUEDOC-ROUSSILLON, LOIRE VALLEY, MIDI, PROVENCE, RHONE VALLEY, ROUSSILLON, SAVOIE, SOUTH-WEST FRANCE; AND INDIVIDUAL WINES AND PRODUCERS.

ITALY

The cultivation of the vine was introduced to Italy over 3000 years ago, by the Greeks (to Sicily and the south) and by the Etruscans (to the north-east and central zones). Despite their great tradition, Italian wines as we know them today are relatively young. New attitudes have resulted, in the last 25 years or so, in a great change in Italian wine. The whole industry has been modernized, and areas like Tuscany are now among the most dynamic of any in the world.

GRAPE VARIETIES AND WINE REGIONS

Vines are grown all over Italy, from the Austrian border in the north to the island of Pantelleria in the far south, nearer to North Africa than to Sicily. The north-west, especially Piedmont, is the home of many of the best Italian red grapes, like Nebbiolo, Dolcetto and Barbera, while the north-east (Friuli-Venezia Giulia and Alto Adige) is more noted for the success of native white varieties like Garganega,

Tocai and Ribolla, as well as imports like Pinot Grigio, Chardonnay and Sauvignon. The central Po Valley is Lambrusco country. Moving south, Tuscany is best known for its red Chianti and Brunello wines from the native Sangiovese grape. South of Rome, where the Mediterranean climate holds sway, the traditional heavy whites and reds are gradually giving way here and there to some admirable wines.

CLASSIFICATIONS

Vino da Tavola, or 'table wine', is used for a wine that is produced either outside the existing laws, or in an area where no delimited zone exists. Both cheap, basic wines and inspired innovative creations like Tignanello and other so-called Super-Tuscans may fall into this anonymous category, but the Italians are gradually coming into line with the rest of Europe. The fancy wines will become either DOC or IGT and the rest will be labelled simply as *bianco*, *rosso* or *rosato* without vintages or geographical indications.

IGT (Indicazione Geografica Tipica) began taking effect with the 1995 vintage to identify wines from certain regions or areas as an equivalent of the French Vin de Pays.

DOC (Denominazione di Origine Controllata) is the fundamental classification for wines from designated zones made following traditions that were historically valid but too often outdated. Recently the laws have become more flexible, encouraging producers to lower yields and modernize techniques, while bringing quality wines under new appellations that allow for recognition of communes, estates and single vineyards. The trend to form new regionwide DOCs – Piedmont is a prime example – will permit classification of many quality table wines.

DOCG (Denominazione di Origine Controllata e Garantita) was conceived as a 'super-league' for DOCs with a guarantee of authenticity that promised high class but didn't always provide it. Still, despite some dubious promotions to this élite category, wines must be made under stricter standards that have favoured improvements. The best guarantee of quality, however, remains the producer's name.

1998 VINTAGE REPORT

It was always going to be hard to try to match 1997 yet it would seem at least here and there it has been achieved. A cool, wet start was followed by a hot summer before the season finished on a damp note again. But the weather pattern is never that consistent throughout Italy. The amount and timing of the heat and rain varied – perfect for some but not all. Many growers in Piedmont, Tuscany and especially Sicily are very confident, Veneto less so. At any rate not the almost uniformly great vintage that 1997 was.

See also ABRUZZO, ALTO ADIGE, CALABRIA, CAMPANIA, EMILIA-ROMAGNA, FRIULI-VENEZIA GIULIA, LAZIO, LIGURIA, LOMBARDY, MARCHE, PIEDMONT, PUGLIA, ROMAGNA, SARDINIA, SICILY, TRENTINO, TUSCANY, UMBRIA, VALLE D'AOSTA, VENETO; AND INDIVIDUAL WINES AND PRODUCERS.

GERMANY

Although exports of German wines are still dominated by semi-sweet Liebfraumilch-type wines, these are falling rapidly. This is focusing attention on the estates more and more, and here quality is significantly better than a decade ago.

GRAPE VARIETIES

The best wines come from Riesling, Scheurebe, Ruländer (also called Grauburgunder or Pinot Gris), Pinot Blanc (Weissburgunder), Gewürztraminer and Silvaner, although the widely planted Müller-Thurgau produces much of the simpler wine. Good reds can be made in the south of the country from Pinot Noir (Spätburgunder), Lemberger and Dornfelder or blends of these.

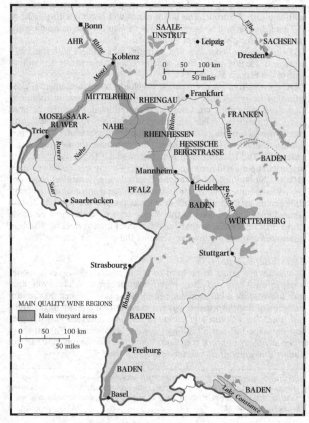

WINE REGIONS

Many of the most delectable Rieslings come from villages such as Bernkastel, Brauneberg, Graach and Ürzig on the Mosel, and Eltville, Johannisberg and Rüdesheim in the Rheingau. The Nahe also makes superb Rieslings in the communes of Schlossböckelheim and Traisen, and Niederhausen has the best vineyards in the entire region. Franken is the one place the Silvaner grape excels, often made in an earthy style. Rheinhessen is unfortunately better known for its sugary Niersteiner Gutes Domtal than it is for the excellent racy Rieslings produced on its steep Rhine slopes in the villages of Nackenheim, Nierstein and Oppenheim. The Pfalz is climatically similar to Alsace and has a similar potential for well-rounded, dry white (and some red) wines. Baden produces wine styles which appeal to an international market increasingly reared on fuller, drier wines. In Württemberg most of the red wines are dull, but there are a few producers who understand the need for weight and flavour in red winemaking. The other smaller wine regions make little wine and little is exported.

CLASSIFICATIONS

Germany's classification system is based on the ripeness of the grapes and therefore potential alcohol level.

Tafelwein (Table Wine) is the most basic term used for any basic blended wine, accounting for only a tiny percentage of production.

Landwein (Country Wine) is a slightly more up-market version, linked to 17 regional areas. These must be Trocken (dry) or Halbtrocken (medium-dry).

QbA (Qualitätswein bestimmter Anbaugebiete) is 'quality' wine from a designated region, but the grapes don't have to be very ripe, and sugar can be added to the juice to increase alcoholic content.

QmP (Qualitätswein mit Prädikat) or 'quality wine with distinction' is the top level. There are 6 levels of QmP (in ascending order of ripeness): Kabinett, Spätlese, Auslese, Beerenauslese, Eiswein and Trockenbeerenauslese.

1998 VINTAGE REPORT

In spite of heavy harvest-time rains, Germany's leading producers brought in another very good vintage in 1998. Indeed, from the Nahe and the Rhein regions it is probably better than the generally over-rated 1997 crop. Although the wines are not big and lush, they have beautiful balance and lovely ripe aromas. Although a very good vintage in the Middle Mosel too, it has been disappointing in the Saar and Ruwer. The prices for good and outstanding quality German Reislings remain low in international comparison.

See also AHR, BADEN, FRANKEN, HESSISCHE BERGSTRASSE, MITTELRHEIN, MOSEL-SAAR-RUWER, NAHE, PFALZ, RHEINGAU, RHEINHESSEN, SAALE-UNSTRUT, SACHSEN, WURTTEMBERG; AND INDIVIDUAL WINE VILLAGES AND PRODUCERS.

SPAIN

From the green, damp north to the arid south, Spain has more land under vine than any other country in the world, yet because of its harsh climate, and outmoded viticultural methods in some regions, the average grape yield in Spain is still small.

WINE REGIONS

Galicia in the green, hilly north-west grows Spain's most aromatic whites. The heartland of the great Spanish reds, Rioja, Ribera del Duero and Navarra, is situated between the central plateau and the northern coast. Catalonia is principally white wine country (much of it sparkling Cava), though there are some great reds in Priorat. The central plateau of La Mancha makes mainly cheap reds and whites; non-DO producers are improving spectacularly though. Valencia in the south-east can rival La Mancha for fresh, unmemorable but inexpensive reds and whites. Andalucía's specialities are the fortified wines, sherry, Montilla and Málaga.

CLASSIFICATIONS

Vino de Mesa, the equivalent of France's Vin de Table, is the lowest level, but is also used for a growing number of non-DO 'Super-Spanish'.
Vino de la Tierra is Spain's equivalent of France's Vin de Pays.
DO (Denominación de Origen) is the equivalent of France's AC, regulating grape varieties and region of origin.
DOC (Denominación de Origen Calificada) is a new super-category. In 1991 Rioja was the first region to be promoted to DOC.

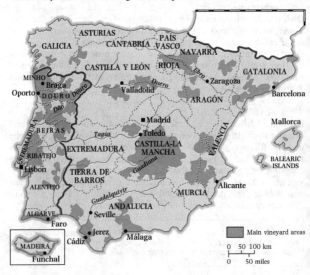

34

1998 VINTAGE REPORT

An uneven vintage due to the heavy September rains in an otherwise drought-stricken year. Very fine in eastern Spain, but disappointing in Rioja and inconsistent in Ribera del Duero where late-ripening varieties such as Cabernet Sauvignon did best.

PORTUGAL

Investment and a new dynamic approach seem to be paying off in this varied and attractive country, with climates that vary from the mild, damp Minho region in the north-west to the subtropical island of Madeira. Innovative use of native grape varieties means that Portugal is now a rich source of inexpensive yet characterful wines.

WINE REGIONS

The lush Vinho Verde country in the north-west gives very different wine from the parched valleys of the neighbouring Douro, with its drier, more continental climate. In Bairrada and Dão, soils are more important in determining the character of the wines. Estremadura and Ribatejo supply generous quantities of wine from regions either close enough to the coast to be influenced by the maritime climate, or softened by the river Tagus. South of Lisbon is the Terras do Sado, home of some exciting table wines. The other dynamic wine region is the Alentejo, with some top-class red wines. And Madeira is unique, a volcanic island 400km (250 miles) out in the Atlantic Ocean.

CLASSIFICATIONS

DOC (Denominação de Origem Controlada) The regions that were formerly classified as Região Demarcada ('demarcated region') are now known as DOC. There are 19 in all.

IPR (Indicação de Proveniência Regulamentada) is the intermediate step for 29 wine regions hoping to move up to DOC status in due course. Their wines are referred to as Vinhos de Qualidade Produzidos em Região Determinada (VQPRD).

Vinho Regional is equivalent to French Vin de Pays with laws and permitted varieties much freer than for DOC and IPR. There are 8 regions and a few sub-regions.

1998 VINTAGE REPORT

A hot summer followed a rain-disrupted flowering and fruit set but there was rain again at the end of September, especially in the Douro. Elsewhere further south, with progressively more precocious vintage dates, some good reds seem likely. Yields are down across the board.

See also (SPAIN) ANDALUCIA, ARAGON, CANARY ISLANDS, CASTILLA-LA MANCHA, CASTILLA Y LEON, CATALONIA, GALICIA; (PORTUGAL) ALENTEJO, ALGARVE, ESTREMADURA, RIBATEJO, TERRAS DO SADO, TRAS-OS-MONTES; AND INDIVIDUAL WINES AND PRODUCERS.

USA

The United States has more varied growing conditions for grapes than any other country in the world, which isn't so surprising when you consider that the 50 states of the Union cover an area that is larger than Western Europe; and although Alaska doesn't grow grapes in the icy far north, Washington State does in the north-west, as does Texas in the south and New York State in the north-east, and even Hawaii, lost in the pounding surf of the Pacific Ocean, manages to grow grapes and make wine. Altogether there are over 40 states that make wine of some sort or another; it ranges from some pretty dire offerings which would have been far better distilled into brandy or used for marinating the sirloin, to some of the greatest and original wine flavours to be found in the world today.

California is far and away the most important state for wine production. In its determination to match the best red Bordeaux and white Burgundy, California proved that it was possible to take the classic European role models and successfully re-interpret them in an area thousands of miles away from their home. However, there is more to California than this. The Central Valley produces the majority of the simple beverage wines that still dominate the American market. Napa and Sonoma counties north of San Francisco Bay do produce great Cabernet and Chardonnay, but grapes like Zinfandel and Merlot are making their mark and Carneros is highly successful for Pinot Noir, Chardonnay and sparkling wines. In the north, Mendocino and Lake Counties manage to produce good grapes, while south of San Francisco, in the cool, foggy valleys between Santa Cruz and

Main vineyard areas

Seattle
WASHINGTON STATE
Portland
OREGON
MENDOCINO
NORTH COAST
LAKE
SONOMA NAPA
San Francisco
CENTRAL COAST
CALIFORNIA
CENTRAL VALLEY
San Luis Obispo
Santa Barbara
Los Angeles
SOUTH COAST

0   150 km
0   100 miles

Santa Barbara, exciting cool-climate flavours are appearing, especially from Pinot Noir and Chardonnay.

There are those that say that much of California is too hot for the best table wines – and many of the critics are based in Oregon and Washington, both keen to wrest the quality crown from California. Oregon, with a cooler but capricious climate, perseveres with Pinot Noir, Chardonnay, Pinot Gris and Riesling with patchy success. Washington, so chilly and misty on the coast, becomes virtual desert east of the Cascade Mountains and it is here in irrigated vineyards that superb reds and whites are made with thrillingly focused fruit. New Yorkers also believe that Long Island has all the makings of a classic region: this warm, temperate claw of land to the east of New York City is well suited to Merlot, Riesling and Chardonnay. Hudson Valley and Finger Lakes can produce good wine but the winters are too cold for many classic vines. Consequently much of New York State's wine comes from hybrid vines, or the native labrusca varieties which can give flavours few people associate with fine wines.

Of the other states, Texas has the most widespread plantings of classic vinifera wine varieties, but producers of excellence exist in Maryland, Virginia and Pennsylvania on the east coast, and Idaho and New Mexico in the west.

CLASSIFICATIONS

The appellation concept is very new in the US and it was only during the 1970s that a rudimentary system was established. AVA (American Viticultural Area) merely defines a spread of land and decrees that at least 85% of the wine's volume must be derived from grapes grown within that AVA.

1998 VINTAGE REPORT

El Niño brought a season of extremes to California. The spring was cold, wet and rainy, and the summer was cool save for those days when it was terribly hot. Carrying a light crop due to the odd spring, coastal vineyards suffered from mildew and fungus problems rarely experienced here. Fruit set was very late, and harvesting stretched into early November. Fears of a miniscule crop proved unfounded – quantity was down in Chardonnay, Merlot, and Pinot Noir but close to the norm for other types. Mild sunny weather in early October allowed Cabernet Sauvignon to come through in fine shape. Other reds and most whites range all over the quality board. In Washington El Niño was kind, giving vintners good reason to celebrate both quality and a record crop size. Following a wetter, slower than normal growing season, Oregon came in with a tiny crop, but the quality of the Pinot Noir has led some to talk about the best vintage in 25 years.

See also CALIFORNIA, NEW YORK STATE, OREGON, WASHINGTON STATE; AND INDIVIDUAL WINE AREAS AND WINERIES.

AUSTRALIA _____

Australian wine today enjoys a reputation well out of proportion to the quantity of wine produced (total output is barely one-twelfth of Italy's). The heavy, alcoholic wines of the past are long gone; sheer volume of fruit aroma and flavour is the hallmark of today's styles. Production of fortified wines has plunged while sparkling wines boom and fine white and red table wines are the bread and butter.

GRAPE VARIETIES AND WINE REGIONS

Most of Australia's wine regions are in the south-east, in South Australia, Victoria and New South Wales. In Western Australia are the other important wine zones, including Margaret River and Lower Great Southern. Semillon and Shiraz have long been key varietals but now Chardonnay and Cabernet Sauvignon are the most fashionable. The use of small oak barrels for aging is important in modern reds as well as Chardonnays. Pinot Noir is yielding occasional success.

CLASSIFICATIONS

Appellation control is unknown except in the tiny regions of Mudgee and Tasmania, and there it is more a guarantee of authenticity than a guide to quality. In a country so keen on inter-regional blending, a system resembling France's Appellation Contrôlée could be problematic

although the Label Integrity Program (LIP) guarantees all claims made on labels. As part of LIP, and also the wine trade treaty between Australia and the EU, regional names must be legislated, but first there's the tricky problem of drawing boundaries and these are still under lively debate.

1999 VINTAGE REPORT
In the Barossa, a dry winter and spring led to lower than usual yields but rain during vintage caused mould problems and low sugar levels. Langhorne Creek fared worse, McLaren Vale perhaps less so, while Clare had a fair to average vintage and in the Riverland it was just about okay. In the cool southern Victorian regions it was touch and go whether the grapes would ripen but in contrast Coonawarra has had an excellent vintage. Hunter had rain at the wrong times and while Semillon should be up to par, it wasn't a good red wine year. Western Australia bore the brunt of a mid-vintage cyclone. No doubt some good wine will be made despite the unseasonal weather, but it's unlikely to be a year for cellaring.

NEW ZEALAND

New Zealand's wines are characterized by intense fruit flavours, zesty acidity and pungent aromatics – the product of cool growing conditions and high-tech winemaking. Styles are diverse due to regional differences, vintage variation and winemaking philosophy.

GRAPE VARIETIES AND WINE REGIONS
Nearly 1600km (1000 miles) of latitude separate New Zealand's northern-most wine region from the country's (and the world's) most southerly region, Central Otago. Warmer northerly climates, especially Waiheke, Matakana and Hawkes Bay, produce New Zealand's best reds from Cabernet, Merlot and Cabernet Franc (or a blend of all three). Pinot Noir is good in Wairarapa and in South Island. Chardonnay performs well in all regions, with riper, fleshier wines in the north and finer, zestier styles to the south. Expect a big difference between pungent, grassy Sauvignon Blanc grown in Marlborough and the more conventional riper stone-fruit flavours of North Island.

1999 VINTAGE REPORT
El Niño giveth and La Niña taketh away. The weather conditions that produced a spectacularly good New Zealand vintage in 1998 created the same hot, dry conditions for the early part of the 1999 vintage before dashing most winemakers' hopes with bouts of heavy rain. Expect a variety of results depending on harvest date and crop load.

See also (AUSTRALIA) NEW SOUTH WALES, SOUTH AUSTRALIA, TASMANIA, VICTORIA, WESTERN AUSTRALIA; (NEW ZEALAND) AUCKLAND, CANTERBURY, CENTRAL OTAGO, GISBORNE, HAWKES BAY, KUMEU/HUAPAI, MARLBOROUGH, NELSON, WAIHEKE ISLAND, WAIRARAPA; AND INDIVIDUAL WINERIES.

SOUTH AMERICA

Several countries in this vast continent have vines, but in only a few places does the climate favour the production of fine wines.

ARGENTINA

Such is foreign faith in this relatively untouched country that even Chileans are investing in MENDOZA vineyards. Yet quality has still to arrive consistently at the top end although encouraging cheap commercial blends are now appearing regularly on the shelves. Watch out for Torrontés, Malbec, Tempranillo, Sangiovese, Barbera and Syrah. There's promising Chardonnay from Tupungato Valley too.

BRAZIL

Winemaking is confined to the southern tip of this huge country, and winemakers have a hard time combating the rot that results from a generally damp, subtropical climate. The fact that hardy labrusca and hybrid varieties still outnumber classic vinifera varieties by 7 to 1 reflects these climatic difficulties. PALOMAS and Vinicola Aurora are the only serious export producers. See also Rio Grande do Sul.

CHILE

Chile is making full use of rejuvenated vineyards and a new self-belief among the indigenous winemaking talent. New projects are sprouting everywhere, helped by a predictable climate, an asset that France and California have been quick to invest in. The search for a second CASABLANCA continues, while for reds, the Rapel region is generating most excitement, particularly with Merlot. And, at last, greater risk-taking is delivering stunning results at the premium end of the market. However, Chile still stands first and foremost for good-value wines, and there are increasing numbers of newcomers to choose from. Drink the most recent vintage available. See also Central Valley.

MEXICO

This is basically brandy country, but in the far north-west in Baja California, some excellent reds are being made by L A CETTO. It is the high-altitude areas in Mexico that have the most potential for producing quality wines, and these include the Parras Valley and Zacatecas. New investment from companies such as González Byass, Seagram and Suntory may be the spur for further improvements. Promising grape varieties include Nebbiolo, Petite Syrah, Barbera, with Viognier and Riesling also being planted.

URUGUAY

With its main wine region sitting on roughly the same latitude as the Barossa in Australia, Uruguay has greater climatic potential than Brazil for producing good wines. Peter Bright's work at Juanico and John Worontschak's wines from Castillo Viejo show that clean, international styles can be made, with best results coming from the tough, black-berried Tannat, smoothed over with some Merlot.

SOUTH AFRICA

South African wine no longer enjoys the special status it was accorded immediately after the country's return to international markets. While producers in all regions have adapted to the modern soft, fruity styles, at the cheaper end of the market, quality is not improving as fast as prices are rising. At the very pinnacle of the quality pyramid, where quantities remain strictly limited, the increase in breadth and depth of quality wines is more noticeable every vintage.

GRAPE VARIETIES AND WINE REGIONS
Due to much uprooting as well as extensive planting, South Africa's vineyards remain close to 100,000 ha (250,000 acres). These invariably fall within the heart of the Cape's winelands, which run roughly 400km (250 miles) north and east of Cape Town, and are divided into districts under the WINE OF ORIGIN system. The major grape varieties are planted over the entire Cape; Chenin Blanc still holds sway with nearly 27% of plantings. Between them, Chardonnay, Sauvignon, Merlot and Shiraz account for just under 19% of vineyard area. There is little typicity of origin, although some areas are historically associated with specific varieties or styles. STELLENBOSCH currently produces some of the best red wines; CONSTANTIA, with its sea-facing slopes, is acknowledged as ideal for Sauvignon Blanc; cooler areas also include Walker Bay in OVERBERG where the focus is Pinot Noir. The inland, warmer areas are noted for fortifieds, both Muscadets and port-styles.

1999 VINTAGE REPORT
Weather was cool and dry up to the end of January when a heatwave struck. The subsequent hot, dry conditions have led to red grapes coming in with high sugars but, in some cases, less fruit than 1998. Despite the heat, better-managed vineyards should produce some flavoursome Sauvignon Blanc and there's early enthusiasm for Chardonnay.

OTHER WINE COUNTRIES

ALGERIA The western coastal province of Oran provides three-quarters of Algeria's wine production, with Alger making up the rest. French traditions live on in the soft but muscular wines of the Coteaux du Tlemcen, near the Moroccan border, while the dark, beefy reds of the Coteaux du Mascara in central Oran recall old-style Rhônes. The Algerians had begun to revive their wine industry by planting noble varieties; what effect the civil war will have remains to be seen.

AUSTRIA Much of Austria's viticulture falls either side of the Danube. The WACHAU produces great Riesling and excellent pepper-dry Grüner Veltliner. Next along the Danube are KAMPTAL and KREMSTAL, also fine dry white regions with a few good reds. Austria's best reds are from BURGENLAND, south of Vienna. Further south, in STEIERMARK, use of oak-aging for Chardonnay and Sauvignon is increasing. In Burgenland, around the Neusiedler See, superb dessert wines in Germanic and Sauternes styles are made. See also Donauland, Thermenregion, Wien.

BULGARIA Eastern Europe's original success story, built mainly on the success of soft, curranty red wine. Classic grape varieties (Cabernet, Merlot, Pinot Noir, Chardonnay, Riesling, Sauvignon), which occupy 75% of the vineyards, are the main attraction but are less successful than they ought to be. Local red varieties, such as the plummy Mavrud, the meaty and toothsome Gamza and the deep though less common Melnik, can be good. The Dimiat can produce gentle, creamy, summer-fruit-bowl whites, while Misket (despite its name and grapy flavour, not a Muscat cousin) combines, if well handled, lively fruit with a haunting muskiness. Whites and lighter reds are mainly from the north and east (the freshest whites are those from the Black Sea coast), while richer, fuller reds come from the mountainous south and south-west. The remaining state-owned wineries were due for privatization but this has been moving slowly. Best wineries include ASSENOVGRAD, IAMBOL, RUSSE, SLIVEN and SUHINDOL.

CANADA The Canada-US Free Trade Agreement, allowing free access for cheap California wine, forced Canadian growers to adopt a more quality-first approach, and the strict VQA (Vintners Quality Alliance) now maintains those standards. There has been enormous progress in the 2 most important regions of OKANAGAN VALLEY in British Columbia and in the NIAGARA PENINSULA in Ontario. Pinot Gris and Chardonnay lead the way in non-sweet wines (ICEWINE still being Canada's main white trump card though it still cannot be imported into the European Union) and Pinot Noir and Merlot show potential in reds.

CHINA The Chinese wine industry is changing rapidly. The official policy promoting wine rather than grain-based alcohol means that the area under vine is expanding rapidly as well as winery capacity. The leading wineries are a mix of Western and Chinese investment (Allied DOMECQ/HUADONG, Rémy-Martin/Dynasty, Pernod Ricard/ Dragon Seal). International grape varieties are being planted, notably Chardonnay, Riesling, Gamay, Cabernet Sauvignon and Merlot.

CROATIA Inland Croatia produces mainly bulk whites; the best vineyards are on the Dalmatian coast, turning out gutsy, mouthfilling Postup, Peljesac and Faros reds.

CYPRUS The island has not had a high reputation for wine since the Crusades, when COMMANDARIA was reputedly a rich, succulent nectar worth risking your neck for. Modern Cyprus has survived on mediocre sherry-style wines and bulk shipments to the old USSR but desperately needs to modernize to find new markets. However, supported by the government, regional press houses and wineries are being built in or near the vineyards, and this should help quality.

THE CZECH REPUBLIC After the division of the former Czechoslovakia, the Czech Republic has been left with only a third of the vineyards, divided between the provinces of Bohemia and Moravia. With mainly cool-climate vineyards, planted with white varieties like Pinot Blanc, Muscat, Grüner Veltliner, Gewürztraminer and the strangely grapy Irsay Oliver, as well as pockets of red, a lack of a sense of direction has been the chief problem. Western investment will help produce good dry, aromatic whites.

ENGLAND With under 1000ha (2470 acres) of vineyards, England remains a statistically insignificant wine-producing nation. Yet no other spot can manage to infuse white wines with such haunting mayflower aromas and slender, graceful, willowy fruit, particularly in vintages like 1995. The most popular winemaking counties are Kent (Biddenden, CHAPEL DOWN, English Vineyard, LAMBERHURST, STAPLE VINE-YARDS, Tenterden) and Sussex (BREAKY BOTTOM, CARR TAYLOR, Hidden Spring, Nutbourne Manor, NYETIMBER, St George's), with other top producers in Berkshire (THAMES VALLEY), Dorset (The Partridge), Gloucestershire (THREE CHOIRS), Oxfordshire (Chiltern Valley), Somerset (Pilton Manor, Wootton) and Surrey (DENBIES). The main problem is an unpredictable weather pattern. The most successful grape varieties – the hybrid Seyval Blanc and German-developed crosses like Schönburger, Huxelrebe, Bacchus, Kerner and Ortega – are those that can hold off disease while waiting for the last rays of October sunshine. Sparkling wines could prove England's best commercial card.

GREECE Production and sales of Greece's best known wine, Retsina, are falling sharply and things are changing fast. Large companies like Boutari, Achais Clauss and Kourtakis are producing clean, modern wines. But the real interest comes from estates like CHATEAU CARRAS, Gerovassilou, CHATEAU LAZARIDI and Skouras. Best results are powerful, concentrated reds, using both native Greek varieties and international ones. The sweet Muscat from SAMOS remains an affordable classic.

HUNGARY The country's great wine traditions did not prosper under the Communists, but inspired winemaking, especially by flying winemakers, has seen a tremendous range in high-quality whites. Foreign investment in TOKAJI, and renewed interest in its native grape varieties make Hungary likely to rejoin the world wine leaders soon.

ISRAEL Wine production began at the end of the 19th century. Nowadays much is sweet red wine, but there are excellent dry wines from the GOLAN HEIGHTS WINERY and CARMEL (near Haifa and Tel Aviv). Askalon's Ben Ami also makes good Cabernet-based reds.

JAPAN Some quality wines have been produced in Japan from homegrown grapes, as those of Chateau Lumière show, but much includes imported grapes, juice or wine.

LEBANON CHATEAU MUSAR is Lebanon's talisman of courage and quality. Watch out also for Chateau Kefraya and the Ksara co-op.

MOLDOVA Most forward-thinking of the ex-USSR wine producers, with Bordeaux-like, mature Rochu and Negru red wines from the Purkar winery. Cabernet from the Krikova winery can also be good.

MOROCCO Known for rich, sweet-fruited reds that found a ready blending market in France, Morocco still produces supple reds – Tarik, Toulal Guerrouane and Chante Bled – as well as refreshing but heady rosés.

ROMANIA An ancient wineland with great traditional vineyards on the Black Sea and the Moldovan border that can provide wonderful sweet wines. The Dealul Mare region can produce good Pinot Noir, Merlot and Cabernet, but quality has been erratic. Good results have been achieved with botrytized Chardonnay and Pinot Gris in the MURFATLAR region.

SLOVAKIA The eastern part of the old Czechoslovakia, with cool-climate vineyards for white wines from Pinot Blanc, Rhine Riesling, Gewürztraminer and Irsay Oliver, plus some reds. Western investment, particularly at the Nitra winery, is rapidly improving quality.

SLOVENIA Many of the old Yugoslav Federation's best vineyards are found here, either on the Italian or the Austrian borders. Lutomer Laski Rizling comes from north-east Slovenia.

SWITZERLAND Fendant (Chasselas) is the main grape for snappy, neutral whites from the VALAIS. Like the fruity DOLE reds, they are best drunk very young. German-speaking cantons produce light reds and rosés from Pinot Noir (Blauburgunder), and whites from Müller-Thurgau (Rivaner). Italian-speaking TICINO concentrates on Merlots, juicy at best but often lean and grassy. Serious wines use Cabernet, Chardonnay and traditional varieties like Arvine and Amigne. See also Neuchâtel, Vaud.

TURKEY The world's fifth-largest grape producer, but 97% ends up as raisins and the rest make pretty poor red and white wines.

UKRAINE Sparkling wine production in Odessa dates back to 1896, when a member of the ROEDERER family established the 'Russian-French Company' to produce fizz from local grapes. See also Crimea.

YUGOSLAVIA What remains of Yugoslavia is predominantly the red wine-producing part of the old federation. The Vranac grape grows full-throated bulky reds in Montenegro.

ZIMBABWE The first wines were produced in 1965 but the industry has only become fully modern in the last decade. There are just two companies: Mukuyu and Stapleford.

A–Z

OF WINES,
PRODUCERS, GRAPES
& WINE REGIONS

In the following pages there are over
1600 entries covering the world's top wines, as well as
leading producers, main wine regions, grape varieties,
wine terms and classifications.

*On page 5 you will find a full explanation of
How to Use the A–Z. On page 299 there is an index
of all wine producers in the book, to help you find the
world's best wines.*

ABRUZZO *Italy* East of Rome, this region stretches from the Adriatic coast to the mountainous Apennine interior. White Trebbiano d'Abruzzo DOC is usually dry and neutral; the MONTEPULCIANO D'ABRUZZO DOC is sometimes rosé called Cerasuolo, but generally a strapping, peppery red of real character. Overproduction is a problem, but there are a number of good producers.

AC/AOC (APPELLATION D'ORIGINE CONTRÔLÉE) The top category of French wines, defined by regulations covering vineyard yields, grape varieties, geographical boundaries and alcohol content. It guarantees the origin and style of a wine, but not its quality, although it ought to!

ACACIA *Carneros AVA, California, USA* A leading producer of Chardonnay and Pinot Noir from the CARNEROS region for almost 2 decades. Reserve Chardonnay★ is consistently exciting and the regular Carneros bottling isn't exactly chopped liver, either. Pinot Noirs include the stunning Reserve★★★ as well as a Beckstoffer Vineyard★ and a Carneros★ – except for the deep, velvety Reserve, they tend to be on the bright cherry fruit side. Acacia also makes an excellent Old Vine Zinfandel★ and a voluptuous Carneros Viognier. The Brut sparkling wine has now moved on from an experimental programme into a commercial venture. Best years: (red) (1997) 96 95 **94 93 92 91 90**; (white) (1997) 96 95 **94 93 92 91**.

TIM ADAMS *Clare Valley, South Australia* Important maker of fine, old-fashioned wine from bought-in grapes. Classic dry Riesling★★, subtly wooded Semillon★★, and rich, full-bodied Shiraz★★ and Cabernet★. The botrytis Semillon★★ can be super stuff, and minty, peppery Aberfeldy Shiraz★★★ is a remarkable, at times unnerving, mouthful of brilliance from 90-year-old vines growing near WENDOUREE. Best years: (Aberfeldy Shiraz) **1996 95 94 93 92**.

ADANTI *Umbria, Italy* Adanti produces a range of characterful wines. The whites, based primarily on the Grechetto grape, are tight, ripe and nutty, but the reds (Montefalco Sagrantino★ and Rosso d'Arquata★) are the real stars, pulsating with dark, unexpected flavours. Best years: (Sagrantino) 1995 94 93 **91 90 88 86 85**.

ADEGA Portuguese for 'winery'.

ADELAIDE HILLS *South Australia* Small, new but exciting region 30 minutes' drive from Adelaide. High altitude affords a cool, moist climate ideal for fine table wines and superb sparkling wine base. Importantly, Australia's finest, most consistently good Sauvignon Blanc. Best producers: Ashton Hills, Chain of Ponds, HENSCHKE★★, Lenswood Vineyards★★, PETALUMA★★, SHAW & SMITH★★, Geoff WEAVER★★.

ADELSHEIM VINEYARD *Willamette Valley AVA, Oregon, USA* This vineyard first hit the headlines with wine labels depicting various local beauties, including the owner's wife. Adelsheim has established a reputation for fine Pinot Noir – especially a rich Reserve★★ – and a rich Chardonnay Reserve★. There is also a Pinot Gris★ with good depth of flavour. Best years: 1997 96 **95 94 92 91 90 89 88 87**; (Reserve) (1996) **95 94 92 90 89 87**.

AGE *Rioja DOC, Rioja, Spain* A huge investment to build Rioja's largest vinification plant may yet improve the whole range. The Siglo Saco★ red Crianza is its best-known wine, perhaps because it comes wrapped in a hessian sack – but, luckily, this does not affect the taste. Best years: (reds) 1995 **94 91 89**.

AGLIANICO DEL VULTURE DOC *Basilicata, Italy*   Red wine from the
Aglianico grape grown on the steep
slopes of Mt Vulture. Despite being one
of Italy's most southerly DOCs, the
harvest is later than in BAROLO, 750km
(470 miles) to the north-west, because
the Aglianico grape ripens very late.
The best wines are structured,
complex and long-lived. Best
producers: D'Angelo★★, Armando
Martino, Paternoster★★, Sasso★, Valle del Trono★. Best years: (1997)
96 **93 90 88**.

AHR *Germany*   The Ahr Valley is a largely red wine region, south of Bonn.
The chief grape varieties are the Spätburgunder (Pinot Noir) and the
(Blauer) Portugieser. Many Ahr reds are made sweet for the day-
trippers from Bonn and Cologne, but this style does not find many
supporters outside Germany. Only Meyer-Näkel has achieved anything
like an international reputation, and that has been won by making
serious dry reds.

AIGLE *Vaud, Switzerland*   Village in the CHABLAIS sub-region of the Vaud,
making white wines from the Dorin (as the locals call the Chasselas
grape) and reds from the Pinot Noir. Best known are the whites, with
their 'flinty' bouquet, light and refreshing from their slight prickle.
Best producers: Badoux, Landolt, Urs Saladin, Testuz.

AIRÉN   Spain's – and indeed the world's – most planted white grape can make
fresh modern white wines, or thick, yellow, old-fashioned brews. Airén
is grown all over the centre and south of Spain, especially in La
MANCHA, VALDEPEÑAS and ANDALUCIA (where it's called Lairén). Any
new plantings are now forbidden in the CASTILLA-LA MANCHA region.

AJACCIO AC *Corsica, France*   Situated in the west of the island around
the town of Ajaccio, this is one of the better Corsican ACs. The reds
often need 2–3 years in bottle to show at their best. Best producers:
Clos d'Alzeto★, Clos Capitoro, Comte Péraldi★.

ALBANA DI ROMAGNA DOCG *Romagna, Italy*   In the hills south of
Bologna and Ravenna, Italy's first white DOCG was a 'political'
appointment that caused outrage among wine enthusiasts because of
the totally forgettable flavours of most Albana wine. Though also
made in dry and sparkling styles, the sweet version is the best.
Especially memorable is the Albana Passito Scacco Matto★★ of Zerbina.
Best producers: Celli, Conti★, Ferrucci★, Paradiso, Riva, Tre Monti★,
Uccellina★, Zerbina★★.

ALBARIÑO   Possibly Spain's most characterful white grape. It grows in
GALICIA in Spain's rainy north-west and, as Alvarinho, in Portugal's
VINHO VERDE region. When well made, Albariño wines have fascinating
flavours of apricot, peach, grapefruit and Muscat grapes, refreshingly
high acidity, highish alcohol – and very high prices.

ALCAMO DOC *Sicily, Italy* One of SICILY's better-known DOCs. Made from the indigenous Catarratto grape of western Sicily, grown between MARSALA and Palermo, the few good examples are dry, nutty and rounded. Drink young. Best producers: Duca di Castelmonte, Principe di Corleone, MID, Rapitalà★, Rincione.

ALEATICO An ancient, native Italian grape that produces sweet after-dinner wines of seriously notable alcoholic strength in PUGLIA, LAZIO, UMBRIA and in TUSCANY, where a small revival is underway. Best producers: AVIGNONESI (Tuscany), Candido (delicious Aleatico di Puglia★).

ALELLA DO *Catalonia, Spain* The city of Barcelona is fast encroaching on this tiny hilly region. Alella wines, mainly white, were traditionally medium-dry, but are now increasingly bone dry. Chardonnay examples can be good, though the unexciting Xarel-lo grape (locally called Pansa Blanca) is still the main staple. There are now some quality Merlots, both reds and rosés. Drink young. Best producers: Parxet, Roura.

ALENQUER IPR *Estremadura, Portugal* Maritime-influenced region of rolling hills, a short drive north of Lisbon. If the lead given by Quinta da Boavista (Quinta das Setencostas) and Quinta de Pancas can be built upon, this will be a region to watch. Some wines are simply labelled ESTREMADURA.

ALENTEJO *Portugal* The 2 provinces, Alto and Baixo Alentejo, making up most of southern Portugal south and east of Lisbon, are Portugal's fastest improving red wine regions. There are 3 IPRs and 5 DOCs. Potential is far from realized but I believe many of Portugal's finest reds will come from here. Best producers: Caves ALIANÇA, Fundação Eugénio de Almeida (Cartuxa★, Pera Manca★★), BORBA co-op, Quinta do CARMO★★, ESPORAO (Reserva★★), José Maria da FONSECA★, J P VINHOS★, Mouchão★, Redondo co-op, Reguengos de Monsaraz co-op★, Roqueval★, SOGRAPE. See also Borba, Reguengos.

ALEXANDER VALLEY AVA *California, USA* Important AVA centred on the Russian River, where the climate is fairly warm with only patchy summer fog. Cabernet Sauvignon is highly successful here, with lovely, juicy fruit not marred by an excess of tannin. Chardonnay may also be good but doesn't give such ripe, round flavours. Zinfandel and Merlot can be outstanding on hillsides. Best producers: Alexander Valley Vineyards★, Chateau Souverain, CLOS DU BOIS★, GEYSER PEAK★, JORDAN★, Murphy-Goode★★, Seghesio★, SILVER OAK★★, SIMI★. See also Sonoma County, Russian River Valley AVA.

ALGARVE *Portugal* It is extraordinary that the predominantly red, feeble-flavoured wines from this holiday region should have not 1 but 4 DOCs – Lagoa, Lagos, Portimão and Tavira. However, these seem likely to be demoted to IPRs. A simple classification such as Vinho Regional Algarve would be sufficient. I'd stick to the beer.

ALIANÇA, CAVES *Beira Litoral, Portugal* Based in BAIRRADA, Aliança makes crisp, fresh whites and soft, approachable red Bairradas. Also made, either from its own vineyards or bought-in grapes or wines, are reds from the DAO, DOURO and ALENTEJO. Best though is a varietal Touriga Nacional, Quinta da Cortesia★, from ESTREMADURA.

ALIGOTÉ French grape, found almost exclusively in Burgundy, whose basic characteristic is a lemony tartness. It can make extremely nice wine, especially from old vines, but is generally rather dull and lean. Traditionally used with local crème de cassis to make the apéritif Kir. In ripe years it can resemble Chardonnay, especially if a little new oak is used. The best comes from Bouzeron in the CÔTE CHALONNAISE. Bouzeron is the only village in Burgundy with its own appellation for Aligoté. Occasionally also found in Moldova and Bulgaria. Best producers: (Burgundy) Jean-Claude Bachelet, COCHE-DURY★, Pierre Cogny, J-J Confuron, JAYER-GILLES★, RION, Villaine★.

ALLEGRINI *Valpolicella, Veneto, Italy* Now a medium-sized and high-profile producer in VALPOLICELLA Classico. Allegrini has concentrated increasingly on quality, and especially on the single-vineyard Valpolicellas La Grola★★ and Palazzo della Torre★★. Barrique-aged La Poja★★, made solely with the Corvina grape, has shown the great potential that exists in Valpolicella. Since 1990, Palazzo della Torre has been made by a new-style *ripasso*, using dried grapes from the vineyard. Makes fine AMARONE★★★ and RECIOTO★ (especially the Giovanni Allegrini★★). Best years: 1997 96 **95 94 93 91 90 88**.

ALL SAINTS *Rutherglen, Victoria, Australia* Old winery revived with great flair since 1992, and recently sold to BROWN BROTHERS family member, Peter Brown. Superb fortifieds Old Tokay★★★, Muscat★★, Tawny★★, Madeira★★ and Amontillado★ have rediscovered past glory. Classic Release fortifieds are good but younger, while table wines can surprise. Pink Aleatico is unusual.

ALOXE-CORTON AC *Côte de Beaune, Burgundy, France* An important village at the northern end of the CÔTE DE BEAUNE producing mostly red wines from Pinot Noir. Its reputation is based on the 2 Grand Crus, CORTON (red and very occasional white) and CORTON-CHARLEMAGNE (white only). The wines from the other vineyards in Aloxe-Corton used to be some of Burgundy's tastiest at a fair price, but nowadays the reds rarely exhibit their characteristically delicious blend of ripe fruit and appetizing savoury dryness. Almost all the white wine is sold as Grand Cru: straight Aloxe-Corton Blanc is very rare. Best producers: Chandon de Briailles★★, M Chapuis★, Marius Delarche★, DROUHIN, Dubreuil-Fontaine★, Antonin Guyon★, R & R Jacob★, JADOT, LATOUR, Rapet Père et Fils★, Comte Senard, TOLLOT-BEAUT★★, Michel Voarick★. Best years: (reds) 1997 96 95 93 90 **89 88**; (whites) 1997 96 95 **92 90 89 88**.

ALSACE AC See pages 50–1.

ALSACE VENDANGE TARDIVE *Alsace, France* Vendange Tardive means 'late-harvest'. The grapes (Riesling, Muscat, Pinot Gris or Gewurztraminer) are picked late and almost overripe, giving higher sugar levels and potentially more intense, exciting flavours. The resulting wines are usually rich and mouthfilling and often need 5 years or more to show their personality. Best producers: Léon Beyer★★, P Blanck★★★, E Burn★★, Rolly Gassmann★★, HUGEL★★, Kreydenweiss★★★, KUENTZ-BAS★★, Schlumberger★★, Schoffit★, TRIMBACH★★, Weinbach★★, ZIND-HUMBRECHT★★★. Best years: (1998) 97 96 95 94 **93 92 90 89 88 85 83 76**. See also pages 50–1.

ALSACE AC

Alsace, France

 Tucked away on France's eastern border with Germany, Alsace produces some of the most individual white wines of all, rich in aroma and full of ripe, distinctive flavours. To the visitor, Alsace appears the most Germanic of France's wine regions – a legacy of intermittent German occupation over the last century and a quarter. The food tastes German, the buildings look German and, perhaps unsurprisingly, there's plenty of beer on offer. As the reputation of German wines has moved down-market this perception has almost certainly restricted the popularity of Alsace wines. In their tall green bottles they could easily be mistaken for something produced in the German Mosel-Saar-Ruwer. The irony of all this is that Alsace is proudly French. More to the point, its wines taste nothing like those from Germany. They're generally drier, richer, less acidic and more alcoholic.

Alsace is almost as far north as Champagne, but its climate is considerably warmer. The key factor is the presence of the Vosges mountains, which act as a natural barrier, protecting the vineyards from rain and westerly winds, and making Alsace one of the drier places in France. In the crucial early autumn months, when the grapes are brought to full ripeness, Alsace is often as warm as Burgundy.

GRANDS CRUS

Since 1975 the best vineyard sites in Alsace can call themselves Grands Crus. There are currently 50 of these, but the list is expanding. There are also an increasing number of very good wines produced from Single Cru vineyards not yet of Grand Cru status. The Grand Cru vineyards are restricted to 1 of 4 grapes – Riesling, Muscat, Gewurztraminer or Pinot Gris (sometimes labelled Tokay-Pinot Gris) – generally considered the finest varieties in Alsace, though Sylvaner and Pinot Blanc can produce good wines. These 4 are also the only grapes permitted for Vendange Tardive and Sélection de Grains Nobles, the late-picked and sometimes sweet wines which are a regional speciality. Pinot Noir, the area's only red grape, is usually confined to less well-appointed vineyards. As a result, it frequently produces wines that are closer to a rosé than a red Burgundy, although in hot vintages Alsace Pinot Noir can be excellent.

Alsace was one of the first regions to label its wines by grape variety – a practice which is now common in Australia and California, but is still frowned upon in France. Apart from Edelzwicker, which is a blend, and Crémant d'Alsace, all Alsace wines are made from a single grape variety.

See also ALSACE VENDANGE TARDIVE, CREMANT D'ALSACE, SELECTION DE GRAINS NOBLES; AND INDIVIDUAL PRODUCERS.

BEST YEARS

(1998) 97 96 95 94 **93 92 90 89 88 85 83 76**

BEST PRODUCERS

Gewurztraminer Albrecht, Léon Beyer, P Blanck, E Burn, Deiss, Dirler, JOSMEYER, HUGEL, Kreydenweiss, KUENTZ-BAS, Ostertag, Pfaffenheim co-op, Schleret, Schlumberger, Schoffit, TRIMBACH, Turckheim co-op, Weinbach, ZIND-HUMBRECHT.

Muscat J Becker, P Blanck, E Burn, Deiss, Dirler, Dopff & Irion, Kreydenweiss, KUENTZ-BAS, Rolly Gassman, Schoffit, Bruno Sorg, TRIMBACH, Weinbach, ZIND-HUMBRECHT.

Pinot Blanc Caves J-B Adam, P Blanck, JOSMEYER, Turckheim co-op, ZIND-HUMBRECHT.

Pinot Gris Albrecht, Léon Beyer, P Blanck, E Burn, Deiss, HUGEL, KUENTZ-BAS, Ostertag, Rolly Gassmann, Schleret, Schlumberger, TRIMBACH, Weinbach, ZIND-HUMBRECHT.

Pinot Noir Albert Hertz, HUGEL, Schleret, Turckheim co-op.

Riesling Albrecht, J Becker, Léon Beyer, P Blanck, Deiss, Dirler, Albert Hertz, HUGEL, JOSMEYER, Kientzler, Kreydenweiss, KUENTZ-BAS, Ostertag, Rolly Gassman, Schlumberger, Schoffit, TRIMBACH, Weinbach, ZIND-HUMBRECHT.

Sylvaner Kientzler, Ostertag, Rolly Gassmann, Martin Schaetzel, Schoffit, Weinbach, ZIND-HUMBRECHT.

51

ALTARE *Barolo DOCG, Piedmont, Italy* Elio Altare crafts some of the most stunning of Alba's wines – excellent Dolcetto d'Alba★★ and BARBERA D'ALBA★ and even finer BAROLO★★ and Barolo Cru Vigneto Arborina★★★. Though a professed modernist, his wines are intense, full and structured while young, but with clearly discernible fruit flavours, thanks largely to tiny yields. He also makes 3 barrique-aged wines under the LANGHE DOC: Arborina★★★ (Nebbiolo), Larigi★★ (Barbera) and La Villa★★ (Nebbiolo-Barbera). Best years: (Barolo) (1997) (96) 95 94 93 **90 89 88 86 85**.

ALTESINO *Brunello di Montalcino DOCG, Tuscany, Italy* One of the pioneers of a more modern style of BRUNELLO. Its range includes a good Brunello★, a more refined Cru (Montosoli★★), a barrique-aged Sangiovese (Palazzo Altesi★) and a Sangiovese-Cabernet blend (Alte d'Altesi★), as well as a varietal Cabernet (Borgo d'Altesi★) and a Merlot (Quarto d'Altesi★). Also a fine VIN SANTO★★. Best years: (Brunello) (1997) (96) (95) 94 93 **90 88**.

ALTO ADIGE *Trentino-Alto Adige, Italy* A largely German-speaking province, originally called Südtirol. The region-wide DOC covers 25 types of wine. A large proportion of its production comes from well-run co-ops producing reliable and sometimes admirable wines. Reds are invariably varietal and range from light and perfumed, when made from the Schiava grape, fruity from Cabernets or Merlot, to dark and velvety if the Lagrein is used. Whites include Chardonnay, Pinot Grigio and Riesling, and are usually fresh and fragrant. There is also some good sparkling wine. Subzones include the previously independent DOCs at SANTA MADDALENA and Terlano. Best producers: Abbazia di Novacella★, Caldaro co-op★, Colterenzio co-op★★, Franz Gojer★, Giorgio Grai★★, Franz Haas★, Haderberg★, Hofstätter★, Graf Kuenberg★, LAGEDER★★, Laimburg★, J Niedermayr★, Ignaz Niedriest★, Heinrich Plattner★, Prima & Nuova/Erste & Neue★, Castel Ringberg and Kastelaz, Hans Rottensteiner★, San Michele Appiano co-op★★, SANTA MADDALENA co-op★, Schwanburg★, Tiefenbrunner★, Baron Widmann★. See also Trentino.

ALVARINHO See Albariño.

AMA, CASTELLO DI *Chianti Classico DOCG, Tuscany, Italy* Model estate of CHIANTI CLASSICO, with outstanding single-vineyard bottlings★★ (Bellavista and La Casuccia). Vigna L'Apparita★★★ is one of Italy's best Merlots; less impressive Vigna Il Chiuso is made from Pinot Nero. Also good VIN SANTO★. Best years: (reds) (1998) (97) (96) 95 **94 93 90 88 85**.

AMARONE DELLA VALPOLICELLA *Valpolicella DOC, Veneto, Italy* A brilliantly individual, bitter-sweet style of VALPOLICELLA made from grapes shrivelled on mats for months after harvest. The wine, which can reach up to 16% of alcohol, differs from the sweet RECIOTO DELLA VALPOLICELLA in that it is fermented to dryness. Classico is generally the best, though an exception can be made for DAL FORNO. It can age impressively for 10 years or longer. Best producers: Stefano Accordini★★, ALLEGRINI★★★, Bertani★★, Bolla★, Brunelli★, Cecilia Beretta (Pasqua)★, Corte Sant'Alda★, DAL FORNO★★★, Guerrieri-Rizzardi★, Lonardi★, MASI★, Mazzi★, QUINTARELLI★★★, Le Ragose★★, Le Salette★, Serègo Alighieri★, Speri★★, Tedeschi★, Tommasi★, Villa Spinosa★, Zenato★★, Fratelli Zeni★. Best years: 1997 95 **93 90 88 86 85 83 81**.

AMIGNE Swiss grape variety that is virtually limited to the region of Vétroz in the VALAIS. The wine has an earthy, nutty intensity and benefits from a few years' aging. Best producers: Jean-René Germanier, Granges Frères (Escalier de la Dame), Caves Imesch.

AMITY VINEYARDS *Willamette Valley AVA, Oregon, USA* Myron Redford was one of the pioneers in Oregon, opening his winery in 1976. The Gewürztraminer★★ is outstanding and the Riesling★★ is almost as good. The showpiece, of course, is the Pinot Noir, notably the Winemakers Reserve★★. Pinot Blanc★, Redford's current obsession, has replaced Chardonnay. Gamay Noir, loaded with berry fruit, remains fine value. Best years: (1998) **97 96**.

AMONTILLADO See Jerez y Manzanilla DO.

AMTLICHE PRÜFUNG See Prüfungsnummer.

ANBAUGEBIET German for 'growing region' and these names will appear on labels of all QbA and QmP wines. In unified Germany there are 13: Ahr, Mosel-Saar-Ruwer, Mittelrhein, Rheingau, Nahe, Rheinhessen, Pfalz, Hessische Bergstrasse, Franken, Württemberg, Baden, Saale-Unstrut and Sachsen.

ANDALUCÍA *Spain* Fortified wines, or wines naturally so strong in alcohol that they don't need fortifying, are the speciality of this southern stretch of Spain. Apart from sherry (JEREZ Y MANZANILLA DO), there are the lesser, sherry-like wines of Condado de Huelva DO and MONTILLA-MORILES DO, and the rich, sometimes treacly-sweet wines of MALAGA DO. These regions now also make some modern but bland dry whites; the best are from Condado de Huelva.

ANDREW WILL WINERY *Washington State, USA* Sourcing the finest grapes and striving for elegance in his wines, winemaker Chris Camarda is making what many critics believe to be the finest Washington Merlots – the Reserve★★ is remarkably tasty. His Cabernets and Sorella, a BORDEAUX blend, are not far behind. A dry Chenin, Cuvée Lulu, has also earned rave reviews. Best years: (reds) (1997) 96 **95 94** 92.

CH. ANGÉLUS★★★ *St-Émilion Grand Cru AC, 1er Grand Cru Classé, Bordeaux, France* One of the biggest and best-known St-Émilion Grands Crus with an energetic owner and talented winemaker. Increasingly gorgeous wines throughout the 80s, recognized by promotion to Premier Grand Cru Classé in 1996. Best years: (1998) 97 96 95 94 **93 92** 90 89 **88 86 85**.

CH. D'ANGLUDET★ *Margaux AC, Cru Bourgeois, Haut-Médoc, Bordeaux, France* This English-owned château makes one of my favourite wines. Always of Classed Growth standard, it has one of the best price–quality ratios in Bordeaux and ages superbly for a decade or more. Best years: (1998) 97 96 95 94 **93 90 89 88 86 85 83 82**.

ANGOVE'S *Riverland, South Australia* Family company making decent varietals, mainly from its Nanya vineyard, one of Australia's largest plantings. Low prices, kept that way by rock-bottom production costs. Chardonnay and Colombard are cheerful cheapies to quaff young.

ANJOU BLANC AC *Loire Valley, France* Ill-defined AC; ranges from bone dry to sweet, from excellent to dreadful. The best are dry and from individual producers. Up to 20% Chardonnay or Sauvignon can be added, but many of the leading producers prefer to use 100% Chenin. Best producers: M Angeli★, Bidet, Cady, C Daviau, Fesles★, Haute Perche, V Lebreton, Ogereau★, Pierre-Bise★, Jo Pithon★, J Renou, RICHOU★, Sauveroy, Soucherie★, Yves Soulez★. Best years: 1998 97 **96 95** 93.

ANJOU MOUSSEUX AC *Loire Valley, France* A rare AC for Anjou sparkling wines, with Chenin Blanc the principal grape. Most producers instead sell their wines as (more prestigious) CREMANT DE LOIRE.

ANJOU ROUGE AC *Loire Valley, France* Anjou is best known for ROSE D'ANJOU but reds (from Cabernets Sauvignon and Franc or Pineau d'Aunis) are increasingly successful. Usually fruity, easy-drinking wine, with less tannin than ANJOU-VILLAGES. Wines made from Gamay are sold as Anjou Gamay. Best producers: M Angeli, Baumard, C Daviau, Fesles, RICHOU★, Sauveroy, Yves Soulez, Touche Noire. Best years: **1998** 97 **96** 95.

ANJOU-VILLAGES AC *Loire Valley, France* As the Anjou AC is such a blanket term, taking in red, white, rosé and fizz of inconsistent quality, the better Anjou red producers asked for a separate AC. Since 1985, 46 villages have been entitled to the AC Anjou-Villages, only for red wine from Cabernet Franc and Cabernet Sauvignon. Some extremely attractive dry, fruity reds are emerging in the region, with better aging potential than ANJOU ROUGE. Best producers: Bidet, Closel★, C Daviau★, P Delesvaux★, Haute Perche★, Laffourcade★, J-Y Lebreton★, V Lebreton★, Ogereau★, Pierre-Bise★, Putille★, RICHOU (Vieilles Vignes★★), Tigné★, Touche Noire. Best years: **1998** 97 **96 95** 93 90 89.

ANSELMI *Soave DOC, Veneto, Italy* Roberto Anselmi, with PIEROPAN, has shown that much-maligned SOAVE can have personality when carefully made. Using ultra-modern methods he has honed the fruit flavours of his Soave Classico and Cru Capitel Foscarino★★ and introduced small-barrel-aging for single-vineyard Capitel Croce★★ and luscious, Sauternes-like Recioto dei Capitelli★★ (sometimes ★★★). Best years: **1995** 93 92 90 88.

ANTINORI *Tuscany, Italy* World-famous Florentine family firm that has been involved in wine since 1385, but it is Piero Antinori, the current head, who has made the Antinori name synonymous with quality and innovation. The quality of its CHIANTI CLASSICO wines like Badia a Passignano★, Pèppoli★, Villa Antinori★ and Tenute Marchese Riserva★★ is

consistently good, but it was its development of the SUPER-TUSCAN concept of superior wines outside the DOC that launched a quality revolution during the 1970s. Introducing small-barrel-aging to Tuscany for the first time, TIGNANELLO★★ (Sangiovese-Cabernet) and Solaia★★★ (Cabernet-based) can be great wines. Other interests include VINO NOBILE, La Braccesca★ and BOLGHERI's Tenute Belvedere (Cabernet-Merlot, Guado al Tasso★★). Ownership further afield includes PRUNOTTO in Piedmont and ATLAS PEAK in California and, most recently, a new development in BRUNELLO DI MONTALCINO. Best years: (reds) 1997 **96 95 94** 93 90 88. See also Castello della Sala.

APPELLATION D'ORIGINE CONTRÔLÉE See AC.

ARAGÓN *Spain* Most of Aragón, stretching from the Pyrenees south to Spain's central plateau, used to be responsible for much of the country's cheap red wine. There have been improvements, especially in the cooler, hilly, northern SOMONTANO DO, which is making some top-quality wines with international grapes. Further south, winemaking technology is improving in Campo de Borja DO, Calatayud DO and, particularly, CARINENA DO.

ARBOIS AC *Jura, France* The largest of the specific ACs in the Jura region. The whites are made from Chardonnay or the local Savagnin, which can give the wines a sherry-like flavour that is most concentrated in VIN JAUNE. There is also a rare, sweet VIN DE PAILLE. Good sparkling wine, now called CREMANT DE JURA, is made mainly from Chardonnay. Some of the best reds and sparklers come from the commune of Pupillon. Best producers: Arbois co-op, Ch. d'Arlay★, Aubin co-op, Aviet, Bourdy★, Désiré, H Maire★, la Pinte, J Puffeney★, Pupillin co-op★, Rolet★, A & M Tissot.

ARGIANO *Brunello di Montalcino DOCG, Tuscany, Italy* A mini-renaissance continues here: renewed investment and the hand of Giacomo Tachis can be seen in radically refashioned BRUNELLO★★ (Riserva★★★) that combines richness and accessibility. New is the scintillating Solengo★★★ (a blend of Cabernet, Merlot, Sangiovese and Syrah). Best years: 1997 96 95 94 **93 90**.

LEONCIO ARIZU *Mendoza, Argentina* Old winery with great potential in reds: solid Syrah★, a powerhouse Malbec★★ and Pinot Noir that swings from elegant to dull, depending on the vintage. There has been a tendency to keep some of the white wines too long before release. Best years: (reds) 1996 **95 94**.

ARNEIS White Italian grape grown in the ROERO hills in PIEDMONT. Arneis is DOC in Roero, producing dry white wines which, at best, have an attractively nutty, herbal perfume. They can be expensive. Best producers: Almondo★, Brovia★, Carretta★, CERETTO, Cascina Chicco★, Correggia★, Deltetto★ GIACOSA★, Malvirà★, Angelo Negro★, Castello di Neive★ (Barbaresco), PRUNOTTO★, Vietti★.

CH. L'ARROSÉE★★ *St-Émilion Grand Cru AC, Grand Cru Classé, Bordeaux, France* This small property, just south-west of the small historic town of St-Émilion, makes really exciting wine: rich, chewy and wonderfully luscious, with a comparatively high proportion (40%) of Cabernet Sauvignon. Drink after 5 years, but may be cellared for 10 or more. Best years: (1998) 97 96 95 94 **90 89 88 86 85 83 82**.

ARROWOOD VINEYARDS WINERY *Sonoma Valley AVA, California, USA* Dick Arrowood was the winemaker at CHATEAU ST JEAN during its glory years of Chardonnay. In 1988 he started his own winery. The wines have mostly been tip-top – beautifully balanced Cabernet★★, superb Merlot★★, lovely, velvety Chardonnay★★ and a crisp, lively Viognier★. Whites should be drunk young, reds with a little age. Best years: (reds) 1997 96 95 **94 93 92 91 90**; (whites) (1998) 97 96 **95 94 91**.

ISMAEL ARROYO *Ribera del Duero DO, Castilla y León, Spain* This family bodega has reached the pinnacle of Ribera del Duero producers in 15 years: long-lived, tannic wines, headed by Val Sotillo Reserva★★★, Gran Reserva★★★ and Crianza★★. Best years: (1996) **95 94 91 89**.

ARRUDA IPR *Estremadura, Portugal* A one-co-op region just north of Lisbon, but luckily that co-op at Arruda dos Vinhos is one of the best in the ESTREMADURA and makes a decent, inexpensive red.

ARVINE Swiss variety from the VALAIS in the communes of Vétroz and Martigny. The best grapes come from Fully and the Mont d'Or of Sion. Arvine has a bouquet of peach and apricot, and develops a spicy, honeyed character with age. Of Switzerland's indigenous grapes, Arvine gives the wines with the best aging potential. Best producers: Chappaz★, Caves Imesch★, Dom. du Mont d'Or★.

ASCHERI *Piedmont, Italy* Winemaker in Piedmont for at least 5 centuries. Ascheri's style is forward and appealingly drinkable, whether it be BAROLO (Vigna Farina★), Dolcetto d'Alba (especially Vigna Nirane★), or NEBBIOLO D'ALBA. A barrique-aged blend of Barbera and Nebbiolo called Bric Mileui★ and a new Freisa, Rocca d'Aucabech★, are particularly good. Best years: (Barolo) 1997 96 **95 93 90 89 88**.

ASSENOVGRAD *Southern Region, Bulgaria* Lush, plummy Cabernet Sauvignon and earthy, mineral-dusted Mavrud are both good from this predominantly red wine winery. The best Assenovgrad Mavrud ages well, but doesn't gain in complexity.

ASTI DOCG *Piedmont, Italy* Asti Spumante, the world's best-selling sweet sparkling wine, was long derided as light and cheap, though promotion to DOCG signalled an upturn in quality. Made in the province of Asti south-east of Turin, under the new appellation (which includes the rarer MOSCATO D'ASTI) the wine may be called simply Asti to avoid confusion with other sparkling wines. Its light sweetness and refreshing sparkle make it ideal with fruit, rich cakes and a wide range of sweet dishes. Drink young. Best producers: (Spumante) Bera★, Cinzano★, Giuseppe Contratto★★, Cascina Fonda★, FONTANAFREDDA, Gancia★ (Camillo Gancia★★), Martini & Rossi★, Cascina Pian d'Or★.

ATA RANGI *Wairarapa, North Island, New Zealand* Small, high-quality winery run by 2 families. Produces concentrated wines with style and individuality, including big, rich Chardonnay★★, seductively soft cherry/plum Pinot Noir★★★ and a Cabernet Sauvignon-Merlot-Syrah blend called Célèbre★★. Best years: (1998) **97 96 94 91 90 89**.

ATLAS PEAK *Atlas Peak AVA, Napa, California, USA* These hillside vineyards, now owned by ANTINORI of Italy, are demonstrating a new sense of direction after several years adrift. From 1990 onwards, the 100% Sangiovese has been improving, as has Consenso, a tasty Sangiovese-Cabernet blend. Each has an aging potential of 5–10 years. Chardonnay and Cabernet are recent additions. Best years: (reds) 1998 97 **96 95**.

AU BON CLIMAT *Santa Maria Valley AVA, California, USA* Pace-setting winery in this cool region, run by the talented Jim Clendenen, who spends much time in the best cellars in BURGUNDY and Italy's PIEDMONT. The result is lush Chardonnay★★, intense Pinot Noir★★ and BORDEAUX styles under the Vita Nova label. Watch out for Italian varietals (Barbera, Tocai, Teroldego) under Il Podere dell' Olivos label and Rhônes under Cold Heaven name. QUPE, a specialist in Rhône varieties, operates from the same winery. Best years: (reds) (1996) 95 94 **91 90 89 87 86**; (whites) (1998) 97 **95 92 90 87**.

AUCKLAND *North Island, New Zealand* Vineyards in the region of Auckland are centred around the small districts of Henderson, KUMEU/HUAPAI and Waimauku. Many of the better wines are made in the recently established districts of WAIHEKE ISLAND and Matakana. Best producers: COLLARDS★, Fenton★★, GOLDWATER★★, Heron's Flight, KUMEU RIVER★, Peninsula★, Providence, STONYRIDGE★★, Te Motu★.

L'AUDE, VIN DE PAYS DE *Languedoc, France* One of the largest VdPs in the region, mainly covering red wines. Quality is generally very ordinary: the best reds are soft, fruity, with a bit of southern spice. Best producers: Boyer, CLOS CENTEILLES, Gourgazaud, Lalande, Nicolas.

AUSBRUCH Both the German and Austrian wine laws rely on precise measurements of sugar content to classify wines in various quality categories. Ausbruch is the Austrian PRADIKAT category used for sweet wines with minimum residual sugar levels of 27 KMW (139 Oechsle), but top producers often sell wines picked at 32–35 KMW as Ausbruch. Traditionally, the wines are fermented to a higher alcohol and lower sugar content than BEERENAUSLESE or TROCKENBEERENAUSLESE. The result is usually closer to SAUTERNES than Germanic sweet styles, with less fruit flavour but richer texture. Best producers: FEILER-ARTINGER★★★, Martin Haider★★, Opitz★★, Schandl★★, Ernst Triebaumer★★, Paul Triebaumer★, Wenzel★★.

AUSLESE German and Austrian QmP category meaning that the grapes were 'selected' for their higher ripeness. A Riesling Auslese from the Mosel can have as little as 83 Oechsle, while most Baden Ausleses are sweeter and start at 105. The Austrian Auslese level is 21 KMW or 105 Oechsle.

CH. AUSONE★★★ *St-Émilion Grand Cru AC, 1er Grand Cru Classé, Bordeaux, France* This elegant property, situated on what are perhaps the best slopes in ST-EMILION, made a much-vaunted return to prominence in the 1980s, and is showing every sign of maintaining a high reputation. The resolution of single ownership in favour of the Vauthier family in 1997 should also inspire confidence. Best years: (1998) 97 96 95 94 93 90 **89 88 86 85 83 81 79 78**.

AUXEY-DURESSES AC *Côte de Beaune, Burgundy, France* Auxey-Duresses is a backwater village up in the hills behind MEURSAULT. The reds should be light and fresh but can often lack ripeness. At its best, and at 3–5 years, the white is dry, soft, nutty and hinting at the creaminess of a good Meursault, but at much lower prices. Of the Premiers Crus, Les Duresses is the most consistent. Best producers: (reds) J-P Diconne★, Jessiaume Père et Fils, Maison LEROY, Duc de Magenta★, M Prunier, P Prunier; (whites) R Ampeau★, J-P Diconne★, J-P Fichet★, Olivier LEFLAIVE★, Maison LEROY, Duc de Magenta★, M Prunier. Best years: (reds) 1997 96 95 **93 90 89 88**; (whites) 1997 96 **95 92 90**.

AVA (AMERICAN VITICULTURAL AREA) System of appellations of origin established for American wines in the 1970s.

L'AVENIR ESTATE *Stellenbosch WO, South Africa* In 7 short vintages owner Marc Wiehe and winemaker François Naude have gained local and international recognition for their wines. While Pinotage★ and Chenin Blanc are Naude's passion, all grapes receive careful attention. The entire range is imbued with stylish individuality, and Cabernet★ looks particularly promising. Best years: **1998 97 96 95 94**.

AVIGNONESI *Vino Nobile di Montepulciano DOCG, Tuscany, Italy* The Falvo brothers of Avignonesi led Montepulciano's revival as one of Tuscany's best zones. Although VINO NOBILE★★ is often the best of the dry wines, the varietals, which include Chardonnay (Il Marzocco★), Sauvignon (Il Vignola★) and Merlot (Toro Desiderio★★), have received more attention. Also famous is the SUPER-TUSCAN Grifi★★ (Sangiovese-Cabernet) and sweet red Aleatico. The VIN SANTO★★★ is the most sought after in Tuscany, and a rare red version from Sangiovese, Occhio di Pernice★★★, is beyond compare. Best years: (premium reds) 1997 96 **95 94 93 90 88 85**.

AYL *Saar, Germany* A top Saar village. The best-known vineyard in Ayl is Kupp, which produces classy, slaty wines on its steep slopes. Best producers: Bischöflicher Konvikt, Peter Lauer, Heinz Wagner. Best years: 1997 **95 94 93 90**.

AZIENDA AGRICOLA Italian for 'estate' or 'farm'. It also indicates wine made from grapes grown by the proprietor.

BABICH *Henderson, North Island, New Zealand* Family-run winery specializing in quality wines. Irongate Chardonnay★★ is an intense, steely wine that needs plenty of cellaring, while intense, strongly varietal reds under the Mara Estate label, including Merlot★★, Syrah★★ and Cabernet Sauvignon★, show even greater potential for development. The newly released Patriarch label now offers the company's top-of-the-line Chardonnay★★ and Cabernet-Merlot★★, both from HAWKES BAY. Best years: (Hawkes Bay) (1998) **97 96 94 91 90 89**.

BACALHÔA, QUINTA DA *Terras do Sado, Portugal* Estate near Azeitão growing Cabernet Sauvignon and Merlot grapes. These are made into rich, oaky, long-lived wine★ at J P VINHOS. Best years: 1996 95 **94 92 91**.

BACKSBERG ESTATE *Paarl WO, South Africa* New partnerships at this family-owned winery have inaugurated two 1998 Sauvignon Blancs. One is the product of worker empowerment; the other, Simonye (Zulu for 'We are one'), results from the private joint venture between the Backs and SIMI's Zelma Long and her viticulturalist husband, Phil Freese. Freese also consults here; his input has benefited reds especially. Klein Babylonstoren★, Cabernet Sauvignon★ and Merlot show denser fruit, more supple tannins. Chardonnay, from old vines, is the top white. The speciality, Sydney Back Estate Brandy★, continues to impress. Best years: (Chardonnay) **1997 96 95 94 93 92**.

BAD DÜRKHEIM *Pfalz, Germany* This spa town may not be as famous as its neighbours but it has some good vineyards and is the headquarters of the dependable Vier Jahreszeiten Kloster Limburg co-op. Best producers: Kurt DARTING★, Fitz-Ritter, Karl Schaefer★. Best years: (whites) **1997 96 93 92**.

BAD KREUZNACH *Nahe, Germany* Spa town with 22 individual vineyard sites, the best wines coming from the steepest sites such as Brückes, Kahlenberg and Krötenpfuhl. Not to be confused with the NAHE district of Bereich Kreuznach. Best producers: Paul Anheuser, Anton Finkenauer, Reichsgraf von Plettenberg. Best years: (whites) **1997 93 90**.

BADEN *Germany* Very large wine region stretching from FRANKEN to the Bodensee. Recently took the lead in making dry whites and reds which show off the fuller, softer flavours Germany is capable of producing in the warmer climate of its southerly regions. Many of the best non-Riesling German wines of the future will come from Baden, as well as many of the best barrel-fermented and barrel-aged wines. Good co-operative cellars at Achkarren, Steinbach, Durbach, Bickensohl, Bötzingen and Königsschaffhausen.

BAGA Important red grape in BAIRRADA, which is one of the few regions in Portugal to rely mainly on one variety. Also planted in much smaller quantities in DAO and the RIBATEJO.

BAILEY'S *North-East Victoria, Australia* Old, traditional winery at Glenrowan, where Australia's most famous bush bandit, Ned Kelly, made his last stand. Now owned by Fosters but still making hearty, thickly textured reds from Shiraz (1920s Block Shiraz is ★★) as well as some of Australia's most luscious fortified Muscat and Tokay (Winemakers Selection★★★) – heavenly and irresistible stickies.

BAIRRADA DOC *Beira Litoral, Portugal* Bairrada has for ages been the source of many of Portugal's best red table wines. These can brim over with intense raspberry and blackberry fruit, though the tannin levels may take a few years to soften. The whites are coming on fast with modern vinification methods. Best producers: (reds) Caves ALIANCA, Quinta das Bágeiras★, Quinta do Carvalhinho★, Gonçalves Faria★★, Luis PATO★★, Caves Primavera (Garrafeira★), Quinta da Rigodeira★, Casa de Saima★, Caves SAO JOAO★★, SOGRAPE; (whites) Quinta da Rigodeira★, Casa de Saima★, SOGRAPE (Reserva★, Quinta de Pedralvites★), Quinta do Voldeiro★★. Best years: (reds) 1997 96 **95 94 92 91 90**.

CH. BALESTARD-LA-TONNELLE★ *St-Émilion Grand Cru AC, Grand Cru Classé, Bordeaux, France* This is a popular ST-EMILION property, making reliable wine, full of strong, chewy fruit. It is decently priced too. Best years: (1998) 96 95 94 **90 89 88 86 85**.

BANDOL AC *Provence, France* Bandol, a lovely fishing port with vineyards high above the Mediterranean, produces some of the best reds and rosés in Provence. The Mourvèdre grape gives Bandol its character – gentle raisin and honey softness with a Provençale herby fragrance. The reds happily age for 10 years, sometimes more, but can be very good at 3–4. The rosés, delicious and spicy but often too pricy, should be drunk young. There is a small amount of white, most of it rather neutral and sold at horrendous prices. Drink as young as possible. Best producers: (reds) Bastide Blanche, Bunan★, Cagueloup, Frégate★, le Gallantin★, l'Hermitage★, Lafran-Veyrolles★, Mas Reclonne★, Pibarnon★★, Pradeaux★★, Ray-Jane★★, Romassan★, Ste-Anne★, TEMPIER★★, la Tour de Bon★, Vannières★. Best years: (1998) 97 96 **95 93 90 89 88 86 85**.

BANFI *Brunello di Montalcino DOCG, Tuscany, Italy* American-owned firm which is now a force in Italian production, with wines of fine quality produced in a high-tech winery, with the aid of noted winemaker Ezio Rivella. Premium wines Brunello★, Chardonnay (Fontanelle★), Cabernet (Tavernelle★★) and Merlot (Mandrielle★★) are very successful, but even better are Brunello Riserva Poggio all'Oro★★ and SUPER-TUSCANS Summus★★ (a blend of Sangiovese, Cabernet and Syrah) and Excelsus★★(Cabernet-Merlot). Also has cellars in PIEDMONT for GAVI and fizz. Best years: (premium reds) 1997 96 **95 94 93 90**.

BANNOCKBURN *Geelong, Victoria, Australia* The experience gleaned from vintage stints at Burgundy's Domaine DUJAC is reflected in Gary Farr's powerful, gamy Pinot Noir★★ and MEURSAULT-like Chardonnay★★★, which are among Australia's best wines. Much-improved Shiraz★ is influenced by Rhône's Alain GRAILLOT. Note that there was no estate-grown wine in 1998 due to a freak hailstorm. Best years: (Chardonnay) **1996** 95 **94** 92 89 88.

BANYULS AC *Roussillon, France* One of the best VIN DOUX NATURELS. Made mainly from Grenache Noir, the strong plum and raisin flavour tastes good in a young, sweet version and the older tawny styles are even better. The wine is generally served as an apéritif in France and deserves a wider audience. Try sampling it mid-afternoon with some macaroons or plain cake. Definitely more exciting than the classic English teatime. Best producers: Casa Blanca, Cellier des Templiers★, Clos des Paulilles★★, l'Étoile★, Mas Blanc★★, la RECTORIE★★, la Tour Vieille★, Vial Magnères.

BARBADILLO *Jerez y Manzanilla DO, Andalucía, Spain* Antonio Barbadillo, the largest sherry company in the coastal town of Sanlúcar de Barrameda, makes a wide range of good to excellent wines, in particular salty, dry manzanilla styles, particularly the Solear★★★ and Principe★★★, and intense, nutty, but dry amontillados and olorosos, led by Oloroso del Tio Río★★. It also produces a neutral-flavoured dry white wine, Castillo de San Diego, which is a best seller in Spain.

BARBARESCO DOCG *Piedmont, Italy* This prestigious red wine, grown near Alba in the LANGHE hills south-east of Turin, is often twinned with its neighbour BAROLO to demonstrate the nobility of the Nebbiolo grape. Barbaresco can be a shade softer and less powerful, due to the slightly warmer climate in its lower altitude position adjacent to the Tanaro river. The wine usually takes less time to mature and is often considered the most approachable of the two, as exemplified by the internationally followed style of GAJA. But, as in Barolo, traditionalists also excel, led by Bruno GIACOSA. The zone covers 475ha (1174 acres) of vineyards in the communes of Barbaresco, Neive and Treiso. Even though the area is relatively compact, wine styles can differ significantly between vineyards and producers. Best vineyards: Asili, Bricco di Neive, Costa Russi, Crichet Pajè, Gallina, Marcorino, Martinenga, Messoirano, Moccagatta, Montestefano, Ovello, Pora, Rabajà, Rio Sordo, San Lorenzo, Santo Stefano, Serraboella, Sorì Paitin, Sorì Tildin. Best producers: Barbaresco co-op★★, CERETTO★★, Cigliuti★★, Cortese, GAJA★★★, GIACOSA★★★, Cantina del Glicine★, Marchesi di Gresy★★, Luigi Minuto★, Moccagatta★, Castello di Neive★★, I Paglieri★★, Paitin★★, Parocco di Neive★, Pelissero★, Pio Cesare★, Punset, Albino Rocca★★, Bruno Rocca★★, La Spinetta★★, Vietti★. Best years: 1998 97 96 95 93 **90 89 88 86 85 82**.

BARBERA A native of north-west Italy, Barbera vies with Sangiovese as the most widely planted red grape in the country. When grown for high yields its natural acidity shows through, producing vibrant quaffers. Low yields from the top PIEDMONT estates create intensely rich and complex wines. When small oak barrels are used the results can be stunning.

BARBERA D'ALBA DOC *Piedmont, Italy* Some of the most outstanding Barbera comes from this appellation. Many producers of BAROLO and BARBARESCO have, in addition to Nebbiolo, planted Barbera. The most modern examples are supple and generous and can be drunk almost at once. More intense, dark-fruited versions require a minimum 3 years' age, but might improve for as much as 8. Best producers: ALTARE★, Azelia★, Boglietti★, Brovia★, Cigliuti★, CLERICO★, Elvio Cogno★★, Aldo

CONTERNO★★, Giacomo CONTERNO★★, Conterno-Fantino★, Corino★★, Correggia★★, Elio Grasso★, Silvio Grasso★, Giuseppe MASCARELLO★, Moccagatta★, Monfalletto-Cordero di Montezemolo★★, Oberto★★, Parusso★, Pelissero★, PRUNOTTO★★, Albino Rocca★, Bruno Rocca★, SANDRONE★, P Scavino★★, Aldo e Riccardo Seghesio★, Vajra★★, Mauro Veglio★★, Giovanni Viberti★, Vietti★★, Giovanni Voerzio★. Best years: (1998) 97 **96 95 93 91 90 89**.

BARBERA D'ASTI DOC *Piedmont, Italy* While Dolcetto d'Asti is usually light and simple, wines made from Barbera show a greater range of quality. Unoaked and barrique-aged examples can compete with the best BARBERA D'ALBA and rival some of the better Nebbiolo-based reds. Best examples can be kept for 5–6 years, occasionally longer. Best producers: La Barbatella★★, Pietro Barbero★★, Bava★, Bertelli★★, Braida★★, Bricco Mondalino★, Cascina Castlèt★, Giuseppe Contratto★, Coppo★, Il Mongetto★★, Martinetti★★, Scarpa★★, F & M Scrimaglio★, La Spinetta★. Best years: (1998) 97 **96 95 93 91 90 89**.

BARCA VELHA★★★ *Douro DOC, Portugal* Portugal's most sought-after red table wine, made by FERREIRA, modelled on fine red BORDEAUX, but using DOURO grape varieties (mainly Tinta Roriz). It is made only in the very finest years – just 12 vintages since 1953, the most recent being 1991. Marginally less good years are sold as Reserva Especial. Best years: (Barca Velha) 1991 **85 83 82 81 78**; (Reserva Especial) 1990 **86 80**.

BARDOLINO DOC *Veneto, Italy* Substantial zone centred on Lake Garda, giving, at best, light, scented red and rosé (CHIARETTO) wines to be drunk young, from the same grape mix as neighbouring VALPOLICELLA. Best producers: Cavalchina★★, Colle dei Cipressi★, Corte Gardoni★, Girasole, Guerrieri-Rizzardi★, MASI★, Le Vigne di San Pietro★, Fratelli Zeni★.

BAROLO DOCG *Piedmont, Italy* Renowned red wine, named after a village south-west of Alba, from the Nebbiolo grape grown in 1175ha (2900 acres) of vineyards in the steep LANGHE hills. Its status as 'king of wines and wine of kings' for a time proved to be more of a burden than a benefit among Italians, who considered its austere power too much for modern palates, with tough, chewy tannins which took years of cask-aging to soften. But for over a decade, many winemakers have applied new methods to make fresher, cleaner wines of greater colour, richer fruit and softer tannins without sacrificing Barolo's noble character. Distinct styles of wine are made in the zone's villages. Barolo and La Morra make the most perfumed wines; Monforte and Serralunga the most structured; Castiglione Falletto strikes a balance between the two. Barolo is nowadays frequently labelled by vineyards, though it is worth remembering that the producer's reputation often carries more weight. Best vineyards: Bricco Boschis, Bricco delle Viole, Brunate, Bussia Soprana, Cannubi, Cerequio, Fiasco, Ginestra, Marcenasco, Monfalleto, Monprivato, Pianpolvere Soprano, Rocche di Castiglione, Rocche di La Morra, Santo Stefano di Perno, La Serra, Vigna Rionda, Villero. Best producers: ALTARE★★, Azelia★★, Batasiolo★, Boglietti★★, Bongiovanni★★, Brovia★★, CERETTO★★, Chiarlo★, CLERICO★★, Aldo CONTERNO★★★, Giacomo CONTERNO★★, Conterno-Fantino★★, Corino★★, R Fenocchio★★, GAJA★★★, E Germano★, GIACOSA★★, Elio Grasso★★, Silvio Grasso★, Marcarini★, Bartolo MASCARELLO★★★, Giuseppe MASCARELLO★★★, Parusso★, Pio Cesare★, F Principiano★★, PRUNOTTO★★, RATTI★★, Rocche dei Manzoni★★, SANDRONE★★★, P Scavino★★, A & R Seghesio★★, Vajra★, M Veglio★★, Vietti★★, G Viberti★, Roberto VOERZIO★★. Best years: 1998 97 96 95 **93 90 89 88 86 85 82**.

BARÓN DE LEY *Rioja DOC, Navarra, Spain* Barón de Ley Reserva and El Mesón Crianza are red RIOJAS made only from grapes grown on the estate, including some 'experimental' Cabernet Sauvignon. Best years: 1996 95 **94 91 87**.

BAROSSA VALLEY *South Australia* Headquarters to such giants as PENFOLDS, SEPPELT, ORLANDO and YALUMBA, this region, noted for port-style wines, Shiraz and Riesling, has less than 10% of the nation's vineyards yet makes 60% of the wine, largely from grapes grown elsewhere in South Australia. A new lease of life for Barossa Valley grapes has come from lively, creative winemakers at Grant BURGE★, Peter LEHMANN★★, Charles Melton★★, ROCKFORD★ and ST HALLETT★★.

JIM BARRY *Clare Valley, South Australia* Initially very much a white wine outfit, with the famous Florita vineyard as the source for perfumed, classy Rieslings★. Now creating bigger waves with reds: a much-improved Cabernet Sauvignon★ and the heady, palate-busting (wallet-busting, too) Armagh Shiraz★★★. Best years: (Armagh Shiraz) 1995 **93 92 90**.

BARSAC AC *Bordeaux, France* Barsac, largest of the 5 communes in the SAUTERNES AC and producing fine sweet wines to similar high standards, also has its own AC, which is used by most of the top properties. In general, the wines are a little less luscious than other Sauternes, but from good estates they can be marvellous. Best producers: (Classed Growths) CLIMENS★★★, COUTET★★, DOISY-DAENE★★, Doisy-Dubroca★, DOISY-VEDRINES★★, Myrat, NAIRAC★★; (others) Liot★, Ménota, Piada. Best years: (1998) 97 96 95 **90 89 88 86 83 81 80 76 75**.

BASSERMANN-JORDAN *Deidesheim, Pfalz, Germany* Since the arrival of winemaker Ulrich Mell with the 1996 vintage, this famous estate has resumed making the rich yet elegant Rieslings which long made its name synonymous with great Deidesheim and FORST wines. Best years: (1998) **97** 96 **90 89 88 86 81 79 76 71**.

CH. BASTOR-LAMONTAGNE★ *Sauternes AC, Cru Bourgeois, Bordeaux, France* Year after year this estate produces luscious, honeyed wine at a price which allows us to enjoy high-class SAUTERNES without taking out a second mortgage. Best years: (1998) 97 96 95 **94 90 89 88 86 85 83 82**.

CH. BATAILLEY★ *Pauillac AC, 5ème Cru Classé, Haut-Médoc, Bordeaux, France* A byword for value for money and reliability among the

Pauillac Classed Growth estates. Marked by a full, obvious blackcurrant fruit, not too much tannin and a luscious overlay of creamy vanilla. Lovely to drink at only 5 years old, the wine continues to age well for up to 15 years. Best years: (1998) (97) 96 95 94 93 **90 89 88 86 85 83 82**.

BÂTARD-MONTRACHET AC *Grand Cru, Côte de Beaune, Burgundy, France* This Grand Cru produces some of the world's greatest whites – they are full, rich and balanced, with a powerful, minerally intensity of fruit and fresh acidity. There are 2 associated Grands Crus: BIENVENUES-BATARD-MONTRACHET and the minuscule Criots-Bâtard-Montrachet. All can age for a decade or more. Best producers: J-N GAGNARD★★, GAGNARD-DELAGRANGE★★, JADOT★★, LATOUR★★, Dom. LEFLAIVE★★★, Olivier LEFLAIVE★★, Pierre Morey★, RAMONET★★, SAUZET★★★, VERGET★★. Best years: 1997 96 95 **92 90 89 88 86 85**.

DOM. DE LA BAUME *Vin de Pays d'Oc, Languedoc, France* The French outpost of BRL HARDY, chiefly making varietal wines. The operation was set up in 1989, when the estate's winemaking equipment was completely renewed with stainless steel and a refrigeration unit replaced concrete. The winery now makes 7 wines. Chardonnay, Sauvignon Blanc, Merlot, Cabernet Sauvignon and Shiraz are sold under the La Baume label, and include contract fruit; there are also 2 premium wines, a Merlot and a Chardonnay-Viognier blend, under the Domaine de la Baume label. For the latter wines, the grapes come exclusively from the surrounding 40-ha (100-acre) estate. The Chai Baumière and Philippe de Baudin labels have now been discontinued after disappointing quality levels being achieved.

LES BAUX-DE-PROVENCE AC *Provence, France* This AC has proved that organic farming can produce spectacular results mainly due to the warm dry climate. Good fruit and inspirational winemaking produce some of the best reds in the south of France. From 1994, TREVALLON is VdP des BOUCHES-DU-RHONE. Best producers: Mas de la Dame★, Mas de Gourgonnier★, Mas Ste Berthe★, Terres Blanches★, TREVALLON★★★. Best years: (1998) **97 96 95 94 93 91 90 89**.

BÉARN AC *South-West France* While the rest of South-West France has been busy producing some unusual and original flavours in recent years, Béarn hasn't managed to cash in. The wines (90% red and rosé) just aren't special enough, despite some decent grape varieties. Best producers: Bellocq co-op, Cauhapé, Clos Lapeyre, Nigri.

CH. DE BEAUCASTEL *Châteauneuf-du-Pape AC, Rhône Valley, France* François Perrin makes some of the richest, most tannic reds★★★ in Châteauneuf-du-Pape, with an unusually high percentage of Mourvèdre and Syrah, which can take at least a decade to show at their best. The white Vieilles Vignes★★★, made almost entirely from Roussanne, is exquisite, too. Best years: (reds) (1998) 97 96 95 94 **93 90 89 88 86 85 83 82 81**; (whites) 1996 95 **94 93 92 90 89 88**. See also la Vieille Ferme.

BEAUJOLAIS AC *Beaujolais, Burgundy, France* Famous red wine from a large area of rolling hills and valleys in southern Burgundy. Much Beaujolais nowadays appears as BEAUJOLAIS NOUVEAU or Beaujolais Primeur, but Beaujolais AC is the basic appellation. In the north, toward Mâcon, most of the reds qualify either as BEAUJOLAIS-VILLAGES or as a single Cru (10 villages which produce better but more expensive wine: BROUILLY, CHENAS, CHIROUBLES, COTE DE BROUILLY, FLEURIE, JULIENAS,

MORGON, MOULIN-A-VENT, REGNIE, ST-AMOUR). In the south, toward Lyon, most of the wine is simple AC Beaujolais, a light red to be drunk within months of the vintage, which should be lovely and fresh but is now too often dilute. Beaujolais Supérieur means wine with a minimum strength of 1% more alcohol than simple Beaujolais. A tiny amount of white is made from Chardonnay. The EVENTAIL DE VIGNERONS PRODUCTEURS is a high-profile marketing group. Best producers: (reds) Bernardin, Michel Carron, Charmet, la Plume, DUBOEUF, H Fessy, Fortières, P Germain, Jambon, Labruyère, Terres Dorées, Texier; (whites) Charmet, Dalissieux, DUBOEUF. Best years: 1998 97 **96**.

BEAUJOLAIS NOUVEAU *Beaujolais AC, Burgundy, France* This is the first release of bouncy, fruity Beaujolais on the third Thursday of November after the harvest. Once a simple celebration of the new vintage, then a much-hyped beano, now increasingly *passé*. Quality is generally reasonably good since much of the best BEAUJOLAIS AC is used for Nouveau. The wine usually improves by Christmas and the New Year, and the best ones are perfect for summer picnics. Best producers: CELLIER DES SAMSONS, la Chevalière, DROUHIN, DUBOEUF, Ferraud, Gauthier, JAFFELIN, Loron, Sapin, Sarrau.

BEAUJOLAIS-VILLAGES AC *Beaujolais, Burgundy, France* Beaujolais-Villages can come from any one of over 40 villages in the north of the region. Carefully made, it can represent all the excitement of the Gamay grape at its best. Best villages: Beaujeu, Lancié, Lantignié, Leynes, Quincié, St-Étienne-des-Ouillières, St-Jean-d'Ardières. Best producers: Aucoeur★, Bel-Air, G Descombes★, DUBOEUF, B Faure, Jaffre, Large, Loron, Miolane★, Dom. Perrier★, Pivot★, J-L Tissier, Verger. Best years: **1997 96** 95.

BEAULIEU VINEYARD *Napa Valley AVA, California, USA* The late André Tchelistcheff had a major role in creating this icon for Napa Cabernet Sauvignon as winemaker in the late 1930s, 40s and 50s. After he left, Beaulieu missed a few beats and lived on its reputation for too long, even though Tchelistcheff continued to consult. However, recent bottlings of the Private Reserve Cabernet Sauvignon★★ signal a return to top form. A meritage red called Tapestry is also promising. Recent bottlings of Chardonnay★ from CARNEROS have been a pleasant surprise. Best years: (Private Reserve) 1995 94 92 91 90 **85 78 70 68**.

BEAUMES-DE-VENISE *Rhône Valley, France* Area famous for its sweet wine: MUSCAT DE BEAUMES-DE-VENISE, France's best-known VIN DOUX NATUREL. The local red wine is also very good, one of the meatier COTES DU RHONE-VILLAGES, with a ripe, plummy fruit in warm years. Best producers: (reds) Bernardins, les Goubert, local co-op.

BEAUNE AC *Côte de Beaune, Burgundy, France* Beaune gives its name to the southern section of the COTE D'OR, the COTE DE BEAUNE. Almost all the wines are red, with delicious, soft red-fruits ripeness. There are no Grands Crus but some excellent Premiers Crus (Boucherottes, Bressandes, Clos des Mouches, Fèves, Grèves, Marconnets, Teurons, Vignes Franches). There's a small amount of white – DROUHIN make an outstandingly good creamy, nutty Clos des Mouches★★. Best producers:

Beaune les Teurons

APPELLATION BEAUNE 1ER CRU CONTROLÉE

DOMAINE JACQUES GERMAIN
PROPRIÉTAIRE AU CHATEAU DE CHOREY-LES-BEAUNE COTE-D'OR 75 d
MISE EN BOUTEILLES AU CHATEAU

(growers) Besancenot-Mathouillet★, GERMAIN★★, LAFARGE★★, Albert Morot★★, André Mussy★, TOLLOT-BEAUT★★; (merchants) Champy★, Chanson Père et Fils★, DROUHIN★★, JADOT★★, Camille Giroud★, JAFFELIN★, LABOURE-ROI★, Thomas-Moillard. Best years: (reds) 1997 96 95 93 **90 89 88 85**; (whites) 1997 96 **95 93 92 90 89**.

CH. BEAU-SÉJOUR BÉCOT★★ *St-Émilion Grand Cru AC, 1er Grand Cru Classé, Bordeaux, France* Demoted from Premier Grand Cru Classé in 1986 and promoted again in 1996, this estate is now back on top form. Brothers Gérard and Dominique Bécot produce firm, ripe, richly textured wines that need at least 8–10 years to develop. Best years: (1998) 97 96 95 94 **90 89 88 86 85 83**.

BEAUX FRÈRES *Willamette Valley AVA, Oregon, USA* A new venture that has already generated much interest due to the participation of wine critic Robert Parker. Grapes are sourced from his brother-in-law's vineyards (hence the name), while the winemaking philosophy is likely to be French. Inspired, perhaps, by Burgundian superstar Henri JAYER, the intention seems to be to make ripe, unfiltered Pinot Noir★★ that expresses the essence of the grape and vineyard. Its immediate success has attracted a cult following. Best years: (1997) 96 95 **94 93 92 91**.

GRAHAM BECK WINERY *Robertson WO, South Africa* This professionally run winery made its name with Cap Classique sparkling, an elegantly rich NV Brut from Pinot Noir and Chardonnay, and a barrel-fermented BLANC DE BLANCS★, toastily fragrant and creamy. Now cellarmaster Pieter Ferreira is determined to prove this predominantly white wine region can produce premium reds too. Early examples of Merlot and Shiraz are encouraging. The flavourful, balanced Lonehill Chardonnay carries the white wine flag.

BEERENAUSLESE German and Austrian Prädikat category applied to wines made from 'individually selected' grapes, which, since the grapes are always overripe and sugar-packed, give wines that have a rich, luscious dessert quality to them. The berries are often affected by noble rot (*Edelfäule* in German). Beerenauslese wines are only produced in the best years in Germany, but in Austria they are a pretty regular occurrence. They start at 110 Oechsle in the MOSEL rising to 128 Oechsle in southern BADEN. Austrian Beerenauslese wines start at 25 KMW or 127 Oechsle.

CH. BELAIR★ *St-Émilion Grand Cru AC, 1er Grand Cru Classé, Bordeaux, France* Belair is located on the limestone plateau next to AUSONE. Under the direction of winemaker Pascal Delbeck the wines have regained their form in recent years. Best years: (1998) 97 96 95 94 **90 89 88 86 85 83 82**.

BELLAVISTA *Franciacorta DOCG, Lombardy, Italy* Winemaker Mattia Vezzola specializes in Franciacorta sparkling wines with a very good Cuvée Brut★★ and 4 distinctive Gran Cuvées★★ (including an excellent rosé). Riserva Vittorio Moretti Extra Brut★★ is made in exceptional years. Also produces still wines, including white Convento dell'Annunciata★★ and red Casotte★ (Pinot Nero) and Solesine★★ (Cabernet-Merlot).

BELLET AC *Provence, France* A tiny AC of usually overpriced wine because of the local tourist market, mostly white, in the hills behind

Nice. Ch. de Crémat and Ch. de Bellet are the most important producers and their wines are worth seeking out.

BENDIGO *Victoria, Australia* Warm, dry, former gold-mining region, which produced some decent wines in the 19th century, then faded away completely. It was triumphantly resurrected by Stuart Anderson, who planted Balgownie in 1969, and other wineries followed (including Chateau Leamon, Water Wheel, Heathcote, Jasper Hill, Passing Clouds and YELLOWGLEN). The best wines are full-bodied Shiraz and Cabernet.

BENZIGER FAMILY WINERY *Sonoma Valley AVA, California, USA* The Benziger family first made its mark with Glen Ellen, a popular brand which grew exponentially until being sold in 1993. That sale allowed the Benzigers to refocus on varietals from their SONOMA VALLEY estate vineyard and from other SONOMA COUNTY areas. Merlot★ and Zinfandel★ are consistently good, but quality is on the rise with CARNEROS Chardonnay★ and Tribute★, meritage blends. Imagery Series wines are often of high quality. Best years: (reds) 1997 95 94 **92 91**.

BERBERANA *Rioja DOC, Rioja, Spain* A dynamic new boss has transformed one of RIOJA's largest companies. Berberana has bought Lagunilla and formed a partnership with MARQUES DE GRINON, and is making lightly oaked Dragon label Berberana red★ and respectable Reservas and Gran Reservas. Best years: (reds) 1996 95 94 **90 89 88**.

BERCHER *Burkheim, Baden, Germany* The Bercher brothers run the top estate of the KAISERSTUHL. The high points are the powerful new oak-aged Spätburgunder reds★ and Weissburgunder and Grauburgunder★★ dry whites, which marry richness with perfect balance. Drink young or cellar for 3–5 years or more. Best years: (1998) 97 **96 94 93 92 90**.

BEREICH German for region or district within a wine region or Anbaugebiet. Bereichs tend to be large, and the use of a Bereich name, such as Bereich BINGEN, without qualification is seldom an indication of quality – in most cases, quite the reverse.

BERGERAC AC *South-West France* Bergerac is the main town of the Dordogne and the overall AC for this underrated area on the eastern edge of Bordeaux. The grape varieties are mostly the same as those used in the BORDEAUX ACs. The red is generally like a light, fresh claret, a bit grassy but with a good, raw blackcurrant fruit and hint of earth. In general drink young although a few aged reds can age for at least 3–5 years. The whites are generally lean and dry for quick drinking. Best producers: (reds) le Barradis, Court-les-Mûts, Gouyat, la JAUBERTIE, Lestignac, Miaudoux, Panisseau, Priorat, la Rayre, Tour des Gendres, Tourmentine. Best years: (reds) 1996 **95 93 90 89 88**.

BERGKELDER *Stellenbosch, South Africa* Wholesaler buying in wine and grapes from contract growers in different regions. Own label, top-of-the-range Stellenryck Cabernet, good-value Fleur-du-Cap Merlot, Cabernet and Shiraz are particularly noteworthy. Well-crafted Cap Classique bubblies include ripe, yeasty Pongracz NV★. Under new SA Wine Cellars umbrella, also provides aging and marketing facilities for 12 estates; MEERLUST★★, La Motte★ and wholly owned Le Bonheur are the best. Best years: (Stellenryck, Fleur-du-Cap reds) **1996** 95 94 93 92 91 90.

BERINGER VINEYARDS *Napa Valley AVA, California, USA* Beringer produces a full range of wine but, in particular, offers a spectacular range of top-class Cabernet Sauvignons. The Private Reserve

Cabernet★★★ is one of NAPA VALLEY's finest yet most approachable; the Lemmon Ranch★★ and Chabot Vineyards★★, when released under their own label, are only slightly less impressive. Beringer makes red and white Alluvium (meritage wines) from Knight's Valley and the red earns high marks. The Reserve Chardonnay★★ is a powerful wine that should age well. HOWELL MOUNTAIN Merlot★★ from Bancroft Vineyard is also good. Best years: (Cabernet Sauvignon) (1996) 95 94 93 **92 91 90 87 86 85 84 81**.

BERNKASTEL *Mosel, Germany* Both a town in the Middle Mosel and the name of a large BEREICH. Top wines, however, will come only from vineyard sites within the town – the most famous of these is the overpriced DOCTOR vineyard. Many wines from the Graben and Lay sites are as good or better and cost a fraction of the price. Best producers: Hansen-Lauer★, Dr LOOSEN★, J J PRUM★★, J WEGELER ERBEN★★.

BERRI RENMANO *Riverland, South Australia* Twin Riverland co-ops which can crush up to 15% of Australia's total grape harvest. Purchased the famous HARDY wine company in 1992. They produce largely bag-in-box wines, but top label Renmano Chairman's Selection is good for buxom Chardonnay★.

BEST'S *Grampians, Victoria, Australia* Small winery run by Viv Thomson, who makes attractive wines from estate vineyards first planted in 1868. Delicious, clear-fruited Shiraz★★ and Cabernet★ are good, and the Riesling shows flashes of brilliance. Tropical-fruity, finely balanced Chardonnay★ is variable, delicious at best; Thomson Reserve is new super-Shiraz label. Best years: (reds) 1996 95 94 **92 91 90 88 87 84 80 76**.

CH. BEYCHEVELLE★ *St-Julien AC, 4ème Cru Classé, Haut-Médoc, Bordeaux, France* Although ranked as a 4th Growth, this beautiful château traditionally made wine of 2nd Growth quality. The wine has a charming softness even when young, but takes at least a decade to mature into the cedarwood and blackcurrant flavour for which ST-JULIEN is famous. Recent vintages have been good but sometimes the price can look too high. Second wine: Réserve de l'Amiral. Best years: (1998) 97 96 95 94 90 **89** 86 **85 83 82**.

BEYERSKLOOF *Stellenbosch WO, South Africa* Red wine maestro Beyers Truter concentrates on only 2 varieties at this property he owns in partnership with the Krige brothers of KANONKOP. The striking yet soft Cabernet★★ is an international award winner. Truter's favourite Pinotage★ has bountiful ripe juiciness; quaffable when young, recent vintages show more aging ability. Grapes are mainly bought in, but 1998 saw the first crop from this small winery's own vineyards.

BIANCO DI CUSTOZA DOC *Veneto, Italy* Dry white from an area overlapping the southern part of BARDOLINO. Similar to neighbouring SOAVE, but the addition of up to 30% Tocai Friulano can give extra breadth and richness. Drink young. Best producers: Arvedi d'Emilei, Cavalchina★, Corte Gardoni, Gorgo★, Lamberti, Le Vigne di San Pietro★.

BIENVENUES-BÂTARD-MONTRACHET AC See Bâtard-Montrachet.

BIERZO DO *Castilla y León, Spain* Sandwiched between the rainy mountains of GALICIA and the arid plains of CASTILLA Y LEON, Bierzo makes mostly commonplace reds. But the best ones, fruity and grassy green, are a revelation and quite unlike any in Spain save for their Galician neighbours. Ideally the wines are made entirely from the Mencía grape. Best producers: Pérez Caramés, Prada a Tope.

JOSEF BIFFAR *Deidesheim, Pfalz, Germany* A father and daughter team runs this 1st-class estate, currently making the best dry and sweet Rieslings from top sites in Deidesheim, Ruppertsberg and WACHENHEIM. Consistent ★ quality recently. Drink young or cellar for 5 years plus. Best years: (1998) 97 96 **94 93 92 90**.

BILLECART-SALMON *Champagne AC, Champagne, France* Top-notch CHAMPAGNE house and one of the few still under family control. The wines are extremely elegant, fresh and delicate, but become simply irresistible with age. The non-vintage Brut★★, non-vintage Brut Rosé★★, Blanc de Blancs★★★, vintage Cuvée N-F Billecart★★★ and Cuvée Elisabeth Salmon★★ are all excellent. Best years: **1991 90 89 88 86 85 82**.

BINGEN *Rheinhessen, Germany* This is a small town and also a BEREICH, the vineyards of which fall in both the NAHE and RHEINHESSEN. The best vineyard in the town is the Scharlachberg, which produces some rather exciting wines, stinging with racy acidity and the whiff of coal smoke. Best producer: VILLA SACHSEN. Best years: (whites) **1997 96 90**.

BINISSALEM DO *Mallorca, Balearic Islands, Spain* Alcoholic reds and rosés are the mainstay of this DO. A few growers make reasonable wines but they are in short supply, even on the island. Best producers: Franja Roja (J L Ferrer), Jaume Mesquida, Herederos de Ribas.

BIONDI SANTI *Brunello di Montalcino DOCG, Tuscany, Italy* Estate that in less than a century created both a legend and an international standing for BRUNELLO DI MONTALCINO. The modern dynamism of the zone owes more to other producers, however, since quality has slipped over the last 2 decades. Yet the very expensive Riserva★★, with formidable levels of extract, tannin and acidity, deserves a minimum 10 years' further aging after release before serious judgement is passed on it. Best years: (Riserva) 1990 88 85 83 82 **75 71 64 55 45 25**.

BLAGNY AC *Côte de Beaune, Burgundy, France* The red wine from this tiny hamlet above MEURSAULT and PULIGNY-MONTRACHET can be fair value, if you like a rustic Burgundy. The white is sold as Puligny-Montrachet, Meursault Premier Cru or Meursault-Blagny. Best producers: JADOT★, J Matrot★. Best years: 1997 96 95 93 **92 90 89 88**.

BLANC DE BLANCS French term used for white wine made from one or more white grape varieties. The term is used all over France, especially for sparkling wines, but is mostly seen in CHAMPAGNE, where it denotes wine made entirely from the Chardonnay grape.

BLANC DE NOIRS French term used for white wine made from black grapes only – the juice is separated from the skins to avoid extracting any colour. Most often seen in CHAMPAGNE, where it is used to describe wine made from Pinot Noir and/or Pinot Meunier grapes.

BLANQUETTE DE LIMOUX AC *Languedoc-Roussillon, France* Most southern white wines are singularly flat and dull, but this fizz is sharp and refreshing. The secret lies in the Mauzac grape, which makes up over 80% of the wine and gives it its striking 'green apple skin' flavour. The Champagne method is used to create the sparkle, although the more rustic *méthode rurale*, finishing off the original fermentation inside the bottle, is also used. Best producers: Collin★, Guinot, Martinolles, SIEUR D'ARQUES co-op, les Terres Blanches. Best years: 1996 **95 94**. See also Crémant de Limoux AC and pages 264–5.

WOLF BLASS *Barossa Valley, South Australia* Wolf Blass stands as one of the most important men in the modern Australian wine world for mastering reds and whites of high quality and consistency which were nonetheless *easy* to enjoy. His reds, blended from many regions and aged mostly in American oak barrels, have a delicious mint and blackcurrant, easy-going charm. His Rieslings are soft and sweetish, while his other whites also possess juicy fruit and sweet oak. Gold Label Riesling★★ from the CLARE and Eden Valleys is impressively intense. Black Label★★, the top label for red wines released at 4 years old, is expensive but good, the Yellow Label cheaper but immensely cheerful. Now owned by MILDARA. Best years: (Black Label) 1996 **94 92 91 90 88 86 82**.

BLAUBURGUNDER See Pinot Noir.

BLAUER LEMBERGER See Blaufränkisch.

BLAUFRÄNKISCH Good, ripe Blaufränkisch has a taste similar to raspberries and white pepper or even beetroot. It does well in Austria, where it is the principal red wine grape of BURGENLAND. The Hungarian vineyards (where it is called Kékfrankos) are mostly just across the border on the other side of the Neusiedler See. Called Lemberger in Germany and almost all of it is grown in WÜRTTEMBERG.

BODEGAS Y BEBIDAS *Spain* The largest wine-producing company in Spain, with wineries including CAMPO VIEJO, AGE and Marqués del Puerto in RIOJA, Vinícola de Navarra, Casa de la Viña in VALDEPEÑAS, Bodegas Alanís in Ribeiro, and others in LA MANCHA and JUMILLA.

JEAN-CLAUDE BOISSET *Burgundy, France* From humble origins, Boisset has become a power in the land, with new acquisitions each year; 1997 saw the addition of Moreau in CHABLIS and L'Héritier Guyot to the range. He has expanded into Beaujolais by taking control of CELLIER DES SAMSONS and Mommessin-Thorin. Others controlled by Boisset include JAFFELIN, Bouchard Aîné, Ropiteau and companies in the RHONE and SAVOIE. Together, the Boisset group markets a vast quantity of Burgundy, but for the most part it is not much better than adequate.

BOLGHERI DOC *Tuscany, Italy* In 1994, this zone near the coast south of Livorno extended its DOC beyond simple white and rosé to cover red wines based on Cabernet, Merlot and Sangiovese in various combinations, while creating a special category for SASSICAIA. The DOC Rosso Superiore now covers wines from the prestigious estates of Grattamacco★★, Le Macchiole★★, ORNELLAIA and Michele Satta★★, and also includes ANTINORI's Guado al Tasso★★. Best years (since 1994): (reds) 1997 96 **95 94**.

BOLLINGER *Champagne AC, Champagne, France* One of the great CHAMPAGNE houses, with good non-vintage (Special Cuvée★★) and vintage wines (Grande Année★★★), made in a full, rich, rather old-fashioned style. (Bollinger is one of the few houses to ferment its base wine in barrels.) It also produces a range of rarer vintage Champagnes, including a Vintage RD★★★ (RD stands for *récemment* *dégorgé*, or recently disgorged, showing that the wine has been on its yeast for longer than usual, picking up loads of flavour on the way) and Vieilles Vignes Françaises Blanc de Noirs★★ from ancient, ungrafted Pinot Noir vines. Best years: **1990 89 88 85 82 79**.

BONNES-MARES AC *Grand Cru, Côte de Nuits, Burgundy, France* A large Grand Cru straddling the communes of CHAMBOLLE-MUSIGNY and MOREY-ST-DENIS and one of the few great Burgundy vineyards to maintain consistency during the turmoil of the last few decades. Bonnes-Mares generally has a deep, ripe, smoky plum fruit, which starts rich and chewy and matures over 10–20 years. Best producers: DROUHIN★★, DUJAC★★, Robert Groffier★★, JADOT★, J-F Mugnier★★, ROUMIER★★★, VOGUE★★★. Best years: 1997 96 95 93 90 89 **85 78**.

BONNEZEAUX AC *Grand Cru, Loire Valley, France* One of France's great sweet wines, Bonnezeaux is a Cru inside the larger COTEAUX DU LAYON AC. Like SAUTERNES the wine is influenced by noble rot but the flavours are different, as only Chenin Blanc is used. Extensive recent plantings have made quality less reliable. It can age very well in vintages like 1990 and 89. Best producers: M Angeli★★★, Fesles★★★, les Grandes Vignes★★, Laffourcade★★, Petits Quarts★★, Petit Val★★, René Renou★★★, Terrebrune★★. Best years: 1997 96 95 94 93 **90 89 88 85 83 76 71 64 59 47**.

BONNY DOON *Santa Cruz Mountains AVA, California, USA* Iconoclastic operation under Randall Grahm, who revels in the unexpected. He has a particular love for RHONE, Italian and Spanish varietals and for fanciful brand names: Le Cigare Volant★★ is a blend of Grenache and Syrah and is Grahm's homage to CHATEAUNEUF-DU-PAPE. Old Telegram★★ is 100% Mourvèdre; Le Sophiste★ is a blend of Rhône white grapes. Particularly delightful are his Ca' del Solo Italianate wines, especially a bone-dry Malvasia Bianca★★ and a white blend, Il Pescatore, his eccentric answer to Verdicchio. He also makes a Syrah from Santa Maria, Cardinal Zinfandel, a pure Riesling from WASHINGTON and eaux de vie. Best years: (Rhônes) (1996) **95 94 92**.

CH. LE BON PASTEUR★★ *Pomerol AC, Bordeaux, France* Small château which has established an excellent reputation under the ownership of Michel Rolland, one of Bordeaux's leading winemakers, and an internationally famous consultant enologist and one of the original Flying Winemakers. Wines from le Bon Pasteur have been expensive in recent years, but they are always deliciously soft and full of lush fruit. Best years: (1998) 97 96 95 94 93 **90 89 88 85 83 82**.

BORBA DOC *Alto Alentejo, Portugal* Promising DOC in the Alto ALENTEJO, specializing in rich, raspberry-fruited reds, best from the local co-op. Best years: **1997 96 95 94**.

BORDEAUX AC *Bordeaux, France* One of the most important ACs in France. It can be applied to straightforward reds and rosés as well as to the dry, medium and sweet white wines of the entire Gironde region. Most of the best wines are allowed more specific geographical ACs (such as MARGAUX or SAUTERNES) but a vast amount of unambitious, yet potentially enjoyable wine is sold as Bordeaux AC. At its best, straight red Bordeaux is marked by bone-dry grassy fruit and an attractive earthy edge. Tannin and astringency, however, can often spoil the effect. Good examples will often benefit from a year or so of aging. Bordeaux Blanc, on the other hand, was once a byword for flabby, fruitless, over-sulphured brews. Fortunately, there is now an increasing number of refreshing, pleasant, clean wines, frequently under a merchant's rather than a château label. Drink as young as possible. Best producers: (reds) Bonnet, Canteloup, Castéra, Ducla, Fontenille, Haut Riot, Roques, Sirius, Thieuley, Tour de Mirambeau, le Trébuchet; (whites) Alpha★, Carsin★, Cayla, DOISY-DAENE★, Dourthe, Grand Mouëys, Ch. du Juge (Dupleich), Lamothe, LYNCH-BAGES★, MARGAUX (Pavillon Blanc)★, Reynon★, Roquefort, Sours★, Thieuley★, Tour de Mirambeau. See also pages 72–5.

BORDEAUX CLAIRET AC *Bordeaux, France* Pale red wine, virtually rosé, making a limited comeback in Bordeaux. The name 'claret', now applied to *any* red wine from the Bordeaux region, derives from *clairet*.

BORDEAUX SUPÉRIEUR AC *Bordeaux, France* This AC covers the same area as the basic BORDEAUX AC but the wines must have an extra ½% of alcohol and a lower yield from the vines, resulting in a greater concentration of flavours. Many of the petits châteaux are labelled Bordeaux Supérieur. The whites under this AC are medium-sweet.

BOSCARELLI *Vino Nobile di Montepulciano DOCG, Tuscany, Italy* Arguably Montepulciano's best producer, Paola de Ferrari and her sons Luca and Niccolò, with guidance from star enologist Maurizio Castelli, craft rich and stylish reds. Most outstanding are VINO NOBILE Riserva del Nocio★★ and the barrique-aged Sangiovese Boscarelli★★.

BOSCHENDAL *Paarl WO, South Africa* The multi-million-rand re-vamp at this huge Anglo-American-owned property already shows improvement in the wines. Shiraz, Merlot and a Merlot-Cabernet Franc blend display elegant concentration. Full flavoursome Chardonnay and Sauvignon Blanc lead a pack, including more commercial whites. Le Grand Pavillon BLANC DE BLANCS NV and rich, vintage Boschendal Brut remain sound Cap Classique bubblies.

BOUCHARD FINLAYSON *Walker Bay, Overberg WO, South Africa* Paul Bouchard's Burgundian know-how and financial support underline this first joint Franco-South African venture. Winemaker Peter Finlayson is committed to Pinot Noir, his 'domaine' Galpin Peak★ elevates Cape Pinots to an international level. Chardonnay★ (several labels, variously sourced grapes, including home-grown Missionvale) and 3 Sauvignon Blancs lack nothing in quality. Best years: (Pinot Noir) 1997 96 95.

BOUCHARD PÈRE ET FILS *Beaune, Burgundy, France* Important merchant and vineyard owner, with vines in some of Burgundy's most spectacular sites, including CORTON, CORTON-CHARLEMAGNE, Chevalier-Montrachet and le MONTRACHET. The firm is owned by Champagne whiz-kid Joseph Henriot, who declassified large chunks of bottled stocks and has greatly raised quality standards. Wines from the company's own vineyards are sold under the Domaines du Château de Beaune label.

BOUCHES-DU-RHÔNE, VIN DE PAYS DES *Provence, France* Wines from 3 areas: the coast, a zone around Aix-en-Provence and the Camargue. Mainly full-bodied, spicy reds, but rosé can be good. Best producers: Château Bas, l'Île St-Pierre, Mas de Rey, TREVALLON★★★, Valdition.

BORDEAUX RED WINES

Bordeaux, France

 This large area of south-west France, centred on the historic city of Bordeaux, produces a larger volume of fine red wine than any other French region. Wonderful Bordeaux-style wines are produced in California, Australia and South America, but the home team's top performers are still unbeatable. Around 580 million bottles of red wine a year are produced here. The best wines, known as the Classed Growths, account for a tiny percentage of this figure, but some of their lustre rubs off on the lesser names, making this one of the most popular wine styles.

GRAPE VARIETIES

Bordeaux's reds are commonly divided into 'right' and 'left' bank wines. On the left bank of the Gironde estuary, the red wines are dominated by the Cabernet Sauvignon grape, with varying proportions of Cabernet Franc, Merlot and Petit Verdot. At best they are austere but perfumed with blackcurrant and cedarwood. The most important left bank areas are the Haut-Médoc (especially the communes of Margaux, St-Julien, Pauillac and St-Estèphe) and, south of the city of Bordeaux, the ACs of Pessac-Léognan and Graves. On the right bank, Merlot is the predominant grape, which generally makes the resulting wines more supple and fleshy than those of the left bank. The key areas for Merlot-based wines are St-Émilion and Pomerol.

CLASSIFICATIONS

Red Bordeaux is made all over the region, from the tip of the Gironde estuary to the southern end of the Entre-Deux-Mers. At its most basic, the wine is simply labelled Bordeaux or Bordeaux Supérieur. Above this are the more specific ACs covering sub-areas (such as the Haut-Médoc) and individual communes (such as Pomerol, St-Émilion or Margaux). Single-estate Crus Bourgeois are the next rung up on the quality ladder, followed by the Classed Growths of the Médoc, Graves and St-Émilion. Many of these châteaux also make 'second wines', which are cheaper versions of their Grands Vins. Curiously Pomerol, home of Château Pétrus, arguably the most famous red wine in the world, has no official pecking order.

See also BORDEAUX, BORDEAUX CLAIRET, BORDEAUX SUPERIEUR, CANON-FRONSAC, COTES DE BOURG, COTES DE CASTILLON, COTES DE FRANCS, FRONSAC, GRAVES, GRAVES SUPERIEURES, HAUT-MEDOC, LALANDE-DE-POMEROL, LISTRAC-MEDOC, LUSSAC-ST-EMILION, MARGAUX, MEDOC, MONTAGNE-ST-EMILION, MOULIS, PAUILLAC, PESSAC-LEOGNAN, POMEROL, PREMIERES COTES DE BLAYE, PREMIERES COTES DE BORDEAUX, PUISSEGUIN-ST-EMILION, ST-EMILION, ST-ESTEPHE, ST-GEORGES-ST-EMILION, ST-JULIEN; AND INDIVIDUAL CHATEAUX.

(1998) 96 95 94 **90 89 88 86 85 83 82 81 79 78 70**

BEST PRODUCERS

Graves, Pessac-Léognan
Dom. de CHEVALIER, FIEUZAL,
HAUT-BAILLY, HAUT-BRION,
la LOUVIERE, la MISSION-HAUT-
BRION, PAPE-CLEMENT, la Tour-
Haut-Brion.

Haut-Médoc CANTEMERLE,
la LAGUNE, SOCIANDO-MALLET.

Margaux FERRIERE, Kirwan, Ch.
MARGAUX, PALMER, RAUZAN-SEGLA.

Médoc POTENSAC, la Tour-de-By.

Pauillac Clerc-Milon, GRAND-
PUY-LACOSTE, HAUT-BATAILLEY,
LAFITE-ROTHSCHILD, LATOUR, LYNCH-
BAGES, MOUTON-ROTHSCHILD,
PICHON-LONGUEVILLE, PICHON-
LONGUEVILLE-LALANDE, PONTET-
CANET.

Pomerol le BON PASTEUR,
Certan-de-May, Clinet,
la CONSEILLANTE, l'EGLISE-CLINET,
l'EVANGILE, GAZIN, LAFLEUR,
PETRUS, le PIN, TROTANOY, VIEUX-
CH.-CERTAN.

St-Émilion ANGELUS, AUSONE,
BEAU-SEJOUR BECOT, CANON,
CANON-LA-GAFFELIERE, CHEVAL
BLANC, FIGEAC, MAGDELAINE, la
Mondotte, TERTRE-ROTEBOEUF,
TROPLONG-MONDOT, VALANDRAUD.

St-Estèphe CALON-SEGUR, COS
D'ESTOURNEL, HAUT-MARBUZET,
LAFON-ROCHET, MONTROSE.

St-Julien BEYCHEVELLE, DUCRU-
BEAUCAILLOU, GRUAUD-LAROSE,
LAGRANGE, LANGOA-BARTON,
LEOVILLE-BARTON, LEOVILLE-LAS-
CASES, LEOVILLE-POYFERRE, TALBOT.

BORDEAUX WHITE WINES
Bordeaux, France

This is France's largest fine wine region but except for the sweet wines of Sauternes and Barsac, Bordeaux's international reputation is based solely on its reds. From 52% of the vineyard area in 1970 white wines now represent only 16% of the present 114,900ha (283,800 acres) of vines. Given the size of the region, the diversity of Bordeaux's white wines should come as no surprise. There are dry, medium and sweet styles, ranging from dreary to some of the most sublime white wines of all. Bordeaux's temperate southern climate – moderated by the influence of the Atlantic and of 2 rivers, the Dordogne and the Garonne, is ideal for white wine production, particularly south of the city along the banks of the Garonne.

GRAPE VARIETIES

Sauvignon Blanc and Sémillon, the most important white grapes, are 2 varieties of considerable character and are usually blended together. They are backed up by smaller quantities of Muscadelle, Ugni Blanc and Colombard.

DRY WINES

The last decade has seen enormous improvements, and the introduction of new technology and new ideas, many of them influenced by the New World, have transformed Bordeaux into one of France's most exciting white wine areas. The white wines, not only of Pessac-Léognan, an AC created for the best areas of the northern Graves in 1987, but also of basic Bordeaux Blanc and Entre-Deux-Mers, the 2 largest white wine ACs in Bordeaux, have improved beyond recognition.

SWEET WINES

Bordeaux's most famous whites are its sweet wines made from grapes affected by noble rot, particularly those from Sauternes and Barsac. Quality improved dramatically during the 1980s as a string of fine vintages brought the wines fame, and the considerable price hike enabled many properties to make long-overdue improvements. On the other side of the Garonne river, Cadillac, Loupiac and Ste-Croix-du-Mont also make sweet wines, but these rarely attain the richness or complexity of a top Sauternes. They are considerably cheaper, however.

See also BARSAC, BORDEAUX, BORDEAUX SUPERIEUR, CADILLAC, CERONS, COTES DE BLAYE, COTES DE BOURG, COTES DE FRANCS, ENTRE-DEUX-MERS, GRAVES, LOUPIAC, PESSAC-LEOGNAN, PREMIERES COTES DE BLAYE, PREMIERES COTES DE BORDEAUX, STE-CROIX-DU-MONT, SAUTERNES; AND INDIVIDUAL CHATEAUX.

(dry) (1998) 96 **95 94 90 89 88
87 86 85 83**; (sweet) (1998) 97
96 95 **90 89 88 86 83 81**

BEST PRODUCERS

Dry wines
(Pessac-Léognan) Dom. de
CHEVALIER, Couhins-Lurton,
FIEUZAL, HAUT-BRION, LAVILLE-
HAUT-BRION, la LOUVIERE,
MALARTIC-LAGRAVIERE, SMITH-HAUT-
LAFITTE, la TOUR-MARTILLAC;
(Graves) Chantegrive, Clos
Floridène; *(Entre-Deux-Mers)*
Bonnet, Fontenille; *(Bordeaux
AC)* Carsin, DOISY-DAENE (Sec),
LYNCH-BAGES, Ch. MARGAUX
(Pavillon Blanc), Reynon,
Thieuley; *(Premières Côtes de
Blaye)* Haut-Bertinerie.

Sweet wines
(Sauternes and Barsac) BASTOR-
LAMONTAGNE, CLIMENS, Clos Haut-
Peyraguey, COUTET, DOISY-DAENE,
DOISY-VEDRINES, FARGUES, GILETTE,
GUIRAUD, LAFAURIE-PEYRAGUEY,
Malle, NAIRAC, Rabaud-Promis,
Raymond-Lafon, RIEUSSEC,
Sigalas-Rabaud, SUDUIRAUT, la
TOUR BLANCHE, YQUEM; *(Graves)*
Clos St-Georges, la Grave;
(Cadillac) Cayla, Manos;
(Cérons) Grand Enclos du Ch.
de Cérons; *(Loupiac)* Clos Jean;
(Ste-Croix-du-Mont) Loubens,
Lousteau-Vieil, la Rame.

BOURGOGNE AC *Burgundy, France* Bourgogne is the French name anglicized as 'Burgundy'. This generic AC mops up all the Burgundian wine with no AC of its own, resulting in massive differences in style and quality. The best wines (red and white) will usually come from a single grower's vineyards just outside the main village ACs of the COTE D'OR. In today's world of high prices such wines may be the only way we can afford the joys of fine Burgundy. If the wine is from a grower, the flavours should follow a regional style. However, if the address on the label is that of a négociant, the wine could be from anywhere in Burgundy. Pinot Noir is the main red grape, with Gamay in the Mâconnais and BEAUJOLAIS. Red Bourgogne is usually light, overtly fruity in an up-front strawberry and cherry way, and should be drunk young (within 2–3 years). The rosé (from Pinot Noir) can be very pleasant but little is produced. Bourgogne Blanc is a bone-dry Chardonnay wine from vineyards not considered quite good enough for a classier AC. Most straight white Burgundy should be drunk within 2 years. Best producers: (reds/growers) COCHE-DURY★, GERMAIN, LAFARGE★, MEO-CAMUZET★★, Pierre Morey, RION★, P Rossignol★; (reds/merchants) DROUHIN, JADOT, LABOURE-ROI; (reds/co-ops) BUXY★, les Caves des Hautes-Côtes★; (whites/growers) M Bouzereau, Boyer-Martenot, COCHE-DURY★★, P Javillier★, F Jobard★, René Manuel, Ch. de Meursault, Guy Roulot; (whites/merchants) DROUHIN, FAIVELEY, JADOT★, JAFFELIN, LABOURE-ROI, Olivier LEFLAIVE; (whites/co-ops) BUXY, les Caves des Hautes-Côtes. Best years: (reds) 1997 96 **95 93** 92 90; (whites) 1997 96 **95 93** 92. See also pages 80–3.

BOURGOGNE ALIGOTÉ AC See Aligoté.

BOURGOGNE-CÔTE CHALONNAISE AC *Côte Chalonnaise, Burgundy, France* These vineyards have gained in importance recently, mainly because of spiralling prices on the COTE D'OR to the north. This recent AC (1990) covers vineyards in the Saône-et-Loire *département* around the villages of Bouzeron, RULLY, MERCUREY, GIVRY and MONTAGNY. Best producers: X Besson, BUXY co-op★, Villaine. Best years: 1997 96 **95** 93.

BOURGOGNE GRAND ORDINAIRE AC *Burgundy, France* This is the bottom rung of the Burgundy AC ladder. You won't find the wine abroad and even in Burgundy it's mostly sold as quaffing wine.

BOURGOGNE-HAUTES-CÔTES DE BEAUNE AC *Burgundy, France* As the supply of affordable Burgundy dwindled in the 1970s, this backwater in the hills behind the great COTE DE BEAUNE came into the spotlight. The red wines are lean but drinkable, as is the slightly sharp Chardonnay. Best producers: Denis Carré, les Caves des Hautes-Côtes★, C Cornu, L Jacob, J-L Joillot, Ch. de Mandelot, Ch. de Mercey. Best years: (reds) 1997 96 **95 93** 90 89; (whites) 1997 96 **95** 94 93 92 90.

BOURGOGNE-HAUTES-CÔTES DE NUITS AC *Burgundy, France* Attractive, lightweight wines from the hills behind the COTE DE NUITS. Best wines are the reds, with an attractive cherry and plum flavour. The whites tend to be rather dry and flinty. In general drink young. Best producers: (reds) les Caves des Hautes-Côtes★, G Dufouleur, B Hudelot★, JAYER-GILLES★★, Thévenot-le-Brun; (whites) les Caves des Hautes-Côtes★, Y Chaley, C Cornu, J-Y Devevey, Dufouleur, Hudelot, JAYER-GILLES★★, Thévenot-le-Brun, Thomas-Moillard, A Verdet★. Best years: (reds) 1997 96 **95 93** 90; (whites) 1997 96 **95** 94 92 90.

BOURGOGNE-IRANCY AC See Irancy AC.

BOURGOGNE PASSE-TOUT-GRAINS AC *Burgundy, France*   Usually
Gamay with a minimum of 33% Pinot Noir. Best producers: BUXY CO-
op, Y Chaley, C Cornu, LEROY, RION★, Taupenot-Merme, G Thomas.

BOURGUEIL AC *Loire Valley, France*   Fine red wine from between Tours
and Angers. Made with Cabernet Franc, topped up with a little Cabernet
Sauvignon; in hot years results can be superb. Given 5–10 years of age,
the wines can develop a wonderful berry fragrance. Best producers:
(reds) Amirault★, Audebert (estate wines), P Breton★, Caslot-Galbrun★,
C Chasle, Max Cognard★, Delaunay Père et Fils★, J-F Demont★,
DRUET★★, Forges★, Lamé-Delille-Boucard★, Morin, Raguenières. Best
years: 1997 96 **95 93 90 89 88 86 85**. See also St-Nicolas-de-Bourgueil.

BOUVET-LADUBAY *Saumur AC, Loire Valley, France*   Owned by the
Champagne house TAITTINGER, Bouvet-Ladubay is not shy of promoting
its wines, nor of charging high prices. The quality of the basic range
(Bouvet Brut, Bouvet Rosé) is good. Cuvée Saphir, the top-selling
wine, is over-sweet, but Trésor (Blanc★ and Rosé★), fermented in oak
casks, is very good. Weird and wonderful Rubis★ sparkling red is
worth trying. Also sells non-sparkling wine from VOUVRAY and SAUMUR.

BOUVIER   Austrian and Slovenian grape short on acidity and so mainly
used for sweet to ultra-sweet wines, where it achieves the richness but
rarely manages to offer any other complexity. Best producers:
Weinkellerei Burgenland, KRACHER★, Opitz★, Unger.

BOUZY *Coteaux Champenois AC, Champagne, France*   A leading
CHAMPAGNE village growing good Pinot Noir, which is used mainly for
white Champagne. However, in outstanding years, a little still red wine
is made. It is light and high in acidity. Best producers: Bara★, Georges
Vesselle, Jean Vesselle. Best years: (1998) 97 95 **93 90 89**.

BOWEN ESTATE *Coonawarra, South Australia*   Doug Bowen makes some
of COONAWARRA's best reds from estate grapes: peppery yet profound
Shiraz★★ and Cabernet★★ with beautifully balanced flavours,
although alcohol levels are on the high side and border on
unbalanced. Chardonnay is improved and now among the best in
Coonawarra. Best years: (reds) 1996 94 **91 90 88 86 84 80 79**.

BRACHETTO   Piedmontese grape revived in dry versions and in sweet,
frothy types with a Muscat-like perfume, as exemplified by Brachetto
d'Acqui DOCG. Best producers: (dry) Correggia★, Scarpa★; (Brachetto
d'Acqui) BANFI★, Braida★, Gatti, Marenco★.

CH. BRANAIRE★ *St-Julien AC, 4ème Cru Classé, Haut-Médoc, Bordeaux,*
France   Recent vintages confirm that Ch. Branaire has returned to
form. It has one of the highest percentages of Cabernet Sauvignon in
the Médoc, and due to the use of old vines and severe selection the
wines from the 90s vintages have a firm structure to match their
seductive fruit. Second wine: Ch. Duluc. Best years: (1998) (97) 96 95
94 **93 90 89 88 86 85 83 82**.

BRAND'S LAIRA *Coonawarra, South Australia*   This is a low-profile
COONAWARRA firm, owned by MCWILLIAMS, that is currently making big
investments in new vineyards. An unsubtle, peachy Chardonnay★ has

77

been the best wine but Cabernet and Cabernet-Merlot are increasingly attractive, ripe and berryish. New life is being breathed into Original Vineyard Shiraz★★, and debut Eric's Blend★★ (after founder Eric Brand) sets an entirely new standard. Best years: (reds) 1997 **96 94 92 90**.

CH. BRANE-CANTENAC★ *Margaux AC, 2ème Cru Classé, Haut-Médoc, Bordeaux, France* Owner Henri Lurton seems to be turning this 2nd Growth around. Recent vintages have shown much improvement with added depth but still that MARGAUX finesse. About time too. It's been an embarrassment for too long. Best years: (1998) 97 96 95 **90 89 88 86**.

BRAUNEBERG *Mosel, Germany* Small village in the Middle Mosel. Its most famous vineyard sites are Juffer and Juffer Sonnenuhr, whose wines have a honeyed richness and creamy gentleness rare in the Mosel. Best producers: Bastgen★, Fritz HAAG★★, Willi Haag★, RICHTER★★. Best years: (1998) **97 95 93 90**.

BREAKY BOTTOM *Sussex, England* Small vineyard tucked in the South Downs near Lewes, towards England's southern coast. Peter Hall is a wonderfully quirky, passionate grower, who makes dry, chunky Seyval Blanc★ that becomes creamy and Burgundy-like after 3–4 years. His crisp Müller-Thurgau★ is full of hedgerow pungency.

BREGANZE DOC *Veneto, Italy* Small DOC in the hills east of Verona and north of Vicenza. A red primarily from Merlot and a dry white based on Tocai Friulano are supplemented by a range of varietals, including Cabernet and Vespaiolo. Best producers: Bartolomeo da Breganze co-op, MACULAN★★, Villa Magna-Novello, Zonta (Vigneto Due Santi).

BODEGAS BRETÓN *Rioja DOC, Rioja, Spain* Pedro Bretón and winery manager Rodolfo Bastida have set this winery apart from the bevy of commercially minded new bodegas launched in the mid-1980s. The single-vineyard Dominio de Conté★★ has become the best expression of their aim to return to RIOJA traditions. Best years: (reds) **1996 95 94 91 90 89**.

GEORG BREUER *Rüdesheim, Rheingau, Germany* Medium-sized estate run by Bernhard Breuer, producing quality dry Riesling from vines on the Rüdesheimer Berg Schlossberg★★ and Rauenthaler Nonnenberg★★. Wines like the Rivaner (Müller-Thurgau, fermented dry) and Grauer Burgunder see a little oak. Best years: (1998) 97 96 **94 93 90**.

BRIDGEHAMPTON *Long Island AVA, New York State, USA* Outstanding Chardonnay★★ and late-harvest Riesling★★ plus a Merlot★★ that has come on fast to become their showcase wine. Best years: 1997 **96 95 93**.

BRIGHT BROTHERS *Ribatejo, Portugal* The Fiúza-Bright winemaking operation is located in the small town of Almeirim in the RIBATEJO but wines are also made from ESTREMADURA and in the BAIRRADA and DOURO. The team is led by Australian Peter Bright, who also makes wines as far afield as SICILY and Argentina; he combines his enthusiasm for native varieties such as the Baga and Sercial-Arinto with familiar names like Chardonnay, Sauvignon Blanc, Cabernet and Merlot.

BROKENWOOD *Hunter Valley, New South Wales, Australia* High-profile winery with delicious, unfashionable Semillon★★ and fashionable Chardonnay★. Best wine is 100% Graveyard Vineyard Shiraz★★; the Rayner Vineyard MCLAREN VALE Shiraz★★ is also a stunner. Cricket Pitch blended reds and whites are cheerful, fruity ready-drinkers. Best years: (Graveyard Vineyard Shiraz) 1996 **94 91 86**.

BROUILLY AC *Beaujolais, Burgundy, France* Largest of the 10 Crus; at its best, the wine is soft, fruity and gluggable. Can also make great BEAUJOLAIS NOUVEAU. Best producers: la Chaize, DUBOEUF (Combillaty, Garanches), H Fessy★, Fouilloux, Hospices de Beaujeu★, A Michaud, Pierreux, Rolland, Ruet, Ch. des Tours★. Best years: 1998 **97 96 95 93 91**.

BROWN BROTHERS *North-East Victoria, Australia* Conservative but highly successful family winery that has outgrown its small producer tag. Big emphasis on varietal table wines – Italian varietals are a new speciality – while vintage fizz is a rapidly rising star. Focusing on cool King Valley and mountain-top Whitlands for its premium grapes.

BRÜNDLMAYER *Kamptal, Niederösterreich, Austria* Top estate in Langenlois: Willi Bründlmayer makes wine in a variety of Austrian and international styles, but his dry Riesling★★ and Grüner Veltliner (Ried Lann★★★) are the best. Good Sekt. Best years: (whites) (1998) 97 95 **94 93 92 91 90 86 83 79**.

BRUNELLO DI MONTALCINO DOCG *Tuscany, Italy* Powerful red wine produced from Sangiovese (known locally as Brunello). Traditionally needed over 10 years to soften, but modern practices result in fruity wines, yet still tannic enough to age into spectacularly complex wine. Best producers: ALTESINO★ (Montesoli★★), ARGIANO★★, BANFI★★, Barbi★, Case Basse-Soldera★★, BIONDI SANTI★, La Campana★★, Caparzo★★, Casanova di Neri★★, CASTELGIOCONDO★★, La Cerbaiola★★, Cerbaiona★★, Ciacci Piccolomini d'Aragona★★, Col d'Orcia★★, COSTANTI★★★, Fuligni★★, La Gerla★, Maurizio Lambardi★★★, Lisini★★, Mastrojanni★★, Siro Pacenti★★, Pieve Santa Restituta★★, Poggio Antico★★, Poggio di Sotto★★, Il Poggiolo★★, Il Poggione★, Livio Sasseti-Pertimali★★, Scopetone★, Talenti★★, Valdicava★. Best years: 1997 96 95 94 **93 91 90 88 85 83 82**.

BRUT French term for dry sparkling wines, especially CHAMPAGNE. Thought of as the driest style of fizz, although Brut Champagne can have up to 15g per litre of sugar added before bottling. Brut Zéro is the driest of all but rare. Extra Dry, Sec and Demi-Sec are all sweeter.

BUÇACO PALACE HOTEL *Beira Litoral, Portugal* Flamboyant 19th-century hotel with its own wines★★, which it lists in a profusion of vintages. They're some of the most interesting in Portugal, subtle and flavoursome, made from grapes from neighbouring DAO and BAIRRADA.

BUCELAS DOC *Estremadura, Portugal* A tiny but historic DOC. The wines are white, have very high acidity and need long aging. The best examples are from Quinta da Murta and Quinta da Romeira.

BUENA VISTA *Carneros AVA, California, USA* Clear, lucid, appealing wines, especially a delicious Pinot Noir and a fairly simple but tasty unoaked Sauvignon. In a Reserve line the Chardonnay★ and Cabernet are capable of aging. Best years: (Cabernet Reserve) 1997 95 **94 91 90**.

BUGEY VDQS, VIN DU *Savoie, France* An area of scattered vineyards halfway between Lyon and Savoie. The best wines are the whites, from Chardonnay, Pinot Gris, Mondeuse Blanche, Altesse and Jacquère. Roussette du Bugey is usually a blend of Altesse and Chardonnay. Best producers: Bel-Air, Crussy, Monin★, Peillot.

VON BUHL *Deidesheim, Pfalz, Germany* Large estate, leased to the Japanese Sanyo group. The wines are rarely subtle, but have stacks of fruit and a confident Riesling character. Best years: (1998) **97 96 94 90**.

BURGUNDY RED WINES

Burgundy, France

 Rich in history and gastronomic tradition, the region of Burgundy (Bourgogne in French) covers a vast tract of eastern France, running from Auxerre, south-east of Paris, to the city of Lyon. As with its white wines, Burgundy's red wines are extremely diverse, sometimes frustratingly so. The explanation for this lies partly in the fickle nature of Pinot Noir, the area's principal red grape, and partly in the historic imbalance of supply and demand between growers – who grow the grapes and make and bottle much of the best wine – and merchants, whose efforts have established the reputation of the wines internationally.

GRAPE VARIETIES

Pinot Noir is one of the world's most ancient varieties, prone to mutation – there are several dozen variations in Burgundy alone – and the range of flavours you get from the grape vividly demonstrates this. A red Épineuil from near Auxerre in the north of the region will be light, chalky, strawberry-flavoured; a Pinot from the Mâconnais toward Lyon will be rough and rooty; and in between in the Côte d'Or – the heartland of red Burgundy – the flavours sweep through strawberry, raspberry, damson and cherry to a wild, magnificent maturity of Oriental spices, chocolate, mushrooms and truffles. Gamay, the grape of Beaujolais to the south, is best at producing juicy fruit flavours of strawberry and plum, demanding in most cases neither aging nor undue respect.

WINE REGIONS

The top red Burgundies come from the Côte d'Or, home to world-famous Grand Cru vineyards such as Clos de Vougeot, Chambertin, Musigny, Richebourg and la Tâche. Givry and Mercurey in the Côte Chalonnaise are up-and-coming, as are the Hautes-Côtes hills behind the Côte d'Or, and light but pleasant reds as well as good pink sparkling Crémant can be found near Chablis in the north. Mâconnais' reds are generally earthy and dull. Beaujolais really is best at producing bright, breezy wines full of fruit, for quaffing at a mere one year old.

See also ALOXE-CORTON, AUXEY-DURESSES, BEAUJOLAIS, BEAUNE, BLAGNY, BONNES-MARES, BOURGOGNE, BOURGOGNE-COTE CHALONNAISE, CHAMBERTIN, CHAMBOLLE-MUSIGNY, CHASSAGNE-MONTRACHET, CHOREY-LES-BEAUNE, CLOS DE LA ROCHE, CLOS ST-DENIS, CLOS DE TART, CLOS DE VOUGEOT, CORTON, COTE DE BEAUNE, COTE DE NUITS, COTE D'OR, CREMANT DE BOURGOGNE, ECHEZEAUX, FIXIN, GEVREY-CHAMBERTIN, GIVRY, LADOIX, MACON, MARSANNAY, MERCUREY, MEURSAULT, MONTHELIE, MOREY-ST-DENIS, MOULIN-A-VENT, MUSIGNY, NUITS-ST-GEORGES, PERNAND-VERGELESSES, PULIGNY-MONTRACHET, RICHEBOURG, LA ROMANEE-CONTI, ROMANEE-ST-VIVANT, RULLY, ST-AUBIN, ST-ROMAIN, SAVIGNY-LES-BEAUNE, LA TACHE, VOLNAY, VOSNE-ROMANEE, VOUGEOT; AND INDIVIDUAL PRODUCERS.

BEST YEARS

1997 96 95 93 **90 89 88 85**

BEST PRODUCERS

Côte de Nuits Dom. l'Arlot, Robert Arnoux, Auvenay, Denis Bachelet, Barthod-Noëllat, Burguet, Charlopin-Parizot, R Chevillon, CLAIR, J-J Confuron, Confuron-Cotéfidot, B Dugat-Py, DUJAC, Engel, Michel Esmonin, Féry-Meunier, Geantet-Pansiot, Gouges, GRIVOT, Anne Gros, Hudelot-Noëllat, JAYER, JAYER-GILLES, Dom. LEROY, H Lignier, MEO-CAMUZET, Mongeard-Mugneret, Denis Mortet, Mugneret-Gibourg, Mugnier, Perrot-Minot, Ponsot, RION, Dom. de la ROMANEE-CONTI, Roty, Rouget, ROUMIER, ROUSSEAU, VOGUE.

Côte de Beaune Ambroise, Ampeau, Angerville, Comte Armand, J-M Boillot, Bonneau du Martray, Chandon de Briailles, COCHE-DURY, Courcel, GERMAIN, V Girardin, Michel LAFARGE, LAFON, Dom. Matrot, MONTILLE, A Morot, Pousse d'Or, RAMONET, TOLLOT-BEAUT.

Côte Chalonnaise Brintet, H & P Jacqueson, Joblot, M Juillot, Thénard, Villaine.

Beaujolais F Calot, Chignard, Lapierre, Ch. du MOULIN-A-VENT, M Tête, Thivin.

Merchants BOUCHARD PERE ET FILS, Champy, DROUHIN, DUBOEUF, FAIVELEY, Camille Giroud, JADOT, LABOURE-ROI, Laurent, Olivier LEFLAIVE, Maison LEROY, A Morot, Remoissenet, RODET.

Co-ops BUXY, les Caves des Hautes-Côtes, Fleurie.

BURGUNDY WHITE WINES

Burgundy, France

 White Burgundy has for generations been thought of as the world's leading dry white wine. The top wines have a remarkable succulent richness of honey and hazelnut, melted butter and sprinkled spice, yet are totally dry. Such wines are all from the Chardonnay grape and the finest are generally grown in the communes of Aloxe-Corton, Meursault, Puligny-Montrachet and Chassagne-Montrachet, where limestone soils and the aspect of the vineyard provide perfect conditions for even ripening of grapes.

WINE STYLES

However, Burgundy encompasses many more wine styles than this, even if no single one quite attains the peaks of quality of those 4 villages on the Côte de Beaune.

Chablis in the north traditionally produces very good steely wines, aggressive and lean when young, but nutty and rounded – though still very dry – after a few years. Modern Chablis is generally a softer, milder wine, easy to drink young, and sometimes enriched with aging in new oak barrels.

There is no doubt that Meursault and the other Côte d'Or villages can produce stupendous wine, but it is in such demand that unscrupulous producers are often tempted to maximize yields and cut corners on quality. Consequently white Burgundy from these famous villages must be approached with caution. Lesser-known villages such as Pernand-Vergelesses and St-Aubin often provide good wine at lower prices.

The Côte Chalonnaise is becoming more interesting for quality white wine now that oak barrels are being used more often for aging. Rully and Montagny are the most important villages, though Givry and Mercurey can produce nice white, too.

The minor Aligoté grape makes some reasonable acidic wine, especially in Bouzeron. Further south the Mâconnais is a large region, two-thirds planted with Chardonnay. The wine used to be dull and flat and not all that cheap, but there is some fair sparkling Crémant de Bourgogne, and some very good vineyard sites, in particular in St-Véran and in Pouilly-Fuissé. Increasingly stunning wines can now be found.

See also ALOXE-CORTON, AUXEY-DURESSES, BATARD-MONTRACHET, BEAUJOLAIS, BEAUNE, BOURGOGNE, BOURGOGNE-COTE CHALONNAISE, CHABLIS, CHASSAGNE-MONTRACHET, CORTON, CORTON-CHARLEMAGNE, COTE DE BEAUNE, COTE DE NUITS, COTE D'OR, CREMANT DE BOURGOGNE, FIXIN, GIVRY, LADOIX, MACON, MARSANNAY, MERCUREY, MEURSAULT, MONTAGNY, MONTHELIE, MONTRACHET, MOREY-ST-DENIS, MUSIGNY, NUITS-ST-GEORGES, PERNAND-VERGELESSES, PETIT CHABLIS, POUILLY-FUISSE, POUILLY-LOCHE, POUILLY-VINZELLES, PULIGNY-MONTRACHET, RULLY, ST-AUBIN, ST-ROMAIN, ST-VERAN, SAVIGNY-LES-BEAUNE, VOUGEOT; AND INDIVIDUAL PRODUCERS.

BUITENVERWACHTING *Constantia WO, South Africa* This beautifully restored property is part of the Cape's original Constantia wine farm. Its history is reflected in the traditional, Old-World-style wines; a graceful, intricate Chardonnay★, penetrating, broad and ageworthy Sauvignon Blanc★★ and light, racily dry Riesling. The aristocratic BORDEAUX-style blend Christine★★ is regularly one of the most complex and elegant. Best years: (whites) **1998** 97 96 95 94 93 92 91; (reds) **1994** **93** 92 91 90 89.

BULL'S BLOOD *Eger, Hungary* Bull's Blood is no longer the barrel-chested red it once was; as Kékfrankos (Blaufränkisch) grapes have replaced Kadarka in the blend, the blood has somewhat thinned, although Cabernet Sauvignon and Merlot are usually in the blend.

GRANT BURGE *Barossa Valley, South Australia* Former Krondorf guiding light is now a leading producer in the BAROSSA VALLEY, producing chocolaty Shiraz★★ and Cabernet★, opulent Chardonnay★ and oaky Semillon. Top label is rich but somewhat oak-dominated Meshach★★. Flagship Cabernet Shadrach★ and RHONE-style blend, Holy Trinity★, are new additions. Best years: (Meshach) 1994 **91** **90**.

BURGENLAND *Austria* 4 regions: Neusiedlersee, including Seewinkel for sweet Prädikat wines; Neusiedlersee-Hügelland, famous for sweet wines, now also big reds and fruity, dry whites; Mittelburgenland, for robust Blaufränkisch reds; and Südburgenland, for good reds and dry whites. Best producers: FEILER-ARTINGER★★★, KRACHER★★★.

BURGUNDY See Bourgogne AC and pages 80–3.

BÜRKLIN-WOLF *Wachenheim, Pfalz, Germany* With nearly 100ha (250 acres) of vineyards, this is one of Germany's largest privately owned estates. Under director Christian von Guradze it has shot back up to the first rank of the region's producers since the 1994 vintage. Regular wines are now ★ to ★★, with the magnificent dessert wines ★★★. Best years: (1998) 97 96 **95** **94** **93** 90 89 86 85.

BURRWEILER *Pfalz, Germany* An exception in the PFALZ, Burrweiler is the region's only wine village with a slate soil like the MOSEL, most notably in the excellent Schäwer site. Produces elegant dry Rieslings and some fine dessert wines. Best producer: Herbert Messmer★. Best years: **1997** **94** 93.

BUXY, CAVE DES VIGNERONS DE *Côte Chalonnaise, Burgundy, France* Based in the Côte Chalonnaise, this ranks among Burgundy's top co-operatives, producing affordable, well-made Chardonnay and Pinot Noir. The light, oak-aged BOURGOGNE Pinot Noir★ and the red and white Clos de Chenôves★, as well as the nutty, white MONTAGNY★, are all good and, hallelujah, reasonably priced.

BUZET AC *South-West France* Good Bordeaux-style red wines from the same mix of grapes and at a lower price. There is very little rosé and the whites are rarely exciting. Best producers: Buzet-sur-Baïse co-op (especially Baron d'Ardeuil★ and Ch. de Gueyze★), Daniel Tissot.

BYRON VINEYARD *Santa Maria Valley AVA, California, USA* After new owner Robert MONDAVI Winery built a new winery and acquired reputable vineyards, founder Ken 'Byron' Brown has been making better than ever Pinot Noir and Chardonnay. His Reserve Pinot★★ is full of spice cherry fruit, and the Reserve Chardonnay★ with mineral notes and fine balance can age for several years. Regular Chardonnay is often good value. Best years: (1998) 97 96 **95** **94** 92.

CA' DEL BOSCO *Franciacorta DOCG, Lombardy, Italy* Model estate, headed by Maurizio Zanella, making some of Italy's finest and most expensive wines: outstanding sparklers in FRANCIACORTA Brut★★, Dosage Zero★★, Satén★ and the prestige Cuvée Annamaria Clementi★★; good Terre di Franciacorta Rosso★, remarkably good Chardonnay★★, Pinero★★ (Pinot Nero) and a BORDEAUX blend, Maurizio Zanella★★.

CABARDÈS AC *Languedoc, France* This wine region neighbours MINERVOIS but, as well as the usual Mediterranean grape varieties, Cabernet Sauvignon and Merlot are allowed. At its best, full-bodied, chewy and rustically attractive. Best producers: Cabrol, Salitis★, Ventenac.

CABERNET D'ANJOU AC *Loire Valley, France* Higher in alcohol than ROSÉ D'ANJOU and generally slightly sweeter. Drink young and fresh as a rule. Best producers: Bertrand, C Daviau, Ogereau, Tigné★.

CABERNET FRANC Often unfairly dismissed as an inferior Cabernet Sauvignon, Cabernet Franc comes into its own in cool zones or areas where the soil is damp and heavy. It can have a grassy freshness linked to raw but tasty blackcurrant-raspberry fruit. In France it thrives in the LOIRE VALLEY and BORDEAUX, especially ST-ÉMILION and POMEROL where it accounts for 19% of the planting. Italy has used the variety with considerable success for generations in the north-east. Experiments with Cabernet Franc on CALIFORNIA's North Coast and in WASHINGTON STATE show promise in blends and as a varietal. There are also some good South African and Australian examples.

CABERNET SAUVIGNON See pages 86–7.

CADILLAC AC *Bordeaux, France* A sweet wine produced in the southern half of the PREMIÈRES CÔTES DE BORDEAUX in close proximity to LOUPIAC and STE-CROIX-DU-MONT. Disappointing in the past, the wines have greatly improved in recent vintages. Styles vary from fresh, semi-sweet to richly botrytized. Drink young. Best producers: Berbec, Carsin, Cayla★, Ch. du Juge (Dupleich), Manos★, Mémoires, Renon, Ste Catherine. Best years: (1998) 97 96 **95 90**.

CAHORS AC *South-West France* Important South-West red wine region. This dark, often tannic wine is made from at least 70% Auxerrois (Bordeaux's Malbec) and has an unforgettable, rich plummy flavour. Ages well. Best producers: la Caminade, Cayrou★, Cèdre★, Clos la Coutale★, Clos de Gamot★, Clos Triguedina★, Côtes d'Olt co-op, Gaudou, Haute-Serre★, Lagrezette★, Lamartine★, Quattre. Best years: (1998) 97 96 **95 92 90 89 88 86 85**.

CAIN CELLARS *Napa Valley AVA, California, USA* This Spring Mountain estate appears to be solidly on track. The Cain Five★★ is a particularly pleasing BORDEAUX blend, which can be a bit slow off the mark but is worth waiting for. Also a lower-priced Cain Cuvée and strongly flavoured Sauvignon Musque are regular items. Best years: (Cain Five) (1996) 95 94 **93 92 91 90 87 86 85**.

CALABRIA *Italy* One of Italy's poorest regions. CIRÒ, Donnici, Savuto and Scavigna reds from the native Gaglioppo grape, and whites from Grecco, are much improved thanks to greater winemaking expertise.

CABERNET SAUVIGNON

 Wine made from Cabernet Sauvignon in places like Bulgaria, Chile, Australia, California, even in parts of southern France, has become so popular now that many people may not realize where it all started – and how Cabernet has managed to become the great, all-purpose, omnipresent red wine grape of the world.

WINE STYLES

Bordeaux Cabernet It all began in Bordeaux. With the exception of a clutch of Merlot-based beauties in St-Émilion and Pomerol, all the greatest red Bordeaux wines are based on Cabernet Sauvignon, with varying amounts of Merlot, Cabernet Franc, and possibly Petit Verdot and Malbec also blended in. The blending is necessary because by itself Cabernet makes such a strong, powerful, aggressive and assertive wine. Dark and tannic when young, the great Bordeaux wines need 10–20 years for the aggression to fade, the fruit becoming sweet and perfumed as fresh blackcurrants, with a fragrance of cedarwood, of cigar boxes mingling magically among the fruit. It is this character which has made red Bordeaux famous for at least 2 centuries.

Cabernet Worldwide When winemakers in other parts of the world sought role models to try to improve their wines, most of them automatically chose Cabernet Sauvignon. It was lucky that they did, because not only is this variety easy to grow in almost all conditions – cool or warm, dry or damp – but that unstoppable personality always powers through. The cheaper wines are generally made to accentuate the blackcurrant fruit and the slightly earthy tannins. They are drinkable young, but able to age surprisingly well. The more ambitious wines are aged in oak barrels, often new ones, to enhance the tannin yet also to add spice and richness capable of developing over a decade or more. Sometimes the Cabernet is blended – usually with Merlot, but occasionally, as in Australia, with Shiraz.

European Cabernets Many vineyards in southern France now produce excellent, affordable Cabernet. Some of the best wines from Spain have been Cabernet, and Portugal has also had success. Italy's red wine quality revolution was sparked off by the success of Cabernet in Tuscany; Austria is beginning to crack the grape's code and even southern Germany is having a go. Eastern Europe, in particular Bulgaria, provides us with some of the most affordable, decent quality reds in the world.

New World Cabernets California's reputation was created by its strong, weighty Cabernets, though in recent vintages winemakers are working with a lighter hand. Both Australia and New Zealand place more emphasis on easy fruit in their Cabernets. Chile has made the juicy, blackcurranty style very much her own, and Argentina and South Africa are showing they want to join in too.

CALERA *San Benito, California, USA*   A pace-setter for California Pinot
Noir with 4 different estate wines: Reed Vineyard★★, Selleck
Vineyard★★★, Jensen Vineyard★★★ and Mills★. They are complex,
balanced wines with power and originality and capable of aging. Mt
Harlan Chardonnay★★ looks set to be excitingly original too. Small
amounts of Viognier★★★ are succulent with sensuous fruit. Best years:
(reds) (1996) 95 94 **92 91 90 88 87 86 85**; (whites) **1997 96 95 94 92 91**.

CALIFORNIA *USA*   California's importance is not simply in being the
leading wine producer in the USA – the state's influence on the world of
wine is far wider than that. Most of the great revolutions in technology
and style that have transformed the expectations and achievements of
winemakers in every country of the world – including France – were born
in the ambitions of a band of Californian winemakers during the 60s and
70s. They challenged the old order with its regulated, self-serving élitism,
democratizing the world of fine wine, to the benefit of every wine drinker.
This revolutionary fervour is less evident now. And there are times
recently when Californians seem too intent on establishing their own
particular New World old order. A few figures: there are 160,000ha
(400,000 acres) of wine grapes, producing over 500 million gallons of
wine annually, about 90% of all wine made in the USA. A large proportion
comes from the hot, inland CENTRAL VALLEY. See also Central Coast, Central
Valley, Mendocino County, Monterey County, Napa County, San Luis
Obispo County, Santa Barbara County, Sonoma County.

CALITERRA *Curicó, Chile*   A joint venture with MONDAVI designed to
promote and sell Caliterra wines in the US. Winemaker Irene Poiva
has built up an impressive portfolio of 1998 wines: sprightly citrus-
edged Chardonnay★★ from CASABLANCA, silky Curicó Merlot★ and an
intense, grassy Sauvignon Blanc★. Whites impress more than reds.

CH. CALON-SÉGUR★ *St-Estèphe AC, 3ème Cru Classé, Haut-Médoc,
Bordeaux, France*   Long considered one of ST-ESTEPHE's leading
châteaux but in the mid-1980s the wines were not as good as they
should have been. Recent vintages have been more impressive, and
the best wines may be cellared for 10 years. Second wine: Marquis de
Ségur. Best years: (1998) 96 95 **90 89 86 82**.

CAMBRIA WINERY *Santa Maria Valley AVA, California, USA*   With over
500ha (1200 acres) at his disposal, owner Jess Jackson developed the
biggest (100,000-case) winery in SANTA BARBARA COUNTY. Most of the
production is Chardonnay (Katherine's Vineyard and Reserve★), with
the remainder devoted to Pinot Noir, Syrah and Sangiovese. Look for
fine Julia's Vineyard Pinot Noir★. Best years: (Chardonnay) (1997) **96 95**.

CAMPANIA *Italy*   Until recently this region was a desert for the wine
lover, but now 3 regions lead the revolution in Italy's south. While many
have been clamouring for the new wines of PUGLIA and SICILY, in Campania
moves toward quality have been underpinned by the likes of enologist
Riccardo Cotarella. Other producers besides the venerable MASTROBERARDINO
have finally begun to realize the potential of its soil, climate and grapes,
especially the red Aglianico. DOCs of note are FALERNO DEL MASSICO, Fiano di
Avellino, Greco di Tufo, Ischia, LACRYMA CHRISTI DEL VESUVIO and TAURASI. The

leading new wine is Montevetrano★★★, made from Cabernet, Merlot and Aglianico at the Montevetrano estate near Salerno.

CAMPILLO *Rioja DOC, País Vasco, Spain* An up-market subsidiary of FAUSTINO MARTINEZ, producing some exciting new red RIOJAS★★. The wines are often Tempranillo-Cabernet Sauvignon blends, with masses of ripe, velvety fruit. Best years: **1996 95 94 89 87 86 85 82 81**.

CAMPO VIEJO *Rioja DOC, Rioja, Spain* The largest producer of RIOJA. The Reservas★ and Gran Reservas★ are reliably good, as are the elegant, all-Tempranillo Reserva Viña Alcorta★ and the barrel-fermented white Viña Alcorta★. Albor is one of the best modern young Riojas, packed with fresh, pastilley fruit. Best years: (reds) **1996 95 94 91 89 88 87 85 83 82 80 78**.

CANARY ISLANDS *Spain* Eight DOs for the Canaries? Yes indeed – Tacoronte-Acentejo, Lanzarote, La Palma, Hierro, Abona, Valle de Güimar, Valle de la Orotava and Ycoden-Daute-Isora. The sweet Malvasia from Lanzarote or La Palma is worth a try, otherwise stick with the young reds, made mostly from Listán Negro. Best producers: Bodegas Monje, Viña Norte.

CANBERRA DISTRICT *New South Wales, Australia* Cool, high altitude (800m/2600ft) may sound good but excessive cold and frost (especially in spring 1998) can be problematic. Lark Hill and Helm's make exciting Riesling, Lark Hill and Brindabella Hills some smart Cabernet-Merlot and Clonakilla increasingly sublime Shiraz (with a dollop of Viognier). BRL HARDY is pouring money in here. Best producers: Brindabella Hills, Clonakilla, Doonkuna, Helm's, Lark Hill.

CANEPA *Maipo, Chile* Family feuds and the departure of talented winemaker Andrés Ilabaca will mean that this MAIPO VALLEY giant will have to be watched closely. Ilabaca's legacy is a grassy, aromatic Sauvignon Blanc, a spicy Zinfandel★ and Merlot★. First results from new winemaker Ernesto Juisan suggest a continuation of quality.

CANNONAU Sardinian grape variety essentially the same as Spain's Garnacha and France's Grenache Noir. In SARDINIA it produces deep, tannic reds but the modern, dry red table wines are gaining in popularity. Traditional sweet and fortified styles can still be found. Best producers: (lighter, modern styles) Argiolas, SELLA & MOSCA★, and Dolianova, Dorgali, Jerzu, Ogliastra, Oliena, Santa Maria La Palma and Trexenta co-ops.

CH. CANON★ *St-Émilion Grand Cru AC, 1er Grand Cru Classé, Bordeaux, France* Canon can make some of the richest, most concentrated ST-EMILIONS. Purchased in 1996 by French fashion and perfume company Chanel, owners of Ch. RAUZAN-SEGLA in MARGAUX, so expect even greater things here. In good vintages wine is tannic to start with but will keep well for 10 years or more. Second wine: Clos J Kanon. Best years: (1998) 96 95 90 **89 88 86 85 83 82 81 79 78**.

CANON-FRONSAC AC *Bordeaux, France* This AC is the heart of the FRONSAC region. The wines are quite strong when young but can age for 10 years or more. Best producers: Barrabaque, Canon★, Canon-de-Brem★, Canon-Moueix, Cassagne-Haut-Canon, la Fleur-Cailleau, Grand

Renouil★, Moulin-Pey-Labrie, Pavillon, Vrai-Canon-Bouché. Best years: (1998) 97 96 95 **94 90 89 88 85 83 82 79 78**.

CH. CANON-LA-GAFFELIÈRE★★ *St-Émilion Grand Cru AC, Grand Cru Classé, Bordeaux, France* Over the last 10 years, Stéphan de Niepperg has placed this property, located at the foot of the town of ST-EMILION, at the top of the list of Grand Crus Classés. The wines are firm, rich and concentrated. Also under the same ownership, Clos l'Oratoire and the remarkable *micro-cuvée* La Mondotte (first vintage 1996). Best years: (1998) 97 96 95 94 93 90 89 **88 85**.

CH. CANTEMERLE★ *Haut-Médoc AC, 5ème Cru Classé, Bordeaux, France* With la LAGUNE, the most southerly of the Crus Classés. The wines are delicate in style and excellent in ripe vintages. Second wine: Villeneuve de Cantemerle. Best years: (1998) 97 96 95 **90 89 83 82**.

CANTERBURY *South Island, New Zealand* The long, cool ripening season of the arid central coast of South Island favours white varieties, particularly Chardonnay, Pinot Gris, Sauvignon Blanc and Riesling, as well as Pinot Noir. The northerly Waipara district produces Canterbury's most exciting wines, especially from Riesling and Pinot Noir. Best producers: GIESEN★, Pegasus Bay★, Mark Rattray, ST HELENA, Sherwood Estate.

CAPEL VALE *Geographe, Western Australia* Radiologist Peter Pratten's winery makes fine Riesling★, Gewürztraminer, Chardonnay★★ and Semillon-Sauvignon Blanc★, often blending Capel fruit with Mount Barker. The reds are increasingly classy. CV is a second label. Best years: (whites) **1997 96 95 93 92 91**.

CAPE MENTELLE *Margaret River, Western Australia* This leading MARGARET RIVER winery, together with New Zealand offshoot CLOUDY BAY, is majority-owned by VEUVE CLICQUOT. Its visionary founder, David Hohnen, produces full-throttle Cabernet★★ and Shiraz★★, impressive Chardonnay★★★, tangy Semillon-Sauvignon Blanc★★★ and wonderfully chewy Zinfandel★★ which effectively expresses Hohnen's CALIFORNIA training. All wines benefit from cellaring – whites up to 5 years, reds 8–10. Best years: (reds) 1996 95 92 91 **90 88 86 83 82 78**.

CH. CARBONNIEUX *Pessac-Léognan AC, Cru Classé de Graves, Bordeaux, France* Carbonnieux is the largest of the GRAVES Classed Growth properties, now part of the PESSAC-LEOGNAN AC. The white wine★ has improved considerably since 1988, profiting from the introduction of 50% new oak. The red★ sometimes seems to lack stuffing, but has also gained in complexity of late. Second wine: la Tour-Léognan. Best years: (whites) (1998) 96 95 **94 90 89 88 85**; (reds) (1998) 96 95 **90 89 88 86**.

CAREMA DOC *Piedmont, Italy* Tiny quantities of wine trickle from Nebbiolo vines grown on the steep, rocky slopes of this small zone in northern Piedmont. Lighter than most other Nebbiolos, these wines can nevertheless have great elegance and perfume. Production is confined to the local co-op and Luigi Ferrando (White Label★, Black Label★★). Best years: 1997 96 **95 93 90 89 88 85**.

CARIGNAN The dominant red grape in the south of France is responsible for much boring, cheap, harsh wine. But when made by carbonic maceration, the wine can have delicious spicy fruit. Old vines are capable of thick, rich, impressive reds now in CALIFORNIA also. Although initially a Spanish grape (as Cariñena or Mazuelo), it is not that widespread there, but is useful for adding colour and acidity in RIOJA and CATALONIA.

CARIGNANO DEL SULCIS DOC *Sardinia, Italy* Carignano is now starting to produce wines of quite startling quality. Rocca Rubia★★, a barrique-aged Riserva from the co-op at Santadi, with rich, fleshy and chocolatey fruit, is one of SARDINIA's best reds. In a similar vein, but more structured and concentrated, is Terre Brune★★. Best producer: Santadi co-op. Best years: (reds) 1997 **96 95 94 93 91 90**.

LOUIS CARILLON & FILS *Puligny-Montrachet AC, Côte de Beaune, Burgundy, France* Excellent, but formerly underrated family-owned estate in PULIGNY-MONTRACHET. The emphasis here is on traditional, slightly savage white wines of great concentration, rather than new oak. Look out for the 3 Premiers Crus – les Referts★★, Champ Canet★★ and les Perrières★★★ – and the tiny but exquisite production of BIENVENUES-BATARD-MONTRACHET★★★. The red wines – from CHASSAGNE-MONTRACHET★, ST-AUBIN★ and MERCUREY★ – are extremely good, too. Best years: (whites) 1997 96 95 **94** 93 **92 90 89**.

CARIÑENA DO *Aragón, Spain* The largest DO of ARAGON, baking under the mercilessly hot sun in inland eastern Spain, Cariñena has traditionally been a land of cheap, deep red, alcoholic wines from the Garnacha grape. However, a switch to Tempranillo grapes has begun, and some growers now pick early. International grape varieties like Cabernet Sauvignon are being planted widely. Best producers: Bodegas San Valero (Monte Ducay, Don Mendo), Señorío de Urbezo.

CARMEL *Israel* Israel's biggest wine-producing company sources grapes from 200 different farmers to make crisp, Sauvignon Blanc from the GOLAN HEIGHTS, jammy Cabernet Sauvignon and aromatic dry Muscat. Other varieties include Sémillon, Chardonnay, Shiraz and Petite Sirah.

CARMEN *Maipo, Chile* Sister winery to SANTA RITA, but worlds apart in terms of quality. Carmen's high-tech winery and innovative young winemaker Alvaro Espinoza are leading the MAIPO VALLEY pack. Best wines include complex, well-structured Cabernet Sauvignon Reserve★★, juicy Merlot★ and the new Grande Vidure Cabernet★. Whites are less successful but the Gewürztraminer-Sauvignon blend shows intelligent innovation and the unoaked Sauvignon Blanc big improvement. Best years: 1997 96.

CARMENET VINEYARD *Sonoma Valley AVA, California, USA* Carmenet sets out to make BORDEAUX-style reds and whites and is probably one of California's most successful exponents of both, producing deep, complex reds★★ and long-lived, barrel-fermented whites★★. Best years: (reds) 1996 95 94 **92 91 90 88 87 86**.

CARMIGNANO DOCG *Tuscany, Italy* Red wine from the west of Florence, renowned since the 16th century and revived in the 1960s by Ugo Contini Bonacossi of Capezzana. The blend (85% Sangiovese, 15% Cabernet) is one of Tuscany's more refined wines and can be very long-lived. Although Carmignano is DOCG for its red wine, notable as Riserva, DOC applies to a lighter red Barco Reale, a rosé called Vin Ruspo and fine VIN SANTO★. Best producers: Ambra, Artimino★, Bacchereto, Capezzana★★, Le Farnete, Il Poggiolo, Villa di Trefiano★. Best years: (1998) 97 96 **95 94 93** 90 88 85.

CARMO, QUINTO DO *Alentejo, Portugal* Well-established estate, part-owned by Domaines Rothschild. Estate red★★ and second label Dom Martinho are complex and ageworthy. Best years: **1995** 94 93 92 90 89 87.

CARNEROS AVA *California, USA* Hugging the northern edge of San Francisco Bay, Carneros includes parts of both NAPA and SONOMA Counties. Windswept and chilly with heavy morning fog off the Bay, it is a top cool-climate area, highly suitable for Chardonnay and Pinot Noir as both table wine and a base for sparkling wine. Merlot is also coming on well. Best producers: ACACIA★, Bouchaine★, Carneros Creek★, DOMAINE CARNEROS★★, MUMM NAPA (Winery Lake)★, RASMUSSEN★★, SAINTSBURY★★.

CARNUNTUM *Niederösterreich, Austria* Wine region south of the Danube and east of Vienna, with a strong red wine tradition. Best producer: Pittnauer★.

CARR TAYLOR *Sussex, England* David Carr Taylor's long-established vineyard and winery north of Hastings has consistently produced good whites from Reichensteiner, Gutenborner and Schönburger, and he now has plans to turn even more attention to his trail-blazing sparkling wines, made from vines on south-facing chalk slopes.

CASABLANCA *Chile* A coastal valley with a distinctly cool climate personality that is Chile's strongest (some say only) proof of regional style. Whites dominate, with best results from the lesser-planted Sauvignon Blanc and Gewürztraminer. Even so, the rare reds are very good. Best producers: CONCHA Y TORO★, ERRAZURIZ★, VINA CASABLANCA★, Veramonte.

CASA LAPOSTOLLE *Rapel, Chile* Joint venture between Marnier-Lapostolle and Chile's Rabat family, with Michel Rolland at the winemaking helm. The Cuvée Alexandre Merlot★★ and Chardonnay★ both have the intensity for several years' aging. All the wines highlight the quality of Rapel fruit. A new Cabernet Rosé★ is one of Chile's best. Best years: (reds) 1997 **96 95**.

CASSIS AC *Provence, France* A picturesque fishing port near Marseille. Because of its situation, its white wine is the most overpriced on the French Riviera. Based on Ugni Blanc and Clairette, the wine can be good if fresh. The red wine is dull but the rosé can be pleasant (especially from a single estate). Best producers: Bagnol★, Clos Ste-Magdelaine★, Ferme Blanche★, Fontblanche, Mas de Boudard, Mas Fontcreuse.

CASTEL DEL MONTE DOC *Puglia, Italy* An arid, hilly zone, and an ideal habitat for the Uva di Troia grape, producing long-lived red wine of astonishing character. There is also varietal Aglianico, some good rosé, and the whites produced from international varieties are improving. Best producers: RIVERA★, Santa Lucia, Torrevento★.

CASTELGIOCONDO *Brunello di Montalcino DOCG, Tuscany, Italy* FRESCOBALDI's estate is the source of fine BRUNELLO★ and Brunello Riserva★★. The vineyards also provide grapes for well-regarded Merlot, Lamaione★★, and the much-heralded joint venture with MONDAVI, Luce★★, a Sangiovese-Merlot blend. Great in 1993 and 94, but even better in 95 when a second wine, Lucente, was added.

CASTELLBLANCH *Cava DO, Catalonia, Spain* One of the world's largest quality sparkling wine companies, owned by another giant CAVA company, FREIXENET. Brut Zero★ and Cristal are fresh and simple fizzes.

CASTELL'IN VILLA *Chianti Classico DOCG, Tuscany, Italy* This is one of Chianti's finest estates, producing notable CHIANTI CLASSICO★★ and

Sangiovese-based Santacroce★★, which combine power, elegance and longevity in a way few Tuscan wines ever manage. Some variation in quality in recent vintages. Best years: (1997) (96) 95 **94** 93 **90** 88.

CASTILLA-LA MANCHA *Spain* Biggest wine region in Spain at over 700,000ha (1.73 million acres); hot, dry country with poor clay-chalk soil. The DOs of the central plateau, La MANCHA and VALDEPEÑAS, make white wines from the Airén grape, and some good reds from the Cencibel (Tempranillo). Méntrida DO and Almansa DO make rustic reds. Most ambitious wines made here fall outside the DOs: those from MARQUES DE GRIÑON's Dominio de Valdepusa estate and the Dehesa de Carrital estate, both in the Toledo mountains, and Manuel Manzaneque's Sierra de Alcaraz vineyards in Albacete province, are of the highest standard.

CASTILLA Y LEÓN *Spain* This is Spain's harsh, high plateau, with long cold winters and hot summers (but always cool nights). A few rivers, notably the Duero, temper this climate and afford fine conditions for viticulture. After many decades of winemaking ignorance, with a few exceptions like VEGA SICILIA, the situation has changed radically for the better in 2 of the region's DOs, RIBERA DEL DUERO and RUEDA, and is fast improving in the other 3, BIERZO, Cigales and TORO.

VIGNERONS CATALANS *Roussillon, France* This Perpignan-based association of growers and co-ops sells a wide range of wines. Founded in 1964, it has encouraged members to invest in modern technology and to experiment with new grape varieties. Its COTES DU ROUSSILLON and COTES DU ROUSSILLON-VILLAGES blends are always consistent. There are now more exciting wines in Roussillon but none more reliable.

CATALONIA *Spain* Standards vary among the region's 8 DOs. PENEDES, between Barcelona and Tarragona, has the greatest number of technically equipped wineries in Spain. ALELLA, up the coast, makes attractive whites, and inland COSTERS DEL SEGRE makes potentially excellent reds and whites at the RAIMAT estate. In the south, in mountainous PRIORAT and the hills of Tarragona and Terra Alta, many producers are still behind the times, while others have made leaps in quality and technique. Ampurdán-Costa Brava, by the French border, has been sadly left in the quality trough. Tourists lap up whatever is made. Catalonia also makes most of Spain's CAVA sparkling wines, many of excellent quality. See also Conca de Barberá.

CATENA *Mendoza, Argentina* Argentina's most progressive and export-orientated wine producer. The Esmeralda winery produces good international-style Chardonnay★, oak-aged Cabernet Sauvignon★, powerful Agrelo vineyard Malbec★ and Catena Alta Malbec★★ from Lunlunta, with second label Alamos Ridge providing  excellent value for money. Catena's takeover of La Rural has delivered an intense new Malbec and soft, jammy Merlot. Latest project is the deeply impressive Alta range of Chardonnay★★, Cabernet★★ and Malbec★★. Best years: 1997 **96 95**.

DOMAINE CAUHAPÉ *Jurançon AC, South-West France*   Henri Ramonteu
has been a major influence in JURANÇON, proving that the area can
make complex dry whites as well as more traditional sweet wines.
Ramonteu is the leading producer of both, but his top wines are sweet
Noblesse du Temps★★ and barrel-fermented Quintessence★★★.

CAVA DO *Spain*   Cava, the Catalan and hence Spanish name for
Champagne-method fizz, is made in 159 towns and villages in northern
Spain, but more than 95% are in CATALONIA. Grapes used are the local trio
of Parellada, Macabeo and Xarel-lo. The best-value, fruitiest Cavas are
generally the youngest, with no more than the minimum 9 months'
aging. Some good Catalan Cavas are made with Chardonnay. A number
of top-quality wines are now produced but are seldom seen abroad,
since their prices are too close to those of CHAMPAGNE to attract
international customers. Best producers: Can Feixes, Castell de
Villarnau, CASTELLBLANCH, CODORNIU (Anna de Codorníu★, Premiere Cuvée
Brut Chardonnay★), FREIXENET, JUVE Y CAMPS★, MARQUES DE MONISTROL★,
Parxet, RAIMAT, Raventós i Blanc, Rovellats★, Agustí Torelló, Jané
Ventura.

CAVE CO-OPÉRATIVE   French for a co-operative cellar, where members
bring their grapes for vinification and bottling under a collective label.
In terms of quantity, the French wine industry is dominated by co-ops.
The best are excellent, but many lack both investment and a director
of sufficient vision to persuade the members that the effort is
worthwhile. Nevertheless, the quality of co-op wines has improved
enormously in the last decade. Often use less workaday titles, such as
Caves des Vignerons, Producteurs Réunis, Union des Producteurs or
Cellier des Samsons. See Buxy, Catalans, Cellier des Samsons, la
Chablisienne, Mont Tauch, Oisly-et-Thésée, Plaimont, Sieur d'Arques.

CAYMUS VINEYARDS *Napa Valley AVA, California, USA*   Caymus Cabernet
Sauvignon is a ripe, intense and generally tannic style that is good in
its regular bottling★ and can be outstanding as a Special Selection★★★.
There is also Conundrum, an exotic, full-flavoured blended white. Mer
& Soleil, a new label for MONTEREY Chardonnay, was an instant success.
Best years: (Special Selection) (1995) 94 92 91 90 **87 86** 85 **84 80**.

DOMAINE CAZES *Rivesaltes, Roussillon, France*   The Cazes brothers
make outstanding MUSCAT DE RIVESALTES★★, RIVESALTES Vieux★★ and the
superb Aimé Cazes★★★, but also produce a wide range of red and
white table wines, mainly as COTES DU ROUSSILLON and Vin de Pays des
Côtes Catalanes. Look out for the soft, fruity le Canon du Maréchal★
and the small production of barrel-fermented Chardonnay. In 1996
they launched the Cabernet-based le Credo★, a VIN DE PAYS grown on
AC land. Best years: (reds) **1996 95 94 93 92 91 90 89 88**.

CELLIER DES SAMSONS *Beaujolais, Burgundy, France*   A group of 10
quality-minded co-ops, producing consistently decent wines from the
Beaujolais and Mâconnais regions. Bought in 1996 by Jean-Claude
BOISSET. The best are sold under the Cuvée Authentique label. Look out
for MOULIN-A-VENT, BEAUJOLAIS-VILLAGES, ST-VERAN and MACON-VILLAGES.

CELLIER LE BRUN *Marlborough, South Island, New Zealand*   Champagne-
method specialist. Vintage BLANC DE BLANCS is ★★, although blended
vintage and non-vintage bubblies are consistently good.

CENCIBEL   See Tempranillo.

CENTRAL COAST AVA *California, USA* Huge AVA covering virtually every vineyard between San Francisco and Los Angeles, with a number of sub-AVAs, such as Santa Cruz, Santa Ynez, SANTA MARIA and MONTEREY, which include some excellent cooler areas for Pinot Noir and Chardonnay. See also Monterey County, San Luis Obispo County, Santa Barbara County.

CENTRAL OTAGO *South Island, New Zealand* The only wine region in New Zealand with a continental rather than maritime climate. The long, cool ripening season may prove to be ideal for flavour development in early-ripening varieties such as Pinot Noir, Gewürztraminer and possibly Chardonnay, even if it's risky for later varieties such as Riesling. Twenty wineries now, another 5 within a year or two, and many more planning vineyards in New Zealand's newest and fastest-growing wine region. Best producers: Black Ridge, Chard Farm, Gibbston Valley, Rippon Vineyards.

CENTRAL VALLEY *Chile* The heart of Chile's wine industry, encompassing the valleys of MAIPO, Rapel, Curicó and Maule. Most major producers are located here and the key factor determining mesoclimate differences is the distance relative to the coastal and Andean Cordilleras. Best producers: CANEPA★, CARMEN★★, CONO SUR★, LA ROSA★, VALDIVIESO★.

CENTRAL VALLEY *California, USA* This vast area grows over 50% of California's wine grapes, used mostly for cheaper styles of wine. Viewed overall, the quality has improved over the past few years, but it is still an overheated area, where irrigated vineyards tend to produce excess tonnage of grapes, much of it siphoned off into production of brandies and grape concentrate. It has often been said that it is virtually impossible to produce exciting wine in the Central Valley, but in fact the climatic conditions in the northern half are not that unlike those in many parts of Spain and southern France. During the 1990s, growers in the Lodi AVA quickly expanded vineyards to 22,000ha (55,000 acres), making Lodi the volume leader for Chardonnay, Merlot, Zinfandel and Cabernet. Lodi Zinfandel shows some potential. Other sub-regions with claims to quality are the Sacramento Valley and the Delta area. Best producers: MONDAVI Woodbridge, Sutter Home.

CERETTO *Piedmont, Italy* This merchant house, run by brothers Bruno and Marcello Ceretto, has gained a reputation as one of the chief modern producers in BAROLO. The style is soft and fragrant, with low tannins. With the help of enologist Donato Lanati, Barolo (from Bricco Rocche★★), BARBARESCO (Bricco Asili★★) and white Arneis Blangè have recently been living up to their reputation. At the La Bernardina estate, Ceretto also produces Chardonnay★, Viognier★, Cabernet★, Pinot Nero, Syrah★ and sparkling Brut.

CÉRONS AC *Bordeaux, France* An AC for sweet wine in the GRAVES region of Bordeaux. The soft, mildly honeyed wine is not quite so sweet as SAUTERNES and for that reason not so well known, nor so highly priced. Most producers now make dry wine under the Graves label. Best producers: Ch. de Cérons★, Grand Enclos du Château de Cérons★, Chantegrive, Seuil. Best years: (1998) 97 **96 95 90 89 86 83**.

L A CETTO *Baja California, Mexico* Mexico's most successful winery, with 1000ha (2470 acres) under vine, relies on mists and cooling Pacific breezes to temper the heat of the Valle de Guadalupe. Italian winemaker Carmelo Magoni is making ripe, fleshy Petite Sirah★, oak-aged Cabernet Sauvignon, Zinfandel and Nebbiolo. Chardonnay lacks acidity and varietal character but, paradoxically, Cetto makes a decent stab at fizz.

CHABLAIS *Vaud, Switzerland*   A sub-region of the VAUD, south-east of Lake Geneva. Most of the vineyards lie on the alluvial plains but 2 villages, Yvorne and AIGLE, benefit from much steeper slopes and produce tangy whites and good reds. Most of the thirst-quenchingly dry whites are made from the Chasselas, or Dorin as it is called locally. The reds are made from Pinot Noir, as is a rosé speciality, Oeil de Perdrix, an enjoyable summer wine. Drink the whites and rosés young. Best producers: Badoux, Delarze, Grognuz, Undermühle.

CHABLIS AC *Burgundy, France*   Chablis, halfway between Paris and Dijon, is Burgundy's northernmost outpost. Chardonnay ripens here with difficulty and there is a dreadful record of frost, which makes pricing volatile. Chablis' other problem is that its name has become synonymous with cheap, dry-to-medium, white-to-off-white wine from any available grape. Real Chablis is always white and dry, but with a steely mineral fruit which can make for delicious drinking. An increasing number of producers are experimenting with oak barrel-aging, resulting in some full, toasty, positively rich dry whites. In general straight Chablis AC should be drunk young, but the better ones can improve for 3–5 years. Best producers: J-C Bessin★, J-M Brocard★, la CHABLISIENNE★, D & E Defaix★★, DROIN★, DROUHIN★★, DURUP, A Geoffroy★, J-P Grossot★★, LABOURE-ROI★, Laroche★, Long-Depaquit★, Malandes★, Marroniers★, MICHEL★★, Pascal Bouchard★, L Pinson★, M Régnard★, Simonnet-Febvre★, Vocoret et Fils★. Best years: 1997 **96 95 92 90 89**.

CHABLIS GRAND CRU AC *Burgundy, France*   The 7 Grands Crus (Bougros, les Preuses, Vaudésir, Grenouilles, Valmur, les Clos and les Blanchots) facing south-west across the town of Chablis are the heart of the AC. Oak barrel-aging takes the edge off taut flavours, adding a rich warmth to these fine wines. DROIN and Fèvre are the most enthusiastic users of new oak, but use it less than they used to. Never drink young: 5–10 years is needed before you begin to see why you spent your money. Best producers: Billaud-Simon★★, J-C Bessin★★★, la CHABLISIENNE★★, DAUVISSAT★★★, D & E Defaix★★, DROIN★★, W Fèvre★★, Laroche★★, Long-Depaquit★, MICHEL★★, RAVENEAU★★★, Guy Robin★★, M Servin★★, Simonnet-Febvre★★, Vocoret et Fils★★. Best years: 1996 95 93 **92 90 89 88 85 83**.

CHABLIS PREMIER CRU AC *Burgundy, France*   Just over a quarter of CHABLIS' vineyards are designated Premier Cru. Some are on splendid slopes (the best are Montée de Tonnerre, Vaillons, Mont de Milieu and Fourchaumes) but many of the newer ones are on slopes of questionable quality. Premiers Crus vary widely in quality, but the good ones are excellent value, at only about 20% above the price of basic Chablis. The wines should taste bigger and more intensely mineral than basic Chablis and may take as long as 5 years to show full potential. Best producers: J-C Bessin★, la CHABLISIENNE★, D Dampt★★, DAUVISSAT★★, D & E Defaix★★, DROIN★★, W Fèvre★, Laroche★, MICHEL★★, RAVENEAU★★, Simonnet-Febvre★, G Tremblay★, Vocoret et Fils★. Best years: 1997 96 **95 93 92 90 89 88**.

LA CHABLISIENNE *Chablis, Burgundy, France*   Substantial co-op producing nearly a third of all CHABLIS. The wines are reliable and can aspire to greatness. The best are the oaky Grands Crus – especially les Preuses★★ and Grenouilles (sold as Ch. Grenouille★★) – but the basic unoaked Chablis★, the Cuvée Vieilles Vignes★ and the numerous Premiers Crus★ are excellent, as is the red BOURGOGNE Épineuil from Pinot Noir. Best years: (whites) 1997 **96 95 92 90**; (reds) 1996 **95 93 90**.

CHALONE *Monterey County, California, USA* Producers of full-blown but slow-developing Chardonnay★★ and concentrated Pinot Noir★★★ from vineyards on the arid eastern slope of the Coastal Range in mid-MONTEREY COUNTY. Also makes very good Pinot Blanc★ and Chenin Blanc★, as well as Reserve bottlings of Pinot Noir★★★ and Chardonnay★★. These are strongly individualistic wines. Wines not making the cut are diverted to the rapidly growing Echelon label. Best years: (Chardonnay) (1997) 96 95 **94 93 92 91 90 89 85**; (Pinot Noir) (1996) 95 94 **92 91 90 88 86 83**.

CHAMBERS *Rutherglen, Victoria, Australia* Family winery making sheer nectar in the form of Muscat and Tokay. The secret is Bill Chambers' ability to draw on ancient stocks put down in wood by earlier generations. His 'Special'★★ and 'Old'★★★ blends are national treasures. The Cabernet is inexpensive and good, the whites pedestrian.

CHAMBERTIN AC *Grand Cru, Côte de Nuits, Burgundy, France* The village of GEVREY-CHAMBERTIN, the largest Côte de Nuits commune, has no fewer than 8 Grands Crus (Chambertin, Chambertin-Clos-de-Bèze, Chapelle-Chambertin, Charmes-Chambertin, Griotte-Chambertin, Latricières-Chambertin, Mazis-Chambertin and Ruchottes-Chambertin) which can produce some of Burgundy's greatest and most intense red wine. Its rough-hewn fruit, seeming to war with fragrant perfumes for its first few years, creates remarkable flavours as the wine ages. Chambertin and Chambertin-Clos-de-Bèze are the greatest sites, but overproduction is a recurrent problem. Even so, the best examples are wonderful and they can age for decades. Best producers: Denis Bachelet★★, CLAIR★★, P Damoy★, DROUHIN★★, FAIVELEY★★★, R Groffier★, JADOT★★, Dom. LEROY★★★, Denis Mortet★★, H Perrot-Minot★★, Ponsot★, Dom. Remy★, Rossignol-Trapet★★, J Roty★, ROUMIER★★, ROUSSEAU★★★. Best years: 1997 96 95 93 **91** 90 89 88 **85**.

CHAMBERTIN-CLOS-DE-BÈZE AC See Chambertin AC.

CHAMBOLLE-MUSIGNY AC *Côte de Nuits, Burgundy, France* AC with the potential to produce the most fragrant, perfumed red Burgundy, when not over-cropped and over-sugared. Encouragingly, more young producers are now bottling their own wines. The 1995s were outstanding. Best producers: Barthod-Noëllat★★, DROUHIN★★, DUJAC, R Groffier★, JADOT, Dom. LEROY, Marchand-Grillot★, J-F Mugnier★, RION, ROUMIER★★, B Serveau★, VOGUE★★. Best years: 1997 96 95 93 **90 89 88**.

CHAMPAGNE See pages 98–9.

CHAMPAGNE ROSÉ *Champagne, France* Good pink CHAMPAGNE has a delicious fragrance of cherries and raspberries. The top wines can age well, but most should be drunk on release. Best producers: BILLECART-SALMON★★, BOLLINGER★★, A Bonnet★, Charbaut★, Charles HEIDSIECK★★, Jacquesson★★, KRUG★★★, LANSON★, LAURENT-PERRIER★★, Mathieu★, MOET & CHANDON★, Nicolas Feuillatte★, PERRIER-JOUET★★, POL ROGER★★, Pommery★, ROEDERER★★, TAITTINGER (Comtes de Champagne)★★. Best years: (1996) (95) **91 90 89 88 86 85 83 82**. See also pages 98–9.

CHAMPAGNE AC

Champagne, France

The Champagne region produces the most celebrated sparkling wines in the world. East of Paris, it is the most northerly AC in France – a place where grapes struggle to ripen fully. Champagne is divided into 5 distinct areas – the best are the Montagne de Reims, where the Pinot Noir grape performs brilliantly, and the Chardonnay-dominated Côte des Blancs south of Épernay. If you buy a bottle of Coteaux Champenois, a still wine from the area, you can see why they decided to make bubbly instead; it tastes mean and tart, but is transformed by the Champagne method into some of the most complex wines of all.

That's the theory anyway, and for 150 years or so the Champenois have suavely persuaded us that their product is second to none. It can be, too, except when it is released too young or sweetened to make up for a lack of richness. A combination of high prices and competition from other sparkling wines has produced a glut of Champagne. But as Champagne expertise begins to turn out exciting sparklers in California, Australia and New Zealand, the Champagne producers must re-focus on quality or lose much of their market for good.

The Champagne trade is dominated by large companies or houses, called négociants-manipulants, recognized by the letters NM on the label. The récoltants-manipulants (recognized by the letters RM) are growers who make their own wine.

STYLES OF CHAMPAGNE

Non-vintage Most Champagne is a blend of 2 or more vintages. Quality varies enormously, depending on who has made the wine and how long it has been aged. Most Champagne is sold as Brut, which is a dry, but not bone-dry style. Interestingly, Extra Dry denotes a style less dry than Brut.

Vintage Denotes Champagne made with grapes from a single vintage. As a rule, it is made only in the best years.

Blanc de Blancs A lighter style of Champagne made solely from the Chardonnay grape.

Blanc de Noirs A white Champagne, but made entirely from black grapes, either Pinor Noir, Pinot Meunier, or a combination of the two. Generally rather solid.

Rosé Pink Champagne, made either from black grapes or (more usually) by mixing a little still red wine into white Champagne.

De luxe cuvée In theory the finest Champagne and certainly always the most expensive, residing in the fanciest bottles.

See also BRUT, CHAMPAGNE ROSE, GRANDES MARQUES; AND INDIVIDUAL PRODUCERS.

BEST PRODUCERS

Houses BILLECART-SALMON, BOLLINGER, de Castellane, Charbaut, Delamotte, DEUTZ, Gosset, Alfred GRATIEN, Charles HEIDSIECK, Henriot, Jacquesson, KRUG, LANSON, LAURENT-PERRIER, Leclerc Briant, Bruno Paillard, Joseph PERRIER, PERRIER-JOUET, Philipponnat, POL ROGER, Pommery, Louis ROEDERER, RUINART, Salon, TAITTINGER, VEUVE CLICQUOT.

Growers Bara, Barnaut, Beaufort, Beerens, Brice, Callot, Cattier, Charpentier, Delbeck, Diebolt Vallois, Egly-Ouriet, Gardet, Gimmonet, A Jaquart, Lamiable, Larmandier, Launois, A Margaine, Mathieu, G Michel, Moncuit, Secondé, Selosse, de Sousa, Soutiran-Pelletier, Tarlant, J Vesselle, Vilmart.

Co-ops Beaumont les Crayères, Mailly co-op, Nicolas Feuillatte, Palmer.

De luxe cuvées Belle Époque (PERRIER-JOUET), N-F Billecart (BILLECART-SALMON), Blanc de Millénaires (Charles HEIDSIECK), Clos de Mesnil (KRUG), Comtes de Champagne (TAITTINGER), Cristal (Louis ROEDERER), Cuvée Josephine (Joseph PERRIER), Cuvée Sir Winston Churchill (POL ROGER), Cuvée William Deutz (DEUTZ), Dom Pérignon (MOET & CHANDON), Dom Ruinart (RUINART), Grand Siècle (LAURENT-PERRIER), Grande Dame (VEUVE CLICQUOT), Noble Cuvée (LANSON), Vintage RD (BOLLINGER).

CHAPEL DOWN *Kent, England* Wines here are from bought-in grapes. Summerhill is the cheapest range; Epoch the most expensive, notably the sparkling Epoch Brut Non-Vintage★ and Vintage★★, though the curious but flavoursome wood-aged red is worth a punt. Now associated with Tenterden Vineyard; David Cowderoy is winemaker.

CHAPEL HILL *McLaren Vale, South Australia* Pam Dunsford has wide winemaking experience (she worked at WYNNS and SEAVIEW for many years). Chapel Hill is no longer a boutique – it doubled its vineyard holdings in 1997, with some great mature MCLAREN VALE vineyards. Pam blends McLaren Vale and COONAWARRA in her Cabernet Sauvignon★★, while Reserve Shiraz★★ is all McLaren Vale. Smart Eden Valley Riesling★ and Chardonnay★ (look for the Reserve★★), as well as rare Verdelho★. Best years: (Shiraz) **1996 94 93 91**.

CHAPELLE-CHAMBERTIN AC See Chambertin AC.

M CHAPOUTIER *Rhône Valley, France* Huge improvements here since Michel Chapoutier took over the winemaking in 1988, but inconsistency is still worrying. The HERMITAGE la Sizeranne★★ and le Pavillon★★★, CROZES-HERMITAGE★★, ST-JOSEPH★★ and COTE-ROTIE★ are all good (these days). Now jointly owns new Provençale property Domaine des Béates. Best years: (1998) 97 96 95 **91 90 89 88**.

CHARDONNAY See pages 102–3.

CHARENTAIS, VIN DE PAYS *France* Wines from the Cognac area of France; Ugni-Blanc-based whites can be good if consumed young. Also increasing amounts of Chardonnay and Sauvignon Blanc. Reds (from Bordeaux varieties) are good value, if you like a grassy tang. Best producers: Aubineau, Blanchard, Ch. de Didonne, Mallinger.

CHARMES-CHAMBERTIN AC See Chambertin AC.

CHARTA A German organization founded in 1984 in order to protect the image of the best RHEINGAU Rieslings. The accent is on dry wines which are thought to go well with food. Many are of high quality but some are rather taut and neutral.

CHASSAGNE-MONTRACHET AC *Côte de Beaune, Burgundy, France* Until recently Chassagne-Montrachet produced more red wine than white, although whites are better. Some of Burgundy's greatest white wine vineyards (part of le MONTRACHET and BATARD-MONTRACHET and all of Criots-Bâtard-Montrachet) are within the village boundary. The white Chassagne Premiers Crus are not as well-known, but can offer nutty, toasty wines. Ordinary white Chassagne-Montrachet is usually enjoyable; the red Chassagne is a little earthy, peppery and plummy and can be an acquired taste. Look out for reds from the following Premiers Crus: Clos de la Boudriotte, Clos St-Jean and Clos de la Chapelle. Best producers: (whites) P Amiot, Blain-Gagnard★★, COLIN★, Fontaine-Gagnard★★, J-N GAGNARD★★, GAGNARD-DELAGRANGE★★, H Lamy★, Duc de Magenta★, Bernard Morey★★, M Niéllon★, RAMONET★★; (reds) Jean-Claude Bachelet, CARILLON★, Raoul Clerget★, Bernard Morey★, RAMONET★. Best years: (whites) 1997 96 95 **92 90 88 88**; (reds) 1997 96 95 **93 92 90 89 88**.

CHASSELAS Chasselas is considered a table grape world-wide. Only in BADEN (where it is called Gutedel) and Switzerland (called Dorin, Perlan or Fendant) is it thought to make decent light, dry wines with a slight prickle for everyday drinking. A few Swiss examples rise above this.

CH. CHASSE-SPLEEN★ *Moulis AC, Cru Bourgeois, Haut-Médoc, Bordeaux, France* Chasse-Spleen is not a Classed Growth – but you'd never have known from the tremendous reputation built during the 1980s by the late proprietor, Bernadette Villars. The château is now run by Villars' daughter Claire and will probably take some time to return to top form. Second wine: l'Ermitage de Chasse-Spleen. Best years: (1998) 96 95 94 **90 89 88 86 83 82 81**.

CHÂTEAU French for 'castle', used to describe a wide variety of wine estates. Some, such as MARGAUX, are truly palatial. Here, all French châteaux are listed under their individual names.

CHATEAU CARRAS *Macedonia, Greece* The reds from this winery are better than the whites, but even so the Greek sun makes itself felt in dryish flavours of coffee and prunes. After a bright start quality became erratic, but is on the up again. The property, however, is now in the administration of the banks and its future uncertain.

CHÂTEAU-CHALON AC *Jura, France* The most prized – and pricy – VIN JAUNE, Jura's great speciality. It is difficult to find, even in the region itself. Best producers: Bourdy★, J-M Courbet★, J Macle★★, Perron★★.

CHÂTEAU-GRILLET AC★★ *Rhône Valley, France* This rare and *very* expensive RHONE white, made from Viognier, has a magic reek of orchard fruit and harvest bloom when young and it can age well. The late 1980s and early 90s were poor, but fortunately this single-property AC has much improved since 1993. Best years: (1998) **97 96 95 93**.

CHÂTEAU LAZARIDI *Thrace, Greece* A pioneering family operation with a long-term plan to repatriate vines planted by ancient Greeks in southern Italy. Production is currently based on noble French varieties with relatively long cask- and bottle-aging. The Lazaridi red★ is very dense and concentrated but still fresh and young, and both white and red Maghiko Vouno★ show great potential. Best years: (reds) 1997 96 **95 94 93 91**.

CHATEAU MONTELENA *Napa Valley AVA, California, USA* Napa winery producing well-balanced Chardonnay and Cabernet★★ that is impressive, if slow to develop. There is also a blended red, St Vincent. Best years: (Cabernet) 1995 94 93 92 91 90 **89 86 85 84 82**; (Chardonnay) (1997) 96 95 **94 93 92 91 90**.

CHATEAU MUSAR *Ghazir, Lebanon* Founded by Gaston Hochar in the 1930s and now run by his Bordeaux-trained son Serge, Musar is famous for having made wine every year bar 2 (1976 and 84) throughout Lebanon's civil war. From an unlikely blend of Cabernet Sauvignon, Cinsaut and Syrah comes a wine of real, if wildly exotic, class – full, with lush, sweet, spicy fruit and deceptively good aging potential. Hochar himself says that red Musar★ 'should be drunk at 15 years'. From the potentially stunning 94 vintage Hochar also made a new rosé and a white, blending Chardonnay and Sémillon. Best years: (reds) **1991** 90 89 **87 85 83 81 77 72 70 69 64**; (whites) **1994**.

CHATEAU ST JEAN *Sonoma Valley AVA, California, USA* Once known almost entirely for its rich Chardonnay★, St Jean has virtually reinvented itself in the past 5 years and has emerged as a producer of delicious Cabernet Sauvignon★ and a meritage-style red called Cinq Cépage★★, which is a champion wine. A Reserve Merlot★★, released for the first time in 1995, is also worth seeking out. Best years: (white) (1997) 96 **95 94 92 91 90**; (reds) (1997) 96 95 94 93 **92 91 90 89**.

CHARDONNAY

I'm always getting asked, 'When will the world tire of Chardonnay?' And I reply 'Not in my lifetime.' The wine critics may pine for something else to write about, and the wine experts may decide that they want to explore the flavours available from other grape varieties, but for the vast majority of wine drinkers the Chardonnay revolution has only just begun, and to many people good dry white wine simply equals Chardonnay. And that's that. The amount of Chardonnay grown has increased dramatically over the last 10 years or so: it is now claimed to be the fourth most-planted white grape variety in the world.

WINE STYLES

France Although a relatively neutral variety if left alone (this is what makes it so suitable as a base wine for top-quality Champagne-method sparkling wine), the grape can ripen in almost any conditions, developing a subtle gradation of flavours going from the sharp apple core greenness of Chardonnay grown in Champagne or the Loire, through the exciting, bone-dry yet succulent flavours of white Burgundy, to a round, perfumed flavour in Languedoc-Roussillon.

Other regions Italy produces Chardonnay that is bone dry and lean as well as fat, spicy and lush. Spain does much the same. A few South African examples are beginning to show what the variety is really capable of there, but California and Australia have virtually created their reputations on great viscous, almost syrupy, tropical fruits and spice-flavoured Chardonnays. They've both toned down the flavours now, though New Zealand is currently producing some wonderfully exotic wine, and Chile and Argentina have found it easy to grow and are rapidly learning how to make fine wine from it too. Add Germany, Canada and New York State and you'll see it can perform almost anywhere.

Using oak The reason for all these different flavours lies in Chardonnay's wonderful susceptibility to the winemaker's aspirations and skills. The most important manipulation is the use of the oak barrel for fermenting and aging the wine. Chardonnay is the grape of the great white Burgundies and these are fermented and matured in oak (not necessarily new oak) but the effect is to give a marvellous round, nutty richness to a wine that is yet savoury and dry. This is enriched still further by aging the wine on its lees.

The New World winemakers sought to emulate the great Burgundies, thus planting Chardonnay and employing thousands of oak barrels (mostly new) and their success – and the enthusiasm with which wine drinkers embraced the wine – has caused winemakers everywhere else to see Chardonnay as the perfect variety – easy to grow, easy to turn into wine and easy to sell to an adoring public.

102

BEST PRODUCERS

France *Chablis* J-C Bessin, DAUVISSAT, DROIN, Laroche, MICHEL, RAVENEAU; *Côte d'Or* G Amiot, J-M Boillot, Bonneau du Martray, BOUCHARD, Michel Bouzereau, CARILLON, COCHE-DURY, Marc COLIN, DROUHIN, J-N GAGNARD, GAGNARD-DELAGRANGE, V Girardin, JADOT, F Jobard, LAFON, Lamy-Pillot, LATOUR, Dom. LEFLAIVE, Dom. LEROY, Matrot, Bernard Morey, Niellon, RAMONET, Roulot, SAUZET, VERGET; *Mâconnais* Barraud, Ferret, Ch. FUISSE, Guffens-Heynen, Merlin, Thévenet, Valette.

Other European Chardonnays

Austria VELICH.

Germany Karl-Heinz JOHNER.

Italy BELLAVISTA, CA' DEL BOSCO, JERMANN, Edi Kante, LAGEDER, Manzano, Vie di Romans.

Spain TORRES.

New World Chardonnays

Australia BANNOCKBURN, Giaconda, Howard Park, LEEUWIN, PENFOLDS, PETALUMA, PIERRO, ROSEMOUNT, TYRRELL'S, Geoff WEAVER, YARRA YERING.

New Zealand CLOUDY BAY, COLLARDS, Isabel, KUMEU RIVER, NEUDORF, TE MATA, Trinity Hill.

USA AU BON CLIMAT, BERINGER, CALERA, CHALONE, FERRARI-CARANO, KISTLER, Landmark, Marcassin, MERRYVALE, MATANZAS CREEK, Peter MICHAEL, Pahlmeyer, SAINTSBURY, STEELE, R Talbott, Villa Mount Eden.

South Africa GLEN CARLOU, HAMILTON RUSSELL, MEERLUST, THELEMA.

South America CATENA, VINA CASABLANCA.

CHATEAU STE MICHELLE *Washington State, USA* A pioneering winery with an enormous range of wines, including several smashing vineyard-designated Chardonnays★★, Cabernet Sauvignons★ and Merlots★★, especially the Cold Creek Vineyard★★ wines. Makes good Riesling, both dry and sweet, and increasingly interesting red Meritage, Syrah and Sauvignon. COLUMBIA CREST began as a budget second label for good-value wines and has blossomed into a stand-alone winery with an excellent range, especially estate-bottled Reserve Chardonnay★, juicy Cabernet Sauvignon and Merlot★. Best years: (reds) (1998) 97 96 95 **94 92 91** 89.

CHATEAU TAHBILK *Goulburn Valley, Victoria, Australia* Wonderfully old-fashioned family company making traditionally big, gumleafy/minty reds, matured only in old wood. Regional speciality white Marsanne★★ is perfumed and attractive. Other whites tend to lack finesse, but Shiraz★ and Cabernet★ are full of character, even if they need years of cellaring. Best years: (reds) 1995 94 91 90 88 **86 84 81 79 78** 76 71 64 62.

CHÂTEAUNEUF-DU-PAPE AC *Rhône Valley, France* A large vineyard area between Orange and Avignon that used to be one of the most abused of all wine names. Now, much Châteauneuf comes from single estates and deservedly ranks as one of France's top reds. Always get an estate wine, and these are distinguished by the papal coat of arms embossed on the neck of the bottle. Only 5% of Châteauneuf is white. Made mainly from Grenache Blanc, Bourboulenc and Clairette, these wines can be surprisingly good. The top reds will age for 8 years or more, while the whites are best drunk young. Best producers: (reds) L Barrot★★, BEAUCASTEL★★★, H Bonneau★★, Bosquet des Papes★★, Dom. du Père Caboche, les Cailloux★★, Chante-Cigale★, Chante-Perdrix★, la Charbonnière★★, G Charvin★★, les Clefs d'Or★★, Clos du Caillou★★, Clos du Mont Olivet★★, CLOS DES PAPES★★★, Crouzet-Feraval★★, Font du Loup★★, FONT DE MICHELLE★, Fortia★★, GRAND TINEL★★, Marcoux★★, Montpertuis★★, Mont Redon★, Nalys★, la Nerthe★★, Pégau★★, RAYAS★★★, Roger Sabon★★, Tardieu-Laurent★, Vieux Donjon★, VIEUX TELEGRAPHE★★, Villen-euve★★; (whites) BEAUCASTEL★★★, CLOS DES PAPES★★, FONT DE MICHELLE★★, la Janasse★, Mont Redon★, la Nerthe★, RAYAS★★, VIEUX TELEGRAPHE★. Best years (reds): (1998) 97 96 95 94 **93 91 90 89 88 86 85 83 81** 78.

CHAVE *Rhône Valley, France* Jean-Louis Chave, son of founder Gérard, has deservedly achieved superstar status in recent years. His red HERMITAGE★★★, produced in exceptional years, is one of the world's great wines, a thick, complex expression of the spicy, peppery Syrah grape at its best, requiring 10 years in bottle to open out. His wonderful white Hermitage★★★ sometimes even outlasts the reds, as it quietly moves toward its honeyed, nutty zenith. Chave also produces a small amount of excellent red ST-JOSEPH★★. Very expensive, but worth the money. Best years: (reds) (1998) (97) 96 95 94 **92** 91 90 89 **88 86 85 83 82 81 79 78**; (whites) (1998) (97) 96 95 94 **93 92 91 90 89 88 82**.

CHÉNAS AC *Beaujolais, Burgundy, France* The smallest of the Beaujolais Crus and its wines, usually quite tough when young, benefit from 2 or more years' aging when they take on chocolaty tones. Best producers: Boccards, G Braillon★, L Champagnon★, Ch. de Chénas, H Lapierre★, P Perrachon, Daniel Robin★, Tremont. Best years: 1998 97 **96 95 94** 91.

CHENIN BLANC One of the most underrated white wine grapes in the world. Found mainly in the LOIRE VALLEY, where it is also called Pineau de la Loire, it is responsible for the great sweet wines of QUARTS DE CHAUME and BONNEZEAUX, as well as being the variety for VOUVRAY, sweet or dry, and much other Anjou white. It is also the main grape for the Loire sparkling wines. In South Africa, Chenin (also known as Steen) accounts for almost one-third of the vineyard area, used for everything from easy-drinking, dryish whites through botrytized desserts to modern barrel-fermented versions. CALIFORNIA, with a few exceptions like Chappellet, only employs it as a useful blender, while New Zealand and Australia have produced the best varietal examples.

CH. CHEVAL BLANC★★★ *St-Émilion Grand Cru AC, 1er Grand Cru Classé, Bordeaux, France* The leading ST-EMILION estate and likely to remain so for the foreseeable future. Right on the border with POMEROL, it seems to share some of its sturdy richness, but with an extra spice and fruit that is impressively, recognizably unique. An unusually high percentage (60%) of Cabernet Franc is used in the blend. Best years: (1998) 97 96 95 94 93 90 89 88 **86 85 83 82 81**.

CHEVALIER-MONTRACHET AC See Montrachet AC.

DOM. DE CHEVALIER *Pessac-Léognan AC, Cru Classé de Graves, Bordeaux, France* This estate mainly devoted to red can produce some of Bordeaux's finest wines. The red★★ always starts out dry and tannic but over 10–20 years gains heavenly cedar, tobacco and blackcurrant flavour. The brilliant white★★★ is both fermented and aged in oak barrels; in the best vintages it will still be improving at 15–20 years. Best years: (reds) (1998) 97 96 95 **93** 90 89 **88 85 83 81 78**; (whites) (1998) 97 96 95 **94 90 89 88** 86 85 83 82 81 76.

CHEVERNY AC *Loire Valley, France* A little-known area south of Blois. The local speciality is the white Romorantin grape, used to make a bone-dry wine with the AC Cour Cheverny, but the best whites are from Chardonnay. Also pleasant Sauvignon, Pinot Noir and Gamay and a bracing Champagne-method fizz. Best producers: Cazin, Cheverny co-op, Courtioux, Gendrier★, Gueritte, Salvard, Sauger, Tessier, Tué Boeuf.

CHIANTI DOCG *Tuscany, Italy* The most famous of all Italian wines, but there are many styles, depending on what grapes are used, where they are grown, and by which producer. It can be a light, fresh, easy-drinking red wine, but with a characteristic hint of bitterness, like a slightly aggressive Beaujolais, or it can be an intense, structured yet sleek wine in the same league as the best Bordeaux. The vineyards are scattered over central Tuscany. In 1932, a law defined 7 zones for Chianti – Classico, Colli Aretini, Colli Fiorentini, Colli Senesi, Colline Pisane, Montalbano and Rufina – and these have been reinforced by modern DOC and DOCG regulations. Sangiovese is the main grape, though it was traditionally blended with the red Canaiolo and the white Malvasia and Trebbiano. Modern winemakers often ignored the others, especially the white, and made Chianti from Sangiovese alone or blended with 10–15% of Cabernet, Merlot or Syrah. The DOCG for Chianti Classico sanctions this, and other zones are now expected to follow suit. See also Chianti Classico, Chianti Colli Fiorentini, Chianti Colli Senesi, Chianti Rufina, Super-Tuscans.

CHIANTI CLASSICO DOCG *Tuscany, Italy* The original (if slightly enlarged) CHIANTI zone from the hills between Florence and Siena. Much of the best Chianti originates here; there are 200-odd named producers and Classico has led the trend in making richer, more structured and better-balanced wines. Nonetheless, many producers use their best grapes for high-profile SUPER-TUSCANS. From the 95 vintage, Classico can be made from 100% Sangiovese; the Riserva (which some Super-Tuscans may become) may now be aged in barrel for 2 instead of 3 years but must only use red grapes. The finest Riserva wines can improve for a decade or more. Many of the estates also offer regular bottlings of red wine, round and fruity, for drinking about 2–5 years after the harvest. Best producers: (Riservas) Castello di AMA★★, ANTINORI★★, Badia a Coltibuono★★, Castello di Bossi★★, Brolio★, Cacchiano★, Capaccia★★, Carobbio★★, Casaloste★★, Castellare★★, CASTELL'IN VILLA★★, Cecchi (Villa Cerna★), Cennatoio★, Le Cinciole★, Dievole★, Casa Emma★★, FELSINA★★, Le Filigare★, FONTERUTOLI★★, FONTODI★★, Gagliole (non-DOCG)★★, ISOLE E OLENA★★, Lilliano★, La Massa★★, Melini, Monsanto★★, Monte Bernardi★, MONTEVERTINE (non-DOCG)★★, Il Palazzino★★, Paneretta★, Poggerino★★, Poggio Scalette (non-DOCG)★★★, Poggio al Sole★★, Querceto★, Querciabella★★, Castello di RAMPOLLA★★, RIECINE★★, Rocca di Castagnoli★, Rocca di Montegrossi★★, RUFFINO★★, San Felice★, San Giusto a Rentennano★★, San Polo in Rosso★, Casa Sola★, Terrabianca★, Valtellina★★, Vecchie Terre di Montefili★★, Verrazzano★, Vicchiomaggio★, Vignamaggio★, Villa Cafaggio★, VOLPAIA★★. Best years: (1998) 97 96 **95 94 93 91 90 88 86 85**. See also Super-Tuscans.

CHIANTI COLLI FIORENTINI *Chianti DOCG, Tuscany, Italy* Colli Fiorentini covers the hills around Florence. The wines traditionally are made to drink young, though some estates make Riservas of real interest. Best producers: (Riservas) Baggiolino★, Le Calvane, Il Corno, Corzano e Paterno★, Dell'Ugo, Lanciola II★, Pasolini dall'Onda★, Petriolo, Poppiano★, La Querce, Sammontana, San Vito in Fior di Selva, Sonnino.

CHIANTI COLLI SENESI *Chianti DOCG, Tuscany, Italy* This CHIANTI sub-zone consists of a vast area of Siena province (including the wine towns of Montalcino, Montepulciano and San Gimignano), with wines ranging from everyday quaffers to some fairly elegant Riservas. Best producers: (Riservas) Casale-Falchini★, Il Colle, Farnetella★, Ficomontanino★, Montemorli, Pacina, Pietraserena, Il Poggiolo, Signano.

CHIANTI RUFINA *Chianti DOCG, Tuscany, Italy* Smallest of the CHIANTI sub-zones, situated in an enclave of the Apennine mountains to the east of Florence, where wines were noted for exceptional strength, structure and longevity long before they joined the ranks of Chianti. Today the wines, particularly the long-lived Riserva from both SELVAPIANA and the ancient FRESCOBALDI estate of Castello di Nipozzano, match the best of CHIANTI CLASSICO. Best producers: (Riservas) Basciano★★, Tenuta di Bossi★, Il Cavaliere, Colognole, FRESCOBALDI★★, SELVAPIANA★★, Travignoli, Villa di Vetrice. Best years: (1998) 97 96 95 **94 93 90 88 86 85**.

CHIARETTO Italian for a rosé or rosato wine of medium pink colour. Used mainly in BARDOLINO and Riviera del Garda Bresciano.

CHIMNEY ROCK *Stags Leap AVA, California, USA* After a shaky start, winemaker Doug Fletcher stepped in to put Chimney Rock on the right track, with powerful yet elegantly shaped Cabernet Sauvignon★★ and a Reserve-style meritage called Elevage★★. The wines are superb, with deep elements of fruit, opening into a long, layered finish. Best years: (1998) 97 96 95 94 **92 91 90 87 86**.

CHINON AC *Loire Valley, France* Best red wine of the Loire Valley, made mainly from Cabernet Franc. Full of raspberry fruit and fresh summer earth when young, can improve for 20 years: always worth buying a single-estate wine. Best producers: Philippe Alliet★★, B Baudry★, J & C Baudry★, COULY-DUTHEIL★, Delaunay Père et Fils★, DRUET★★, la Grille★, JOGUET★★, Lenoir★, Noblaie★, J-M Raffault★, Olga Raffault★, Raifault. Best years: (reds) (1998) 97 **96 95 93 90 89 88 85 83 82 78 76**.

CHIROUBLES AC *Beaujolais, Burgundy, France* Lightest, most delicately fragrant of the BEAUJOLAIS Crus; expensive for only a slightly superior BEAUJOLAIS-VILLAGES. Best producers: Chiroubles co-op, DUBOEUF, la Grosse Pierre, Javernand, Alain Passot★. Best years: 1998 **97 96 95**.

CHIVITE *Navarra DO, Navarra, Spain* The longtime leader in wine exports from NAVARRA, owned and run by the Chivite family. The wine is reliable to very good. The Colección 125 red★, Moscatel★★ and Chardonnay★★ are its top wines. Best years: (reds) **1996 95 94 92**; (whites) 1996 **95 94**.

CHOREY-LÈS-BEAUNE AC *Côte de Beaune, Burgundy, France* One of those tiny, forgotten villages that make good, if not great, Burgundy at prices most of us can still afford, with some committed producers too. Can age for 5–8 years. Best producers: Arnoux Père et Fils, DROUHIN, GERMAIN★, Maillard Père et Fils, TOLLOT-BEAUT★. Best years: 1997 **96 95 93 90**.

CHURCHILL *Port DOC, Douro, Portugal* Johnny and Caroline Graham started Churchill (her maiden name) in 1981; it was the first new port shipper for 50 years. The wines are good, notably vintage★★, LBV★, Crusted★★, single quinta Agua Alta★★ and well-aged dry white★ ports. Best years: (vintage) 1994 **91 85**; (Agua Alta) 1995 92 87.

CINQUETERRE DOC *Liguria, Italy* From hills that rise steeply above the sea west of La Spezia, this white wine sells to the tourists, no matter what the quality. At its best, it is dry and crisp: the sweet white, called Sciacchetrà and made from PASSITO grapes, can be excellent. Best producers: De Battè★, Forlini e Cappellini, Gasparini, Riomaggiore co-op★.

CINSAUT Found mainly in France's southern RHONE, PROVENCE and the MIDI, giving a light wine with fresh, but rather fleeting, neutral fruit. Popular as a blender in South Africa and Lebanon's CHATEAU MUSAR.

CIRÒ DOC *Calabria, Italy* The fact that this was the wine offered to champions in the ancient Olympics seemed a more potent reason to buy it than for quality. Yet Cirò Rosso, a full-bodied red from the Gaglioppo grape, has improved remarkably of late. New wines, such as Librandi's Gravello★★ (an oak-aged blend with Cabernet), are even better. The DOC also covers a dry white from Greco and a rare dry rosé. Best producers: Caparra & Siciliani, Librandi★, San Francesco★. Best years: (reds) (1998) 97 **96 95 93 90 88**.

CH. CISSAC★ *Haut-Médoc AC, Cru Bourgeois, Bordeaux, France* High-quality wines made by proudly traditional methods: old vines, lots of wood and meticulous selection for the final blend. The wines are deeply coloured, with a high proportion of Cabernet, and are very slow to mature. Best years: (1998) 96 95 94 90 89 **88 86 85 83 82 81 78**.

BRUNO CLAIR *Marsannay, Côte de Nuits, Burgundy, France* A highly competent winemaker based in unfashionable Marsannay, Bruno Clair produces a large range of excellent wines from a broad span of vineyards there, as well as in FIXIN, GEVREY-CHAMBERTIN, GIVRY, SAVIGNY and VOSNE-ROMANEE. Most of his wine is red, but there is a small amount of white★ and a delicious Marsannay rosé★. Top wines are CHAMBERTIN Clos de Bèze★★, SAVIGNY La Dominode★★ from very old vines and vineyard-designated Marsannay reds★. Best years: 1997 96 95 93 **92 90 89 88**.

CLAIRETTE DE DIE AC *Rhône Valley, France* One of the undeservedly forgotten sparkling wines of France, made from a minimum of 75% Muscat, off-dry with a creamy bubble and an orchard-fresh fragrance. The *méthode Dioise* is used, which preserves the Muscat scent. By this method the bottle re-fermentation is stopped before all the sugar is converted to carbon dioxide and alcohol and the wine is filtered and re-bottled under pressure. Drink young. Best producers: Achard-Vincent★, A Andrieux, Clairette de Die co-op★, Jacques Faure.

A CLAPE *Cornas, Rhône Valley, France* The leading estate in CORNAS. Clape's wines★★★ are consistently among the best in the RHONE – dense, tannic and full of rich, roasted fruit. Clape also makes fine COTES DU RHONE, both red★ and white★. Best years: (1998) 96 95 94 91 **90 89 88 86 85 82**.

LA CLAPE *Coteaux du Languedoc AC, Languedoc, France* The mountain of La Clape rears unexpectedly from the flat coastal fields south-east of Narbonne. The vineyards here are a Cru within the COTEAUX DU LANGUEDOC AC and produce some of the best Aude wines. There are excellent whites from Bourboulenc and Clairette, plus some good reds and rosés, mainly from Carignan. The whites and reds can age. Best producers: Mire l'Étang, Pech-Celeyran, Pech-Redon★★, Vires. Best years: (1998) 96 **95 94 93 91 90**.

CLARET English for red Bordeaux wines, from the French *clairet*, which was traditionally used to describe a lighter style of red Bordeaux. See also Bordeaux Clairet.

CLARE VALLEY *South Australia* Upland valley north of Adelaide with a deceptively moderate climate, able to grow fine, aromatic Riesling, marvellously textured Semillon, and rich, robust Shiraz and Cabernet-based reds. More recently several voluptuous Grenaches. Best producers: (whites) ADAMS★★, Jim BARRY★★, BLASS★★ (Gold Label), Leo Buring (Leonay★★★), GROSSET★★★, KNAPPSTEIN★★, LEASINGHAM★, MITCHELL★, Mount Horrocks, PETALUMA★★★, Pike; (reds) ADAMS★★, Jim BARRY★, LEASINGHAM★★, MITCHELL★★, WENDOUREE★★★.

CH. CLARKE *Listrac-Médoc AC, Bordeaux, France* Owned by the late Baron Edmond de Rothschild, this property had millions spent on it during the late 1970s and the wines are reaping the benefit. From the 98 vintage, Michel Rolland has been consultant enologist. The wines have an attractive blackcurrant fruit, though they never quite escape the typical Listrac earthiness. And with a name like Clarke, how could they possibly fail to be seductive? There is also a small production of dry white wine, le Merle Blanc. Best years: (1998) 96 95 **90 89 88 86 85 83**.

DOMENICO CLERICO *Barolo DOCG, Piedmont, Italy* Domenico Clerico is one of the best of the younger generation of BAROLO producers. He produces impressive Barolos (Pajana★★, Ciabot Mentin Ginestra★★★) and one of the best Barberas★★, all wonderfully balanced. His range also includes LANGHE Arte★★, a barrique-aged blend of Nebbiolo and Barbera. Best years: (Barolo) (1998) (97) (96) (95) 94 93 **92** 90 89 **88.**

CH. CLIMENS★★★ *Barsac AC, 1er Cru Classé, Bordeaux, France* The leading estate in BARSAC, with a deserved reputation for rich, elegant wines with a light, lemony acidity that keeps them fresh. Easy to drink at 5 years, a good vintage will be richer and more satisfying after 10–15 years. Second wine: les Cypres (and delicious too). Best years: (1998) 97 96 95 **91 90 89 88 86 83 76 75.**

CLOS French for a walled vineyard – as in Burgundy's CLOS DE VOUGEOT. Traditionally a sign of quality, today also commonly incorporated into the names of estates (CLOS DES PAPES), regardless of whether they are actually walled or not.

CLOS DU BOIS *Alexander Valley AVA, California, USA* Winery showcasing gentle, fruit-dominated flavours of SONOMA Chardonnay, Merlot and Cabernet. Top vineyard selections can be decidedly exciting, especially the Calcaire Chardonnay★, as well as the rich, strong Briarcrest Cabernet Sauvignon★ and Marlstone★, a red BORDEAUX blend. Best years: (reds) (1997) 96 95 **94 91 90 88 87 86.**

CLOS CENTEILLES *Minervois AC, Languedoc, France* Although labels still feature the name Domergue, this estate has been retitled. From vineyards close to Caunes-Minervois, Daniel Domergue and his wife Patricia Boyer are producing both excellent MINERVOIS and innovative VIN DE PAYS. The impressive Clos de Centeilles★★ is their top wine; Cuvée Capitelle★ and Carignanissime★ are 100% Cinsaut and Carignan respectively. Best years: (1997) 96 **95 94 93.**

CLOS DES PAPES *Châteauneuf-du-Pape AC, Rhône Valley, France* Paul Avril is one of the outstanding Châteauneuf-du-Pape producers. His reds★★★ have an unusually high proportion of Mourvèdre, which explains their longevity, but enough Grenache to be approachable in their youth and provide the initial blast of fruit. The whites★★ take on the nutty character of aged Burgundy after a decade. Best years: (reds) (1997) 96 95 94 **93 90 89 88 86 85 83 82 79.**

CLOS RENÉ★ *Pomerol AC, Bordeaux, France* This is wonderfully plummy, juicy, fleshy wine from the less fashionable western side of the POMEROL AC. You can drink Clos René young, but it also ages well for at least 10 years. Sometimes sold under the label Moulinet-Lasserre. Best years: (1998) 96 95 94 **93 90 89 88 85 83 82 81.**

CLOS DE LA ROCHE AC *Grand Cru, Côte de Nuits, Burgundy, France* The best and biggest of the 5 MOREY-ST-DENIS Grands Crus. It has a lovely, bright, red-fruits flavour when young, which should get richly chocolaty or gamy as it ages. Best producers: Guy Castagnier★★, DROUHIN★★, DUJAC★★, H Lignier, Henri Perrot-Minot★, Ponsot★★, ROUSSEAU★★. Best years: 1997 96 95 93 90 **89 88 85.**

CLOS ST-DENIS AC *Grand Cru, Côte de Nuits, Burgundy, France* This small (6.5ha/16 acres) Grand Cru, which gave its name to the village of MOREY-ST-DENIS, produces wines which are often on the light side, but should be wonderfully silky, with the texture that only great Burgundy, so far, can give. Best with 10 years or more. Best producers: DUJAC★★, Georges Lignier★★, Ponsot★★. Best years: 1997 96 95 93 90 **89** 88 85.

CLOS DE TART AC★★ *Grand Cru, Côte de Nuits, Burgundy, France* Grand Cru in the village of MOREY-ST-DENIS, and entirely owned by one firm – the Burgundy merchant Mommessin. The wine, light and elegant at first, can develop a delicious savoury richness as it ages. Best years: 1997 96 95 93 90 **89** 88 85.

CLOS DU VAL *Napa Valley AVA, California, USA* A sometimes overlooked producer of elegant Cabernet Sauvignon★, Chardonnay★, Merlot, Pinot Noir and Zinfandel★. The Reserve Cabernet★★ can age with the best. Best years: (Cabernet) 1996 95 94 92 **91 90** 87 86 85 84.

CLOS DE VOUGEOT AC *Grand Cru, Côte de Nuits, Burgundy, France* Enclosed by Cistercian monks in the 14th century, and today a considerable tourist attraction, this large vineyard is now divided among 82 owners. As a result of this division, Clos de Vougeot has become one of the most unreliable Grand Cru Burgundies, but the better wine tends to come from the upper and middle parts. When it is good it is wonderfully fleshy, turning dark and exotic with 10 years' age or more. Best producers: B Ambroise★, Amiot-Servelle★★, Chopin-Groffier★★, J-J Confuron★, R Engel★★, FAIVELEY★, GRIVOT★★, Anne Gros★★, Haegelin-Jayer★, JADOT★★, Dom. LEROY★★, MEO-CAMUZET★★, D Mortet★★, ROUMIER★★. Best years: 1997 96 95 93 **92** 90 **89** 88 85.

CLOUDY BAY *Marlborough, South Island, New Zealand* New Zealand's most successful winery, Cloudy Bay achieved cult status with the first release of the zesty, herbaceous Sauvignon Blanc★★★ in 1985. Now controlled by the Champagne house VEUVE CLICQUOT, Cloudy Bay also makes Chardonnay★★, Cabernet-Merlot★, a late-harvest Riesling★★, Pinor Noir★★ and Pelorus★★, a high-quality old-style Champagne-method fizz. Best years: (1998) **97 96 94 91**.

J-F COCHE-DURY *Meursault, Côte de Beaune, Burgundy, France* Jean-François Coche-Dury is a modest superstar, quietly turning out some of the finest wines on the COTE DE BEAUNE. His best wines are his CORTON-CHARLEMAGNE★★★ and MEURSAULT Perrières★★★, but everything he makes is excellent, even his BOURGOGNE Blanc★★. His red wines, from VOLNAY★★ and MONTHELIE★★, tend to be significantly cheaper than the whites and should be drunk younger, too. Best years: (whites) 1997 96 95 94 93 **92 90** 89 88 86 85.

COCKBURN *Port DOC, Douro, Portugal* Best known for its Special Reserve Ruby, Cockburns has much more than that to offer. Cockburns Vintage★★ is stylishly cedary and Quinta dos Canais★★ is a fine single quinta while the aged tawnies★★ are creamy and nutty. Best years: (vintage) 1994 91 **70 63**; (Quinta dos Canais) 1995 92.

CODORNÍU *Cava DO, Catalonia, Spain* The biggest Champagne-method sparkling wine company in the world. Anna de Codorníu★ and Première Cuvée Brut★, both with 85% Chardonnay, are especially good but all the sparklers are better than the CAVA average. The spectacular Art Nouveau winery and 30km (19 miles) of underground cellars in San Sadurní de Noya are really worth a visit and are an easy drive from Barcelona. Codorníu also owns the top-quality RAIMAT estate in COSTERS DEL SEGRE and the still wine company of Masía Bach in the PENEDES, in addition to the quality-conscious California winery Codorníu Napa. Drink young for freshness.

COLARES DOC *Estremadura, Portugal* The vineyards of this archaic DOC are phylloxera-free and ungrafted with the Ramisco vines planted on sand-dunes. The wines are tooth-curdlingly tannic and are *said* to soften with age, but in fact generally just wither away.

COLDSTREAM HILLS *Yarra Valley, Victoria, Australia* Although Southcorp purchased this formerly public company in 1996, James Halliday still holds the reins. Only YARRA VALLEY grapes are used, with the exception of the James Halliday export range. Pinot Noir★ is one of Australia's best: sappy and smoky with cherry fruit and clever use of oak. Chardonnay★ has subtlety and delicacy but real depth as well. Reserve labels of both can be outstanding (Chardonnay sometimes★★). Cabernet Sauvignon★ and Cabernet-Merlot★ blend are increasingly good. Best years: (Pinot Noir) **1997** 96 94 92 91 90 88.

COLHEITA Aged tawny port from a single vintage. See Port.

MARC COLIN *St-Aubin, Côte de Beaune, Burgundy, France* An excellent but often underrated domaine specializing in reds and whites from CHASSAGNE-MONTRACHET★ and ST-AUBIN★★. The St-Aubin Premiers Crus★★ are fine value, but Colin's most exquisite wine is his tiny production of le MONTRACHET★★★. All the wines are ageworthy. Best years: (whites) 1997 96 95 93 **92 90 89 88**.

COLLARDS *Henderson, Auckland, New Zealand* A small family winery that produces some of the country's finest white wines, including Rothesay Chardonnay★★ and Sauvignon Blanc★, HAWKES BAY Chardonnay★★, and MARLBOROUGH Chardonnay★, Sauvignon★★ and Riesling★. The dry Chenin Blanc is one of New Zealand's few premium examples of this grape variety. Red wines are less interesting, with the exception of a light, fruity Pinot Noir★. Best years: (whites) (1998) **96 94 91 90 89**.

COLLI BOLOGNESI DOC *Emilia, Italy* Wines from this zone in the Apennine foothills near Bologna were traditionally slightly sweet and frothy in style. Today some winemaking concessions have begun to be made to international taste, resulting in a fine Cabernet★★ from Terre Rosse. Other good red wines are produced from Merlot, and increasing amounts of dry white wine are made from Sauvignon, Pignoletto and Pinot Bianco. Best producers: Bonzara (Cabernet★★, Merlot★★), Gaggioli (Vigneto Bagazzana), San Vito, Terre Rosse★★, Vallona★. Best years: (reds) (1998) 97 **96 95 94 93**.

COLLI EUGANEI DOC *Veneto, Italy* The sheer hills south of Padova produce an array of DOC wines, still and sparkling, that are mainly taken lightly. One serious exception to this rule is the Vignalta estate, for Cabernet Riserva★★ and Merlot-Cabernet blend Gemola★★. Best producers: Ca' Lustra★, Vignalta★★, Villa Sceriman. Best years: (reds) (1998) 97 **95 94 93 90**.

COLLI ORIENTALI DEL FRIULI DOC *Friuli-Venezia Giulia, Italy* North-east Italian DOC, covering 20 different types of wine. Best known for its sweet whites from the Ramandolo sub-zone and the delicate Picolit, but it is the reds, from the indigenous Refosco and Schioppettino, as well as imports like Cabernet and dry whites, from Tocai, Ribolla, Pinot Bianco and Malvasia Istriana, that show how exciting the wines can be. Prices are high. Best producers: Bosco Romagno★, Ca' Ronesca★, Dario Coos★, Dorigo★, Dri★, Livio Felluga★★, Adriano Gigante★, Livon★, Davino Meroi★, Miani★, Rocca Bernarda★, Rodaro★, Ronchi di Cialla★★, Ronco delle Betulle★, Ronco del Gnemiz★★, Ronco dei Roseti★, Roberto Scubla★, Specogna★, Torre Rosazza★, La Viarte★, Vigne dal Leon★, Zamò e Zamò★. Best years: (whites) (1998) **97 96 95 93 90**.

COLLI PIACENTINI DOC *Emilia-Romagna, Italy* Home to some of Emilia-Romagna's best wines, this DOC covers 11 different types, the best of which are Cabernet Sauvignon and the red Gutturnio (an appealing blend of Barbera and Bonarda) as well as the medium-sweet white and bubbly Malvasia. Best producers: Campominosi, Fugazza★, Montessissa (Gutturnio Riserva Bosca del Sole★), Mossi★, Romagnoli, La Stoppa★ (Cabernet★★), La Tosa (Cabernet Sauvignon★). Best years: (reds) (1998) **97 96 95 94 93**.

COLLINES RHODANIENNES, VIN DE PAYS DES *Rhône Valley, France* From this region, between Vienne and Valence, the best wines are varietal Gamay and Syrah, although there are some good juicy Merlots, too. Best producers: Colombo★, ST-DESIRAT co-op★, Tain-Hermitage co-op, Vernay★, les Vignerons Ardèchois.

COLLIO DOC *Friuli-Venezia Giulia, Italy* These hills are the home of some of the country's best and most expensive dry white wines. The zone produces 19 types of wine, including 17 varietals, which range from the local Tocai and Malvasia Istriana to the more international: Chardonnay, Sauvignon, Pinots Bianco and Grigio, Cabernet Sauvignon, Merlot and Pinot Nero. The best white and red wines are ageworthy. Best producers: Borgo Conventi★, Borgo del Tiglio★★, Paolo Caccese, La Castellada★, Fiegl★, Livio Felluga★★, Mario Felluga★, Gradnik, GRAVNER★★★, JERMANN★★, Edi Keber★, Renato Keber★★, Livon★, Matijaz Tercic★, Primosic★, Princic★, PUIATTI★, Stanislao Radikon★, Ronco dei Tassi, Russiz Superiore★, SCHIOPETTO★★, Castello di Spessa★, Subido di Monte★, Vazzoler★, Venica & Venica★, Villa Russiz★★. Best years: (whites) (1998) **97 96 95 93 90**.

COLLIOURE AC *Roussillon, France* This tiny fishing port tucked away in the Pyrenean foothills only a few miles from the Spanish border is also an AC, and makes a throat-warming red wine that is capable of aging for a decade but is marvellously aggressive when young. Best producers: (reds) Dom. de Baillaury★, Casa Blanca, Cellier des Templiers★, Clos des Paulilles, Mas Blanc★★, la RECTORIE★★, la Tour Vieille★. Best years: (1998) 97 **96 95 94 93 90 89 88 86 85**.

COLOMBARD In France, Colombard traditionally has been distilled to make Armagnac and Cognac, but is now emerging as a table wine grape in its own right, notably as a Vin de Pays des COTES DE GASCOGNE. At its best, it has a lovely, crisp acidity and fresh, aromatic fruit. The largest plantings of the grape are in CALIFORNIA, where it generally produces rather less distinguished wines. Australia has some fair examples, and South Africa can also produce very attractive basic whites.

COLUMBIA CREST *Washington State, USA* Columbia Crest started life as a second label for CHATEAU STE MICHELLE but has evolved into a full-scale producer of good-value, top-quality wines. The Chardonnay and Estate Merlot★ are the strong suits. For fruit intensity, drink both with 2–3 years' age. There is also a promising, intense Syrah.

COLUMBIA WINERY *Columbia Valley AVA, Washington, USA* Under the guidance of David Lake MW, Columbia manages to produce an assortment of serviceable wines along with several standouts from Red Willow Vineyard. His best include deeply fruited, built-to-last Cabernet Sauvignon★★ and a fruity, smoky styled Syrah★. Merlot has improved in recent vintages. Best years: (reds) 1998 97 **95 94**.

COMMANDARIA *Cyprus* The Crusaders went batty about this dark brown, challengingly treacly wine made from red Mavro and white Xynisteri grapes, sun-dried for 2 weeks before vinification and solera aging. Still pretty decent stuff but only potentially one of the world's great rich wines.

COMTÉS RHODANIENS, VIN DE PAYS DES *Rhône Valley and Savoie, France* Most of the wines are red, from Syrah, Gamay, Cinsaut and Grenache, but the whites, particularly those from Viognier, Sauvignon Blanc and Chardonnay, are good too. Best producers: Rouoms co-op, ST-DESIRAT co-op★, Tain-Hermitage co-op, les Vignerons Ardèchois.

COMTÉ TOLOSAN, VIN DE PAYS DU *South-West France* A VIN DE PAYS covering most of the area to the south and east of Bordeaux. The reds, using local varieties such as Duras, Tannat and Fer Servadou blended with Cabernet Sauvignon, Cabernet Franc and Merlot, are your best bet, but don't overlook the rosés. Best producers: Labastide-de-Levis co-op, Ribonnet.

CONCA DE BARBERÁ DO *Catalonia, Spain* Quality wine area, but most of its production is sold to CAVA producers. Cool climate here is ideal and TORRES and CODORNIU grow excellent Chardonnay, Cabernet Sauvignon, Pinot Noir, Merlot and Tempranillo. Best producers: Concavins-Ryman★, Sanstravé (Gasset Chardonnay★★), TORRES (Milmanda★).

CONCHA Y TORO *Maipo, Chile* Chile's biggest winery has over 1500ha (3700 acres) of vineyard resources but has lost winemaker Pablo Morandé to his own project in the Rapel Valley. Top whites include Amelia Chardonnay★★, CASABLANCA Sauvignon Blanc★★ and Trio Chardonnay. Don Melchor Cabernet Sauvignon★ leads the reds, along with vibrant Merlots★ under the Casillero del Diablo and Trio labels.

CONDRIEU AC *Rhône Valley, France* Because of the demand for this wonderfully fragrant wine made entirely from Viognier, Condrieu is decidedly expensive. Unfortunately, quality is alarmingly variable. Condrieu is a sensation everyone should try at least once, but make sure you choose a good producer. Best drunk young. Best producers: G Barge★★, P & C Bonnefond★★, L Chèze★★, Y Cuilleron★★★, DELAS★★, P Dumazet★★, GUIGAL★★, Montelier★★, Niéro-Pinchon★★, A Perret★★, R Rostaing★★, G & L Vernay★★, F Villard★★. Best years: (1998) **97 96 95**.

CONO SUR *Rapel, Chile* Dynamic sister winery to CONCHA Y TORO, whose Chimbarongo Pinot Noir★ put both grape and region on the Chilean map. The new CASABLANCA Pinot★★ is more austere than the sweet, fleshy Rapel versions. Second labels Tocornal and Isla Negra offer easy-drinking blended wines. Best years: **1996 95**.

CH. LA CONSEILLANTE★★ *Pomerol AC, Bordeaux, France* Elegant, exotic, velvety textured wine that develops after 5 to 6 years but can age longer. Best years: (1998) 96 95 94 **90 89 88 86 85**.

CONSTANTIA WO *South Africa* The historic heart of South African wine now flying the flag of New World quality. The land originally granted to Simon van der Stel in 1685 was divided into 3 on his death; 2 estates, Groot Constantia and KLEIN CONSTANTIA, still exist, while BUITENVERWACHTING is partly carved from the third portion. Further along the same slopes historic Steenberg and Uitsig are chasing the quality of their illustrious neighbours. While the 2 'Constantia' estates continue tradition with some wines based on the famed 18th-century sweet Constantias, white varieties, especially Sauvignon, are thrusting this cool-climate area into the limelight. Best producers: BUITENVERWACHTING★★, KLEIN CONSTANTIA★★, Steenberg★.

ALDO CONTERNO *Barolo DOCG, Piedmont, Italy* Arguably BAROLO's finest producer. Good Freisa★, Grignolino and Dolcetto, excellent Barbera d'Alba Conca Tre Pile★★, a barrique-aged Nebbiolo Il Favot★★ and 2 Chardonnays, a young, non-oaked version called Printaniè, and Bussia d'Or★, fermented and aged in new wood. Pride of the range, though, are his Barolos from the hill of Bussia. In top vintages produces Barolos Vigna Colonello★★★, Vigna Cicala★★★ and excellent Granbussia★★★, as well as a blended Barolo called Bussia Soprana★★. All these Barolos, though accessible when young, need several years to show their true majesty, but retain a remarkable freshness of fruit. Best years: (Barolos) (1998) (97) (96) 95 93 **90 89 88 86 85 82**.

GIACOMO CONTERNO *Barolo DOCG, Piedmont, Italy* Aldo's elder brother Giovanni has always taken a more traditional approach to winemaking. His flagship wine is Barolo Monfortino★★★, but Barolo Cascina Francia★★★ is also superb. Powerful, earthy Dolcetto★ and Barbera★ are also made. Best years: (Monfortino) 1990 89 88 **87 86 85 82 79 78 74 71 70**.

CONTINO *Rioja DOC, Rioja, Spain* An estate on some of the finest RIOJA land, half-owned by CVNE. The wine is made by CVNE; the winery skipped the 1992 and 93 vintages to solve cellar problems. Best years: 1996 **95 94 86 85 82**.

COONAWARRA *South Australia* On a limestone belt thinly veneered with terra rossa soil, this flat patch of land can produce sublime Cabernet with blackcurrant leafy flavours and spicy Shiraz that age for many years. Chardonnay and Riesling can be good. An export-led boom has seen hundreds of new vineyards planted and, in view of some disappointing light reds, I wonder if Coonawarra's great reputation is not at risk. Best producers:  BOWEN★★, HOLLICK★ (Ravenswood★★), KATNOOK★, LECONFIELD★, LINDEMANS★★, MILDARA★, ORLANDO★, PARKER★, PENFOLDS★★, PENLEY★★, PETALUMA★★★, ROSEMOUNT★★, ROUGE HOMME★, WYNNS★★★.

COOPERS CREEK *Auckland, New Zealand* A small winery specializing in wines from HAWKES BAY and MARLBOROUGH grapes. Successful producer of Chardonnay★, especially Swamp Road Chardonnay★★ and luscious Marlborough Sauvignon Blanc★★. Dry Riesling★ and

Late Harvest Riesling★★ styles are also very good. Separate company Obsidian is making red from WAIHEKE. Best years: (1998) **96 94 91**.

COPERTINO DOC *Puglia, Italy* Based primarily on the Negroamaro grape, with a small percentage of Malvasia Nera, Copertino produces elegant wines. Best producers: Copertino co-op★, Leone De Castris, Monaci.

CORBANS *Auckland, Gisborne and Marlborough, New Zealand* New Zealand's second-largest wine company behind MONTANA and whose brand names include Cooks, Stoneleigh and Robard & Butler. Stoneleigh Sauvignon Blanc★ and Rhine Riesling★★, both made with MARLBOROUGH fruit, capture the best of each variety and display their regional styles well. Private Bin Chardonnay★★, Noble Rhine Riesling★★★ and Merlot★ are fine, small production wines. Consistently good Champagne-method sparkler called Amadeus★. Flagship wines from top varieties and all major wine regions are now produced under the Cottage Block label. Best years: (Marlborough whites excluding Sauvignon Blanc) (1998) **97 96**; (Marlborough reds) (1998) **97 96 94**; (Hawkes Bay whites) (1998) **96 95**; (Hawkes Bay reds) (1998) **96 95 94**.

CORBIÈRES AC *Languedoc, France* This AC now produces some of the best reds in the LANGUEDOC, with juicy fruit and more than a hint of wild hillside herbs. Excellent young, they age for years when from the best estates. White Corbières is adequate – drink as young as possible. Best producers: (reds) Bel Eveques★, Caraguilhes★, Ch. Cascadais★, Étang des Colombes★, Fontsainte★, Grand Moulin★, Hélène★, LASTOURS★, Mansenoble★, MONT TAUCH co-op★, les Palais★, St-Auriol★, VOULTE-GASPARETS★. Best years: (reds) (1997) 96 **95 94 93 91 90 89**.

CORNAS AC *Rhône Valley, France* Northern Rhône's up-and-coming star, whose wines are especially attractive since those of neighbouring HERMITAGE and COTE-ROTIE have spiralled upward in price in recent years. When young, the wine is a thick, impenetrable red, almost black in the ripest years. Most need 10 years' aging. Best producers: T Allemand★, Guy de Barjac★, CLAPE★★★, J-L Colombo★★, DELAS★, JABOULET★★, M Juge★, J Lemencier★★, LIONNET★, R Michel★, Tardieu-Laurent★★, A Voge★, VERSET★★. Best years: (1998) 97 96 95 94 **91 90 89 88 85 83 80 78**.

CORSE AC, VIN DE *Corsica, France* The overall AC for Corsica with 5 superior sub-regions (Calvi, Cap Corse, Figari, Porto Vecchio and Sartène). PATRIMONIO and AJACCIO are entitled to their own ACs. Things are improving on this lovely island but slowly. The most distinctive wines, mainly red, come from local grapes (Nielluccio and Sciacarello for reds and Vermentino for whites). There are some rich sweet Muscats – especially from MUSCAT DE CAP CORSE. Best producers: Cantone, Clos Landry, Couvent d'Alzipratu, Gentile, Leccia, Péraldi★, Torraccia, UVAL.

CORSICA *France* This Mediterranean island has made some pretty dull and undistinguished wines in the past. The last decade has seen a welcome trend toward quality, with co-ops and local growers investing in better equipment and planting noble grape varieties – such as Syrah, Merlot, Cabernet Sauvignon and Mourvèdre for reds, and Chardonnay and Sauvignon Blanc for whites – to complement the local Nielluccio, Sciacarello and Vermentino. Whites and rosés are pleasant for drinking young; reds are more exciting and can age for 3–4 years. See also Ajaccio, l'Île de Beauté, Muscat de Cap Corse, Patrimonio, Vin de Corse AC.

CORTESE White grape variety planted primarily in south-eastern PIEDMONT in Italy. It is also used in the Colli Tortonesi and Alto Monferrato DOCs as well as for GAVI, and can be labelled simply as Cortese del Piemonte. The grape can produce good, fairly acidic, dry whites.

CORTON AC *Grand Cru, Côte de Beaune, Burgundy, France* The AC covers both red and white wine. It is the only red Grand Cru in the CÔTE DE BEAUNE and ideally the wines should have the burliness and savoury power of the top CÔTE DE NUITS wines, combined with the more seductively perfumed fruit of Côte de Beaune. Red Corton should take 10 years to mature, but too many modern examples never make it. Very little white Corton is made. Best producers: Bonneau du Martray★★, Chandon de Briailles★★, Dubreuil-Fontaine★★, JADOT★★★, LATOUR★, MEO-CAMUZET★★★, Rapet Père et Fils★, Senard★, TOLLOT-BEAUT★★, M Voarick★. Best years: (reds) 1997 96 95 93 90 **89 88 85**.

CORTON-CHARLEMAGNE AC *Grand Cru, Côte de Beaune, Burgundy, France* Corton-Charlemagne, at the top of the famous Corton hill, is the largest of Burgundy's white Grands Crus. It can produce some of the most impressive white Burgundies – rich, buttery and nutty with a fine mineral quality. The best wines show their real worth only at 10 years or more. Best producers: Bonneau du Martray★★, COCHE-DURY★★★, DROUHIN★, Dubreuil-Fontaine★, FAIVELEY★★, JADOT★★, LATOUR★★, Rapet Père et Fils★, ROUMIER★★, TOLLOT-BEAUT★★, VERGET★★. Best years: 1997 96 95 94 **92 90 89 88 86 85**.

CH. COS D'ESTOURNEL★★★ *St-Estèphe AC, 2ème Cru Classé, Haut-Médoc, Bordeaux, France* Now the top name in ST-ESTÈPHE, and one of the leading châteaux in all Bordeaux. Despite a high proportion of Merlot (just under 40%) the wine is classically made for aging and usually needs 10 years to show really well. Recent vintages have been dark, brooding and packed with long-term potential. Second wine: les Pagodes de Cos (from 1994). Best years: (1998) 97 96 95 94 **93** 90 89 **88 86 85** 83 82 81 79 78 76.

COSTANTI *Brunello di Montalcino DOCG, Tuscany, Italy* One of the original, highly respected Montalcino estates, run by Andrea Costanti, making first-rate BRUNELLO★★★ and Rosso★★, as well as a tasty partially barrique-aged Sangiovese called Vermiglio★. The archetypal Brunello of this zone is austere, elegant and long-lived, epitomized by the Costanti Riserva★★★. Best years: 1990 **88 86 85 82**.

COSTERS DEL SEGRE DO *Catalonia, Spain* Originally created to cope with the huge RAIMAT estate near Lérida in western CATALONIA. A great array of grape varieties is grown, with the accent on French varieties. Quality is generally good and prices moderate. Best producers: Castell del Remei, RAIMAT★ (Mas Castell Cabernet Sauvignon★★). Best years: (reds) 1996 95 **93 92 91**.

COSTIÈRES DE NÎMES AC *Languedoc, France* A large improving AC between Nîmes and Arles in the Gard. The reds are often soft and make attractively easy drinking, and the rosés are at their best when really young. Only a little white is produced, which can be light and appley. Best producers: l'Amarine★, Beaubois, Belle-Coste, Campuget★, Mas des Bressailles★, Mourgues du Grés★, Nages★, Roubaud, la Tuilerie★. Best years: (1998) **97 96 95 94 93 91 90**.

CÔTE French word for a slope or hillside, which is where many, but not all, of the country's best vineyards are to be found. The names of specific slopes have been adopted as ACs (CÔTE-ROTIE, CÔTE DE BROUILLY) and even whole regions (CÔTE D'OR).

CÔTE DE BEAUNE *Côte d'Or, Burgundy, France* Southern part of the CÔTE D'OR; beginning at the hill of Corton, north of the town of BEAUNE, the Côte de Beaune progresses south as far as les Maranges, with white wines gradually taking over from red. A separate Côte de Beaune AC only refers to rare reds and whites from the vineyards on the hill to the west of the town of Beaune.

CÔTE DE BEAUNE-VILLAGES AC *Côte de Beaune, Burgundy, France* The general AC covering 16 villages for Pinot Noir reds. Most producers use their own village name nowadays but if the wine is a blend from several villages it is sold as Côte de Beaune-Villages and most merchants produce a relatively undistinguished version.

CÔTE DE BROUILLY AC *Beaujolais, Burgundy, France* A steep hill in the middle of the BROUILLY AC, producing extra-ripe grapes. The wine, a 'Super-Brouilly', is good young but can age well for several years. Best producers: Conroy★, DUBOEUF, Henry Fessy, Geoffray★, O Ravier★, Ch. Thivin★★, L & R Verger. Best years: 1998 97 96 **95 94 93**.

CÔTE CHALONNAISE See Bourgogne-Côte Chalonnaise.

CÔTE DE NUITS *Côte d'Or, Burgundy, France* This is the northern part of the great CÔTE D'OR and is *not* an AC. Almost entirely red wine country, the vineyards start in the southern suburbs of Dijon and continue south in a narrow swath to below the town of NUITS-ST-GEORGES. The villages are some of the greatest wine names in the world – GEVREY-CHAMBERTIN, VOUGEOT and VOSNE-ROMANEE etc.

CÔTE DE NUITS-VILLAGES AC *Côte de Nuits, Burgundy, France* This appellation is specific to the villages of Corgoloin, Comblanchien and Prémeaux in the south of the Côte de Nuits and Brochon and FIXIN in the north. Although not much seen, the wines are often good, not very deep in colour but with a nice cherry fruit. There is also a tiny amount of white. Best producers: (reds) René Durand, JAYER-GILLES★, Gérard Julien★, RION★★, P Rossignol★.

CÔTE D'OR *Burgundy, France* Europe's most northern great red wine area and also the home of some of the world's best dry white wines. The name, meaning 'golden slope', refers to a 48-km (30-mile) stretch between Dijon and Chagny which divides into the CÔTE DE NUITS in the north and the CÔTE DE BEAUNE in the south.

CÔTE ROANNAISE AC *Loire Valley, France* In the upper Loire; the nearest large town is Lyon, the capital of BEAUJOLAIS, and so it is quite logical that the chief grape variety here is Gamay. Most of the wine produced is red and should generally be drunk young. Best producers: R Chaucesse, Demon★, Lapandéry★, M Lutz, Montroussier★, J Plasse★, Serol★ & M Vial★.

CÔTE-RÔTIE AC *Rhône Valley, France* The Côte-Rôtie, or 'roasted slope', produces one of France's greatest red wines. The Syrah grape bakes to super-ripeness on these steep slopes and the small amount of white Viognier sometimes included in the blend gives an unexpected exotic fragrance in a red wine. Lovely young, it is better aged for 10 years. Best producers: Gilles Barge★★, B Burgaud★★, E & J Champet★, Clusel-Roch★★, Y Cuilleron★, DELAS★, J-M Gérin★★, GUIGAL★★, JAMET★,

117

JASMIN★, R Rostaing★★, M Ogier★★, Tardieu-Laurent★★, G & L Vernay★, Vidal-Fleury★★. Best years: (1998) 97 96 95 94 **91 90 89 88 85 83 78**.

COTEAUX D'AIX-EN-PROVENCE AC *Provence, France* This AC was the first in the south to acknowledge that Cabernet Sauvignon can enormously enhance the traditional, local grape varieties such as Grenache, Cinsaut, Mourvèdre, Syrah and Carignan. The red wines produced here can age, but it is best to catch them young. Some quite good fresh rosé is made while the white wines, mostly still traditionally made, are pleasant but hardly riveting. Best producers: (reds) Ch. Bas★, les Bastides★, Beaupré, Calisanne★, Fonscolombe★, Revelette★, Mas Ste-Berthe, Salen, Ch. du Seuil, la Vallongue, Vignelaure★; (whites) Beaupré, Calisanne, Camaissette, Fonscolombe, Ch. du Seuil. Best years: (1998) **97 96 95 94 93 91 90 89**.

COTEAUX DE L'ARDÈCHE, VIN DE PAYS DES *Rhône Valley, France* Wines from the southern part of the Ardèche. Look out for the increasingly good varietal red wines made from Cabernet Sauvignon, Syrah, Merlot or Gamay and dry, fresh white wines from Chardonnay, Viognier or Sauvignon Blanc. Best producers: Colombier, Louis LATOUR, Pradel, ST-DESIRAT co-op, les Vignerons Ardèchois.

COTEAUX DE L'AUBANCE AC *Loire Valley, France* Smallish AC located parallel to the COTEAUX DU LAYON AC. It is now enjoying a renaissance for its sweet or semi-sweet white wines made from Chenin Blanc. Most producers also make red, rosé or dry white ANJOU AC, which is easier to sell. Sweet styles can improve for 10–25 years. Best producers: Bablut★, Haute Perche★, J-Y Lebreton★★, Montgilet★★, RICHOU★★, la Varière★. Best years: (1997) 96 95 **94 93 90 89 88 86 85 83**.

COTEAUX CHAMPENOIS AC *Champagne, France* The AC for still wines from Champagne. Fairly acid with a few exceptions, notably from BOUZY and Ay. The best age for 5 years or more. Best producers: Bara, BOLLINGER★, Ch. de Saran★ (MOET & CHANDON), LAURENT-PERRIER, Joseph PERRIER, G Vesselle. Best years: (1998) 97 96 95 **90 89 88 85 82**.

COTEAUX DU LANGUEDOC AC *Languedoc, France* A large and increasingly successful AC situated between Montpellier and Narbonne in the Languedoc, producing over 40 million bottles of beefy red and tasty rosé wines. Eleven of the best villages (crus) can now add their own names to the AC name, including Cabrières, la CLAPE, Montpeyroux, PIC ST-LOUP, St-Drézery and St-Georges-d'Orques. Best producers: Abbaye de Valmagne, l'Aiguelière★★, Auphilhac★, Calage★, Carignano co-op★, Cazeneuve★, la Coste★, l'Hortus★, Jougla★, Lascaux★, Lavabre★, Mas Bruguière★, Mas des Chimères★, MAS JULLIEN★, Mas de Mortes★, Peyre Rose★, Prieuré de St-Jean de Bébian★, la Sauvageonne★. Best years: (1998) **96 95 94 93 91**.

COTEAUX DU LAYON AC *Loire Valley, France* Sweet wine from the Layon Valley south of Angers. The wine is made from Chenin Blanc grapes that, ideally, are attacked by noble rot. In great years like 1990 and 89, and from a talented grower, this can be one of the world's exceptional sweet wines. Seven villages are entitled to use the Coteaux du Layon-Villages AC (one of the best is Chaume) and put their own name on the label, and these wines, in particular, are definitely underpriced for the quality. Two small sub-areas, BONNEZEAUX and QUARTS DE CHAUME, have their own ACs. Can be aged for 5, 10 or 15 years or more. Best producers: P Baudouin★★, Baumard★★, Bidet★, Breuil★★, Cady★★, P Delesvaux★★, Forges★★, Ogereau★★, Pierre-Bise★★, Jo Pithon★★★, Plaisance★★, Joseph Renou★★, Robineau★, Sauveroy★, Soucherie★★, Yves Soulez★★★, Touche Noire★. Best years: (1998) 97 96 95 **94 93** 90 89 88 85 83 82 76 75.

COTEAUX DU LYONNAIS AC *Burgundy, France*   Good, light, Beaujolais-style reds and a few whites and rosés from scattered vineyards between Villefranche and Lyon. Drink young. Best producers: Régis Descotes, Fayolle, P & J-M Jomard, Caves des Vignerons de Sain Bel.

COTEAUX DU TRICASTIN AC *Rhône Valley, France*   From the southern Drôme these are light, fresh reds and rosés with attractive juicy fruit. Only a little white is made but is worth looking out for as a fairly good, nutty drink to consume within the year. Best producers: Grangeneuve, Lônes, la Tour d'Elyssas, Vieux Micocoulier. Best years: (1998) **97 96 95**.

COTEAUX VAROIS AC *Provence, France*   An area to watch with new plantings of classic grapes. Best producers: Alysses★, Bremond, Deffends★, Garbelle, Routus★, Ch. St-Estève, St-Jean-le-Vieux, St-Jean-de-Villecroze★, Triennes★. Best years: (1998) **97 96 95** 94 93 91 90 88.

CÔTES DE BERGERAC AC *South-West France*   The AC covers good-quality reds made from the same grapes as BERGERAC AC but with a higher minimum alcohol level. Côtes de Bergerac Moelleux AC is the name for sweet wines. Best producers: Belingard-Chayne, Combrillac, le Mayne, Tour des Gendres★. Best years: (1998) **97 96 95 94 93** 91 90 88.

CÔTES DE BLAYE AC *Bordeaux, France*   The main AC for white wines from the right bank of the Gironde estuary. Almost all the best whites of the area are now dry. Drink young. Best producer: Cave de Marcillac.

CÔTES DE BOURG AC *Bordeaux, France*   Mainly a red wine area to the south of the CÔTES DE BLAYE, where the best producers and the local co-op at Tauriac make great efforts. The reds are earthy but blackcurranty and can age for 6–10 years, though most are drunk at 3–5. Very little white is made, most of which is dry and dull. Best producers: Barbe, Brulesécaille★, Bujan, Falfas★, Fougas, Guerry, Haut-Guiraud, Haut-Macô, Macay, Nodoz, Roc-de-Cambes★, Rousset, Tauriac co-op, Tayac. Best years: (1998) 96 **95 94 90** 89 88.

CÔTES DE CASTILLON AC *Bordeaux, France*   Red wine area just to the east of ST-EMILION. As the price of decent red Bordeaux climbs ever upward, Côtes de Castillon wines have remained an excellent, reasonably priced alternative – a little earthy but full and round. Depending on the vintage the wine is enjoyable between 3 and 10 years after the vintage. Best producers: Aiguilhe, Belcier★, Cantegrive, Cap-de-Faugères, Côte-Montpezat★, Lapeyronie★, Parenchère, Pitray, Poupille★, Robin, Vieux-Ch.-Champs-de-Mars. Best years: (1998) 96 95 **94 90** 89 88 86 85.

CÔTES DE DURAS AC *South-West France*   AC between ENTRE-DEUX-MERS and BERGERAC in the Lot-et-Garonne, with 2 very active co-ops which offer extremely good, fresh, grassy reds and whites from traditional Bordeaux grapes but at distinctly lower prices. Drink the wines young. Best producers: Amblard, L de Conti, Cours, Duras co-op, Landerrouat co-op, Lapiarre, Laulan. Best years: (1998) **97 96 95** 94.

CÔTES DE FRANCS AC *Bordeaux, France*   Mainly red wine from a tiny but quality-orientated area east of ST-EMILION. The Thienpont family (Puygueraud) continue to be the driving force in the appellation. Already impressive, you can expect more fine wines from here in the future. Best producers: les Charmes-Godard, Laclaverie★, Francs★, Marsau, Moulin la Pitié, la Prade, Puygueraud★★. Best years: (1998) 97 96 95 **94 90 89 88 86 85 83**.

CÔTES DU FRONTONNAIS AC *South-West France*   From north of Toulouse, some of the most distinctive reds in South-West France. Négrette is the chief grape and the wine can be superb and positively silky in texture. It can age well but I prefer it young. There is also a little fairly good rosé. Best producers: Baudare, Bellevue-la-Forêt★, la Colombière, Ferran, Flotis, Laurou, Montauriol, la Palme, le Roc★. Best years: (1998) **97 96 95**.

CÔTES DE GASCOGNE, VIN DE PAYS DES *South-West France*   Mainly white wines from the Gers *département*. This is Armagnac country, but the tangy-fresh, fruity table wines are tremendously good – especially when you consider that they were condemned as unfit for anything but distillation a decade ago. Best producers: Aurin, Brumont, GRASSA★, Union des Producteurs PLAIMONT, Hugh Ryman, Dom. de Joy, Dom. St-Lannes.

CÔTES DU JURA AC *Jura, France*   The regional AC for Jura covers a wide variety of wines, including local specialities VIN JAUNE and VIN DE PAILLE. The Savagnin makes strong-tasting whites and Chardonnay is used for some good dry whites and Champagne-method fizz. The reds and rosés can be good when made from Pinot Noir, but when the local varieties Poulsard and Trousseau are used, the wines can be a bit weird. Drink young. Best producers: Ch. d'Arlay★, Bourdy★, Clavelin★, Durand-Perron★, Gréa, Joly★, Pupillin co-op, Reverchon★, Rolet, A & M Tissot★. Best years: (whites) (1998) 97 **96 95 94 92 90 89 88 86 85**.

CÔTES DU LUBÉRON AC *Rhône Valley, France*   Wine production is dominated by the co-ops east of Avignon. The light, easy wines are for drinking young, when they are refreshing and enjoyable. Best producers: Ch. la Canorgue, Ch. de l'Isolette★, Val Joanis, Ch. de Mille, la Sable, la Tour-d'Aigues co-op, Vendran. Best years: (1998) **97 96 95 94**.

CÔTES DU MARMANDAIS AC *South-West France*   The Marmandais producers have always set out to make Bordeaux look-alikes and the red wines achieve a fair amount of success. Syrah is also permitted. Best producers: Boissonneau, Cave de Beaupuy, Cocumont co-op.

CÔTES DE MONTRAVEL AC *South-West France*   Area within the BERGERAC AC for sweeter whites from Sémillon, Sauvignon Blanc and Muscadelle. Best producers: Gourgueil, Perreau, Pique-Sègue.

CÔTES DE PROVENCE AC *Provence, France*   Large AC for mainly reds and rosés, showing signs of improvement in recent years. Now generally much fruitier but should still be drunk young. The whites are forgettable. Best producers: Barbeyrolles, la Bernade★, Berne, Commanderie de Bargemore★, Commanderie de Peyrassol, la Courtade★, Coussin Ste-Victoire★, Dragon★, Esclans★, l'Estandon, Féraud★, Gavoty★, Hauts de St-Jean, Maravenne★, Mentone, Minuty, Ott★, Pampelonne, Rabiega★, Real Martin★, RICHEAUME★, Rimauresq★, St-Baillon★, St-Maur, les Maîtres Vignerons de St-Tropez, Sorin★. Best years: (reds) (1998) 97 **96 95 94 93 91 90**.

CÔTES DU RHÔNE AC *Rhône Valley, France* The general AC for the whole Rhône Valley. Over 90% is red and rosé mainly from Grenache with some Cinsaut, Syrah, Carignan and Mourvèdre to add lots of warm, spicy southern personality. Modern winemaking has revolutionized the style and today's wines are generally juicy, spicy and easy to drink, ideally within 2 years. Most wine is made by the co-ops and there are now many examples with depth and structure. Best producers: (reds) les Aussellons, BEAUCASTEL, A Brunel★, la Cantharide, CLAPE★, Colombo★, Coudoulet de Beaucastel★, Cros de la Mure★, Fonsalette★★, les Goubert, Gramenon★★, GRAND MOULAS★, Grand Prebois★, GUIGAL★, JABOULET, Mont Redon, la Mordoree★, l'Oratoire St-Martin★, M Richaud★, Ruth, St-Estève d'Uchaux, STE-ANNE★, Tardieu-Laurent★; (whites) Chusclan co-op, CLAPE★, Laudun co-op, Pélaquié★, Rabasse-Charavin, la Remejeanne, STE-ANNE★. Best years: (reds) (1998) 97 **95 94 93 91** 90.

CÔTES DU RHÔNE-VILLAGES AC *Rhône Valley, France* AC for wines with a higher minimum alcohol content than straightforward CÔTES DU RHÔNE, covering 16 villages in the southern Rhône that have traditionally made superior wine (especially Cairanne, Séguret, Valréas, Sablet, Visan, Chusclan, Laudun). Almost all the best Villages wines are red – they have a marvellous spicy flavour and can age for up to 10 years. Best producers: l'Ameillaud★, BEAUMES-DE-VENISE co-op, Beaurenard★, Boisson, Bressy-Masson★, Daniel Brusset★, Cairanne co-op, Chamfort, Roger Combe★, les Goubert★, GRAND MOULAS★, les Hautes Cances★, JABOULET★, l'Oratoire St-Martin★, Pélaquié★, Piaugier★, Rabasse Charavin★, M Richaud★, STE-ANNE★, St-Gayan, la Soumade★, Trapadis★, Trignon★, Vacqueyras co-op, Verquière. Best years: (1998) 97 **95 94 93 90 89** 88.

CÔTES DU ROUSSILLON AC *Roussillon, France* Large AC, with reds dominant, covering much of ROUSSILLON. Villages Caramany, Latour-de-France and Lesquerde may add their own name, but wines from Caramany and Latour have been poor lately. The small amount of white is mainly unmemorable. Production is dominated by the co-ops, some with enlightened winemakers, but estates are starting to make their presence felt. Best producers: (reds) Vignerons CATALANS, Casenove★, CAZES, Charmettes, J-L Colombo, Forca Real, GAUBY★★, Jau, Joliette, Laporte, Mas Crémat★, Mas Rous, Piquemal, Rey, Rivesaltes co-op, Rombeau, Salvat, Sarda-Malet★. Best years: (1998) **96 95 94** 93.

CÔTES DU ROUSSILLON-VILLAGES AC *Roussillon, France* Appellation covering red wines from the best sites in the northern part of CÔTES DU ROUSSILLON. The wine from villages like Caramany and Latour-de-France is wonderfully juicy when young but also has potential for age. Best producers: Agly co-op, Cap de Fouste, Vignerons CATALANS, CAZES, Chênes★, Forca Real, GAUBY★, Jau★, Joliette, Mas Crémat★, Maury co-op, Ch. Montner, Sabazin★, St-Martin, Vingrau. Best years: (1998) 96 **95 94** 93.

CÔTES DE ST-MONT VDQS *South-West France* A good VDQS for firm but fruity reds and some fair rosés and dry whites. Best producer: Union des Producteurs PLAIMONT (especially Château de Sabazan).

CÔTES DU TARN, VIN DE PAYS DES *South-West France* Wines from around Toulouse-Lautrec's home town of Albi. The whites should be sharp but fruity and the young reds are enjoyable too. Best producers: Chaumet-Lagrange, Gayrel, Labastide-de-Levis co-op.

CÔTES DE THAU, VIN DE PAYS DES *Languedoc, France* Wines from the shores of Lake Thau to the west of the Mediterranean town of Sète. Whites are often surprisingly good for the MIDI. Best producers: Gaujal, Genson, UCA Vignerons Garrigues, Pinet co-op, Pomérols co-op.

CÔTES DE THONGUE, VIN DE PAYS DES *Languedoc, France* Mainly red wines, from north-east of Béziers. Most are dull quaffers made from Carignan, but recent plantings of classic grapes by dynamic estates can produce excellent results. Best producers: l'Arjolle★, Bellevue, Condamine l'Evêque, Croix Belle.

CÔTES DU VENTOUX AC *Rhône Valley, France* Increasingly successful AC, with vineyards on the slopes of Mt Ventoux in the RHONE VALLEY near Carpentras. When the wine is well made from a single estate or blended by a serious merchant, the reds can have a lovely juicy fruit, or in the case of JABOULET and la VIEILLE FERME, some real stuffing. There is only a little white. Best producers: Anges★, Champ-Long, JABOULET, Pesquié, Union des Caves du Ventoux, la VIEILLE FERME.

CÔTES DU VIVARAIS VDQS *Rhône Valley, France* In the Ardèche and northern Gard, typical southern Rhône grapes produce light, fresh reds and rosés for drinking young, but plantings of classic varieties (Cabernet Sauvignon and Syrah) are producing deep-flavoured wines of surprising quality and irresistible price. Best producers: Chais du Vivarais, Vigier, les Vignerons Ardèchois.

COTNARI *Romania* A hilly region close to the border with Moldova, whose warm mesoclimate is well suited to the development of noble rot. Romania's finest sweet wines are made here using a blend of Grasa, Tamiîoasă, Francusa and Fetească Albă grapes.

CÔTTO, QUINTA DO *Douro DOC and Port DOC, Douro, Portugal* Table wine expert in Lower DOURO. Basic red and white Quinta do Côtto are reasonable, and Grande Escolha★★ is one of Portugal's best reds, oaky and powerful when young, rich and cedary when mature. Best years: (Grande Escolha) 1995 94 **90 87 85 82**.

COULY-DUTHEIL *Chinon, Loire Valley, France* Large merchant house responsible for 10% of the CHINON AC. Uses its own vineyards for the best wines, particularly Clos de l'Écho★★ and Clos de l'Olive★. Top négociant blend is la Baronnie Madeleine★, which combines delicious raspberry fruit with a considerable capacity to age. Also sells a range of other Touraine wines. Best years: (1998) 97 96 **95 93 90 89 88 86 85**.

PIERRE COURSODON *St-Joseph AC, Rhône Valley, France* A good family-owned domaine producing rich ST-JOSEPH from very old vines. The red wines★ need up to 5 years to show all the magnificent cassis and truffle and violety richness of the best Rhône reds, especially the top wine, called le Paradis St-Pierre★★. Pierre Coursodon also produces white St-Joseph★ and a tiny amount of white le Paradis St-Pierre★★. Best years: (reds) (1998) 97 96 **95 94 90 89 88 86 85 83**.

CH. COUTET★★ *Barsac AC, 1er Cru Classé, Bordeaux, France* BARSAC'S largest Classed Growth property is not usually as rich as the AC's other First Growth, CLIMENS. The wines are aromatic, with a lively fruit character, and age well. Since 1981 a special Cuvée Madame★★★ is

made in exceptional years, which ranks with the greatest sweet wines.
Best years: (1998) 97 96 95 **90 89 88 86 83 81 76 75**.

COWRA *New South Wales, Australia* Very promising district with a reliable warm climate and good water supplies for irrigation. It produces soft, peachy Chardonnay and spicy, cool-tasting Shiraz. Best producers: Arrowfield, Hungerford Hill, Richmond Grove, ROTHBURY, Charles Sturt University.

CRASTO, QUINTA DO *Douro DOC and Port DOC, Douro, Portugal* Well-situated property belonging to the Roquette family. Very good LBV★ and vintage★★ port and even better table wines, especially the Reservas★★. Best years: (vintage ports) 1995 94; (table wines) 1997 96 **95 94**.

CRÉMANT French term for up-market sparkling wine from Alsace, Bordeaux, Burgundy, Die, Jura, Limoux, Loire and Luxembourg, imposing stricter regulations than those for ordinary fizz. The term was used for Champagnes with less pressure (3 atmospheres instead of 6) but it was banned in 1994.

CRÉMANT D'ALSACE AC *Alsace, France* Good Champagne-method sparkling wine from Alsace, usually made from Pinot Blanc, Chardonnay, Auxerrois, Pinot Gris and Pinot Noir are also permitted. Reasonable quality, if not great value for money. Best producers: Joseph Cattin, Dopff au Moulin, Dopff & Irion, Ginglinger, Willy Gisselbrecht, KUENTZ-BAS, Muré, Ostertag, Turckheim co-op, Willm, Wolfberger.

CRÉMANT DE BOURGOGNE AC *Burgundy, France* Most Burgundian Crémant is white and is made either from Chardonnay alone or blended with Pinot Noir. The result, especially in ripe years, can be full, soft, almost honey-flavoured – if you give the wine the 2–3 years' aging needed for

mellowness to develop. The best rosé comes from the Chablis and Auxerre regions in northern Burgundy. Best producers: A Delorme, Lucius-Grégoire, Parigot-Richard, Simonnet-Febvre; and the co-ops at Bailly (the best for rosé), Lugny★, St-Gengoux-de-Scissé and Viré.

CRÉMANT DE DIE AC *Rhône Valley, France* AC for fizz made entirely from the Clairette Blanche grape. Less aromatic than CLAIRETTE DE DIE.

CRÉMANT DE JURA AC *Jura, France* AC created in 1995 for fizz from Jura. Annual production is expected to be around 2 million bottles, largely Chardonnay-based, with Poulsard for the pinks.

CRÉMANT DE LIMOUX AC *South-West France* Sparkling wine AC dating from 1990. The blend includes Chardonnay, Chenin Blanc and Mauzac and the wines generally have more complexity than straight BLANQUETTE DE LIMOUX. Drink young. Best producers: l'Aigle★, Antech, Delmas, Guinot, Laurens★, Martinolles★, SIEUR D'ARQUES★, Vadent. Best years: **1996 95 94**.

CRÉMANT DE LOIRE AC *Loire Valley, France* The AC for Champagne-method sparkling wine in Anjou and Touraine, created in 1975 in an effort to improve Loire fizz. With stricter regulations than VOUVRAY and SAUMUR, the result is an attractive wine, with more fruit and yeast character. The wine is good to drink as soon as it is released and can be excellent value. Best producers: Baumard★, Berger Frères★, Brizé★, la Gabillière, Girault, GRATIEN & MEYER★, Lambert★, Langlois-Château★, Michaud★, OISLY-ET-THESEE co-op★, Passavant★.

CRIANZA Spanish term for the youngest official category of oak-matured wine. A red Crianza wine must have had at least 2 years' aging (1 in oak, 1 in bottle) before sale; a white or rosé, 1 year.

CRIMEA *Ukraine* This Black Sea peninsula has been an important centre of wine production since the early 19th century. Its greatest wines are the historical treasures of the Massandra winery: superb dessert and fortified wines, originally destined for the Tsar's summer palace at Livadia. Winemaking today seems understandably but regrettably aimless.

CRIOTS-BÂTARD-MONTRACHET AC See Bâtard-Montrachet AC.

CROFT *Port DOC, Douro, Portugal* Croft's vintage ports★★ can be deceptively light in their youth, but they develop into subtle, elegant wines. The 1995 single Quinta da Roêda is excellent. Best years: (vintage) 1994 91 **77 70 66 63 60 45 35**.

CROZES-HERMITAGE AC *Rhône Valley, France* The largest of the northern Rhône ACs. Ideally the reds should have a full colour with a strong, meaty but rich flavour. You can drink it young but in ripe years from a hillside site it improves greatly for 2–5 years. The quality has improved dramatically since the late 1980s. The best whites are extremely fresh, clean and racy. In general drink white Crozes young before the floral perfume disappears. Best producers: (reds) Albert Belle★, CHAPOUTIER★, B Chave★, Caves des Clairmonts, Colombier★, Laurent Combier★, DELAS★, O Dumaine★, Fayolle★, GRAILLOT★★, JABOULET★ (Thalabert★★), Pavillon★, Pochon★, Tardieu-Laurent★, L de Vaillouit; (whites) B Chave★, Colombier★, Laurent Combier★, DELAS★, O Dumaine, Entrefaux★, Fayolle★, GRAILLOT★, JABOULET, Pochon★, Pradelle★, M Sorrel★. Best years: (reds) (1998) 97 **96 95 94 91 90 89 88 85**; (whites) (1998) 97 **96 95 94 91 90 89**.

CRU French for a specific plot of land or particular estate. Bordeaux, Burgundy and Champagne use the term for individual vineyard sites, or the estates which own them. In Burgundy, growths are divided into Grands (great) and Premiers (first) Crus, and apply solely to the actual land. In Champagne the same terms are used for whole villages. In Bordeaux there are various hierarchical levels of Cru referring to estates rather than their vineyards.

CRU BOURGEOIS French term for wines from the MEDOC and SAUTERNES that are ranked immediately below the Crus Classés. Many are excellent value for money. The best of the Crus Bourgeois, such as ANGLUDET in MARGAUX and CHASSE-SPLEEN in MOULIS, make very fine drinking and are a match for many a Classed Growth.

CRU CLASSÉ The Classed Growths are the aristocracy of Bordeaux, ennobled by the classifications of 1855 (for the MEDOC, BARSAC and SAUTERNES), 1955, 1969, 1986 and 1996 (for ST-EMILION) and 1947, 1953 and 1959 (for GRAVES). Curiously, POMEROL has never been classified. The modern classifications are more reliable than the 1855 version, which was based solely on the price of the wines at the time of the Great Exhibition in Paris, but in terms of prestige, the 1855 classification remains the most important. With the exception of a single alteration in 1973, when Ch. MOUTON-ROTHSCHILD was elevated to First Growth status, the list has not changed since 1855. It is certainly in need of revision.

HANS CRUSIUS *Traisen, Nahe, Germany* Hans and Peter Crusius, father and son, produce Rieslings at their Traiser Bastei★ and Schlossböckelheimer Felsenberg★ vineyards, which manage to be both rich and flinty. Best years: (1998) 97 **96 95 94 89 88 86 85 83**.

CULLEN *Margaret River, Western Australia* One of the original and best MARGARET RIVER vineyards, run by the Cullen women (winemakers are Vanya and her mother Diana). The Chardonnay★★★ is one of the region's richest and most complex; Semillon★ (Reserve Semillon★★) and Sauvignon Blanc★ are made deliberately non-herbaceous. The Cabernet-Merlot★★★ is gloriously soft, deep and scented; prospects for this wine have risen even higher now the Reserve bottling has been discontinued. Best years: (reds) 1996 95 94 93 **92 91 90 86 84 82**.

CUVAISON *Napa Valley AVA, California, USA* Cuvaison built a reputation for brooding red wines in the 1970s but has taken a while to modernize styles. Now it produces tasty, focused Merlot★, and good but less thrilling Chardonnay. Most should be drunk young. A budget label, Calistope Cellars, was launched in 1993. Best years: (Merlot) (1997) 96 95 **94 92 91 90 88**.

CUVÉE French for the contents of a single vat or tank, but more commonly used to describe a wine selected by an individual producer for reasons of style or quality.

CVNE *Rioja DOC, Rioja, Spain* Compañía Vinícola del Norte de España is the full name of this firm, but it's usually known as 'coonay'. Monopole★ is one of RIOJA's only remaining well-oaked whites; the Reserva and Gran Reserva reds easily surpass the rather commercial Crianzas; the Viña Real can be rich and meaty, and the top Imperial Gran Reserva★ long-lived and impressive. Best years: (reds) 1996 **95 94 92 91 90 89 88 87 86 85 81**.

DIDIER DAGUENEAU *Pouilly-Fumé AC, Loire Valley, France* Didier Dagueneau is known as the wild man of POUILLY-FUME. In fact he is a much-needed innovator and quality fanatic in what is a decidedly complacent region. His wines generally benefit from 4 or 5 years' aging and, although at times unpredictable, are generally intense and complex. Probably best-known for the barrel-fermented Sauvignon Blanc called Silex★★★ and another entitled Pur Sang★★. Best years: (1998) 97 **96 95 94 93 90 89 88**.

ROMANO DAL FORNO *Valpolicella DOC, Veneto, Italy* On his small estate at Illasi, outside the VALPOLICELLA classico area, Romano Dal Forno makes one of the most impressive wines of the appellation. His Valpolicella Superiore★★ from the Monte Lodoletta vineyard is a model of power and grace, though his RECIOTO DELLA VALPOLICELLA★★★ and AMARONE★★★, from the same source, are even more voluptuous. Best years: (Amarone) 1990 **89 88 86 85**.

DÃO DOC *Beira Alta, Portugal* Dão has steep slopes ideal for vineyards, and a great climate for growing local grape varieties; yet only in the last decade have white wines been freshened up, and reds begun to realize their long-promised potential. Best producers: (reds) Caves ALIANCA, Boas Quintas (Fonte do Ouro★★), Quinta das Maias★, Quinta da

Pellada (Tinta Roriz, Touriga Nacional★), Quinta dos Roques (Tinta Roriz★, Touriga Nacional★★), Quinta de Sães★, Casa de Santar★, Caves SAO JOAO, SOGRAPE★; (whites) Quinta das Maias★, Quinta dos Roques★, Quinta de Sães★, Casa de Santar★, SOGRAPE★. Best years: (reds) (1998) 97 **96 95 94 92**.

D'ARENBERG *McLaren Vale, South Australia* Chester Osborn makes blockbuster Dead Arm Shiraz★★, Footbolt Old Vine Shiraz★, Custodian Grenache★★ and blends from very low-yielding old vines, most of which are family-held. These are some of Australia's most character-filled wines, bursting with terroir. Best years: (reds) **1996 95 92 91 90**.

KURT DARTING *Bad Dürkheim, Pfalz, Germany* Darting makes full, four-square wines in Bad Dürkheim (Spielberg), Ungstein (Ungsteiner Herrenberg 1996 Riesling Spätlese★★) and WACHENHEIM (Mandelgarten), including rich, peachy Kabinett★ from Dürkheim. Best years: **1997 96 93 92**.

VINCENT DAUVISSAT *Chablis AC, Burgundy, France* One of the top 3 domaines in Chablis, specializing in concentrated wines from 2 Grand Cru and 3 Premier Cru sites. This is Chablis at its most complex – refreshing, seductive and beautifully structured with the fruit balancing the subtle influence of mostly older oak. Look out in particular for la Forêt★★ and the more aromatic Vaillons★★. Best years: 1997 96 95 **94** 93 **92 90 89** 88.

MARCO DE BARTOLI *Sicily, Italy* Marco De Bartoli is most noted for a dry but unfortified MARSALA-style wine called Vecchio Samperi; his version of what he believes Marsala was before the first English merchant, John Woodhouse, fortified it for export. Released as 10★-, 20★★- and 30-year-old★★ wines, these are dry, intense and redolent of candied peel, dates and old, old raisins. Some of the finest wines of this style in the world. Also excellent is the MOSCATO PASSITO DI PANTELLERIA Bukkuram★★.

DE BORTOLI *Riverina, New South Wales, Australia* Large family-owned winery producing a truly sublime botrytized Semillon★★★ that is head and shoulders above the rest of its vast range of inexpensive RIVERINA quaffers. De Bortoli is also crafting some of the YARRA VALLEY's best Chardonnay★★, Shiraz★★, Cabernet★ and Pinot Noir★. Good second labels are Windy Peak and Gulf Station. Best years: (Botrytis Semillon) **1995 94 93 90 87 82**.

DEHLINGER *Russian River AVA, California, USA* Outstanding Pinot Noir★★★ from estate vineyards in the cool Russian River region a few miles from the Pacific, best at 5–10 years old. Also makes solid Chardonnay★ and bold, peppery Syrah★★. Best years: (reds) (1997) 96 95 94 93 **92 91 90 87 86**.

DELAS FRÈRES *Rhône Valley, France* An underrated merchant based near Tournon, now part of DEUTZ, selling wines from the entire Rhône Valley. Wines from its own northern Rhône vineyards have improved greatly in recent vintages. Look out for the aromatic CONDRIEU★★, best drunk young, as well as its single-vineyard, dense, powerful HERMITAGE★★, which needs as much as a decade to reach its peak, and the perfumed single-vineyard COTE-ROTIE★★. In a lighter style, the CROZES-HERMITAGE★ is a good bet. Best years: (premium reds) (1998) 97 96 95 94 91 90 89 **88 86 85 83 78**; (whites) (1998) 97 **96 95 94 93 90 89**.

DELATITE *Mansfield, Victoria, Australia* The Ritchies were graziers who got involved in wine when diversifying their farm. Their high-altitude vineyard in sight of VICTORIA's snowfields grows delicate, aromatic Riesling★★ and Traminer★★; there is also subtle Chardonnay★ and extravagantly fruity reds. The Pinot Noir★ is perfumed, and Devil's River★★ is a very smart, minty Bordeaux blend. Best years: (Riesling) **1996 94 93 92 90 87 86 82**.

DELEGAT'S *Henderson, Auckland, North Island, New Zealand* Family winery specializing in Chardonnay, Cabernet-Merlot and Sauvignon Blanc from the HAWKES BAY and MARLBOROUGH (under Oyster Bay★ label) regions. Until recently it was a reliable producer rather than a memorable one, but prices are keen and quality is improving, which is reflected in very good Reserve Chardonnay★★ and good Merlot★. Best years: (1998) **96 94 92 91**.

DEMI-SEC French for medium-dry.

DENBIES *Surrey, England* This is the giant among English vineyards, with 102ha (253 acres) planted since 1986 on the chalky soils outside Dorking. Twenty different varieties have produced, so far, a range of wines from the adequate to the truly exciting. The Dornfelder red is memorable for an English effort, the Pinot Noir, sparklers and botrytized whites★ are good, and the dry white wines show a perfume that almost makes you forgive them their rather exalted prices. They were badly hit by spring frosts in 1997.

DEUTZ *Champagne AC, Champagne, France* A Champagne house that is probably better known for its CALIFORNIA and New Zealand fizz than for its Champagne. Unfairly so, perhaps, because this small company, now owned by ROEDERER, produces excellent, medium-priced Champagne. The non-vintage★ is always reliable, but the top wine is the weightier Cuvée William Deutz★★. Best years: **1990 89 88 85 82**.

DE WETSHOF ESTATE *Robertson WO, South Africa* Pioneer Chardonnay specialist of the region, although wines seem to have lost a little momentum of late. This whites-only estate is now experimenting with a small block of Pinot Noir under the expert guidance of Californian viticulturalist, Phil Freese. Pick of the range are the elegant, toasty Bateleur and spicy, citrusy d'Honneur, both barrel-fermented. Best years: (Chardonnay) **1998 97 96 95**.

DÉZALEY *Vaud, Switzerland* The top wine communes in the VAUD, making surprisingly powerful mineraly wines from the white Chasselas grape. Best producers: Bovard, Conne, Dubois Fils, J D Fonjallaz (l'Arbalète)★, Pinget★, Testuz.

DIAMOND CREEK VINEYARDS *Napa Valley AVA, California, USA* Small estate specializing in Cabernet: Volcanic Hill★★★, Red Rock Terrace★★ and Gravelly Meadow★. Huge, tannic wines; when tasted young I swear they won't ever come round. Yet there's usually a sweet inner core of fruit that envelops the tannin over 5–10 years, for one of California's great Cabernet experiences. Best years: 1997 96 95 94 92 91 90 **87 86 85 84 80 75**.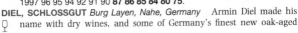

DIEL, SCHLOSSGUT *Burg Layen, Nahe, Germany* Armin Diel made his name with dry wines, and some of Germany's finest new oak-aged whites during the 1980s. However, since 1990 it has been classic style Rieslings which have been attracting headlines. Spätlese and Auslese from Dorsheim's top sites are regularly ★★, EISWEIN★★★. Best years: (1998) 97 96 95 **93 92 90 89 88**.

DO (DENOMINACIÓN DE ORIGEN) Spain's equivalent of the French quality wine category AC, regulating origin and production methods. Some Spanish DOs frankly don't deserve the title.

DOC (DENOMINAÇÃO DE ORIGEM CONTROLADA) The top regional classification for Portuguese wines since 1990. Formerly called *Região Demarcada* or RD.

DOC (DENOMINACIÓN DE ORIGEN CALIFICADA) Recent Spanish quality wine category, intended to be one step up from DO. So far only RIOJA qualifies.

DOC (DENOMINAZIONE DI ORIGINE CONTROLLATA) Italian quality wine category, regulating origin, grape varieties, yield and production methods. Covers more than 250 zones, which seems excessive since many wines are obscure and characterless. But a commitment to raise the proportion of DOC wines in Italy's total from 15% to 50% in the near future (while bringing some of the VINO DA TAVOLAS under new regional appellations) may help to give the system some much-needed credibility.

DOCG (DENOMINAZIONE DI ORIGINE CONTROLLATA E GARANTITA) The highest tier of the Italian classification system. It is a guarantee of authenticity, and supposedly quality, since wines are made under strict regulations and are approved by tasting panels. For such established wines as BAROLO, BARBARESCO and BRUNELLO DI MONTALCINO the DOCG label serves mainly as a further mark of prestige. But for others its main purpose seems to be to stimulate improvement, as witnessed in CHIANTI, VINO NOBILE DI MONTEPULCIANO, ALBANA DI ROMAGNA, ASTI and VERNACCIA DI SAN GIMIGNANO.

DOCTOR *Bernkastel, Mosel, Germany* Famous vineyard at Bernkastel (not to be confused with the Doktor vineyard in the RHEINHESSEN). Rather overrated and overpriced. Best producer: J WEGELER ERBEN★★. Best years: (1998) 97 **95 93 92 90 88**.

CH. DOISY-DAËNE★★ *Barsac AC, 2ème Cru Classé, Bordeaux, France* A consistently good BARSAC property and unusual in that the sweet wine is made exclusively from Sémillon, giving it extra richness. It ages well for 10 years or more. Doisy-Daëne Sec★ is a good, perfumed, dry white Bordeaux. Drink young. Best years: (sweet) (1998) 97 96 95 **90 89 88** 86 83 82 79; (dry) (1998) 96 **95 94 90 89 88 87**.

CH. DOISY-VÉDRINES★★ *Barsac AC, 2ème Cru Classé, Bordeaux, France* Next door to DOISY-DAENE, Doisy-Védrines is a richly botrytized wine, fatter and more syrupy than most BARSAC wines. Best years: (sweet) (1998) 97 96 95 **90 89 88 86 85 83 82 76 75**.

DOLCETTO One of Italy's most charming native grapes, producing purple wines bursting at the seams with fruit. Virtually exclusive to PIEDMONT, it is DOC in 7 zones, with styles ranging from the intense and rich in Alba, Ovada and Dogliani, to the lighter, more perfumed versions in Acqui and ASTI. Usually best drunk within a year or two, top wines can age up to 4 years. Best producers: (Alba) ALTARE★★, Brovia★, Giacomo CONTERNO★, Conterno-Fantino★, Marcarini★, Bartolo

MASCARELLO★, Giuseppe MASCARELLO★, Renato RATTI★, Albino Rocca★★, Luciano SANDRONE★★, Vajra★★, Vietti★, Roberto VOERZIO★★; (Dogliani) Francesco Boshis★, Chionetti★★, Luigi Einaudi★★, Gillardi★, Pecchenino★.

DÔLE *Valais, Switzerland*   Red wine from the Swiss VALAIS that must be made from at least 51% Pinot Noir, the rest being Gamay. Dôle is generally a light wine – the deeper, richer (100% Pinot Noir) styles have the right to call themselves Pinot Noir. Best producers: M Clavien, J Germanier, Caves Imesch, Mathier, Orsat.

DOMAINE CARNEROS *Carneros AVA, California, USA*   From its founding in 1987, this TAITTINGER-owned sparkling wine house has shown great promise. Both the Brut★ and the BLANC DE BLANCS★★ now match the French Taittinger fizz from Champagne. Domaine Carneros also produces Le Rêve, a deluxe Blanc de Blancs, and a very tasty Pinot Noir★ still wine.

DOMAINE CHANDON *Napa Valley AVA, California, USA*   The first of what turned out to be many French-owned (in this case, by MOET & CHANDON) sparkling wine producers in California. Has shown remarkable consistency and good quality over the years with non-vintage bubblies that stay reasonably priced. The Reserve★ bottlings, rich and creamy, are especially worth seeking out. BLANC DE BLANCS★ made entirely from CARNEROS Chardonnay is a welcome addition to the line. The super Reserve Étoile★ has reached ★★ on occasion. Shadow Creek is the budget line. Long-aged alambic brandies are the latest star attraction.

DOMAINE DROUHIN *Willamette Valley AVA, Oregon, USA*   Burgundy wine merchant Robert DROUHIN bought 40ha (100 acres) in OREGON in 1987, with plans to make great Pinot Noir★★★, and this has certainly been achieved already. The first vintage, 1988, made from bought-in grapes, was already more than adequate. Since then the regular Pinot Noir★ has been silky smooth, and the deluxe Pinot Noir Laurene★★ is supple, voluptuous, and one of Oregon's finest. Chardonnay is new to the roster. Best years: (1997) 96 95 **94 93 92 91 90**.

DOMAINE PAUL BRUNO *Maipo, Chile*   Pontallier and Prats are the surnames behind this small premium project close to Santiago. After a disappointing start, the new vintages of the Cabernet blend show more promise (but still at a price). Given their experience, 'could do better' should still be pinned to the winery wall. Best year: **1996**.

DOMECQ *Jerez y Manzanilla DO, Andalucía and Rioja DOC, País Vasco, Spain*   The largest of the sherry companies, best known for its reliable fino, La Ina★. However, the top-of-the-range wines, dry Amontillado 51-1A★★★, Sibarita Palo Cortado★★★ and Venerable Pedro Ximénez★★, are spectacular. Domecq is also the world's biggest brandy producer, and makes light, elegant red RIOJA★ from its own vineyards.

DOMINUS *Napa Valley AVA, California, USA*   Red wine only from this property owned by Christian MOUEIX, director of Bordeaux's PETRUS. Wines are based on Cabernet with leavenings of Merlot and Cabernet Franc. The dense, rich 1990 and 94 (both ★★) are the finest yet. Early vintages were mercilessly tannic, but recent ones show improvement. In recent vintages Moueix has relied on winemaking expertise from Pétrus. Best years: 1996 95 94 91 **90**.

DONAULAND *Niederösterreich, Austria* Amorphous wine region on both
banks of the Danube stretching from just north of Vienna west to
St Polten. Best are the dry Grüner Veltliners from the Wagram area.

HERMANN DÖNNHOFF *Oberhausen, Nahe, Germany* Great NAHE estate
with sites in Oberhausen, Niederhausen and BAD KREUZNACH. Kabinett and
Spätlese are usually ★★, anything from the Hermannshöhle vineyard
★★★; also makes sensational Auslese★★★ and EISWEIN★★★ in top
years. Best years: (1998) 97 96 95 **94 93** 92 90 89 88 86 83 76 75 71 69 66

DORDOGNE, VIN DE PAYS DE LA *South-West France* Good-value
wines from an attractive area of France; Sémillon-based whites best
drunk young, some Chardonnay (Ch. la JAUBERTIE), and various fruity
BERGERAC-style reds that can age for 1–2 years.

DOURO DOC *Douro, Portugal* As well as a flood of port and basic table
wine, some of Portugal's top, soft-textured red wines come from here.
There are good whites, made from the more aromatic white port grape
varieties. White wines are best young, but red wines may improve for
10 years or even more. Best producers: (reds) Quinta do COTTO (Grande
Escolha★★), Quinta do CRASTO★★, FERREIRA (BARCA VELHA★★★), Quinta do
Fojo★★, Quinta da Gaivosa★★, RAMOS PINTO (Duas Quintas★★), Quinta
de la ROSA★, SOGRAPE (Reserva★), Quinta do Vale da Raposa (single
varietals★). Best years: (reds) 1997 **96 95 94 92 91 90.**

DOW *Port DOC, Douro, Portugal* The grapes for Dow's vintage ports★★★
come mostly from the Quinta do Bomfim, which is also the name of
the excellent single quinta★★. Dow ports are all relatively dry, and
there are some excellent aged tawnies★★. Best years: (vintage) 1994 **91**
85 83 80 77 70 66 63 60 55 45; (Bomfim) 1995 **92 90** 87 86 84.

JEAN-PAUL DROIN *Chablis AC, Burgundy, France* Jean-Paul Droin sells
some of his production to the NUITS-ST-GEORGES merchant LABOURE-ROI,
but still manages to bottle no fewer than 14 different wines under his
own label. Apart from his CHABLIS★ and PETIT CHABLIS, all of Droin's
wines are fermented and/or aged in oak barrels. The best wines are
the big, buttery Chablis Premiers Crus – Montmains★★ and
Vosgros★★ – and Grands Crus – Vaudésir★★ and Grenouille★★. Best
years: 1997 96 95 **93 92 90.**

DROMANA ESTATE *Mornington Peninsula, Victoria, Australia* Garry
Crittenden went against the trend when he chose low-fertility soils in
a wind-protected site for his first Dromana plantings in 1982. The
pay-off can be tasted in fragrant, restrained Pinot Noir★ and
Chardonnay★★ and elegant if rather leafy Cabernet-Merlot★. Italian
varietals under the Garry Crittenden 'I' label, mostly from King Valley
grapes, are of special interest. Schinus is a popular second label.

JOSEPH DROUHIN *Beaune, Burgundy, France* One of the best
Burgundian merchants, now Japanese-owned, with substantial
vineyard holdings in CHABLIS and the COTE D'OR, and DOMAINE DROUHIN in
OREGON, USA. Drouhin makes a consistently good, if expensive, range
of wines from all over Burgundy. Look for BONNES-MARES★★, ROMANEE-
ST-VIVANT★★, BEAUNE Clos des Mouches (red★ and white★★), le
Musigny★★ and le MONTRACHET★★★ from the Domaine du Marquis de
Laguiche. Drouhin offers better value in Chablis★★ and less
glamorous Burgundian ACs, such as RULLY★ and ST-AUBIN★. The
BEAUJOLAIS is always good, but overall Drouhin's whites are (just)

better than the reds. Quality reds and whites should be aged for at least 5 years, often better nearer 10. Best years: (reds) 1997 96 95 93 **92** 90 89 88 85; (whites) 1997 96 **95 93** 92 90 89.

PIERRE-JACQUES DRUET *Bourgueil, Loire Valley, France* A passionate producer of top-notch BOURGUEIL and small quantities of CHINON. Druet makes 5 Bourgueils, les Cent Boisselées★, Cuvée Beauvais★★, Cuvée Reservée★★, Cuvée Grand Mont★★ and Vaumoreau (★★ in good years only), each a complex expression of the Cabernet Franc grape, but lacking obvious, upfront fruit. Best aged for 3–5 years. Best years: (1998) 97 96 **95 93 91** 90 89 88 85 83.

DRY CREEK VALLEY AVA *Sonoma, California, USA* Best known for Sauvignon Blanc, Zinfandel and Cabernet Sauvignon, this valley runs west of ALEXANDER VALLEY AVA, and similarly becomes hotter moving northwards. Best producers: DRY CREEK VINEYARDS★, Duxoup★, FERRARI-CARANO★★, GALLO (Chardonnay★), NALLE★★, Pezzi King★, Preston★, QUIVIRA★★, Rafanelli (Zinfandel★★), Michel Schlumberger★.

DRY CREEK VINEYARDS *Dry Creek Valley AVA, California, USA* An early advocate of Fumé Blanc, Dave Stare now offers a range of friendly wines but remains faithful to the brisk racy style of Fumé. A drink-young Chardonnay is solid, but the stars here are Merlot★, Old Vine Zinfandel★, and red Meritage along with compact Reserve Fumé Blanc★ which improves with aging. Best years: (reds) 1997 95 94 **92** 91.

DRY RIVER WINES *Wairarapa, North Island, New Zealand* Low yields, careful selection and an uncompromising attitude to quality at this tiny winery, owned by the meticulous Dr Neil McCallum, have helped create some of the country's top Gewürztraminer★★★ and Pinot Gris★★★, together with an intense and seductively smooth Pinot Noir★★, a sleek Chardonnay★★ and powerful, long-lived Riesling★★. Best years: 1998 97 **96** 94.

GEORGES DUBOEUF *Beaujolais, Burgundy, France* Known, with some justification, as the King of Beaujolais, Duboeuf is responsible for more than 10% of the wine produced in the region. Given the size of his operation, the quality of the wines is high. Duboeuf also makes and blends wine from the Mâconnais and the RHONE VALLEY. His BEAUJOLAIS NOUVEAU is usually one of the best, but his top wines are those he bottles for small growers, particularly Jean Descombes★★ in MORGON, Domaine des Quatre Vents★, la Madone★ in FLEURIE and Domaine de la Tour du Bief★★ in MOULIN-A-VENT. His ST-VERAN★ is also worth a try.

DUCKHORN *Napa Valley AVA, California, USA* This Californian winery has earned a well-deserved reputation for its Merlot★, if you like a chunky, tannic style, but the Cabernet Sauvignon★ and Sauvignon Blanc★ provide easier drinking. Paraduxx, a Zinfandel-Cabernet blend, is new to the range; Decoy is the budget line. Best years: (Merlot) (1997) 96 95 94 93 **92** 91 90; (Cabernet Sauvignon) (1996) 95 94 **93 92 91 90** 87 86.

CH. DUCRU-BEAUCAILLOU★★★ *St-Julien AC, 2ème Cru Classé, Haut-Médoc, Bordeaux, France* Traditionally the epitome of ST-JULIEN, mixing charm and austerity, fruit and firm tannins. In the 1970s, it was effortlessly ahead of other Second Growths, but vintages in the mid-80s and early 90s were flawed. Recent vintages show vast improvement, praise be. Second wine: la Croix de Beaucaillou. Best years: (1998) 97 96 95 94 **86 85 83 82 81 79** 78.

131

DUJAC *Morey-St-Denis AC, Côte de Nuits, Burgundy, France* One of Burgundy's leading winemakers, based in MOREY-ST-DENIS, but also with some choice vineyards in VOSNE-ROMANEE, CHAMBOLLE-MUSIGNY and GEVREY-CHAMBERTIN. The wines are all perfumed and elegant, including the small quantity of Morey-St-Denis white wine, but the outstanding Dujac bottlings are the 3 Grands Crus – CLOS DE LA ROCHE★★, BONNES-MARES★★ and CLOS ST-DENIS★★ – all of which will age for a decade or more. Owner Jacques Seysses has also had a very positive quality influence on many young Burgundian winemakers. Best years: 1997 96 95 93 **92** 90 **89 88 85**.

DUNN VINEYARDS *Howell Mountain AVA, California, USA* Massive, concentrated, hauntingly perfumed, long-lived Cabernet Sauvignon★★★ is the trademark of Randy Dunn's wines from HOWELL MOUNTAIN. His NAPA VALLEY Cabernets★★ are more elegant but less memorable. Best years: 1996 95 94 93 92 91 90 **88 87 86 85 84 82**.

DURBACH *Baden, Germany* Unusually for BADEN, Riesling (here called Klingelberger) is something of a speciality in Durbach. Another speciality is Traminer, here called Klevner (normally a synonym for Pinot Blanc!). Best producers: Durbach co-op, Andreas Laible★★, Heinrich Männle, Wolff-Metternich. Best years: **1997 96 94**.

DURIF See Petite Sirah.

JEAN DURUP *Chablis, Burgundy, France* The largest vineyard owner in CHABLIS, Jean Durup is a great believer in unoaked Chablis, and his wines tend to be clean and well made without any great complexity. His top Chablis is the Premier Cru Fourchaume★. Wines appear under a variety of labels, including l'Eglantière, Ch. de Maligny and Valéry.

ÉCHÉZEAUX AC *Grand Cru, Côte de Nuits, Burgundy, France* The village of Flagey-Échézeaux, hidden down in the plain away from the vineyards, is best known for its 2 Grands Crus, Échézeaux and the smaller and more prestigious Grands-Échézeaux, which are sandwiched between the world-famous CLOS DE VOUGEOT and VOSNE-ROMANEE. Few of the 80 growers here have really made a name for themselves but there are some fine wines with a lovely, smoky, plum richness, and a soft texture that age well over 10–15 years to a gamy, chocolaty depth. Best producers: Cacheux-Sirugue★, C Clerget★, DROUHIN★, R Engel★★, GRIVOT★★, JAYER-GILLES★★, Mongeard-Mugneret★, Dom. de la ROMANEE-CONTI★★, E Rouget★★. Best years: 1997 96 95 93 **92** 90 **89 88 85**.

EDELZWICKER See Alsace AC.

CH. L'ÉGLISE-CLINET★★ *Pomerol AC, Bordeaux, France* A tiny 5.5-ha domaine in the heart of the POMEROL plateau, l'Église-Clinet has a very old vineyard – one of the reasons for the depth and elegance of the wines. The other is the winemaking ability of owner Denis Durantou. The wine is expensive and in limited supply, but worth seeking out. It can be enjoyed young, though the best examples should be cellared 10 years or more. Best years: (1998) 97 96 95 94 93 **90 89 86 85**.

EIKENDAL VINEYARDS *Stellenbosch WO, South Africa* Winemakers Josef Krammer and Anneke Burger are a modest pair; their wines are also unflamboyant, though individual and complex. The deep, well-drained slopes of Helderberg produce an elegant, balanced Chardonnay★ with an aging ability unusual in South Africa, and a light-textured but flavoursome Merlot★. Best years: (Chardonnay) **1998 97 96 95 94**.

EINZELLAGE German for an individual vineyard site or slope which is generally farmed by several growers. The name is preceded on the label by that of the village; for example, the Wehlener Sonnenuhr is the Sonnenuhr vineyard in WEHLEN. The mention of a particular site should signify a superior wine. Sadly it often does not, and even the name of a top vineyard site is no guarantee of top quality. The demands of some leading growers for a vineyard classification have as yet been ignored by the politicians.

EISWEIN Rare, chiefly German and Austrian late-harvested wine made by waiting for winter frosts, picking the grapes and pressing them while frozen. This concentrates the sweetness of the grape as most of the liquid is removed as ice. Any grape variety may be used, but healthy grapes unaffected by rot are the ones that give the best results. Canadian examples, called ICEWINE, are showing some potential too.

NEIL ELLIS *Stellenbosch WO, South Africa* This leading winemaker/négociant has consolidated his far-flung operations under a modernized STELLENBOSCH cellar. Long-recognized for full, vigorous Sauvignon Blancs★ from cooler areas and striking Stellenbosch reds, a blackcurranty Cabernet Sauvignon★★ and supple Cabernet-Merlot, Neil Ellis has now turned his attention to Shiraz. A silky Pinot Noir from cool Elgin confirms this winemaker is short of neither versatility nor ability. Best years: (whites) **1998 97 96 95**; (reds) **1996 95 94 93 92**.

ELTVILLE *Rheingau, Germany* This large wine town makes some of the RHEINGAU's most racy Riesling wines. Best producers: J B Becker★, J Fischer, Hans Hulbert. Best years: (1998) 97 **96 95 90** 89.

EMILIA-ROMAGNA *Italy* Central-eastern region in Italy, divided into the provinces of Emilia (in the west) and ROMAGNA (in the east). It is chiefly infamous for LAMBRUSCO in Emilia. See also Colli Bolognesi, Colli Piacentini.

ENTRE-DEUX-MERS AC *Bordeaux, France* This AC increasingly represents some of the freshest, brightest, snappiest dry white wine in France. Behind the revival lie the techniques of cold fermentation and of leaving skins in contact with juice for a few hours before fermentation. In general, drink the wine of the latest vintage, though the better wines will last a year or two. The sweet wines are sold as PREMIERES COTES DE BORDEAUX, St-Macaire, LOUPIAC and STE-CROIX-DU-MONT. Best producers: Bel Air, Bonnet★, Castelneau, Fontenille, Launay, Moulin-de-Launay, Nardique-la-Gravière, Ste-Marie, Tour-de-Mirambeau, Turcaud.

ERATH VINEYARDS *Willamette Valley AVA, Oregon, USA* OREGON's third-largest producer, formerly known as Knudsen Erath before the partnership dissolved in 1996. Makes stylish Pinot Noirs, a Vintage Select★★ and a Willamette Valley★ that have been gaining greater concentration of fruit in recent vintages. Erath's Chardonnay can be good, and the Pinot Gris is very attractive. Best years: (Pinot Noir Vintage Select) (1996) 95 94 **93 92** 91 86; (Willamette Valley) 1996 95 **94 93 92 90**.

ERBACH *Rheingau, Germany* Erbach's famous Marcobrunn vineyard is one of the top spots for Riesling on the Rhine. The village wines are elegant, off-dry; those from Marcobrunn more powerful and imposing.

Best producers: von Knyphausen★, SCHLOSS REINHARTSHAUSEN★★, Schloss Schönborn★. Best years: (1998) 96 95 **94 93** 92.

ERBALUCE DI CALUSO DOC *Piedmont, Italy* Usually a dry or sparkling white from the Erbaluce grape; Caluso Passito, where the grapes are semi-dried before fermenting, can be a great sweet wine. Best producers: (dry) Giuseppe Bianchi★, Cieck★, Ferrando★, Orsolani★, Massimo Pachié; (Caluso Passito) Cieck★, Ferrando★★, Orsolani.

ERDEN *Mosel, Germany* Village in the Middle MOSEL, whose most famous vineyards are Prälat and Treppchen. The wines are rich and succulent with a strong mineral character and are among the region's finest. Best producers: J J Christoffel★★, Dr LOOSEN★★★, Mönchhof. Best years: (1998) 97 96 95 **94 93** 92 90.

ERMITAGE Swiss name for the Marsanne grape of the northern RHONE VALLEY. Mostly found in the central VALAIS where the wines stop short of fermenting out dry, producing a range of wines from slightly sweet to lovely honeyed dessert wines. Best producers: Chappaz★, Dom. du Mont d'Or★, Orsat (Marsanne Blanche★).

ERRÁZURIZ *Aconcagua, Chile* Suffering a lack of continuity on the winemaking front, but the signing of ex-CONO SUR wonderkid Ed Flaherty is bringing results. Using some red grapes from the cool Aconcagua Valley north of Santiago, as well as traditional supplies from south of Santiago, it produces the reliably concentrated Don Maximiano Cabernet Sauvignon★★ and Merlot★. Slick-textured, citrus Chardonnay★★ from CASABLANCA heads the whites. A new top-quality BORDEAUX blend, Seña★, is the result of a joint venture with Robert MONDAVI. Best years: (reds) 1997 **96** 95.

ESPORÃO *Reguengos DOC, Alentejo, Portugal* Huge estate in the heart of the Alentejo, with Australian David Baverstock producing a broad range of wines. The principal labels are Esporão (red★★ and white★ reservas) Monte Velho and Alandra, and there are some excellent varietals: Trincadeira★★, Aragonês★, Cabernet Sauvignon★ and Touriga Nacional★★. Best years: (reds) 1997 96 **95 94** 92.

EST! EST!! EST!!! DI MONTEFIASCONE DOC *Lazio, Italy* Modest white from the shores of Lake Bolsena accorded its undeserved reputation because of an apocryphal story of a bishop's servant sent ahead to scout out good wines. Getting so excited about this one, he reiterated the thumbs-up code 3 times. Perhaps it had been a long day. The most credible exception is Falesco's Poggio dei Gelsi★. Far better though is the same producer's barrique-aged Merlot Montiano★★★. Best producers: Bigi (Graffiti), Falesco★, Mazziotti.

CH. DES ESTANILLES *Faugères AC, Languedoc, France* Don't be deceived by Michel Louison's *enfant terrible* appearance: he and his wife are completely serious about making the best wine they can. The Louisons know that quality begins in the vineyard. Their best site is the Clos de Fou, with its very steep schistous slope planted with Syrah; the grape 'dominates' his top red cuvée★★ (i.e. 100% – but the AC regulations do not allow him to say so). They also make a wood-fermented and aged rosé, plus a fine COTEAUX DU LANGUEDOC white★. Best years: (reds) 1996 **95 94** 91.

ESTREMADURA *Portugal* A regional designation for IPRs of Alcobaça, ALENQUER, ARRUDA, Encostas d'Aire, Obidas and Torres Vedras. More wine is produced here than in any other Portuguese region, but only Alenquer and Arruda are producing anything of real quality. Most of this region's wine is instantly forgettable, although a number of co-ops and new small estates are beginning to produce some fresher reds and whites. Much is sold as Vinho Regional Estremadura. Best producers: Quinta da Abrigada, Arruda co-op, Quinta da Boavista (Espiga, Palha Canas★), Quinta das Setencostas★ and exciting new single varietals★), D F J Vinhos (Alta Mesa, Ramada), José Neiva, Quinta de Pancas★. See also Bucelas, Colares.

ETNA DOC *Sicily, Italy* This wine zone around the famous volcano manages to produce some good wine. The red wine is based on varieties of Nerello and Nero d'Avole, and the white is a blend using the local Carricante. Best producers: Benanti★, Barone Scammacca del Murgo★, Barone di Villagrande.

L'ÉTOILE AC *Jura, France* A tiny area within the COTES DU JURA which has its own AC for whites, mainly Chardonnay and Savagnin, and for VIN JAUNE. There is good Champagne-method fizz too. Best producers: Ch. de l'Étoile★, l'Étoile co-op, Geneletti, Dom. de Montbourgeau★★.

CH. L'ÉVANGILE★★ *Pomerol AC, Bordeaux, France* Made by one of Bordeaux's most talented winemakers, Michel Rolland, the wine can be rich, fat and exotic. But I still remain unconvinced it's worth the high asking price. Now owned by the Rothschilds of LAFITE-ROTHSCHILD. Best years: (1998) 97 96 95 94 93 **90 89 88 85 83 82 79 75**.

EVANS FAMILY *Hunter Valley, New South Wales, Australia* Len Evans' tiny HUNTER vineyard grows majestic Chardonnay★★, highly regarded sparkling wine (PETALUMA-made), as well as Gamay and Pinot Noir. Nearly all the wine is sold privately or ex-winery; or drunk by Len with his friends. Following the 1997 sale of ROTHBURY, Evans created 2 new labels: Evans Wine Company for regional varietals, and Bulletin Place for budget-priced blends. Best years: (Chardonnay) **1996 95 93 88**.

EVANS & TATE *Margaret River, Western Australia* Important Western Australian winery originally in the SWAN VALLEY. Producer of fruit-driven MARGARET RIVER Chardonnay★★, Two-Vineyards Chardonnay★, curranty Cabernet★ and a Shiraz of real substance. Barrel-fermented Semillon is ★★, but drink it young. Signs of substantial improvement since the 1996 vintage. Brian Fletcher (ex-ST HUBERTS and SEPPELT) is the dynamic winemaker. Best years: (Cabernet) 1996 95 **93 90 88**.

ÉVENTAIL DE VIGNERONS PRODUCTEURS *Beaujolais, Burgundy, France* The most successful and powerful of the BEAUJOLAIS growers' associations, formed to improve quality and marketing of their wines. The standard is generally high. Look out for Louis Desvignes★ in MORGON, Georges Passot★ in CHIROUBLES and Domaine M Pelletier★ in JULIENAS.

EYRIE VINEYARDS *Willamette Valley AVA, Oregon, USA* One of the leading Pinot Noir★ producers in Oregon, especially the Reserve★★, but in poor years the wines can be withdrawn and thin. Chardonnay★ shows nice varietal fruit, while the popular Pinot Gris flies off the shelves. Best years: (Pinot Noir) 1996 95 **94 92 90 89 88**.

FAIRVIEW ESTATE *Paarl WO, South Africa* Charles Back is constantly on the move: keeping tabs on the maiden harvest of The Spice Route

Wine Company, a joint West Coast venture with John Platter, THELEMA's Gyles Webb and Jabulani Ntshangase; initiating a workers-empowerment project and producing South Africa's first Viognier★★, richly textured and delicious, and Mourvèdre. These are but the main new directions this confirmed workaholic busied himself with in 1998. Fairview is certainly not neglected – a sound team produces good Shiraz★, Pinotage, Cabernet Sauvignon★, Merlot, Chardonnay★ and Sémillon. Zinfandel-Cinsaut (Zin-Cin)★ and Zinfandel Carignan remain delightful idiosyncracies. Best years: **1998 97 96 95 94 93 92 91 90**.

JOSEPH FAIVELEY *Nuits-St-Georges, Côtes de Nuits, Burgundy, France*
This Burgundian merchant makes excellent red wines (especially CHAMBERTIN-Clos-de-Bèze★★★ and Mazis-Chambertin★★), principally from its own substantial vineyard holdings. Indeed, Faiveley is more like an outsize grower than a négociant. The much cheaper MERCUREY reds★ are also attractive if on the lean side. The Côte Chalonnaise whites from RULLY★ and MERCUREY★, and the oak-aged BOURGOGNE Blanc represent good value. Best years: (premium reds) 1997 96 95 93 **92 91 90 88 85**; (whites) 1997 96 **95 93 92 90 89**.

FALERNO DEL MASSICO DOC *Campania, Italy* Falernian, from north of Naples, was one of the ancient Romans' superstar wines. The revived DOC, with a white Falanghina and reds from Aglianico and Piedirosso, or Primitivo, looks promising. Best producers: Michele Moio, Villa Matilde★. Best years: (reds) (1998) 97 **96 95 93**.

CH. DE FARGUES★★ *Sauternes AC, Cru Bourgeois, Bordeaux, France*
Property run by the Lur-Saluces family, who until recently also owned Ch. d'YQUEM. The quality of this fine, rich wine is more a tribute to their commitment than to the inherent quality of the vineyard. Best years: (1998) 97 96 95 90 89 88 86 83.

FAUGÈRES AC *Languedoc, France* Faugères, with its hilly vineyards stretching up into the mountains north of Béziers in the Hérault, was the first of the LANGUEDOC communes to make a reputation of its own. What marks it out from other Languedoc reds is its ripe, soft, rather plummy flavour, and though it is a little more expensive than neighbouring wines, the extra money is generally worth it. Best producers: Alquier★, ESTANILLES★, Faugères co-op, Fraisse, Grézan, Haut-Fabrègues, la Liquière, Ollier-Taillefer★, Raymond Roque★, St-Aimé. Best years: 1998 **96 95 94 93 91 90 89**.

FAUSTINO MARTÍNEZ *Rioja DOC, País Vasco and Rioja, and Cava DO, Spain* Family-owned and technically very well equipped, this RIOJA company makes good Reserva★ and Gran Reserva★ red Riojas in distinctive dark, frosted bottles, as well as a fruity, Beaujolais-style Vino Joven or Viña Faustina★, and pleasant whites and rosés. Best years: (reds) 1996 **95 94 92 91 90 89 87 85 82 81**.

FEILER-ARTINGER *Rust, Neusiedlersee, Burgenland, Austria* Father and son team Hans and Kurt Feiler make Ausbruch-style dessert wines★★★ of great elegance at this medium-sized estate housed in a fine Baroque building. Their dry whites★ and reds★ from a range of traditional Austrian and French grapes are also worthy of attention. Best years: (dessert wines) (1998) 96 95 **94 93 91**; (dry whites, reds) (1997) **94 93 92**.

FELSINA, FATTORIA DI *Chianti Classico DOCG, Tuscany, Italy* Leading estate making full, chunky CHIANTI CLASSICO★★ wines which improve with several years' bottle age. Quality is generally outstanding, though most notable are the single-vineyard Riserva Rancia★★★ and Sangiovese Fontalloro★★★. Also good VIN SANTO★★. Best years: (reds) (1998) 97 96 **95 94 93 91 90 88 85**.

FENDANT *Valais, Switzerland* Chasselas wine from the steep slopes of the Swiss VALAIS. Good Fendant should be ever so slightly *spritzig* with a spicy character. However, the average Fendant is thin and virtually characterless. It is best drunk *very* young, but a good example can age for years. The best is said to come from the slopes above Molignon and Montibeux, or from around Sion or Uvrier. Best producers: Chappaz, J Germanier, Gilliard, Caves Imesch, Maye & Fils, Orsat.

FERRARI *Trento DOC, Trentino, Italy* Founded in 1902, the firm is a leader for sparkling wine. Consistent, classy wines include Ferrari Brut★, Maximum Brut★, Perlé★, Rosé★ and the elegant vintage Giulio Ferrari Riserva del Fondatore★★, aged 8 years on its lees and an Italian classic.

FERRARI-CARANO VINEYARDS *Dry Creek Valley AVA, California, USA* Really lovely Chardonnay★★, with balanced, elegant fruit made in a regular and a Reserve style. The Reserve is deeply flavoured with more than a touch of oak, while the regular bottling has delicious apple-spice fruit. A new red wine, Siena★★ (a blend of Cabernet Sauvignon and Sangiovese), shows great promise and could outshine the Chardonnay. Merlot★ and Fumé Blanc★ are also good. Reds can improve for 5–10 years. Best years: (reds) 1996 95 94 **92 91 88 87**.

FERREIRA *Port DOC, Douro DOC, Douro, Portugal* Old port house owned by SOGRAPE, who have taken a major role in modernizing Portugal's wine production. Ferreira produces the famous BARCA VELHA★★★ table wine, but is best known for excellent tawny ports: creamy, nutty Quinta do Porto 10-year-old★ or the Duque de Braganza 20-year-old★★. The vintage port★★ is increasingly good. Best years: (vintage) 1995 94 91 **85 83 78 77 70 66 63**.

CH. FERRIÈRE★★ *Margaux AC, 3ème Cru Classé, Bordeaux, France* The smallest classified growth in MARGAUX, Ferrière was leased to its larger neighbour Ch. LASCOMBES until 1992, when it was purchased by the Merlaut family, owners of Ch. CHASSE-SPLEEN. It is now managed by Claire Villars, and the wines, ripe, rich and elegant, have become the revelation of the Margaux AC. Best years: (1998) 96 95 94 **93**.

FETZER VINEYARDS *Mendocino County, California, USA* Winery making drinkable, fair-priced wines. The Reserve wines, Barrel Select Cabernet Sauvignon and Chardonnay, are a step up. The Zinfandel Special Reserves★ are concentrated, fruity wines with staying power. Chardonnay, Cabernet, Sangiovese, Syrah and Viognier from organically grown grapes have been released under the Bonterra label and they have been enthusiastically received. Best years: (1997) 96 95 94 **92 91**.

FIANO Distinctive, low-yielding southern Italian white grape variety. Best producers: (Molise) Di Majo Norante; (Fiano di Avellino DOC in Campania) Colli di Lapio★, Feudi di San Gregorio★, Marianna, MASTROBERARDINO★, Nicola Romano★, Struzziero, Terre Dora di Paolo★ (formerly Vignadora), Vadiaperti★, Vega-D'Antiche Terre.

CH. DE FIEUZAL *Pessac-Léognan AC, Cru Classé de Graves, Bordeaux, France* One of the most up-to-date properties in the region and the delicious, oaky wine sells at a high price. The rich, complex red★ is drinkable almost immediately because of its succulent fruit, but it will age for a decade or more. Less than 10% of the wine is white★★ but it is stupendous stuff. Second wine: l'Abeille de Fieuzal. Best years: (reds) (1998) 97 96 95 **94 90 89 88 87 86 85 83 82 78**; (whites) (1998) 97 96 **95 94 93 90 89** 88 87 86 85.

CH. FIGEAC★★ *St-Émilion Grand Cru AC, 1er Grand Cru Classé, Bordeaux, France* Leading property whose wine has a delightful fragrance and gentleness of texture. There is an unusually high percentage of Cabernets Franc and Sauvignon (70%) in the wine. Lovely young yet, ideally, should age for at least 10–12 years. Second wine: la Grange-neuve de Figeac. Best years: (1998) 97 96 95 94 90 89 **88 86 85 83 82 78**.

FILLIATREAU *Saumur-Champigny, Loire Valley, France* The leading grower in SAUMUR-CHAMPIGNY, producing 4 different, richly flavoured Cabernet Francs – Jeunes Vignes★, Lena Filliatreau★, la Grande Vignolle★★ and Vieilles Vignes★★ – as well as SAUMUR Rouge, called Château Fouquet★. In a good vintage, Filliatreau's top reds can age for up to 15 years. Best years: (1998) 97 96 **95 94 93 90 89 88 85**.

FINGER LAKES AVA *New York State, USA* Cool region in central NEW YORK STATE. Riesling and Chardonnay are the trump cards here, but a few growers are having success with Pinot Noir. Best producers: FOX RUN VINEYARDS, Heron Hill, LAMOUREAUX LANDING, Lucas, Wagner.

FINO See Jerez y Manzanilla DO.

FITOU AC *Languedoc-Roussillon, France* Dark red Fitou was one of the success stories of the 1980s – its burly flavour comes from Carignan and the wine will age well for at least 5–6 years. Best producers: Colomer, les Fenals★, MONT TAUCH CO-OP★, des Nouvelles★, Dom. de Rolland, Roudène★. Best years: **1995 94** 93 91 90 89 88.

FIXIN AC *Côte de Nuits, Burgundy, France* Despite being next door to GEVREY-CHAMBERTIN, Fixin rarely produces anything really magical. The wines are worthy enough to last, but rarely taste exciting and are often sold off under COTE DE NUITS-VILLAGES label. Recent vintages, though, have shown distinct improvements. Best producers: V & D Berthaut, CLAIR, Pierre Gelin, Alain Guyard★, Philippe Joliet. Best years: (reds) 1997 96 95 **93 92 90** 89 88.

FLEURIE AC *Beaujolais, Burgundy, France* The third-largest, but best-known BEAUJOLAIS Cru. Good Fleurie reveals the happy, carefree flavours of the Gamay grape at its best, plus heady perfumes and a juicy sweetness that can leave you gasping with delight. Not surprisingly, demand has meant that many wines are overpriced and ordinary. Best producers: J-M Aujoux, P Bernard, Berrod, Michel Chignard, DUBOEUF★ (named vineyards), H Fessy★, Fleurie co-op★, la Grand Cour, Montgénas, Quatre Vents. Best years: 1998 97 **96 95** 93.

CH. LA FLEUR-PÉTRUS★★ *Pomerol AC, Bordeaux, France* Like the better-known PETRUS and TROTANOY, this is owned by the dynamic MOUEIX family. But, unlike its stablemates, la Fleur-Pétrus is situated entirely on gravel soil and tends to produce tighter wines with less immediate fruit flavours but considerable elegance and cellar potential. Among POMEROL's top dozen properties. Best years: (1998) 97 96 95 94 93 90 89 **88 85 82**.

FLORA SPRINGS *Napa Valley AVA, California, USA* This NAPA VALLEY winery started life as a white wine specialist, but after recent replanting is now best known for Cabernet Reserve★★, a BORDEAUX blend called Trilogy★★ and Merlot. Chardonnay Reserve★★ tops the whites. Best years: (Chardonnay) (1998) 97 **96 95 94 92 91**; (Trilogy) (1996) 95 94 93 **92 91**.

ÉMILE FLORENTIN *St-Joseph AC, Rhône Valley, France* Traditional, organically produced ST-JOSEPH, both red★ and white★, from very old vines. The wines are rather rustic, and can seem to lack fruit when young, but they age well. Best years: (reds) (1998) 97 96 95 94 **91 90 89 88 85 83**; (whites) (1998) 97 96 **95 94 91 90 89 85**.

FONSECA *Port DOC, Douro, Portugal* Owned by the same group as TAYLOR FLADGATE & YEATMAN, Fonseca makes ports in a rich, densely plummy style. Fonseca vintage★★★ is magnificent, the aged tawnies★★ uniformly superb – even its Late Bottled Vintage★ is way better than most. Fonseca Guimaraens★★ is the name of the 'off-vintage'. Best years: (vintage) 1994 92 **85 83 77 70 66 63**.

JOSÉ MARIA DA FONSECA *Arrábida IPR, Terras do Sado, Portugal* One of Portugal's most go-ahead wineries. Its most exciting red wines come from the ALENTEJO, in particular the fleshy, oaky d'Avillez★ from Portalegre. From the Setúbal Peninsula, south of Lisbon, it produces the round, fruity red Periquita, as well as good red and dry white Quinta de Camarate★, even better Primum white★ and red★★ and the famous sweet fortified Moscatel de SETUBAL, ★★ in its 20-year-old and vintage-dated 'superior' versions.

FONTANAFREDDA *Barolo DOCG, Piedmont, Italy* This is one of the most important PIEDMONT estates, based in the old BAROLO hunting lodge of the King of Italy. As well as a commercial Barolo, it also produces a range of Piedmont varietals, several single-vineyard Barolos★, 4 million bottles of ASTI and a good dry sparkler, Contessa Rosa. Best years: (Barolo) (1998) (97) 96 95 90 89 **88 85**.

FONT DE MICHELLE *Châteauneuf-du-Pape AC, Rhône Valley, France* This much-improved estate is currently among the top performers in CHATEAUNEUF-DU-PAPE. The reds★, in particular Cuvée Etienne Gonnet★★, and whites★ are stylish but still heady, with richness and southern herb fragrance – and not too expensive. Best years: (1997) 95 94 **93 90 89 88**.

FONTERUTOLI, CASTELLO DI *Chianti Classico DOCG, Tuscany, Italy* This eminent estate has belonged to the Mazzei family since the 15th century. Now in a dramatic gesture, it has focused production on CHIANTI CLASSICO Riserva★★★. The new wine replaces the fine SUPER-TUSCAN Concerto★★ (Sangiovese with 20% Cabernet) and previously outstanding Riserva Ser Lapo★★. The Sangiovese-Merlot Siepi★★ is being retained.

FONTODI *Chianti Classico DOCG, Tuscany, Italy* The Manetti family has steadily built this superbly sited estate into one of the most admired in the CHIANTI CLASSICO area, with a consistent *normale*★, richer Riserva★ and fine Riserva Vigna del Sorbo★★. Exemplary SUPER-TUSCAN Flaccianello della Pieve★★★ is produced from a single vineyard of old vines and though now better than ever, it has served as a shining example to other producers of how excellent Sangiovese can be when it stands alone, without the addition of other native or foreign varieties. Two varietals are made under the new Case Via label; of these, the Syrah★ is most promising. Best years: (Flaccianello) 1995 94 **93 91 90 88 86 85**.

FORST *Pfalz, Germany* Small village with 6 individual vineyard sites, including the Ungeheuer or 'Monster'; wines from the Monster can indeed be quite savage, with a marvellous mineral intensity and richness in the best years. Equally good are the Kirchenstück, Jesuitengarten, Freundstück and Pechstein. Best producers: VON BUHL★, BURKLIN-WOLF★, Georg Mosbacher★★, J WEGELER ERBEN★, Werlé★, WOLF★★. Best years: (whites) (1998) 97 96 **95 94 93 90**.

FOX RUN VINEYARDS *Finger Lakes AVA, New York State, USA* The Reserve Chardonnay★ produced here is very attractive, with well-integrated oak and fruit in an elegant style. The just off-dry Riesling is also a treat, as is the vintage-dated Brut bubbly. Merlot and Pinot Noir both show great promise. There was a good Meritage★ (red wine produced from classic BORDEAUX grape varieties) made in 1996. Best years: (1998) 97 **95 94**.

FRANCIACORTA DOCG *Lombardy, Italy* The 14th wine to achieve 'guaranteed' status is the Champagne-method sparkler Franciacorta, made from Pinot and Chardonnay grapes. The former DOC applied to still as well as sparkling wines: Bianco from Pinot Bianco and Chardonnay; Rosso from Cabernet, Barbera, Nebbiolo and Merlot. These remain DOC under the appellation Terre di Franciacorta. Best producers: BELLAVISTA★★, CA' DEL BOSCO★★, Castellino★, Cavalleri★, La Ferghettina★, Enrico Gatti★, Monte Rossa★, Principe-Banfi★, Ricci Curbastro★, Uberti★.

FRANCISCAN VINEYARD *Napa Valley AVA, California, USA* Consistently good wines at fair prices, from the heart of the NAPA VALLEY. The Cuvée Sauvage Chardonnay★★★ is an absolutely blockbusting, courageous mouthful, but the Cabernet Sauvignon-based Meritage Red★ is developing a very attractive style. Estancia is a second label, with remarkably good-value Chardonnay from CENTRAL COAST and Cabernet Sauvignon from ALEXANDER VALLEY, as well as its own Meritage★. Franciscan also owns Mount Veeder Winery, where lean but intense Cabernet Sauvignon★★ of great minerally depth and complexity is made. Best years: (Chardonnay) (1997) 96 95 **94 92 91 90**; (Cabernet Sauvignon) (1996) 95 94 93 **91 88 87**.

FRANKEN *Germany* Wine region incorporated into the kingdom of Bavaria at the beginning of the 19th century and specializing in dry wines. Easily recognizable by their squat, green Bocksbeutel bottles (now more familiar because of the Portuguese wine Mateus Rosé). Silvaner is the traditional grape variety, although Müller-Thurgau now predominates. The most famous vineyards are on the hillsides around WÜRZBURG and IPHOFEN.

FRANSCHHOEK WO *South Africa* A picturesque valley encircled by breathtaking mountain peaks. The Huguenot refugees settled here in the 17th century and many of the wineries still bear French names. Sémillon is a local speciality (a few vines are close to 100 years old) and the valley is best-known for its white wines. However, a diverse range of reds are now showing promise, including Cabrière's Pinot Noir★, La Motte's Shiraz and Optima, a Cabernet-Merlot blend from L'Ormarins. Best producers: Cabrière Estate★, Dieu Donné, La Motte★, L'Ormarins.

FRASCATI DOC *Lazio, Italy* One of Italy's most famous whites, frequently referred to as Rome's quaffing wine. The wine is a blend of Trebbiano and Malvasia; the better examples have a higher proportion of Malvasia. Good Frascati is worth seeking out, most notably from the revelationary Castel de Paolis, who also makes a good example of a sweet late-harvest style called Cannellino. Other light, dry Frascati-like wines come from neighbouring DOCs in the hills of the Castelli Romani and Colli Albani, including Marino, Montecompatri, Velletri and Zagarolo. Best producers: Casale Marchese★, Castel de Paolis★★, Colli di Catone★, Villa Simone★, Zandotti★.

FREISA Italian PIEDMONT grape making sweet, foaming, 'happy juice' reds, now sadly rather out of fashion. Some producers are now making a dry style which is very tasty after 3 or 4 years. Best producers: ASCHERI, Aldo CONTERNO★, Giacomo CONTERNO, Bartolo MASCARELLO★, Scarpa★, Aldo Vajra★★.

FREIXENET *Cava DO, Catalonia, Spain* The second-biggest Spanish sparkling wine company (after CODORNIU) makes fresh, young Cordon Negro Brut CAVA in a vast network of cellars in San Sadurní de Noya. However, most of its other Cavas are unexciting.

FRESCOBALDI *Tuscany, Italy* Florentine company selling large quantities of inexpensive blended CHIANTIS, but from its own vineyards (some 800 ha in total) it produces good to very good wines at Nipozzano (especially CHIANTI RUFINA Castello di Nipozzano Riserva★★ and Montesodi★★), Tenuta di Pomino★ in POMINO and from CASTELGIOCONDO★★ in BRUNELLO DI MONTALCINO. Castelgiocondo is also the early source for the much-heralded new wine, Luce★★ – a joint venture with MONDAVI. Best years: (premium reds) (1998) (97) 96 95 **94 93 91 90 88 85**.

FRIULI GRAVE DOC *Friuli-Venezia Giulia, Italy* DOC covering 19 wine types in western Friuli. Good affordable Merlot, Refosco, Chardonnay, Pinot Grigio, Traminer and Tocai. Best producers: Borgo Magredo★, La Delizia co-op, Fantinel★, Le Fredis★, Di Leonardo★, Organi★, Pighin★, Pittaro★, Plozner★, Pradio★, Russolo★, Vigneti Le Monde★, Villa Chiopris★. Best years: (whites) (1998) **97 96 95 93**.

FRIULI ISONZO DOC *Friuli-Venezia Giulia, Italy* Classy southern neighbour of COLLIO with wines of outstanding value. The DOC covers 20 styles, including Merlot, Chardonnay, Pinot Grigio and Sauvignon. The best from neighbouring Carso are also good. Best producers: (Isonzo) Borgo San Daniele★, Colmello di Grotta★, Drius★, Masùt da Rive★ (Silvano Gallo), Lis Neris-Pecorari★★, Pierpaolo Pecorari★, Giovanni Puiatti★, Ronco del Gelso★★, Tenuta Villanova★, Vie di Romans★★; (Carso) Castelvecchio, Edi Kante. Best years: (whites) (1998) **97 96 95**.

FRIULI-VENEZIA GIULIA *Italy*   Located in north-east Italy, this region borders Slovenia and Austria. The hilly DOC zones of COLLIO and COLLI ORIENTALI produce some of Italy's finest whites from Chardonnay, Pinot Bianco, Pinot Grigio, Sauvignon and Tocai, and the reds can also be excellent mainly from Cabernet, Merlot and Refosco. The DOCs of Friuli Aquileia, FRIULI ISONZO, Friuli Latisana and FRIULI GRAVE, in the rolling hills and plains, produce good-value wines.

FRIZZANTE   Italian for semi-sparkling wine, usually made dry, but sometimes sweet.

FRONSAC AC *Bordeaux, France*   A small area west of POMEROL making Merlot-based wines that are among the best value in Bordeaux today. The top producers have made a considerable effort to improve in recent years and it shows in the wines. Firmly structured, occasionally perfumed, they are better with at least 5 years' age. Best producers: Carles, Dalem★, la Dauphine★, Fontenil★, la Grave, Mayne-Vieil, Moulin-Haut-Laroque★, Puy Guilhem, la Rivière★, la Rousselle, Tour du Moulin, les Trois Croix, la Vieille-Cure, Villars★. Best years: (1998) 97 96 95 **94 90 89 88 86 85 83 82**.

CH. FUISSÉ *Pouilly-Fuissé, Mâconnais, Burgundy, France*   Owner Jean-Jacques Vincent is the leading grower in POUILLY-FUISSÉ, producing rich, ripe, concentrated Chardonnays. Top wines are the 3 Pouilly-Fuissés – Jeunes Vignes Cuvée Première★, the oak-fermented Ch. Fuissé★★ and the memorable, richly textured Ch. Fuissé Vieilles Vignes★★★. He also makes a fine ST-VÉRAN★, BEAUJOLAIS and has a négociant business specializing in wines of the Mâconnais.

FUMÉ BLANC   See Sauvignon Blanc.

RUDOLF FÜRST *Bürgstadt, Franken, Germany*   Paul Fürst's dry Rieslings★★ are unusually elegant for a region renowned for its earthy white wines, and his Spätburgunder reds★ are some of the best in Germany. Wines as intellectual and sensual as their maker, with excellent aging potential. Best years: (1998) 97 95 94 **93 92 90 89 88**.

JEAN-NOËL GAGNARD *Chassagne-Montrachet AC, Côte de Beaune, Burgundy, France*   One of many Gagnards in CHASSAGNE-MONTRACHET, Jean-Noël and his daughter Caroline consistently make some of the best wines. His top wine is rich, toasty BATARD-MONTRACHET★★, but his other whites are first rate, too, particularly Caillerets and Morgeot Premiers Crus★★. Gagnard's reds★ are not quite as good as his whites, but are still among the most enjoyable in Chassagne. All whites are capable of extended cellaring. Best years: (whites) 1997 96 95 93 **92 90 89**.

GAGNARD-DELAGRANGE *Chassagne-Montrachet AC, Côte de Beaune, Burgundy, France*   Jacques Gagnard-Delagrange heads a distinguished family of interrelated winemakers – Jacques' brother is Jean-Noël GAGNARD, and the source of many of his vineyards was Jacques' father-in-law, Edmond Delagrange-Bachelet. Jacques makes excellent BATARD-MONTRACHET★★ and CHASSAGNE-MONTRACHET Premiers Crus Boudriottes★★ and Morgeot★★. His 2 daughters and their husbands are responsible for Domaines Blain-Gagnard (look out for Criots-Bâtard-Montrachet★★) and Fontaine Gagnard (also Criots-Bâtard-Montrachet★★ and several Chassagne-Montrachet Premiers Crus★★). Best years: (whites) 1997 96 95 94 93 **92 90 89**.

GAILLAC AC *South-West France*   The whites, mainly from Mauzac with its sharp but attractive green apple bite, are rather stern but, from a decent grower or the revitalized co-ops, can be extremely refreshing. Some more serious reds are now being made, which require some aging. The star of Gaillac at the moment is the outstanding fizz, made by either the Champagne method or the *méthode rurale*, and ideally not quite dry and packed with fruit. Tecou co-op makes oak-aged Cuvée Passion and Cuvée Séduction, but the labels don't say in which order they should be consumed. Drink as young as possible. **Best producers:** Albert, Boissel-Rhodes, Bosc-Long, L Brun, Causses Marines★, Ch. Clément Termes, J Cros, Gayrel, Labarthe, Labastide-de-Lévis co-op, Larroze, Mas Pignou, Plageoles★, Técou co-op★.

GAJA *Barbaresco DOCG, Piedmont, Italy*   Angelo Gaja brought about the transformation of PIEDMONT from a sleepy, old-fashioned region that Italians swore made the finest red wine in the world yet the rest of the world disdained, to an area buzzing with excitement. He introduced international standards into what was a parochial, backward area and charged staggeringly high prices, thus giving other Piedmont growers the chance at last to get a decent return for their labours. Into this fiercely conservative area, full of fascinating grape varieties but proudest of the native Nebbiolo, he also introduced French grapes like Cabernet Sauvignon (Darmagi★★), Sauvignon Blanc (Alteni di Brassica★) and Chardonnay (Gaia & Rey★★). Gaja's traditional strength has been in single-vineyard BARBARESCO (his Sorì San Lorenzo★★★, Sorì Tildìn★★★ and Costa Russi★★★ are often cited as Barbaresco's best). His BAROLO Sperss★★★, introduced from the 1988 vintage, made with grapes from his estate at Serralunga d'Alba, is outstanding. Gaja has also invested in BRUNELLO DI MONTALCINO and BOLGHERI. **Best years:** (Barbaresco) (1998) (97) (96) 95 93 90 89 88 **85 82 79 78 71 61**.

GALICIA *Spain*   Up in Spain's hilly, verdant north-west, Galicia is renowned for its fine but expensive Albariño whites. There are 5 DOs: RIAS BAIXAS can make excellent, fragrant Albariño whites, with modern equipment and serious winemaking; Ribeiro has also invested heavily in new equipment, and better local white grapes are now being used, as is the case in the mountainous Valdeorras DO. Some young reds from the Mencía grape are also made there and in the new Ribeira Sacra DO. Monterrei DO, also new, is technically backward but shows some potential with its native white grape variety, Doña Blanca. Most wines are best consumed young.

E & J GALLO *Central Valley, California, USA*   With the release of its upscale, expensive Sonoma Estate Chardonnay and Cabernet Sauvignon in the mid-1990s, Gallo, the world's biggest winery known for cheap wines, is at last convincing doubters it can make fine wine. Both limited production wines came from Gallo's 800ha (2000 acres) of premium vineyards in key SONOMA COUNTY AVAs. These vineyards led to Gallo of Sonoma, a new label for varietals such as Zinfandel and Merlot from DRY CREEK VALLEY, Cabernet from ALEXANDER VALLEY and Chardonnay from several vineyards. New vineyards in RUSSIAN RIVER VALLEY have been planted to Pinot Noir. These Sonoma wines, both regular and Reserve-style, represent a giant step up in quality, but

Gallo continues to produce oceans of low-priced, ordinary wine. New labels such as Turning Leaf have been launched in the 90s, followed by Gossamer Bay (for Chardonnay), Anapamu (Central Coast Chardonnay), Zabaco (Sonoma County wines), Marcelina (Napa wines), and Indigo Hills (Mendocino wines).

GAMAY The only grape allowed for red BEAUJOLAIS. In general Gamay wine is rather rough-edged and quite high in raspy acidity, but in Beaujolais, so long as the yield is not too high, it can achieve a wonderful, juicy-fruit gluggability, almost unmatched in the world of wine. Elsewhere in France, it is successful in the Ardèche and the Loire and less so in the Mâconnais. In CALIFORNIA, the grape sold under the name of Gamay has now been identified as Valdiguie and in future the name Gamay won't be used. South Africa's very limited production has yielded mixed results.

GARD, VIN DE PAYS DU *Languedoc, France* Mainly reds and rosés from the western side of the RHONE delta. Most Gard red is light and spicy and increasingly attractive. Rosés can be fresh when young. With modern winemaking the whites can be good. **Best producers: Barud★, Christin, la Coste, Maillac, Mas des Bressades★★, St-Gilles co-op.**

GARGANEGA Italian white grape from the VENETO in north-east Italy; main component of SOAVE. Grown on hillsides, it can have class, but its reputation is tainted by excessive yields from the Veronese plain.

GARNACHA BLANCA See Grenache Blanc.
GARNACHA TINTA See Grenache Noir.
GARRAFEIRA Portuguese term for wine from an outstanding vintage, with ½% more alcohol than the minimum required, and 2 years' aging in vat or barrel, followed by 1 year in bottle for reds, and 6 months of each for whites. Also used by merchants for their best blended and aged wines. Use of the term is in decline as producers opt for the more readily recognized Reserva as an alternative on the label.
GATTINARA DOCG *Piedmont, Italy* One of the most capricious of Italy's top red wine areas, capable of both great things and dross. Situated in northern PIEDMONT and recently elevated to DOCG, the Nebbiolo wines should be softer and lighter than BAROLO but with a delicious, black plums, tar and roses flavour – if you're lucky, but few producers have shown much consistency yet. Vintages follow those for Barolo, but the wines should be drunk within 10 years. **Best producers: Antoniolo★, Le Colline★, Nervi★, Travaglini★. Best years: (1998) (97) (96) 95 90 88 85.**
DOMAINE GAUBY *Côtes du Roussillon-Villages AC, Roussillon, France* Gérard Gauby used to make wines as burly as himself. The fruit was there but it was hidden by very hard tannins. In the last 3 vintages the wines have been softer while still retaining concentration, and Gauby is now a hot property in ROUSSILLON. Highlights include powerful COTES DU ROUSSILLON-VILLAGES★★ and a VIN DE PAYS Viognier★★. **Best years: (1997) 96 95 94 93.**
GAVI DOCG *Piedmont, Italy* Fashionable, expensive PIEDMONT white wine. This Cortese-based, steely lemony white can age up to 5 years or more,

providing it starts life with sufficient fruit. La Scolca's Spumante Brut Soldati★ is an admirable sparkling wine. Best producers: BANFI, Nicola Bergaglio★, Broglia★, Chiarlo★, FONTANAFREDDA, La Giustiniana★, Pio Cesare, San Pietro★, Santa Seraffa★, La Scolca★, Tassarolo★, Villa Sparina★. Best years: **1998 97 96 95**.

CH. GAZIN★★ *Pomerol AC, Bordeaux, France* One of the largest châteaux in POMEROL, next to the legendary PETRUS. The wine, traditionally a succulent, sweet-textured Pomerol, wonderful to drink young but capable of long aging, has been a disappointing performer over the years, but has achieved top form since 1988, as Christian MOUEIX of Petrus has taken an interest in the estate. Now one of the most improved Pomerol properties. Best years: (1998) 96 95 94 93 **90 89 88**.

GEELONG *Victoria, Australia* Another wine region revived in the 1960s after its destruction by phylloxera in the 19th century, but expansion has been erratic so far. The climate and wine potential match up to those of the YARRA VALLEY. Pinot Noir is exciting, but Chardonnay, Riesling, Sauvignon Blanc and Shiraz are also impressive. Best producers: BANNOCKBURN★★, Idyll, Innisfail, Scotchmans Hill★.

GEISENHEIM *Rheingau, Germany* Village famous for its wine school, founded in 1872. It was here that the Müller-Thurgau grape, now one of Germany's most widely planted grapes, was bred in 1882. Geisenheim's most famous vineyard is the Rothenberg, the name indicating the vineyard's red soils, which produce strong, earthy wines. Best producers: Johannishof, J WEGELER ERBEN. Best years: (1998) 96 **94 93 92 90**.

JACQUES GERMAIN *Chorey-lès-Beaune, Côte de Beaune, Burgundy, France* The sleepy village of Chorey-lès-Beaune is the source of some of the COTE D'OR's best-value reds and, along with TOLLOT-BEAUT, François Germain is the AC's best-known producer. As well as an elegant red, called Ch. de Chorey★, he makes a series of richer BEAUNE Premiers Crus (Teurons★★ and Vignes Franches★★ are both superb) and reasonably priced PERNAND-VERGELESSES Blanc★. The reds are best drunk after 2–6 years in bottle. Best years: 1997 96 95 **93 92 90 89**.

GEVREY-CHAMBERTIN AC *Côte de Nuits, Burgundy, France* In boom times, the wines of Gevrey-Chambertin too often disappoint, as growers cash in on the fame of the AC. However, a new generation of growers has restored the reputation of Gevrey as a source of well-coloured, firmly structured, powerful, perfumed wines that become rich and gamy with age. Village wines should be kept for at least 5 years, Premiers Crus and the 8 Grands Crus for 10 years or more, especially Chambertin and Clos-de-Bèze. Look for the Premier Cru Clos St-Jacques, a wine worthy of promotion to Grand Cru. Best producers: Denis Bachelet★★, L Boillot★, A Burguet★★, CLAIR★★, P Damoy★, DROUHIN★, C Dugat★★, B Dugat-Py★★, DUJAC★, M Esmonin★★, FAIVELEY★★, JADOT★, LABOURE-ROI★, Philippe Leclerc★, Denis Mortet★★, Rossignol★★, J Roty★, ROUSSEAU★★, J & J-L Trapet★. Best years: 1997 96 95 93 **92 90 89 88 85**.

145

GEWÜRZTRAMINER A popular grape all over the world, but reaching its peak in France's ALSACE; also impressive in the Styria region of Austria. Also grown, with mixed results, in Australia, New Zealand, OREGON CALIFORNIA, the Czech Republic, Germany, South Africa and Italy's ALTO ADIGE (where it is called Traminer or Aromatico) and Romania. As Heida it is grown in Switzerland. *Gewürz* means spice, and the wine certainly can be spicy and exotically perfumed as well as being typically low in acidity but remarkably, in Alsace, while they exude sensuality, the wines generally show delightful balance. Styles vary enormously, from the fresh, light, florally perfumed wines produced in Italy to the rich, luscious, late-harvest ALSACE VENDANGE TARDIVE.

GEYSER PEAK *Alexander Valley AVA, California, USA* The arrival of Australian winemaker Daryl Groom raised Geyser Peak from the dead. The winery had been limping along for years, producing mediocre (at best) wines. Groom's wines tend to be accessible, fruity and fun to drink. Best is the Cabernet★ in a light, fruity style. The Reserve★, a blend of Cabernet Sauvignon, Merlot, Cabernet Franc and Malbec, is made for aging, and the Shiraz Reserve★★ has quite a cult following. (Note that Shiraz is usually known as Syrah in California.) Venezia is a label for vineyard-specific Chardonnay, Cabernet, Sangiovese, Syrah and special blends. Best years: (reds) 1997 **95 94 92 91**.

GHEMME DOCG *Piedmont, Italy* Red, Nebbiolo-based wine, from vines on the opposite bank of the Sesia to GATTINARA. The top examples are Cantalupo's Collis Breclemae and Collis Carellae. Best producers Antichi Vigneti di Cantalupo★★, Giuseppe Bianchi★, Le Colline. Best years: (1998) (97) 96 95 **93 90 89 88 85**.

BRUNO GIACOSA *Barbaresco DOCG, Piedmont, Italy* One of the great intuitive winemakers of the LANGHE hills south of Alba. He is an unashamed traditionalist, leaving his BARBARESCOS and BAROLOS in cask for up to 6 years. His Barbaresco Santo Stefano★★★ and Barolo Collina Rionda★★★ are superb, but also excellent are Dolcetto d'Alba★, Roero Arneis★, Moscato d'Asti★★ and the sparkling Extra Brut★★.

GIESEN *Canterbury, South Island, New Zealand* CANTERBURY's largest winery makes outstanding botrytized Riesling★★★, as well as fine dry Riesling★, complex, oaky Chardonnay★, and an attractive Sauvignon Blanc★. Best years: (1998) **97 96 95 94 91**.

GIGONDAS AC *Rhône Valley, France* Gigondas gained its own AC in 1971. The wines, mostly red with a little rosé and made mainly from the Grenache grape, have fistfuls of chunky personality. Most drink well with 5 years' age, some a little more. Best producers: D Brusset★★, Cayron★★, F Chastan, Clos des Cazaux★, R Combe★, Cros de la Mure★, DELAS★, M Faraud, Font-Sanc★, les Goubert★, Gour de Chaule★, Grapillon d'Or★, GUIGAL★, JABOULET★, Longue-Toque★, Christian Meffre Grand Montmirail, les Pallières★, Piaugier★, Raspail-Ay★, Ch. de St-Cosme★, St-Gayan★, Santa-Duc★, Tardieu-Laurent★, Trignon★. Best years: (1998) 97 95 94 **93 90 89 88 86 85**.

CH. GILETTE★★ *Sauternes AC, Bordeaux, France* These astonishing wines are stored in concrete vats as opposed to the more normal wooden barrels. This virtually precludes any oxygen contact, and it is oxygen that ages a wine. Consequently, when released at up to 30 years old, they are bursting with life and lusciousness. Best years: **1978 76 75 70 67 61 59 55**.

GIPPSLAND *Victoria, Australia* Diverse wineries along the southern Victoria coast, all tiny but with massive potential, are led by Nicholson River with its brooding Burgundy-style Chardonnay★★. Pinot Noir from Nicholson River★ is very good and McAlister★, a BORDEAUX blend, has also produced some tasty flavours. Bass Phillip Reserve★★★ and Premium★★★ Pinots are among the very best in Australia, with a cult following – in years like 1995 and 97 they approached the silky charm of the COTE DE NUITS.

GISBORNE *North Island, New Zealand* Gisborne, with its hot, humid climate and fertile soils, has shown that it is capable of producing quality as well as quantity. Local growers have christened their region 'The Chardonnay Capital of New Zealand' and Gewürztraminer and Chenin Blanc are also a success. Good reds, however, are hard to find. Best producers: CORBANS, MILLTON★★, MONTANA, Revington.

CH. GISCOURS★ *Margaux AC, 3ème Cru Classé, Haut-Médoc, Bordeaux, France* This is a large MARGAUX property with enormous potential that is not always realized. Giscours' magic is that it can produce wines of delectable scent yet also with a pretty solid structure. After a dull patch, recent vintages are definitely picking up. Best years: (1998) 96 90 **86 83 82 81 80 79**.

GIVRY AC *Côte Chalonnaise, Burgundy, France* An important COTE CHALONNAISE village. The reds have an intensity of fruit and ability to age that are unusual in the region. In recent years the whites have improved considerably, and there are now some attractive fairly full, nutty examples. Best producers: Chofflet-Valdenaire, Joblot, F Lumpp, J-P Ragot, Sarrazin, Thénard★. Best years: (reds) 1997 96 95 **93 90**; (whites) 1997 96 **95 93 92 90**.

GLEN CARLOU *Paarl WO, South Africa* Extensive new Chardonnay vineyards reveal the bullish mood in this successful partnership between the Finlaysons and Donald Hess, international businessman and owner of CALIFORNIA winery THE HESS COLLECTION. David Finlayson is proving himself the equal of his father Walter; his elegant standard Chardonnay★ and richer toasty Reserve★ version are widely acclaimed, as are the Pinot Noir★, full of spicy, silky fruit, and Grande Classique★, a fine BORDEAUX blend with excellent aging potential. Best years: (Chardonnay) **1998 97 96 95 94**.

CH. GLORIA★ *St-Julien AC, Cru Bourgeois, Haut-Médoc, Bordeaux, France* A fascinating property, created by one of Bordeaux's grand old men, the late Henri Martin, out of tiny plots of Classed Growth land scattered all round ST-JULIEN. His obsession raised Gloria's wine during the 1960s and 70s to both Classed Growth quality and price. Generally very soft and sweet-centred, the wine nonetheless ages well. But Martin desperately wanted to own a Classed Growth and finally succeeded when he bought ST-PIERRE in 1982. Second wine: Peymartin. Best years: (1998) 97 96 95 94 **93 90 89 88 86 85 83 82 81**.

GOLAN HEIGHTS WINERY *Golan Heights, Israel* Israel's leading quality wine producer. Cool summers, well-drained, high-altitude vineyards and winemaking that combines the latest Californian techniques with kosher strictures have all resulted in good Sauvignon Blanc★ and Cabernet Sauvignon★, excellent, oaky Chardonnay★★ and, recently, good bottle-fermented fizz★. Yarden is the label used for top-of-the-range wines, while Golan and Gamla are mid-range labels.

GOLDENMUSKATELLER The Moscato Giallo grape is known as Golden-muskateller in Italy's ALTO ADIGE. Here and elsewhere in Italy's north-east it is made in both highly scented and dry, and slightly sweet versions. Best producers: LAGEDER★, Conti Martini, Tiefenbrunner★.

GOLDWATER ESTATE *Waiheke Island, Auckland, New Zealand* The founding vineyard established by Kim and Jeanette Goldwater on WAIHEKE ISLAND, New Zealand's premium and very fashionable red wine district. A red wine specialist, therefore, producing intense, long-lived Cabernet-Merlot★★ and Merlot★★, made in an elegant, cedary style with considerable depth and structure. Also makes an intense and luscious MARLBOROUGH Sauvignon Blanc★★ and Chardonnay★ from grapes grown under contract. Best years: (Waiheke reds) (1998) 96 **94** 93.

GONZÁLEZ BYASS *Jerez y Manzanilla DO, Andalucía, Spain* Tio Pepe★★, the high-quality fino brand of this huge top sherry firm, is the world's biggest-selling sherry. The top range of old sherries is superb: intense, dry Amontillado del Duque★★★, and 2 rich, complex olorosos, sweet Matusalem★★★ and medium Apostoles★★. One step down is the Alfonso Dry Oloroso★. The firm has pioneered the rediscovery of single-vintage (non-solera) dry olorosos★★★, reviving what was a common practice in Jerez until the late 19th century.

DEL DUQUE
Amontillado Muy Viejo
Jerez · Xérès · Sherry
GONZALEZ BYASS

GOULBURN VALLEY *Victoria, Australia* The Goulburn river is a serene, beautiful thread of contentment running through VICTORIA's parched grazing lands. Surprisingly few vineyards have been established here but these do produce some very individual wines. The region's speciality is Marsanne white. Best producers: CHATEAU TAHBILK★, MITCHELTON★★, Osicka, Plunkett, David Traeger.

GRAACH *Mosel, Germany* Important Middle MOSEL wine village with 4 vineyard sites, the most famous being Domprobst (also the best) and Himmelreich. A third, the Josephshöfer, is wholly owned by the von KESSELSTATT estate in Trier. The wines have an attractive fullness to balance their steely acidity. Best producers: von KESSELSTATT★★, Dr LOOSEN★★, J J PRUM★★, W Schaefer★★, SELBACH-OSTER★★. Best years: (1998) 97 96 95 **94** 93 90.

GRACIANO A rare but excellent Spanish grape, traditional in RIOJA and NAVARRA, but low-yielding. It makes dense, highly structured, fragrant reds, and its high acidity adds life when blended with the good-quality, but low-acid Tempranillo.

GRAHAM *Port DOC, Douro, Portugal* Another port shipper in the Symington empire, making rich, florally scented Vintage Port★★★

sweeter than DOW's and WARRE's, 2 other major Symington brands, but with enough backbone to age. When a vintage is not declared, it makes a fine wine called Malvedos★. Best years: (vintage) 1994 **91** 85 83 **80 77 75 70 66 63 60**; (Malvedos) 1995 92 **90 87 86 84**.

ALAIN GRAILLOT *Crozes-Hermitage AC, Rhône Valley, France* This excellent estate, established in 1985, stands out as a producer of powerfully concentrated rich, fruity reds. The top wine is called la Guiraude★★, but the basic Crozes★★ is wonderful too, as is the Hermitage★★. Keep for 5 years, though the best will become even finer with longer aging. Best years: (1998) 97 96 **95 94** 91 90 89 88.

GRAMPIANS *Victoria, Australia* This recently renamed area centres on Great Western, a distinguished old viticultural area in central-western Victoria, historically known for its sparkling wine. Grampians has not expanded in the 1990s like the other southern Victoria regions but still produces some of Australia's greatest Shiraz – as table wine, sparkling red and even port-style. Best producers: BEST'S★★, Garden Gully, Montara★★, MOUNT LANGI GHIRAN★★★, SEPPELT★★.

GRAN RESERVA Top category of Spanish wines from a top vintage, with at least 5 years' aging (2 of them in cask) for reds and 4 for whites.

GRAND CRU French for 'great growth', or a vineyard. These are supposedly the best sites in ALSACE, BURGUNDY, CHAMPAGNE and parts of BORDEAUX and should produce the most exciting wines. However, the term applies only to the vineyard site. What the grower decides to do, and what the winemaker then does with the grapes, is another matter.

GRANDES MARQUES Great brands – this was once CHAMPAGNE's self-appointed élite. After several years of attempted reform, the Syndicat des Grandes Marques finally admitted defeat and disbanded in 1997. Quality differences between the various Champagne houses were just too great to resolve.

CH. DU GRAND MOULAS *Côtes du Rhône, Rhône Valley, France* Marc Ryckwaert makes first-rate COTES DU RHONE★ from Grenache and a lick of Syrah that is delicious young but will age for 2–4 years. He also produces very rich COTES DU RHONE-VILLAGES★ (red and white) and a rich, Syrah-based Grande Reserve red wine called Cuvée de l'Écu★. Best years: (1998) 97 **95 94 93** 91 90 89 88.

CH. GRAND-PUY-DUCASSE★ *Pauillac AC, 5ème Cru Classé, Haut-Médoc, Bordeaux, France* This used to be one of the duller PAUILLAC Classed Growths, but the wines have improved enormously since the mid-80s. Recent vintages have been consistently pleasurable, with lots of supple, blackcurrant fruit, which makes them approachable after 5 years, but allows the wines to improve for considerably longer. Second wine: Artigues-Arnaud. Best years: (1998) 96 95 94 **92 90 89 88 86 85**.

CH. GRAND-PUY-LACOSTE★★ *Pauillac AC, 5ème Cru Classé, Haut-Médoc, Bordeaux, France* This wine is classic PAUILLAC, with lots of blackcurrant and cigar-box perfume. As the wine develops, the flavours mingle with the sweetness of new oak into one of Pauillac's most memorable taste sensations. Second wine: Lacoste-Borie. Best years: (1998) 97 96 95 94 93 90 89 88 **86 85 83 82 81 79 78**.

GRAND TINEL *Châteauneuf-du-Pape AC, Rhône Valley, France* One of the Rhône's most undervalued producers, Elie Jeune makes big, Grenache-dominated reds★★ with a piercing aroma of cassis that age superbly. The vines are very old and it shows in the concentration of the wine. Best years: (1997) 96 95 94 93 **91 90 89 88 86 85 83 81 79 78**.

GRANDS-ÉCHÉZEAUX AC See Échézeaux AC.

GRANGEHUST *Stellenbosch WO, South Africa* Production is growing at this boutique winery – it will top out at 9000 cases – but quality remains paramount. Using bought-in grapes, owner/winemaker Jeremy Walker hand crafts only 2 wines: a modern Pinotage★★, savoury and ripe, and a Cabernet-Merlot★★ with powerful clarety appeal. Best years: **1995 94 93 92**.

YVES GRASSA *Vin de Pays des Côtes de Gascogne, South-West France* The most innovative producer of COTES DE GASCOGNE, who transformed Gascony's thin raw whites into some of the snappiest, fruitiest, almost-dry wines in France. Grassa has also been experimenting with oak-aged★ and late-harvest★ styles.

ALFRED GRATIEN *Champagne AC, Champagne, France* This small company makes some of my favourite CHAMPAGNE. Unusually in the modern world, Gratien declares that its image is the quality of the wine and nothing else. Its wines are made in wooden casks, which is very rare nowadays. The non-vintage★★ blend is usually 4 years old when sold, rather than the normal 3 years. The vintage★★★ wine is deliciously ripe and toasty when released but can age for another 10 years. Best years: **1990 89 88 87 85 83 82**.

GRATIEN & MEYER *Loire Valley, France* Owner of the quality-minded CHAMPAGNE house Alfred GRATIEN, Gratien & Meyer is an important Loire producer too. The company's reputation rests on its quality, Champagne-method SAUMUR MOUSSEUX, particularly its attractively rich, biscuity Cuvée Flamme★ and the Cuvée Flamme Rosé. Also a producer of still SAUMUR white wine and the red SAUMUR-CHAMPIGNY, it produces a little CREMANT DE LOIRE★ – and the sparkling red Cuvée Cardinal★ is unusual and fun.

GRAVES AC *Bordeaux, France* The Graves region covers the area south of Bordeaux to Langon, but the generally superior villages in the northern half broke away in 1987 to form the PESSAC-LEOGNAN AC. However, all is not lost, as a new wave of winemaking is sweeping through the southern Graves. Nowadays, there are plenty of clean, bone-dry white wines, with lots of snappy freshness, as well as more complex soft, nutty barrel-aged white wines, and some juicy, quick-drinking red wines. Best producers: Archambeau, Ardennes, le Bonnat, Brondelle★, Chantegrive★, Clos Floridène★, Dom. la Grave★, l'Hospital, Landiras, Magence, Rahoul, Respide-Médeville, Seuil, Vieux-Ch.-Gaubert, Villa Bel Air. Best years: (reds) (1998) 96 95 **94 90 89 88 86 85 83 82**; (whites) (1998) 96 **95 94 90 89 88 87**.

GRAVES SUPÉRIEURES AC *Bordeaux, France* White Graves, dry, medium or sweet, with a minimum alcohol level of 12% as opposed to 11% for Graves. The AC has never really caught on because of the confusion between dry and sweet wines, but the sweet wines can, in good years, make decent substitutes for the more expensive SAUTERNES. Best producers: (sweet) Clos St-Georges, Lehoul. Best years: (sweet) 1997 96 **95 90 89 88 86**.

GRAVINA DOC *Puglia, Italy* This small DOC produces a rarity in PUGLIA: a dry white wine of real character. A blend of the native grape varieties Greco and Malvasia, grown in the hills of central Puglia, the wine has an intense peachy perfume combined with a hint of apricot. Botromagno, the only producer, has salvaged the region's potential.

GRAVNER *Friuli-Venezia Giulia, Italy* Josko Gravner, Friuli's most zealous winemaker, sets styles with wood-aged wines of uncommon stature, though some remain outside the COLLIO DOC. Along with prized and high-priced Chardonnay★★, Sauvignon★★ and Ribolla Gialla★, he combines 6 white varieties in Breg★★. Reds are Rosso Gravner★ (predominantly Merlot) and Rujno★★ (Merlot-Cabernet Sauvignon).

GRECHETTO An attractive Italian white grape variety centred on UMBRIA, making tasty, anise-tinged dry whites. It also contributes to VIN SANTO in Tuscany. Best producers: ADANTI, Antonelli, Caprai, Rocca di Fabbri.

GREEN POINT VINEYARDS *Yarra Valley, Victoria, Australia* MOET & CHANDON's Aussie offshoot makes leading Pinot Noir-Chardonnay Champagne-method fizz★★ and occasional BLANC DE BLANCS and BLANC DE NOIRS. The latest adventure is still wines from Chardonnay★★ and Pinot Noir, in a fairly oaky style. The DOMAINE CHANDON label is used in the Australian market and is the name of the winery.

GRENACHE BLANC A common white grape in the south of France, but without many admirers. Except me, that is, because I love the pear-scented wine flecked with anise that a good producer can achieve. Best at 6–12 months old. Also grown as Garnacha Blanca in Spain.

GRENACHE NOIR Among the world's most widely planted red grapes – the bulk of it in Spain, where it is called Garnacha Tinta. It is a hot-climate grape and in France it reaches its peak in the southern RHONE, especially in CHATEAUNEUF-DU-PAPE, where it combines great alcoholic strength with rich raspberry fruit and a perfume hot from the herb-strewn hills. It is generally given more tannin and acid by blending with Syrah, Cinsaut or other southern French grapes. It can make wonderful rosé in TAVEL, LIRAC and COTES DE PROVENCE, as well as in NAVARRA in Spain. It forms the backbone of the impressive, newly rediscovered reds of PRIORAT and in RIOJA it adds weight to the Tempranillo. It is also the basis for the VINS DOUX NATURELS of BANYULS and MAURY. Also widely grown in CALIFORNIA and Australia. It has only recently been recorded much respect as imaginative winemakers realized there was a great resource of century-old vines capable of making wild and massively enjoyable reds that no one was taking any notice of. See also Cannonau.

GRGICH HILLS CELLAR *Napa Valley AVA, California, USA* Mike Grgich was winemaker at CHATEAU MONTELENA when its Chardonnay shocked the Paris judges by finishing ahead of French versions in the famous 1976 tasting. At his own winery he makes ripe, tannic Cabernet and a huge, old-style Zinfandel★, but his reputation has been made by big, ripe, oaky Chardonnay★★ that proves to be one of NAPA's best-selling, high-priced wines. Best years: (Chardonnay) (1997) 96 **95 94 92 91 90 88 87**.

GRIGNOLINO An Italian red grape native to PIEDMONT that can produce light-coloured but intensely flavoured wines. It is DOC in the Monferrato Casalese and Asti hills, and is also made in Alba. HEITZ makes a rare version in CALIFORNIA. Best producers: Braida, Bricco Mondalino★, Aldo CONTERNO, Pavese, Scarpa, La Tenaglia, Viarengo.

GRIOTTE-CHAMBERTIN AC See Chambertin AC.

JEAN GRIVOT *Vosne-Romanée, Côte de Nuits, Burgundy, France* Winemaker Étienne Grivot took time to settle down but has now reconciled both his father's traditional styles and former consultant Accad's experimentation into a high-quality interpretation of his own. He has made brilliant wines since 1995, especially RICHEBOURG★★ and NUITS-ST-GEORGES les Boudots★★. Expensive. Best years: 1997 96 95 93 **90**.

GROS PLANT DU PAYS NANTAIS VDQS *Loire Valley, France* From the marshy salt-flats around Nantes, Gros Plant can be searing stuff, but this acidic wine is well suited to the seafood guzzled in the region. Look out for a *sur lie* bottling. Best producers: Chiron, J Guindon, J Hallereau, Herbauges, Ch. de la Preuille, Sauvion. Best years: (1998) **97** 96.

GROSSET *Clare Valley, South Australia* Jeffrey Grosset is a stubborn perfectionist, crafting tiny quantities of truly hand-made wines in his Auburn winery. A Riesling specialist, he bottles Watervale★★ separately from Polish Hill★★. Both are supremely good and age well, while Cabernet-blend Gaia★★ is smooth and seamless. Piccadilly (ADELAIDE HILLS) Chardonnay★★★, Pinot Noir★★★ and Semillon-Sauvignon★ are the new buzz. Best years: (Riesling) 1998 97 **96 95 94 92 90 87 86**.

GROSSLAGE German term for a grouping of vineyards. Some are not too big, and have the advantage of allowing small amounts of higher QmP wines to be made from the grapes from several vineyards. But sometimes the use of vast Grosslage names (for example, Niersteiner Gutes Domtal) only deceives consumers into believing that they are buying something special. Also an Austrian term, where a single Grosslage refers to an even larger vineyard area than in Germany.

GROVE MILL *Marlborough, New Zealand* Mid-sized producer with a strong quality focus. Consistently top Sauvignon Blanc★★ is a feature of their range, together with a ripe, rich and remarkably smooth Chardonnay★. Best years: (1998) 97 **96 94**.

CH. GRUAUD-LAROSE★★★ *St-Julien AC, 2ème Cru Classé, Haut-Médoc, Bordeaux, France* One of the largest ST-JULIEN estates, now owned by the same family as CHASSE-SPLEEN and HAUT-BAGES-LIBÉRAL. Until the 1970s these wines were classic, cedary St-Juliens. Since the early 80s, the wines have been darker, richer and coated with new oak, yet have also shown an unnerving animal quality. They're certainly impressive, but it is hard to say whether the animal or the cedar will prevail after 20 years or so of aging in bottle. Second wine: Sarget de Gruaud-Larose. Best years: (1998) 97 96 95 94 91 90 89 **88 86 85 84 83 82 81**.

GRÜNER VELTLINER Grown in every Austrian wine region with the exception of Styria. The grape is at its best, however, in KAMPTAL, KREMSTAL, and the WACHAU, where the soil and cool climate bring out all the lentilly, white-peppery aromas in the fruit. Can also be good in the Czech Republic.

GUELBENZU *Navarra DO, Spain* Family-owned bodega making good Guelbenzu Crianza★, from Tempranillo, Cabernet and Merlot, and rich concentrated Evo★★, made mostly from Cabernet Sauvignon. In 1995 it introduced the unoaked Jardin cuvée (100% Garnacha) with considerable success. Best years: **1996 95 94 93 92 90**.

GUIGAL *Côte-Rôtie AC, Rhône Valley, France* Marcel Guigal is among the most famous names in the Rhône, producing wines from his company's own vineyards in COTE-ROTIE under the Château d'Ampuis label as well as from purchased grapes. Guigal's top wines – la Mouline★★★, la Turque★★★ and la Landonne★★★ – are expensive but superb, if you don't mind an oaky sweetness masking the wines' fruit for the first few years of its life. CONDRIEU★★ is also very fine, if oaky, HERMITAGE★★ is also good, while the cheaper COTES DU RHONE★ is a delicious wine outperforming its humble AC with ease. His GIGONDAS★ is good, too. All reds can be cellared, the famous trio of Côte-Rôties for perhaps 20 years or more. Best years: (top reds) 1997 95 94 **91 90 89 88 85 83 82**.

CH. GUIRAUD★★ *Sauternes AC, 1er Cru Classé, Bordeaux, France* A property that was hauled up from near extinction by the Canadian Narby family, convinced that Guiraud could be one of SAUTERNES' greatest wines. Selecting only the best grapes and using 50% new oak each year, they have returned Guiraud to the top-quality fold. Keep best vintages for 10 years or more. Second wine (dry): G de Guiraud. Best years: (1998) 97 96 95 **90 89 88 86 83 82 81**.

GUNDERLOCH *Nackenheim, Rheinhessen, Germany* One of the nation's new stars, producing rich, dramatic wines with explosive fruit aromas. Has been making some of the best Rieslings★★ anywhere on the Rhine since 1989, and since 1992 dessert wines have been ★★★. Best years: (1998) 97 **95 94 93 92 90 89**.

GUNDLACH-BUNDSCHU *Sonoma Valley AVA, California, USA* This family-owned winery was founded in 1858. Since then it has had its ups and downs but for the last couple of decades it has been all up. The Cabernet Sauvignon★★ (Rhine Farm Vineyard) is outstanding, with lean herbal tones opening up to big, juicy, fruity centres. The Chardonnay is rich but not over the top and a Riesling is delightfully different. The Zinfandel★ and Cabernet merit at least short-term cellaring. Best years: (reds) 1997 95 **94 92 91 87 86 85**.

GYÖNGYÖS ESTATE *Gyöngyös, Hungary* The wines from this Hungarian estate appeared on the shelves out of the blue and were brought to prominence by British winemaker Hugh Ryman who left his base in France to produce Sauvignon Blanc and Chardonnay in one of the most forward-looking of the old eastern bloc countries. The winery was bought in 1995 by the German company St-Ursula and Ryman is no longer involved. Drink current vintage.

FRITZ HAAG *Brauneberg, Mosel, Germany* Top MOSEL grower with vineyards in the Brauneberger Juffer and Brauneberger Juffer Sonnenuhr. Extremely pure, elegant Rieslings always at least ★ quality, with Auslese reaching ★★ or ★★★. Best years: (1998) 97 **96 95 94 93 92 91 90 88 85 83 79 76 75 71**.

HALBTROCKEN German for medium dry. In Germany and Austria medium-dry wine has 9–18g per litre of residual sugar, though sparkling wine is allowed up to 50g per litre. But the high acid levels in German wines can make them seem rather dry and lean.

HALLAU *Schaffhausen, Switzerland* Important wine commune situated in German-speaking eastern Switzerland, best known for Müller-Thurgau, very light Blauburgunder (Pinot Noir), especially from Max Baumann, and also Sekt from Hans Schlatter.

HAMILTON RUSSELL VINEYARDS *Walker Bay, Overberg WO, South Africa*

Proprietor Anthony Hamilton-Russell and winemaker Kevin Grant are a determined duo. Pinot Noir and Chardonnay are their holy grails, individuality their philosophy. New clones are providing a fruitier profile to the regular Pinot Noir★; after a slight hiccup, the single-vineyard Ashbourne should regain ★★ status with 1997. Ashbourne and regular Chardonnays★★ show typical house-style classic restraint. Southern Right is a new label focusing on Pinotage, Chenin Blanc and Sauvignon Blanc from bought-in grapes. Best years: (Pinot Noir) **1997 96 95**; (Chardonnay) **1997 96 95 94.**

HANDLEY CELLARS *Mendocino County, California, USA* Outstanding producer of hand-crafted sparkling wines, including one of California's best Brut Rosés★★ and a delicious, mouthwatering BLANC DE BLANCS★★. Two bottlings of Chardonnay, one from the DRY CREEK VALLEY★ and an Anderson Valley, are worth seeking out. Best years: 1997 **95 94 92**.

HANGING ROCK *Macedon Ranges, Victoria, Australia* Highly individual gutsy sparkling wine, Macedon non-vintage★★★ is the stand-out at John and Anne (née Tyrrell) Ellis' ultra-cool-climate vineyard high in the Macedon Ranges. Tangy, high-acid estate-grown Sauvignon Blanc★★ is mouthwatering stuff, while Heathcote Shiraz★, from a warmer neighbouring region, is the best red.

HARDY *McLaren Vale, South Australia* Fine quality across the board comes from the flagship label of the BRL Hardy group. Varietals under the Siegersdorf and Nottage Hill labels are tasty and affordable everyday wines, among Australia's most reliably good gluggers. Top of the tree are the commemorative Eileen Hardy Shiraz★★★ and Thomas Hardy Cabernet★★, both dense reds for hedonists. Eileen Hardy Chardonnay★★★ is rich, heady, oak-perfumed and complex. New releases include the attractively packaged Tintara Shiraz★★ and Grenache★★, plus 'ecologically aware' Banrock Station, the inexpensive Insignia wines and great value sparkling wine under the Omni label. Premium sparklings received a big boost with Ed Carr's arrival from Southcorp. Best years: (Eileen Hardy Shiraz) 1995 **93 91 90 88 87 81 79 70**. See also Reynell.

HARTENBERG ESTATE *Stellenbosch WO, South Africa* An old winery making a strong return to the Cape super-league under a young and enthusiastic team. The warmer Bottelary Hills area favours reds especially Shiraz★, Merlot★ and Cabernet★. More unusual are Zinfandel and the Cape's sole Pontac; both reflect winemaker Carl Schultz' high standards. Whites are well served by a firm, flavoursome

Chardonnay and, unusually for these north-facing slopes, a vigorous, limy Riesling. Best years: (reds) **1996 95 94**.

HARVEYS *Jerez y Manzanilla DO, Andalucía, Spain* Harveys is the biggest of the sherry firms, thanks to Bristol Cream. The standard range is unexciting, but the up-market 1796 wines are much better.

HATTENHEIM *Rheingau, Germany* Fine Rheingau village with 13 vineyard sites, including a share of the famous Marcobrunn vineyard. Best producers: RESS, SCHLOSS REINHARTSHAUSEN★★, Schloss Schönborn★. Best years: (1998) 96 **95 94 93 92 90**.

CH. HAUT-BAGES-LIBÉRAL★ *Pauillac AC, 5ème Cru Classé, Haut-Médoc, Bordeaux, France* This obscure property is fast becoming one of my favourite PAUILLACs: loads of unbridled delicious fruit, positively hedonistic style – and I can afford it! The wines will age well but are ready to drink at 5 years. Best years: (1998) 97 96 95 94 **93 90** 89 86 85 83 82.

CH. HAUT-BAILLY★★ *Pessac-Léognan AC, Cru Classé de Graves, Bordeaux, France* The softest and most charming wines among the GRAVES Classed Growths, which showed welcome improvement in the late 1980s. Drinkable very early, but can age. Second wine: la Parde-de-Haut-Bailly. Best years: (1998) 97 96 95 **94 93 90 89** 88 86 85 83 82 81.

CH. HAUT-BATAILLEY★ *Pauillac AC, 5ème Cru Classé, Haut-Médoc, Bordeaux, France* Despite being owned by the Borie family of DUCRU-BEAUCAILLOU, this small estate has made too many wines that are light and pleasant, attractively spicy, but lacking any real class and concentration. Recent vintages have improved and it is at last becoming more substantial. Best years: (1998) 97 96 95 **90 89 85 83 82**.

CH. HAUT-BRION *Pessac-Léognan AC, 1er Cru Classé, Graves, Bordeaux, France* The only Bordeaux property outside the MEDOC and SAUTERNES to be included in the great 1855 Classification, when it was accorded First Growth status. The excellent gravel-based vineyard is now part of Bordeaux's suburbs and the red wine★★★ frequently, but by no means always, deserves its exalted status. There is also a small amount of white★★★. At its best it is fabulous wine, magically rich yet marvellously dry, blossoming out over 5–10 years. Second wine: (red) Bahans-Haut-Brion. Best years: (reds) (1998) 97 96 95 94 93 90 89 88 86 **85 83 81 78**; (whites) (1998) 97 96 95 **94 92 90 89** 88 87 85 83 82 81.

CH. HAUT-MARBUZET★★ *St-Estèphe AC, Cru Bourgeois, Haut-Médoc, Bordeaux, France* Impressive ST-ESTEPHE wine with great, rich, mouthfilling blasts of flavour and lots of new oak. Best years: (1998) 97 96 95 94 **93 90** 89 88 86 85 83 82 81 78.

HAUT-MÉDOC AC *Bordeaux, France* Appellation for the southern half of the Médoc peninsula. All the finest gravelly soil is here, and Haut-Médoc AC covers all the decent vineyard land not included in the 6 separate village ACs (MARGAUX, MOULIS, LISTRAC, ST-JULIEN, PAUILLAC and ST-ESTEPHE). The wines tend to vary somewhat in quality and style. Best producers: Beaumont, Belgrave★, Camensac, CANTEMERLE★, Charmail, CISSAC★, Citran★, Coufran★, Hanteillan, la LAGUNE★★, LANESSAN★, Malescasse, Maucamps, Ramage-la-Batisse, SOCIANDO-MALLET★★, la Tour-Carnet, la Tour-du-Haut-Moulin, Villegeorge. Best years: (1998) 96 95 **94 90 89 88 86 85**.

HAUT-MONTRAVEL AC *South-West France* Pleasant, sweet white wines from hillside vineyards at the western limit of the BERGERAC region. The wines are sweeter than straight MONTRAVEL and CÔTES DE MONTRAVEL. Best producers: le Bondieu, Gourgueil, Puy-Servain.

HAUT-POITOU VDQS *Loire Valley, France* Wines from south of the Loire Valley on the way to Poitiers. Crisp, zingy Sauvignons and Chardonnays, slightly green Cabernet and Gamay reds and fresh rosés also good sparkling Diane de Poitiers. In general drink young. The Haut-Poitou co-op, now run by Georges DUBOEUF, dominates production.

HAUTE VALLÉE DE L'AUDE, VIN DE PAYS DE L' *Languedoc-Roussillon, France* The best still wines from the LIMOUX sparkling wine district. Most of the wine is white, with an emphasis on Chardonnay. Barrel-fermented white wines are entitled to the new Limoux AC. Best producers: l'Aigle★, Astruc, Buoro, SIEUR D'ARQUES co-op, Vialade.

HAUTES-CÔTES DE BEAUNE AC See Bourgogne-Hautes-Côtes de Beaune AC.
HAUTES-CÔTES DE NUITS AC See Bourgogne-Hautes-Côtes de Nuits AC.

HAWKES BAY *North Island, New Zealand* One of New Zealand's oldest and most prestigious wine regions. The high number of sunshine hours, moderately predictable weather during ripening and a complex array of soil patterns make it ideal for a wide range of winemaking styles. Chardonnay, Cabernet Sauvignon and Merlot are the area's greatest strengths, although Pinot Gris and Syrah could be rising stars. Sauvignon Blanc is generally a bit flat. Best producers: Clearview, Esk Valley★, MATUA VALLEY★★, MISSION, MONTANA (The MacDonald Winery★★), MORTON ESTATE★★, NGATARAWA★, C J Pask, Sacred Hill, TE MATA★★★, Trinity Hill★★, Vidal★, VILLA MARIA★★.

HEEMSKERK *Northern Tasmania, Australia* Major changes here, as the Tasmanian group which included Heemskerk, Rochecombe and Jansz was sold to PIPERS BROOK lock, stock and French oak barrel, and the Jansz bubbly brand (and vineyard) was quickly shuffled off to YALUMBA. The Heemskerk brand, with superb Chardonnay★★, up-and-down Pinot and Riesling, will continue.

DR HEGER *Ihringen, Baden, Germany* Joachim Heger specializes in powerful, dry Grauburgunder, Weissburgunder and red Spätburgunder★ with Riesling a sideline. The Grauburgunder wines from the Winklerberg★★ are serious stuff. Best years: (1998) 97 **96 94** 93 90 89 88.

HEIDA Swiss name for the grape thought to be either the Savagnin of the French Jura or the Gewürztraminer. In the Swiss VALAIS it is known as the Païen. Above the town of Visp at Visperterminen, Heida is grown at heights of around 1000m (3280ft), the highest-altitude vineyards in Europe, and the wine is correspondingly pungent and mountain mad. Best producers: Chanton, St Jodern.

CHARLES HEIDSIECK *Champagne AC, Champagne, France* Charles Heidsieck, under Rémy Martin ownership, has transformed itself in the last decade and is now the most consistently fine of all the major houses. The non-vintage★★ is regularly of vintage quality especially those cuvées★★ marked by a bottling date. In a time when many vintage wines have been degraded by millennium fever, Charles Heidsieck Vintage★★★ stands out. Best years: **1990** 89 85.

HEITZ CELLARS *Napa Valley AVA, California, USA*   The star attraction here is the Martha's Vineyard Cabernet Sauvignon★★. Heitz recently added a Trailside Vineyard Cabernet and continues offering a Bella Oaks Vineyard Cabernet Sauvignon★, which has its fans, and a straight Cabernet★ that takes time to understand but can be good. After 1992, phylloxera forced the replanting of Martha's Vineyard and bottling only resumed in 1996. Many in CALIFORNIA believe that early bottlings of Martha's Vineyard are among the best wines ever produced in the state. Grignolino Rosé is an attractive picnic wine. Best years: (Martha's Vineyard) 1992 91 **86 85 75**; (Bella Oaks) (1995) 93 **91 87 86**.

HENSCHKE *Eden Valley, South Australia*   Fifth-generation winemaker Stephen Henschke and his viticulturist wife Prue make some of Australia's grandest reds from old vines in Eden Valley. Hill of Grace★★★, a stunning wine with dark exotic flavours, comes from a single, century-old plot of Shiraz. Mount Edelstone Shiraz★★★ and Cyril Henschke Cabernet★★ are also brilliant wines. The whites★★ are full and intensely flavoured too, and a conscious move to lower alcohols is a refreshing and welcome change. Best years: (reds) 1996 **94 92 91 90 88 86 84 82 80 78 72**.

HÉRAULT, VIN DE PAYS DE L' *Languedoc, France*   A huge VIN DE PAYS, covering the entire Hérault *département*. Red wines predominate, based on Carignan, Grenache and Cinsaut, and most of the wine is sold in bulk. But things are changing. There are lots of hilly vineyards with great potential, and MAS DE DAUMAS GASSAC is merely the first of many exciting reds from the region. The whites are improving too. Best producers: Bosc, Capion★, la Fadéze★, les Granges des Pères★★, Jany, Limbardie★, MAS DE DAUMAS GASSAC★★, Moulines.

HERMITAGE AC *Rhône Valley, France*   Great Hermitage, from steep vineyards above the town of Tain l'Hermitage in the northern RHÔNE, is revered throughout the world as a rare, rich red wine – expensive, memorable and classic. Not all Hermitage achieves such an exciting blend of flavours because the vineyard area is not large and some merchants will take any grapes just to list Hermitage. But the best growers, with mature red Syrah vines, can create superbly original wine, needing 5–10 years' ageing even in a light year and a minimum of 15 years in a ripe vintage. White Hermitage, from Marsanne and Roussanne, is rather less famous but the best wines, made by traditionalists, can outlive the reds, sometimes lasting as long as 40 years. Some winemakers are making modern, fruity, fragrant whites that are attractive at 1–2 years old. Best producers: A Belle★★, CHAPOUTIER★★ (since 1988), CHAVE★★★, B Chave★★, Colombier★★, DELAS★★ (single vineyard), A Desmeure★, B Faurie★★, Fayolle★, M Ferraton★★, A Graillot★★, J-L Grippat★★, GUIGAL★★, JABOULET★★★ (since 1988), J-M Sorrel★★, M Sorrel★★, Cave Tain l'Hermitage★, Tardieu-Laurent★★. Best years: (1998) 97 96 95 94 **92** 91 90 **89 88 85 83 82 80 78 76 71 70**.

JAMES HERRICK *Vin de Pays d'Oc, Languedoc, France*   When Herrick and his Aussie partners planted 175ha (435 acres) of Chardonnay between Narbonne and Béziers, many locals thought he was mad. His neatly trellised rows with drip-feed irrigation are a real contrast to his neighbours' traditionally straggling vines. Chardonnay is an attractive blend of exuberant fruit and French elegance. A reserve bottling★ is more concentrated. A red, Cuvée Simone, started out OK in 1995 but has been very patchy since.

THE HESS COLLECTION *Mount Veeder AVA, California, USA* This NAPA VALLEY producer is earning rave reviews for its Cabernet Sauvignon★★ which is showing all the intense lime and black cherry originality of its MOUNT VEEDER

fruit, without coating it with impenetrable tannins. Hess Select is the budget label. Best years: (Cabernet) 1995 94 93 91 **90**.

HESSISCHE BERGSTRASSE *Germany* Small, warm wine region near Darmstadt. Much of the winemaking here is by the local co-op, although the Staatdomäne also makes some good wines. There has been less flirtation with new grape varieties here than elsewhere in Germany, and Riesling is still the most prized grape. EISWEINS are a speciality.

HEURIGER *Austria* Fresh, young wine drunk in the many taverns in the Viennese hills. Once the wine is a year old it is called der Alte, or 'old chap'. No really good wine is sold as Heuriger, yet a few swift jugs of it can make for a great evening – but keep the aspirin handy.

HEYL ZU HERRNSHEIM *Nierstein, Rheinhessen, Germany* Top estate on the Rhine practising organic farming. It always produces some fine Rieslings★★ especially from the Brudersberg, Pettenthal, Hipping and Ölberg sites but the wines are rather inconsistent lower down the scale. Best years: (1998) 97 **96 93 90** 89 88.

HIDALGO *Jerez y Manzanilla DO, Andalucía, Spain* Hidalgo's Manzanilla La Gitana★★ is deservedly the best-selling manzanilla in Spain. Hidalgo is still family-owned, and only uses grapes from its own vineyards. Brands include Mariscal★, Fino Especial and Miraflores, Amontillado Napoleon★★, Oloroso Viejo★★ and Jerez Cortado★★.

HILLTOPS *New South Wales, Australia* Promising high-altitude cherry-growing region with a small but fast-growing area of vineyards around the town of Young. Special potential for reds from Cabernet Sauvignon and Shiraz. Best producers: Demondrille, Hungerford Hill★, MCWILLIAMS (Barwang vineyard).

FRANZ HIRTZBERGER *Wachau, Niederösterreich, Austria* One of the Wachau's top growers. Hirtzberger's finest wines are the Rieslings from Singerriedel★★★ and Hochrain★★. The best Grüner Veltliner comes from the Honivogl site★★. Best years: (1998) 97 96 **95 94 93** 92 91 90 88 86 83 79 77 71.

HOCHHEIM *Rheingau, Germany* Village best known for having given the English the word 'Hock' for Rhine wine, but with good individual vineyard sites, especially Domdechaney, Hölle (or Hell!) and Kirchenstück. On the Königin Victoria Berg there is even a statue of the 19th-century British Queen who swore by the therapeutic qualities of Hock after she'd stopped off there for a picnic. Best producers: Franz KUNSTLER★★, Domdechant WERNER. Best years: (1998) 97 96 **93 92 90**.

HOGUE CELLARS *Washington State, USA* Really splendid ripe, brambly Reserve Cabernet Sauvignon★★, often blended with Merlot, and a supple, elegant Reserve Merlot★★ that has hit ★★★ on occasion. The Chardonnay★ looks likely to emulate this high standard. Best years: (reds) 1996 **95 94 92 91 90 89 87 86**.

HOLLICK *Coonawarra, South Australia*   Run by viticulturalist Ian Hollick, this winery makes a broader range of good wines than is usually found in COONAWARRA: a much-improved Champagne-method Pinot-Chardonnay★ fizz, subtle Chardonnay★, tobaccoey Cabernet-Merlot★ and a richer Ravenswood Cabernet Sauvignon★★. In all but the best vintages, spicy Shiraz and limy Riesling go into the second label Terra. Best years: (reds) 1996 **94 93 91 90 88**.

HOSPICES DE BEAUNE *Côte de Beaune, Burgundy, France*   Scene of a theatrical auction on the third Sunday in November each year, the Hospices is an historic foundation which sells wine from its holdings in the CÔTE D'OR to finance its charitable works. The quality of the wine-making has increased immeasurably since 1994, after former winemaker André Porcheret returned to the helm at a new state-of-the-art winery. The wines are matured and bottled by the purchaser, which can cause variations in quality, and pricing reflects charitable status rather than common sense. Best years: (reds) 1997 96 95 94 **85**; (whites) 1997 96 95 **94**.

HOUGHTON *Swan Valley, Western Australia*   WESTERN AUSTRALIA's biggest winery, with a huge output of 'White Burgundy★' (called Houghton's 'Supreme' in the EU). Good Semillon★, Verdelho★ and Chenin Blanc★; also greatly improved Chardonnay★★ and excellent Riesling★★. Reliable budget label is Wildflower Ridge. With the inclusion of more grapes from the south of the state, the reds have improved, especially Houghton and Moondah Brook Cabernets★ and Shiraz★. Super-duper Reserve Shiraz★★ and Jack Mann Commemorative Cabernet★★ were released in 1997 to a well-deserved fanfare.

VON HÖVEL *Konz-Oberemmel, Saar, Germany*   Jovial Eberhard von Kunow has always made classic Saar Riesling, but since 1993 quality has taken another jump up. The rich, racy new wines are almost all ★★. Best years: 1997 96 **95 94 93 90 89 88 85**.

HOWELL MOUNTAIN AVA *Napa Valley, USA*   This mountainous, somewhat magical area in Napa's north-east corner is noted for its extra-strength, powerhouse Cabernet Sauvignon and Zinfandel as well as exotic, full-flavoured Merlot. Best producers: BERINGER (Merlot)★★, DUCKHORN★, DUNN★★★, La Jota★, Liparita★.

HUADONG WINERY *Shandong Province, China*   The first producer of varietal and vintage wines in China, Huadong has received massive investments from its multinational joint owners (Allied DOMECQ). But money can't change climates, and excessive moisture from the summer rainy season can cause problems. Riesling and Chardonnay (under the Tsingtao label) were the first wines to be exported, but most of the noble varieties have been planted.

HUET SA *Vouvray AC, Loire Valley, France*   Gaston Huet has passed this famous estate to his son-in-law, Noël Pinguet, but still takes a keen interest in the wines; complex, traditional Vouvrays which can age for up to 50 years. As well as a good Vouvray Mousseux★★, the estate produces wines from 3 excellent sites – le Haut Lieu, Clos du Bourg and le Mont – which can be dry★★, medium-dry★★ or sweet★★★, depending on the vintage. Best years: (1998) 97 96 95 **93 90 89 88 85 76 64 61 59 47**.

HUGEL ET FILS *Alsace AC, Alsace, France* Arguably the most famous name in Alsace, thanks to marketing and (sometimes) the quality of its wines. As well as wines from its own vineyards, Hugel buys in grapes for basic wines. Best wines are sweet ALSACE VENDANGE TARDIVE★★ and SELECTION DE GRAINS NOBLES★★★. Ordinary releases have improved dramatically of late. Best years: (1998) 97 96 **95 94 93 92 90 89 85 83**.

HUNTER VALLEY *New South Wales, Australia* NEW SOUTH WALES' oldest wine region overcomes a tricky climate to make fascinating, ageworthy Semillon and rich, buttery Chardonnay. The reds meet less universal approval. Shiraz is the mainstay, aging well but often developing a leathery overtone. Cabernet can deliver occasional success but Pinot Noir is less suited. Premium region is the Lower Hunter Valley; the Upper Hunter has few wineries but extensive vineyards. Best producers: Allandale, Briar Ridge, BROKENWOOD★★, LAKE'S FOLLY★★, LINDEMANS★★, MCWILLIAMS★★, ROSEMOUNT★★, ROTHBURY★, Thalgara, TYRRELL'S★.

HUNTER'S *Marlborough, South Island, New Zealand* One of MARLBOROUGH's star winemakers, with superlative Sauvignon★★★, lean and elegant Chardonnay★★, vibrant Riesling★ and a renowned luscious, botrytized Chardonnay★★. Also produce attractive fizz★ with technical input from Tony Jordan, DOMAINE CHANDON's ex-general manager. Best years: (1998) **97 96 94 91 89**.

IAMBOL *Southern Region, Bulgaria* Since privatization in 1995, the Iambol winery (5th largest in the country) has formed a partnership with Domaine Boyar. It concentrates on making reds for the export market and can draw on some of the best grapes in Bulgaria. There is good Merlot★, either by itself or blended with Cabernet or Pamid. Starting to develop some premium-level Cabernet Sauvignon★. Definitely a winery to watch.

ICEWINE *Canada* A speciality of Canada produced from juice squeezed from ripe grapes that have frozen on the vine. Very expensive, very sweet, extremely complex, these are undoubtedly some of the world's greatest dessert wines. Best producers: Chateau des Charmes, Henry of Pelham, INNISKILLIN★, Marynissen, MISSION HILL. See also Eiswein.

IGT (INDICAZIONE GEOGRAFICA TIPICA) The Italian equivalent of the French VIN DE PAYS. As in the MIDI, both premium and everyday wines may share the same appellation. Many of the super VINO DA TAVOLAS are now being sold under a regional IGT.

ÎLE DE BEAUTÉ, VIN DE PAYS DE L' *Corsica, France* Some increasingly good wines are being made here from Syrah, Cabernet Sauvignon, Nielluccio, Sciaccarello and Merlot (for reds); Grenache and Barbarossa (for rosés); Chardonnay and Vermentino (for whites). Best producers: Aleria, Casinca, Marana co-op, Samuletto, UVAL co-op.

INNISKILLIN *Niagara Peninsula, Ontario, Canada* Leading Canadian winery producing good Pinot Noir★, a beautifully rounded Klose Vineyard Chardonnay★ full of bananas, vanilla and cinnamon toast, and thick, rich, Vidal ICEWINE★★. Winemaker Karl Kaiser is also achieving good results with Cabernet Franc and Merlot. Another Inniskillin winery is in the somewhat drier Okanagan Valley in British Columbia, a partnership between the winery and the Inkameep Indian Band. Best years: 1998 **96 94**.

IPHOFEN *Franken, Germany* One of the 2 best wine towns in FRANKEN (the other is WURZBURG) for dry Riesling and Silvaner. Both are powerful, with a pronounced earthiness. Best producers: JULIUSSPITAL★★, Johann Ruck★, Wirsching★. Best years: (1998) 97 **94 93 92 90**.

IPR (INDICAÇÃO DE PROVENIÊNCIA REGULAMENTADA) The second tier in the Portuguese wine classification regulations, covering grape varieties, yields and aging requirements.

IRANCY AC *Burgundy, France* Formerly known as Bourgogne-Irancy and labelled simply Irancy from 1996, this northern outpost of vineyards, just south-west of CHABLIS, is an unlikely champion of the clear, pure flavours of the Pinot Noir grape. But red Irancy can be delicate and lightly touched by the ripeness of plums and strawberries, and can age well. There is also a little rosé. Best producers: Bienvenu, J-M Brocard, Cantin, A & J-P Colinot, Delaloge, Patrice Fort, Simonnet-Febvre. Best years: 1997 96 **95 93 92 90**.

IRON HORSE VINEYARDS *Sonoma, California, USA* Producer of outstanding sparkling wines with Brut★★ and the BLANC DE BLANCS★★★ delicious on release but capable of aging. A BLANC DE NOIRS★ called 'Wedding Cuvée' and a Brut Rosé★ complete the line-up. Often overlooked are the Iron Horse table wines including a Cabernet★ (Cabernet Sauvignon-Cabernet Franc blend), a good Pinot Noir★, a barrel-fermented Chardonnay★, a zesty Sauvignon and a vigorous Viognier. Best years: (reds) (1997) 96 95 94 **92** 91 **90 88 87 86 85 84 83**; (whites) (1998) 97 96 **95 92 91 90**.

IROULÉGUY AC *South-West France* A small AC in the Basque Pyrenees, reviving after its virtual disappearance in the 1950s and 60s. Cabernet Sauvignon, Cabernet Franc and Tannat give robust reds that are softer than MADIRAN. Production of white from Courbu and Manseng has recently restarted. Best producers: Abotia, Brana★, Ilarria★, Irouléguy co-op, Mignaberry★. Best years: (reds) (1998) 97 **96 95 94**.

ISOLE E OLENA *Chianti Classico DOCG, Tuscany, Italy* Long one of the pacesetters in Chianti Classico, this fine estate is run by Paolo De Marchi. His CHIANTI CLASSICO★★, characterized by a clean, elegant and spicily perfumed fruit, excels in every vintage. The powerful SUPER-TUSCAN Cepparello★★★, made from 100% Sangiovese, is the top wine, and there is also excellent Syrah★★, Cabernet Sauvignon★★ and Chardonnay★★, as well as great VIN SANTO★★★. Best years: (Cepparello) (1998) (97) **96 95 94 93 91 90 88 86 85**.

CH. D'ISSAN★ *Margaux AC, 3ème Cru Classé, Haut-Médoc, Bordeaux, France* This lovely moated property has rather underperformed over the last few years, although recent vintages show improvement. When successful, the wine can be one of the most elegant but delicate in the MARGAUX AC, with a fragrant violet and cassis fruit bouquet. The second wine is labelled le Moulin d'Issan. Best years: (1998) 97 96 95 **90 89 85 83 82 78**.

PAUL JABOULET AÎNÉ *Rhône Valley, France* During the 1970s, Jaboulet led the way in raising the world's awareness of the great quality of Rhône wines, yet during the 80s the quality of wine faltered. But recent vintages, fuller of fruit, less manipulated and proud of their origins, make it look as though Jaboulet is back on the quality bandwagon, despite the tragic early death of Gérard Jaboulet in 97. Best wines are top red HERMITAGE la Chapelle★★★ and white Chevalier de Stérimberg★★. Also good CÔTE-RÔTIE★, excellent CROZES-HERMITAGE Thalabert★★, fine juicy ST-JOSEPH le Grand Pompée★ from 94, concentrated CORNAS★★ and sweet, perfumed MUSCAT DE BEAUMES-DE-VENISE★. Best years: (top reds) (1997) 96 95 94 **91 90 89 88 78**.

JACKSON ESTATE *Marlborough, South Island, New Zealand* Established grapegrower with vineyards in MARLBOROUGH's most prestigious district, Jackson Estate turned its hand to winemaking in 91 with the help of a local contract winemaker. Unirrigated vineyards help produce a concentrated and very ripe Sauvignon Blanc★★ with an equally concentrated Chardonnay★★ and, more recently, a complex traditional-method fizz★. One of New Zealand's most successful 'winemakers without a grape press'. Best years: (1998) **97 96 94**.

LOUIS JADOT *Beaune, Burgundy, France* A leading merchant based in Beaune with a broad range only matched by DROUHIN, and with rights to some estate wines of the Duc de Magenta★★. Jadot has particularly extensive vineyard holdings for red wines, but it is the firm's whites which have earned its reputation. Good in Grands Crus like BÂTARD-MONTRACHET★★ and CORTON-CHARLEMAGNE★★ but it is in lesser ACs like ST-AUBIN★★ and RULLY★ that Jadot really shows what it can do. After leading white Burgundy in quality during the 1970s, the 80s were less thrilling, but in the 90s Jadot returned to form. Best years: (top reds) 1997 96 95 94 93 **90 89 88**.

JAFFELIN *Beaune, Burgundy, France* Now owned by BOISSET, Jaffelin sells a large range of wine from the CÔTE D'OR, the CÔTE CHALONNAISE and BEAUJOLAIS. The lesser ACs – RULLY★, ST-ROMAIN★, BOURGOGNE Blanc and Beaujolais – are the best value but don't overlook the Beaune les Avaux★★. Despite introducing a sound range of Village wines, Boisset has yet to prove its quality credentials here. Best years: **1997 96 95 92 90**.

JAMET *Côte-Rôtie AC, Rhône Valley, France* Jean-Paul and Jean-Luc Jamet are 2 of the most talented young growers of CÔTE-RÔTIE. If anything, the wines★★ from this excellent estate have improved since they took over from their father, Joseph. The wines age well for a decade or more. Best years: 1997 96 95 94 **91 90 89 88 87 85 83 82**.

JARDIN DE LA FRANCE, VIN DE PAYS DU *Loire Valley, France* This VIN DE PAYS covers most of the LOIRE VALLEY, and production often exceeds 50 million bottles – mostly white wine, from Chenin Blanc and Sauvignon Blanc, and usually very cheap to buy. There is an increasing amount of good Chardonnay made here, too. The few reds and rosés are generally light and sharp in style. Best producers: Couillaud, C Daviau, Forges, Hauts de Sanziers, Touche Noire.

ROBERT JASMIN *Côte-Rôtie AC, Rhône Valley, France* The good-quality CÔTE-RÔTIES★★ made by Robert Jasmin and his son Patrick are some of the most aromatic red wines produced in this northern section of the RHÔNE VALLEY. The wines have an exuberance of gluggable young fruit and a beguiling scent. They are at their best after 4–5 years, but are capable of keeping for longer. Best years: (1997) 96 95 94 **91 90 89 88 87 85 83**.

JASNIÈRES AC *Loire Valley, France* Tiny AC north of Tours making long-lived, bone-dry whites from Chenin Blanc. Best producers: F Fresneau, J Gigou★, Renard-Potaire★. Best years: (1998) 97 96 95 **93 92 90 89**.

CH. LA JAUBERTIE *Bergerac, South-West France* The most innovative domaine in BERGERAC, run since 1973 by the Ryman family, producing fresh, aromatic wines with lots of fruit. The rosé★ and dry white★ wines should be drunk young, but the red★ can age for up to 5 years. The estate is currently up for sale. Best years: (red) (1998) 97 **96 95 94 93 91 90**.

HENRI JAYER *Vosne-Romanée, Côte de Nuits, Burgundy, France* In 1988, the vineyards of this famous estate were divided between MEO-CAMUZET, Jayer himself and his nephew Emmanuel Rouget. Since 1995 Jayer's own vineyards in VOSNE-ROMANEE★★★ and NUITS-ST-GEORGES★★★ have been cultivated by Rouget, with kindly advice from his uncle. These truly great wines show the heady perfume and exhilarating, oak-enriched fruit that top Burgundy is supposed to be all about. Best years: 1997 96 95 93 92 **90 89 88 85 80 78**.

ROBERT JAYER-GILLES *Côtes de Nuits, Burgundy, France* Robert Jayer-Gilles produces expensive but sought-after wines, heavily dominated by new oak. Good ALIGOTE★ and wonderful Hautes-Côtes de Nuits Blanc★★, as well as a range of structured reds, including ECHEZEAUX★★ and NUITS-ST-GEORGES les Damodes★★. Best years: (reds) 1997 96 95 93 **90 88**.

JEREZ Y MANZANILLA DO/ SHERRY See pages 164–5.

JERMANN *Friuli-Venezia Giulia, Italy* Silvio Jermann, in the COLLIO zone of north-east Italy, produces non-DOC Chardonnay★, Sauvignon Blanc★, Pinot Bianco★ and Pinot Grigio. Vintage Tunina★★ is based on Sauvignon-Chardonnay, and barrel-fermented Chardonnay★★ was called 'Where the dreams have no end' and has now, incredibly, been renamed 'Were dreams, now it is just wine'. The wines are plump but pricy. Vinnae★ is based on Ribolla; Cabernet★ blends the 2 Cabernet grapes.

CHARLES JOGUET *Chinon AC, Loire Valley, France* Until recently, Joguet was the leading winemaker in CHINON. However, he has virtually retired now and the wines are not as outstanding as they were. There are 4 different reds – Cuvée du Clos de la Curé★, Clos du Chêne Vert★★, les Varennes du Grand Clos★★ and Clos de la Dioterie★★ – all of which require aging for 5–10 years or more for the full beauty to show. There is also a little rosé. Best years: (1997) 96 95 **93 92 90 89 88 85 82 81 76**.

JOHANNISBERG *Rheingau, Germany* Just about the most famous of all the Rhine villages with 10 individual vineyard sites, including the famous Schloss Johannisberg where standards have improved recently. Best producer: Johannishof★. Best years: (1998) 97 **96 94 93 90**.

KARL-HEINZ JOHNER *Bischoffingen, Baden, Germany* Johner specializes in new oak-aged wines from his native BADEN. The vividly fruity Pinot Noir★ and Pinot Blanc★ are excellent, the rich silky Pinot Noir SJ★★ one of Germany's finest reds and the Chardonnay SJ★★ its best example of this varietal. Best years: (reds) (1997) **96 93 92 90 89 88 86**.

JORDAN *Alexander Valley AVA, Sonoma, California, USA* Ripe, fruity Cabernet Sauvignon★★ with a cedar character that is rare in California. The Chardonnay★ has improved markedly during the last few years. The sparkling wine, J★★, has also been improving. Best years: (reds) 1996 95 94 **91 90 87 86**.

JEREZ Y MANZANILLA DO/SHERRY

Andalucía, Spain

The Spanish have won the battle. From 1 January 1996 'British sherry' and 'Irish sherry' ceased to exist. At least in the EU, the only wines that can be sold as sherry come from the triangle of vineyard land between the Andalucian towns of inland Jerez de la Frontera, and Sanlúcar de Barrameda and Puerto de Santa María by the sea.

The best sherries can be spectacular. Three main factors contribute to the high quality potential of wines from this region: the chalky-spongy albariza soil where the best vines grow, the Palomino Fino grape – unexciting for table wines but potentially great once transformed by the sherry-making processes – and a natural yeast called flor. All sherry must be a minimum of 3 years old, but fine sherries age in barrel for much longer. Sherries must be blended through a solera system. About a third of the wine from the oldest barrels is bottled, and the barrels topped up with slightly younger wine from another set of barrels and so on, for a minimum of 3 sets of barrels. The idea is that the younger wine takes on the character of older wine, as well as keeping the blend refreshed.

MAIN SHERRY STYLES

Finos, manzanillas and amontillados These sherries derive their extraordinary, tangy, pungent flavours from flor. Young, newly fermented wines destined for these styles of sherry are deliberately fortified very sparingly to just 15–15.5% alcohol before being put in barrels for their minimum of 3 years' maturation. The thin, soft, oatmeal-coloured mush of flor grows on the surface of the wines, protecting them from the air (and therefore keeping them pale) and giving them a characteristic sharp, pungent tang. Manzanillas are fino-style wines that have matured in the cooler seaside conditions of Sanlúcar de Barrameda, where the flor grows thickest and the fine tang is most accentuated. True amontillados are simply fino sherries that have continued to age after the flor has died (after about 5 years) and so finish their aging period in contact with air. These should all be bone dry. Medium-sweet amontillados are merely concoctions for the export market.

Oloroso This type of sherry is strongly fortified after fermentation to deter the growth of flor. Olorosos therefore mature in barrel in contact with the air, which gradually darkens them while they develop rich, intense, nutty and raisiny flavours.

Other styles Palo cortado is an unusual, deliciously nutty, dry style somewhere in between amontillado and oloroso. Sweet oloroso creams and pale creams are almost without exception enriched solely for the export market.

See also INDIVIDUAL PRODUCERS.

BEST PRODUCERS AND WINES

Argüeso (Manzanilla San Léon, Manzanilla Fina Las Medallas).

BARBADILLO (Manzanilla Eva, Manzanilla Príncipe, Solear Manzanilla Fina Vieja, Amontillado Príncipe, Amontillado de Sanlúcar, Oloroso del Tio Río, Oloroso Seco).

Delgado Zuleta (Manzanilla La Goya).

Díez Mérito (Don Zoilo Imperial Amontillado and Fino, Victoria Regina Oloroso).

DOMECQ (Amontillado 51-1A, Sibarita Palo Cortado, Venerable Pedro Ximénez).

Garvey (Palo Cortado, Amontillado Tio Guillermo, Pedro Ximénez).

GONZALEZ BYASS (Tio Pepe Fino, Matusalem Oloroso Muy Viejo, Apostoles Oloroso Viejo, Amontillado del Duque Seco y Muy Viejo, Noé Pedro Ximénez, Oloroso Viejo de Añado).

HARVEYS (1796 range).

HIDALGO (Manzanilla La Gitana, Manzanilla Pasada, Jerez Cortado).

LUSTAU (Almacenista single-producer wines, Old East India Cream, Puerto Fino).

OSBORNE (Fino Quinta, Bailén Oloroso, Solera India Pedro Ximénez).

Sánchez Romate (Pedro Ximénez Cardenal Cisneros).

VALDESPINO (Amontillado Coliseo, Tio Diego Amontillado, Pedro Ximénez Solera Superior).

Williams & Humbert (Pando Fino, Manzanilla Alegria).

165

JORDAN VINEYARDS *Stellenbosch WO, South Africa* Ted and Shelagh Jordan purchased this farm in the early 1980s and planted premium varieties on its many different slopes. Son and daughter-in-law, Gary and Kathy, took full advantage of this forward thinking on their return from studying and working in California. A nutty Chardonnay★ heads the strong white range; improving Cabernet Sauvignon★ and Merlot are modern but understated. Best years: (whites) **1998 97 96 95 94**.

JOSMEYER ET FILS *Alsace AC, Alsace, France* Known for excellent wine, whether as a merchant or as a producer in its own right. The top wines are Gewurztraminer (particularly les Archenets★★) and Pinot Blanc (les Lutins★). Best years: (1998) 97 **96 95 94 93 92 90 89 86 85 83**.

TONI JOST *Bacharach, Mittelrhein, Germany* Producer that lends the Mittelrhein an international dimension. From the Bacharacher Hahn site come some delicious, racy Rieslings★ including well-structured Halbtrockens★; Auslese★★ adds creaminess without losing that pine-needle scent. Best years: (1998) 97 **94 93 90 89 88**.

J P VINHOS *Terras do Sado, Portugal* The name has changed since the João Pires Muscat brand was sold to IDV, but the winemaking is as forward-looking as ever, using Portuguese and foreign grapes with equal ease. Quinta da BACALHOA★ is an oaky, meaty Cabernet-Merlot blend, Tinto da Anfora★★ rich and figgy, white Herdade de Santa Marta★ rich, greengagey and mouthfilling, and Cova da Ursa★ a tasty, toasty rich Chardonnay that walks on the wild side. For fizz, there is Portugal's finest sparkling wine, the vintaged Loridos Extra Bruto★. Made from Chardonnay, it can compete with similarly prized examples from elsewhere. There is also decent Moscatel de SETUBAL★.

JULIÉNAS AC *Beaujolais, Burgundy, France* One of the more northerly BEAUJOLAIS Crus, Juliénas makes delicious, 'serious' Beaujolais which can be big and tannic enough to develop in bottle. Best producers: G Descombes★, DUBOEUF★, Ch. de Juliénas, Juliénas co-op, Pelletier★. Best years: 1998 97 96 **95 94 93**.

JULIUSSPITAL WEINGUT *Würzburg, Franken, Germany* A 16th-century charitable foundation known for its dry wines – very good Silvaners, especially from IPHOFEN and WURZBURG, and the occasional Riesling that's pretty special. Look out for the wines from the estate's holdings in the Würzburger Stein vineyard, sappy Müller-Thurgau, grapefruity Silvaners★★ and petrolly Rieslings★★. Best years: 1995 **94 93 92 90 89**.

JUMILLA DO *Murcia and Castilla-La Mancha, Spain* Jumilla's reputation in Spain is for big alcoholic reds. Reds and fruity rosés are made from Monastrell (Mourvèdre), giving them great potential if not always great current quality, and there are also a few boring whites. Best producers: Rico Agapito, Julia Roch Melgares (Casa Castillo), San Isidro.

JURA See Arbois, Château-Chalon, Côtes du Jura, l'Étoile.

JURANÇON AC *South-West France* The sweet white wine made from late-harvested and occasionally botrytized grapes can be heavenly. The rapidly improving dry wine, Jurançon Sec, can be ageworthy. Best producers: Bellegarde★, Bru-Baché★★, Castira★, CAUHAPE★, Clos Lapeyre★, Clos Uroulat★★, Clos Thou★★, Larrédya, Souch★. Best years: 1996 **95 94 93 90**.

JUVÉ Y CAMPS *Cava DO and Penedès DO, Catalonia, Spain* Juvé y Camps is ultra-traditional – and expensive. Unusually among the

Catalan companies, most of the grapes come from its own vineyards. Fruitiest CAVA is Reserva de la Familia Extra Brut★, but the rosé and the top brand white Cava Gran Juvé are also good.

KABINETT Term used for the lowest level of QmP wines in Germany, with Oechsle levels ranging from 67 in the MOSEL to 85 for a BADEN Ruländer. In Austria, Kabinett wines must be produced in the dry style, with 17 KMW or 84 Oechsle.

KAISERSTUHL *Baden, Germany* A 4000-ha (10,000-acre) volcanic stump rising to 600m (2000ft) and overlooking the Rhine plain and south BADEN. Best producers: BERCHER★, Bickensohl co-op, Dr HEGER★★, JOHNER★, Königsschaffhausen co-op, Salwey★. Best years: (1998) **97 96 93**.

KALLSTADT *Pfalz, Germany* A warm climate combined with the excellent Saumagen site results in the richest dry Rieslings in Germany. These, and the dry Weissburgunder and Muskateller, can stand beside the very best from ALSACE, while Pinot Noir is also showing it likes the limestone soil. Best producer: KOEHLER-RUPRECHT★★. Best years: (1998) 97 96 **95 93 92** 90 89 88 85 83.

KAMPTAL *Niederösterreich, Austria* Wine region centred around the town of Langenlois, making some impressive dry whites, particularly Riesling and Grüner Veltliner. Best producer: BRUNDLMAYER★★. Best years: (1998) **97 95 94 93**.

KANONKOP ESTATE *Stellenbosch WO, South Africa* Beyers Truter has proved he is a red wine supremo with several international awards; Pinotage, however, remains his first love. Some of the world's first Pinotage vines, planted in the 1950s, produce his standard Pinotage★ and lavishly new-oaked Auction Reserve★★. The BORDEAUX blend, Paul Sauer★★, Auction Reserve★★ and Cabernet Sauvignon★ uphold an enviable red wine reputation. The Krige brothers, owners of the estate, are partners in Truter's other winery, nearby BEYERSKLOOF★ and have also purchased more land to experiment with a more Burgundian style of Pinotage. Best years: **1996 95 94 93 92 91 90 89**.

KARTHÄUSERHOF *Trier, Ruwer, Germany* Top Ruwer estate which has gone from strength to strength since Christoph Tyrell and winemaker Ludwig Breiling took charge from the 1986 vintage. Since 93 most wines are ★★, some Auslese and EISWEIN ★★★. Best years: 1997 96 95 **94 93 92 90 89 88 86**.

KATNOOK ESTATE *Coonawarra, South Australia* Expensive, often exceptional Chardonnay★★, Sauvignon Blanc★★ and much-improved Cabernet Sauvignon★★ plus new flagship red, Odyssey★★. Second label, Riddoch, often throws up a bargain. Best years: (red) 1996 **94 93 91 90 88**.

KÉKFRANKOS See Blaufränkisch.

KENDALL-JACKSON *Lake County, California, USA* Jess Jackson founded KJ in bucolic Lake County in 1982 after buying a vineyard there. The winery has since grown from under 10,000 cases to over 2 million. Early success with Chardonnay was fuelled by a style of winemaking favouring sweetness, but in the 1990s Jackson redirected energies toward consistency and value. Today's Chardonnays are 100% barrel fermented and oak aged. Most varietals, including ambitious Grand Reserves, are blends from several AVAs. The line-up has experienced a complete quality makeover, exemplified by Cabernet Sauvignon and

Pinot Noir. Jackson currently owns a dozen wineries, including Cambria, Stonestreet, Edmeades and Robert Pepi.

KENWOOD VINEYARDS *Sonoma Valley AVA, California, USA* From humble beginnings, this winery is now home to one of California's best Sauvignon Blancs★★, and news of its expanded Zinfandel programme is welcome to Zin fans. Kenwood Zinfandels★ have always been first rate, with the Jack London Ranch★★ often getting rave reviews for its rich, spicy flavours. Kenwood also releases 2 more single-vineyard Zinfandels – Mazzoni Vineyard★ and Nuns Canyon★. Best years: (1997) 96 95 **94 93 91 90**.

VON KESSELSTATT *Trier, Mosel, Germany* Estate making good Riesling★ and the best Spätlese and Auslese★★ wines from some top sites at GRAACH (Josephshöfer) in the MOSEL, Scharzhofberg in the Saar and at Kasel in the Ruwer. Best years: (1998) 97 96 95 **94 93 91 90 89**.

KHAN KRUM *Eastern Region, Bulgaria* Winery producing some of Bulgaria's rare good whites, like oaky Reserve Chardonnay and delicate, apricoty Riesling-Dimiat Country Wine, but below par recently, probably because of the need to reconstruct the vineyard.

KIEDRICH *Rheingau, Germany* Small village whose first vineyard is the Gräfenberg, giving extremely long-lived, minerally wines. Wines from Sandgrub and Wasserose are also good. Best producer: WEIL★★★. Best years: (1998) 97 96 **95 94 93 92 90**.

KING ESTATE *Oregon, USA* It took only 3 years for the King Estate to become OREGON's biggest producer of Pinot Noir and Pinot Gris. Both wines are made in a user-friendly style. The Reserve Pinot and Reserve Pinot Gris★ offer greater depth. A surprisingly tasty Zinfandel is also made. Best years: (1998) **97 96 94 93**.

KIONA *Yakima Valley AVA, Washington State, USA* A small operation in sagebrush country, Kiona has a young but growing reputation for its barrel-fermented Chardonnay★, big, rich Cabernet Sauvignon★ and delightful sweet or dry Riesling★. Kiona also has a Lemberger★, a juicy red wine that has achieved a cult status in the Pacific Northwest.

KISTLER *Sonoma, California, USA* One of California's hottest Chardonnay producers. Wines are made from many different vineyards (Kistler Estate and Dutton Ranch can be ★★★, Durell Vineyard and McCrea Vineyard ★★), and they all possess great complexity with good aging potential. Kistler also makes a number of single-vineyard Pinot Noirs that go from good to very good. Best years: (Dutton) (1997) **96 95 94 93 92 91 90 87**; (Durell) (1997) 96 95 94 **93 91 90 89 87**; (Kistler) 1996 95 94 **91 90 88**; (McCrea) (1997) **96 95 94 93 92 91 90 88**.

KLEIN CONSTANTIA *Constantia WO, South Africa* Since 1980, the Jooste family have turned this winery into a South African show-piece. Sauvignon Blanc★★, crisp and vivid, benefits from winemaker Ross Gower's experience in New Zealand. A toasty butterscotch Chardonnay★, often botrytis-brushed Riesling★ and Vin de Constance★★, a beautifully packaged Muscat dessert wine based on the celebrated 18th-century CONSTANTIA examples, also highlight the area's aptitude for white wine. Reds have not risen to the same level, a shortcoming which should be rectified by the recent purchase of prime STELLENBOSCH vineyards. Best years: (whites) **1998 97 96 95 93 92 91**.

KNAPPSTEIN *Clare Valley, South Australia* In 1995 Tim Knappstein quit the company, now part of PETALUMA, to focus on his own Lenswood Vineyards, high in the ADELAIDE HILLS. However, the Knappstein brand continues as a market leader, with fine Riesling★★ and Traminer★, subtly-oaked Fumé Blanc★, Cabernet★, Cabernet-Merlot★ and Chardonnay★. Former Petaluma winemaker Andrew Hardy has been in charge since the 1996 vintage, and he has been pumping new enthusiasm into the wines. Best years: (Cabernet Sauvignon) **1994 90 86**.

KOEHLER-RUPRECHT *Kallstadt, Pfalz, Germany* Bernd Philippi makes dry Rieslings★★★ from the Kallstadter Saumagen site, the oak-aged botrytized Elysium★★ and, since 1991, Burgundian-style Pinot Noirs★★. Best years: (Riesling) (1998) 97 96 **95 94 93 92 90 89 88 83** 79.

ALOIS KRACHER *Illmitz, Burgenland, Austria* Austria's greatest sweet winemaker. Nouvelle Vague wines are aged in barriques while Zwischen den Seen wines are spared oak. The Sämling (Scheurebe) Beerenauslesen and Trockenbeerenauslesen, and the Muskat-Ottonels, Welschrieslings and Chardonnay-Welschrieslings are all ★★★. The Bouviers★ are good. Best years: **1996 95 94 93 91 89 86 81**.

KREMSTAL *Niederösterreich, Austria* Wine region on both sides of the Danube around the town of Krems, producing some of Austria's best whites, particularly dry Riesling and Grüner Veltliner. Best producers: Nigl★, NIKOLAIHOF★★, Salomon★. Best years: (1998) **97 95 94 93**.

KRUG *Champagne AC, Champagne, France* Krug is a serious CHAMPAGNE house. The non-vintage, Grande Cuvée★★, knocks spots off most other de luxe brands but has begun to get a bit too cumbersome for its own good. There is also an impressive vintage wine★, a rosé★★★ and an ethereal single-vineyard Clos du Mesnil BLANC DE BLANCS★★★. Now bought by Moet-Hennessy so the style may change. Best years: **1989 85 82 81 79**.

KUENTZ-BAS *Alsace AC, Alsace, France* A small négociant, with high-quality wines from its own vineyards (labelled Réserve Personnelle) and from purchased grapes (Cuvée Tradition). Look out for the Eichberg Grand Cru★★ and the excellent ALSACE VENDANGE TARDIVE★★ wines. Best years: (1998) 97 96 **95 94 93 92 90 89 88 86 85**.

KUMEU/HUAPAI *Auckland, North Island, New Zealand* A small but significant viticultural area north-west of Auckland. The 11 wineries profit from their proximity to New Zealand's capital. Most producers make little or no wine from their home region. Best producers: COOPERS CREEK★, Harrier Rise, KUMEU RIVER★, MATUA VALLEY★★, NOBILO, SELAKS★.

KUMEU RIVER *Kumeu, Auckland, North Island, New Zealand* This family winery has been transformed by New Zealand's first Master of Wine, Michael Brajkovich, who has created a range of adventurous, high-quality wines. Unconventional oak-aged Sauvignon Blanc★, intense Chardonnay★★★ and softly stylish Merlot-Cabernet Sauvignon★ blend are Kumeu River's most obvious successes. Pinot Gris is a recent addition to the range. Best years: 1997 **96 95 94 93 91 90**.

KUNDE ESTATE *Sonoma Valley, California, USA*   The Kunde family have been wine-grape growers for at least 100 years in SONOMA COUNTY, and in 1990 they decided to start producing wines with spectacular results. A powerful, buttery Reserve Chardonnay★★ gets rave reviews and an explosively fruity Viognier★ is a real beauty. Best years: (Chardonnay) (1998) 97 **96 95** 94.

FRANZ KÜNSTLER *Hochheim, Rheingau, Germany*   Gunter Künstler makes the best dry and sweet Rieslings in the RHEINGAU. This estate is based in HOCHHEIM on the river Main. They are powerful, minerally wines★★, with everything from the Hölle site worthy of ★★★. In 1996 he bought the run-down Aschrott estate, which more than doubled his vineyard area. Best years: (1998) 97 96 **95 94 93 92** 90 89 88.

KWV *Paarl, South Africa*   Huge investment is paying dividends for this recently formed company. The KWV standard range has been rationalized, while the flagship Cathedral Cellar line-up has been enlarged with more premium varietals; both moves have advanced overall quality and allow Cellarmaster Kosie Muller, to treat each wine as an individual. This is shown to best advantage in Cathedral Cellar's bright-fruited, well-oaked Triptych★ BORDEAUX-style blend, rich bold Cabernet★★ and modern-style Pinotage, all international award winners. Reds in the standard range also have a more modern touch. Whites are generally less exciting, though Cathedral Cellar barrel-fermented Chardonnay shows pleasing fruit/oak balance and the standard Chenin Blanc is a consistent, fruity, off-dry crowd-pleaser. Dessert, sherry and port-style fortifieds remain superb value, particularly the dated Vintage★★, and Colheita-style Late Bottled Vintage★. The KWV brand has been retained even though the initials stand for its erstwhile status as a co-operative. KWV International still buys and markets a considerable range of wines and brandies.

CH. LABÉGORCE-ZÉDÉ★ *Margaux AC, Bordeaux, France*   One of the most improved domaines in the MARGAUX AC. Much of the credit goes to manager Luc Thienpont, whose family purchased the estate in 1979. The balance between concentration and finesse is always good. Age for 5 years or more. Second wine: Domaine Zédé. Best years: (1998) 97 96 95 **90 89 88** 86 85 83 82 81.

LABOURÉ-ROI *Nuits-St-Georges, Burgundy, France*   Price-conscious and generally reliable merchant, yet no longer so consistent as before as supply struggles to keep up with demand. The CHABLIS★ and MEURSAULT★ are very correct wines and NUITS-ST-GEORGES★, CHAMBOLLE-MUSIGNY, GEVREY-CHAMBERTIN★, BEAUNE★ and MARSANNAY★ are usually good. Best years: (reds) 1997 96 95 93 **91 90** 89 88.

LACRYMA CHRISTI DEL VESUVIO DOC *Campania, Italy*   Since DOC was introduced in 1983, things have improved for the red based on Piedirosso and the white from Coda di Volpe and Verdeca – but the name is still more evocative than the wine. Best producers: Cantine Caputo, MASTROBERARDINO, Sorrentino.

LADOIX AC *Côte de Beaune, Burgundy, France*   Most northerly village in the COTE DE BEAUNE and one of the least known. Best wines sell under the ACs CORTON, ALOXE-CORTON or Aloxe-Corton Premier Cru, and the less good ones as Ladoix-Côte de Beaune or COTE DE BEAUNE-VILLAGES. There are several good growers in the village and Ladoix wine, mainly red, quite light in colour and a little lean in style, is reasonably priced. Best producers: (reds) F Capitain, E Cornu★, M Mallard, A & J-R Nudant; (whites) E Cornu, M Mallard. Best years: (reds) 1997 96 95 **93 92 90**.

MICHEL LAFARGE *Côte de Beaune, Burgundy, France* The doyen of VOLNAY, Michel Lafarge has now virtually handed over to his son, Frédéric. The MEURSAULT produced under this label is not thrilling, but all the red wines are truly outstanding, notably Volnay Clos des Chênes★★★, Volnay Clos du Château des Ducs★★★ (a monopole) and less fashionable Beaune Grèves★★. Bourgogne Rouge★ is excellent value. Top wines are accessible when young but can age up to 10 years or more. Best years: (reds) 1997 96 95 93 92 91 **90 89 88 85.**

CH. LAFAURIE-PEYRAGUEY★★★ *Sauternes AC, 1er Cru Classé, Bordeaux, France* This was one of the most improved SAUTERNES properties of the 1980s and nowadays is frequently one of the best Sauternes of all. The wines can age well too. Best years: (1998) 97 96 95 **90 89 88 86 85 83.**

CH. LAFITE-ROTHSCHILD★★★ *Pauillac AC, 1er Cru Classé, Haut-Médoc, Bordeaux, France* This PAUILLAC First Growth is frequently cited as the epitome of elegance, indulgence and expense – but, unfortunately, the wine used to be sadly inconsistent. There have been great improvements of late but as this wine often needs 15 years and can take 30 years or more to achieve the magical and unlikely marriage of cedar fragrance and lean but lovely blackcurrant fruit, we are only gradually learning how good these 'new' Lafites are going to be. So it does get ★★★, but not without sóme reservations. Second wine: les Carruades de Lafite-Rothschild. Best years: (1998) 97 96 95 94 90 89 88 86 **85 82 81 79 76.**

CH. LAFLEUR★★★ *Pomerol AC, Bordeaux, France* Using some of POMEROL'S most traditional winemaking, this tiny estate makes Pomerols that seriously rival those from the great PETRUS for sheer power and flavour, and indeed in recent years has begun to pull ahead of Pétrus for hedonistic richness and concentration. Best years: (1998) 97 96 95 94 93 **90 89 88 86 85.**

LAFON *Meursault, Côte de Beaune, Burgundy, France* A leading producer in MEURSAULT and one of Burgundy's current superstars, with a reputation and prices to match. Dominique Lafon produces rich, powerful Meursaults that spend as long as 2 years in barrel and age superbly in bottle. As well as excellent Meursault, especially Clos de la Barre★★, les Charmes★★ and les Perrières★★★, Lafon makes a tiny amount of le MONTRACHET★★★ and some really individual and exciting red wines from VOLNAY★★ (Santenots du Milieu) and MONTHELIE★. Best years: 1997 96 95 **94** 93 **92 90 89 88 85.**

CH. LAFON-ROCHET ★★ *St-Estèphe AC, 4ème Cru Classé, Haut-Médoc, Bordeaux, France* Good-value, affordable Classed Growth claret. Recent vintages have seen an increase of Merlot in the blend, making the wine less austere. Delicious and blackcurranty after 10 years. Best years: (1998) 97 96 95 94 93 90 89 88 **86 85 83 82 79**.

LAGEDER *Alto Adige DOC, Trentino-Alto Adige, Italy* Leading producer in ALTO ADIGE. Produces medium-priced varietals under the Lageder label, and pricy estate and single-vineyard wines including Cabernet★ and Chardonnay★★ under the Löwengang label, Sauvignon Lehenhof★,

Cabernet Cor Römigberg★★ and Pinot Grigio Benefizium Porer★★. Also own the Cason Hirschprunn estate, source of excellent Alto Adige varietals, including Chardonnay★, Pinot Grigio★ and Sauvignon★, and blended red Casòn★★ (Merlot-Cabernet) and whites Etelle★ and Contest★.

LAGO DI CALDARO DOC *Trentino-Alto Adige, Italy*   At its best a lovely, delicate, barely red, youthful glugger from the Schiava grape in Italy's mountainous north, tasting of strawberries and cream and bacon smoke. However, much overproduced Caldaro scarcely passes muster as red wine at all. Known in German as Kalterersee. Kalterersee Auslese (or Lago di Caldaro Scelto) is not sweet, but has 0.5% more alcohol. Best producers: Brigl, Castel Ringberg & Kastelaz, Baron Dürfeld de Giovanelli★, LAGEDER★, Karl Martini, J Niedermayr, Prima & Nuova/Erste & Neue co-op★, San Michele Appiano co-op, Schloss Sallegg★.

CH. LAGRANGE★★ *St-Julien AC, 3ème Cru Classé, Haut-Médoc, Bordeaux, France*   Since the Japanese company Suntory purchased this estate in 1983, the leap in quality has been astonishing. No longer an amiable, shambling ST-JULIEN, this has become a single-minded wine of good fruit, meticulous winemaking and fine quality. Second wine: les Fiefs de Lagrange. Best years: (1998) 97 96 95 94 90 89 **88 86 85**.

LAGREIN   Highly individual black grape variety, planted only in Italy's Trentino-Alto Adige region, producing deep-coloured, brambly, chocolaty reds called Lagrein Dunkel, and full-bodied yet attractively scented rosé (known as Kretzer). Best producers: Franz Gojer★, Gries co-op★, Hofstätter★, LAGEDER★, Laimburg★, Muri-Gries★, J Niedermayr★, Plattner-Waldgries★, Hans Rottensteiner★, Tiefenbrunner★.

CH. LA LAGUNE ★★ *Haut-Médoc AC, 3ème Cru Classé, Haut-Médoc, Bordeaux, France*   Consistently excellent Classed Growth – full of the charry, chestnut warmth of good oak and a deep, cherry-blackcurrant-and-plums sweetness which, after 10 years or so, becomes outstanding claret. Best years: (1997) 96 95 90 89 **88 86 85 83 82 78 76 75**.

LAKE'S FOLLY *Hunter Valley, New South Wales, Australia*   Erratic wines with an eager following, thanks to charismatic Dr Max Lake. In best years, austere Chardonnay ★★ ages slowly to a masterly antipodean yet Burgundy-like peak. The Cabernet can be ★★, supple and beautifully balanced at best, but doesn't always live up to its reputation. Best years: (red) **1995 94 91 89 87 85 83 81**; (white) **1996 94 92 91 86**.

LALANDE-DE-POMEROL AC *Bordeaux, France*   To the north of its more famous neighbour POMEROL, this AC produces full, ripe wines with an unmistakable mineral edge that are very attractive to drink at 3–4 years old, but age reasonably well too. Even though they lack the concentration of top Pomerols the wines are not particularly cheap. Best producers: Annereaux★, Belles-Graves, Bertineau-St-Vincent★, Clos de l'Église, la Croix-Chenevelle, la Croix-St-André★, Fougeailles, Garraud★, Grand-Ormeau, Haut-Chaigneau, Haut-Surget, les Hauts Conseillants, Sergant, Siaurac ★, Tournefeuille, Viaud. Best years: (1998) 96 **95 94 90 89 88 85 83 82**.

LAMBERHURST *Kent, England*   Once a leading English vineyard, but changed hands in 1995. Very badly hit by frost in 1997, the vineyard is now in administration and its future must be uncertain.

LAMBRUSCO *Emilia-Romagna, Italy* Lambrusco is actually a black grape variety, grown in 4 DOC zones on the plains of Emilia and 1 around Mantova in LOMBARDY, but it is the red and white screwcap bottles labelled as non-DOC Lambrusco that have made the name famous, even though some of them may contain no wine from the Lambrusco grape at all. Originally a dry or semi-sweet fizzy red wine, whose high acidity naturally partnered the rich local food, good dry Lambrusco (especially Lambrusco di Sorbaia and Grasparossa di Castelvetro) is worth trying. However, technology has led to huge quantities of anonymous, sweetened FRIZZANTE wines being let loose on the unsuspecting public. Best producers: Barbolini★, Francesco Bellei★, Casali, Cavicchioli★, Chiarli, Giacobazzi, Vittorio Graziano★, Oreste Lini, Stefano Spezia, Venturini Baldini.

LAMOUREAUX LANDING *Finger Lakes AVA, New York State, USA* Lamoreaux Landing, established in 1990, has rapidly become one of the most important wineries in this top-quality Eastern region. Its Chardonnay★★ is a consistent medal winner at competitions, and the Pinot Noir improves with each vintage. Also look for the Riesling★, Gewürztraminer and a limited-production BLANC DE BLANCS. Best years: (1998) 97 **95**.

LANDWEIN German or Austrian country wine and the equivalent of French VIN DE PAYS. The wine must have a territorial definition and may be chaptalized to give it more body.

CH. LANESSAN ★ *Haut-Médoc AC, Cru Bourgeois, Haut-Médoc, Bordeaux, France* Attractive but occasionally austere Cru Bourgeois from the commune of Cussac-Fort-Médoc. Hardly ever uses new oak barrels, yet often achieves Fifth Growth standard and is never overpriced. Tends to be at its best in top vintages and can easily age for 8–10 years. Second wine: Dom. de Ste-Gemme. Best years: (1998) 96 95 **90 89 88 85 83 82**.

LANGHE DOC *Piedmont, Italy* Important new DOC covering wines from the Langhe hills around Alba. The range of varietals such as Chardonnay, Barbera and Nebbiolo include many former VINO DA TAVOLA blends of the highest order. Best years: (reds) (1998) 97 96 **95 93 90**.

CH. LANGOA-BARTON ★★ *St-Julien AC, 3ème Cru Classé, Haut-Médoc, Bordeaux, France* Owned by the Barton family since the 1820s, Langoa-Barton is usually lighter in style than its ST-JULIEN stablemate LÉOVILLE-BARTON, but it is still an extremely impressive and reasonably priced wine. Drink after 7 or 8 years, although it may keep for 15. Second wine: Lady Langoa. Best years: (1998) 96 95 94 90 89 **88 86 85 83 82 81**.

LANGUEDOC-ROUSSILLON *Midi, France* Traditionally a source of undistinguished cheap wine, this area of southern France, running from Nîmes to the Spanish border and covering the *départements* of the GARD, HÉRAULT, AUDE and Pyrénées-Orientales, is now turning out many exciting reds. Temperature-controlled vinification and a growing sense of regional pride have wrought the transformation, hand in hand with better grape varieties and ambitious producers, from the heights of MAS DE DAUMAS GASSAC to very good local co-ops. The best wines are the reds, particularly those from CORBIÈRES, FAUGÈRES, MINERVOIS and PIC ST-LOUP, and some new-wave Cabernets, Merlots and Syrahs, as well as the more traditional VIN DOUX

NATURELS, such as BANYULS, MAURY and MUSCAT DE RIVESALTES; but we are now seeing exciting whites as well, particularly as new plantings of Chardonnay, Marsanne, Viognier and Sauvignon Blanc mature. See also Aude, Bouches-du-Rhône, Collioure, Costières de Nîmes, Coteaux du Languedoc, Côtes du Roussillon, Côtes du Roussillon-Villages, Côtes de Thau, Côtes de Thongue, Faugères, Fitou, Gard, Haute Vallée de l'Aude, Hérault, Muscat de Frontignan, Muscat de Mireval, Oc, St-Chinian, Vallée du Paradis.

LANSON *Champagne AC, Champagne, France* A mass-market fizz whose brilliant 'Why Not?' advertising campaign did so much to democratize Champagne's image. The non-vintage Black Label is reliable stuff, while the rosé ★ and vintage ★★ wines, especially the de luxe blend called Noble Cuvée ★★, aspire to greater things. New owners Marne & Champagne are the dominant force in own-label cheap Champagne, but fortunately seem determined to make Lanson their quality flagship. Best years: 1993 **90 89 88 85 83 82 79**.

LA ROSA *Cachapoal, Chile* Old family operation rejuvenated by a new winery and the magic hand of Ignacio Recabarren in the La Palma range. The unoaked Chardonnay is pure apricots and figs, and the Merlot★★ one of the best from the Rapel appellation.

CH. LASCOMBES ★ *Margaux AC, 2ème Cru Classé, Haut-Médoc, Bordeaux, France* This important Margaux Second Growth was very inconsistent during the 1970s and early 80s but the early 90s have shown a return to better things. There's still a way to go, though, before we see the best of Lascombes. The Chevalier de Lascombes rosé is rather good. Second wine: Ségonnes. Best years: (1998) 96 95 94 **90 89 88 86 85**.

CH. DE LASTOURS *Corbières AC, Languedoc, France* A large estate in CORBIERES, producing some of the most exciting wines in the MIDI. The top white is Dry de Lastours★, an interesting blend of Muscat, Malvoisie and Grenache Blanc. But the best wines are the reds – particularly the Cuvée Simon Descamps★ and the oaky Cuvée Boisée★. Best years: (reds) 1996 **95 94 93 90 89 88 86 85**.

CH. LATOUR ★★★ *Pauillac AC, 1er Cru Classé, Haut-Médoc, Bordeaux, France* Latour's great reputation is based on powerful, long-lasting classic wines. Throughout the 1950s, 60s and 70s the property stood for consistency and a refusal to compromise in the face of financial pressure. Strangely, however, in the early 80s there was an attempt to make lighter, more fashionable wines with mixed results. The late 80s saw a return to classic Latour, much to my relief. Its reputation for making fine wine in less successful vintages is well deserved. After 30 years in British hands, it is now French-owned. Second wine: les Forts de Latour. Best years: (1998) 97 96 95 94 93 90 89 88 **82 79 78 75 70**.

LOUIS LATOUR *Beaune, Burgundy, France* Controversial merchant almost as well known for his COTEAUX DE L'ARDECHE Chardonnays as for his Burgundies. Latour's white Burgundies are much better than the reds, although the red CORTON-Grancey ★ can be good. Latour's oaky CORTON-CHARLEMAGNE ★★, from his own vineyard, is his top wine, but there is also good CHEVALIER-MONTRACHET ★★, BATARD-MONTRACHET ★★ and le MONTRACHET ★★. Even so, as these are the greatest white vineyards in Burgundy, there really should be a higher rating in there somewhere. Best years: (top whites) 1997 96 95 93 **92 90 89 88 85**.

CH. LATOUR-À-POMEROL★★ *Pomerol AC, Bordeaux, France* Now directed by Christian MOUEIX of PETRUS fame, this property makes luscious wines, with loads of gorgeous fruit, and enough tannin to age well. Best years: (1998) 97 96 95 94 **90 89 88 85 83 82 81 79**.

LATRICIÈRES-CHAMBERTIN AC See Chambertin AC.

LAUREL GLEN *Sonoma Mountain AVA, California, USA* Owner wine-maker Patrick Campbell makes only Cabernet ★★★ at his mountaintop winery. This is rich wine with deep fruit flavours, aging after 6–10 years to a perfumed, complex BORDEAUX style, rare in CALIFORNIA. Second label: Counterpoint. Two other labels, Terra Rosa and Reds, are made from blended wines, with recent vintages from Chile and Argentina. Best years: 1996 95 94 93 92 **91 90 87 86 85**.

LAURENT-PERRIER *Champagne AC, Champagne, France* Large, family-owned CHAMPAGNE house, with wines offering flavour and quality at reasonable prices. Non-vintage★ is now leaner and drier, but the vintage★★ is delicious, and the top wine, Cuvée Grand Siècle★★★, is among the finest Champagnes of all. Also good rosé, as non-vintage★ and Vintage Alexandra Grand Siècle★★. Best years: **1990 88 85 82 79**.

CH. LAVILLE-HAUT-BRION★★★ *Pessac-Léognan AC, Cru Classé de Graves, Bordeaux, France* This is the white wine of the MISSION-HAUT-BRION and is one of the finest white GRAVES, with a price tag to match. The wine is fermented in barrel and needs 10 years' aging or more to reach its savoury but luscious peak. Best years: (1998) 97 96 95 94 93 92 **90 89 88 85 83 82 79 78**.

LAZIO *Italy* Region best known for FRASCATI, Rome's white glugger. There are also various bland whites from Trebbiano and Malvasia, such as EST! EST!! EST!!! DI MONTEFIASCONE, and unmemorable red wine from Cesanese, but the region's best are red table wines based on Cabernet and Merlot from the likes of Castel de Paolis or Paolo di Mauro.

LEASINGHAM *Clare Valley, South Australia* Another wing of the BRL HARDY group, Leasingham is CLARE VALLEY's biggest winery, with a senior and respected position. Once prostituted on 4-litre casks, the Stanley Leasingham name now stands for rich, chocolaty reds laced with coconutty American oak that are better than ever under the hand of Richard Rowe. Bin 56 Cabernet-Malbec★★ and Bin 61 Shiraz★★, once great bargains, are rising in price, while newly minted Classic Clare Shiraz★★ and Cabernet★★ are high-alcohol but overpriced blockbusters. Riesling★★ can be among the area's best; respectable Chardonnay and Semillon-Sauvignon as well.

L'ECOLE NO 41 *Washington State, USA* The velvety and deeply flavoured Merlot★★ from this fine winery is marvellous, and Cabernet★★ runs it a close second. A rich, intense Semillon★ is very good and the Chardonnay★ has now reached a similar level. Best years: (reds) (1998) 97 **96 95**.

LECONFIELD *Coonawarra, South Australia* Ralph Fowler, who re-invented Leconfield in the 1990s with elegant, distinctive lighter-bodied reds, left to do his own thing in late 1998. The Cabernet★ is finely crafted, the Merlot★ is a stunner and peppery Shiraz★ can also hit the heights. Best years: (reds) 1996 **95 94 93 91**.

LEEUWIN ESTATE *Margaret River, Western Australia*
MARGARET RIVER's high-flier, with pricy Chardonnay (at best ★★★) that could well prove to be Australia's nearest thing to le MONTRACHET. The Cabernets have been patchy, but since 1994 at best are ★★, blackcurrant yet with a cool lean edge. Best years: (white) **1995** 94 93 92 91 89 87 86 85 82 80.

DOM. LEFLAIVE *Puligny-Montrachet, Côte de Beaune, Burgundy, France*
The most famous white Burgundy producer of all, with extensive holdings in some of the world's greatest vineyards (BATARD-MONTRACHET, CHEVALIER-MONTRACHET and, since 1990, le MONTRACHET itself). The price of the wines is correspondingly high, but 1986–92 produced a number of disappointing wines. A new winemaking team, led by Anne-Claude Leflaive and including the talented Pierre Morey, and the adoption of biodynamic growing soon turned things around. The top wines here – Pucelles★★, Chevalier-Montrachet★★ and Bâtard-Montrachet★★★ – are consistently delicious. Capable of aging for up to 20 years. Best years: 1997 96 95 94 93 **85 83**.

OLIVIER LEFLAIVE FRÈRES *Puligny-Montrachet, Côte de Beaune, Burgundy, France* Former co-manager of Dom. LEFLAIVE, négociant Olivier Leflaive specializes in crisp, modern white wines from the COTE D'OR and the COTE CHALONNAISE that are good examples of international-standard Chardonnay. The best-value wines are those from lesser ACs – ST-ROMAIN, MONTAGNY★, ST-AUBIN★ and RULLY★ – but the rich, oaky BATARD-MONTRACHET★★ is the star turn of talented winemaker Franck Grux. Best years: 1997 96 **95 93 92 90 89**.

PETER LEHMANN *Barossa Valley, South Australia* Lehmann buys grapes from many BAROSSA smallholders, but we can no longer say he owns no vineyards, as he bought the superb Stonewell plot in 1994, subsequently source of his best Shiraz★★★. The company, public since 1993, makes splendidly juicy reds, old-fashioned but packed with fruit. Also tasty Chardonnay★, lemony Semillon★★ and dry, long-lived Riesling★★ from Eden Valley. Best years: (Stonewell Shiraz) **1994** 93 91 90 89.

LENZ VINEYARDS *Long Island AVA, New York State, USA* Leading LONG ISLAND winery still going from strength to strength. The Merlot★ is elegant and powerful with soft, balanced tannins; dry Gewürztraminer★ is spicy and tasty – a good apéritif. In good vintages the Pinot Noir★ has deep, ripe fruit. Chardonnay★ is mostly excellent and a new Cabernet Franc is appealing. The brut-style sparkling wine★ is hard to find, but well worth the search. Best years: 1998 96 **95**.

JEAN LEÓN *Penedès DO, Catalonia, Spain* Jean León, who died in 1996, established vineyards to supply wine for his Californian restaurant, before selling to TORRES in 1995. The style is Californian; the reds★★ rich and blackcurranty, made from Cabernet Sauvignon with Cabernet Franc and Merlot, the Chardonnay★★ rich, biscuity and pineappley, fermented in oak. Best years: (reds) 1996 **95 92 91 90 87 85 82 79**.

LEONETTI CELLAR *Washington State, USA* The Cabernet★★★ and Merlot★★★ produced here have won praise from many critics, and the tiny production is usually sold out within hours. The wines are immense with concentrated fruit and enough tannin to chew on but not be blasted by; the Sangiovese also impresses. Best years: (1997) 96 95 94 93 **92 91 90 89 88 87**.

CH. LÉOVILLE-BARTON★★★ *St-Julien AC, 2ème Cru Classé, Haut-Médoc, Bordeaux, France* Made by Anthony Barton, whose family has run this ST-JULIEN property since 1821, this excellent claret is a traditionalist's delight. Dark, dry and tannic, the wines are difficult to taste young and therefore often underestimated, but over 10–15 years they achieve a lean yet sensitively proportioned classical beauty rarely equalled in Bordeaux. Moreover, they are extremely fairly priced. Praise be. Best years: (1998) 97 96 95 94 93 90 89 88 **86 85 82 81 78**.

CH. LÉOVILLE-LAS-CASES★★★ *St-Julien AC, 2ème Cru Classé, Haut-Médoc, Bordeaux, France* This is the largest of the 3 Léoville properties and probably now the most exciting of all the ST-JULIEN wines. A direct neighbour of the great LATOUR, there are certain similarities in the wines. Since 1975 Las-Cases has been making wines of startlingly deep, dark concentration. From a good year the wine really needs 15 years of aging and should last happily for up to 30 years. Second wine: Clos du Marquis. Best years: (1998) 97 96 95 94 90 89 88 **86 85 83 82 81 79 78 75**.

CH. LÉOVILLE-POYFERRÉ★★ *St-Julien AC, 2ème Cru Classé, Haut-Médoc, Bordeaux, France* Until comparatively recently, this was the weakest of the 3 Léoville properties. The 1980s saw a marked improvement with a string of excellent wines produced under Didier Cuvelier, who has gradually increased the richness of the wine without wavering from its austere style. Since the 1986 vintage these are approaching the top level and need 8–10 years' aging to blossom. Second wine: Moulin-Riche. Best years: (1998) 97 96 95 94 93 90 89 **86 85 83 82**.

DOMAINE LEROY *Vosne-Romanée, Côte de Nuits, Burgundy, France* In 1988 Lalou Bize-Leroy bought the former Domaine Noëllat in VOSNE-ROMANEE, renaming it Domaine Leroy which should not be confused with her négociant house, Maison LEROY, or the Dom. d'Auvenay, a small estate she owns in St-Romain. Here she produces some fiendishly expensive, though fabulously concentrated, wines with biodynamic methods and almost ludicrously low yields from top vineyards such as CLOS DE VOUGEOT★★, RICHEBOURG★★★ and ROMANEE-ST-VIVANT★★. Best years: (reds) 1997 96 95 93 **92 91** 90 **89 88**.

MAISON LEROY *Auxey-Duresses, Côte de Beaune, Burgundy, France* Négociant tucked away in the back streets of AUXEY-DURESSES, Leroy co-owns Domaine de la ROMANEE-CONTI, though is no longer involved in the distribution of the wines. However, its own cellar contains an extraordinary range of gems, often terrifyingly expensive, dating back to the beginning of the century. Best years: (reds) **1971 59 49 47 45 37**.

LIEBFRAUMILCH *Pfalz, Rheinhessen, Nahe and Rheingau, Germany* A legally designated wine from the PFALZ, RHEINHESSEN, NAHE or the RHEINGAU that must be made of 70% Riesling, Silvaner, Müller-Thurgau or Kerner grapes. Liebfraumilch is sweetish and low in acidity. At best it is a well-constructed wine that appeals to the uninitiated wine drinker. Liebfraumilch was an important factor in introducing millions to wine during the 1980s, but now it has a down-market image. Best producers: Sichel (Blue Nun), Valckenberg (Madonna).

LIGURIA *Italy* Thin coastal strip of north-west Italy, running from the French border at Ventimiglia to the Tuscan border. Best-known wines are the Riviera Ligure di Ponente, CINQUETERRE and Rossese di Dolceacqua DOCs.

LIMOUX AC *Languedoc, France* The first AC in the LANGUEDOC where producers are allowed to use Chardonnay and Chenin Blanc, which must be vinified in oak. Production is dominated by the SIEUR D'ARQUES co-op, whose best wines, Toques et Clochers★, fetch high prices at the annual charity auction.

LINDEMANS *Murray River, Victoria, Australia* Large, historic company now part of Southcorp Wines Pty Ltd. Best wines are old-fashioned HUNTER VALLEY Shiraz★★ (Steven Vineyard), Chardonnay★ and Semillon★★ although quality is not what it was and lags behind the Hunter leaders today. There is a trio of increasingly impressive oaky COONAWARRA red wines: St George Cabernet★★, spicy Limestone Ridge Shiraz-Cabernet★★ and multi-variety Pyrus★★. PADTHAWAY Chardonnay★ is keenly priced, but no longer the fruit-packed flagwaver it once was. The mass-market Bin 65 Chardonnay★ is a benchmark for affordable Australian Chardonnay abroad. Best years: (Hunter Shiraz) **1995 93 91 87 86 83 82 80 79 73 70 65**; (Semillon) **1996 95 93 91 90 89 87 86 80 79 78 75 72 70 68**; (Coonawarra reds) **1994 93 91 90 88 86 85 82**.

LINGENFELDER *Grosskarlbach, Pfalz, Germany* Rainer Lingenfelder's talent is indisputable as is clear from his Spätlese wines from the Scheurebe grape with their aromas of grapefruit, pine and apricots. Good vintages of Spätburgunder can be among Germany's best red wines and there's also good Dornfelder. To top it all is heavenly Riesling, especially Auslese from the Freinsheimer Goldberg site★★★. Dry wines should be drunk during the first 3–4 years, dessert wines benefit from 5 years' cellaring or more. Best years: **1998 97 93 90 89 88**.

JEAN LIONNET *Cornas, Rhône Valley, France* Jean Lionnet produces dense, tannic CORNAS★ in a fairly modern style. The emphasis here is on new oak aging. Because the wines can seem closed when young, it's worth waiting for 6–7 years, especially for his Domaine de Rochepertuis★★. Lionnet also produces impressive COTES DU RHONE★ from his younger Cornas vines, and a little white ST-PERAY★. Best years: (reds) 1997 96 95 94 **91 90 89 88 85 83**.

LIRAC AC *Rhône Valley, France* An excellent but underrated AC between TAVEL and CHATEAUNEUF-DU-PAPE. The reds have the dusty, spicy fruit of Châteauneuf without quite achieving the intensity of the best examples. They age well but are delicious young. The rosé is refreshing with a lovely strawberry fruit and the white can be good – drink them both young before the perfume goes. Best producers: Aquéria★, Assémat, Devoy, la Fermade, la Genestière, Lafond-Roc-Epine★, Maby, la Mordorée★★, Roger Sabon★, St-Roch★, Ségriès★, la Tour. Best years: (1998) 97 **95 94 91 90**.

LISTEL *Golfe de Lion, Languedoc, France* Listel is best known for its Gris de Gris (a rather dull rosé), Brut de Listel, an equally dull fizz, and a sweet grapy concoction called Pétillant de Listel. Its varietal wines, particularly Sauvignon and Cabernet Sauvignon, are much better. Now part of the VAL D'ORBIEU group.

LISTRAC-MÉDOC AC *Haut-Médoc, Bordeaux, France* Set back from the
Gironde and away from the best gravel ridges, Listrac is 1 of the 6
specific ACs within the HAUT-MÉDOC. The wines can be good without ever
being thrilling, and are marked by solid fruit, a slightly coarse tannin and
an earthy flavour. **Best producers:** CLARKE, Ducluzeau, Fonréaud, Fourcas-
Dupré, Fourcas-Hosten, Fourcas-Loubaney, Grand Listrac co-op, Mayne-
Lalande, Saransot-Dupré. **Best years:** (1998) 96 95 **90 89 88 86 85 83**.

LOCOROTONDO DOC *Puglia, Italy* Nutty, crisp, dry white from the
south. Drink young. Neighbouring Martina Franca DOC is essentially
the same. **Best producers:** Borgo Canale, Cardone, Locorotondo co-op,
Torrevento.

LOIRE VALLEY *France* The Loire river cuts right through the heart of
France. The upper reaches are the home of world-famous SANCERRE and
POUILLY-FUMÉ. The region of TOURAINE makes good Sauvignon Blanc and
Gamay, while at VOUVRAY and MONTLOUIS the Chenin Blanc makes some pretty
good fizz and still whites, ranging from sweet to very dry. The Loire's best reds
are made in SAUMUR-CHAMPIGNY, CHINON and BOURGUEIL, mainly from Cabernet
Franc, with ANJOU-VILLAGES improving fast. Anjou is famous for ROSÉ D'ANJOU
but the best wines are white, either sweet from the Layon Valley or very
dry Chenin from SAVENNIÈRES. Near the mouth of the river around Nantes is
MUSCADET. See also Anjou Blanc, Anjou Mousseux, Anjou Rouge, Bonnezeaux,
Cabernet d'Anjou, Cheverny, Côte Roannaise, Coteaux de l'Aubance,
Coteaux du Layon, Crémant de Loire, Gros Plant du Pays Nantais, Haut-
Poitou, Jardin de la France, Menetou-Salon, Muscadet des Coteaux de la
Loire, Muscadet Côtes de Grand Lieu, Muscadet de Sèvre-et-Maine, Pouilly-
sur-Loire, Quarts de Chaume, Quincy, Rosé de Loire, St-Nicolas-de-
Bourgueil, Saumur, Saumur Mousseux, Touraine, Touraine Mousseux.

LOMBARDY *Italy* Lombardy, richest and most populous of Italian regions,
is a larger consumer than producer. The Milanese drink vast quantities
from the OLTREPÒ PAVESE zone, as well as imports from France. Many of the
best grapes go to provide base wine for Italy's thriving SPUMANTE industry.
However, there are some interesting wines in Oltrepò Pavese, VALTELLINA,
LUGANA and high-quality sparkling and still wines in FRANCIACORTA.

DR LOOSEN *Bernkastel, Mosel, Germany* Loosen's estate has portions of
some of the MOSEL's most famous vineyards: Treppchen and Prälat in
ERDEN, Würzgarten in URZIG, Sonnenuhr in WEHLEN, Himmelreich in
GRAACH and Lay in BERNKASTEL. Ernst Loosen took over in 1988 and
since then the wines have gone from strength to strength, with most
wines achieving ★★, and Spätlese and Auslese from Wehlen, Ürzig
and Erden frequently ★★★. One of Germany's foremost protagonists of
organic methods, his simple Riesling is great, year in year out. **Best
years:** (1998) 97 96 95 **94 93 92 90 89 88 85 76**. See also J L Wolf.

LONG ISLAND *New York State, USA* Long Island has 2 AVAs: North
Fork, which has more maritime exposure, and the Hamptons, of jetset
fame. This cool region has a long growing season and concentration
of fruit in the wines can be wonderful in a good year. However,
hurricanes have ruined some vintages. Best grapes are Chardonnay,
Riesling, Merlot and Pinot Noir, with some success also for Cabernets

Franc and Sauvignon. Best producers: Bedell, BRIDGEHAMPTON, Gristina, Hargrave, LENZ, Palmer, Paumanok, PECONIC BAY, Pellegrini, Pindar.

LÓPEZ DE HEREDIA *Rioja DOC, Rioja, Spain* Family-owned RIOJA company, still aging wines in old oak casks. Younger red wines are called Viña Cubillo★, and mature wines Viña Tondonia★ and Viña Bosconia★. Good, oaky whites, especially Viña Gravonia. Best years: (reds) **1994 91 90 89 87 86 85 78 76 73**.

LOS LLANOS *Valdepeñas DO, Castilla-La Mancha, Spain* Huge, scrupulously clean, well-equipped winery in central Spain, renowned for an excellent-value, oak-aged red Señorio de Los Llanos★ in both Reserva and Gran Reserva qualities. Best years: (reds) 1995 **92 87 85 84**.

CH. LOUDENNE *Médoc AC, Cru Bourgeois, Bordeaux, France* This lovely pink château on the banks of the Gironde river has been owned by the English firm Gilbeys since 1875. The wines, both red and white, are gentle in style, but tend to lack excitement. Recent vintages are showing more character. Best years: (1998) 97 96 95 **90 89 88 86**.

LOUISVALE *Stellenbosch WO, South Africa* This property enjoys a climate well suited to Chardonnay; it remains the sole variety on this farm and is produced in 3 guises: a barrel-fermented version★ impresses with buttery, biscuity richness and oak balance; Chavant (lightly oaked) and Chavant (unwooded) complete the line-up. Best among the reds, from bought-in grapes, is dense, spicy, minty Cabernet-Merlot★. Best years: (Chardonnays) **1997** 96 95 94 93.

LOUPIAC AC *Bordeaux, France* A sweet wine area across the Garonne river from BARSAC. The wines are attractively sweet without being gooey. Drink young in general, though they can age. Best producers: Clos Jean★, Cros, Loupiac-Gaudiet, Mazarin, Mémoires, Dom. du Noble, Ricaud, les Roques. Best years: (1998) 97 96 **95 90 89 88 86 85 83**.

CH. LA LOUVIÈRE *Pessac-Léognan AC, Bordeaux, France* The star of PESSAC-LEOGNAN's non-classified estates; its reputation almost entirely due to the presence of André Lurton, who revitalized the property over the last 30 years. The well-structured reds★★ and fresh, Sauvignon-based whites★★ are excellent value for money. Best years: (reds) (1998) 96 95 94 93 **90 89 88 86 85**; (whites) (1998) 97 96 **95 94 93 90 89 88**.

LUGANA DOC *Lombardy, Italy* Medium-bodied white (occasionally sparkling) from the Trebbiano di Lugana grape. Well-structured wines from the better producers can develop excitingly over several years. Best producers: Ca' dei Frati★★, Ottella★, Roveglia★, Visconti★, Zenato★.

LUNA *Napa Valley, California, USA* Led by winemaker John Kongsgaard (ex-NEWTON), Luna has been attracting attention recently with its ambitious SUPER-TUSCAN-style Sangiovese★, stylish Pinot Grigio and attractive Merlot. Best years: (reds) (1998) 97 **96**.

PIERRE LUNEAU *Muscadet de Sèvre-et-Maine AC and Muscadet des Coteaux de la Loire AC, Loire Valley, France* Meticulous Muscadet producer who specializes in unoaked Muscadets for the long haul – his top wine, le 'L' d'Or★, ages brilliantly – but his oak-fermented wines, although interesting, are variable. Best years: ('L' d'Or) **1997** 96 95 90.

LUNGAROTTI *Torgiano DOC, Umbria, Italy* Leading producer of TORGIANO. Also makes fine red San Giorgio★★ (Cabernet-Sangiovese), white Torgiano, Chardonnays Miralduolo and Palazzi★, and even a good sherry-style Solleone. His Torgiano Riserva Rubesco★★ is now DOCG.

LUSSAC-ST-ÉMILION AC *Bordeaux, France* Much of the wine from this AC, which tastes like a lighter ST-EMILION, is made by the first-rate local co-op and should be drunk within 4 years of the vintage; certain properties are worth seeking out. Best producers: Barbe-Blanche, Bel-Air, Courlat, Croix-de-Rambeau, la Grenière, Haut-Milon, Lyonnat, Vieux-Ch.-Chambeau, Villadière. Best years: (1998) 96 **95 90 89 88**.

EMILIO LUSTAU *Jerez y Manzanilla DO, Andalucía, Spain* Specializes in supplying 'own-label' wines to supermarkets. Quality is generally good, and there are some real stars at the top, especially the Almacenista range★★, very individual sherries from small, private producers.

CH. LYNCH-BAGES *Pauillac AC, 5ème Cru Classé, Haut-Médoc, Bordeaux, France* I am a great fan of Lynch-Bages red★★★ – with its almost succulent richness, its gentle texture and its starburst of flavours, all butter, blackcurrants and mint, and it is now one of PAUILLAC's most popular wines. Because of its Fifth Growth status, it was inclined to be underpriced; I couldn't say that now, but it's still excellent value. It is impressive at 5 years, beautiful at 10 years and irresistible at 20. Second wine: Haut-Bages-Avérous. White wine: Blanc de Lynch-Bages★. Best years: (reds) (1998) 97 96 95 94 90 89 **88 86 85 83 82 81**.

MÂCON AC *Mâconnais, Burgundy, France* The basic Mâconnais AC, but most whites in the region are labelled under the superior MACON-VILLAGES AC. The wines are rarely exciting. Chardonnay-based Mâcon-Blanc, especially, is a rather expensive basic quaffer. Drink young. Mâcon Supérieur has a slightly higher minimum alcohol level. Best producers: Bertillonnes, Bruyère, DUBOEUF. Best years: **1997 96 95**.

MÂCON-VILLAGES AC *Mâconnais, Burgundy, France* Mâcon-Villages should be an enjoyable, fruity, fresh wine for everyday drinking at a fair price, but because it comes from Chardonnay, the wines are often overpriced. Forty-three villages in the region can call their wine Mâcon-Villages or add their own name, as in Mâcon-Viré. Co-ops dominate production. Best villages: Chaintré, Chardonnay, Charnay, Clessé, Davayé, Igé, Lugny, Prissé, la Roche Vineuse, St-Gengoux-de-Scissé, Uchizy, Viré. Best producers: Barraud★★, A Bonhomme★★, Denogent★★, Deux Roches★, la Greffière★★, J-J Litaud★, Manciat-Poncet★, O Merlin★★, Roally★, Saumaize★, J Thévenet★★, Valette★★, VERGET★, J-J Vincent★. Best years: 1997 96 **95 94 93**.

MACULAN *Breganze DOC, Veneto, Italy* Fausto Maculan makes an impressive range of BREGANZE DOC led by Cabernet Fratta★★ and Palazzotto★, along with excellent non-DOC reds★★ and whites★★ from the Ferrata vineyards, but his most impressive wines are sweet Torcolato★★ and outstanding Acininobili★★★ made from botrytized Vespaiola, Garganega and Tocai grapes.

MADEIRA DOC *Madeira, Portugal* The subtropical island of Madeira seems an unlikely place to find a serious wine. However, Madeiras are very serious indeed and the best can survive to a great age. Internationally famous by the 17th century, modern Madeira was shaped by the phylloxera epidemic 100 years ago, which wiped out the vineyards. Replantation was with hybrid vines inferior to the 'noble' and traditional Malvasia (or Malmsey), Boal (or Bual), Verdelho and Sercial varieties. There are incentives to replant with noble grapes, but progress is slow (having now crept up to 15% of total plantage). The

181

typically burnt, tangy taste of inexpensive Madeira comes from the process of heating in huge vats. The better wines are aged naturally in the subtropical warmth. All the wines are fortified early on and may be sweetened with fortified grape juice before bottling. Basic 3-year-old Madeira is made mainly from Tinta Negra Mole, whereas higher-quality 5-year-old (Reserva), 10-year-old (Reserva Velha), 15-year-old (Extra Reserva) and vintage wines (from a single year, aged in cask for at least 20 years) tend to be made from 1 of the 4 'noble' grapes. Under European labelling restrictions any wine with a varietal designation must be made from at least 85% of the grape stated on the label. The best Madeira can survive to a great age but it's a rare beast in modern times. Best producers: Barbeito, Barros e Souza, H M Borges, Henriques & Henriques, MADEIRA WINE COMPANY, d'Oliveira, Pereira.

MADEIRA WINE COMPANY *Madeira DOC, Madeira, Portugal* This company ships more than half of all Madeira exported in bottle. Among the brand names are Blandy's, Cossart Gordon, Leacock and Rutherford & Miles. Now controlled by the Symington family from the mainland. Big improvements are taking place especially at the 5-year-old level.

MADIRAN AC *South-West France* In the gentle hills of Vic-Bilh, north of Pau, there has been a steady revival of the Madiran AC as viticulturalists have gradually discovered ways to propagate the difficult Tannat vine successfully. Several of the best producers are now using new oak, and this certainly helps to soften the rather aggressive wine. Best producers: Aydie★★, Barréjat, Berthoumieu, Bouscassé★★, Capmartin★, la Chapelle-Lenclos★★, Caves de Crouseilles, Laffitte-Teston★, MONTUS★★, Mouréou★, Union des Producteurs PLAIMONT. Best years: 1996 95 **94 93 92 90 89 88 85**.

CH. MAGDELAINE★ *St-Émilion Grand Cru AC, 1er Grand Cru Classé, Bordeaux, France* Owned by the quality-conscious company of MOUEIX, these are dark, rich, aggressive wines, yet with a load of luscious fruit and oaky spice. In lighter years the wine has a gushing, easy, tender fruit and can be enjoyed at 5–10 years. Best years: (1998) 97 95 94 **90 89 88 86 85 83 82 75**.

MAIPO VALLEY *Chile* Birthplace of the Chilean wine industry and closest winemaking region to the capital city of Santiago. Cabernet is king in this valley and most of Chile's premium-priced reds come from here. Good Chardonnay is produced from vineyards close to the Andes. Best producers: CARMEN★★, CONCHA Y TORO★★, SANTA RITA★.

MÁLAGA DO *Andalucía, Spain* Málaga is a curious blend of sweet wine, alcohol and juices (some boiled up and concentrated, some fortified, some made from dried grapes) and production is dwindling. The label generally states colour and sweetness. The best Málagas are intensely nutty, raisiny and caramelly. The traditional, much-admired Scholtz Hermanos ceased operations in 1996. Best producer: Larios.

CH. MALARTIC-LAGRAVIÈRE *Pessac-Léognan AC, Cru Classé de Graves, Bordeaux, France* A change of ownership in 1997 and massive investment in the vineyard and cellars should lead to improvements at this underperforming GRAVES Classed Growth. The tiny amount of white★ is made from 100% Sauvignon Blanc and usually softens after 3–4 years into a lovely nutty wine. Best years: (reds) (1998) 97 96 95 **93 89 88 85 83 82**; (whites) (1998) 97 **95**.

MALBEC A red grape, rich in tannin and flavour, from South-West France. A major ingredient in CAHORS wines, it is also known as Cot or Auxerrois. Also important in Argentina and Chile where it produces ripe, peppery, approachable reds. In CALIFORNIA, it plays a minor supporting role in red meritage blends. Further plantings exist in Australia and South Africa.

MALVASIA This grape is widely planted in Italy and is found there in many guises, both white and red. In Friuli, it is known as the Malvasia Istriana and produces tight, fragrant wines of great charm, while in TUSCANY, UMBRIA and the rest of central Italy, it is used to improve the blend for wines like ORVIETO and FRASCATI. On the islands, Malvasia is used in the production of rich, dry or sweet wines in Bosa and Cagliari (in SARDINIA) and in Lipari off the coast of SICILY to make really tasty, apricoty sweet wines. As a black grape, Malvasia Nera is blended with Negroamaro in southern PUGLIA, while in PIEDMONT a paler-skinned relation produces frothing light reds in Castelnuovo Don Bosco, just outside Turin. Variants of Malvasia also grow in Spain and mainland Portugal. On the island of MADEIRA it produces sweet, varietal fortified wine, often known by its English name: Malmsey.

LA MANCHA DO *Castilla-La Mancha, Spain* Spain's vast central plateau is Europe's biggest delimited wine area. Whites are never exciting (the dominant Airén grape has little character) but nowadays are often fresh and attractive. Reds, from Cencibel (Tempranillo), and without the traditional addition of white grapes, can be light and fruity, or richer, sometimes with a dash of Cabernet Sauvignon. New DO regulations in 1995 allow for much-needed irrigation and the planting of new grape varieties, including Viura, Chardonnay, Syrah, Cabernet Sauvignon, Petit Verdot and Merlot. There is still much rough, old-style wine, but progress is fast. Best producers: Fermín Ayuso Roig (Viña Q Estola), Vinícola de Castilla (Castillo de Alhambra, Señorío de Guadianeja★), Nuestra Señora de la Cabeza co-op (Casa Gualda), Nuestra Señora de Manjavacas co-op, Rodriguez y Berger (Viña Santa Elena★), Julian Santos Aguado (Don Fadrique), Torres Filoso (Arboles de Castillejo★), Casa de la Viña.

MANZANILLA See Jerez y Manzanilla DO.

MARANGES AC *Côte de Beaune, Burgundy, France* AC created in 1989 to cover the Cheilly, Dezize and Sampigny ACs in the southern CÔTE DE BEAUNE. Attractive light wines, though many growers still sell them as CÔTE DE BEAUNE-VILLAGES. Best producers: Bernard Bachelet, Maurice Charleux, Contat-Grange, DROUHIN. Best years: (reds) 1997 96 **95 93 90**.

MARCHE *Italy* Adriatic region producing good white VERDICCHIO and reds from Montepulciano and Sangiovese led by ROSSO CONERO and ROSSO PICENO.

MARCILLAC AC *South-West France* Strong, dry red wines (there is a little rosé), largely made from the local grape Fer. The reds are rustic but full of fruit and should be drunk between 2 and 5 years. Best producers: Marcillac-Vallon co-op, Philippe Teulier.

MARGARET RIVER *Western Australia* First Australian region planted on the advice of scientists in the late 1960s. Quickly established its name as a leading area for Cabernet, with marvellously deep, BORDEAUX-like structured reds. Now Chardonnay, concentrated and opulent, is arguably the star turn, but there is also fine grassy Semillon, tropical Sauvignon and spicy Verdelho. Best producers: CAPE MENTELLE★★★, Chateau Xanadu, CULLEN★★★, EVANS & TATE★, LEEUWIN ESTATE★★★ (Chardonnay), MOSS WOOD★★ (Cabernet★★★), PIERRO★★ (Chardonnay), VASSE FELIX★.

MARGAUX AC *Haut-Médoc, Bordeaux, France*   AC centred on the village of Margaux but including Soussans and Cantenac, Labarde and Arsac in the south. The gravel banks dotted through the vineyards mean that the wines are rarely heavy and should have a divine perfume when mature at 7–12 years. Best producers: (Classed Growths) BRANE-CANTENAC★, Dauzac★, FERRIERE★★, GISCOURS★, ISSAN★, Kirwan★, LASCOMBES★, MARGAUX★★★, PALMER★★, PRIEURÉ-LICHINE★, RAUZAN-SEGLA★★, TERTRE★; (others) ANGLUDET★, Bel-Air Marquis d'Aligre★, la Gurgue★, Labégorce-Zédé★, Monbrison★, SIRAN★. Best years: (1998) 96 95 94 90 89 **88 86 85 83 82**.

CH. MARGAUX★★★ *Margaux AC, 1er Cru Classé, Haut-Médoc, Bordeaux, France*   The greatest wine in the MEDOC. Has produced almost flawless wines since 1978, as great as any MARGAUX ever made. Inspired winemaker Paul Pontallier continues to produce the best from this great terroir. There is also some delicious white, Pavillon Blanc★, made from Sauvignon Blanc, but it must be the most expensive wine sold under the BORDEAUX AC label by a mile. Second wine: (red) Pavillon Rouge. Best years: (reds) (1998) 97 96 95 94 93 90 89 88 86 **85 83 82 81 80 79 78**; (whites) (1998) 97 96 **95 94 90 89 88 85**.

MARLBOROUGH *South Island, New Zealand*   Marlborough has enjoyed such spectacular success as a quality wine region that it is difficult to imagine that the first vines were planted as recently as 1973. Long, cool and relatively dry ripening and free-draining stony soils are the major assets. Its snappy, aromatic Sauvignon Blanc first brought the region fame worldwide. Fine-flavoured Chardonnay, steely Riesling, elegant Champagne-method fizz and luscious botrytized wines are the other successes. Best producers: CELLIER LE BRUN, CLOUDY BAY★★, CORBANS★ (Stoneleigh), DELEGAT'S (Oyster Bay★), Fromm, GROVE MILL★, HUNTER'S★, JACKSON ESTATE★, Lawson's Dry Hills★, MONTANA, NAUTILUS★★, Allan Scott★, Seresin★, VAVASOUR★★, Wairau River, Whitehaven, Wither Hills. See also Goldwater.

MARNE ET CHAMPAGNE *Champagne AC, Champagne, France*   Family firm, the second-largest producer in CHAMPAGNE, selling over 20 million bottles, mainly for supermarkets, under dozens of different labels. The best known is Alfred Rothschild, which is the second-biggest-selling Champagne in France. The company bought the house of LANSON in 1991.

MARQUÉS DE CÁCERES *Rioja DOC, Rioja, Spain*   Go-ahead RIOJA winery making crisp, aromatic, modern whites★ and rosés★, and fleshy, fruity reds★ with the emphasis on aging in bottle, not barrel. Best years: (reds) 1996 **95 94 92 91 90 89 87 85 82 78**.

MARQUÉS DE GRIÑÓN *Rioja DOC, Rioja and Rueda DO, Castilla y León, Spain*   From his home, non-DO estate at Malpica, near Toledo and

Madrid, Carlos Falcó (the eponymous Marqués de Griñón) has expanded into RUEDA and now into RIOJA, after selling a stake in his company to BERBERANA and forming a partnership with the giant concern. Minty Cabernet de Valdepusa★★ and Durius red★ (blended from TORO and RIBERA DEL DUERO) have been joined by a barrel-fermented Chardonnay, a Petit Verdot★★ and a Syrah★ from his own estate, 2 Marqués de Griñón red Riojas (a lightly oaked young wine★ and a Reserva★), and white non-DO Durius. Best years: (reds) **1995 94 92 91 90 89 86.**

MARQUÉS DE MONISTROL *Cava DO and Penedès DO, Catalonia, Spain* The Arco group (led by BERBERANA) now owns this winery. The young Brut Selección★ is the freshest and fruitiest CAVA. The still whites, BLANC DE BLANCS★ and Blanc en Noirs★, are good; the reds, long unexceptional, have gained from the introduction of a young Merlot. Drink the youngest available.

MARQUÉS DE MURRIETA *Rioja DOC, Rioja, Spain* The RIOJA bodega that most faithfully preserves the traditional style of long aging. Ultra-conservative, yet sporting glistening new fermentation vats and a Californian bottling line. The latest move has been to release more wines under their splendidly ornate Castillo de Ygay★★ label. No longer do these wait 20 years for release. A new, more modern-styled, up-market cuvée was introduced in 1999: Dalmau★★. Whites are dauntingly oaky, reds packed with savoury, mulberry fruit. Best years: (reds) **1995 94 92 91 89 87 85 68 64**; (whites) **1992 91 86 85 78.**

MARQUÉS DE RISCAL *Rioja DOC, País Vasco, and Rueda DO, Castilla y León, Spain* When the families who own RIOJA's oldest bodega recaptured control of management in 1988 they installed one of their own as cellar master: Francisco Hurtado de Amézaga, who had been behind the huge success of Riscal's RUEDA winery. Old musty vats were promptly cleared out, and the classic pungent reds★★ reappeared. The expensive, Cabernet-based Barón de Chirel cuvée is an important addition. In Rueda, the consultancy of Hugh Ryman has translated into increasingly aromatic whites★. Best years: (reds) **1992 91 90 89.**

MARSALA DOC *Sicily, Italy* Fortified wines, once as esteemed as sherry or Madeira. A taste of an old Vergine (unsweetened) Marsala, fine and complex, will show why. Today most is sweetened. Purists say this mars its delicate nuances, but DOC regulations allow for sweetening Fine and Superiore versions. Best producers: (Vergine) Florio★, Pellegrino★; also DE BARTOLI (Vecchio Samperi★★, Il Marsala Superiore★).

MARSANNAY AC *Côte de Nuits, Burgundy, France* Village almost in Dijon, best known for its rosé, pleasant but a little too austere and dry. The red is rapidly proving itself as one of Burgundy's most fragrant wines. There is little white but it is dry and nutty and good. Best producers: R Bouvier, P Charlopin, CLAIR★, B Coillot, Fougeray, A Guyard, JADOT, LABOURE-ROI★, J & J-L Trapet. Best years: (reds) 1996 **95 93 90.**

MARSANNE Undervalued grape yielding rich, nutty wines in the northern Rhône (HERMITAGE, CROZES-HERMITAGE, ST-JOSEPH and ST-PERAY), often with the more lively Roussanne. Also planted in Switzerland, and performs well in Australia at CHATEAU TAHBILK★★ and MITCHELTON★★.

MARTINBOROUGH VINEYARD *Wairarapa, North Island, New Zealand*
Since 1986 many of the country's best Pinot Noirs come from here, although they now have many challengers. Winemaker Larry McKenna's heart may be in Pinot Noir★★ (Reserve★★★) but he also makes impressive Chardonnay★★, strong spicy Riesling★, and luscious botrytized styles★★ when vintage conditions allow. 1999 will be McKenna's last vintage – he is leaving to start another winery in the region. Best years: (1998) **97 96 94 91 90 89**.

MARTÍNEZ BUJANDA *Rioja DOC, País Vasco, Spain* Family-owned firm that makes some of the best 'modern' RIOJAS. Whites and rosés are young and crisp, reds★ are full of fruit *and* age well. The single-vineyard Valpiedra★★ is a major newcomer. Best years: (reds) (1996) **95 94 92 91 90 87 86 85**.

LOUIS M MARTINI *Napa Valley, California, USA* During the 1980s the wines from this well-respected NAPA winery changed from being deep and rich to relatively light, though pleasant and cheap. Recently it has returned to a more concentrated style based on single vineyards and a range of Reserve wines, so far with mixed results. The Monte Rosso Zinfandel and Cabernet Sauvignon★ can be very good, the Chardonnays are coming along nicely and the Merlot shows most improvement. Best years: (reds) 1997 96 **95 94 91**.

MARZEMINO This red grape of northern Italy's TRENTINO province makes deep-coloured, plummy and zesty reds that are best drunk within 3–5 years. Best producers: Battistotti★, Bossi Fedrigotti, Casata Monfort, La Cadalora★, Cavit★, Concilio Vini★, Isera co-op★, Letrari★, Mezzacorona, Simoncelli★, Spagnolli★, De Tarczal★, Vallarom★, Vallis Agri★.

MAS DE DAUMAS GASSAC *Vin de Pays de l'Hérault, Languedoc, France*
Ebullient Aimé Guibert is the longest established quality producer in the Languedoc, proving that the HERAULT, normally associated with cheap table wine, is capable of producing great red wines that can age in bottle. The Daumas Gassac rosé is dull; however, the tannic yet rich Cabernet Sauvignon-based red★★ and the fabulously scented white★★ (Viognier, Muscat, Chardonnay and Petit Manseng) are brilliant, if expensive. Best years: (reds) 1996 95 94 93 **92 91 90 89 88 87 85**.

MAS JULLIEN *Coteaux du Languedoc AC, Languedoc, France* Olivier Jullien makes superb wines from traditional MIDI varieties, with such success that bottles have to be rationed. Reds include les Cailloutis★ and les Depierre★★. White les Vignes Oubliées★ (Terret Bouret, Carignan and Grenache) is memorable. Also late-harvest Clairette Beaudille. Best years: (reds) **1996 95 94 93 91**.

BARTOLO MASCARELLO *Barolo DOCG, Piedmont, Italy* One of the great old-fashioned producers of BAROLO★★★, yet the wines have an exquisite perfume and balance. The Dolcetto★★ and Freisa★ are good. Best years: (Barolo) 1993 90 89 **88 86 85 82 79 78**.

GIUSEPPE MASCARELLO *Barolo DOCG, Piedmont, Italy* The old house of Giuseppe Mascarello (now run by grandson Mauro) is renowned for dense, vibrant Dolcetto d'Alba (Bricco★★) and intense Barbera★, but the pride of the house is BAROLO from the Monprivato★★★ vineyard. Best years: (Monprivato) 1996 95 **93** 91 90 89 **88 85 82 78 74**.

MASI *Veneto, Italy* Family firm, one of the driving forces in VALPOLICELLA★ and SOAVE★. Campo Fiorin★, a Ripasso Valpolicella, is worth looking out for, as is AMARONE from the Mazzano★★ vineyard. The oaky Toar is a blend of Corvina and other native varieties. The wines of Serègo Alighieri★★ are also produced by Masi.

MASTROBERARDINO *Campania, Italy* This family firm has long flown the flag for southern Italy, though it has now been joined by others. Best known for red TAURASI★ and white Greco di Tufo★ and Fiano di Avellino★. Best years: (Taurasi Radici) 1993 92 90 **89 88 86 85 83 82 81 79**.

MATANZAS CREEK *Sonoma Valley AVA, California, USA* Sauvignon Blanc★★ is taken very seriously here, and the results show in a complex, pleasing wine; Chardonnay★★ is rich and toasty but not overblown. Limited-edition Chardonnay and Merlot under the Journey label are opulent but pricy and controversial. In recent years, Merlot★★ has established a high reputation, with a silky richness that fills the mouth with ripe flavour. Best years: (Chardonnay) **1997 96 95 94 93 92 91 90**; (Merlot) 1996 **95** 94 **93 92 91 90** 88.

MATUA VALLEY *Waimauku, Auckland, North Island, New Zealand* A mid-sized family company producing a wide range of often adventurous and usually good-value wines from 4 regions. Best wines include the sensuous, scented Ararimu Chardonnay★★, lush and strongly varietal Gewürztraminer, a creamy oak-aged Sauvignon Blanc★★, tangy MARLBOROUGH Shingle Peak Sauvignon Blanc★★, fine Merlot★ and thrilling Ararimu Cabernet Sauvignon★★. Best years: (reds) (1998) **96** 94.

CH. MAUCAILLOU *Moulis AC, Cru Bourgeois, Haut-Médoc, Bordeaux, France* Maucaillou shows that you don't have to be a Classed Growth to make high-quality claret. Expertly made by the Dourthe family, it is soft but classically flavoured. It matures quickly but ages well for 10–12 years. Best years: (1998) 96 95 **90 89 88 86 85 83 82 81**.

MAURY AC *Roussillon, France* A VIN DOUX NATUREL made mainly from Grenache Noir. This strong, sweetish wine can be made in either a young, fresh style or the locally revered old RANCIO style. Best producers: Mas Amiel★★, la Coume du Roy★, Maury co-op★, Maurydoré★, la Pleiade★.

MAXIMIN GRÜNHAUS *Grünhaus, Ruwer, Germany* The best estate in the Ruwer valley and one of Germany's greatest. Carl von Schubert vinifies separately the wines of his 3 vineyards under sole ownership (Abtsberg, Bruderberg and Herrenberg), making chiefly dry and medium-dry wines of great subtlety and distinction. In good vintages the wines are easily ★★★ and the Auslese will age for decades. Best years: (1998) 97 96 95 **94 93 92 90 89 88 85 83 79 76 75 71**.

MAZIS-CHAMBERTIN AC See Chambertin AC.

MAZOYÈRES-CHAMBERTIN AC See Chambertin AC.

McLAREN VALE *South Australia* Sunny maritime region just south of Adelaide, with about 45 small wineries, plus big boys HARDY and SEAVIEW. Once a 'port' area, nowadays it produces full-bodied wines from Chardonnay, Sauvignon Blanc, Shiraz, Grenache and Cabernet. Best producers: CHAPEL HILL★★, Coriole, D'ARENBERG★★, Fox Creek, Andrew Garrett, HARDY★★, Ingoldby, Maxwell, Geoff MERRILL★, REYNELL★★, ROSEMOUNT★★, SEAVIEW★, Tatachilla, WIRRA WIRRA★★.

McWILLIAMS *Riverina, New South Wales, Australia* Large family winery whose best wines are the Mount Pleasant range from the Lower HUNTER VALLEY: classic bottle-aged Semillons, including Elizabeth★★★ and Lovedale★★, buttery Chardonnays★★ and special-vineyard Shirazes★ – Old Paddock, Old Hill and Rose Hill. Also classy liqueur Muscat★★ and 'sherries'★ from RIVERINA, and exciting table wines from Barwang★ vineyard near HILLTOPS. Best years: (Hunter Semillon) 1997 96 **95 93 91 87 86 84 82 80 79**.

MÉDOC AC *Bordeaux, France* The Médoc peninsula north of Bordeaux on the left bank of the Gironde river produces a good fistful of the world's most famous reds. These are all situated in the HAUT-MEDOC, the southern, more gravelly half of the area. The Médoc AC, for reds only, covers the northern part. Here, in these flat clay vineyards, the Merlot grape dominates. The wines can be attractive, dry but juicy and most are best to drink at 3–5 years old. Best producers: la Cardonne, les Grands Chênes, Greysac, Lacombe-Noaillac, Lafon, Lestage-Simon, LOUDENNE, les Ormes-Sorbet, Patache d'Aux, Plagnac, POTENSAC★, Rollan-de-By, la Tour-de-By★, la Tour-Haut-Caussan★, la Tour-St-Bonnet, Vieux-Robin. Best years: (1998) 96 95 **94 90 89 88 86 85 83 82 81**.

MEERLUST *Stellenbosch WO, South Africa* Current owner Hannes Myburgh maintains his late father's faith in the Bordeaux varieties: his complex Rubicon★★ was one of the Cape's first Bordeaux blends. Italian cellarmaster Giorgio Dalla Cia's passion is Merlot★; refined with good aging potential. Chardonnay★★ is made in an impressive full, toasty style. Best years: (Rubicon) **1995 94 93 91**; (Chardonnay) **1997 96 95**.

MENDOCINO COUNTY *California, USA* The northernmost county of the North Coast AVA. The best growing areas are Anderson Valley AVA, a cool east–west valley opening up to the Pacific Ocean and an excellent area for sparkling wines and the occasional Pinot Noir; and Redwood Valley AVA, a warmer area with good results from Zinfandel and Cabernet. Best producers: FETZER, HANDLEY CELLARS★★, Hidden Cellars, Jepson, Lazy Creek★, McDowell Valley★, Navarro★★, PACIFIC ECHO★, Parducci, Pepperwood Springs, ROEDERER★★.

MENDOZA *Argentina* The most important wine region in Argentina, accounting for about 90% of fine wine production. Situated in the eastern foothills of the Andes on a similar latitude to Chile's Santiago, the region's bone-dry continental climate produces powerful, high-alcohol red wines. High-altitude sub-regions like Tupungato are now producing better whites, particularly Chardonnay. Further from the mountains, the sub-regions of Maipú and Luján are proving ideal for Malbec, Syrah and Cabernet. Best producers: CATENA★, La Agricola, NORTON★.

MENETOU-SALON AC *Loire Valley, France* Extremely attractive, chalky-clean Sauvignon white wines and cherry-fresh Pinot Noir reds and rosés from west of SANCERRE. Best producers: Chatenoy★, Chavet★, J-P Gilbert★, H Pellé★, J-M Roger★, J Teiller★. Best years: (1998) **97 96 95**.

MÉO-CAMUZET *Vosne-Romanée, Côte de Nuits, Burgundy, France* Super-quality estate, thanks in no small measure to the advice of Henri JAYER, a third of whose property it gained in 1988. The style is heavily influenced by Jayer – new oak barrels and luscious, rich fruit combining to produce superb wines, which also age well. The CORTON★★★ and CLOS DE VOUGEOT★★★ are the top wines here, but don't miss the VOSNE-ROMANEE Premiers Crus, aux Brulées★★, Cros Parantoux★★★ and les Chaumes★★. Best years: 1997 96 95 93 **92 90 89 88**.

MERCUREY AC *Côte Chalonnaise, Burgundy, France* Most important of the 4 main COTE CHALONNAISE villages. The red is usually pleasant and strawberry-flavoured, sometimes rustic, and can take some aging. There is not much white but I like its buttery, even spicy taste. It is best drunk at 3–4 years old. Best producers: (reds) Chanzy, FAIVELEY★, E Juillot★, M Juillot★★, Meix-Foulot★, RODET★, H & Y de Suremain★, E Voarick; (whites) FAIVELEY (Clos Rochette)★, Genot-Boulanger★, M Juillot★, Olivier LEFLAIVE, RODET (Chamirey★). Best years: (reds) 1996 95 **93 90**.

MERLOT See pages 190–1.

GEOFF MERRILL *McLaren Vale, South Australia* A high-profile winemaker who combines an instinctive feel for wine with canny marketing ability. Under the Geoff Merrill brand he fields nicely bottle-aged Cabernet, a light early-picked style which seems slightly eccentric these days, plus a Chardonnay★ (Reserve is ★★). The cheaper Mount Hurtle brand has a moreish Grenache rosé★ and a surprisingly zippy Sauvignon Blanc★.

MERRYVALE *Napa Valley, California, USA* Late-blooming winery is now a Chardonnay powerhouse with its Reserve★★, Silhouette★★ and Starmont★. Reds are not far behind, with fine BORDEAUX-blend Profile★★ and juicy Merlot★. Best years: (Chardonnay) 1997 96 95 **94**.

LOUIS MÉTAIREAU *Muscadet de Sèvre-et-Maine AC, Loire Valley, France* Classic Muscadets with considerable intensity, due to low yields and careful winemaking. Styles range from lighter Petit Mouton to concentrated Cuvée LM★ and Cuvée One★.

MEURSAULT AC *Côte de Beaune, Burgundy, France* The biggest and most popular white wine village in the COTE D'OR. There are no Grands Crus, but a whole cluster of Premiers Crus. The general standard of wine is variable due to the worldwide demand. The deep-golden wine is lovely to drink young but better aged for 5–8 years. Virtually no Meursault red is now made. Best producers: R Ampeau★, Michel Bouzereau★, Boyer-Martenot★, COCHE-DURY★★★, DROUHIN, J-P Fichet★★, Grivault★★, JADOT, P Javillier★★, Charles & Rémi Jobard, François Jobard★★, LAFON★★★, Dom. Matrot★★, Michelot-Buisson★, Pierre Morey★★, Potinet-Ampeau★, J Prieur★, G Roulot★★. Best years: 1996 95 94 93 **92 90 89**.

CH. MEYNEY★ *St-Estèphe AC, Cru Bourgeois, Haut-Médoc, Bordeaux, France* One of the most reliable ST-ESTEPHES, producing broad-flavoured wine with dark, plummy fruit. Second wine: Prieur de Meyney. Best years: (1998) 95 94 **90 89 88 86 85 83 82 81 78 75**.

PETER MICHAEL WINERY *Knights Valley AVA, California, USA* British-born Sir Peter Michael caught the wine bug and turned a country retreat into an impressive winery known for its small batch wines with fanciful names. Les Pavots★ is the estate BORDEAUX blend, and Mon Plaisir★ and Cuvée Indigne are his top Chardonnays, both noted for their deep, layered flavours. Best years: (Chardonnay) 1998 97 **95 94 92**.

MERLOT

Red wine without tears. That's the reason Merlot has vaulted from being merely Bordeaux's red wine support act, well behind Cabernet Sauvignon in terms of class, to being the darling of the 1990s, planted like fury all over the world. It is able to claim some seriousness and pedigree, but – crucially – can make wine of a fat, juicy character mercifully low in tannic bitterness, which can be glugged with gay abandon almost as soon as the juice has squirted from the press. Yet this doesn't mean that Merlot is the jelly baby of red wine grapes. Far from it.

WINE STYLES

Bordeaux Merlot The great wines of Pomerol and St-Émilion are largely based on Merlot and the best of these can mature for 20–30 years. In fact there is more Merlot than Cabernet Sauvignon planted in Bordeaux, and I doubt if there is a single red wine property that does not have some growing, because the variety ripens early, can cope with cool conditions and is able to bear a heavy crop of fruit. In a cool, damp area like Bordeaux Cabernet Sauvignon cannot always ripen, so the soft, mellow character of Merlot is a fundamental component of the blend even in the best Médoc estates.

Other European Merlots The south of France has briskly adopted the variety, but in the hot Languedoc the grape often ripens too fast to express its full personality and can seem a little simple and even raw-edged. Italy has long used very high-crop Merlot to produce a simple, light quaffer in the north, particularly in the Veneto, though Friuli and Alto Adige make fuller styles and there are some impressive Tuscan examples. The Italian-speaking Swiss canton of Ticino is often unjustly overlooked for concentrated, oak-aged versions. Eastern Europe should provide fertile pastures for Merlot and so far the most convincing, albeit simple, styles have come from Hungary and Bulgaria, although the younger examples are almost invariably better than the old. The improvement in Merlots has been one of the most striking developments in Spain in the mid-1990s.

New World Merlots Youth is also important in the New World, nowhere more so than in Chile. Chilean Merlot has leapt to the front of the pack of New World examples with gorgeous garnet-red wines of unbelievable crunchy fruit richness that cry out to be drunk virtually in their infancy. California Merlots often have more serious pretensions, but the nature of the grape is such that its soft, juicy quality still shines through. The cooler conditions in Washington State have produced some thrilling wines, and even the east coast of the US has produced good examples from places such as Long Island. With some French input, South Africa is starting to get Merlot right, and in New Zealand, despite the cool, damp conditions, some gorgeous rich examples have been made. Only Australia seems to find Merlot problematic – but there's so much other ripe fruit in Australian reds that maybe Merlot isn't a necessity there.

190

BEST PRODUCERS

France

Bordeaux (St-Émilion) ANGELUS, AUSONE, BEAU-SEJOUR BECOT, CANON, MAGDELAINE, le TERTRE-ROTEBOEUF, TROPLONG-MONDOT; (Pomerol) le BON PASTEUR, l'EGLISE-CLINET, l'EVANGILE, la FLEUR-PETRUS, LAFLEUR, PETRUS, le PIN, TROTANOY, VIEUX-CHATEAU-CERTAN.

Other European Merlots

Italy (Veneto) MACULAN; (Friuli) Livio Felluga; (Tuscany) AMA, AVIGNONESI, ORNELLAIA, Tua Rita; (Lazio) Falesco.

Spain (Penedès) Can Ràfols dels Caus.

New World Merlots

USA (California) ARROWOOD, BERINGER, CHATEAU ST JEAN, FERRARI-CARANO, MATANZAS CREEK, NEWTON, Pahlmeyer, Paloma, SHAFER, Swanson; (Washington) ANDREW WILL, CHATEAU STE MICHELLE, COLUMBIA WINERY, LEONETTI; (New York) Bedell.

Australia Clarendon Hills, KATNOOK Estate, Pepper Tree, PETALUMA, Tatachilla, YARRA YERING.

New Zealand Esk Valley, GOLDWATER, VILLA MARIA.

South Africa MEERLUST, Morgenhof, SAXENBURG, THELEMA, VEENWOUDEN, VERGELEGEN.

Chile CARMEN, CASA LAPOSTOLLE, La Palma, VINA CASABLANCA.

LOUIS MICHEL & FILS *Chablis AC, Burgundy, France* The prime exponent of unoaked CHABLIS. The top Crus – les Clos★★, Montmains★★ and Montée de Tonnerre★★ – are fresh-flavoured and long-lived. Best years: 1997 96 95 93 **92 90 89 88**.

MIDI *France* A loose geographical term, virtually synonymous with LANGUEDOC-ROUSSILLON, covering the vast, sunbaked area of southern France between the Pyrenees and the RHONE VALLEY.

MILDARA *Murray River, Victoria, Australia* Based on the Murray River, but the best wines are from large COONAWARRA vineyards including the hugely popular and fairly priced Jamieson's Run★ (blended red and Chardonnay and Sauvignon Blanc whites) and Saltram in the BAROSSA. Also owns BAILEY'S, Balgownie, Wolf BLASS, Andrew Garrett, Ingoldby, Krondorf, ROTHBURY, Mount Ida, Yarra Ridge, YELLOWGLEN, and was itself bought in 1996 by Fosters, the lager lads.

MILLTON *Gisborne, North Island, New Zealand* Organic vineyard using biodynamic methods, whose top wines include the sophisticated and individual Clos St Anne Chardonnay★, botrytized Opou Vineyard Riesling★★ and ambitiously complex barrel-fermented Chenin Blanc★. Best years: (1998) **96 95 94 91 90**.

MINERVOIS AC *Languedoc, France* Attractive, mostly red wines from north-east of Carcassonne. The area's great strength is organization, and big companies like Nicolas have worked hard with local co-ops to produce good-quality, juicy, quaffing wine at reasonable prices. The best wines are made by the estates: full of ripe, red fruit and pine-dust perfume, for drinking young. It can age, especially if a little new oak has been used. Best producers: (reds) Abbaye de Tholomies★, CLOS CENTEILLES★, Fabas★, Festiano, Gourgazaud, Maris★, Meyzonnier, Nicolas, Paraza, Piccinini★, Ste-Eulalie★, la Tour Boisée★, Vassière, Villerambert-Julien★, Violet★. Best years: (1998) **96 95 94 93**.

MISSION *Hawkes Bay, North Island, New Zealand* New Zealand's oldest continuous winery is owned by the Society of Mary. Established in HAWKES BAY 147 years ago, the Mission has recently been revitalized with new vineyards and a winery upgrade. Significantly improved wines have resulted, particularly with the top level Jewelstone label – stylish Chardonnay★, medium-dry Gewürztraminer★, and an off-dry, succulent Pinot Gris★. Best years: (1998) **96 95 94 91**.

CH. LA MISSION-HAUT-BRION★★ *Pessac-Léognan AC, Cru Classé de Graves, Bordeaux, France* I always find la Mission wines powerful but, unlike its neighbour HAUT-BRION, never charming. Their strength is in massive, dark fruit and oak flavours, and they often need 20 years' age or so. Best years: (1998) 97 96 95 94 93 90 89 **88 85 82 81 79 78 75**.

MISSION HILL *British Columbia, Canada* British Columbia's most progressive producer, employing the full-time services of New Zealand winemaker John Simes. Antipodean style is clearly evident in the passion-fruit aromas of the Chardonnay★★, and the Pinot Blanc★ shows equally good fruit retention. Grand Reserve Pinot Noir★★ is a real stunner in reds. Best years: 1997 96 **95 94**.

MITCHELL *Clare Valley, South Australia* The effervescent Jane and winemaker husband Andrew Mitchell turn out some of CLARE VALLEY's fruitiest, cellarable Riesling★★ and a much-improved barrel-fermented Growers Semillon★★ which both deserve a wider audience. Growers

Grenache is a huge unwooded and inelegant lump of fruit, but if you're in the mood... Peppertree Vineyard Shiraz★ and Cabernet Sauvignon★ are plump, chocolaty and typical of the region. Best years: **1995 94 93 92 90**.

MITCHELTON *Goulburn Valley, Victoria, Australia* Victoria's most consistently fine Riesling★★. Oaked Marsanne★★, released at 4 years old, is a speciality; new Mitchelton III red★★ and white★★ are character-filled RHONE-style blends designed to partner Mediterranean food. Reds from Shiraz★★ and Cabernet★★ are increasingly deep and structured. Best years: (Print Label) 1995 **94 92 90**.

MITTELRHEIN *Germany* Small, unsung (as far as great wine is concerned, that is) northerly wine region. About 75% of the wine here is Riesling but, unlike other German regions, the Mittelrhein has been in decline over the last few decades. The vineyard sites are steep and difficult to work – although breathtaking. Some wines are successfully turned into Sekt. The best growers (like Toni JOST★★) cluster around Bacharach in the south, and produce wines of a striking mineral tang and dry, fruity intensity.

MOELLEUX French for soft or mellow, used to describe sweet or medium-sweet wines.

MOËT & CHANDON *Champagne AC, Champagne, France* Moët & Chandon's enormous production of more than 25 million bottles a year dominates the CHAMPAGNE market. Good non-vintage can be absolutely delightful – soft, creamy and a little spicy, and consistency is pretty good. The vintage★ is more consistent, and usually has a reasonable style to it, while the rosé★ shows a Pinot Noir floral fragrance depressingly rare in modern Champagne. Dom Pérignon★★★ is the de luxe CUVÉE. It can be one of the greatest Champagnes of all, but you've got to age it for a number of years or else you're wasting your money on the fancy bottle. Best years: **1992 90 88 86 85 83 82**.

MONBAZILLAC AC *South-West France* BERGERAC's leading sweet wine. Most of it is light, vaguely sweet and entirely forgettable, usually from the efficient but unadventurous co-op. This style won't age, but a real, truly rich, late-harvested Monbazillac can happily last 10 years. Best producers: la Borderie★, le Fagé, Grande Maison★, Haut-Bernasse, Hébras★, Ch. Monbazillac (co-op made), Theulet★, Tirecul-la-Gravière★, Treuil-de-Nailhac★. Best years: (1998) 97 96 **95 93 91 90 89 88 86**.

ROBERT MONDAVI *Napa Valley, California, USA* Robert Mondavi is a Californian institution, spreading the gospel of California wine from his NAPA home base. Best known for the regular bottling Cabernet Sauvignon★, open and fruity with the emphasis on early drinkability, and the Reserve Cabernet★★, possessing enormous depth and power. Winemaker Tim Mondavi has put a great deal of energy into Pinot Noir over the past few years and the results are easy to see. A regular bottling of Pinot Noir★ and a Reserve Pinot Noir★★ are improving with every vintage: velvety smooth and supple wines with great style, perfume and balance. For many years the Mondavi trademark wine was Fumé (Sauvignon) Blanc, but in recent years Chardonnay has become the winery leader (the Reserve★★ can be superb), although the quality is inconsistent. The Mondavis also own

BYRON VINEYARD in SANTA BARBARA COUNTY, OPUS ONE in Napa in partnership with the Rothschilds, as well as the Mondavi Woodbridge winery, where inexpensive varietal wines are produced. La Famiglia, made in Napa, is a range aimed at a younger market, based chiefly on Italian varietals. Mondavi is involved in a joint venture with ERRAZURIZ in Chile, and is also making wines in France's LANGUEDOC to sell under the Vichon Mediterranean label, as well as having an association with FRESCOBALDI (CASTELGIOCONDO) producing a SUPER-TUSCAN named Luce. Best years: (Cabernet Sauvignon Reserve) (1996) 95 94 93 **92 91 88 87 86 85 84 82**; (Pinot Noir Reserve) 1997 96 95 **94 92 91 90 88 87**; (Chardonnay Reserve) 1997 96 95 **94 92 91 90 87**.

MONTAGNE-ST-ÉMILION AC *Bordeaux, France* A ST-EMILION satellite which can produce rather good red wines. The wines are normally ready to drink in 4 years but age quite well in their slightly earthy way. Best producers: Bonneau, Calon, Corbin, Faizeau, Laurets, Moines, Montaiguillon, Négrit, Roc-de-Calon, Rocher Corbin, Roudier, Vieux-Ch.-St-André. Best years: (1998) 96 95 **94 90 89 88 85 83 82**.

MONTAGNY AC *Côte Chalonnaise, Burgundy, France* This is the most southerly of the 4 Côte Chalonnaise village ACs. The wines are dry and rather lean, but now that some producers are aging their wines for a few months in new oak, there has been a great improvement. Generally best with 2 years' age or more. Best producers: BUXY CO-op★, Davenay★, FAIVELEY, Louis LATOUR★, Olivier LEFLAIVE★, B Michel★, A Roy, Steinmaier, J Vachet★. Best years: 1997 **96 95 93 92**.

MONTALCINO See Brunello di Montalcino DOCG.

MONTANA *Auckland, Gisborne, Hawkes Bay and Marlborough, New Zealand* Montana is easily the country's largest winemaker, and it has consistently made some of New Zealand's best-value wines. The Sauvignon Blanc★ and Chardonnay★ are in a considerable way to thank for putting New Zealand on the international map. The company now wants to prove that big can be best. To achieve that goal it has established The McDonald Winery, a small (by Montana standards) winery in HAWKES BAY from which it produces top Chardonnay★★ and good Merlot★★ and Cabernet-Merlot★. Church Road Reserve Chardonnay★★ and Cabernet★★ are among New Zealand's finest. Montana's Special 'Estate' bottlings, particularly Ormond Estate Chardonnay★★★ in GISBORNE, also bode well. Montana make consistent Lindauer fizz and, with the help of the CHAMPAGNE house DEUTZ, produce the austere, yet full-bodied Deutz MARLBOROUGH Cuvée NV Brut★★. Best years: (1998) **96 94 91**.

MONTECARLO DOC *Tuscany, Italy* Both reds (Sangiovese with Syrah) and whites (Trebbiano with Sémillon and Pinot Grigio) are distinctive. But other non-DOC wines can include Cabernet, Merlot, Pinot Bianco, Vermentino and Roussanne. Best producers: Buonamico★, Carmignani★, Michi, Wandanna★. Best years: (reds) (1998) 97 96 **95 94 93 90**.

MONTECILLO *Rioja DOC, Rioja, Spain* Owned by sherry firm OSBORNE, Montecillo makes high-quality RIOJAS in young and mature styles. Red and white Viña Cumbrero★ is young and fruity. Rich, fruity Viña Monty★ red Gran Reservas are aged in French oak barrels and combine delicacy with flavour. Best years: (reds) (1996) **95 94 91 88 87 86 82 81 78 73**.

MONTEFALCO DOC *Umbria, Italy* The often good Sangiovese-based
Montefalco Rosso is outclassed by the dry Sagrantino di Montefalco (now
DOCG) and Sagrantino Passito, a glorious sweet red made from dried
grapes. Best producers: (Sagrantino) ADANTI★, Antonelli, Caprai★★,
Colpetrone, Rocca di Fabbri. Best years: (1998) (97) 96 **95 94 93 91 90 88 85**.

MONTEPULCIANO This grape, grown mostly in eastern Italy (and
unconnected with TUSCANY's Sangiovese-based wine VINO NOBILE DI
MONTEPULCIANO), can produce deep-coloured, fleshy, spicy wines with
moderate tannin and acidity. Besides MONTEPULCIANO D'ABRUZZO, it is
used in ROSSO CONERO and ROSSO PICENO in the MARCHE and also in UMBRIA,
Molise and PUGLIA.

MONTEPULCIANO D'ABRUZZO DOC *Abruzzo, Italy* The Montepulciano
grape's most important manifestation. Quality varies from the insipid
or rustic to concentrated and characterful. Best producers: Cataldi
Madonna, Cornacchia★, Filomusi Guelfi★, Illuminati★, Masciarelli★,
Elio Monti★★, Montori★, Nicodemi, Cantina Tollo★, Umani Ronchi★,
Valentini★★★, Ciccio Zaccagnini★. Best years: (1998) **97 95 94 93 90 88 85**.

MONTEREY COUNTY *California, USA* Large CENTRAL COAST county south
of San Francisco Bay. The most important AVAs are Arroyo Seco,
CHALONE, Carmel Valley and Salinas Valley. Best grapes are
Chardonnay, Riesling and Pinot Blanc, with some good Cabernet
Sauvignon, Merlot in Carmel Valley and Pinot Noir in the cool north
of the county. Best producers: Bernardus, CHALONE★★, Durney, Galante,
Mer et Soleil★★, The Monterey Vineyard, Morgan★, Ventana★.

MONTES *Curicó, Chile* This has to be one of Chile's most frustratingly
erratic producers, but the Malbec★★ really does show what
winemaker Aurelio Montes can do at his best. The Sauvignon
Blanc★ has improved dramatically recently and is good, and Montes
Alpha Cabernet Sauvignon★ and Merlot★ are slowly revealing a
very satisfying mixture of fruit ripeness and structure. Aurelio
Montes is also kept busy acting as consultant to many other Chilean
wineries.

MONTEVERTINE *Tuscany, Italy* Based in the heart of CHIANTI CLASSICO,
Montevertine is famous for its non-DOC wines, particularly Le Pergole
Torte★★★. This was the first of the new-style SUPER-TUSCANS made
solely with the Sangiovese grape variety, and it remains one of the
best. Owner Sergio Manetti includes a little Canaiolo in the excellent
Il Sodaccio★★ and Montevertine Riserva★★. Best years: (1998) (97) (96)
95 **93 90 88 86 85**.

MONTHELIE AC *Côte de Beaune, Burgundy, France* Attractive, mainly
red wine village lying halfway along the COTE DE BEAUNE behind
MEURSAULT and VOLNAY. The wines generally have a lovely, cherry fruit
and make pleasant drinking at a good price. Best producers: J-F COCHE-
DURY★★, J Garaudet, P Garaudet, JAFFELIN, LAFON★, Olivier LEFLAIVE,
Maison LEROY, Monthelie-Douhairet★, Potinet-Ampeau, G Roulot★, E de
Suremain★. Best years: (reds) 1997 96 95 **93 90 89**; (whites) 1997 96 **95** 92.

MONTILLA-MORILES DO *Andalucía, Spain* Sherry-style wines that are
sold almost entirely as lower-priced sherry substitutes. However, the
wines *can* be superb, particularly the top dry amontillado, oloroso and

195

rich Pedro Ximénez styles. And if you think top sherry is underpriced, they're almost giving this stuff away. Also light and uncharacterful dry whites. Best producers: Alvear★ (top labels only), Aragón, Gracia Hermanos, Pérez Barquero★, Toro Albalá★.

HUBERT DE MONTILLE *Volnay, Burgundy, France* Estate producing some of the most concentrated, ageworthy red wines on the CÔTE DE BEAUNE. If you're willing to wait for 10 years or more, de Montille's VOLNAYS and POMMARDS are very rewarding wines. The Volnay Champans★★, Pommard les Épenots★★★ and Pommard les Pezerolles★★ are all well worth their high prices. Best years: 1997 96 95 93 92 **90 89 88 85**.

MONTLOUIS AC *Loire Valley, France* Situated on the opposite bank of the Loire river to the VOUVRAY AC, Montlouis wines are made from the same Chenin grape and in similar styles (dry, medium and sweet and Champagne-method fizz) but tend to be a touch more rustic than its neighbour's since the grapes rarely ripen quite as well. Two-thirds of the production is Mousseux, a green, appley fizz which is best drunk young. The still wines need aging for 5–10 years, particularly the sweet or Moelleux version. Best producers: Berger Frères★, Y & F Chidaine★, Delétang★★, Levasseur, Moyer★, Taille aux Loups★★. Best years: (1998) 97 96 95 **93 90 89 88 86 85 83 82 78 76 70**.

MONTRACHET AC *Côte de Beaune, Burgundy, France* This world-famous Grand Cru straddles the boundary between the villages of CHASSAGNE-MONTRACHET and PULIGNY-MONTRACHET, with another Grand Cru, Chevalier-Montrachet, immediately above it on the slope. Le Montrachet produces wines with a unique combination of concentration, finesse and perfume; white Burgundy at its most sublime. Chevalier's higher elevation yields a slightly leaner wine that is less explosive in its youth, but good examples will become ever more fascinating over 20 years or more. Best producers: COLIN★★★, DROUHIN (Laguiche)★★★, LAFON★★★, LATOUR★★, Dom. LEFLAIVE★★, RAMONET★★★, Dom. de la ROMANÉE-CONTI★★★, Thénard★★. Best years: 1997 96 95 93 **92** 90 **89 88 86 85**.

MONTRAVEL AC *South-West France* Dry, medium-dry and sweet white wines from the western end of the BERGERAC region. Production is declining. Best producers: Gouyat, Krevel, le Raz, Roque Peyre.

CH. MONTROSE★★★ *St-Estèphe AC, 2ème Cru Classé, Haut-Médoc, Bordeaux, France* Used to be thought of as the leading ST-ESTÈPHE property, famous for its dark, brooding wine that would take around 30 years of aging before it was at its prime. Following a period in the late 1970s and early 80s when the wines became lighter and easier, Montrose has now returned to its original firm, dense, powerful style. Recent vintages have mostly been exceptional. Second wine: la Dame de Montrose. Best years: (1998) 97 96 95 94 90 89 88 **86**.

MONT TAUCH, LES PRODUCTEURS DU *Fitou, Languedoc-Roussillon, France* A big, quality-conscious co-op based in the Fitou region, but producing a large range of MIDI wines, from good gutsy FITOU★ and CORBIÈRES★ to rich MUSCAT DE RIVESALTES★ and light but gluggable Vin de Pays du Torgan. Its top red wine, called Terroir de Tuchan★, is a good example of the quality now being achieved in the Midi. Best years: (whites and rosés) **1997**; (reds) (1998) 97 96 **95 94 93 91 90 89**.

CH. MONTUS *Madiran AC, South-West France*   Alain Brumont has
led MADIRAN's revival using 100% Tannat and deft public relations.
The top wine is aged in new oak. He has 3 properties: Montus★★★,
Bouscassé★★ and Meinjarre★. Montus and Bouscassé make a
drinkable dry PACHERENC DU VIC-BILH★, while Bouscassé has fine
Moelleux★★. Best years: (reds) (1997) 96 95 94 93 **91 90 89 88 85**.

MOREY-ST-DENIS AC *Côte de Nuits, Burgundy, France*   Morey has 5
Grands Crus (Clos des Lambrays, CLOS DE LA ROCHE, CLOS DE TART, CLOS
ST-DENIS and a share of BONNES-MARES) as well as some very good
Premiers Crus. Basic village wine tends to be dilute and dull, but from
a quality grower the wine has good strawberry or redcurrant fruit and
acquires an attractive depth as it ages. A tiny amount of startling
nutty white wine is also made. Best producers: Pierre Amiot,
Castagnier-Vadey★, CLAIR★★, DUJAC★★, FAIVELEY★, Georges Lignier★★,
Hubert Lignier★★, H Perrot-Minot★, Ponsot★★, Rossignol-Trapet★,
ROUMIER★★, ROUSSEAU★★, J Tardy★. Best years: 1997 96 95 93 **90 89 88**.

MORGON AC *Beaujolais, Burgundy, France*   A BEAUJOLAIS Cru around the
commune of Villié-Morgon. Most of the wine produced has a soft, cherry
fruit for very easy drinking, but from a good grower and from the slopes
of the Mont du Py the wine can be thick and dark, acquiring a perfume
of cherries as it ages. Classic Morgon is the most tannic of the Beaujolais
Crus. Best producers: N Aucoeur, Georges Brun, la Chanaise, G Charvet★,
L-C Desvignes★, DUBOEUF (J Descombes★★), M Lapierre★, P Savoye★, J-J
Vincent. Best years: 1997 96 **95 93 91 90**.

MORNINGTON PENINSULA *Victoria, Australia*   Exciting
new cool-climate maritime region dotted with small
vineyards, often owned by monied Melbourne
hobbyists. Chardonnay here is tantalizing and
honeyed, and Pinot Noir shows great promise. Best
producers: Craig Avon, DROMANA★, King's Creek, Main
Ridge, Massoni, Moorooduc Estate, Paringa★★, Port
Phillip Estate, STONIER's★★, T'gallant★.

MORRIS *Rutherglen, Victoria, Australia*   Historic winery, ORLANDO-
owned, making traditional regional favourites like liqueur
Muscat★★ and Tokay★★ (Old Premium is ★★★), 'ports', 'sherries'
and robust table wines from Shiraz★, Cabernet★, Durif and Blue
Imperial (Cinsaut). Mick Morris retired in 1993, handing over the
reins to his son David.

MORTON ESTATE *Katikati, North Island, New Zealand*   Katikati is the
tiny town where Morton Estate built their winery in Dutch Cape of
Good Hope style. Their vineyards, however, are in HAWKES BAY. Best
wines are the robust, complex Black Label Chardonnay★★,
nectarine/tropical fruit Black Label Fumé Blanc★, intense berries and
cedar Black Label Cabernet Sauvignon-Merlot★★, as well as successful
fizz★. Best years: (whites) 1998 **96 95 94 91**.

MOSCATO D'ASTI DOCG *Piedmont, Italy*   The Moscato (Muscat) grape
comes in a seemingly infinite number of styles, but not one is as
beguiling as this delicately scented and gently bubbling version, made
from Moscato Bianco grapes grown in the hills between Asti and Alba
in north-west Italy. The DOCG is the same as for ASTI Spumante, but
only select grapes go into this wine, which is frizzante (semi-sparkling)

rather than spumante (fully sparkling). The best are thrillingly grapy and low in alcohol. Drink the wines while still bubbling with youthful fragrance. Best producers: ASCHERI★, Bava★, Fratelli Bera★, Braida★, Caudrina★★, Cascina Fonda★, Fortello della Luja★, Icardi★, Marenco★, Beppe Marino★, La Morandina★, Perrone★, Cascina Pian d'Or★, Saracco★★, Scagliola★, La Spinetta★★, I Vignaioli di Santo Stefano★; (Moscato del Piemonte) Marco Negri★.

MOSCATO PASSITO DI PANTELLERIA DOC *Sicily, Italy* The Muscat of Alexandria grape is used to make this powerful dessert wine. Pantelleria is a small island south-west of SICILY, closer to Africa than it is to Italy. The grapes are picked in mid-August and laid out in the hot sun to dry and shrivel for a fortnight. They are then crushed and fermented to give an amber-coloured, intensely flavoured sweet Muscat that is one of the best produced. The wines are best drunk within 5–7 years of the vintage, though they can age gracefully for a decade or more. Best producers: D'Ancona★, DE BARTOLI (Bukkuram★★), MID (Tanit), Murana (Martingana★★, Khamma★), Nuova Agricoltura co-op, Pellegrino★.

MOSEL-SAAR-RUWER *Germany* Not a coherent wine region, but a collection of vineyard areas on the Mosel and its tributaries, the Saar and the Ruwer. The Mosel river itself rises in the French Vosges before forming the border between Germany and Luxembourg. In its first German incarnation in the Upper Mosel the fairly dire Elbling grape holds sway but with the Middle Mosel begins a series of villages responsible for some of the world's very best Riesling wines: PIESPORT, BRAUNEBERG, BERNKASTEL, GRAACH, URZIG and ERDEN. The wines are not big or powerful, but in good years they have tremendous 'slaty' breed and an ability to blend the greenness of perfumes and fruits with the golden warmth of honey. Great wines are rarer in the lower part of the valley as the Mosel swings round into Koblenz. The Saar can produce wonderful, piercing wines in villages such as Serrig, Ockfen and Wiltingen. The Ruwer is north of Trier and produces slightly softer wines; if no village names stand out here there are a few estates (MAXIMIN GRUNHAUS, KARTHAUSERHOF) which are on every list of the best in Germany. See also Ayl, Bernkastel, Brauneberg, Erden, Graach, Ockfen, Piesport, Ürzig, Wehlen.

LENZ MOSER *Rohrendorf-bei-Krems, Kremstal, Austria* Important merchant buying growers' wines and bottling them as 'Selection'. Also fine Burgenland wines from the Klosterkeller Siegendorf and Weinviertel wines (including Cabernet Sauvignon!) from the Malteser Ritterorden estate. Don't confuse with the Sepp Moser★ estate of the KREMSTAL region.

MOSS WOOD *Margaret River, Western Australia* Pioneer winery producing outstanding silky smooth, rich but structured Cabernet★★★. The Chardonnay★★ can be rich and peachy and the Pinot Noir★ erratic but magical at best. Semillon★★, both oaked and unoaked, is a consistently fascinating wine. Best years: (reds) 1995 94 **93 92 91 90 87 86 85 83 80 77 75**.

J P MOUEIX *Bordeaux, France* As well as owning PETRUS, la FLEUR-PETRUS, MAGDELAINE, TROTANOY and other properties, the Moueix family runs a thriving merchant business specializing in the wines of the right bank, particularly POMEROL and FRONSAC. Quality is generally high. Christian Moueix (son of Jean-Pierre) also runs the California winery DOMINUS.

MOULIN-À-VENT AC *Beaujolais, Burgundy, France* BEAUJOLAIS Cru that can resemble a full, chocolaty Burgundy, tasting more of Pinot Noir than Gamay, if you leave the wine to age for 6–10 years. Best producers: J Brugne, L Champagnon★, J Charvet★, Chauvet★, Desperrier Père et Fils★, DUBOEUF (single domaines★), Ch. des Jacques★★, Janodet, Ch. du Moulin-à-Vent★★, R Siffert, la Tour du Bief★★, R Trichard. Best years: 1998 97 96 95 **93 91 90** 88.

MOULIS AC *Haut-Médoc, Bordeaux, France* The smallest of the specific ACs within the HAUT-MEDOC area. Much of the wine is excellent – delicious at 5–6 years old, though good examples should age 10–20 years – and not overpriced. Best producers: Anthonic, Biston-Brillette, Brillette★, CHASSE-SPLEEN★, Duplessis, Dutruch-Grand-Poujeau, Gressier-Grand-Poujeaux, MAUCAILLOU★, Ch. du Moulin-à-Vent★, POUJEAUX★★. Best years: (1998) 96 95 **94 90 89 88 86** 85 83 82.

MOUNTADAM *Eden Valley, South Australia* The late David Wynn and his Bordeaux-educated son Adam selected this property on one of the highest points of the Mount Lofty Ranges and planted the vineyards from scratch. Mountadam's rich, buttery Chardonnay★★ has a worldwide reputation. There is also sumptuous Pinot★★, leaner Cabernet★, and fruity David Wynn unoaked and Eden Ridge organic labels. Best years: (reds) 1996 94 93 **91 90** 87 84; (Chardonnay) **1997** 96 94 92 91 90.

MOUNT LANGI GHIRAN *Grampians, Victoria, Australia* Rapidly rising star turning out powerful, peppery Shiraz★★, well-structured Cabernet★★, fragrant Riesling★★ and decent unwooded Chardonnay. Restrained Pinot Gris is a new tangent; Sangiovese is among the recent plantings. Best years: (reds) 1995 **94 93 92 91 90** 89 86 84.

MOUNT MARY *Yarra Valley, Victoria, Australia* Classic property using only estate-grown grapes along Bordeaux lines, with dry white 'Triolet'★ blended from Sauvignon Blanc, Semillon and Muscadelle, and 'Cabernets'★★ from all 5 Bordeaux red grapes (Cabernet Sauvignon, Cabernet Franc, Merlot, Petit Verdot and Malbec) that ages beautifully. The Pinot Noir★★ is almost as good. Best years: ('Cabernets') 1995 94 **92 91 90 88** 84 80.

MOUNT VEEDER AVA *Napa Valley, USA* Cabernet Sauvignon and Zinfandel wines, made in a typical rough-hewn style, come from this small mountain AVA in NAPA's south-west corner. Best producers: Chateau Potelle★, HESS COLLECTION★★, Lokoya, Mayacamas, Mount Veeder Vineyards★.

MOURVÈDRE The variety originates from south-eastern Spain, where it is called Monastrell. In southern French grape variety needs lots of sunshine to ripen, which is why it performs well on the Mediterranean coast at BANDOL, producing wines that can age for 20 years or more. It is increasingly important as a source of colour, body and tarry, pine-needle flavour in the wines of CHATEAUNEUF-DU-PAPE and parts of the MIDI. It is now beginning to make a reputation in Australia and CALIFORNIA, where it is frequently known as Mataro.

MOUSSEUX French for sparkling wine.

MOUTON-CADET *Bordeaux AC, Bordeaux, France*   The most widely sold red BORDEAUX in the world was created by Baron Philippe de Rothschild in the 1930s. The wine is blended and comes from the entire Bordeaux region, is perfectly correct but uninspiring – and never cheap. There is also a white and rosé.

CH. MOUTON-ROTHSCHILD *Pauillac AC, 1er Cru Classé, Haut-Médoc, Bordeaux, France*   Baron Philippe de Rothschild died in 1988 after 65 years of managing Mouton, raising it from a run-down Second Growth to its promotion to First Growth status in 1973, and a reputation as one of the greatest wines★★★ in the world. It can still be the most magnificently rich and indulgent of the great MEDOC reds but recent signs of inconsistency are beginning to hurt its tip-top status. When young, this wine is rich and indulgent on the palate, aging after 15–20 years to a complex bouquet of blackcurrant and cigar box. There is also a white wine, Aile d'Argent. Best years: (red) (1998) 97 96 95 94 93 91 89 88 86 **85 83 82 78 70**.

MUDGEE *New South Wales, Australia*   Small, long-established but overlooked region neighbouring HUNTER VALLEY, with higher altitude and cooler temperatures. Major new plantings are giving it a fresh lease of life; in 1996, ROSEMOUNT unveiled the most exciting Mudgee newcomer in ages, an impressive Shiraz-Cabernet called Mountain Blue★★. Best producers: Huntington, Miramar, Montrose, ROSEMOUNT★★, Thistle Hill.

MUGA *Rioja DOC, Rioja, Spain*   A traditional family winery making high-quality, rich red RIOJAS★, especially the Gran Reserva, Prado Enea★. It is the only bodega in Rioja where every step of red winemaking is still carried out in oak containers. In recent years, the whites and rosés have been good too. The modern Torre Muga Reserva★ marks a major stylistic change. Best years: (reds) (1996) 95 **94 92 90 89 87 85 82 81**.

MULDERBOSCH *Stellenbosch WO, South Africa*   Any fears that new (corporate) ownership of this small property might lead to a drop in standards and individuality of both wines and winemaker Mike Dobrovic are unfounded. A sleek, gooseberry-infused Sauvignon Blanc★★ is a model of consistency and a deserved cult wine. Purity with intensity are also the hallmarks of Chardonnay★★ and new Steen-op-Hout★ (Chenin Blanc brushed with oak). Faithful Hound, a Cabernet-Merlot blend and the sole red, is claret-like, though easy-drinking. Best years: (whites) **1998** 97 96 95 94.

EGON MÜLLER *Scharzhofberg, Saar, Germany*   Not only some of the greatest German wines but also the most expensive (the TBA can cost £1000/$1600 per bottle at the time it is released). The ultimate sweet versions are the estate's Auslese, Beerenauslese, Trocken-beerenauslese and EISWEIN, all ★★★. Regular Kabinett and Spätlese wines are pricy but classic. Best years: 1997 96 95 94 93 **91 90 89 88 83 79 76 75 71**.

MÜLLER-CATOIR *Neustadt-Haardt, Pfalz, Germany*   Müller-Catoir is an eye-opener for those who are sceptical about Germany's ability to make wines in a more international idiom. From vineyards in the PFALZ region it produces wine of a piercing fruit flavour and powerful structure unexcelled in Germany, including Riesling, Scheurebe, Gewürztraminer, Rieslaner (all frequently ★★★), Muskateller★★ and Weissburgunder★. Best years: (1997) 96 **94 93 92 90 89 88**.

MÜLLER-THURGAU The workhorse grape of Germany, largely responsible for LIEBFRAUMILCH. Once thought to be a crossing of Riesling and Sylvaner, new research proves that it is, in fact, Sylvaner and Chasselas, which explains its saltiness and non-Riesling aromas. When yields are low it produces pleasant floral wines; but this is rare since it was bred for productivity. It is occasionally better in England – though the odd good examples, with a slightly green edge to the grapy flavour, come from Austria, Switzerland, Luxembourg and northern Italy. New Zealand used to pride itself on making the world's best Müller-Thurgau, although acreage is in rapid decline.

G H MUMM *Champagne AC, Champagne, France* Mumm's top-selling non-vintage brand, Cordon Rouge, is usually one of the least impressive Grande Marque Champagnes, frequently out-performed by its Californian counterpart, MUMM NAPA. The de luxe cuvée, René Lalou★, is rather better, but the best wine is the elegant Mumm de Cramant★★. Best years: **1990 89 88 85**.

MUMM NAPA *Napa Valley AVA, California, USA* The French CHAMPAGNE house MUMM and Seagram Classic Wines of California started Mumm Napa in 1983. Some reports have it that the French owners are sorry they did because the bubbly coming out of California has been superb. Cuvée Napa Brut Prestige★★ is one of California's classiest sparklers, although the more expensive Vintage Reserve★ runs a close second. A BLANC DE NOIRS★ is far better than most pink Champagnes. A Tête de Cuvée DVX★ has righted itself after a weak debut vintage.

MURFATLAR *Romania* Lying to the west of the Black Sea, Murfatlar produces excellent late-harvest wines from Chardonnay, Muscat Ottonel and, in particular, Pinot Gris★. Sparkling wines are now being made, too. The maritime influence can create the problem of warm nights with resultant low acidity levels, often a fault in the Cabernet Sauvignon and Merlot made here. When they work it out, Murfatlar should be a good source of ripe, soft reds. Best producer: Murfatlar Winery.

MUSCADET AC *Loire Valley, France* All change in 1994 with Muscadet becoming the base AC for the whole region with 3 high-quality zones: MUSCADET DES COTEAUX DE LA LOIRE, MUSCADET COTES DE GRAND LIEU and MUSCADET DE SEVRE-ET-MAINE. Producers who make basic Muscadet AC are allowed higher yields but cannot use the term *sur lie* on the labels. Inexpensive and best drunk young and fresh. Best producers: Chereau-Carré, Donatien Bahuaud, Ch. de la Preuille★, Sauvion.

MUSCADET DES COTEAUX DE LA LOIRE AC *Loire Valley, France* East of Nantes and on both sides of the Loire river, this is the smallest of the 3 high-quality zones. Yields are lower than for basic MUSCADET AC and producers can use *sur lie* on their labels. Best producers: Jacques Guindon, Luneau-Papin.

MUSCAT

It's strange, but there's hardly a wine grape in the world which makes wine that actually tastes of the grape itself. Yet there's one variety which is so joyously, exultantly grapy that it more than makes up for all the others – the Muscat, generally thought to be the original wine vine. In fact there seem to be about 200 different branches of the Muscat family, but the one that always makes the most exciting wine is called Muscat à Petits Grains. These berries can be crunchily green, golden yellow, pink or even brown, and the wines they make may be pale and dry, rich and golden, subtly aromatic or as dark and sweet as treacle.

WINE STYLES

France Muscat is grown from the far north-east right down to the Spanish border, yet is rarely accorded great respect in France. This is a pity because the dry, light, hauntingly grapy Muscats of Alsace are some of France's most delicately beautiful wines. (These are sometimes blended with the crossbreed Muscat Ottonel.) It pops up sporadically in the Rhône Valley, especially in the sparkling wine enclave of Die. Mixed with Clairette, the Clairette de Die Tradition is a fragrant grapy fizz that should be better known. Muscat de Beaumes-de-Venise could do with being less well known because quality has suffered in recent years. But its success has encouraged the traditional fortified winemakers of Languedoc-Roussillon, especially in Frontignan and Rivesaltes, to make fresher, more perfumed wines rather than the usual flat and syrupy ones.

Italy Muscat is grown in Italy for fragrantly sweet or (rarely) dry table wines in the north and for *passito*-style wines (though the less fine Muscat of Alexandria makes most of the rich southern Moscato). Yet the greatest Muscats in Italy are those of Asti, where it is called Moscato Bianco. As either Asti Spumante or Moscato d'Asti, this brilliantly fresh fizz can be a blissful drink. Italy also has red varieties: the Moscato Nero for rare sweet wines in Lazio, Lombardy and Piedmont; and Moscato Rosa and Moscato Giallo for delicately sweet wines in Trentino-Alto Adige and Friuli-Venezia Giulia.

Other regions Hungary still grows some Muscat, Crimea has shown how good it can be in the Massandra fortified wines, and Greece's finest wines are the Muscats of Samos and Patras. As Muskateller in Austria and Germany it makes both sweet and dry subtly aromatic wines. In Spain, Moscatel de Valencia is sweet, light and sensational value. Moscatel de Grano Menudo is on the resurgence in Navarra and has been introduced in Mallorca. Portugal's Moscatel de Setúbal is also wonderfully rich and complex. California grows Muscat, often calling it Muscat Canelli, but South Africa and Australia make better use of it. With darker berries, and called Brown Muscat in Australia and Muscadel in South Africa, it makes some of the world's most sweet and luscious fortified wines, especially in north-east Victoria in Australia.

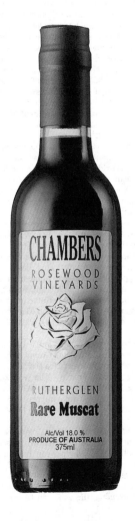

Sparkling Muscat

France (Clairette de Die) Achard-Vincent, Clairette de Die co-op.

*Italy (*Asti) G Contratto, Gancia; (Moscato d'Asti) Fratelli Bera, Braida, Caudrina, Saracco, La Spinetta.

Dry Muscat

Austria (Muskateller) F X PICHLER, E & M TEMENT.

France (Muscat d'Alsace) J Becker, Dirler, KUENTZ-BAS, Rolly Gassmann, Schleret, Schoffit, TRIMBACH, ZIND-HUMBRECHT.

Germany (Muskateller) BERCHER, MULLER-CATOIR, Rebholz.

Spain (Alicante) Bocopa co-op.

Italy (Goldenmuskateller) LAGEDER, Tiefenbrunner.

Sweet Muscat

Australia (Liqueur Muscat) ALL SAINTS, BAILEY'S, Campbells, CHAMBERS, MCWILLIAMS, MORRIS, SEPPELT, Stanton & Killeen.

France (Muscat d'Alsace) René Muré, Schoffit; (Muscat de Beaumes-de-Venise) Durban, Paul JABOULET, Vidal-Fleury; (Muscat de Frontignan) Peyrade; (Muscat de Rivesaltes) CAZES, Jau, Laporte.

Greece Samos co-op.

Italy (Moscato Passito di Pantelleria) DE BARTOLI, Murana; (Moscato di Strevi Passito) Ivaldi; (Moscato Rosa) Franz Haas.

Portugal (Moscatel de Setúbal) J M da FONSECA, J P VINHOS.

South Africa KLEIN CONSTANTIA.

Spain (Navarra) Camilo Castilla; (Alicante) Gutiérrez de la Vega.

MUSCADET CÔTES DE GRAND LIEU AC *Loire Valley, France*   A new AC
for the best vineyards around Lac de Grand Lieu, south-west of
Nantes. The vines have to be 7 years old before they merit the AC.
Some of these wines can age for up to 5 years. The first vintage was
1994. Best producers: Serge Bâtard★, Bel-Air, Herbauges★.

MUSCADET DE SÈVRE-ET-MAINE AC *Loire Valley, France*   The Maine
and Sèvre rivers converge south of Nantes in north-west France and
give their name to this AC. Look out for the term *sur lie* on a label as
it describes the traditional method of bottling – the wine is bottled
directly off its sediment or lees, retaining a creamy, yeasty flavour and
a slight prickle of carbon dioxide. Good Muscadet perfectly matches
the local seafood. Most is drunk young but the best wines can age for
several years. Best producers: Michel Bahuaud (estate bottlings), Bideau-
Giraud, G Bossard★, Chasseloir★, Chéreau-Carré, Dorices★, Marquis de
Goulaine, l'Hyvernière★, LUNEAU★, METAIREAU★, Quatre Routes★, la
Ragotière★, Sauvion★, la Touché★. Best years: (1998) 97 **96 95 89**.

MUSCAT See pages 202–3.

MUSCAT OF ALEXANDRIA   Not to be confused with the superior Muscat
Blanc à Petits Grains, Muscat of Alexandria rarely shines in its own
right but performs a useful job worldwide, adding perfume and fruit to
what would otherwise be dull, neutral white wines. It is common for
sweet and fortified wines throughout the Mediterranean basin and in
South Africa (where it is also known as Hanepoot), as well as being a
fruity, perfumed bulk producer there and in Australia.

MUSCAT DE BEAUMES-DE-VENISE AC *Rhône Valley, France*   Some of
the best Muscat VIN DOUX NATUREL in France comes from the attractive
village of BEAUMES-DE-VENISE in the southern Rhône. In the 1980s the
wine achieved phenomenal success as a 'sophisticated' dessert wine
though you'll find the locals supping it on the way home from work.
It is certainly sweet but with a fruity acidity and a bright fresh feel to
it. Best drunk young to get all that lovely grapy perfume at its peak.
Best producers: Baumalric★, Beaumes-de-Venise co-op, Bernardins★,
CHAPOUTIER★, Coyeux, Durban★★, Fenouillet★, JABOULET★★, Vidal-Fleury★.

MUSCAT BLANC À PETITS GRAINS See Muscat.

MUSCAT DE CAP CORSE AC *Corsica, France*   New fortified wine AC
covering 17 communes on CORSICA. Muscat à Petits Grains is the only
permitted grape variety. Best producers: Arena★, Clos Nicrosi★.

MUSCAT DE FRONTIGNAN AC *Languedoc, France*   The well-known
Muscat VIN DOUX NATUREL on the Mediterranean coast. With colours
ranging from bright gold to deep orange, it is quite impressive but can
seem rather cloying. Best producers: Cave du Muscat de Frontignan,
la Peyrade★, Robiscau.

MUSCAT DE MIREVAL AC *Languedoc, France*   An AC for VIN DOUX
NATUREL, a little further inland to the much better-known MUSCAT DE
FRONTIGNAN. The wines, while still sweet and ripe, can have a little
more acid freshness, and quite an alcoholic kick as well. Best
producers: la Capelle, Mas des Pigeonniers, Moulinas.

MUSCAT DE RIVESALTES AC *Roussillon, France*   Made from Muscat Blanc
à Petits Grains and Muscat of Alexandria, the wine can be very good

indeed, especially since several go-ahead producers are now allowing the skins to stay in the juice for longer periods, thereby gaining perfume and fruit. Best producers: Casenove★, CAZES★★, Chênes★, Destavel, Fontanel★, Forca Real, Jau★, Laporte★, Mas Rous, Maurydoré★, MONT TAUCH CO-OP★, Piquemal★, Sarda-Malet.

MUSCAT DE ST-JEAN-DE-MINERVOIS AC *Languedoc, France* Up in the remote and wild Minervois hills is the little village of St-Jean-de-Minervois with its small appellation for fortified Muscat, made only from the superior Muscat à Petits Grains. It is less cloying than some Muscats from the plains of LANGUEDOC-ROUSSILLON, more tangerine and floral. Best producers: Barroubio, Vignerons de Septimanie★.

MUSIGNY AC *Grand Cru, Côte de Nuits, Burgundy, France* One of a handful of truly great Grands Crus, combining power with an exceptional depth of fruit and lacy elegance – an iron fist in a velvet glove. Understandably expensive. A tiny amount of white Musigny is produced by de VOGUE. Best producers: DROUHIN★★, JADOT★★★, Dom. LEROY★★, J-F Mugnier★★★, Jacques Prieur★, ROUMIER★★, VOGUE★★★. Best years: 1997 96 95 93 90 **89** 88 **85**.

NAHE *Germany* Wine region named after the River Nahe which rises below Birkenfeld and joins the Rhine by BINGEN, just opposite RUDESHEIM in the RHEINGAU. Riesling, Müller-Thurgau and Silvaner are the main grapes, but the Rieslings from this geologically complex region are considered some of Germany's best. The finest vineyards are those of Niederhausen and SCHLOSSBÖCKELHEIM, situated in the dramatic, rocky Upper Nahe Valley, and at Dorheim and Münster in the lower Nahe.

CH. NAIRAC★★ *Barsac AC, 2ème Cru Classé, Bordeaux, France* This Second Growth estate is an established star in BARSAC which, by dint of enormous effort and considerable investment, produces a wine sometimes on a par with the First Growths. The influence of aging in new oak casks, adding spice and even a little tannin, makes this sweet wine a good candidate for aging 10–15 years. Best years: (1998) 97 96 95 90 **89** 88 86 83 82 81 80 76.

NALLE WINERY *Dry Creek Valley AVA, California, USA* Owner and winemaker Doug Nalle is one of the leading producers of Zinfandel in California. He is one of that rare breed that would rather not talk to the press. 'All I'm doing is making the best Zinfandel I can make', he once explained. Nalle's superb Zinfandel★★ just keeps getting better and more expensive. Best years: (1997) 96 95 **94 93 92 91 90**.

NAPA COUNTY *California, USA* Home to some of California's best traditional wineries as well as many of its more determined newcomers, Napa has made itself synonymous with quality California wine. The county is viticulturally diverse, with about 20 major sub-areas already identified, but no proof as yet that they offer 20 genuinely diverse styles. Napa's reputation rests on its Cabernet, Merlot and Chardonnay, with Pinot Noir important in the CARNEROS district. Many feel that in the long run, Chardonnay will become less important in Napa and plantings of Cabernet and Merlot will increase. See also Napa Valley.

NAPA VALLEY AVA *California, USA* An AVA designed to be so inclusive that it is almost completely irrelevant. It includes vineyards that are outside the Napa River drainage system – such as Pope Valley and Chiles Valley. Because of this a number of sub-AVAs have been and are in the process of being created, but few of them have any real claim to being discernibly different from their neighbours, and many fear that these sub-AVAs will simply serve to dilute the magic of Napa's name. Best producers: BEAULIEU★, BERINGER★★, CAIN★, CAYMUS★★, CHATEAU MONTELENA★, CHIMNEY ROCK★, Clos Pegase★, CLOS DU VAL★, CUVAISON, DIAMOND CREEK★★, DOMAINE CHANDON★, DUCKHORN★, DUNN★, FLORA SPRINGS★★, FRANCISCAN★, HEITZ CELLARS★, HESS COLLECTION★★, MONDAVI★★, MUMM NAPA★, NEWTON★★, OPUS ONE★★, Joseph PHELPS★, PINE RIDGE★, SCHRAMSBERG★★, SHAFER★★, SILVERADO★, STAG'S LEAP★★, STERLING★, TREFETHEN, Turley★★, ZD Wines★. See also Carneros, Howell Mountain, Mount Veeder, Oakville, Rutherford.

NAUTILUS *Marlborough, South Island, New Zealand* Australian-owned company controlled by S Smith & Sons (YALUMBA) with vineyards, a retail outlet and a share in the winery Raupara Vintners, making one of the better examples of MARLBOROUGH Sauvignon Blanc★, stylish Chardonnay★★ and superb fizz★★. Best years: (1998) **97 96 94**.

NAVARRA DO *Navarra, Spain* This buzzing region is Spain's answer to the New World, with growing numbers of vineyards planted to Cabernet Sauvignon, Merlot and Chardonnay in addition to Tempranillo, Garnacha and Moscatel de Grano Menudo (Muscat à Petits Grains). This translates into a wealth of juicy reds, barrel-fermented whites, unoaked young Garnacha reds and modern sweet Muscats. Best producers: Camilo Castilla (Capricho de Goya Muscat★★), CHIVITE★, (Colección 125★★), GUELBENZU★, Magaña★, Vicente Malumbres, Alvaro Marino★, Castillo de Monjardin★, Vinícola Navarra, Nekeas co-op (Merlot★★), OCHOA★, Palacio de la Vega★, Piedemonte Olite co-op★, Señorío de Sarría★, Príncipe de Viana★ (formerly Cenalsa). Best years: (reds) 1996 95 **94 93 89**.

NEBBIOLO See pages 208–9.

NEBBIOLO D'ALBA DOC *Piedmont, Italy* Red wine from Nebbiolo grown around Alba, but excluding the BAROLO and BARBARESCO zones. Vineyards in the LANGHE and ROERO hills, by the Tanaro river, are noted for sandy soils that produce a fragrant, fruity style for early drinking, though some growers make wines of real character that improve for 5 years or more. Best producers: Alario★, ALTARE★, ASCHERI★, Brovia★, CERETTO★, Correggia★★, GIACOSA★, Giuseppe MASCARELLO★, PRUNOTTO★, RATTI★, SANDRONE, Vietti★. Best years: (1998) **97 96 95 93**.

NELSON *South Island, New Zealand* A range of mountains separates Nelson from MARLBOROUGH at the northern end of South Island. Nelson is made up of a series of small hills and valleys with a wide range of mesoclimates, supporting most of the grape varieties grown in New Zealand: Chardonnay, Riesling and Sauvignon Blanc do well. Best producers: Greenhough, NEUDORF★★, Ruby Bay, SEIFRIED★ (Redwood Valley).

NEUCHÂTEL *Switzerland* Swiss canton with high-altitude vineyards, mainly Chasselas for whites and Pinot Noir for reds. Three small areas (Schloss Vaumarcus, Hôpital Poutalès and Domaine de

Champrevèyres) have the right to a special AC. Best producers: Ch. d'Auvernier, Porret.

NEUDORF *Nelson, South Island, New Zealand* Owners Tim and Judy Finn make stylish and often innovative wines and have resisted the temptation to expand production, preferring instead to fine-tune the quality of their wines by careful vineyard and winery management. Best wines are Chardonnay★★★, Sauvignon Blanc★, Pinot Noir★★ and Riesling★★. Best years: (1998) **96 94 91**.

NEW SOUTH WALES *Australia* Australia's most populous state. The RIVERINA, a hot, irrigated area of 9000ha (22,000 acres) grows 14% of Australia's grapes and is definitely showing signs of improvement. The HUNTER VALLEY, MUDGEE, COWRA and HILLTOPS are smaller, premium-quality regions hugging the coastal highlands. Orange is a high-altitude inland district. Fashionable CANBERRA is an area of tiny vineyards at chilly altitudes.

NEWTON VINEYARDS *Napa Valley AVA, California, USA* Spectacular winery and vineyards above St Helena. Estate Cabernet Sauvignon★★, Merlot★★ and Claret★ are some of California's most balanced and ageworthy examples. Recent release of an unfiltered, unfined Chardonnay★★★ played to rave reviews. Newtonian★ is the excellent second label for Cabernet blends and Chardonnay and sold chiefly in export markets. Age the Chardonnays for up to 5 years, reds for 10–15. Best years: (Cabernet Sauvignon) 1996 95 94 92 91 **90 85**; (Merlot) 1996 95 93 92 91 **90 88 87 86**; (Chardonnay) 1997 96 **95 94 93 91 90**.

NEW WORLD When used as a geographical term, New World includes all the Americas, South Africa, Australia and New Zealand. By extension, it is also a term used to describe the clean, fruity, upfront style now in evidence all over the world, but pioneered by winemakers in the USA, Australia and New Zealand.

NEW YORK STATE *USA* Wine grapes were first planted on Manhattan Island in the mid-17th century but it wasn't until the early 1950s that a serious wine industry began to develop in the state as vinifera grapes were planted to replace natives such as *Vitis labrusca*. The most important region is the FINGER LAKES in the north of the state, with the Hudson River also showing some form, but LONG ISLAND is the most exciting area. New York wines, in general, have well-developed varietal fruit character and show good balance, but the erratic weather patterns of the East Coast can pose ripeness problems. Best producers: Benmarl, Brotherhood, Four Chimneys Farm Winery, FOX RUN, Heron Hill, LAMOUREAUX LANDING★, Millbrook★, Vinifera, Wagner, Wiemer Vineyard.

NGATARAWA *Hawkes Bay, North Island, New Zealand* One of Hawkes Bay's top estates and small producer of premium wines, notably Chardonnay★ and botrytized Riesling★★. Cabernet Sauvignon-Merlot can also be good but lacks consistency. Special Selections, bottled under the Glazebrook label★ (Chardonnay and Cabernet-Merlot) can be delicious. Best years: (1998) **96 95 94 91**.

NEBBIOLO

It seems almost bizarre that the grape that makes such great red wines as Nebbiolo should be so limited in its geographical spread. Yet the variety that is responsible for the majestic wines of Barolo and Barbaresco is found almost nowhere outside north-west Italy. Its name derives from the Italian for fog, *nebbia*, because it ripens late when the hills are shrouded in autumn mists. It needs a thick skin to withstand this fog, so often gives wines with a very tannic character that needs years to soften. When grown in the limestone soils of the Langhe hills around Alba, Nebbiolo produces wines that are only moderately deep in colour but have a wonderful array of perfumes and an ability to develop great complexity with age – rivalled only by Pinot Noir and Syrah.

So far efforts to grow Nebbiolo elsewhere haven't been that successful, partly because high, cool, fog-shrouded vineyards are rare in the New World, where most producers like to have their harvest safely gathered long before autumn mists descend. Even so, because of the fame of Barolo and Barbaresco, and because many vineyards were created by Italian emigrants, there are a few examples.

WINE STYLES

Barolo Usually considered the best and longest-lived of the Nebbiolo wines, though the myth that it needs a decade or more to be drinkable has been dispelled by new-style Barolo that is better balanced, softer and ready sooner. Yet the best of the traditional styles are more than worth the wait.

Barbaresco Barolo's neighbour is somewhat more approachable though styles vary between the traditional and the new.

Nebbiolo d'Alba and Roero Lighter types of Nebbiolo are produced here. The variety is also used for special barrique-aged Nebbiolos in the Alba area, such as Altare's Vigna Arborina and Aldo Conterno's Il Favot, now in the Langhe DOC.

Nebbiolo-Barbera blends The 2 varieties combine in table wines such as Clerico's Arte and Rocche dei Manzoni's Bricco Manzoni.

Northern Piedmont Nebbiolo is also the principal grape for reds of northern Piedmont – Carema, Gattinara and Ghemme.

Lombardy Known locally as Chiavennasca, it is the main variety of the Valtellina and Valtellina Superiore DOC wines.

New World There remains little outside of Italy which has really notable quality, but Australia shows the greatest potential. Trials in California have not been encouraging. The major problem for the small number of enthusiastic producers is being able to obtain virus-free planting material of a sufficiently high standard to ensure a good result.

See also BARBARESCO, BAROLO, CAREMA, GATTINARA, GHEMME, NEBBIOLO D'ALBA, VALTELLINA; AND INDIVIDUAL PRODUCERS.

BEST PRODUCERS

Italy

Barolo ALTARE, Azelia, Batasiolo, Boglietti, Bongiovanni, Brovia, CERETTO, Chiarlo, Domenico CLERICO, Aldo CONTERNO, Giacomo CONTERNO, Conterno-Fantino, Corino, R Fenocchio, GAJA, E Germano, Bruno GIACOSA, Elio Grasso, Silvio Grasso, Marcarini, Bartolo MASCARELLO, Giuseppe MASCARELLO, Parusso, Pio Cesare, F Principiano, PRUNOTTO, Renato RATTI, Rocche dei Manzoni, Luciano SANDRONE, Paolo Scavino, A & R Seghesio, Vajra, Mauro Veglio, Giovanni Viberti, Vietti, Roberto VOERZIO.

Barbaresco Barbaresco co-op, CERETTO, Cigliuti, GAJA, Bruno GIACOSA, Cantina del Glicine, Marchesi di Gresy, Moccagatta, Castello di Neive, I Paglieri, Paitin, Pelissero, Albino Rocca, Bruno Rocca, La Spinetta.

Nebbiolo d'Alba and Roero Alario, ALTARE, ASCHERI, Correggia, Deltetto, Malvirà, PRUNOTTO, Renato RATTI, Vietti.

Northern Piedmont (Carema) Ferrando; (Gattinara) Antoniolo, Le Colline, Travaglini; (Ghemme) Antichi Vigneti di Cantalupo.

Valtellina Enologica Valtellinese, Fay, Nino Negri, Rainoldi, Conti Sertoli Salis, Triacca.

New World Nebbiolos

USA (California) BONNY DOON, Martin Brothers, Il Podere dell'Olivos, Viansa.

Mexico L A CETTO.

Australia BROWN BROTHERS.

NIAGARA PENINSULA *Ontario, Canada*   Sandwiched between lakes Erie and Ontario, the Niagara Peninsula benefits from regular through-breezes created by the Niagara escarpment, the cool climate bringing out distinctive characteristics in the wine. Chardonnay leads the way in dry whites, with Riesling and Vidal making good ICEWINE. Pinot Noir is proving the most successful red grape, but Merlot and Cabernet Franc have made leaps in quality in recent vintages. Best producers: Cave Spring★, Chateau des Charmes, Henry of Pelham, Hillebrand, INNISKILLIN, Marynissen★, Southbrook Farm, Vineland Estates.

NIEBAUM COPPOLA ESTATE *Rutherford AVA, California, USA*   Movie director Coppola has turned the historic Inglenook Niebaum winery into an elaborate tourist destination. Rubicon★, a BORDEAUX blend, lacked grace in the early vintages but with Coppola's greater involvement in the 90s the wine has taken on a more elegant personality. It still needs 5–6 years of aging. As his favourite pizza wine, Coppola offers Zinfandel under the Edizione Pennino label and Cabernet Franc under Coppola Family Wines. Best years: (Rubicon) (1996) 95 94 **93 91 87 86**.

NIEPOORT *Port DOC, Douro, Portugal*   Small port shipper of Dutch origin, now run by the fifth generation of the Niepoort family. Produces outstanding vintage ports★★★, old tawnies and Colheitas★★★ and a new single-quinta wine: Quinta do Passadouro★★★. Unfiltered LBVs★★ are among the best in their class – intense and complex. Dirk Niepoort also produces good red and white DOURO Redoma★. Best years: (vintage) 1994 92 91 87 85 83 **82 80 77 70 66 63 55 45 27**; (Passadouro) 1992.

NIERSTEIN *Rheinhessen, Germany*   Both a small town and a large BEREICH which includes the infamous Grosslage Gutes Domtal. The town boasts 23 vineyard sites and the top ones (such as Ölberg, Orbel, Hipping and Pettenthal) are some of the best in the whole Rhine Valley. Best producers: GUNDERLOCH★★★, HEYL ZU HERRNSHEIM★★, St Antony★★. Best years: (1998) 97 96 **94 93 90**.

NIKOLAIHOF *Wachau, Niederösterreich, Austria*   The Saahs family of Mautern makes some of the best wines in the WACHAU as well as in nearby Krems-Stein in KREMSTAL, including one of Austria's finest Rieslings from their small plot in the famous Steiner Hund vineyard, always ★★. Best years: 1998 97 96 **95 94 92 91 90 86 79 77**.

NOBILO *Kumeu/Huapai, Auckland, North Island, New Zealand*   A family winery which produces a wide range of wines from popular medium-dry White Cloud to single-vineyard varietals. Dixon Vineyard Chardonnay★★, a lush, intensely flavoured wine, is Nobilo's 'prestige' label. Sleek Sauvignon Blanc★ and Chardonnay★ from Nobilo's newly developed MARLBOROUGH vineyard are rapidly moving toward centre-stage. In 1998 Nobilo bought SELAKS, a mid-sized company with wineries in AUCKLAND and MARLBOROUGH. The largest Australian winemaker, BRL HARDY, subsequently bought a 25% stake in Nobilo. Best years: (1998) **96 95 94 91**.

NORTON *Mendoza, Argentina*   Austrian-owned winery, with one of the country's best viticulturists, Carlos Tizio Mayer, delivering superb-quality fruit. Good new aromatic Torrontés and clean, crisp Sémillon-Chenin Blanc blend★. A thumping blockbuster Malbec★★ heads the reds with top-of-the-range Privada★★ blend needing at least 5 years' cellaring. Best years: (reds) **1996 94**.

NOVAL, QUINTA DO *Port DOC, Douro, Portugal* Bought by French insurance giant AXA subsidiary's AXA-Millésimes in 1993, this immaculate property, perched above Pinhão, is the source of an extraordinary port, Quinta do Noval Nacional★★★, made from ungrafted vines. This is probably the best vintage port made, but it is virtually unobtainable except at auction. Other Noval ports (including vintage Quinta do Noval★★ and single-quintas do Silval★★ and do Roriz★★) are now excellent too. Also makes fine Colheitas★★. Best years: (Nacional) 1994 91 87 85 **70 66 63 31**; (vintage) 1995 94.

NUITS-ST-GEORGES AC *Côte de Nuits, Burgundy, France* This large AC for mainly red wine is one of the few relatively reliable 'village' names in Burgundy. Although it has no Grands Crus, many of its Premiers Crus (it has 38!) are extremely good. The red can be rather slow to open out, often needing at least 5 years. There are also minuscule amounts of white made by Gouges★, l'Arlot, Chevillon, and RION. Best producers: l'Arlot★★, Chauvenet★, R Chevillon★★, J-J Confuron★, R Dubois★★, FAIVELEY★, Gouges★★, GRIVOT★★, JAYER★★★, JAYER-GILLES★★, LABOURE-ROI★, MEO-CAMUZET★★, A Michelot★, Remoriquet★, RION★★, Thomas-Moillard★. Best years: (reds) 1997 96 95 93 **91** 90 **89 88 85**.

NYETIMBER *West Sussex, England* Brainchild of two expatriate Chicagoans, making top-quality, trophy-winning, traditional-method sparkling wines, clearly showing England's potential in this field. First production Première Cuvée 1992 is all Chardonnay. The 1993 Classic Cuvée★★ has 30% Pinot Noir and Meunier in the blend.

OAKVILLE AVA *Napa Valley, USA* Made official in 1996, this region is similar in just about every respect to RUTHERFORD, which lies immediately to the north. Planted primarily to Cabernet Sauvignon, the area contains some of the best vineyards (MONDAVI, Martha's Vineyard, OPUS ONE), but no discernible regional style has made itself known.

OC, VIN DE PAYS D' *Languedoc-Roussillon, France* Increasingly exciting VIN DE PAYS concentrating on New-World-style red and white wines. Local producers such as SKALLI-FORTANT and VAL D'ORBIEU have been complemented by the arrival of talented winemakers from Australia, England and Switzerland. Best producers: Dom. de la BAUME, HERRICK, Lalaurie, J Lurton★, Mas Cremant★, Pech-Céleyran (Viognier★), Quatre Sous★, Hugh Ryman, SKALLI-FORTANT, VAL D'ORBIEU★ (top reds), Virginie★ (top cuvées).

OCHOA *Navarra DO, Navarra, Spain* Javier Ochoa has clearly taken his own advice as the former chief winemaker of the experimental wine research station by completely modernizing the family bodega and its 68ha (168 acres) of vineyards. The resulting wines are fresh, clean and fruity, with particularly good Merlot★★, Cabernet Sauvignon★, Tempranillo★ and sweet Muscat★. Best years: (reds) 1996 **95 94 93 92 91** 90 89 87 86 85.

OCKFEN *Saar, Germany* Village with one famous individual vineyard site, the Bockstein. The wines can be superb in a sunny year, never losing their cold steely streak but packing in delightful full-flavoured fruit as well. Best producers: Dr Fischer, Heinz Wagner★★, ZILLIKEN★★. Best years: 1997 95 **93** 90.

OISLY-ET-THÉSÉE, CONFRÉRIE DES VIGNERONS D' *Touraine, Loire Valley, France* This innovative co-op established itself as one of the leading names in TOURAINE under the directorship of the late Jacques Choquet. Choquet's vision lives on in the fresh but richly flavoured wines, especially the Sauvignon-based whites★, Gamay-based reds and CREMANT DE LOIRE★, all sold under the Baronnie d'Aignan label. Except for their Sauvignon Cuvée Excellence★, the best single varietals come from Château de Vallagon★.

OKANAGAN VALLEY *British Columbia, Canada* The most important wine-producing region of British Columbia and first home of Canada's rich, honeyed ICEWINE. The Okanagan Lake's warmth helps temper the bitterly cold nights but October frosts can be a problem here. Pinot Blanc and Pinot Noir are the top performing grapes. South of the lake, Cabernet and Merlot are now being grown successfully. Best producers: Blue Mountain, Gray Monk, MISSION HILL★, Quail's Gate★, Sumac Ridge.

OLOROSO See Jerez y Manzanilla DO/Sherry.

OLTREPÒ PAVESE DOC *Lombardy, Italy* Oltrepò Pavese is Italy's main source of Pinot Nero, used mainly for sparkling wines that may be called Classese when made by the Champagne method here, though base wines supply SPUMANTE industries elsewhere. The hills have long furnished Milan with daily wines, often fizzy, though still reds from Barbera, Bonarda and Pinot Nero and whites from the Pinots, Riesling and, lately, Chardonnay can be impressive. Best producers: Anteo, Cà di Frara★, Le Fracce★, Frecciarossa★, Fugazza, Mazzolino★, Monsupello★, Montelio★, Piccolo Bacco dei Quaroni, Santa Maria della Versa co-op★, Vercesi del Castellazzo★, Bruno Verdi★. Best years: (reds) (1998) 97 **96 95 93 90**.

OMAR KHAYYAM *Maharashtra, India* Champagne-method sparkling wine produced from a blend of Chardonnay, Ugni Blanc, Pinot Noir, Pinot Meunier – and Thompson Seedless. The Thompson is now being used less and less as plantings of the other varieties come on stream. Technology, thanks to CHAMPAGNE consultants PIPER-HEIDSIECK, together with high-sited, irrigated vineyards, generally produce a firm, fresh, chunky sparkler – though quality is somewhat erratic. A demi-sec style, Marquise de Pompadour, is also made.

OPPENHEIM *Rheinhessen, Germany* Village whose reputation has suffered from the sale of much inferior wine under the Oppenheimer Krötenbrunnen label. In its steepest sites, such as Sackträger, it can be one of the best villages in RHEINHESSEN, where the deep soils give relatively earthy, weighty wines. Best producers: Guntrum, Koch, Kühling-Gillot. Best years: (1998) **96 93**.

OPUS ONE *Napa Valley AVA, California, USA* Widely publicized joint venture between Robert MONDAVI and the late Baron Philippe de Rothschild of MOUTON-ROTHSCHILD. The first vintage (1979) was released in 1983. At that time, the $50 price was the most expensive for any California wine, though others have reached beyond it now. The various Opus bottlings since 1979 have been in the ★★ range but have just recently reached the standard of the Mondavi Reserve Cabernet★★★. Best years: (1996) 95 94 93 92 91 **90 88 87 84 80**.

OREGON *USA* Oregon shot to international stardom in the early 1980s following some perhaps overly generous praise of its Pinot Noir, but the state has failed to consolidate this position. Not that Oregon Pinot Noir can't be attractive, but at its best it rarely offers more than a black cherry fruit generally without much complexity. Chardonnay can be quite good in an austere, understated style. The rising star is Pinot Gris which, in Oregon's cool climate, can be delicious with surprising complexity. Pinot Blanc is also gaining some momentum. The Willamette Valley is considered the best growing region and the Dundee hills area the best sub-region. Best producers: ADELSHEIM★★, AMITY★★, Archery Summit★, Argyle, BEAUX FRERES★★, Bethel Heights★, Cameron★, DOMAINE DROUHIN★★, Elk Cove★, Eola Hills, ERATH, EYRIE★★, Henry Estate, KING ESTATE, PONZI★, Rex Hill★, SOKOL BLOSSER★★, Yamhill Valley★.

ORLANDO *Barossa Valley, South Australia* Australia's second-biggest wine company is owned by Pernod-Ricard and encompasses MORRIS, Wickham Hill, Gramps, Richmond Grove and WYNDHAM ESTATE. Top wines under the Orlando name are consistent COONAWARRA reds St Hugo★ and Jacaranda Ridge★; individualistic Eden Valley Rieslings St Helga★ and Steingarten★★. Jacobs Creek basics are deservedly Australia's most successful brand abroad, but these days Orlando lacks strength at the premium end. Pricy but rich Centenary Hill Shiraz★ promises to change that. Best years: (St Hugo Cabernet) **1994 92 90 86 82**.

ORNELLAIA, TENUTA DELL' *Bolgheri, Italy* This beautiful property was developed by Lodovico Antinori, brother of Piero, after he left the family firm, ANTINORI, to strike out on his own. The red Ornellaia★★★, a Cabernet-Merlot blend, can be interestingly compared with neighbouring SASSICAIA. The white Poggio alle Gazze★★ is made solely with Sauvignon. An outstanding Merlot, Masseto★★★, is produced in small quantities. Best years: (Ornellaia) (1998) (97) (96) 95 94 **93 92 91 90 88**.

ORVIETO DOC *Umbria, Italy* Traditionally a lightly sweet abboccato white wine, Orvieto is now usually a dry characterless white. In the superior Classico zone, however, the potential for richer and more biscuity wines exists. Not generally a wine for aging, Palazzone's Riserva★ is an exception. There are also several very good noble-rot-affected examples. Best producers: (dry) Barberani★, La Carraia, Decugnano dei Barbi★, Palazzone★, Castello della SALA★, Salviano★, Conte Vaselli★, Le Velette★; (sweet) Barberani★, Decugnano dei Barbi★, Palazzone★★, Castello della SALA★★.

OSBORNE *Jerez y Manzanilla DO, Andalucía, Spain* The biggest drinks company in Spain, Osborne does most of its business in brandy and other spirits. Its sherry arm in Puerto de Santa María specializes in the light Fino Quinta★. Amontillado Coquinero★, rich, intense Bailén Oloroso★★ and Solera India★★ are very good indeed.

OVERBERG WO *South Africa* South Africa's most southerly wine region, much prized for cool-climate viticulture; embracing the upland area of Elgin as well as the coastal ward of Walker Bay. Sauvignon, Chardonnay, Riesling and Pinot Noir vindicate the decision to replace valuable apple orchards. Walker Bay was opened up (at the time illegally) by HAMILTON RUSSELL in the mid-1970s, who remained the only producer until BOUCHARD FINLAYSON started in the early 90s. The number of producers, currently 11, is growing steadily. Pinot Noir is the holy grail of the majority, although Pinotage is also doing well. Best producers: (Elgin) Paul Cluver; (Walker Bay) BOUCHARD FINLAYSON★★, HAMILTON RUSSELL VINEYARDS★★, Wildekrans★.

213

PAARL WO *South Africa* Paarl is South Africa's second most densely planted region after Worcester, accounting for nearly 19% of all vineyards. There is great diversity of soil and climate here, favouring everything from Cap Classique sparkling wines to sherry styles. Wellington and FRANSCHHOEK are smaller designated areas within the Paarl region. Wineries are also varied: KWV's 22-ha (55-acre) complex is said to be the largest winery facility in the world; Claridge (Wellington) represents the boutique end of the scale. Best producers: (Paarl) BACKSBERG★, BOSCHENDAL, FAIRVIEW★★, GLEN CARLOU★★, STELLENBOSCH FARMERS' WINERY (Plaisir de Merle★★, Nederburg), VEENWOUDEN★★, VILLIERA★★, Welgemeend★; (Wellington) Claridge.

PACHERENC DU VIC-BILH AC *South-West France* Small amount of individual whites from an area overlapping the MADIRAN AC in north-east Béarn. The wines are mainly dry but there are some medium-sweet/sweet late-harvest wines. Most Pacherenc is best drunk young. Best producers: Aydie, Berthoumieu★, Brumont★, Crampilh, Damiens, Laffitte-Teston, PLAIMONT co-op. Best years: (1998) **97 96 95**.

PACIFIC ECHO *Anderson Valley AVA, California, USA* Known until 1998 as Scharffenberger Cellars, this winery was erratic in its early vintages, but money from Pommery and its parent LVMH has upgraded the facility and recent vintages have been greatly improved. The Brut★, with finely focused fruit, and the exuberant Rose★ are lovely. The BLANC DE BLANCS Prestige Cuvée★★ is one of California's finest sparklers.

PADTHAWAY *South Australia* This wine region has always been the alter-ego of nearby COONAWARRA, growing whites to complement Coonawarra's reds. But today some excellent reds are made, and even PENFOLDS Grange now has some Padthaway grapes. ORLANDO's premium Shirazes, Centenary Hill★ and Lawson's★, are all Padthaway. HARDY's Eileen Hardy Shiraz★★★ is half Padthaway and LINDEMANS Padthaway Chardonnay★ is a serious white. Padthaway Sauvignon Blanc is also some of Australia's tastiest. Best producers: Browns of Padthaway, HARDY★, LINDEMANS★, ORLANDO★, Padthaway Estate, SEPPELT.

BODEGAS PALACIO *Rioja DOC, País Vasco, Spain* Founded in 1894 by Don Cosme Palacio, then the owner of VEGA SICILIA. Relaunched in the late 1980s by then owner Jean Gervais and POMEROL winemaker Michel Rolland, whose Cosme Palacio y Hermanos★★ has become a cult wine in Spain. Sold in 1998 to the owners of Viña Mayor, a RIBERA DEL DUERO winery. Best years: (reds) 1995 **94 92 91 90 89**.

ALVARO PALACIOS *Priorat DO, Catalonia, Spain* Although he was only in his 20s, Alvaro Palacios was already a veteran with Bordeaux and Napa experience when he launched his boutique winery in the rough hills of southern CATALONIA in the late 1980s. He is now one of the driving forces of the area's sensational rebirth. His expensive, highly concentrated reds★★★ from old Garnacha vines and a dollop of Cabernet Sauvignon, Merlot and Syrah have won a cult following. Best years: 1996 95 94 93 **92 90**.

PALETTE AC *Provence, France* Tiny AC just east of Aix-en-Provence. Even though the local market pays high prices, I find the reds and rosés rather tough and charmless. However, Ch. Simone, the only producer of white Palette, manages to achieve a wine of some flavour from basic southern grapes. Best producers: Crémade, Ch. Simone★★.

PALLISER ESTATE *Wairarapa, North Island, New Zealand* State-of-the-art winery producing some of New Zealand's best Sauvignon★★★ (certainly the best outside MARLBOROUGH) and Riesling, with some impressive but less consistent Pinot Noir★. Exciting botrytized dessert wines appear in favourable vintages. It may be small but it's still one of the largest in WAIRARAPA. Best years: (1998) **97 96 94 91**.

CH. PALMER★★ *Margaux AC, 3ème Cru Classé, Haut-Médoc, Bordeaux, France* This estate was named after a British major-general who fought in the Napoleonic Wars. Palmer was the leading property in MARGAUX AC during the 1960s and 70s until the Mentzelopolous family took over at Ch. MARGAUX in 1977. Although only a Third Growth, the wine, with its wonderful perfume and irresistible plump fruit, often manages to be as good as the top Second Growths but sometimes would benefit from rather more body and intensity. The very best vintages can age for 30 years or more. Second wine: Réserve-du-Général. Best years: (1998) 97 96 95 90 89 **88 86 85 83 82 79 78 75 70**.

PALOMAS *Rio Grande do Sul, Brazil* Winery just north of the Uruguay border, in the one area of Brazil where the climate at least tolerates the cultivation of classic vinifera varieties. Its simple, ramshackle wines satisfy curiosity rather than titillate.

CH. PAPE-CLÉMENT *Pessac-Léognan AC, Cru Classé de Graves, Bordeaux, France* This expensive and famous GRAVES Classed Growth mainly for red wine★★ has not always been as consistent as it should be – but things have looked up considerably since the exciting 1986 vintage. In style it is mid-way between the refinement of HAUT-BRION and the firmness of la MISSION-HAUT-BRION. There is also a small production of a much-improved

white wine★★. Second wine: (red) Clémentin. Best years: (1998) 97 96 95 94 93 90 89 88 **86 85**.

PARELLADA This Catalan exclusivity is the lightest of the trio of simple white grapes that go to make CAVA wines in north-eastern Spain. It also makes still wines, light, fresh and gently floral, with good acidity and (for Spain) lowish alcohol (between 9 and 11%). Drink it as young as possible – and I mean *young* – while it still has the benefit of freshness.

PARKER ESTATE *Coonawarra, South Australia* Recent arrival on the premium market, a red specialist impressing with its first efforts made by the experienced Ralph Fowler (formerly at LECONFIELD), and latterly by Chris Cameron at Pepper Tree. The top label is the cheekily named Terra Rossa First Growth★★, which drinks well at 3 years but promises to age well.

PARRINA DOC *Tuscany, Italy* On the coast in southern TUSCANY, the Sangiovese-Canaiolo red is minty and robust; the white is from

Trebbiano and Ansonica. Drink within 3–5 years, Riserva★ will keep a little longer. Best producer: La Parrina. Best years: (1998) **97 96 95 94 93**.

PASSITO Italian term for wine made from dried grapes. The result is usually a sweet wine with a raisiny intensity of fruit. See also Moscato Passito di Pantelleria, Recioto di Soave, Recioto della Valpolicella, Vin Santo.

LUIS PATO *Bairrada, Beira Litoral, Portugal* Leading 'modernist' in BAIRRADA, passionately convinced of the Baga grape's ability to make great reds on clay soil. From 1995, wines such as the Vinhas Velhas★★, Vinha Barrosa★★ and Quinta do Ribeirinho Primera Escolha★ rank among Portugal's finest new red wines. Best years: (reds) 1997 **96 95 92**.

PATRIMONIO AC *Corsica, France* Good, underrated wines from the northern end of the island. The reds and rosés, based on the local Nielluccio grape, are your best bet; Malvasia is becoming the exclusive variety for whites. Best producers: Arena★, Gentile, Leccia★, Orenga de Gaffory★. Best years: (reds) (1998) 97 96 **95 94 93 92 91 90 89**.

PAUILLAC AC *Haut-Médoc, Bordeaux, France* The deep gravel banks around the town of Pauillac in the HAUT-MEDOC are the true heartland of Cabernet Sauvignon. For many wine lovers, the king of red wine grapes finds its ultimate expression in the 3 Pauillac First Growths (LATOUR, LAFITE-ROTHSCHILD and MOUTON-ROTHSCHILD). The large AC also contains 15 other Classed Growths, including world-famous PICHON-LONGUEVILLE-LALANDE, PICHON-LONGUEVILLE and LYNCH-BAGES. The uniting characteristic of Pauillac wines is their intense blackcurrant fruit flavour and heady cedar and pencil-shavings perfume. These are the longest-lived of Bordeaux's great red wines. Best producers: BATAILLEY★, Clerc-Milon★★, Fonbadet★, GRAND-PUY-DUCASSE★, GRAND-PUY-LACOSTE★★, HAUT-BAGES-LIBERAL★, HAUT-BATAILLEY★, LAFITE-ROTHSCHILD★★★, LATOUR★★★, LYNCH-BAGES★★★, MOUTON-ROTHSCHILD★★★, Pibran★, PICHON-LONGUEVILLE★★★, PICHON-LONGUEVILLE-LALANDE★★★, PONTET-CANET★★. Best years: (1998) 96 95 94 90 89 88 86 **85 83 82 81 79 78**.

CH. PAVIE★ *St-Émilion Grand Cru AC, 1er Grand Cru Classé, Bordeaux, France* The 2nd-largest of the ST-EMILION Premiers Grands Crus (after FIGEAC), Pavie produces supple, aromatic wines. The wines will happily evolve for a decade yet never lose the soft, unctuous charm of the fruit and the sweet oak. Recent vintages have lacked guts but a change of ownership in 1998 should signal a rapid improvement. Best years: (1998) 96 95 **90 89 88 86 85 83 82 81**.

PÉCHARMANT AC *South-West France* Lovely red wines from this small AC north-east of BERGERAC. The wines are quite light in body but have a delicious, full, piercing flavour of blackcurrants and a most attractive grassy acidity. Good vintages will easily last 10 years and end up indistinguishable from a good HAUT-MEDOC wine. Best producers: Bertranoux, Champarel, Clos Peyrelevade, Corbiac, Costes, Haut-Pécharmant, la Métairie, Tiregand★. Best years: (1998) 97 96 **95 90 89 88 86 85 83**.

PECONIC BAY VINEYARDS *Long Island AVA, New York State, USA* Peconic Bay has a well-deserved reputation for Chardonnay, which it makes in a light oaked style and as barrel-fermented single-vineyard Chardonnays★★ (Sandy Hill, Rolling Ridge) that are complex and buttery. But don't bypass the Merlot, especially the Epic Hill bottling and the intense Cabernet Sauvignon. Best years: (1998) 96 95.

PEDROSA *Ribera del Duero DO, Castilla y León, Spain* Delicious, elegant reds★ (Pérez Pascuas Reserva★★), both young and oak-aged, from a family winery in the little hill village of Pedrosa del Duero. The wines are not cheap, but far less pricy than some stars of this fashionable region. Best years: (reds) 1996 **95 94 92 91 90 89 86.**

PEMBERTON *Western Australia* Exciting new region, deep in the karri forests of the south-west; full of promise for cool-climate Pinot Noir, Chardonnay and who knows what else. Leading wineries include Salitage, run by Denis (LEEUWIN ESTATE) Horgan's brother John; Picardy, founded by Bill Pannell of MOSS WOOD fame; Chestnut Grove, part-owned by the Langes from Alkoomi, and Bronzewing Estate, owned by John Kosovich of SWAN VALLEY winery Westfield. Kosovich makes a fine Verdelho and Pannell has high hopes for Shiraz.

PEÑAFLOR *Mendoza, Argentina* The biggest producer of wine in Argentina sends millions of litres of cheap Termidor brand to Buenos Aires each month. Investment in its fine wine arm, Trapiche, along with the recent hiring of Bordeaux enologist Michel Rolland, is beginning to deliver results. Grassy Chenin Blanc★, rich, melony Chardonnay and punchy Sauvignon★ from high-altitude vineyards show promise. Oak-aged Cabernet-Malbec blend★ is a mouthfilling red.

PENEDÈS DO *Catalonia, Spain* The wealthy CAVA industry is based in Penedès, and the majority of the still wines are white, made from the Cava trio of Parellada, Macabeo and Xarel-lo, clean and fresh when young, but never exciting. Better whites are made from Chardonnay. The reds are variable, the best made from Cabernet Sauvignon and/or Tempranillo and Merlot. Best producers: Albet i Noya★, Can Feixes★, Can Ráfols des Caus★ (Caus Lubis Merlot★★), Cavas Hill, JUVE Y CAMPS★, Jean LEON★★, MARQUES DE MONISTROL★, Masía Bach★, Albert Milá i Mallofré, Puig i Roca★, TORRES★, Vallformosa, Jané Ventura.

PENFOLDS *Barossa Valley, South Australia* Part of Australia's Southcorp Wines group, Penfolds proves that quality *can* go in hand with quantity and is regarded as the dominant force in Australian wine. Makes the country's greatest red wine, Grange★★★, and a welter of superbly rich, structured reds from Magill Estate★ through St Henri★, Bin 707 Cabernet★★★, Bin 389 Cabernet-Shiraz★★, Bin 28 Kalimna★★ and Bin 128 Coonawarra Shiraz★ to Koonunga Hill★ and Rawson's Retreat cheapies. Still very much a red wine name, although making a spirited bid for Chardonnay fame with new Chardonnay★★★ and Semillon★★★ from ADELAIDE HILLS, led by overpriced Yattarna★★★, which set new heights for PR hype in 1998. Also makes tasty wooded Semillon★★ and lemony Semillon-Chardonnay★★. Best years: (Grange) 1993 92 91 90 88 86 83 **80 76 71 66 65 63 62 56 55 53;** (other reds) 1996 **94 93 92 91 90 88 86 84 83 82 80 78 76 71.**

PENLEY ESTATE *Coonawarra, South Australia* Kym Tolley, a member of the PENFOLD family, combined the names when he left Southcorp and launched Penley Estate in 1991. The Cabernet Sauvignon★★★ is outstanding and matches its lavish packaging. Chardonnay and Hyland Shiraz can reach ★★; sparkling★ is also worth a try. Best years: (Cabernet) **1994 93 92 91 90.**

PERLWEIN German for lightly sparkling wine.

PERNAND-VERGELESSES AC *Côte de Beaune, Burgundy, France* The little-known village of Pernand-Vergelesses contains a decent chunk of the great Corton hill, including much of the best white CORTON-CHARLEMAGNE Grand Cru vineyard. The red wines sold under the village name are very attractive when young with a nice raspberry pastille fruit and a slight earthiness, and will age for 6–10 years. As no one ever links poor old Pernand with the heady heights of Corton-Charlemagne, the whites sold under the village name can be a bargain – quite a rarity in Burgundy. The wines can be a bit lean and dry to start with but fatten up beautifully after 2–4 years in bottle. Best producers: (reds) Besancenot-Mathouillet★, Chandon de Briailles★★, C Cornu★, Denis Père et Fils★, Dubreuil-Fontaine★, Laleure-Piot★, Rapet★, Rollin★; (whites) Chandon de Briailles★, Dubreuil-Fontaine★, GERMAIN★, A Guyon, JADOT, Laleure-Piot★, J-M Pavelot★, Rapet★, Rollin. Best years: (reds) 1997 96 95 **93 90 89 88**; (whites) 1997 96 95 **92 90**.

JOSEPH PERRIER *Champagne AC, Champagne, France* This is the sole CHAMPAGNE house left in Châlons-en-Champagne (previously called Châlons-sur-Marne) and is still family-run. The NV Cuvée★ is biscuity and creamy, the Prestige Cuvée Josephine★★ has length and complexity, but the much cheaper Cuvée Royale Vintage★ is the best deal. Best years: **1990 89 88 85 82 79 75**.

PERRIER-JOUËT *Champagne AC, Champagne, France* This is supposedly the best of the CHAMPAGNE houses owned by the Canadian multi-national Seagram. The non-vintage is variable, but the vintage is still a good rich style★★. A de luxe cuvée, Belle Époque★★★, famous for its embossed Art Nouveau label, has, for once, in the image-obsessed world of Champagne, an exciting flavour to match the exterior fol-de-rols. Belle Époque rosé★★ is excellent, too. Best years: **1992 90 89 88 85 82**.

PESQUERA *Ribera del Duero DO, Castilla y León, Spain* Viña Pesquera reds, richly coloured, firm, fragrant and plummy-tobaccoey, are among Spain's best. Made by the small firm of Alejandro Fernández, they are 100% Tempranillo and sold as Crianzas★★, with Reservas★★ and Pesquera Janus★★★ in the best years. Best years: 1996 **95 94 93 92 91 90 89 86 85**.

PESSAC-LÉOGNAN AC *Bordeaux, France* New AC, created in 1987, for the northern (and best) part of the GRAVES region and including all the Graves Classed Growths. The supremely gravelly soil tends to favour red wines over the rest of the Graves. Now this is also one of the most exciting areas of France for top-class white wines, the standard has vastly improved, thanks to the advent of cool fermentation, controlled yeast selection and the use of new oak barrels. Best producers: (reds) CARBONNIEUX★, Dom. de CHEVALIER★★, FIEUZAL★, HAUT-BAILLY★★, HAUT-BRION★★★, la LOUVIERE★★, MALARTIC-LAGRAVIERE, la MISSION-HAUT-BRION★★, PAPE-CLEMENT★★, SMITH-HAUT-LAFITTE★, la Tour-Haut-Brion★★, la TOUR-MARTILLAC★; (whites) CARBONNIEUX★, Dom. de CHEVALIER★★★, Couhins-Lurton★★, FIEUZAL★★, HAUT-BRION★★★, LAVILLE-HAUT-BRION★★, la LOUVIERE★★, MALARTIC-LAGRAVIERE★, Rochemorin★, SMITH-HAUT-LAFITTE★★, la TOUR-MARTILLAC★★. Best years: (reds) (1998) 96 95 94 90 89 **88 86 85 83 82 81 79 78**; (whites) (1998) 96 **95 94 93 90 89 88 86 85 83 82**.

PETALUMA *Adelaide Hills, South Australia* This publicly listed company, which includes KNAPPSTEIN and MITCHELTON, is run by Brian Croser.

probably Australia's most influential and thoughtful winemaker. Champagne-method Croser★★ has at last mellowed in style but is dry and lean. The Chardonnay★★★ and COONAWARRA Cabernet-Merlot★★★ are consistently outstanding and CLARE Riesling★★★ is at the fuller end of the spectrum and matures superbly. Vineyard Selection Tiers Chardonnay★★★ set a new price record with its debut 1996 vintage. Best years: (reds) 1996 94 93 **92 91 90 88**.

PÉTILLANT French for a slightly sparkling wine, often one which has been purposely bottled with a bit of carbon dioxide.

PETIT CHABLIS AC *Chablis, Burgundy, France* Once this denoted the outlying parts of the CHABLIS region. Then the vineyards were upgraded to full Chablis. Now more land has been planted even further away. The wine is often thin but can be appealing when drunk young. Too close to regular Chablis in price, though.

PETITE SIRAH Long used as a blending grape in California but used also for varietal wines, Petite Sirah is supposed to be the Durif of southern France, although there is now some doubt about that. At its best in California and Mexico, the wine has great depth and strength; at worst it can be monstrously huge and unfriendly. Best producers: L A CETTO★ (Mexico), Fife, FETZER, Foppiano, RIDGE★, Turley★★★.

PETIT VERDOT A rich, tannic red variety, grown mainly in Bordeaux's HAUT-MEDOC to add depth, colour and violet fragrance to top wines. Late-ripening and erratic yield limits its popularity, but warmer-climate plantings in Australia, Spain and California are giving exciting results.

CH. PETIT-VILLAGE★★ *Pomerol AC, Bordeaux, France* This top POMEROL wine, traditionally much sterner in style than its neighbours, is now made by Jean-Michel Cazes, who also runs PICHON-LONGUEVILLE in PAUILLAC. In general it is worth aging the wine for 8–10 years at least. Best years: (1998) 96 95 94 90 89 88 **85 83 82 81 79 78**.

CH. PÉTRUS★★★ *Pomerol AC, Bordeaux, France* Now one of the most expensive red wines in the world, but only 30 years ago Pétrus was virtually unknown. Today it regularly fetches astronomical prices at auction, as do several other fine wines from POMEROL, such as le PIN. The powerful, concentrated wine produced here is the result of the caring genius of Pétrus' co-owners since 1962, the MOUEIX family, who have maximized the potential of the vineyard of almost solid clay and remarkably old vines, which, in places, are up to 70 years of age. Drinkable for its astonishingly rich, dizzying blend of fruit and spice flavours after a decade, but top years will age for much longer, developing exotic scents of tobacco and chocolate and truffles as they mature. Best years: (1998) 97 96 95 94 93 90 89 88 **86 85 82 79 75 71**.

CH. DE PEZ★ *St-Estèphe AC, Cru Bourgeois, Haut-Médoc, Bordeaux, France* One of ST-ESTEPHE's leading non-Classed Growths, de Pez makes mouthfilling, satisfying claret with sturdy fruit. Slow to evolve, good vintages often need 10 years or more to mature. Best years: (1998) 97 96 95 94 90 89 **88 86 85 83 82 79 78**.

PFALZ *Germany* Germany's most productive wine region makes a lot of mediocre wine, but the quality estates are capable of matching the best that Germany has to offer. The Mittelhaardt has a reputation for Riesling, especially round the villages of WACHENHEIM, FORST and Deidesheim, though Freinsheim, Ungstein, KALLSTADT, Gimmeldingen and Haardt also produce fine Riesling as well as Scheurebe, Pinot Gris and Dornfelder. In the Südliche Weinstrasse the warm climate makes the area an ideal testing ground for the so-called Burgunders (Pinot Noir, Pinot Blanc and Pinot Gris), as well as Gewürztraminer, Scheurebe, Muscat and Dornfelder, usually made dry but rich. See also Bad Dürkheim, Burrweiler, Kallstadt.

JOSEPH PHELPS *Napa Valley AVA, California, USA* Joseph Phelps' Insignia★★ red (Cabernet, Merlot and Cabernet Franc) is consistently one of California's top reds, strongly fruit-driven with a lively spicy background. Phelps makes 2 Cabernets: Napa Valley★, a medium-weight wine, and Backus Vineyard★; each has solid fruit with good balance. Best years: (Insignia) (1996) 95 94 93 92 91 **89 87 85 84 80.**

PIAT D'OR An inexorably popular, off-dry VIN DE TABLE made in red and white versions. These wines are dull and ludicrously overpriced – but then someone has to pay for the extremely effective advertising. Now also playing the MIDI varietal card.

FRANZ X PICHLER *Wachau, Niederösterreich, Austria* A leading WACHAU superstar whose Kellerberg and Steinertal Rieslings★★★ are extremely concentrated. There are also excellent Grüner Veltliners★★ from the Loibner Berg. Best years: (1998) 97 **95 94 93 92 91 90 86 75.**

CH. PICHON-LONGUEVILLE★★★ *Pauillac AC, 2ème Cru Classé, Haut-Médoc, Bordeaux, France* Despite its superb vineyards with the potential for making great PAUILLAC, Pichon-Longueville (called Pichon-Baron until 1988) wines were 'also-rans' for a long time. In 1987 the management was taken over by Jean-Michel Cazes of LYNCH-BAGES and, since then, there has been a remarkable change in fortune. Recent vintages have been of First Growth standard, with firm tannic structure and rich dark fruit. Cellar for at least 10 years, although it is likely to keep for 30. Second wine: les Tourelles de Pichon. Best years: (1998) 97 96 95 94 90 89 **88 86 82.**

CH. PICHON-LONGUEVILLE-LALANDE★★★ *(on recent form) Pauillac AC, 2ème Cru Classé, Haut-Médoc, Bordeaux, France* Pichon-Longueville-Lalande has been run since 1978 by the inspirational figure of Madame de Lencquesaing, who has led the property ever upwards on a wave of passion and involvement, through her superlative vineyard management and winemaking sensitivity. Divinely scented and lush at 6–7 years, the wines usually last for 20 at least. Things dipped at the end of the 1980s, but recent efforts have been excellent. Second wine: Réserve de la Comtesse. Best years: (1998) 97 96 95 94 93 **89 88 86 85 83 82 81 79 78 75.**

PIC ST-LOUP *Coteaux du Languedoc AC, Languedoc, France* The vineyards of this Cru, arranged around a steep outcrop of limestone north of Montpellier, produce some of the best reds in the Languedoc. This is one of the coolest growing zones in the MIDI. Syrah does particularly well and, along with Grenache and Mourvèdre, it is the dominant variety. Whites from Marsanne, Roussanne, Rolle and Viognier are beginning to show promise. Best producers: l'Hortus★, Lascaux★, Mas Bruguière★, la Roque. Best years: (reds) (1998) **96 95 94 93 91**.

PIEDMONT *Italy* This is the most important Italian region for the tradition of quality wines. In the north, there is CAREMA, GHEMME and GATTINARA. To the south, in the LANGHE hills, there's BAROLO and BARBARESCO, both masterful examples of the Nebbiolo grape, and other wines from Dolcetto and Barbera grapes. In the Monferrato hills, in the provinces of Asti and Alessandria, the Barbera, Moscato and Cortese grapes hold sway. Recent changes in the system have created the broad new DOCs of Colline Novaresi in the north, Langhe and Monferrato in the south and the regionwide Piemonte appellation designed to classify all wines of quality from a great range of grape varieties. See also Asti, Erbaluce di Caluso, Gavi, Moscato d'Asti, Nebbiolo d'Alba, Roero.

PIEROPAN *Veneto, Italy* Leonildo and Teresita Pieropan produce excellent SOAVE Classico★ and, from 2 single vineyards, Calvarino★★ and La Rocca★★, the definitive wines of this zone. There is an excellent Recioto di Soave Le Colombare★★, and an opulent Passito della Rocca★★, a barrique-aged blend of Sauvignon, Riesling Italico and Trebbiano di Soave. Single-vineyard Soaves can improve for 5 years or more, as can the Recioto and other sweet styles.

PIERRO *Margaret River, Western Australia* Yet another of MARGARET RIVER's winemaking doctors, Mike Peterkin makes Pierro Chardonnay★★★ by the hatful, yet still it is a masterpiece of power and complexity. The Semillon-Sauvignon blend★ is full and less grassy than most, while Pinot Noir is above average. A dark, dense Cabernet is a new addition. Fire Gully is the second label with bought-in grapes. Best years: (Chardonnay) **1997 96 95 94 93 92 91 90 87 86**.

PIESPORT *Mosel, Germany* Best known for the generic Piesporter Michelsberg wines, soft, sweet and easy-drinking, which have nothing to do with the excellent Rieslings from the top Goldtröpfchen site. With their intense blackcurrant and peach aromas they are unique among MOSEL wines. Best producers: Grans-Fassian, Reinhold Haart★★, Kurt Hain★, von KESSELSTATT★, Weller-Lehnert. Best years: (1998) 97 96 **95 93 92 90 89 88 83**.

CH. LE PIN★★★ *Pomerol AC, Bordeaux, France* Now one of the most expensive wines in the world, with prices at auction overtaking those for PETRUS. The 1979 was the first vintage and the wines, which are concentrated but elegant, are produced from 100% Merlot. The tiny 2-ha (5-acre) vineyard lies close to those of TROTANOY and VIEUX-CH.-CERTAN. Best years: (1998) 97 96 95 94 **90 89 88 86 85 83 82 81**.

PINE RIDGE WINERY *Stags Leap District AVA, California, USA* Within an ever-changing roster, Pine Ridge offers wines from several NAPA AVAs, but its flagship Cabernet remains the supple, plummy Stags Leap District★. For sheer power and richness, the Andrus Reserve Cabernet★★ goes over the top. Lately, the winery has zeroed in on CARNEROS District Merlot★ capturing lovely spice and cherry fruit in a seamless package. Also, showing well of late is the Carneros Chardonnay made from a variety of French clones. OREGON's Achery Summit is a sister label. Best years: (reds) (1997) 96 95 **94 92 91**.

PINGUS, DOMINIO DE *Ribera del Duero DO, Castilla y León, Spain* Peter Sisseck's tiny vineyard and winery have attracted worldwide attention since 1995 due to the extraordinary depth and character of the cult wine they produce, Pingus★★★. Best years: **1996 95**.

PINOT BIANCO See Pinot Blanc.

PINOT BLANC Wine made from the Pinot Blanc grape has a clear, yeasty, appley taste and good examples can age to a delicious honeyed fullness. In France its chief power-base is in ALSACE, where it is taking over the 'workhorse' role from Sylvaner and Chasselas. In fact, most CREMANT D'ALSACE now uses Pinot Blanc as the principal variety. Important in northern Italy as Pinot Bianco, in Germany and Austria as Weissburgunder and is successful in Hungary, Slovakia, Slovenia and the Czech Republic. Promising new plantings in CALIFORNIA, OREGON and Canada.

PINOT GRIGIO See Pinot Gris.

PINOT GRIS At its finest in France's ALSACE, where it is now called Tokay-Pinot Gris; with reasonable acidity and a deep colour the grape produces fat, rich wines that will often mature wonderfully. It is occasionally used in BURGUNDY to add fatness to a wine. As Pinot Grigio it is also grown in northern Italy, where it produces some of the country's most popular and often boring dry whites. Also successful in Austria and Germany as Ruländer or Grauer Burgunder, and as Malvoisie in the Swiss VALAIS. There are some good Romanian and Czech examples, as well as spirited ones in Hungary (as Szurkebarat). Made in a crisp style, it is very successful in OREGON and, to a lesser extent, in CALIFORNIA.

PINOT MEUNIER The most widely planted grape in the CHAMPAGNE region. A vital ingredient in Champagne, along with Pinot Noir and Chardonnay – though it is the least well known of the 3.

PINOT NERO See Pinot Noir.
PINOT NOIR See pages 224–5.

PINOTAGE A Pinot Noir x Cinsaut cross, conceived in South Africa in 1925 but not widely planted until the 1950s. Despite its current popularity on the international market, it remains a love-or-hate grape among Cape winemakers. The variety's champion and driving force behind the Pinotage Producers' Association is Beyers Truter of KANONKOP. New-style Pinotage, wooded or unwooded, is more refined; plums, bananas and redcurrants are hallmarks of its flavour. Also grown in New Zealand, CALIFORNIA (rare), Germany and Zimbabwe. Best producers: l'AVENIR★, BACKSBERG, Bellingham Premium★, BEYERSKLOOF★, Clos Malverne Reserve, FAIRVIEW, GRANGEHURST★★, KANONKOP★★, SIMONSIG★, WARWICK★★, Wildekrans.

PIPER-HEIDSIECK *Champagne AC, Champagne, France* Traditionally one of CHAMPAGNE's least distinguished brands, though the owners, Remy, seem to be trying to improve things. The Piper non-vintage is gentler than it used to be, and can develop complexity. The best wines are the de luxe cuvée, Champagne Rare★★, and the ultra-dry Sauvage★★. Also has a CALIFORNIA outpost, Piper-Sonoma. Best years: 1989 **85 82**.

PIPERS BROOK VINEYARDS *Northern Tasmania, Australia* Keenly sought wines combining classy design, high prices, clever marketing and skilled winemaking by Andrew Pirie. Steely Riesling★★, classically reserved Chardonnay★★, fragrant Gewürztraminer★ and refreshing Pinot Gris are highlights. Purchased the HEEMSKERK-Rochecombe group in 1998. Considerable expansion in 1998 will test Piper's metal, but initial signs are good. Best years: 1995 **94 92 91 90 88 86 84 82**.

PLAIMONT, L'UNION DES PRODUCTEURS *Madiran AC, Côtes de St-Mont VDQS and Vin de Pays des Côtes de Gascogne, South-West France* This grouping of 3 Gascon co-ops is the largest, most reliable and most go-ahead producer of COTES DE GASCOGNE and COTES DE ST-MONT. The whites, full of crisp fruit, are reasonably priced and are best drunk young. The reds, especially Ch. St-Go★ and de Sabazan★, are very good too. Also good MADIRAN and PACHERENC DU VIC-BILH.

PLANTAGENET *Great Southern, Western Australia* An apple-packing shed in chilly Mount Barker seems an unlikely place to make fine table wines, but Tony Smith and his winemaker Gavin Berry are achieving great results. Noted for spicy Shiraz★★★, melony/nutty Chardonnay★★, limy Riesling★, plump Pinot★★ and increasingly classy Cabernet Sauvignon★★. Best years: 1996 **95 94 93 91 90 88 86 85**.

POLIZIANO *Vino Nobile di Montepulciano, Tuscany, Italy* A leading light in Montepulciano. VINO NOBILE★ is far better than average, especially the Riserva Vigna Asinone★★ and Vigneto Caggiole★★, while the SUPER-TUSCANS Elegia★★ (Sangiovese) and Le Stanze★★ (Cabernet Sauvignon) are packed with fruit and sweet oak. VIN SANTO★★ is unctuous.

POL ROGER *Champagne AC, Champagne, France* Makers of Winston Churchill's favourite CHAMPAGNE and challenging for the title of Champagne's leading quality producer. The non-vintage White Foil★ is a little richer than usual right now. Pol Roger also produces a vintage★★, a rosé★, a vintage Chardonnay★★ and a vintage Réserve Spécial★★. Its top Champagne, called Cuvée Sir Winston Churchill★★, is a deliciously refined drink. All vintage wines are ready on release but will improve with another 5 years' keeping or more. Best years: **1990 89 88 86 85 82 79**.

POMEROL AC *Bordeaux, France* Now one of the most famous and expensive of the BORDEAUX ACs, Pomerol includes some of the world's most sought-after red wines. The AC's unique quality lies in its deep clay in which the Merlot grape flourishes. The result is seductively rich, almost creamy wine with wonderful mouthfilling fruit flavours. Best producers: Beauregard★, Bonalgue, le BON-PASTEUR★★, Certan-de-May★★, Clinet★★, Clos l'Eglise, CLOS RENE★, la CONSEILLANTE★★, l'EGLISE-CLINET★★, l'EVANGILE★★, la FLEUR-PETRUS★★, GAZIN★★, LAFLEUR★★★, LATOUR-A-POMEROL★★, Mazeyres, Montviel, PETIT-VILLAGE★★, PETRUS★★★, le PIN★★★, SALES★★, TROTANOY★★, VIEUX-CHATEAU-CERTAN★★. Best years: (1998) 96 95 94 **90 89 88 86 85 83 82 81 79 78**.

PINOT NOIR

There's this myth about Pinot Noir that I think I'd better lay to rest. It goes something like this. Pinot Noir is an incredibly tricky grape to grow; in fact Pinot Noir is such a difficult customer that the only place that regularly achieves magical results is the thin stretch of land known as the Côte d'Or, between Dijon and Chagny in France, where mesoclimate, soil conditions and 2000 years of experience weave an inimitable web of pleasure.

This just isn't so. The thin-skinned, early-ripening Pinot Noir is undoubtedly more difficult to grow than other great varieties like Cabernet or Chardonnay, but that doesn't mean that it's impossible to grow elsewhere – you just have to work at it with more sensitivity and seek out the right growing conditions. And although great red Burgundy is a hauntingly beautiful wine, many Burgundians completely fail to deliver the magic, and the glorious thing about places like New Zealand, California, Oregon, Australia and Germany is that we are seeing an ever increasing number of wines that are thrillingly different to anything produced in Burgundy, yet with flavours that are unique to Pinot Noir.

WINE STYLES
France All France's great Pinot Noir wines do come from Burgundy's Côte d'Or. Rarely deep in colour, they should nonetheless possess a wonderful fruit quality when young – raspberry, strawberry, cherry or plum that becomes more scented and exotic with age, the plums turning to figs and pine, and the richness of chocolate mingling perilously with truffles and well-hung game. Strange, challenging, hedonistic. France's other Pinots – in north and south Burgundy, the Loire, Jura, Savoie, Alsace and now occasionally in the south of France – are lighter and milder, and in Champagne its pale, thin wine is used to make sparkling wine.
Other European regions The great 1993, 90 and 89 vintages have allowed German winemakers to produce impressive, perfumed wines (generally called Spätburgunder). Italy, where it is called Pinot Nero, and Switzerland (where it is known as Blauburgunder) both have fair success with the variety. Austria and Spain have produced a couple of good examples, and Romania, the Czech Republic and Hungary produce significant amounts of variable quality.
New World Light, fragrant wines have bestowed upon Oregon in America's Pacific Northwest the greatest reputation for being 'another Burgundy'; but I get more excited about the marvellously fruity, erotically scented wines of California's Carneros and Russian River Valley regions, and the original offerings from the outposts, particularly Santa Maria Valley, south of San Francisco. New Zealand is the most important southern hemisphere producer with wines of thrilling fruit and individuality, while Australia is slowly finding its way and even South Africa and Chile have a few fine producers.

BEST PRODUCERS

France *Burgundy* (growers) Ambroise, Angerville, Comte Armand, Denis Bachelet, Barthod-Noëllat, J-M Boillot, R Chevillon, CLAIR, J-J Confuron, DUJAC, Engel, H Gouges, Anne Gros, GRIVOT, Hudelot-Noëllat, LAFARGE, LAFON, H Lignier, MEO-CAMUZET, MONTILLE, Denis Mortet, J-F Mugnier, Ponsot, RION, Dom. de la ROMANEE-CONTI, E Rouget, ROUMIER, ROUSSEAU, TOLLOT-BEAUT, VOGUE; (merchants) DROUHIN, FAIVELEY, JADOT, V Girardin, LABOURE-ROI, D Laurent, Maison LEROY, RODET; (co-ops) BUXY, les Caves des Hautes-Côtes.

Germany K-H JOHNER.

Italy CA' DEL BOSCO (Pinèro), Marchesi Pancrazi (Villa di Bagnolo), SALA.

New World Pinot Noirs
USA (California) AU BON CLIMAT, CALERA, CHALONE, DEHLINGER, Etude, Gary Farrell, Landmark, Littorai, Lane Tanner, J ROCHIOLI VINEYARDS, SAINTSBURY, SANFORD, WILLIAMS SELYEM; (Oregon) Archery Summit, BEAUX FRERES, Broadley, Criston, DOMAINE DROUHIN, Panther Creek, PONZI, Talley, Torii Mor, WillaKenzie, Ken Wright.

Australia BANNOCKBURN, Bass Phillip, COLDSTREAM HILLS, Diamond Valley, Giaconda, Lenswood Vineyards, Paringa Estate, YARRA YERING.

New Zealand ATA RANGI, DRY RIVER, Isabel, MARTINBOROUGH VINEYARD, NEUDORF, Rippon.

South Africa BOUCHARD FINLAYSON, HAMILTON RUSSELL (Ashbourne).

POMINO DOC *Tuscany, Italy* Small zone, east of Florence in the hills above CHIANTI RUFINA, noted for its historical use of French varieties in both red (Merlot and Cabernet blended with Sangiovese) and white (where, unusually, Trebbiano plays a supporting role to Pinot Bianco and Chardonnay). FRESCOBALDI's Pomino Il Benefizio★ (a barrique-fermented Chardonnay) was a trendsetting Tuscan white. Best producers: FRESCOBALDI★, SELVAPIANA (Petrognano★). Best years: (reds) (1998) 97 96 95 **94 93 90 88 85**.

POMMARD AC *Côte de Beaune, Burgundy, France* The first village south of Beaune. At their best, the wines should have full, round, beefy flavours. Can age well, often for 10 years or more. There are no Grands Crus but les Rugiens Bas, les Épenots and les Arvelets (all Premiers Crus) occupy the best sites. Best producers: Comte Armand★★, Jean-Marc Boillot, Courcel★★, J Garaudet★, P Garaudet★, M Gaunoux★, LAFARGE, Lejeune★, MONTILLE★★, A Mussy★, J & A Parent★, Ch. de Pommard★, Pothier-Rieusset★, Pousse d'Or★. Best years: 1997 96 95 93 **92 90 89 88**.

CH. PONTET-CANET★★ *Pauillac AC, 5ème Cru Classé, Haut-Médoc, Bordeaux, France* The vineyards of this property are located close to those of MOUTON-ROTHSCHILD. The wines used to be rather lean and uninteresting but since 1979, when the Tesserons of LAFON-ROCHET bought the property, there has been a gradual return to form – big, chewy, intense claret which develops a beautiful blackcurrant fruit. Now one of the best-value of the Classed Growths. Best years: (1998) 97 96 95 94 90 89 **86 85 83 82**.

PONZI *Willamette Valley AVA, Oregon, USA* A minty Pinot Noir★ in both a regular and Reserve bottling gets the attention but Ponzi was also one of the first in OREGON to make Pinot Gris. The Riesling★ is usually successful – and Ponzi also brews great beer★★. Best years: (reds) (1998) 97 **94 92**.

PORT See pages 228–9.

PORTA *Rapel, Chile* Boutique winery formed in 1993, making small quantities of elegant, oak-aged Cabernet Sauvignon★ and Chardonnay★★. Recent large investment in new plantings has obviated the need to buy in grapes. French winemaker Yves Pouzet is getting the maximum out of the Cachapoal Valley fruit and a new low-yield Merlot★★ hints at even better things to come. Best years: 1997 **96 94**.

CH. POTENSAC★ *Médoc AC, Cru Bourgeois, Bordeaux, France* Potensac's fabulous success is based on quality, consistency and value for money. Owned and run by Michel Delon, the genius of LEOVILLE-LAS-CASES, the wine can be drunk at 4–5 years old, but fine vintages will improve for at least 10 years, and the 1982 for up to twice that. Best years: (1998) 97 96 95 **94 93 90 89 88 86 85 83 82 81**.

POUILLY-FUISSÉ AC *Mâconnais, Burgundy, France* Dry white Chardonnay from 5 villages surrounding the Solutré rock, including Pouilly and Fuissé. For several years high prices and low quality meant this was a wine to avoid, but now it is beginning to find a sensible price level and there are some committed growers producing buttery, creamy wines that can be delicious at 2 years, but will often develop beautifully for up to 10. Best producers: Corsin★★, R Denogent★★, J-M Drouin★, T Drouin★, J-A Ferret★★, M Forest★★,

Ch. FUISSE★★★, Guffens-Heynen (VERGET)★★, R Lassarat★★, Léger-Plumet★, R Luquet★, Valette★★. Best years: 1997 96 **95 94 93 92 90**.

POUILLY-FUMÉ AC *Loire Valley, France* Fumé means 'smoked' in French and a good Pouilly-Fumé has a strong, pungent smell that is often likened to gunflint. The only grape allowed is the Sauvignon Blanc and what gives these wines their extra smokiness is that many of the vineyards are planted on slopes of flinty soil called silex. Despite the efforts of a few producers, this is a seriously underperforming appellation: overcropped and overpriced. The word 'fumé' was also annexed by Californian producers such as MONDAVI to attach to their Sauvignon Blanc varietal wines. Best producers: Berthiers★, Henri Bourgeois★, A Cailbourdin★, J-C Chatelain★, Didier DAGUENEAU★★, Serge Dagueneau★, M Deschamps★, Ladoucette★, Landrat-Guyollot★, Masson-Blondelet★, R Pabiot, M Redde, G Saget, Tinel-Blondelet★, Ch. de Tracy★. Best years: (1998) 97 **96 95 93 90 89 88**.

POUILLY-LOCHÉ AC *Mâconnais, Burgundy, France* Loché is a village to the east of Fuissé which has added the name of Pouilly to its own. The wines are no better than many MACON-VILLAGES and certainly not a patch on POUILLY-FUISSE, but the magic name of Pouilly commands higher prices. The wine can be labelled as POUILLY-VINZELLES. Best producer: Cave des Grands Crus Blancs. Best years: 1997 **96 95**.

POUILLY-SUR-LOIRE AC *Loire Valley, France* Light appley wines from the Chasselas grape from vineyards around Pouilly-sur-Loire, the town which gave its name to POUILLY-FUME. Drink as young as possible.

POUILLY-VINZELLES AC *Mâconnais, Burgundy, France* Like POUILLY-LOCHE, the village of Vinzelles adds the name of Pouilly to its own. Best producers: Cave des Grands Crus Blancs, Valette, Ch. de Vinzelles. Best years: 1997 **96 95**.

CH. POUJEAUX★★ *Moulis AC, Cru Bourgeois, Haut-Médoc, Bordeaux, France* Poujeaux is one reason why MOULIS AC is attracting attention: the wines have a delicious chunky fruit and new-oak sweetness. Attractive at 6–7 years old, good vintages can easily last for 20–30 years. Best years: (1998) 97 96 95 **94 93 90 89 88 86 85 83 82 81 79 78**.

PRÄDIKAT Grades defining quality wines in Germany and Austria. These are (in ascending order) KABINETT (not considered as Prädikat in Austria), SPATLESE, AUSLESE, BEERENAUSLESE, the Austrian-only category Ausbruch, and TROCKENBEERENAUSLESE. Strohwein and EISWEIN are also Prädikat wines. The drawback of a system that grades wine according to the amount of sugar in the unfermented grape juice or must is that it implies that the sweeter the wine, the better it is. Some Spätleses and even a few Ausleses are now made as dry wines.

FRANZ PRAGER *Wachau, Niederösterreich, Austria* One of the pioneers of the region, who produced the first Riesling Trockenbeerenauslese in the WACHAU in 1993. Also top dry Rieslings from the Achleiten and Klaus vineyards★★★ and excellent Grüner Veltliners from the Achleiten vineyard★. Best years: (1998) 97 **96 95 93 92 90 86**.

PREMIER CRU The quality level below Grand Cru in the French appellation system. Premier Cru vineyards are usually less well-sited than the Grands Crus. But Premier Grand Cru is the very top level in BORDEAUX.

PORT DOC

Douro, Portugal

The Douro region in northern Portugal, where the grapes for port are grown, is wild and beautiful. Steep hills covered in vineyard terraces plunge dramatically down to the Douro river. Grapes are one of the only crops that will grow in the inhospitable climate, which gets progressively drier the further inland you travel. But not all the Douro's grapes qualify to be made into increasingly good port. A quota is established every year, and the rest are made into table wines.

Port grapes (including Touriga Nacional, Tinta Roriz, Tinta Barroca, Tinta Cão and Touriga Francesca) are partially fermented, and then *aguardente* (grape spirit) is added – fortifying the wine, stopping the fermentation and leaving sweet, unfermented grape sugar in the finished port.

PORT STYLES

Vintage Finest of the ports matured in bottle, made from grapes from the best vineyards. Vintage port is not 'declared' every year, but during the second year in cask, if the shipper thinks the standard is high enough. It is bottled after 2 years, and may be consumed not long afterwards, not uncommon in the USA; at this stage it packs quite a punch. The British custom of aging for 20 years or more can yield exceptional mellowness.

Single quinta A true single quinta wine comes from an individual estate; however, many shippers sell their vintage port under a quinta name in years which are not declared as a vintage. In the latter case, the wines may come from several vineyards. It is quite possible for these 'off vintage' ports to equal or even surpass the vintage wines from the same house.

Tawny Matured in cask for 10, 20 or 30 years before bottling and sale, older tawnies have delicious nut and fig flavours. Cheap tawny is a blend of ruby and white port and is both dilute and raw.

Colheita Tawny from a single vintage, matured in cask for at least 7 years – potentially the finest of the aged tawnies.

Late Bottled Vintage/Late Bottled Port matured for 4–6 years in cask then usually filtered to avoid sediment forming in the bottle. Traditional unfiltered examples have much more flavour.

Crusted Rarely seen today, this is a blend of good ports from 2–3 vintages, bottled without filtration after 3–4 years in cask. A deposit (crust) forms in the bottle and the wine should be decanted.

Ruby The youngest red port. Ruby port should be bursting with young, almost peppery fruit but rarely achieves this level of quality.

Vintage Character Usually little more than expensive ruby, with no vintage character at all, though maybe a bit more age.

White Only the best taste dry and nutty from wood-aging; most are coarse and alcoholic, best drunk chilled with tonic water.

1994 92 **91 85 83 80 77 70 66 63 60 55 48 47 45 35 34 27**

BEST PRODUCERS

Vintage CHURCHILL, COCKBURN, Quinta do CRASTO, CROFT, Delaforce, DOW, FERREIRA, FONSECA, Gould Campbell, GRAHAM, Quarles Harris, Quinta do Infantado, Martinez, NIEPOORT, Quinta do NOVAL (including Nacional), Offley, RAMOS PINTO, Quinta de la ROSA, SMITH WOODHOUSE, TAYLOR, Quinta do VESUVIO, WARRE.

Single quinta CHURCHILL (Agua Alta), COCKBURN (Quinta dos Canais), CROFT (Quinta da Roêda), DOW (Quinta do Bomfim), FONSECA (Guimaraens, Quinta do Panascal), GRAHAM (Malvedos), Martinez (Quinta da Eira Velha), NIEPOORT (Quinta do Passadouro), Quinta do NOVAL (Quinta do Silval, Quinta do Roriz), RAMOS PINTO (Quinta da Ervamoira), SMITH WOODHOUSE (Madalena), TAYLOR (Quinta de Vargellas), WARRE (Quinta da Cavadinha).

Aged tawny Barros, Cálem, COCKBURN, DOW, FERREIRA, FONSECA, GRAHAM, Krohn, NIEPOORT, RAMOS PINTO, Quinta de la ROSA, SANDEMAN, TAYLOR, WARRE.

Colheita Barros, Feist, Krohn, NIEPOORT, Quinta do NOVAL.

Traditional Late Bottled Vintage CHURCHILL, Quinta do CRASTO, NIEPOORT, RAMOS PINTO, Quinta de la ROSA, SMITH WOODHOUSE, WARRE.

White CHURCHILL, NIEPOORT.

PREMIÈRES CÔTES DE BLAYE AC *Bordeaux, France* An improving AC mainly for reds on the right bank of the Gironde. The fresh, Merlot-based reds are ready at 2–3 years but will age for more. The whites are usually sold under the COTES DE BLAYE AC. Best producers: Haut-Bertinerie★, Haut-Grelot, Haut-Sociando, Jonqueyres, Loumède, Mondésir Gazin, Segonzac, Sociando, Tourtes. Best years: (1998) 96 **95 94 90 89 88**.

PREMIÈRES CÔTES DE BORDEAUX AC *Bordeaux, France* Hilly region with views overlooking GRAVES and SAUTERNES across the Garonne. For a long time the AC was best known for its Sauternes-style sweet wines, particularly from the communes of CADILLAC, LOUPIAC and STE-CROIX-DU-MONT, but in recent years the attractive, juicy reds and rosés have forged ahead. These are usually delicious at 2–3 years old but should last for 5–6 years. Dry whites are designated BORDEAUX AC. Best producers: (reds) Brethous★, Carsin★, Chelivette, Clos Ste-Anne, Grand-Mouëys★, Haux, Jonchet, Ch. du Juge (Dupleich), Lamothe-de-Haux, Langoiran, Melin, Puy-Bardens★, Reynon★, le Sens, Suau, Tanesse. Best years: (reds) (1998) 96 **95 94 90** 89 88 88 86 85; (whites) (1998) 97 96 **95 94 90**.

CH. PRIEURÉ-LICHINE★ *Margaux AC, 4ème Cru Classé, Haut-Médoc, Bordeaux, France* Owned by Alexis Lichine, possibly the greatest promoter of high-quality French wines this century, until his death in 1989, and now by his son, Sacha. The wine has a gentle, perfumed style, though it does not lack tannin and keeps well for 10–15 years. Best years: (1998) 96 95 **90 89 88 86** 85 83 82.

PRIMEUR French term for a young wine, often released for sale within weeks of the harvest. BEAUJOLAIS NOUVEAU is the best-known example.

PRIMO ESTATE *Adelaide Plains, South Australia* Innovative Joe Grilli stuck his winery in one of Australia's hottest climates but works miracles with his own grapes and those from outlying areas. The premium label is Joseph: Grilli adapts the AMARONE method for Cabernet-Merlot★, uncorks aged still reds to throw into the Shiraz blend for Sparkling Red★, and uses a novel pruning technique to achieve 'cooler' flavours in Double Pruned Cabernet★. He also does a juicy Botrytis Riesling★★, surprising dry white Colombard – and superb olive oil★★★. Best years: (Cabernet-Merlot Joseph) **1996 95 93 92 90**.

PRIORAT DO *Catalonia, Spain* This beautiful hilly, isolated district is characterized by vineyards planted on deep, pure slate, precipitous slopes. Yields of Garnacha and Cariñena are minuscule. Old-style fortified RANCIO wines used to attract little attention. Then in the 1980s a group of young winemakers revolutionized the area, bringing in state-of-the-art winemaking methods and some French grape varieties to back up native varieties. Their rare, expensive wines have taken Spain, and now other parts of the world, by storm. Drink with at least 5 years' age; the best will last much longer. Best producers: René Barbier Fill (Clos Mogador★★★), Clos i Terrasses★★★ (Clos Erasmus), Costers del Siurana★, Joset Maria Fuentes★★, Mas Martinet★★★, Alvaro PALACIOS★★★, Pasanau Germans★, Scala Dei★, Rotllan Torra★, Vall-Llach★★. Best years: (reds) 1996 95 94 **93 92 90**.

PROSECCO DI CONEGLIANO-VALDOBBIADENE DOC *Veneto, Italy* The all-purpose fizz of Venice, though Prosecco can also be still (tranquillo). The Prosecco grape gives soft, scented wine made sparkling by a second fermentation in tank. Though not for aging, it can be a delicious sipping SPUMANTE or FRIZZANTE. Cartizze, from a vineyard area of that name, is the most refined. Best producers: Adami★, Bernardi★, Case Bianche, Bisol★, Carpenè Malvolti★, Le Colture, Col Vetoraz★, Nino Franco★, Merotto, Mionetto, Ruggeri & C★, Tanorè, Zardetto★.

PROVENCE *France* Provence is home to France's oldest vineyards but the region is better known for its nudist beaches and arts festivals than for its wines. However, it seems even Provence is caught up in the revolution sweeping through the vineyards of southern France. The area has 5 small, high-quality ACs (BANDOL, les BAUX-DE-PROVENCE, BELLET, CASSIS and PALETTE), but most of the wine comes from the much larger areas of the COTES DE PROVENCE, COTEAUX VAROIS, Coteaux de Pierrevert and COTEAUX D'AIX-EN-PROVENCE. Provençal reds and rosés are generally better than whites.

PRÜFUNGSNUMMER In Germany and Austria this means literally the 'test number' or 'official examination', which all quality wines must undergo. In Germany it is also called *Amtliche Prüfung*, and on labels is generally shortened to AP and followed by a number. In reality the number means nothing because the test is not strenuous enough.

J J PRÜM *Bernkastel, Mosel, Germany* Estate making some of Germany's best Riesling in sites like the Sonnenuhr★★★ in WEHLEN, Himmelreich★★ in GRAACH and Lay★★ and Badstube★★ in BERNKASTEL. All have great aging potential. Best years: (1997) 96 95 94 **93 91** 90 89 88 86 85 83 79 76 75 71.

S A PRÜM *Wehlen, Mosel, Germany* There are a confusing number of Prüms in the MOSEL – the best known is J J PRÜM, but Raimund Prüm of S A Prüm makes a decent second. The estate's most interesting wine is Riesling from Wehlener Sonnenuhr★★, especially Auslese★★★, but it also makes good wine from sites in BERNKASTEL★, GRAACH★ and Zeltingen★. Best years: (1997) 95 **93 90 88 86 85**.

PRUNOTTO *Barolo DOCG, Piedmont, Italy* One of the great BAROLO producers, whose winemaker Giuseppe Colla pioneered the concept of single vineyards in the zone. The company was bought by ANTINORI in 1989. Since the sale quality has, if anything, improved, as shown by Barbera Pian Romualdo★★, Nebbiolo Occhetti★ and Barolo from the Bussia★★, Cannubi★★ and Montestefano★★ vineyards. Also produce good MOSCATO D'ASTI★.

PUGLIA *Italy* This southern region is a prolific source of blending wines, but recently exciting progress has been made with native varieties: Uva di Troia in CASTEL DEL MONTE; Negroamaro in SALICE SALENTINO, COPERTINO, and other reds and rosés of the Salento peninsula; the white Greco for GRAVINA; and Verdeca and Bianco d'Alessano for LOCOROTONDO and Martina Franca. But it is Puglia's Primitivo grape (CALIFORNIA's Zinfandel) led by examples from Pervine and Felline that is set to make the biggest impact.

PUIATTI *Collio DOC, Friuli-Venezia Giulia, Italy* Notable for whites made without oak. Pinot Grigio★, Pinot Bianco★, Chardonnay★, Sauvignon★ and Tocai★ have, at their best, a clearly defined varietal character, good concentration, and are good to drink young but better with age. The Archetipi★★ range is the finest selection; the Enofriulia label is for a less expensive but consistent varietal range.

PUISSEGUIN-ST-ÉMILION AC *Bordeaux, France* Small ST-EMILION satellite AC. The wines are usually fairly solid but with an attractive chunky fruit and usually make good drinking at 3–5 years. Best producers: Bel-Air, Branda, Durand-Laplagne, Guibeau, Laurets, Producteurs Réunis, Soleil. Best years: (1998) 96 95 94 **90 89 88**.

PULIGNY-MONTRACHET AC *Côte de Beaune, Burgundy, France* Puligny is one of the finest white wine villages in the world and long ago added the name of its greatest Grand Cru, le MONTRACHET, to its own. There are 3 other Grands Crus which are almost as good (BATARD-MONTRACHET, BIENVENUES-BATARD-MONTRACHET and CHEVALIER-MONTRACHET), and no fewer than 11 Premiers Crus. Wines from the flatter vineyards use the simple Puligny-Montrachet AC. Good vintages really need 5 years' aging, while the Premiers Crus and Grands Crus may need 10 years and can last for 20 years or more. Only about 3% of the AC is red wine. Best producers: J-M Boillot★, CARILLON★★★, Jean Chartron★, Gérard Chavy★, H Clerc★, DROUHIN★, JADOT★, LABOURE-ROI★, Louis LATOUR★, Dom. LEFLAIVE★, Olivier LEFLAIVE★, P Pernot★, Ch. de Puligny-Montrachet★, RAMONET★★★, RODET, SAUZET★★★, G Thomas★. Best years: 1997 96 95 93 **92 90 89 88 86**.

PYRENEES *Victoria, Australia* Robust, often eucalyptus-scented reds from Shiraz and Cabernet Sauvignon are the trademark of this hilly central Victoria district, but ripe Sauvignon Blanc and Chardonnay can also impress. Champagne-method bubblies from TALTARNI and French-owned Blue Pyrenees Estate are improving. Best producers: Blue Pyrenees★, Dalwhinnie★, Redbank★★, TALTARNI★.

QbA (QUALITÄTSWEIN BESTIMMTER ANBAUGEBIETE) German for 'quality wine from designated regions'. Sugar can be added to the juice when natural levels are low, and permitted yields are high. Usually pretty ordinary, but some estates downgrade good wines when necessary. In Austria *Qualitätswein* is equivalent to the German QbA.

QmP (QUALITÄTSWEIN MIT PRÄDIKAT) German for 'quality wine with distinction'. A higher category than QbA: with controlled yields and no sugar addition. QmP covers 6 levels based on the ripeness of the grapes (in ascending order): KABINETT, SPATLESE, AUSLESE, BEERENAUSLESE, EISWEIN and TROCKENBEERENAUSLESE.

QUARTS DE CHAUME AC *Grand Cru, Loire Valley, France* The Chenin grape finds one of its most rewarding mesoclimates here in the Layon Valley. Quarts de Chaume is a 40-ha (100-acre) Cru within the larger COTEAUX DU LAYON AC and, as autumn mists begin to curl off the river Layon, noble rot attacks the grapes. The result is intense, sweet wines which can last for longer than almost any in the world. Best producers: Baumard★★, Bellerive★★, Clos des Maurières★, Laffourcade★, Pierre-Bise★★, Joseph Renou★★. Best years: (1998) 97 95 94 **93 90 89 88 85 83** 81 78 76 70 69 64 59 47.

QUEENSLAND *Australia* Queensland has the smallest production of all Australia's wine-producing states. About 12 wineries perch on rocky hills in the main region, the Granite Belt, near the NEW SOUTH WALES border. Best producers: Bald Mountain, Kominos, Robinson's, Stone Ridge.

QUILCEDA CREEK VINTNERS *Washington State, USA* This tiny winery has built a cult following in Washington because of a big, rich Cabernet Sauvignon★★, the primary wine made here. The wine can be a bit overpowering and closed, but it does open up after a few minutes in the glass and has good aging potential. Ditto for the Merlot. Best years: (1998) 97 96 95 **94 92 89**.

QUINCY AC *Loire Valley, France* Intensely flavoured, dry white wine from Sauvignon Blanc vineyards west of Bourges. You can age the wine for a year or two but it will always keep its rather aggressive gooseberry flavour. Best producers: D & N Jaumier, Mardon, Jacques Rouzé. Best years: **1997 96 95**.

QUINTA Portuguese for 'farm' or 'estate'.

QUINTARELLI *Valpolicella DOC, Veneto, Italy* Giuseppe Quintarelli is the great traditional winemaker of VALPOLICELLO, and his distinctive handwritten labels herald some remarkable wines. His philosophy is one of vinifying only the very best grapes and leaving nature to do the rest. His Classico Superiore★★ is left in cask for about 4 years and his famed AMARONE★★★ and RECIOTO★★ for 7 years or more before release. There is also Alzero★★, a spectacular Amarone-style wine from Cabernet Franc and Cabernet Sauvignon. Best years: (Amarone) 1990 **88 86 85 83**.

QUIVIRA *Dry Creek Valley DO, California, USA* Amongst the best of the new-wave Zinfandel★★ producers. Under former winemaker Doug Nalle (now at NALLE WINERY) the mid-1980s Zinfandels quickly established the trend for bright, fruity wine made for short-term consumption. The wines are immediately delicious and will age well because of their balance. A new bottling, Dry Creek Cuvée (Grenache, Mourvèdre, Syrah and Zinfandel), is fruity and delightful. Lively Sauvignon Blanc is another crowd-pleaser. Best years: (Zinfandel) 1997 96 95 **94 91 90**.

QUPÉ *Santa Maria Valley AVA, California, USA* Owner Bob Lindquist, an iconoclastic winemaker with a bent for the unusual, makes a gorgeously tasty Reserve Syrah★★★. His Santa Maria Chardonnay★★★ and Bien Macido Cuvée (two-thirds Chardonnay, one-third Viognier) have sublime appley fruit and perfume. Lindquist, a leading exponent of RHÔNE-based wines, also produces Viognier, Mourvèdre and Marsanne. Best years: (Rhônes) (1998) 97 **96 95 94 92**.

RAÏMAT *Costers del Segre DO, Catalonia, Spain* Owned by the CAVA company CODORNIU, this large, irrigated estate can make good to excellent fruity wines from Spanish and foreign grapes such as Cabernet Sauvignon★ (Mas Castell vineyard★★), Merlot★ and Chardonnay. Best years: (reds) **1996 95 94 92 91 90**.

RAMONET *Chassagne-Montrachet, Côte de Beaune, Burgundy, France* The Ramonets (father and sons) produce some of the most complex of all white Burgundies from 3 Grands Crus (BATARD-MONTRACHET★★★, BIENVENUES-BATARD-MONTRACHET★★★ and le MONTRACHET★★★) and 5 Premiers Crus (les Ruchottes★★★, les Caillerets★★, les Vergers★, Morgeot★★ and les Chaumées★★). The wines are very expensive, so if you want to spare your wallet try the ST-AUBIN★★ or the CHASSAGNE-MONTRACHET white★★ or red★. Generally the whites are in a higher league than the reds. Best years: (whites) 1997 96 95 94 93 **92 90 89 86 85**.

RAMOS PINTO *Port DOC, Douro, Portugal* Innovative port company now controlled by ROEDERER making complex, full-bodied Late Bottled

Vintage★ and aged tawny (Quinta do Bom Retiro★★). The 1994 Vintage★★ and Quinta da Ervamoira★★ are of a different order to older vintage efforts. New table wines Duas Quintas★ (Reserva★★) and Bon Ares★ (Reserva★★) are already most impressive. Best years: (vintage ports) 1995 94 **85 83 82**; (table wines) **1995 94 92 91**.

RAMPOLLA, CASTELLO DEI *Chianti Classico DOCG, Tuscany, Italy* Located in the 'golden shell' of Panzano, one of the outstanding CHIANTI CLASSICO★★ estates. Sammarco, sometimes ★★★, is mostly Cabernet with some Sangiovese, while the new Vigna d'Alceo★★ adds Petit Verdot to Cabernet Sauvignon. Best years: (1998) (97) (96) 95 94 93 **90 88 86**.

RANCIO A fortified wine deliberately exposed to the effects of oxidation, found mainly in LANGUEDOC-ROUSSILLON, CATALONIA and southern Spain.

RANDERSACKER *Franken, Germany* One of the most important wine villages in FRANKEN, producing excellent medium-bodied dry Rieslings, dry Silvaners, spicy Traminer and piercingly intense Rieslaner. Best producers: Martin Göbel, JULIUSSPITAL★★, Robert Schmitt★, Schmitt's Kinder★★. Best years: (1998) 97 **94 93 92 90**.

KENT RASMUSSEN *Carneros AVA, California, USA* Tightly structured Burgundian-style Chardonnay★★ capable of considerable bottle age and a fascinating juicy Pinot Noir★★ are made by ultra-traditional methods. Rasmussen makes occasional small batches of odd wines like Pinotage, Alicante and Dolcetto, which he releases under the Ramsay label. Best years: 1997 95 94 **92 91 90 88**.

RASTEAU AC *Rhône Valley, France* Rasteau is one of the original 16 villages entitled to the COTES DU RHONE-VILLAGES AC. The AC is for a fortified red or white and a RANCIO version which is left in barrel for 2 or more years. Best producers: Cave des Vignerons, Rabasse-Charavin, St-Gayan. Best years: (fortified reds) (1998) 97 95 94 **90 89**.

RENATO RATTI *Barolo DOCG, Piedmont, Italy* The late Renato Ratti led the revolution in winemaking in the Alba area with BAROLO and BARBARESCO of better balance, colour and richness and softer in tannins than the traditional models. Today his son Pietro and nephew Massimo Martinelli produce exemplary modern Barolo★★ from the Marcenasco vineyards at La Morra, as well as fine BARBERA D'ALBA★, Dolcetto d'Alba★ and NEBBIOLO D'ALBA★, from choice vineyards in the zone. Villa Pattono★ is a blend of Barbera and Freisa from ASTI.

RAUENTHAL *Rheingau, Germany* This most famous wine village of the RHEINGAU produces some of the region's most overpriced wines from the great Baiken and Gehrn sites. Sadly few of the Rieslings made here today have the intense spice and mineral character for which they are renowned. Best producers: J B Becker, Georg BREUER★★, August Eser. Best years: (1998) 97 96 **94 93 90**.

CH. RAUZAN-SÉGLA★★ *Margaux AC, 2ème Cru Classé, Haut-Médoc, Bordeaux, France* A dynamic change of winemaking regime in 1982 brought about a startling change for the better. This has been further improved by new owners Chanel from 1994. Now the wines have a rich blackcurrant fruit, almost tarry, thick tannins and weight, excellent woody spice and superb concentration. Second wine: Ségla. Best years: (1998) 97 96 95 94 90 89 88 **86 85 83**.

JEAN-MARIE RAVENEAU *Chablis AC, Burgundy, France* One of the outstanding growers in CHABLIS, producing beautifully nuanced wines from 3 Grands Crus (Blanchot★★, les Clos★★★ and Valmur★★★) and 4 Premiers Crus (Montée de Tonnerre★★, Vaillons★★, Butteaux★★ and Chapelots★★), using a combination of oak and stainless-steel fermentation. The wines can easily age for a decade or more. Best years: 1997 96 95 93 **92 90 89 88 86**.

RAVENSWOOD *Sonoma Valley AVA, California, USA*

Joel Peterson, one of California's leading Zin masters, established Ravenswood in 1976 with the sole purpose of making Zinfandel. During the lean years, when most California Zinfandel was pink and sweet, Peterson added a serviceable Chardonnay, a sometimes very good Cabernet Sauvignon★ and a tasty Merlot. But Zinfandel remains the trump card. Peterson makes several, varying the menu from year to year: the Dickerson Vineyard★★, Old Hill★★ and Old Vines★★★ are super Zins, with ripe, concentrated fruit – bold and beautiful wines. Most should be drunk 5–15 years from the vintage. Best years: 1997 96 95 94 **92 91 90 87 86 85**.

CH. RAYAS *Châteauneuf-du-Pape, Rhône Valley, France* The most famous estate in CHATEAUNEUF-DU-PAPE. The eccentric Jacques Reynaud produced big, alcoholic, exotically rich reds★★★ and whites★★ which also age well. However, prices are not cheap and the wines are not consistent, but at its best Rayas is worth the money. The red is made entirely from low-yielding Grenache vines – the only such wine in the AC – while the white's a blend of Clairette, Grenache Blanc and (so rumour has it) Chardonnay. The COTES DU RHONE Ch. de Fonsalette★★ is wonderful stuff. Pierre Reynaud, Jacques' nephew, is now running the estate in his uncle's inimitable rule-breaking style. Best years: (Châteauneuf-du-Pape) (1997) 96 95 94 93 91 90 89 88 **86**; (whites) (1998) 97 96 95 94 **93 91 90 89 86**.

RECIOTO DELLA VALPOLICELLA DOC *Veneto, Italy* The great sweet wine of VALPOLICELLA, made from grapes picked earlier than usual and left to dry on straw mats until the end of January. The wines are deep in colour, with a rich, bitter-sweet cherryish fruit. They age well for 5–8 years, but most are best drunk young. As with Valpolicella, the Classico tag is all important. SOAVE makes its own version of Recioto. Best producers: Accordini★, ALLEGRINI★★, Bolla (Spumante★), Brigaldara★, Brunelli★, Tommaso Bussola★★, Ca' La Bionda★, Michele Castellani★, DAL FORNO★★★, Degani★, Aleardo Ferrari★, Giuseppe Lonardi★, MASI★, Giacomo Montresor★, QUINTARELLI★, Le Ragose★, Le Salette★, Serègo Alighieri★★, Speri★, Tedeschi★, Villa Bellini★, Villa Spinosa★, Viviani★, Fratelli Zeni★. Best years: 1997 **95 93 90 88 85**.

RECIOTO DI SOAVE DOCG *Veneto, Italy* Sweet white wine made in the SOAVE zone from dried grapes, like RECIOTO DELLA VALPOLICELLA. Garganega grapes give wonderfully delicate yet intense wines that age well for up to a decade. Two outstanding examples are ANSELMI's Recioto I Capitelli★★★ and PIEROPAN's le Colombare★★. Best producers: ANSELMI★★★, La Cappuccina★★, Cantina del Castello, Cà Rugate★, Coffele★, Gini★, PIEROPAN★★, Soave co-op, Suavia. Best years: **1995 93 90 88**.

DOM. DE LA RECTORIE *Banyuls AC and Collioure AC, Roussillon, France*
Parcé is a famous name in BANYULS. For many years Dr A Parcé (Mas

235

Blanc) kept the Banyuls flag flying. Now his distant relations Marc and Thierry Parcé are leading the way. Their COLLIOURE★★ is made for keeping, while the Banyuls Cuvée Léon Parcé★★ can be enjoyed for its youthful fruit or kept for future pleasure. The VIN DE PAYS Cuvée l'Argile★ made from Grenache Blanc is one of the best whites in ROUSSILLON. Best years: (reds) (1997) 96 95 94 **93**.

REGALEALI *Sicily, Italy* The estate of the Conte Tasca d'Almerita in the highlands of central SICILY makes some of Italy's most admired wines. From native grape varieties come excellent Rosso del Conte★★ (based on Nero d'Avola) and white Nozze d'Oro★ (based on Inzolia), but the range extends to Chardonnay★★ and Cabernet Sauvignon★★ of extraordinary intensity and elegance. Almerita Brut★ (Chardonnay) may well be the finest Italian Champagne-method sparkler south of the Alpine regions.

RÉGNIÉ AC *Beaujolais, Burgundy, France* In 1988 the village of Régnié and its neighbour Durette were promoted to BEAUJOLAIS' 10th Cru. The wines are generally light and attractive but in poor years not up to scratch. Best producers: P Cinquin, Crêt des Bruyères, DUBOEUF★, J-M Laforest, R Magrin, J-P Rampon, J Trichard. Best years: 1998 97 **96** 95.

REGUENGOS DOC *Alentejo, Portugal* One of the most promising of the new ALENTEJO DOCs with good, flavoursome reds epitomizing the excitingly juicy flavours of southern Portugal. Best producers: ESPORAO★★, José Maria de FONSECA★, Reguengos de Monsaraz co-op. Best years: **1997** 96 95.

REMELLURI *Rioja DOC, País Vasco, Spain* Organic RIOJA estate producing wines with far more fruit than usual and good concentration for aging. Best are ★★. Best years: 1996 **95 94** 91 89.

RESERVA Spanish wines of above-average quality that have fulfilled certain aging requirements: reds must have at least 3 years' aging before sale, of which one must be in oak barrels; whites and rosés must have at least 2 years' aging, of which 6 months must be in oak.

RÉSERVE French for what is, in theory at least, a winemaker's finest wine. The word has no legal definition in France.

BALTHASAR RESS *Eltville-Hattenheim, Rheingau, Germany* Stefan Ress cleared out his cellar and replaced wooden casks with stainless steel and fibreglass. Currently wines are not as good as during the late 1980s and early 90s. Basically a Riesling producer, he also produces sound Scheurebe. Best years: **1993** 92 90.

RETSINA *Greece* Resinated white and rosé wine now common all over Greece. The best are deliciously oily and piny, while the resin produces a mild cooling effect on the tongue. For this reason, Retsina need not be overchilled. The younger the better is a good rule here. Both production and sales are falling. Best producers: Achaia-Clauss, Cambas, Kourtakis.

REUILLY AC *Loire Valley, France* Extremely dry but attractive Sauvignon from west of the world-famous SANCERRE. Also some pale Pinot Noir red and Pinot Gris rosé. Best producers: H Beurdin★, G Cordier, C Lafond★, G Malbête, D Martin, Sorbe. Best years: (1998) **97 96 95** 93.

REYNELLA *McLaren Vale, South Australia* Pioneer John Reynell established Chateau Reynella in 1838. Now part of the BRL HARDY empire, wines have been labelled Reynell since 97. Some of the grapes for these rich, sumptuous, fleshy reds still come from the original Ch.

Reynella vines. Prices have shot up lately, but they're not unreasonable given the quality. Cabernet★★, Merlot★★ and Shiraz★★★ are all memorably concentrated, tannic, ageworthy reds from low-yielding vines. Best years: 1996 95 94 **92 91 90 88 86**.

RHEINGAU *Germany* Wine region occupying a south-facing stretch of the Rhine flanking the city of Wiesbaden. Considered Germany's most aristocratic wine region, both in terms of the racy, slow-maturing 'breed' of the wines and because of the number of noble estate owners. Unfortunately many of the most famous names here are no longer a guarantee of top quality, and a new generation of winemakers now produces the best wines. See also Eltville, Geisenheim, Hattenheim, Hochheim, Johannisberg, Kiedrich, Rüdesheim, Winkel.

RHEINHESSEN *Germany* Large wine region to the south and west of Mainz. On the Rheinterrasse between Mainz and Worms are a number of very famous top-quality estates, especially at Nackenheim, NIERSTEIN, OPPENHEIM and Bodenheim. BINGEN, to the north-west, also has a fine vineyard area along the left bank of the Rhine.

RHÔNE VALLEY *France* The Rhône starts out as a river in Switzerland, ambling through Lake Geneva before hurtling southwards into France. In the area south of Lyon, between Vienne and Avignon, the valley becomes one of France's great wine regions. In the northern part, where vertigo-inducing slopes overhang the river, there is not much wine produced but the little that is made is of remarkable individuality. The Syrah grape reigns here in COTE-ROTIE and on the great hill of HERMITAGE. ST-JOSEPH, CROZES-HERMITAGE and CORNAS also make excellent reds, while the white Viognier grape yields perfumed, delicate wine at CONDRIEU and at the tiny AC CHATEAU-GRILLET. In the southern part the steep slopes give way to wide plains, where the vines swelter in the hot sun, with hills both in the west and east. Most of these vineyards are either COTES DU RHONE or COTES DU RHONE-VILLAGES, reds, whites and rosés, but there are also specific ACs. The most well known of these are CHATEAUNEUF-DU-PAPE and the luscious, golden dessert wine, MUSCAT DE BEAUMES-DE-VENISE. See also Clairette de Die, Coteaux de l'Ardèche, Coteaux du Tricastin, Côtes du Lubéron, Côtes du Vivarais, Gigondas, Lirac, Rasteau, St-Péray, Tavel, Vacqueyras.

RÍAS BAIXAS DO *Galicia, Spain* The best of Galicia's 5 DOs, Rías Baixas is making increasing quantities of Spain's best whites (apart from a few Chardonnays in the north-east). The magic ingredient is the characterful Albariño grape, making creamy-rich, fruity whites with a glorious fragrance. Drink young or with short aging. Best producers: Adegas Galegas★, Agro de Bazan★★, Quinta de Couselo★, Granxa Fillaboa★, Lagar de Fornelos★ (La RIOJA ALTA), Lusco do Miño★★, Martin Códax★★, Pazo de Barrantes★ (MARQUES DE MURRIETA), Pazo de Señorans★, Bodegas Salnesur (Condes de Albarei)★★, Santiago Ruiz★★ (Lan), Terras Gauda★★.

RIBATEJO *Portugal* Portugal's second-largest wine region straddles the river Tagus (Tejo) upstream from Lisbon. Hotter and drier than ESTREMADURA to the west, prolific vineyards on the fertile soils alongside the river are producing volumes of improving everyday reds and whites. There are 5 IPRs, of which Almeirim, with its giant co-op, is probably the best known. The Ribatejo is also the traditional source of some good GARRAFEIRAS. Best producers: Almeirim co-op, BRIGHT BROTHERS, Casa Cadaval, Quinta do Casal Branco, Falua, Quinta Grande, Quinta da Lagoalva★.

RIBERA DEL DUERO DO *Castilla y León, Spain* The dark elegant reds in this DO, from Tinto Fino (Tempranillo) sometimes with Cabernet Sauvignon and Merlot, are as good as those of RIOJA. Also a few light rosés. New names are rising to join the top ranks of quality. Best producers: Alión★★, Ismael ARROYO★★★, Arzuaga★, Balbás★, Hijos de Antonio Barceló★, Felix Callejo★, Hermanos Cuadrado García C B★★, Dehesa de los Canonigos★, Del Campo★, Fuentespina★, Grandes Bodegas, Hacienda Monasterio★, Emilio Moro★, Pago de Carraovejas, PEDROSA★★, PESQUERA★★★, PINGUS★★★, Protos★, Teófilo Reyes★★, Rodero★, Hermanos Sastre★★, Señorio de Nava, Valduero★, Valtravieso★★, VEGA SICILIA★★★, Viñedos y Bodegas★, Virgen de Fátima co-op★, Winner Wines★. Best years: 1996 95 **94** 91 **90 89 86 85 82**.

DOMAINE RICHEAUME *Côtes de Provence AC, Provence, France* German-owned property close to Cézanne's favourite Mont Ste-Victoire. The estate is run on organic principles and is planted with a mix of Mediterranean varieties (Cinsaut, Grenache, Syrah) and Cabernet Sauvignon, which produce impressively deep-coloured wines★ full of smoky spice and power. Best years: (1998) 97 95 **93 92 91** 90 89 88.

RICHEBOURG AC *Grand Cru, Côte de Nuits, Burgundy, France* Rich, fleshy wine from the northern end of VOSNE-ROMANÉE. Most domaine-bottlings are exceptional. Best producers: GRIVOT★★, Gros Frère et Soeur★★★, Anne Gros★★★, A-F Gros★★, JAYER★★★, LEROY★★★, MEO-CAMUZET★★, Dom. de la ROMANÉE-CONTI★★★. Best years: 1997 96 95 93 **92** 90 **89 88** 85.

RICHOU *Loire Valley, France* One of the leading domaines in the LOIRE, producing a large, consistently good range of wines. The best are the ANJOU-VILLAGES Vieilles Vignes★★ and the sweet COTEAUX DE L'AUBANCE Cuvée les Trois Demoiselles★★. Best years: (1998) 97 **96 95 94** 93 90 89 88.

MAX FERD RICHTER *Mülheim, Mosel-Saar-Ruwer, Germany* Dr Richter makes Riesling wines in some of the best sites in the MOSEL, including Wehlener Sonnenuhr★★, Brauneberger Juffer★★ and Graacher Domprobst★★. His wines are marked out by splendid racy acidity balanced by fragrant Riesling fruit. His Mülheimer Helenenkloster vineyard is unique in Germany for producing a magical EISWEIN★★★ virtually every year. Best years: (1998) 97 96 95 **94 93 92 90 89 88** 83.

RIDGE VINEYARDS *Santa Clara, California, USA* Established as a Zinfandel-only winery in 1962, winemaker Paul Draper moved into Cabernet Sauvignon★★ and Petite Sirah★ in the late 1960s. The Zinfandels★★★, made with grapes from various sources, have great intensity and long life, and the reds, led by the flagship Monte Bello Cabernet★★★, display ageability, impressive concentration of fruit and originality. There is some good Chardonnay★, too. Best years: (Zinfandel) 1997 96 95 **94 92 91** 90 88 85 84.

RIECINE *Chianti DOCG, Tuscany, Italy* Small estate in Gaiole, made famous by Englishman John Dunkley, that makes some of the most exquisite CHIANTI. Yields are low, so there is a great intensity of fruit and a superb definition of spiced cherry flavours. New American owners have retained Irish winemaker Sean O'Callaghan, so CHIANTI CLASSICO★★, Riserva★★★ and the barrique-aged La Gioia★★★, already outstanding, could get even better. Best years: (1998) (97) (96) 95 94 **93 90 88 86 85**.

RIESLING See pages 240–1.

RIESLING ITALICO Known as Welschriesling in the rest of Europe, and not in any way related to the great Riesling of the Rhine, this grape is widely planted in Italy, especially in the north, where it produces decent dry whites. In Austria it makes some of the very best sweet wines, but tends to be rather dull and thin as a dry wine. Watch out for a revival in Hungary where, as Olasz Rizling, it is highly esteemed.

CH. RIEUSSEC★★ *Sauternes AC, 1er Cru Classé, Bordeaux, France*
Apart from the peerless and scarcely affordable Ch. d'YQUEM, Rieussec often used to be the richest, most succulent wine of SAUTERNES. Other estates now rival in quality but at its best it is still a big, extravagant wine. The 1996 is excellent, showing plenty of botrytized richness. Cellar for at least 10 years, though it may be kept for another decade or more. The dry white wine, called 'R', is inexplicably dull. Second wine: Clos Labère. Owned since 1984 by LAFITE-ROTHSCHILD. Best years: (1998) 97 96 95 **90 89 88 86 85 83 81 75**.

RIO GRANDE DO SUL *Brazil* High rainfall and humidity in this southern-most region of Brazil mean that fungal diseases and ripening can be a problem for winemakers here. The main grape-growing area is the Serra Gaucha, a hilly zone at an altitude of over 700m (over 200ft). Flying winemaker John Worontschak has made progress with Cabernet Sauvignon and Merlot at Vinicola Aurora, but Chardonnay is still his most drinkable wine.

RIOJA DOC *Rioja, Navarra, País Vasco and Castilla y León, Spain* Rioja, in the centre of northern Spain, is not all oaky, creamy white wines and elegant, barrel-aged reds, combining oak flavours with wild strawberry and prune fruit. Over half Rioja's red wine is sold young, never having seen the inside of a barrel, and most of the white is fairly anonymous. But wine quality is still maddeningly inconsistent (though the best producers are improving all the time), and prices for grapes – and wine – have shot up in the last 3 years, despite large harvests in 1995, 96 and 97. Stick with the good guys. A bevy of new producers with great ambitions is changing the regional hierarchy fast. Best producers: (reds) Allende★★, Amézola de la Mora, Artadi★★, BARON DE LEY★, BERBERANA★, Berceo, Beronia, BRETON★★, CAMPILLO★★, CAMPO VIEJO★, Luis Cañas, CONTINO★★, El Coto★, CVNE, DOMECQ★, FAUSTINO MARTINEZ★, Herencia Lasanta, LOPEZ DE HEREDIA★, MARQUES DE CACERES★, MARQUES DE GRINON★, MARQUES DE MURRIETA★, MARQUES DE RISCAL★★, Marqués de Vargas★, MARTINEZ BUJANDA★★, MONTECILLO★, MUGA★, Navajas, PALACIO★★, REMELLURI★★, Fernando Remírez de Ganuza★★, La RIOJA ALTA★★, RIOJANAS★, Roda★★, Señorío de San Vicente★★, Sierra Cantabria, Torre de Oña, Viña Ijalba; (whites) Artadi★★, Beronia, BRETON★★, CAMPO VIEJO★, CVNE★, LOPEZ DE HEREDIA★, MARQUES DE CACERES★, MARQUES DE MURRIETA★, MARTINEZ BUJANDA★★, MONTECILLO★, La RIOJA ALTA★, RIOJANAS★. Best years: 1995 94 **91 89 87 86 85 83 82 81 78**.

RIESLING

I'm sad to have to make this bald statement at the start, but I feel I must. If you have tasted wines with names like Laski Riesling, Olasz Riesling, Welschriesling, Gray Riesling, Riesling Italico and the like and found them unappetizing – do not blame the Riesling grape. These wines have filched Riesling's name, but have nothing whatsoever to do with the great grape itself.

Riesling is Germany's finest contribution to the world of wine – and herein lies the second problem. German wines have fallen to such a low level of general esteem through the proliferation of wines like Liebfraumilch that Riesling, even true German Riesling, has been dragged down with it.

So what *is* true Riesling? It is a very ancient German grape, probably the descendant of wild vines growing in the Rhine Valley. It certainly performs best in the cool vineyard regions of Germany's Rhine and Mosel Valleys, but also does well in New Zealand and cool parts of Australia; yet it is widely planted in California, South Africa and Italy, and the warmer parts of Australia also grow it to good effect.

WINE STYLES

Germany These wines are based on a marvellous perfume and an ability to hold on to a piercing acidity, even at high ripeness levels, so long as the ripening period has been warm and gradual rather than broiling or rushed. German Rieslings can be bone dry, through to medium and even lusciously sweet, but if they are dry, they must be made from fully ripe grapes, otherwise the acidity is excessive and the wine's body insufficient.

Young Rieslings often show a delightful floral perfume, sometimes blended with the crispness of green apples, often lime, sometimes even peach, raisin or honey, depending upon the ripeness of the grapes. As the wines age, the lime often intensifies, and a flavour perhaps of slate, perhaps of petrol/kerosene intrudes.

Other regions The rather heavier, petrolly style is typical of Australia's warmer areas, while California generally produces a grapy style which is usually best when sweet. In the valleys of the Danube in Austria, Riesling gives stunning dry wines that combine richness with elegance. The mountain vineyards of northern Italy, and the cool vineyards of the Czech Republic, Slovakia and Switzerland can show a floral sharp style, but the most fragrant wines come from Germany, from France's Alsace, and from New Zealand, with some success from America's Pacific Northwest and New York State, and from the odd cool spot in Australia. South Africa's cooler regions produce delicate drier styles; there are also good late harvest and botrytized Rieslings.

In general Rieslings may be drunk young, but top dry wines can improve for many years, and the truly sweet German styles can age for generations.

BEST PRODUCERS

Dry Rieslings

Austria BRUNDLMAYER, HIRTZBERGER, Knoll, Nigl, NIKOLAIHOF, F-X PICHLER, Rudi Pichler, PRAGER, Freie Weingärtner WACHAU.

France (Alsace) P Blanck, A Boxler, Deiss, Dirler, Rolly Gassmann, HUGEL ET FILS, Kientzler, Kreydenweiss, KUENTZ-BAS, Ostertag, TRIMBACH, Weinbach, ZIND-HUMBRECHT.

Germany Georg BREUER, BURKLIN-WOLF, GUNDERLOCH, Heymann-Löwenstein, JULIUSSPITAL, KOEHLER-RUPRECHT, Franz KUNSTLER, J Leitz, MULLER-CATOIR, St Antony, J L WOLF.

Non-dry Rieslings

Germany BURKLIN-WOLF, DONNHOFF, Heymann-Löwenstein, GUNDERLOCH, HAAG, JOST, KARTHAUSERHOF, C Loewen, von KESSELSTATT, Franz KUNSTLER, Dr LOOSEN, MAXIMIN GRUNHAUS, MULLER-CATOIR, Egon MULLER-SCHARZHOF, J J PRUM, RICHTER, Willi Schaefer, DIEL, WEIL, ZILLIKEN.

France (Alsace) L Beyer, Deiss, HUGEL ET FILS, TRIMBACH, Weinbach, ZIND-HUMBRECHT.

New World Rieslings

Australia Tim ADAMS, Alkoomi, Wolf BLASS, Leo Buring, DELATITE, GROSSET, HENSCHKE, Howard Park, LEEUWIN, MITCHELL, MITCHELTON, ORLANDO, PETALUMA, PIPERS BROOK, PLANTAGENET, Geoff WEAVER, Wilson Vineyard.

New Zealand CLOUDY BAY, CORBANS, DRY RIVER, GIESEN, MILLTON, NEUDORF, VILLA MARIA.

South Africa Neethlingshof.

USA (Washington) KIONA; (New York) LAMOUREAUX LANDING.

LA RIOJA ALTA *Rioja DOC, Rioja, Spain* One of the best of the older RIOJA producers, making mainly Reservas and Gran Reservas. Its only Crianza, Viña Alberdi, fulfils the minimum age requirements for a Reserva anyway. There is a little good, lemony-oaky Viña Ardanza Reserva★ white. Red Reservas, Viña Arana★ and Viña Ardanza★★, age splendidly, and Gran Reservas, Reserva 904★★ and Reserva 890★★★ (made only in exceptional years), are among the very best of Rioja wines. Best years: (reds) 1996 95 **94 92 89 88 87 86 85 82 81 78 76 73**.

RIOJANAS *Rioja DOC, Rioja, Spain* Quality winery producing Reservas and Gran Reservas in 2 styles: elegant Viña Albina★ and richer Monte Real★. White Monte Real Blanco Crianza★ is one of RIOJA's best. The whites and Reservas can be kept for 5 years after release, Gran Reservas for 10 or more. Best years: (reds) 1995 **94 91 90 89 87 83 82 73 64**.

DANIEL RION *Nuits-St-Georges, Côte de Nuits, Burgundy, France* One of Burgundy's most consistent performers, producing concentrated but slightly austere reds from Pinot Noir, and a little bit of crisp, white Aligoté. Also white NUITS-ST-GEORGES les Terres Blanches from 1994. The best wines are the VOSNE-ROMANEE les Beaux Monts★★ and les Chaumes★★, Nuits-St-Georges Clos de Argillières★★ and the village level VOSNE-ROMANEE★. Best years: (reds) 1997 96 95 94 93 **90 89 88 85**.

RISERVA An Italian term, recognized in many DOCs and DOCGs, for a special selection of superior-quality wine that has been aged longer before release. Quite often, it is also destined for longer aging. It is only a promise of a more pleasurable drink if the wine had enough fruit and structure in the first place. Losing favour in BAROLO, it is still important in CHIANTI and CHIANTI CLASSICO.

RIVERA *Puglia, Italy* One of southern Italy's most dynamic producers. In the traditional mould, the CASTEL DEL MONTE Riserva Il Falcone★★ is an excellent, full-blooded southern red. There is also a series of varietals sold under the Terre al Monte label, best of which are Aglianico★, Pinot Bianco and Sauvignon Blanc.

RIVERINA *New South Wales, Australia* Along with South Australia's RIVERLAND, this extensive irrigated region, fed by the Murrumbidgee River, provides the bulk of Australia's basic table wines. Many of Australia's best-known brands, from companies like PENFOLDS, HARDY, ORLANDO and MCWILLIAMS, though not mentioning either Riverina or Riverland on the label, will in fact be based on wines from these areas. There are also some remarkable sweet wines such as the botrytis Semillon from DE BORTOLI★★★, Gramps★, Lillypilly★, MCWILLIAMS★, Miranda★★ and Wilton Estate★★.

RIVERLAND *Australia* A vast irrigated region along the Murray River, straddling 3 states (NEW SOUTH WALES, SOUTH AUSTRALIA and VICTORIA), and producing 27% of the national grape crush. Mainly given over to casks and cheaper bottles of table and fortified wine, though an increasing number of producers are bringing out high-quality special selections. Best producers: ANGOVE'S, BERRI RENMANO, Deakin Estate, Kingston Estate, Trentham Estate, YALUMBA (Oxford Landing).

RIVESALTES AC *Languedoc-Roussillon, France* VIN DOUX NATUREL from a large area around the town of Rivesaltes. These fortified wines are some of southern France's best and can be made from an assortment of grapes, mainly white Muscat (when it is called MUSCAT DE RIVESALTES) and Grenache Noir, Gris and Blanc. There is also a RANCIO style which ages well. Best producers: Ch. Cap de Fouste, Vignerons CATALANS, CAZES★★, Chênes★, Ch. de Corneilla, Forca Real, Ch. de Jau★, Laporte, Mas Rancoure★, Rivesaltes co-op, Sarda-Malet★, Terrats co-op, Troillas co-op.

ROBERTSON WO *South Africa* Hot, dry inland area with lime-rich soils, uncommon in the Cape, that are ideal for wines. Chenin Blanc and Colombard are the major varieties in this predominantly white wine region; used mainly for distilling, they also produce tasty everyday wines. Chardonnay performs very well (for both still and sparkling styles), as does the traditional Muscadel (Muscat Blanc à Petits Grains) yielding a benchmark fortified wine. Shiraz, Merlot and Cabernet show promise for reds. Best producers: Bon Courage, Graham BECK★, DE WETSHOF★, Robertson Winery, Springfield★, Van Loveren, Zandvliet.

J ROCHIOLI VINEYARDS *Russian River Valley AVA. California, USA* Pinot Noir from Rochioli's vineyard was largely responsible for placing RUSSIAN RIVER VALLEY on the wine map. Meticulous growers still selling grapes, the Rochioli family are equally good at winemaking, offering silky, black cherry Pinot Noir★★ and a richer, dramatic Reserve Pinot★★. All wines stand out, including a fine Sauvignon Blanc Reserve★★ and a solid Chardonnay★★. Best years: (Pinot Noir) (1998) 97 **95 94 92**.

ROCKFORD *Barossa Valley, South Australia* Wonderfully nostalgic wines from the stone winery of Robert 'Rocky' O'Callaghan, who has a great respect for the old vines so plentiful in the BAROSSA, and delights in using antique machinery. Produces masterful Basket Press Shiraz★★, EDEN VALLEY Riesling★, Dry Country Grenache★ and red sparkling cult wine, Black Shiraz★★. Best years: (reds) 1996 94 93 **92 91 90 87 85**.

ANTONIN RODET *Mercurey, Côte Chalonnaise, Burgundy, France* Merchant based in the village of MERCUREY, specializing in COTE CHALONNAISE, but also producing an excellent range from throughout Burgundy. Rodet owns or co-owns 5 domaines – Ch. de Rully★★, Ch. de Chamirey★, Ch. de Mercurey★★, Dom. de Perdrix★ and Jacques Prieur★★ – which are the source of the best wines. Don't miss the BOURGOGNE Vieilles Vignes★, one of the best inexpensive Chardonnays available. Best years: (reds) 1997 96 95 93 **92** 90 **89 88**; (whites) 1997 96 **95 92 90 89**.

LOUIS ROEDERER *Champagne AC, Champagne, France* Good-quality firm making some of the best, full-flavoured CHAMPAGNES around. As well as the excellent non-vintage★★ and pale rosé★ it also makes a big, exciting vintage★★, and the famous Roederer Cristal★★★, a de luxe cuvée which is pretty nearly always delicious. Both the vintage version and Cristal can usually be aged for 10 years or more. Best years: **1993 90 89 88 86 85**.

ROEDERER ESTATE *Anderson Valley AVA, California, USA* Californian off-shoot of French CHAMPAGNE house Louis ROEDERER. The Brut★★ (sold in the UK as Quartet) is somewhat austere, a step back from the upfront fruit of many California sparklers, but it should age well if you can wait. L'Ermitage★★, a tête de cuvée first released in 1994, is a stunning addition to the range of California fizz. Best years: (L'Ermitage) **1994 92 91**.

ROERO DOC *Piedmont, Italy* The Roero hills lie across the Tanaro river from the LANGHE hills, home of BAROLO and BARBARESCO. Long noted as a source of Nebbiolo in supple, fruity red wines to drink in 2–5 years, Roero has recently made its mark with the white Arneis grape. The red wine is called simply Roero and the white Roero Arneis. Best producers: (reds) Almondo★, Cascino Ca' Rossa★, Carretta★, Cascina Chico, Cornarea, Correggia★, Deltetto★, Malabaila, Malvirà★, Monchiero Carbone★, Angelo Negro, Porello★, Giovanni Voerzio. Best years: (reds) (1998) **97 96 95**. Also see Arneis.

ROMAGNA *Emilia-Romagna, Italy* Romagna's wine production is centred on 4 DOCs and 1 DOCG. The whites are from Trebbiano (ineffably dull), Pagadebit (showing promise as both a dry and sweet wine) and Albana (ALBANA DI ROMAGNA was upgraded to DOCG in 1987 and can be made in either dry or sweet versions). The reds are dominated by the Sangiovese grape, which ranges from young and fresh through to wines that can rival a good CHIANTI. Castelluccio makes outstanding Sangiovese, such as Ronco delle Ginestre★★ or Ronco della Simia★★. Best producers: (Sangiovese) La Berta★, Le Calbane★, Casetto dei Mandorli★, Castelluccio★★, Celli★, Conti★, Ferrucci★, La Palazza★, Paradiso★, San Patrignano co-op (Riserva★), Spalletti, Tre Monti★, Trerè★, Zerbina★★.

LA ROMANÉE-CONTI AC *Grand Cru, Côte de Nuits, Burgundy, France* For many extremely wealthy wine lovers this is the pinnacle of red Burgundy★★★. It is an incredibly complex wine with great structure and pure, clearly defined fruit flavour, but you've got to age it two dozen years to see what all the fuss is about. The vineyard covers only 1.8ha (4½ acres), which is one reason for the high prices. Wholly owned by Dom. de la ROMANÉE-CONTI. Best years: 1996 95 93 90 89 88 **85 78 76 71**.

DOM. DE LA ROMANÉE-CONTI *Vosne-Romanée, Côte de Nuits, Burgundy, France* This famous red wine domaine owns a string of Grands Crus in VOSNE-ROMANÉE (la TACHE★★★, RICHEBOURG★★★, ROMANÉE-CONTI★★★, ROMANÉE-ST-VIVANT★★, ECHEZEAUX★★ and Grands-Échézeaux★★) as well as a small parcel of le MONTRACHET★★★. The wines are all ludicrously expensive but they can be quite sublime – full of fruit when young, but capable of aging for 15 years or more to an astonishing marriage made in the heaven and hell of richness and decay. Recent vintages seem to show a necessary return to consistency. At these prices they'd better! Best years: 1996 95 93 90 89 88 **85 78 71**.

ROMANÉE-ST-VIVANT AC *Grand Cru, Côte de Nuits, Burgundy, France* By far the largest of VOSNE-ROMANÉE's 6 Grands Crus. At 10–15 years old, the wines should reveal the keenly balanced brilliance of which the vineyard is capable but a surly, rough edge sometimes gets in the way. Best producers: Robert Arnoux★, J-J Confuron★★, DROUHIN★★, Louis LATOUR★, Dom LEROY★★, Hudelot-Noëllat★★, Dom. de la ROMANÉE-CONTI★★. Best years: 1997 96 95 93 90 **89 88 85**.

RONGOPAI *Te Kauwhata, Auckland, North Island, New Zealand* Small winery doing well with bunch- and berry-selected sweet botrytis styles, which include Riesling, Müller-Thurgau and Chardonnay★★. There is also distinctive dry Sauvignon Blanc, Chardonnay★, Riesling and Cabernet Sauvignon. Best years: (1998) **96 94 91**.

ROSA, QUINTA DE LA *Douro DOC and Port DOC, Douro, Portugal* The Bergqvist family have transformed this spectacular property into a small but serious independent producer of both PORT and DOURO table wines★. The vintage port★ (1992★★) is excellent. Best years: (vintage ports) 1995 94 92 **91**.

ROSÉ D'ANJOU AC *Loire Valley, France* AC for cheap ANJOU rosé that is usually somewhere between off-dry and quite sweet. Produced predominantly from the Groslot grape, which doesn't give much colour or flavour. Most of the top producers prefer to use ROSE DE LOIRE or CABERNET D'ANJOU titles. Drink young. Best producer: Caves de la Loire.

ROSÉ DE LOIRE AC *Loire Valley, France* AC for dry rosé wine from SAUMUR and TOURAINE but mainly from ANJOU. It can be a lovely drink, full of red berry fruits, but drink as young as possible and chill well. Best producers: l'Echalier, Haute Perche, Ogereau, Passavant, RICHOU, Sauveroy.

ROSÉ DES RICEYS AC *Champagne, France* This is a curiosity and an expensive one at that. It's a still, dark pink wine made from Pinot Noir grapes in the southern part of the CHAMPAGNE region. Best producers: Alexandre Bonnet, Horiot.

ROSEMOUNT ESTATE *Hunter Valley, New South Wales, Australia* Model winery buying and growing grapes in several regions to produce some of Australia's best, most popular wines. Top are complex, weighty Roxburgh★★ and Show Reserve★★ Chardonnays; blackcurranty COONAWARRA Cabernet★★ and gutsy Balmoral Syrah★★. New Rose label Chardonnay★★ from the Orange region is very fine; MCLAREN VALE Orange Syrah★★ is too. Mountain Blue Shiraz-Cabernet★★ is the most exciting new wine to come out of MUDGEE for a long time, and GSM★★ (Grenache, Syrah, Mourvèdre) blend is a knockout, but prices of all these premium reds have soared lately. 'Split label' Semillon-Chardonnay and Shiraz-Cabernet★ are among Australia's best inexpensive gluggers. Best years: (whites) 1996 **95 94 93** 91 90 89 87.

ROSSO CÒNERO DOC *Marche, Italy* The best wines in this zone, on the Adriatic coast just south of Ancona, are made solely from Montepulciano, and have a wonderfully spicy richness undiluted by the addition of Sangiovese. Winemaking has improved greatly of late. Best producers: Garofoli★★, Lanari★, Leopardi Dittajuti★, Marchetti (Villa Bonomi★), Mecella (Rubelliano★), Monarco, Moroder★ (Dorico★★), Le Terrazze (Sassi Neri★), Umani Ronchi★ (Cumaro★★), La Vite. Best years: (1998) 97 **96 95 94 93 92 90**.

ROSSO DI MONTALCINO DOC *Tuscany, Italy* The little brother of BRUNELLO DI MONTALCINO spends much less time aging in wood, so enabling the wines to retain a wonderful exuberance of flavour that Brunello may lose through its longer cask-aging. Best producers: ALTESINO★, ARGIANO★, BANFI★, Barbi★, Canalicchio di Sopra★, Caparzo★, Casanova di Neri★, CASTELGIOCONDO, Ciacci Piccolomini d'Aragona★★, Col d'Orcia★, COSTANTI★, La Fortuna★, Fuligni★, La Gerla★, Maurizio Lambardi★★, Lisini★, Mocali★, Silvio Nardi★, Siro Pacenti★, Agostina Pieri★, Poggio Antico★, Il Poggiolo★, Il Poggione★, Duc Portine-Gorelli★, San Filippo★, Talenti★, Uccelliera★, Valdicava★, Val di Suga★. Best years: (1997) 96 **95 94 93** 91 90.

ROSSO DI MONTEPULCIANO DOC *Tuscany, Italy* This DOC, created in 1989, gives producers the option of honing the production of their grander VINO NOBILE DI MONTEPULCIANO DOCG by diverting some of the younger, juicier vats into bottle at an earlier stage. Some producers turn out a fresh, jammy, rather innocuous style, but the best give the drinker a mouthful of plummy, chocolaty flavours that is pure delight. Best producers: La Braccesca★, Buracchi, Le Casalte, Contucci, Dei★, Del Cerro★, Fassati★, Gracciano della Seta, Antonio Lombardo, Il Macchione, Nottola, POLIZIANO★, Massimo Romeo★, Valdipiatta★. Best years: 1998 **97 96 95**.

ROSSO PICENO DOC *Marche, Italy* Though related to ROSSO CONERO, this red is often considered a poor relative, since Sangiovese tends to be lean and harsh in the Marche. But when the full complement of Montepulciano is used at 40%, Rosso Piceno can be rich and seductive. Best producers: Boccadigabbia★, Bucci, Cocci Grifoni★, Saladini Pilastri★, Velenosi★, Villa Pigna, Villamagna★. Best years: (1998) 97 **95 94 93 90**.

ROTHBURY ESTATE *Hunter Valley, New South Wales, Australia* After a protracted fight, Len Evans' brainchild was sold in 1996 to the Fosters brewery, which adds it to its MILDARA-BLASS group of brands. What effect this will have on the wines is uncertain, but early signs are encouraging. Rothbury has a great name for sturdy HUNTER Shiraz★ (Reserve★★) and barrel-fermented Chardonnay★★ as well as quaffing COWRA Chardonnay★ and some of the Hunter's greatest Semillons★★★. Best years: (whites) 1998 **96 95** 93 91 90 86 84 79; (reds) 1996 **95** 93 91 89 87 86 83 81 79.

ROUGE HOMME *Coonawarra, South Australia* Came to the Southcorp stable as part of LINDEMANS, which bought it from the pioneer Redman family (red-man, geddit?) in 1965. Now blossoming in the hands of winemaker Paul Gordon, a whiz with reds. He's smartened up the Cabernet Sauvignon★★, Shiraz-Cabernet★ and Pinot Noir★ so they're among the best value for money in the country. New Cabernet blend Richardson's Red Block★ is a moreish award-winning drop; Chardonnay★ is terrific value, the unoaked version not bad either. Best years: (reds): 1996 **94 93 91 90** 88 86.

GEORGES ROUMIER *Chambolle-Musigny AC, Côte de Nuits, Burgundy, France* Although barely 40 years of age, Christophe Roumier who is now in charge has long been recognized as one of Burgundy's top winemakers, yet he devotes as much attention to his vineyards as to cellar technique, believing in severe pruning, low yields, and stringent grape selection. Roumier never uses more than one-third new oak. His best wine is often BONNES-MARES★★★, but his other Grands Crus include MUSIGNY★★, CLOS DE VOUGEOT★★ and CORTON-CHARLEMAGNE★★. The best value is usually the exclusively owned Premier Cru in MOREY-ST-DENIS, Clos de la Bussière★★. Best years: (reds) 1997 96 95 93 **92 91** 90 **89** 88 85.

ROUSSANNE The RHÔNE VALLEY's best white grape variety, Roussanne is frequently blended with Marsanne. Roussanne is the more aromatic and elegant of the 2, less prone to oxidation and with better acidity, but growers usually prefer Marsanne due to its higher yields. Now being planted in the MIDI.

ARMAND ROUSSEAU *Gevrey-Chambertin AC, Côte de Nuits, Burgundy, France* One of the most highly respected and important CHAMBERTIN estates, with vineyards in Clos-de-Bèze, Mazis-Chambertin and Charmes-Chambertin as well as CLOS DE LA ROCHE★★ in MOREY-ST-DENIS and GEVREY-CHAMBERTIN Clos St-Jacques★★. The outstandingly harmonious, elegant, yet rich wines are made in a traditional style and enjoy an enviable reputation for longevity. The Chambertin★★★ is exceptionally fine. Best years: 1997 96 95 93 **92 91** 90 **89 88 85**.

ROUSSILLON *France* The snow-covered peaks of the Pyrenees form a spectacular backdrop to the ancient region of Roussillon, now the Pyrénées-Orientales *département*. The vineyards produce a wide range of fairly priced wines, mainly red, ranging from the ripe, raisin-rich VINS DOUX NATURELS to light, fruity-fresh VINS DE PAYS. After spending several years in the shadow of the LANGUEDOC renaissance, there are now some really exciting table wines, both white and red, being made in Roussillon, especially by individual estates. See also Banyuls, Collioure, Côtes du Roussillon, Côtes du Roussillon-Villages, Maury, Muscat de Rivesaltes, Rivesaltes.

RUCHOTTES-CHAMBERTIN AC See Chambertin AC.

RÜDESHEIM *Rheingau, Germany* Village producing silky, aromatic wines from some famous sites (Berg Schlossberg, Berg Rottland, Berg Roseneck and Bischofsberg). Not to be confused with the NAHE village of the same name. During the 1980s a group of young winemakers dramatically improved standards here. Best producers: Georg BREUER★★, Johannishof★, J Leitz★★. Best years: (1998) 96 **94 93 90**.

RUEDA DO *Castilla y León, Spain* The RIOJA firm of MARQUES DE RISCAL launched the reputation of this white-wine-only region in the 1970s, first by rescuing the almost extinct local grape, Verdejo, then by introducing Sauvignon Blanc. Fresh young whites have been joined by barrel-fermented wines aiming for a longer life, particularly those made by an immigrant from Bordeaux, Brigitte Lurton. Best producers: Alvarez y Diez, Antaño (Viña Mocén★), Belondrade y Lurton★★, Cerro Sol (Doña Beatriz), Hermanos Lurton★★, MARQUES DE RISCAL (Sauvignon Blanc★★), Angel Rodríguez Vidal (Martinsancho), Castilla La Vieja (Mirador), Viños Sanz.

RUFFINO *Tuscany, Italy* Huge winemaking concern, whose main business is still centred on basic CHIANTI, though it has succeeded in establishing some fine wines. CHIANTI CLASSICO comes from estates at Zano★, Nozzole★ and Santedame★, though the classic is Riserva Ducale★★. SUPER-TUSCANS include Chardonnay Cabreo La Pietra★★, Cabernet Cabreo Il Borgo★★, Pinot Noir Nero del Tondo★ and the unique blend of Colorino and Sangiovese in Romitorio di Santedame★. VINO NOBILE estate Lodola Nuova and BRUNELLO Il Greppone Mazzi are also owned by Ruffino.

RUINART *Champagne AC, Champagne, France* This is one of the oldest CHAMPAGNE houses. Ruinart has a surprisingly low profile, given the quality of its wines. The non-vintage★★ is very good, but the top wines here are the excellent, classy Dom Ruinart BLANC DE BLANCS★★★ and the Dom Ruinart Rosé★★★. Best years: **1993** 92 90 88 86 85 83 82.

RULLY AC *Côte Chalonnaise, Burgundy, France* One of Burgundy's most improved ACs with good-quality, reasonably priced wine. Once famous for sparkling wines, it is now best known for its still whites, often oak-aged. Reds are light, with a fleeting strawberry and cherry perfume. Best producers: (whites) J-C Brelière★, A Delorme, DROUHIN★, Duvernay, FAIVELEY★, JADOT★, JAFFELIN★, Olivier LEFLAIVE★, RODET★★, E de Suremain; (reds) A Delorme, Dureuil-Janthial★, Duvernay, la Folie, H & P Jacqueson★. Best years: (whites) 1997 **96 95 94 92 90**; (reds) 1997 **96 95 93 90**.

RUSSE *Northern Region, Bulgaria* One of Bulgaria's largest wineries and an up-and-coming star, achieving vibrant, zesty results with Cabernet Sauvignon★ and Merlot★. The low-priced 'country' blends are good. To date, this winery has not been privatized.

RUSSIAN RIVER VALLEY AVA *Sonoma, USA* Beginning south of Healdsburg along the Russian River as it flows south-west, this wine valley cools as it meanders south-westerly towards the Pacific. Seemingly coming from nowhere, it is now challenging CARNEROS as the top spot for Pinot Noir and Chardonnay. Best producers: DEHLINGER★★★, De Loach★, IRON HORSE★★, J ROCHIOLI VINEYARDS★★, SONOMA-CUTRER★, Rodney Strong★, Joseph SWAN★, Marimar TORRES★, WILLIAMS SELYEM★★.

RUSTENBERG ESTATE *Stellenbosch WO, South Africa* A new cellar in the old dairy is part of the extensive overhaul that has brought this magnificent old farm technically up to date without losing the ambiance of its national monument status. New Zealand winemaker Rod Easthorpe's first new-look, classically styled Rustenberg wines are no less impressive: the single-vineyard Five Soldiers Chardonnay★, Rustenberg★, a BORDEAUX-style blend and a majestic Cabernet★★ Peter Barlow, named after owner Simon Barlow's late father, restores the estate to the super-league. The Brampton range, focusing on varietal fruit, remains good value. Best years: (reds) **1996**; (whites) **1997**.

RUST-EN-VREDE ESTATE *Stellenbosch WO, South Africa* Owner Jannie Engelbracht has adopted the 'new broom' approach at this premium red estate. Louis Strydom, previously at Shiraz specialist SAXENBURG, has been appointed winemaker; a new underground cellar, several hundred new oak wine barrels and a surge of replanting complete the picture. It leaves few excuses for the already suppler, fruitier Shiraz★ and Rust-en-Vrede★, a Cabernet-Shiraz vintage blend, designed to show off the terroir. Best years: **1995 94 92 91 89**.

RUTHERFORD AVA *California, USA* This recently defined viticultural area in mid-NAPA VALLEY has inspired endless hours of argument and acrimony. The heart of the area – known as the Rutherford Bench – does seem to be a prime Cabernet Sauvignon production zone, and many of the traditional old Napa Cabernets have come from Rutherford and exhibit the 'Rutherford Dust' flavour. Best producers: BEAULIEU★★, Cakebread, FLORA SPRINGS★★, Freemark Abbey, NIEBAUM COPPOLA★.

RUTHERGLEN *Victoria, Australia* This district in north-east Victoria is the home of heroic reds from Shiraz, Cabernet and Durif, and luscious, world-beating fortifieds from Muscat and Tokay (Muscadelle). There are also good sherry-style and ultra-ripe vintage port-style wines. The whites from Chardonnay and Semillon are tasty but unsubtle. Best producers: (fortifieds) ALL SAINTS★★, Campbells★★, CHAMBERS★★★, MORRIS★★★, Stanton & Killeen★.

SAALE-UNSTRUT *Germany* Located in the former East Germany, Saale Unstrut wines used to be virtually reserved for Party members, and their chief reputation was for rarity. But there has been considerable improvement since reunification in 1989. Best producer: Lützkendorf★.

SACHSEN *Germany* Until recently one of Europe's forgotten wine regions on the river Elbe in former East Germany. During the last couple of years some good wines have started coming out of Sachsen. Best producers: Schloss Proschwitz, Klaus Seifert, Klaus Zimmerling★.

CH. ST-AMAND★ *Sauternes AC, Bordeaux, France* One of the few non-Classed Growth properties regularly producing big, rich, classic SAUTERNES, although the price is verging on the high side. The wine is also sold as Ch. la Chartreuse. Best years: (1998) 97 96 95 **90 89 88 86 83**.

ST-AMOUR *AC Beaujolais, Burgundy, France* The northernmost BEAUJOLAIS Cru, producing juicy, soft-fruited wine which lasts well for 2–3 years. Best producers: Billards (Loron et Fils)★, DUBOEUF, J Patissier★, A Poitevin, J-G Revillon★, Ch. de St-Amour. Best years: 1998 **97 96 95**.

ST-AUBIN AC *Côte de Beaune, Burgundy, France* Some of Burgundy's best-value wines. Good reds, especially from Premiers Crus like les Frionnes and les Murgers des Dents de Chien. Also reasonably priced, oak-aged white wines. Best producers: Jean-Claude Bachelet, Raoul Clerget★, COLIN★★, DROUHIN★, GERMAIN★, JADOT★★, JAFFELIN, Lamy-Pillot★, Olivier LEFLAIVE★, Bernard Morey★, H Prudhon, RAMONET★★, Roux★, G Thomas. Best years: 1997 96 **95 93 92 90**.

ST-CHINIAN AC *Languedoc, France* Large AC for strong, spicy red wines with more personality than run-of-the-mill HERAULT, especially when carbonic maceration has been used to extract lots of fruit and colour from the grapes. Best producers: Berlou co-op★, Canet Valette★★, Cazal-Viel★, Clos Bagatelle, Coujan, la Dournie, Jougla★, Maurel Fonsalade★, Prieuré des Mourges★, Roquebrun co-op★, St-Chinian co-op, la Vitarele★. Best years: (1998) 96 **95 94 93 91 90 89**.

ST-DÉSIRAT, CAVE CO-OPERATIVE DE *St-Joseph, Rhône Valley, France* St-Désirat is the largest single producer of ST-JOSEPH wines and one of the best co-ops in the RHONE VALLEY. The intense, smoky red St-Joseph★ is a fantastic bargain, as are local VINS DE PAYS. Best years: (1998) 97 96 95 **92 91 90 89**.

ST-ÉMILION AC *Bordeaux, France* The scenic Roman hill town of St-Émilion is the centre of Bordeaux's most historic wine region. Tourists flock in their thousands for the wine and the sights. The finest vineyards are on the côtes, or steep slopes, around the town, although a second area to the west, called the *graves*, contains 2 of St-Émilion's most famous properties, CHEVAL BLANC and FIGEAC. It is a region of smallholdings, with over 1000 different properties, and consequently the co-operative plays an important part. The dominant early-ripening Merlot grape gives wines with a 'come hither' softness and sweetness rare in red Bordeaux. St-Émilion AC is the basic generic AC, with 4 so-called satellites (LUSSAC, MONTAGNE, PUISSEGUIN, ST-GEORGES) allowed to annex their name to it. The best producers, including the Classed Growths, are found in the more controlled ST-EMILION GRAND CRU AC category. Best years: (1998) 96 **95 94 90 89 88 86 85**.

ST-ÉMILION GRAND CRU AC *Bordeaux, France*   St-Émilion's top-quality AC, which includes the estates classified as Grand Cru Classé and Premier Grand Cru Classé. The 1996 classification lists 55 Grands Crus Classés. Top wines in this category are better value than Premiers Grands Crus Classés and can age for 10–15 years. Best producers: (Grands Crus Classés) l'ARROSEE★★, BALESTARD-LA-TONNELLE★, CANON-LA-GAFFELIERE★★, la Dominique★★, Grand Mayne★, Grand Pontet★, Larmande★, Pavie-Decesse★, Pavie-Macquin★, Soutard★, TROPLONG-MONDOT★★; (others) Faugères, Fleur Cardinale, Fombrauge, la Mondotte★, Monbousquet★, Moulin St-Georges★, TERTRE-ROTEBOEUF★★, Teyssier, VALANDRAUD★★. Best years: (1998) 97 96 95 94 **90 89 88 86 85 83 82**. See also St-Émilion Premier Grand Cru Classé.

ST-ÉMILION PREMIER GRAND CRU CLASSÉ *Bordeaux, France*   The St-Émilion élite level, divided into 2 categories – 'A' and 'B', with only the much more expensive CHEVAL BLANC and AUSONE in category 'A'. There are 11 'B' châteaux, with ANGELUS and BEAU-SEJOUR BECOT added in the 1996 Classification. Best producers: ANGELUS★★★, AUSONE★★, BEAU-SEJOUR BECOT★★, Beauséjour★★, BELAIR★, CANON★, CHEVAL BLANC★★★, Clos Fourtet★★, FIGEAC★★, MAGDELAINE★, PAVIE★. Best years: (1998) 97 96 95 94 90 89 **88 86 85 83 82 79 78 75**.

ST-ESTÈPHE AC *Haut-Médoc, Bordeaux, France*   Large AC north of PAUILLAC with 5 Classed Growths. St-Estèphe wines have high tannin levels, but less weight. They are drinkable at 2–3 years, but given time (10–20 years) those sought-after flavours of blackcurrant and cedarwood can peek out. More Merlot has been planted to soften the wines. Best producers: CALON-SEGUR★, COS D'ESTOURNEL★★★, Cos Labory★, HAUT-MARBUZET★, LAFON-ROCHET★, Lilian-Ladouys★, Marbuzet★, MEYNEY★, MONTROSE★★★, les Ormes-de-Pez★, PEZ★, Phelan Ségur★. Best years: (1998) 96 95 94 90 89 **88 86 85 83 82 78 75**.

ST-GEORGES-ST-ÉMILION AC *Bordeaux, France*   The best satellite of ST-EMILION, with lovely, soft wines that can nevertheless age for 6–10 years. Best producers: Calon, Ch. St-Georges★, Macquin St-Georges★, St-André Corbin, Tour-du-Pas-St-Georges★, Vieux-Montaiguillon. Best years: (1998) 96 95 **94 90 89 88 85 83**.

ST HALLETT *Barossa Valley, South Australia*   Bob McLean manages this revitalized winery which makes Old Block Shiraz★★★, one of BAROSSA's best reds, using very old vines and open fermenters. Two other lovely Shirazes have slotted in below it recently: Blackwell★★ (named after the winemaker) and Faith★★. Semillon-Sauvignon Blanc★ and Chardonnay★ are excellent modern whites. Best years: (reds) 1996 **94 93 92 91 90 88 86**.

ST HELENA *Canterbury, South Island, New Zealand*   This winery achieved fame with New Zealand's first outstanding Pinot Noir in 1982, though quality has been variable since; also good Pinot Blanc★ and Pinot Gris★. Best years: (Pinot Noir) (1998) **96 95 94 91 90 89**.

ST HUBERTS *Yarra Valley, Victoria, Australia*   Dating back to the 1860s, this winery is glamorous now in name only. Quality has wavered since being swallowed up by Fosters/MILDARA-BLASS in 1996. Traditionally respected for its crystal-clean Chardonnay★, fragrant Pinot Noir★ and elegant, modern Cabernet★★ and Cabernet-Merlot★. Best years: (Cabernet) 1995 94 **93 92 91 90 88 87 82**.

ST-JOSEPH AC *Rhône Valley, France* Large, mainly red AC, on the opposite bank of the Rhône to HERMITAGE. Made from Syrah, the reds have mouthfilling fruit with irresistible blackcurrant richness. Brilliant at 1–2 years, they can last for up to 8. There is only a little white made and, with up-to-date winemaking, these are usually pleasant, flowery wines for drinking without too much ceremony at a year or so old, although an increasing number are ageworthy. Best producers: (reds) G Barge★, CHAPOUTIER★, CHAVE★★, L Chèze★, COURSODON★★, Y Cuilleron★, FLORENTIN★, P Gaillard★★, P Gonon★, GRAILLOT★, B Gripa★★, J-L Grippat★★, JABOULET★, Monteillet★★, Paret★, A Perret★, P Pinchon★, ST-DESIRAT CO-op★, F Villard★; (whites) L Chèze★, Y Cuilleron★, FLORENTIN★, P Gaillard★, JABOULET★, B Gripa★★, J-L Grippat★, Monteillet★, A Perret★. Best years: (reds) (1998) 97 **96 95 92 91 90 89**; (whites) (1998) **97 96 95**.

ST-JULIEN AC *Haut-Médoc, Bordeaux, France* For many, St-Julien produces perfect claret, with an ideal balance between opulence and austerity and between the brashness of youth and the genius of maturity. It is the smallest of the HAUT-MEDOC ACs but almost all is first-rate vineyard land and quality is high. Best producers: BEYCHEVELLE★, BRANAIRE★★, DUCRU-BEAUCAILLOU★★★, GLORIA★, GRUAUD-LAROSE★★★, LAGRANGE★★, LANGOA-BARTON★★, LEOVILLE-BARTON★★★, LEOVILLE-LAS-CASES★★★, LEOVILLE-POYFERRE★★, ST-PIERRE★, TALBOT★★. Best years: (1998) 97 96 95 94 **93** 90 89 **88 86 85 83 82 81 79 78**.

ST-NICOLAS-DE-BOURGUEIL AC *Loire Valley, France* An enclave of just under 500ha (1250 acres) within the larger BOURGUEIL AC. Almost all the wine is red and with the same piercing red fruit flavours of Bourgueil, and are much better after 7–10 years, especially in warm vintages. Best producers: Audebert, P Jamet★★, Lorieux, Mabileau★, Taluau★, Vallée★. Best years: 1995 **93 90 89 88 86 85**.

ST-PÉRAY AC *Rhône Valley, France* Rather hefty, Champagne-method fizz from Marsanne and Roussanne grapes from vineyards across the river from Valence, plua a little still white, which is usually dry and stolid. Best producers: J-F Chaboud★, CLAPE★, DELAS, Fauterie★, B Gripa★, J Lemencier★, LIONNET, J-L Thiers★, A Voge★. Best years: (1998) 97 **96 95 94**.

CH. ST-PIERRE★★ *St-Julien AC, 4ème Cru Classé, Haut-Médoc, Bordeaux, France* Small ST-JULIEN property making wines that have become much lusher and richer since 1982, with far more new oak spice. Drinkable early, but top vintages can improve for 20 years. Best years: (1998) 97 96 95 94 93 **90 89 88 86 83 81 79 78 75**.

ST-ROMAIN AC *Côte de Beaune, Burgundy, France* Out-of-the-way village producing red wines with a firm, bitter-sweet cherrystone fruit and flinty-dry whites varying between the austerely acid and the quirkily old-style. Both are usually good value by Burgundian standards, and may take at least 5 years to open out. Best producers: (reds) A Gras, Thévenin-Monthélie★; (whites) Bazenet★, H & G Buisson, A Gras★, JAFFELIN★, Olivier LEFLAIVE, P Taupenot, Thévenin-Monthélie★. Best years: (reds) 1997 96 **95 93 90**; (whites) 1997 96 **95 93 92 90**.

ST-VÉRAN AC *Mâconnais, Burgundy, France* Often thought of as a POUILLY-FUISSE understudy. This is gentle, fairly fruity, normally unoaked Mâconnais Chardonnay at its best, and the overall quality is good. The price is fair, too. Best to drink young. Best producers: G Chagny, Corsin★★, Deux Roches★, B & J-M Drouin★, DUBOEUF★,

E Loron, R Luquet, Lycée Agricole de Davayé, O Merlin★, Prissé co-op, J-L Tissier★, J-J Vincent★. Best years: 1997 **96 95 94 93 92**.

DOM. STE-ANNE *Côtes du Rhône AC, Rhône Valley, France* Top-notch COTES DU RHONE and COTES DU RHONE-VILLAGES produced by Burgundian expatriate Guy Steinmaier. There are several reasonably priced and marvellously full-throttle reds; COTES DU RHONE★, COTES DU RHONE-VILLAGES★, Cuvée Notre Dame des Cellettes★ and Cuvée St-Gervais★, as well as very good Viognier★★. Best years: (1998) **97 95 94 93 91 90 89**.

STE-CROIX-DU-MONT AC *Bordeaux, France* Best of the 3 sweet wine ACs that gaze jealously at SAUTERNES and BARSAC across the Garonne river (the others are CADILLAC and LOUPIAC). The wine is mildly sweet rather than splendidly rich, best drunk as an apéritif or with hors d'oeuvre. The top wines can age for at least a decade. Best producers: Bertranon, Crabitan-Bellevue, Loubens★, Lousteau-Vieil★, Mailles, Mont, la Rame★. Best years: (1998) 97 96 **95 90 89 88 86 85 83**.

SAINTSBURY *Carneros AVA, California, USA* New wave, deeply committed winery using only CARNEROS fruit. Its Pinot Noirs★★ are brilliant examples of the perfume and fruit quality of Carneros. The Reserve★★★ is deeper and oakier, while Garnet★ is a delicious, lighter style. Chardonnay★ and Reserve

Chardonnay★★ are also impressive, best drunk after 2–3 years. Best years: (Chardonnay) 1997 **96 95 94 92 91** 90; (Chardonnay Reserve) **1997 95 94 93 92** 90; (Pinot Noir Reserve) 1996 95 94 **92 91** 90; (Pinot Noir Carneros) 1997 96 95 **94 93 92 91** 90.

SALA, CASTELLO DELLA *Orvieto DOC, Umbria, Italy* Belongs to the ANTINORI family, making good ORVIETO★ and outstanding oak-aged Cervaro della Sala★★★ (90% Chardonnay-10% Grechetto). Also impressive Pinot Nero. The sweet Muffato della Sala★ is also good.

SALAPARUTA, DUCA DI *Sicily, Italy* Corvo is the brand name for Sicilian wines made by this firm. Red and white Corvo are pretty basic, but there are superior whites, Colomba Platino and Bianca di Valguarnera★, and 2 fine reds, Terre d'Agala★ and Duca Enrico★★.

CH. DE SALES★ *Pomerol AC, Bordeaux, France* Tucked in the north-western tip of the AC where the soil is sandier, the wines never have the tingling excitement of the best POMEROLS but are reasonably priced. Quick to mature, they are still capable of aging for 10 years in bottle. Best years: (1998) 96 95 94 **90 89 88 82**.

SALICE SALENTINO DOC *Puglia, Italy* Probably the best of the DOCs in this area, turning out wines (made with Negroamaro and tempered with a dash of perfumed Malvasia Nera) that are ripe and chocolaty, acquiring hints of roast chestnuts and prunes with age. Drink after 3 or 4 years, although they may last as long again. Neighbouring Squinzano turns out a similar Rosso and Rosato – La Mea and the Santa Barbera co-op produce reasonable examples. The DOCs of Alezio, Brindisi (Taurino★★ and Vallone★ are noted producers), COPERTINO and Leverano are similar. Best producers: Candido★, Leone De Castris★, Taurino★, Vallone★, Conti Zecca. Best years: (reds) (1998) 97 **96** 95 94 93 91 90.

SALM-DALBERG, PRINZ ZU *Wallhausen, Nahe, Germany* Germany's oldest estate produces good wines, including Scheurebe and a very pale Spätburgunder. In 1995 Prinz zu Salm-Dalberg bought the well-known VILLA SACHSEN estate in BINGEN (RHEINHESSEN). Riesling Beerenauslese★ from the Wallhauser Pfarrgarten shows skill with that grape too. Best years: 1997 95 **93 92 90 89**.

SAMOS *Greece* The island of Samos was granted an appellation in 1982, but its reputation for producing rich, sweet dessert wines from the Muscat grape stretches back centuries. The 2 wineries of the Samos co-op make similar wines. Pale green Samena dry white is made from early-picked Muscat; deep gold, honeyed Samos Nectar★★ is made from sundried grapes, with an even rarer version, Palaio, aged for up to 20 years, very apricoty in nature; and seductively complex Samos Anthemis★, cask-aged for up to 5 years.

SANCERRE AC *Loire Valley, France* Sancerre mania broke out in the 1970s, firstly with the white wine which can provide the perfect expression of the bright green tang of the Sauvignon grape, then with the reds and rosés which are made from Pinot Noir. The whites, from a good grower in one of the best villages like Bué, Chavignol, Verdigny or Ménétréol in the chalky rolling land around the hill town of Sancerre, can be deliciously refreshing; so too can the rare Pinot Noir rosé. Reds, also from Pinot Noir, really need hot years like 1989 and 90 to be good. The wines are now more consistent than those of neighbouring POUILLY, with an enthusiastic younger generation emerging. Drink the wines young. Best producers: F & J Bailly★, Bailly-Reverdy★, Henri Bourgeois★★, Champault★, F & P Cotat★, L Crochet★★, Alain & Pierre Dezat★, Fouassier, Gitton★, P Jolivet, A Mellot★, J Mellot★, Millérioux★, Natter★, Roger Neveu★, A & F Neveu★, V Pinard★★, N & P Reverdy★, Reverdy-Cadet★, Jean-Max Roger★, Vacheron★, André Vatan★. Best years: (1998) **97 96 95 93 90 89**.

SANDEMAN *Port DOC, Douro, Portugal and Jerez y Manzanilla DO, Spain* No longer one of the leading port houses, Sandeman vintage port continues to disappoint. Best now are the aged tawnies, Imperial Aged Reserve Tawny★ and 20-year-old★★. Major sherry export markets are Germany and the Netherlands. Best years: (vintage ports) **1982 80 77 67 66 63**.

LUCIANO SANDRONE *Barolo DOCG, Piedmont, Italy* Luciano Sandrone has become one of PIEDMONT's leading wine stylists, renowned for his BAROLO Cannubi Boschis★★★ and Le Vigne★★★, as well as BARBERA D'ALBA★★ and Dolcetto d'Alba★★, which rank with the best of breed.

SANFORD *Santa Ynez Valley AVA, California, USA* Richard Sanford was one of the first Californians to appreciate the importance of matching specific slow-ripening conditions especially for Pinot Noir. He planted the great Benedict vineyard in the Santa Ynez Valley in 1971, thus establishing Santa Ynez and SANTA BARBARA as potentially top-quality vineyard regions. Sanford now makes sharply focused, green-edged Pinot Noir★★, Chardonnay★★ and Sauvignon Blanc★. A new series of 'Signature' Pinot Noir★★ is especially impressive. Best years: (Pinot Noir) (1998) 97 **96 95 94 92 91**.

SANGIOVESE Sangiovese rivals Trebbiano as the most widely planted grape variety in Italy. It is grown throughout the country but reaches its greatest heights in central TUSCANY. This grape has produced a wide variety of clones that make generalization difficult. Furthermore, recent research has shown that there is no close correlation between grape size and quality. Much care is being taken in the current wave of replanting, whether in CHIANTI CLASSICO, BRUNELLO DI MONTALCINO or VINO NOBILE DI MONTEPULCIANO. Styles range from pale, lively and cherryish, through the vivacious, mid-range Chiantis, to excellent top Riservas and SUPER-TUSCANS. At the latter level, Sangiovese shows itself to be one of the great grapes of the world. CALIFORNIA producers like ATLAS PEAK, SHAFER, Robert Pepi and Seghesio are now working some of their magic on this grape. Some interesting examples are also grown in Australia and Argentina.

SAN LUIS OBISPO COUNTY *California, USA* CENTRAL COAST county best known for Chardonnay, Pinot Noir, a bit of old-vine Zinfandel and Cabernet Sauvignon. There are 5 AVAs – Edna Valley, Paso Robles, SANTA MARIA VALLEY (shared with SANTA BARBARA COUNTY), Arroyo Grande Valley and York Mountain, each of which has already grown some outstanding grapes and will surely grow a lot more. Best producers: Clairborne & Churchill, Corbett Canyon, Creston Vineyards, Eberle★★, Edna Valley, Justin, Martin Brothers, Meridian, Talley★, Wild Horse.

SAN PEDRO *Curicó, Chile* A take-over by Chile's biggest brewer, along with Jacques Lurton as consultant since 1994, has turned the fortunes of San Pedro around, leading to another 1000ha (2470 acres) of planting and construction of new facilities and equipment. The quality of the Gato range, both red and white, has improved steadily since 1994; but the Castillo de Molina range shows just what a little more money can buy. Crisp, clean Sauvignon Blanc★, Chardonnay Reserve★ and Merlot★ are the wines to watch.

SANTA BARBARA COUNTY *California, USA* CENTRAL COAST county, just north of Los Angeles, which is best known for Chardonnay, Riesling and Pinot Noir. The main AVAs are Santa Ynez Valley and most of SANTA MARIA VALLEY (the remainder is in SAN LUIS OBISPO COUNTY), both leading areas for Pinot Noir. Best producers: AU BON CLIMAT★★, Babcock★, BYRON★, CAMBRIA, Firestone, Foxen★, Lane Tanner (Pinot Noir★★★), QUPE★★, SANFORD★★ Whitcraft, Zaca Mesa★.

SANTA MADDALENA *Alto Adige, Italy* Light, delicate wine from the Schiava grape grown in the hills above Bolzano. It has a perfume of black cherries, cream and bacon smoke, and can be improved with the addition of up to 10% of Lagrein. The best wines are generally from the original Classico zone. Drink young but some vintages will age. Best producers: Egger-Ramer★, Franz Gojer★, Gries CO-OP, LAGEDER★, Josephus Mayr, Josef Niedermayr★, Heinrich Plattner★, Hans Rottensteiner★, Heinrich Rottensteiner★, Santa Maddalena co-op★, Thurnhof.

SANTA MARIA VALLEY AVA *California, USA* Cool Santa Maria Valley is coming on strong as a producer of Chardonnay and Pinot Noir. Look for wines made from grapes grown in Bien Nacido vineyards by several small wineries. Best producers: AU BON CLIMAT★★, BYRON★, CAMBRIA, Foxen★, Lane Tanner (Pinot Noir★★★), QUPE★★.

SANTA RITA *Maipo, Chile* Signs are emerging that this MAIPO giant is climbing out of the doldrums. CANEPA's Andrés Ilabaca has joined up as winemaker and has some great fruit to work with. Juicy, plump-packed CASABLANCA Merlot★★ shows what he can do. The Medalla Real range is currently more reliable than the 120 portfolio.

SANTENAY AC *Côte de Beaune, Burgundy, France* There are some good wines here. The reds often promise good ripe flavour, but are usually disappointing, although worth aging for 4–6 years in the hope that the wine will open out. The best whites, as with the reds, come from les Gravières Premier Cru on the border with CHASSAGNE-MONTRACHET. Best producers: (reds) R Belland, D & F Clair★, COLIN★, Fleurot-Larose, GERMAIN, J Girardin★, V Girardin★, Mestre Père et Fils, Bernard Morey★, L Muzard, Pousse d'Or★, Prieur-Brunet, Roux Père et Fils★; (whites) JAFFELIN, Lequin-Roussot, Prosper Maufoux, Prieur-Brunet. Best years: (reds) 1997 96 95 **93 90 89 88**; (whites) 1997 96 **95 93 92 90 89**.

SÃO JOÃO, CAVES *Beira Litoral, Portugal* A traditional-seeming but discreetly modernist company. It was a pioneer of cool-fermented, white BAIRRADA, and has made some very good Cabernet Sauvignons from its own vines. It is best known for its rich, complex reds, including outstanding Reserva★★ and Frei João★ from Bairrada and Porta dos Cavalheiros★★ from DAO – they demand at least a decade of aging to show their quality.

SARDINIA *Italy* Grapes of Spanish origin, like the white Vermentino and Torbato and the red Monica, Cannonau and Carignano, dominate production on this huge, hilly Mediterranean island, but they vie with a Malvasia of Greek origin and natives like Nuragus and Vernaccia. The cooler northern part favours whites, especially Vermentino, while the southern and eastern parts are best suited to reds from Cannonau and Monica. The wines were powerful, alcoholic monsters, but the current trend is for a lighter, modern, more international style. Foremost among those in pursuit of quality are Argiolas, SELLA & MOSCA and the Santadi co-op. See also Carignano del Sulcis, Vermentino, Vernaccia di Oristano.

SASSICAIA DOC★★★ *Tuscany, Italy* This Cabernet Sauvignon-Cabernet Franc blend from the coast has done more than any other wine to gain credibility abroad for Italy. Vines were planted in 1944 to satisfy the Marchese Incisa della Rochetta's thirst for fine red Bordeaux, which was in short supply during the war. The wine remained purely for family consumption until nephew Piero Antinori (of ANTINORI) and winemaker Giacomo Tachis persuaded the Marchese to refine production practices and to release several thousand bottles from the 1968 vintage. Since then, Sassicaia's fame has increased as it consistently proved itself to be one of the world's great Cabernets, combining a blackcurrant power of blistering intensity with a heavenly scent of cigars. It is the first Italian single-owner estate wine to have its own DOC, within the BOLGHERI appellation, from the 1995 vintage. Best years: (1998) (97) (96) 95 90 88 **85 82 81 78 75 71 68**.

SAUMUR AC *Loire Valley, France* Improving dry white wines from around Saumur, made mainly from Chenin Blanc, but 20% of Chardonnay can be added. The reds are lighter than those of SAUMUR-CHAMPIGNY. There is a little dry to off-dry Cabernet rosé and sweet

Coteaux de Saumur in good vintages. Best producers: Clos Rougeard★★, FILLIATREAU★, A Fourrier, Hureau★★, Langlois-Château★, la Paleine, J-M Reclu, la Renière★, Roches Neuves★, St-Cyr-en-Bourg co-op, P Vatan★★, Villeneuve★★. Best years: (whites) (1998) 97 **96 95 90**.

SAUMUR-CHAMPIGNY AC *Loire Valley, France* Saumur's best red wine. Cabernet Franc is the main grape, and in hot years the wine can be superb, with a piercing scent of blackcurrants and raspberries easily overpowering the earthy finish. Delicious young, it can age for 6–10 years. Best producers: Clos Rougeard★, Cordeliers★, Drouineau★, FILLIATREAU★★, Hureau★, Nerleux, Roches Neuves★★, Val Brun★, P Vatan★, Villeneuve★★. Best years: (1998) 97 96 **95 90 89**.

SAUMUR MOUSSEUX AC *Loire Valley, France* Reasonable Champagne-method sparkling wines made mainly from Chenin Blanc. Adding Chardonnay and Cabernet Franc makes Saumur Mousseux softer and more interesting. Usually non-vintage. Small quantities of rosé are also made. Best producers: BOUVET-LADUBAY★, GRATIEN & MEYER★, Grenelle★, Lambert, Nerleux, St-Cyr-en-Bourg co-op★.

SAUTERNES AC *Bordeaux, France* The name Sauternes is synonymous with the best sweet wines in the world. Sauternes and BARSAC both lie on the banks of the little river Ciron and are 2 of the very few areas in France where noble rot occurs naturally. Production of these intense, sweet, luscious wines from botrytized grapes is a risk-laden and extremely expensive affair, and the wines are never going to be cheap. From good producers (most of which are Crus Classés) the wines are worth their high price – with 14% alcohol they have a richness full of flavours of pineapples, peaches, syrup and spice. Good vintages should be aged for 5–10 years, and they can often last twice as long. Best producers: BASTOR-LAMONTAGNE★, Clos Haut-Peyraguey★, DOISY-DAENE★★, DOISY-VEDRINES★★, FARGUES★★, GILETTE★★, GUIRAUD★★, les Justices★, LAFAURIE-PEYRAGUEY★★★, Lamothe-Guignard★, Malle★★, Rabaud-Promis★, Raymond-Lafon★, Rayne-Vigneau★, RIEUSSEC★★, ST-AMAND★, Sigalas Rabaud★, SUDUIRAUT★★, la TOUR BLANCHE★★, YQUEM★★★. Best years: (1998) 97 96 95 **90 89 88 86 83 81 80 76 75 71 70**.

SAUVIGNON BLANC See pages 258–9.

SAUZET *Côte d'Or, Burgundy, France* A producer with a reputation for classic, rich, full-flavoured white Burgundies, made in an opulent, fat style. Sauzet supplements grapes from its own vineyards with bought-in supplies; its actual holdings include prime sites in PULIGNY-MONTRACHET★★ and CHASSAGNE-MONTRACHET★ as well as small parcels of BATARD-MONTRACHET★★★ and BIENVENUES-BATARD-MONTRACHET★★★. The wines are at their best 5–12 years after the vintage. Best years: 1997 96 95 93 **92 90 89 88 86 85**.

SAVENNIÈRES AC *Loire Valley, France* The AC for wines from Chenin Blanc, produced on steep vineyards above the Loire south of Anjou and which have always been thought of as steely and dry. They also used to appear in semi-sweet and sweet styles, and with the great 1989 and 90 vintages we've seen a revival of these. The top wines usually need at least 8 years to mature, and can age for longer. There are 2 extremely good Grand Cru vineyards with their own ACs, la Coulée-de-Serrant and la Roche-aux-Moines. Best producers:

Baumard★★, Clos de Coulaine★, Clos de la Coulée-de-Serrant★★, Closel★★, Clos des Maurières★, Épiré★★, Forges★, Laffourcade★, Laroche★, Pierre-Bise, P Soulez★, P-Y Tijou★. Best years: (1998) 97 96 95 **93 91 90 89 88 85 83 82 78 76 71 70 69 66**.

SAVIGNY-LÈS-BEAUNE AC *Côte de Beaune, Burgundy, France* This large village concentrates its production on red wines; they are usually middle weight and are best drunk 4–10 years from the vintage. The top Premiers Crus are more substantial yet rarely shed their rather earthy core. The white wines manage to show a bit of dry, nutty class after 3–4 years. All the wines are generally reasonably priced. Best producers: S Bize★, Camus-Bruchon★, Chandon de Briailles★, B CLAIR★★, M Écard★, Girard-Vollot★, V Girardin★, L Jacob★, Dominique Laurent★★, C Maréchal★, J-M Pavelot★★, TOLLOT-BEAUT★★, Terregelesses★★. Best years: (reds) 1996 95 **93 92 90 89 88**; (whites) 1996 **95 92**.

SAVOIE *France* Savoie's high Alpine vineyards, which are scattered between Lake Geneva and Grenoble and on the banks of the Rhône and Isère rivers, produce fresh, snappy white wines with loads of flavour, when made from the Altesse (or Roussette) grape. There are some attractive light reds and rosés, too, mainly from a group of villages south of Chambéry and, in hot years, some positively Rhône-like reds from the Mondeuse grape. Most of the better wines use the Vin de SAVOIE AC and should be drunk young or with 3–4 years' age. See also Seyssel.

SAVOIE AC, VIN DE *Savoie, France* The general AC for the Alpine region of Savoie. The 15 best villages, including Abymes, Apremont, Arbin, Chignin, Cruet and Montmélian, can add their own name to the AC name. The best wines are white and to enjoy the thrilling snap of their tangy fruit drink them young. Occasional good Pinot Noir and excellent beefy Mondeuse reds. Best producers: Blard, Boniface★, Bouvet★, Cavaillé, Genoux, Gonnet, Magnin★, Monin, Montermined, Neyroud, Perret, Jean Perrier, R Quénard, Ripaille★, Rocailles★. Best years: (1998) **97 95**.

SAXENBURG *Stellenbosch WO, South Africa* Two harvests a year are now a feature of winemaker Nico van der Merwe's life. Locally, he creates some of the Cape's most sought-after reds, led by a headily scented and, at times, burly Private Collection Shiraz★★. The Cabernet★★, Merlot★ and Sauvignon Blanc★★ under the same label are also excellent, as is the standard Chardonnay★. Nico is producing equally good results at Swiss magnate owner Adrian Bührer's other estate, Ch. Capion in the LANGUEDOC. Two Capion/Saxenburg intercontinental blends, a red and white, unite the 2 hemispheres. Drink whites young; reds will improve for 5–8 years. Best years: (reds) **1996 95 94 93 92 91**; (whites) **1998 97 96 95**.

SCHEUREBE Very popular Silvaner x Riesling crossing most widespread in Germany's RHEINHESSEN and PFALZ. Also planted in Austria, where it is frequently sold under the name Sämling 88. Gives of its best in higher Prädikat dessert styles such as Trockenbeerenauslese and EISWEIN. When ripe, it has a marvellous flavour of honey and the pinkest of pink grapefruit.

SAUVIGNON BLANC

Of all the world's grapes, the Sauvignon Blanc is leader of the 'love it or loathe it' pack. It veers from being wildly fashionable to totally out of favour depending upon where it is grown and which country's consumers are being consulted. But Sauvignon is always at its best when full rein is allowed to its very particular talents because this grape does give intense, sometimes shocking flavours, and doesn't take kindly to being put into a straitjacket.

WINE STYLES

Sancerre-style Sauvignon Although initially used largely as a blending grape in Bordeaux, where its characteristic green tang injected a bit of life into the blander, waxier Sémillon, Sauvignon first became trendy as the grape used for Sancerre, a bone-dry Loire white whose green gooseberry fruit and slightly smoky perfume inspired the winemakers of other countries to try to emulate, then often surpass the original model.

But Sauvignon is only successful where it is respected. The grape is not as easy to grow as Chardonnay, and the flavours are not so adaptable. Yet the range of styles Sauvignon produces is as wide, if less subtly nuanced, as those of Chardonnay. It is highly successful when picked not too ripe, fermented cool in stainless steel, and bottled early. This is the Sancerre model followed by growers elsewhere in France, in Italy, Portugal, Spain and Eastern Europe, increasingly in South Africa and Chile, but above all in New Zealand.

Using oak Sauvignon also lends itself to fermentation in barrel and aging in new oak, though less happily than does Chardonnay. This is the model of the Graves region of Bordeaux, although generally here Sémillon would be blended in with Sauvignon to good effect.

New Zealand again excels at this style, though there are good examples from California, Australia, northern Italy and South Africa. In southern Styria (Steiermark) a handful of producers make powerful, aromatic versions with a touch of oak. In all these regions the acidity that is Sauvignon's great strength should ideally remain, but there should be a dried apricots kind of fruit and a spicy, biscuity softness from the oak. These oaky styles are best drunk either within about a year, or after aging for 5 years or so, and can produce remarkable, strongly individual flavours that you'll either love or loathe.

Sweet wines Sauvignon is also a crucial ingredient in the great sweet wines of Sauternes and Barsac from Bordeaux, though it is less susceptible than its partner Sémillon to the sweetness-enhancing 'noble rot' fungus or botrytis.

Sweet wines from the USA, South Africa, Australia and, inevitably, New Zealand range from the interesting to the outstanding – but the characteristic green tang of the Sauvignon should stay in the wine even at ultra-sweet levels.

Top-class Sauvignons

France (Pouilly-Fumé)
Chatelaine, Didier DAGUENEAU,
Ladoucette, Masson-Blondelet,
Tracy; (Sancerre) A Mellot,
Bourgeois, Cotat, Crochet,
Pinard, Jean-Max Roger;
(Pessac-Léognan) Dom. de
CHEVALIER, Couhins-Lurton,
FIEUZAL, HAUT-BRION, SMITH-HAUT-
LAFITTE.

New Zealand CLOUDY BAY,
COLLARDS, GOLDWATER, GROVE
MILL, HUNTER'S, Isabel, JACKSON
ESTATE, Lawson's Dry Hills,
NEUDORF, PALLISER, SELAKS,
Seresin, VAVASOUR, VILLA MARIA.

Italy GRAVNER, Edi Kante,
LAGEDER, ORNELLAIA, SCHIOPETTO,
Vie di Romans, Villa Russiz.

Other good Sauvignons

Australia Bridgewater Mill,
Chain of Ponds, HANGING ROCK,
Karina, KATNOOK, Lenswood
Vineyards, SHAW & SMITH, Geoff
WEAVER.

Austria Polz, Gross, E & M
TEMENT.

Chile VINA CASABLANCA.

New Zealand Cairnbrae,
MONTANA, NAUTILUS, NOBILO, Allan
Scott, SEIFRIED.

South Africa BUITENVERWACHTING,
KLEIN CONSTANTIA, MULDERBOSCH,
SAXENBURG, VILLIERA.

Spain (Rueda) MARQUES DE
RISCAL, Hermanos Lurton.

USA (California) KENWOOD,
MATANZAS CREEK, Murphy-Goode,
QUIVIRA, J ROCHIOLI VINEYARDS.

SCHIOPETTO *Friuli-Venezia Giulia, Italy* Mario Schiopetto is one of the legends of Italian viniculture, pioneering the development of scented varietals and, above all, high-quality, intensely concentrated white wines from COLLIO. Most outstanding are Tocai★★, Pinot Bianco★★ and Sauvignon★★ which begin life as intense but closed wines, opening out with age to display a myriad range of flavours. New COLLIO ORIENTALI vineyards Poderidei Blumeri can only add further prestige.

SCHLOSSBÖCKELHEIM *Nahe, Germany* This NAHE village's top sites are the Felsenberg and Kupfergrübe, but good wines also come from Mühlberg and Königsfels. Best producers: CRUSIUS★, Hermann DONNHOFF★★, Weingutsverwaltung Niederhausen-Schlossböckelheim. Best years: (1998) **96 95 94**.

SCHLOSS REINHARTSHAUSEN *Erbach, Rheingau, Germany* Estate formerly owned by the Hohenzollern family, which ruled Prussia, then Germany until 1918. There are several fine vineyard sites, including the great Erbacher Marcobrunn. There is an interesting organic Weissburgunder-Chardonnay blend from its vines in Erbacher Rheinhall, an island in the middle of the Rhine. Superb Rieslings★★ (Auslese, BA, TBA ★★★) and good Sekt★. Best years: (1998) 97 96 95 **94 93 92 90 89**.

SCHLOSS SAARSTEIN *Serrig, Saar, Germany* Fine Saar estate whose Riesling Dry can taste a little austere; better balanced are wines like the Serriger Riesling Kabinett★ or Spätlese★ and Auslese★★, which keep the startling acidity but coat it with fruit, often with the aromas of slightly unripe white peaches. Saarstein makes the occasional spectacular EISWEIN★★★. Best years: 1997 **95 93 92 90 89 88 86 85**.

SCHLOSS VOLLRADS *Oestrich-Winkel, Rheingau, Germany* Following the sudden death of owner Erwein Graf Matuschka-Greiffenclau before the 1997 harvest, the running of this historic estate was taken up by its banker, who continues to direct it. Though wines of recent years have been less severe than the piercingly dry wines of the late 80s and early 90s, they still do not impress; change could be a good thing.

SCHRAMSBERG *Napa Valley AVA, California, USA* The first CALIFORNIA winery to make really excellent CHAMPAGNE-method sparklers from the classic grapes. Though all releases do not achieve the same heights, the best of these wines can be unequalled in California – and in most of Champagne too. The Crémant★ is an attractive sweetish sparkler, the BLANC DE NOIRS★ and the BLANC DE BLANCS★★ stand out. Top of the line is the Reserve Brut★★★, which is frequently world class. In a bold, powerful style is J Schram – rich and flavoursome and increasingly good. Recent releases have achieved ★★ status. Vintage-dated wines can be drunk with as much as 10 years' age. Following the death of Jack Davies, who had been at Schramsberg since 1965, the company is now run by his wife Jamie and children.

SEAVIEW *McLaren Vale, South Australia* Best known for good, mass-market fizz★ and excellent Pinot-Chardonnay★★ and BLANC DE BLANCS★★ but, along with value-for-money commercial reds and whites, occasionally produces super export selection Cabernet★. Edwards & Chaffey★★ is the Reserve label for top fizz, rich Shiraz, Cabernet and unfiltered Chardonnay.

SEIFRIED ESTATE *Nelson, South Island, New Zealand* Established in 1974 by Austrian Hermann Seifried and his New Zealand wife Agnes.

The best wines include botrytized Riesling★ and Gewürztraminer★ and Sauvignon Blanc★. The Redwood Valley label is used in export markets. Best years: (1998) **96 94 91**.

SEKT German for sparkling wine. The wine will be entirely German only if it is called 'Deutscher Sekt' or 'Sekt bA'. The best wines are CHAMPAGNE method and will occasionally be 100% Riesling. Best producers: Bergdolt, Rudolf FURST★, KOEHLER-RUPRECHT★, Max Ferd RICHTER, SCHLOSS REINHARTSHAUSEN★, Dr Wagner★.

SELAKS *Kumeu/Huapai, Auckland, North Island, New Zealand* A long-established winery making New Zealand's best Sauvignon Blanc-Semillon★★ and an increasingly good Sauvignon Blanc★★; also Chardonnay★ and Riesling★. Selaks was purchased by NOBILO in 1998. Best years: (1998) **97 96 94 91**.

SELBACH-OSTER *Zeltingen, Mosel, Germany* Johannes Selbach is one of the MOSEL's new generation of star winemakers, producing very pure, elegant Riesling★. Best years: (1998) **97 96 95 94 93 92 91 90 89 88 85**.

SÉLECTION DE GRAINS NOBLES *Alsace AC, Alsace, France* This term is used for late-harvest wines made exclusively from super-ripe Muscat, Riesling, Gewurztraminer or Pinot Gris grapes. Invariably sweet and should be affected by noble rot, they are among ALSACE's finest, but are very expensive to produce (and to buy). Now also being widely used in the LOIRE, especially for sweet COTEAUX DU LAYON. Best producers: M Deiss★★★, HUGEL★★★, Mann★★★, Schlumberger★★, Schoffit★★★, TRIMBACH★★, Weinbach★★★, ZIND-HUMBRECHT★★★. Best years: 1997 96 95 92 **90 89 83 76**.

SELLA & MOSCA *Sardinia, Italy* Apart from the rich, port-like Anghelu Ruju★ made from semi-dried Cannonau grapes, this much-modernized old firm produces excellent dry whites, Terra Bianche★ (Torbato), La Cala★ (Vermentino) and oak-aged reds, Marchese di Villamarina★★ (Cabernet) and Tanca Farrà★★ (Cannonau-Cabernet). Best years: (premium reds) (1998) (97) (96) 95 **94 93 90 89 88**.

SELVAPIANA *Chianti DOCG, Tuscany, Italy* This 25-ha (62-acre) estate in CHIANTI RUFINA has always produced excellent wines that are typical of the zone. But since 1990 it has vaulted into the top rank of Tuscan estates, particularly with the Riserva★★ and single-vineyard Riserva, Vigneto Bucerchiale★★★. New is another single-vineyard Riserva, Fornace★★.

SÉMILLON Found mainly in South-West France, especially in the sweet wines of SAUTERNES and BARSAC where, because of its thin skin, it is prone to noble rot. Also blended with Sauvignon to make dry wine – almost all the great GRAVES Classed Growths are based on this blend. Performs well in Australia (aged Semillon from the HUNTER and Clare Valley can be wonderful) on its own or as a blender with Chardonnay (note that the accent over the é is dropped on New World labels). This variety is blended with Sauvignon in New Zealand, Australia, CALIFORNIA and WASHINGTON STATE; it is also enjoying a revival in the South African Cape, where it is primarily a bulk blender, but barrel-fermented varietals and blends with Sauvignon can produce outstanding results.

SEPPELT *Barossa Valley, South Australia and Grampians, Victoria* Leading Australian fizz factory, from mass-produced Great Western tank-fermented, up to excellent Fleur de Lys★, and on to Drumborg★★, Harpers Range★ and Salinger★★, all made by the Champagne method from Pinot Noir and Chardonnay, all pristine and fruity with minor yeast influence. A Sauvignon fizz called Rhymney is the latest addition. Table wines are generally good, especially Great Western Shiraz★★ and Chardonnay★, Dorrien Cabernet★, Partalunga Riesling★, and wines from super-cool Drumborg. Mid-priced 'Victorian Portfolio' stars Chalambar Shiraz★ and Sheoak Spring Riesling. Also makes wonderful sparkling Show Reserve Shiraz★★ (the 85, 86 and 87 are ★★★) and top-notch fortifieds (some ★★★).

SETÚBAL DOC *Terras do Sado, Portugal* Fortified wine from the Setúbal Peninsula south of Lisbon, which is called 'Moscatel de Setúbal' when made from at least 85% Moscatel, and 'Setúbal' when it's not. Best producers: José Maria da FONSECA★★, J P VINHOS★.

SEYSSEL AC *Savoie, France* Known for its feather-light, sparkling wine, Seyssel Mousseux. With the lovely sharp, peppery bite of the Molette and Altesse grapes smoothed out with a creamy yeast, it is an ideal summer gulper. The still white is light and floral, and made only from Altesse. Best producers: Mollex, Varichon & Clerc★.

SEYVAL BLANC Hybrid grape (Seibel 5656 x Rayon d'Or) whose disease resistance and ability to continue ripening in a damp autumn make it a useful variety in England, Canada and NEW YORK STATE and other areas in the eastern US. Gives clean, sappy, grapefruit-edged wines that are sometimes a very passable imitation of bone-dry CHABLIS.

SHAFER *Stags Leap AVA, California, USA* One of the best NAPA wineries, making unusually fruity Stags Leap District Cabernet★★ and a Reserve-style Hillside Select★★★. Merlot★★ and Firebreak★ (Sangiovese-Cabernet) are increasingly important. Chardonnay★★, from Red Shoulder Vineyard in CARNEROS, is greatly improved. Best years: (Cabernet Hillside Select) 1996 95 94 **93 92 91 90** 85 84.

SHAW & SMITH *Adelaide Hills, South Australia* Cousins Michael Hill Smith – Australia's first MW and operator of a noted wine bar – and Martin Shaw, an ex-flying winemaker, had a runaway success with their deep, tangy Sauvignon Blanc★★ from the first vintage in 1989. Not a pair to rush in, they have gradually added a wooded Reserve★★ and unwooded Chardonnay★ to the list but, as yet, no red wines. Drink the Sauvignon and unoaked Chardonnay very young, but the Reserve Chardonnay will keep. Best years: 1997 96 **95 94 93 92 91**.

SHERRY See Jerez y Manzanilla DO, pages 164–5.

SHIRAZ See Syrah, pages 272–3.

SICILY *Italy* Sicily is emerging with a renewed spirit and attitude to wine production. The three leading estates for table wines, Planeta, REGALEALI and Duca di SALAPARUTA, are now certain to be joined by others including the revitalized Spadafora, Donnafugata and transformed Settesoli (headed by Diego Planeta) as well as other exciting estates such as Abbazia Santa Anastasia (whose Cabernet Sauvignon Litra★★ has been shaped by the great Giacamo Tachis). A new internal dynamism is being matched by outside investment and expertise – nowhere better illustrated than in the dynamic Maurizio Miccichè's (Calatrasi) joint venture with BRL HARDY. Zonin's new 200-ha (495-acre) estate in the Caltanissetta region is set to have a major impact over the next decade. See also Alcamo, Etna, Marsala, Moscato Passito di Pantelleria.

SIEUR D'ARQUES, LES CAVES DU *Limoux AC and Blanquette de Limoux AC, Languedoc, France* This well-organized and modern co-op dominates the production of the still and sparkling wines of LIMOUX, making around 90% of the area's wines. The BLANQUETTE DE LIMOUX and CREMANT DE LIMOUX★ are both reliable, but the real excitement comes with the Toques et Clochers Chardonnays★. The co-op also makes a range of white and red varietal VINS DE PAYS.

SILVER OAK CELLARS *Napa Valley, California, USA* One of California's best Cabernet Sauvignon producers, with bottlings from ALEXANDER VALLEY★★ grapes and NAPA VALLEY★ as well as a superlative limited release Bonny's Vineyard★★★, last produced in 1991. Forward, generous, fruity wines, impossible not to enjoy young, yet with great staying power. Best years: (Alexander Valley) 1995 **94 93 92 91 90 88 87 85**; (Napa Valley) 1995 **94 93 92 91 90 88 87 86 85 84 82**; (Bonny's Vineyard) **1991 90 86**.

SILVERADO *Napa Valley AVA, California, USA* Owned by a branch of the Disney family, there's nothing Mickey Mouse about the splendid Cabernet Sauvignon★ and Chardonnay★★ from this estate winery. The regular bottling of Cabernet has intense yet playful fruit and is drinkable fairly young. A Limited Reserve bottling★★ has more depth and is capable of some aging. The Chardonnay has soft, inviting fruit and a silky finish and is best within 2–3 years of the vintage. A fruity Merlot and SUPER-TUSCAN-style Sangiovese are also much in demand. Best years: (Reserve) 1995 94 **93 91 90 87 86**.

SIMI *Alexander Valley AVA, California, USA* Historic winery which was revitalized by the arrival of Zelma Long as winemaker in 1979 and the purchase by Moët-Hennessy in 1981. Recently sold to Canandaigua. Through improved vineyard sites, Long has brought the Cabernet Sauvignon★, Chardonnay★★ and Sauvignon Blanc★ up to high standards, and the Chardonnay Reserve has occasionally reached ★★★. Best years: (reds) 1997 95 94 **92 91 90**.

SIMONSIG ESTATE *Stellenbosch WO, South Africa* A family-owned estate with winemaker Johan Malan orchestrating an extensive quality range including a Pinotage-Cabernet blend under the Frans Malan Reserve label which is highly individual; Tiara★, a BORDEAUX blend; a fruity unwooded Pinotage★; dry Riesling; Chardonnay★; Gewürztraminer dessert wine★; and the Cape's first commercially produced Cap Classique (Champagne-method) sparkler, Kaapse Vonkel★. Best years: **1998 97 96 95 94 93 92 91 90**.

SION *Valais, Switzerland* Considered one of the top wine villages in the VALAIS and best known for its pure Chasselas Fendant. Best producers: Michel Clavien★, Dom. du Mont d'Or★.

CH. SIRAN★ *Margaux AC, Cru Bourgeois, Haut-Médoc, Bordeaux, France* Consistently good claret, approachable young, but with enough structure to last for as long as 20 years. Second wine: Ch. Bellegarde. Best years: (1998) 97 96 95 **90 89 86 85 83 82**.

SPARKLING WINES OF THE WORLD

Made by the Traditional (Champagne) Method

Although Champagne is still the benchmark for top-class sparkling wines all over the world, the Champagne houses themselves have taken the message to California, Australia and New Zealand via wineries they've established in these regions. However, Champagne-method fizz doesn't necessarily have to feature the original grape varieties, and this allows a host of other places to join the party. Describing a wine as Champagne method is now strictly speaking no longer allowed (only original Champagne from France is officially sanctioned to do this), but the use of a phrase like Traditional Method should not distract from the fact that these wines are still painstakingly produced using the complex system of secondary fermentation in the bottle itself.

STYLES OF SPARKLING WINE

French Sparklers Non-Champagne French fizz ranges from the sublime to the near-ridiculous. Some of the best examples have great finesse and include grapy Crémant d'Alsace, produced from Pinot Blanc and Riesling; often inexpensive yet eminently drinkable Crémant de Bourgogne, based mainly on Chardonnay, and some stylish examples of the genre from Loire producers, notably in Saumur and Vouvray. Clairette de Die and Blanquette de Limoux in the south confuse the issue by following their own idiosyncratic method of production but the end result is delicious.

Rest of Europe Franciacorta DOCG is a success story for Italy; Asti and Lambrusco don't qualify for inclusion here as they are not Champagne-method wines. In Spain, the Cava wines of Catalonia offer an earthy and affordable style for everyday drinking. Fruity German Sekt has its followers; even England is now producing some well-reviewed sparklers.

Australia and New Zealand Australia picked just the right moment to start producing clean, fresh fizz, and as a result its international popularity must be one of the vinous success stories of the past decade or so. There is a wide range of style here, with no particular regional character; blends are produced using fruit from a variety of areas. Tasmania is an exception to this and makes some interesting fizz from its own local grapes. Red sparklers are a fun Australian curiosity, notably the Shiraz. Cool-climate New Zealand is coming up fast for fizz with some premium and pricy examples; as in Australia and California, some have Champagne connections.

USA Some magnificent quality examples are produced – the best ones using grapes from Carneros or the Anderson Valley. Quality has been transformed by the efforts of French Champagne houses. Oregon is also a contender in the sparkling stakes.

See also BRUT AND INDIVIDUAL PRODUCERS.

BEST PRODUCERS

Australia BROWN BROTHERS, Cope-Williams, GREEN POINT, Hanging Rock, PETALUMA (Croser), ROCKFORD (Sparkling Shiraz), SEAVIEW, SEPPELT, TALTARNI (Clover Hill).

Austria BRUNDLMAYER.

France (Alsace) Ostertag; (Burgundy) Caves de Lugny; (Saumur) BOUVET-LADUBAY, GRATIEN & MEYER; (Die) Clairette de Die co-op; (Limoux) Les Caves du SIEUR D'ARQUES; (Vouvray) Clos Naudin, HUET.

Germany (Pfalz) Bergdolt, Rudolf FURST, KOEHLER-RUPRECHT; (Saar) Dr Wagner.

Italy (Franciacorta) BELLAVISTA, CA' DEL BOSCO; (Piedmont) Rocche dei Manzone; (Trento) FERRARI.

New Zealand CELLIER LE BRUN, CLOUDY BAY (Pelorus), CORBANS (Amadeus), Deutz, MORTON ESTATE, NAUTILUS.

Portugal J P VINHOS (Lorridos Extra Bruto).

South Africa Graham BECK, Cabrière Estate.

Spain (Cava) CASTELLBLANCH, CODORNIU, FREIXENET, JUVE Y CAMPS, MARQUES DE MONISTROL, Raventos y Blanc.

UK CHAPEL DOWN, NYETIMBER, THAMES VALLEY, THREE CHOIRS, Warden Vineyard.

USA (California) S Anderson, DOMAINE CARNEROS, DOMAINE CHANDON, HANDLEY CELLARS, IRON HORSE, JORDAN, Laetitia, MUMM NAPA, PACIFIC ECHO, ROEDERER, SCHRAMSBERG; (Oregon) Argyle.

SKALLI-FORTANT DE FRANCE *Languedoc-Roussillon, France* It has not been a happy time recently for the self-styled 'king of varietal wines' from the LANGUEDOC. The new Fortant range, launched in 1996, was a flop. Now only the Fortant de France label is being sold in the UK; the Grenache is best. Skalli seems to be losing its way while others like Foncalieu, la BAUME and Laroche are finding theirs.

SLIVEN *Southern Region, Bulgaria* This winery is now providing some of Bulgaria's best, cleanest Chardonnay. The reds, like the juicy Merlot-Pinot Noir Country Wine, deliver the goods, too.

CH. SMITH-HAUT-LAFITTE *Pessac-Léognan AC, Cru Classé de Graves, Bordeaux, France* Large property best known for its reds★, now one of the most improved and innovative estates in PESSAC-LEOGNAN AC since a change of ownership in 1990. There is only a little white★★ (from 100% Sauvignon) but it is a shining example of tip-top modern white Bordeaux. Best years: (reds) (1998) 97 96 95 94 90 **89 88 86 85 83**; (whites) (1998) 97 96 **95 94 93 92 90**.

SMITH WOODHOUSE *Port DOC, Portugal* Underrated but consistently satisfying port from this shipper in the Symington group. The Smith Woodhouse vintage★★ is worth looking out for, and its Late Bottled Vintage Port★★ is the rich and characterful, figgy, unfiltered type. Best years: (vintage) 1994 92 91 **85 83 80 77 70 63**.

SOAVE DOC *Veneto, Italy* In the hilly Soave Classico zone near Verona, the Garganega and Trebbiano di Soave grapes can produce ripe, nutty, scented wines of great quality. However, 70% of all Soave comes from the flat fertile plains, and much of this is cynically blended by merchants into a limp, tasteless white. Since 1992, the legal addition of 30% of Chardonnay was supposed to help, and good examples are definitely on the increase. Best producers: ANSELMI★★, Bertani★, Bolla★, Ca' Rugate★, La Cappuccina★, Cantina del Castello★, Cecilia Beretta (Pasqua)★, Coffele★, Gini★, Inama★★, MASI★, PIEROPAN★★, Portinari★, Prà★, Soave co-op, Suavia★. See also Recioto di Soave DOCG.

CH. SOCIANDO-MALLET★★ *Haut-Médoc AC, Cru Bourgeois, Haut-Médoc, Bordeaux, France* Owner Jean Gautreau has made this one of BORDEAUX's star Crus Bourgeois now worthy of classification. The wine has every sign of great red Bordeaux flavours to come if you can hang on for 10–15 years. Best years: (1998) 97 96 95 94 **93** 90 89 **88 86 85 83 78**.

SOGRAPE *Portugal* Sogrape proves that it is possible to be the biggest *and* among the best, and can be credited with revolutionizing quality in some of Portugal's most reactionary wine regions. Mateus Rosé is still the company's golden egg, but Sogrape makes good to very good wines in BAIRRADA (Reserva Branco★), DAO★, DOURO (Reserva Tinto★) and VINHO VERDE as well, and subsidiary FERREIRA provides top-flight ports and BARCA VELHA★★★, one of Portugal's best reds. Quinta dos Carvalhais Branco★ is oaky and characterful; the Duque de Viseu red is ripe and fruity. The first vintage (1995) of the Carvalhais red (based on Touriga Nacional) shows great promise, while Vinha do Monte is a new red from the ALENTEJO.

SOKOL BLOSSER WINERY *Willamette Valley AVA, Oregon, USA* Consistently good Chardonnay★★ (Redland) and sometimes outstanding, though not as consistent, Pinot Noir★★ (Redland). The Chardonnay tends to the buttery, toasty style, while the several versions of Pinot Noir emphasize a soft, rather elegant fruit. Best years: (1998) 97 **94 92 90**.

SOMONTANO DO *Aragón, Spain* In the foothills of the Pyrenees, this region is an up-and-coming star. Reds and rosés from the local grapes (Moristel and Tempranillo) can be light, fresh and flavourful, and new plantings of international varieties such as Chardonnay and Gewürztraminer are already yielding promising wines. An interesting development is the rediscovery of the soft native red grape, Moristel. Best producers: Enate★★, Bodega Pirineos★, Viñas del Vero★. Best years: (reds) 1996 95 **94**.

SONOMA COUNTY *California, USA* Sonoma's vine-growing area is big and sprawling, with dozens of soil types and mesoclimates, from the fairly warm SONOMA VALLEY/ALEXANDER VALLEY region to the cool Green Valley and lower RUSSIAN RIVER VALLEY. The best wines are from Chardonnay, Sauvignon Blanc, Cabernet Sauvignon, Pinot Noir and Zinfandel. Catching up with rival NAPA in quality and originality of flavours. See also Carneros, Dry Creek Valley.

SONOMA-CUTRER *Russian River Valley AVA, California, USA* Crisp, pleasant but often overrated Chardonnay from 3 vineyards. Les Pierres is the most complex and richest of the 3, often worth ★★. Cutrer★ can also have a complexity worth waiting for though the Russian River Ranches can be rather flat and ordinary, but is much improved in recent releases. Best years: 1997 **95 94 92 91 90**.

SONOMA VALLEY AVA *Sonoma, USA* The oldest wine region north of San Francisco, Sonoma Valley is situated on the western side of the Mayacamas Mountains, which separate it from NAPA VALLEY. Best varieties are Chardonnay and Zinfandel, with Cabernet and Merlot from hillside sites coming on strong. Best producers: ARROWOOD★★, BUENA VISTA, CARMENET★★, CHATEAU ST JEAN★, B R Cohn, Fisher★, GUNDLACH-BUNDSCHU★, KENWOOD★, KUNDE★, LAUREL GLEN★★★, MATANZAS CREEK★★, RAVENSWOOD★★, St Francis★, Sebastiani.

SOUTH AUSTRALIA Australia's biggest grape-growing state, with 38,000ha (94,000 acres) of vineyards. Covers many climates and most wine styles from bulk wines to the very best. Old established areas are BAROSSA, CLARE and Eden valleys, MCLAREN VALE, Langhorne Creek, COONAWARRA, Adelaide Plains and RIVERLAND. Newer districts creating excitement are ADELAIDE HILLS and PADTHAWAY, and the recently planted Wrattonbully, already producing promising red wines, like COONAWARRA, made up of *terra rossa* soil over limestone.

SOUTH-WEST FRANCE As well as the world-famous wines of BORDEAUX, South-West France has many lesser-known, inexpensive ACs, VDQS and VdPs, over 10 different *départements* from the Atlantic coast to LANGUEDOC-ROUSSILLON. Bordeaux grapes (Cabernet, Merlot and Cabernet Franc for reds; Sauvignon, Sémillon and Muscadelle for whites) are common, but there are lots of interesting local varieties as well, such as Tannat (in MADIRAN), Petit Manseng (in JURANCON) and Mauzac (in GAILLAC). See also Bergerac, Cahors, Côtes de Duras, Côtes du Frontonnais, Côtes de Montravel, Gaillac, Irouléguy, Monbazillac, Montravel, Pacherenc du Vic-Bilh.

SUPER-TUSCANS
Tuscany, Italy

The term 'Super-Tuscans', first used by English and American writers, has now been adopted by Italians themselves to describe the new-style red wines of Tuscany. The 1970s and 80s were a time when enormous strides were being made in Bordeaux, Australia and California, yet these changes threatened to bypass Italy completely because of its restrictive wine laws. A group of winemakers, led by Piero Antinori, abandoned tradition to put their best efforts and best grapes into creative wines styled for modern tastes, replacing old casks with barriques, while planting Cabernet and other trendy varieties, such as Merlot, Pinot Noir and Syrah, alongside Sangiovese in vineyards that emerged with sudden grandeur as crus. Since the DOC specifically forbade such innovations, producers were forced to label their wines as plain Vino da Tavola. The 'Super-Tuscan' Vino da Tavolas, as they were quickly dubbed, were a phenomenal success: brilliant in flavour with an approachable, upfront style, although foreigners found it hard to believe that table wines with no official credentials could outrank DOCG Chianti in prestige and price. A single mouthful was usually enough to convince them.

WINE STYLES
Sangiovese and Cabernet Sauvignon are the basis for most Super-Tuscans, one usually making up the balance with the other. Both also appear varietally with Sangiovese forming the largest group of top-quality Super-Tuscans. To some Sangiovese-based wines, a small percentage of other native varieties such as Colorino, Canaiolo or Malvasia Nera is added. Merlot has long been used as the complement to Cabernet in the Bordeaux mould but more recently has been combined with Sangiovese in exactly the same way. Syrah is of growing importance, mostly varietally, but also in innovative new blends such as Argiano's Solenga. Super-Tuscan wines also show considerable differences in vinification and aging. Top wines are invariably based on ripe, concentrated grapes from a site with special attributes.

CLASSIFICATIONS
A law passed in 1992 should bring most Super-Tuscans into line with official classifications. Sassicaia now has its own DOC under Bolgheri; Chianti Classico's newly independent DOCG would cover many a Sangiovese-based Super-Tuscan; and plans for a regional Toscana DOC would create niches for superior wines from the international varieties.

See also BOLGHERI, CHIANTI CLASSICO, SASSICAIA, TIGNANELLO, VINO DA TAVOLA; AND INDIVIDUAL PRODUCERS.

BEST PRODUCERS

Sangiovese and other Tuscan varieties Badia a Coltibuono (Sangioveto), BOSCARELLI (Boscarelli), Castellare (I Sodi di San Niccolò), Fattoria di FELSINA (Fontalloro), FONTODI (Flaccianello della Pieve), ISOLE E OLENA (Cepparello), MONTEVERTINE (Le Pergole Torte, Il Sodaccio), Poggio Scalette (Il Carbonaione), POLIZIANO (Elegia), Querceto (La Corte), RIECINE (La Gioia), San Giusto a Rentennano (Percarlo), VOLPAIA (Coltassala).

Sangiovese-Cabernet blends ANTINORI (Tignanello), ARGIANO (Solengo), AVIGNONESI (Grifi), BANFI (Summus), Gagliole, Montepeloso (Nardo), Querciabella (Camartina).

Cabernet ANTINORI (Solaia), Col d'Orcia (Olmaia), ISOLE E OLENA (Collezione), Nozzole (Il Pareto), POLIZIANO (Le Stanze), Castello dei RAMPOLLA (Sammarco, Vigna d'Alceo).

Sangiovese-Merlot blends FONTERUTOLI (Siepi), FRESCOBALDI-MONDAVI (Luce).

Merlot Castello di AMA (Vigna L'Apparita), AVIGNONESI, ORNELLAIA (Masseto), Tua Rita (Redigaffi).

Cabernet-Merlot blends ANTINORI (Guado al Tasso), BANFI (Excelsus), Capezzana (Ghiaie della Furba), ORNELLAIA (Ornellaia), Le Pupille (Saffredi), TERRICCIO (Lupicaia, Tassinaia), Tua Rita (Giusto di Notri).

SPÄTBURGUNDER See Pinot Noir.

SPÄTLESE German for literally 'late-picked' and therefore riper grapes, but this is a question of must weight of the juice. In Germany the Oechsle level runs from 76 for a MOSEL Riesling to 92 for a BADEN Ruländer. In Austria a Spätlese must be 19 KMW or 94 Oechsle.

SPUMANTE Italian for 'sparkling'. Bottle-fermented wines are often referred to as *metodo classico* or *metodo tradizionale*.

STAG'S LEAP WINE CELLARS *Stags Leap AVA, California, USA* The winery's fame was made when the Cabernet Sauvignon 1973 came first at the Paris tasting of 1976. At its best, Cabernet Sauvignon★★ can be a stunning wine, particularly the SLV Reserve★★★ from estate vineyards; the Cask 23 Cabernet Sauvignon★ is good, sometimes very good, but is overhyped. Recent vintages haven't measured up to earlier standards. A lot of work has gone into the Chardonnay and the style is one of NAPA's most successful. Best years: (reds) 1996 95 94 93 **92 91 90 89 88 84 81 79**; (whites) 1997 96 95 **94 93 91 90**.

THE STAPLE VINEYARDS *Kent, England* A small but well-run vineyard near the Kent coast, whose vibrantly fruity Huxelrebe★ is consistently one of England's best bone-dry whites.

STEELE WINES *Lake County, California, USA* Owner and winemaker Jed Steele is a master blender. He sources grapes from vineyards all over California and shapes them into exciting wines, usually featuring vivid fruit with supple mouthfeel. But he also offers single-vineyard wines and has, in current release, 4 Chardonnays★. His Zinfandels★ are often superb and his Pinot Noirs (CARNEROS, SANTA MARIA VALLEY) are better than most. Shooting Star is a budget second label, which provides remarkable value in a ready-to-drink style. Best years: (Zinfandels) (1998) 97 **95 94 93**.

STEIERMARK *Austria* Known as Styria in English, this wine region in south-east Austria formerly covered much of Slovenia's vineyards, too. It includes the regions of Süd-Oststeiermark, Süd-Steiermark and West-Steiermark, and has a continental climate, the warmest of the 4 Austrian wine zones. The best wines are Morillon (unoaked Chardonnay, though oak is catching on here as well), Sauvignon Blanc and Gelber Muskateller. Best producers: Gross★, Lackner-Tinnacher★, Polz★, TEMENT★★.

STELLENBOSCH WO *South Africa* Considered the hub of the South African wine industry, this fine red wine region boasts the greatest concentration of wineries in the Cape, with vineyards straddling valley floors and stretching up the many mountain slopes. Climates and soils are as diverse as wine styles; the renowned reds are matched by some excellent Sauvignon Blanc and Chardonnay. The major wholesalers and the Enological and Viticultural Research Station have their headquarters here. Best producers: L'AVENIR★, Avontuur, BEYERSKLOOF★, Blaauwklippen, Le Bonheur, J P Bredell, Cordoba, Delheim, EIKENDAL★, Neil ELLIS★★, GRANGEHURST★★, HARTENBERG★, JORDAN★, Kaapzicht, KANONKOP★★, Lievland★, LOUISVALE★, MEERLUST★★, Morgenhof★, MULDERBOSCH★★, Neethlingshof★, Overgaauw★, RUSTENBERG★★, RUST-EN-VREDE★, SAXENBURG★★, SIMONSIG★, STELLENZICHT★★, THELEMA★★★, Uiterwyk, VERGELEGEN★★, Vriesenhof, WARWICK★.

STELLENBOSCH FARMERS' WINERY *Stellenbosch, South Africa* South Africa's largest merchant-producer, buying in wine and grapes and with leading brands in every sector. Top-of-the-range Zonnebloem has agreeable, if simple, reds and whites. Two wineries in PAARL, Nederburg and Plaisir de Merle★★, also fall under SFW's wing, but are run separately. Nederburg's standard range is sound if unexciting. Its best-known botrytized dessert, Edelkeur★, is sold only through annual auction. Plaisir de Merle is the company's showpiece: winemaker Neil Bester was tutored at Ch. MARGAUX by Paul Pontallier, hence reds are his forte. Beautifully structured Cabernet Sauvignon★★ is an award winner and ageworthy Merlot★ looks likely to follow its example.

STELLENZICHT *Stellenbosch WO, South Africa* A hopefully temporary lull in excitement at this high-profile winery, while Guy Webber settles in as the new, permanent winemaker. His predecessor, dynamic, hugely talented Andre van Rensburg, now at VERGELEGEN, established an excellent range. Most notable is a rich, spicy Syrah★★, which beat PENFOLDS Grange in the controversial 1995 South Africa/Australia wine test match. Sauvignon Blanc★★, a fine Sémillon★, botrytized desserts★★, Riesling in particular, rivalled only by those from sister winery Neethlingshof, carry the white wine flag.

STERLING VINEYARDS *Napa Valley AVA, California, USA* After more than 20 vintages as winemaker, Bill Dyer was replaced by Rob Hunter of Markham Vineyards. Reserve Cabernet★★ is good to very good, while the regular bottling is at last showing signs of improvement. Winery Lake Pinot Noir★ is now beginning to hit its stride. The NAPA VALLEY Chardonnay★ can be rich and intense, yet balanced. Best years: (reds) (1997) 95 94 **92 91 90 87 86 85.**

STONIER'S *Mornington Peninsula, Victoria, Australia* PETALUMA recently became part-owner of this winery which is still run by the Stonier family and winemaker Ted Dexter. The peninsula's biggest winery and one of its best has usually outstanding Reserve Chardonnay★★ and Reserve Pinot★★ as well as fine standard bottlings in warm vintages. Cabernets are rather herbaceous, in the regional style.

STONYRIDGE *Waiheke Island, Auckland, North Island, New Zealand* The leading winery on WAIHEKE ISLAND, Stonyridge specializes in reds made from Cabernet Sauvignon, Merlot, Petit Verdot, Malbec and Cabernet Franc. The top label, Larose★★★, is a remarkably BORDEAUX-like red of real intensity. Best years: (1997) **96** 94 93 **91 89 87.**

CH. SUDUIRAUT★★ *Sauternes AC, 1er Cru Classé, Bordeaux, France* Together with RIEUSSEC, Suduiraut is regarded as a close runner-up to d'YQUEM. Although the wines are delicious at only a few years old, the richness and excitement increase enormously after a decade or so. Very expensive and seemed to be under-performing since the mid-1980s but now owned by AXA of PICHON-LONGUEVILLE fame, so watch out! Best years: (1998) 97 96 95 **90 89 88 82 79 76.**

SUHINDOL *Northern Region, Bulgaria* This winery is the old warhorse among Bulgarian wineries, established in 1909, and was the first to be privatized in 1991. It perfected the creamy, curranty, throat-soothing style of Cabernet Sauvignon then synonymous with Bulgaria, and is now developing some premium Cabernet and Merlot reds, and trades today as Lovico Suhindol. Despite its efforts, progress is erratic.

SYRAH/SHIRAZ

Syrah now produces world-class wines in 3 countries. In France, where Hermitage and Côte-Rôtie are 2 of the world's great reds; in Australia, where as Shiraz it produces some of the New World's most remarkable reds; and now in California, too. And wherever Syrah appears it trumpets a proud and wilful personality based on loads of flavour and unmistakable originality.

Syrah's spread round the warmer wine regions of the world has been limited, however. Syrah's heartland – Hermitage and Côte-Rôtie in the Rhône Valley – comprises a mere 270ha (670 acres) of steeply terraced vineyards, producing hardly enough wine to make more than a very rarefied reputation for themselves. For long, growers in other countries simply had no idea as to what kind of flavour the Syrah grape produced, so didn't copy it. But the situation is rapidly changing.

WINE STYLES

French Syrah The flavours of Syrah are most individual, but with modern vineyard practices and modern winemaking techniques they are far less daunting than they used to be. Traditional Syrah had a savage, almost coarse, throaty roar of a flavour. And from the very low-yielding Hermitage vineyards, the small grapes often showed a bitter tannic quality. But better selections of clones in the vineyard and improved winemaking have revealed that Syrah in fact gives a wine with a majestic depth of fruit, all blackberry and damson, loganberry and plum, some quite strong tannin, and some tangy smoke, but also a warm creamy aftertaste, and a promise of chocolate and occasionally a scent of violets. It is these characteristics that have made Syrah popular throughout the south of France as an 'improving' variety for its rather rustic red wines.

Australian Shiraz Australia's most widely planted red variety is often used for light, soft, bulk wines but it can give spectacularly good results when taken seriously – especially in the Clare, Eden Valley, Barossa and McLaren Vale regions of South Australia. An increasingly diverse range of high-quality examples also includes those from Victoria's warmer vineyards (especially in the Grampians region), more traditional examples from New South Wales' Hunter Valley and Mudgee, and more recently exciting elegant styles from Western Australia's Margaret River and Great Southern regions. The flavours are rich, intense, thick sweet fruit coated with chocolate, and seasoned with leather, herbs and spice. It is frequently blended with Cabernet Sauvignon to add a little richness to Cabernet's angular frame.

Other regions In California more producers are turning out superb southern-Rhône-like blends as well as varietal examples modelled closely on Côte-Rôtie or Hermitage. In South Africa, too, some exciting wines are appearing and even New Zealand seems to have the potential for refined examples, at the cool end of the spectrum.

BEST PRODUCERS

Top Syrah
France (Rhône) Allemand, Gilles Barge, Belle, Burgaud, CHAPOUTIER, CHAVE, A CLAPE, B Faurie, J-M Gerin, A GRAILLOT, Jean-Louis Grippat, GUIGAL, JABOULET, JAMET, JASMIN, Rostaing, M Sorrel, Tardieu-Laurent, Verset.

USA (California) Araujo, Christopher Creek, DEHLINGER, Edmunds St John, Jade Mountain, Ojai, Joseph PHELPS, QUPE, Sine Qua Non, Swanson, THACKREY, Zaca Mesa.

Top Shiraz
Australia Tim ADAMS, Jim BARRY, Charles Cimicky, Clarendon Hills, Coriole, Craiglee, Dalwhinnie, HARDY, Jasper Hill, HENSCHKE, Peter LEHMANN, Charles Melton, MOUNT LANGI GHIRAN, PENFOLDS, PLANTAGENET, ROCKFORD, ROSEMOUNT, ST HALLETT, WENDOUREE, WYNNS, YARRA YERING.

Other good Syrah
France (Languedoc) Ch. des Estanilles, l'Hortus; (Rhône) Pierre Barge, COURSODON, DELAS.
Italy Bertelli, Fontodi, ISOLE E OLENA, Le Macchiole, Manzano.

Other good Shiraz
Australia BAILEY'S, BEST'S, BROKENWOOD, Grant BURGE, CAPE MENTELLE, CHAPEL HILL, D'ARENBERG, DE BORTOLI, LECONFIELD, LINDEMANS, MITCHELTON, Redbank, ROTHBURY, SEPPELT, Seville Estate, TALTARNI, TYRRELL'S, VASSE FELIX, WIRRA WIRRA, Zema Estate.
New Zealand Stonecroft, TE MATA.
South Africa SAXENBURG, STELLENZICHT.

SUPÉRIEUR French for a wine with a higher alcohol content than the basic AC. Bordeaux Supérieur, for example, has a minimum of 10.5% alcohol by volume, compared with 10% for straight Bordeaux.

SUPERIORE Italian DOC wines with higher alcohol or more age potential.

SUPER-TUSCANS See pages 268–9.

SUTTER HOME *Napa Valley AVA, California, USA* Now known for White Zinfandel, Sutter Home still makes a very drinkable Amador County Zinfandel, although it doesn't achieve the intensity and richness of its Zins of the 1970s and early 80s. Reserve Cabernet is a recent hit.

SWAN VALLEY *Western Australia* The original WESTERN AUSTRALIA wine region and the hottest stretch of vineyards in Australia, spread along the torrid, fertile silty flats of Perth's Swan River. It used to specialize in fortified wines, but SOUTH AUSTRALIA and north-east VICTORIA both do them better. New-wave whites and reds, especially from Moondah Brook and HOUGHTON, are encouraging. Best producers: Paul Conti, HOUGHTON★, Moondah Brook, Talijancich, Westfield.

JOSEPH SWAN VINEYARDS *Russian River Valley AVA, California, USA* Joseph Swan made legendary Zinfandel in the 1970s and was one of the first to age Zinfandel★★ in French oak. In the 1980s he turned to Pinot Noir★★ which is now probably the winery's best offering. After Swan's death in 1989, his son-in-law, Rod Berglund, took over as winemaker. Best years: (1997) 96 95 94 **93 92 91**.

SYRAH See pages 272–3.

LA TÂCHE AC★★★ *Grand Cru, Côte de Nuits, Burgundy, France* Along with la ROMANÉE-CONTI, la Tâche is the greatest of the great VOSNE-ROMANÉE Grands Crus and it is owned by Dom. de la ROMANÉE-CONTI. The wine has the rare ability to provide layer on layer of flavours; keep it for 10 years or you'll only experience a fraction of the pleasure you paid big money for. Best years: 1996 95 93 91 90 89 88 **85 78**.

TAFELWEIN German for table wine.

TAITTINGER *Champagne AC, Champagne, France* One of the few large independently owned CHAMPAGNE houses. The top wine, Comtes de Champagne BLANC DE BLANCS★★, used to be memorable for its creamy, foaming pleasures, but hasn't been so hot recently. Ordinary non-vintage★ is soft and honeyed but again has been unusually inconsistent for the last few years. The Comtes de Champagne rosé★ is elegant and always enjoyable. Another de luxe cuvée, called Vintage Collection★, is certainly good, but sells at a silly price. Best years: **1991 90 89 88 86 85 82 79**. See also Bouvet-Ladubay.

CH. TALBOT★★ *St-Julien AC, 4ème Cru Classé, Haut-Médoc, Bordeaux, France* Chunky, soft-centred but sturdy, capable of aging well for 10–20 years. Recent vintages have been superb. There is also an interesting white wine, Caillou Blanc de Talbot. Second wine: Connétable Talbot. Best years: (1998) 97 96 95 94 90 89 **88 86 85 83 82 81 79 78**.

TALTARNI *Pyrenees, Victoria, Australia* Biggest winery in this region, specializing in classic, deep-flavoured, European-style Cabernet★, Syrah★★, Merlot and Malbec; also good and improving fizz, especially new Clover Hill★★ from TASMANIA. Fumé Blanc★ is full yet tangy and gooseberry-like. Best years: (reds) 1996 94 93 **92 91 90 88 86 84 82**.

TARRAWARRA *Yarra Valley, Victoria, Australia* Clothing magnate and arts patron Marc Besen wanted to make a MONTRACHET, and hang the expense. His winemakers are on the right track: Tarrawarra Chardonnay★★ is deep and multi-faceted, but Pinot Noir★★ is just as good, with almost COTE DE NUITS flavour and concentration. Tunnel Hill is a less costly brand of both, but no other varieties are planted or planned. Best years: 1997 96 95 **94 92 90 89 88**.

TASMANIA *Australia* Tasmania is a minor state viticulturally, with only 500ha (1200 acres) of vines. The cool climate has attracted seekers of greatness in Pinot Noir and Chardonnay, but doesn't always deliver. Top Pinots are great but in a minority, Chardonnay can be superb, and there is some delicious Riesling. An important supplier of grapes for sparkling wine. Best producers: Delamere, Freycinet★★, HEEMSKERK★, Iron Pot Bay, Moorilla★, Notley Gorge, PIPERS BROOK★, Spring Vale, Stoney, Wellington.

TAURASI DOCG *Campania, Italy* Remarkably, it was a single producer, MASTROBERARDINO, and a single vintage, 1968, that created the reputation for this red. The 68 was a fabulous, deep autumnal wine, never again repeated, showing the great potential of the Aglianico grape. But the wines do need 5–10 years' aging. Best producers: Feudi di San Gregorio★★, MASTROBERARDINO (single-vineyard Radici★), Struzziero, Terre Dora di Paolo★. Best years: (recent) 1995 94 **93 92 90 89 88 86**.

TAVEL AC *Rhône Valley, France* Big, alcoholic rosé from north-west of Avignon. Grenache and Cinsaut are the main grapes. Drink Tavel at one year old if you want it cheerful, heady, yet refreshing. Best producers: Aquéria★, la Forcadière★, Genestière, GUIGAL★, la Mordorée★, Vignerons de Tavel, Trinquevedel, Vieux Moulin.

TAYLOR FLADGATE & YEATMAN *Port DOC, Douro, Portugal* The aristocrat of the port industry, 300 years old and still going strong. Its vintage port★★★ is superb; long-lived and high-priced and generally among the best around. Quinta de Vargellas★★ is an elegant, cedary, single-quinta vintage port made in the best of the 'off-vintages'. Taylor's 20-year-old★ is an excellent aged tawny. The best vintage ports from this house may be kept for at least 25 years. Best years: (vintage) 1994 92 85 83 **80** 77 **75 70 66 63 60 55 48 45 27**; (Vargellas) 1995 91 88 87 **82 78 67 64 61**.

TE MATA *Hawkes Bay, North Island, New Zealand* HAWKES BAY's glamour winery and still probably its best, though now facing increasing local competition. The best-known wines are the Te Mata reds, Coleraine★★★ and Awatea★★, both based on Cabernet Sauvignon with varying proportions of Merlot and Cabernet Franc. Also outstanding Elston Chardonnay★★★, a superbly crafted, toasty, spicy wine, capable of long aging. Exceptional vintages of all 3 wines might be aged for 5–10 years. A new addition to the range is Bullnose Shiraz★, an elegant, peppery red that does not quite match the quality of the winery's more robust blends. Best years: (1998) 96 95 **94 91 90 89 83 82**.

E & M TEMENT *Ehrenhausen, Steiermark, Austria* Manfred Tement is a fanatic who makes Austria's best Sauvignon Blanc★★ and

Chardonnay★★ in a cellar that looks like a Heath Robinson cartoon. Both varieties are fermented and aged in oak, giving wines with lots of power and depth but subtle oak character. The Sauvignon Blanc from the Zieregg site is ★★★ in the best vintages. Drink young or after brief keeping. Best years: (1998) 97 96 **95 94 93 92 90 88**.

DOM. TEMPIER *Bandol AC, Provence, France* Leading BANDOL estate, run by the Péyraud family and making rich, ageworthy reds from a high percentage of Mourvèdre. The top wines are Migoua★★, Cabassou★★ and la Tourtine★★. The rosé★ is one of Provence's best. Best years: (1998) (97) 96 95 **93 92 90 89 88 85 84 83 82**.

TEMPRANILLO Spain's best-quality native red grape can make wonderful red wine, with wild strawberry and spicy, tobaccoey flavours. It is important in RIOJA, PENEDES (as Ull de Llebre), RIBERA DEL DUERO (as Tinto Fino or Tinta del País), La MANCHA and VALDEPENAS (as Cencibel), NAVARRA, SOMONTANO, UTIEL-REQUENA and TORO (as Tinta de Toro). In Portugal it is found in the DOURO and DAO (as Tinta Roriz or Aragonês). Wines can be deliciously fruity for drinking young, but Tempranillo also matures well, and its flavours blend happily with oak. Plantings have been made in CALIFORNIA and OREGON in the past few years.

TEROLDEGO ROTALIANO DOC *Trentino-Alto Adige, Italy* Teroldego is a native TRENTINO variety, producing deep-coloured, grassy, blackberry-flavoured wine on the gravel soils of the Rotaliano plain. Best producers: Barone de Cles★, Dorigati★, Foradori★★, Gaierhof, Conti Martini★, Mezzacorona (Riserva★), Cantina Rotaliana★, Sebastiani★, A & R Zeni★. Best years: 1997 96 **95 94 93** 91 90 89 88 86 85.

TERRA NOBLE *Maule, Chile* Small Talca-based winery making only 2 wines: a grassy, mineral-edged Sauvignon Blanc and a light Nouveau-style Merlot. Loire wizard Henri Marionnet acts as consultant.

TERRAS DO SADO *Setúbal Peninsula, Portugal* Area south of Lisbon with 2 IPR regions, Arrábida and Palmela. SETUBAL produces fine sweet fortified, best from José Maria da FONSECA; the same producer has quality table wines, particularly Quinta de Camarate★ and Primum reds★★ and whites★ and red Periquita★. Tinta da Anfora★ by J P VINHOS and Pegos Claros★ are other good reds. Best years: (1998) 97 96 **95 94 92 91**.

TERRICCIO, TENUTA DEL *Tuscany, Italy* High in the hills south of Livorno, this producer has transformed itself from bulk red and white wines to the status of Tuscan superstar; new plantings have meant development of international-style reds and dry whites. The top red is Lupicaia★★★ (Cabernet-Merlot), rich and concentrated with a hint of eucalyptus and already very expensive. Tassinaia★★ is a second red, again from Bordeaux varieties, ready to drink sooner. The Chardonnay-based Saluccio★★ and Con Vento★, based on Sauvignon Blanc, are the most interesting whites. Best years: (reds) 1997 96 **95 94 93**.

CH. DU TERTRE★ *Margaux AC, 5ème Cru Classé, Haut-Médoc, Bordeaux, France* Obscure MARGAUX property at last gaining the recognition it deserves. With lots of fruit and tannin, the wine is usually delicious at 5–6 years old, but will happily age for 10–15 years. Hopefully the new ownership in 1997 will continue the progression. Best years: (1998) 96 95 94 **90 89 88 86 85 82 80 79 78**.

CH. LE TERTRE-RÔTEBOEUF★★ *St-Émilion Grand Cru AC, Bordeaux, France* ST-EMILION's most exceptional unclassified estate. The richly seductive, Merlot-based wines sell at the same price as the Premiers Grands Crus Classés. Best years: (1998) 97 96 95 94 90 89 **88 86 85**.

THACKREY & CO. *Marin County, California, USA* A tiny winery (1500 cases) with a cult following for huge RHONE-style red wines, especially the Orion★★, made from Syrah grapes grown in NAPA, and a Mourvèdre called Taurus★. The wines are well thought of by those who prefer power over elegance. All can age for 5 years or more. Best years: 1997 **95 94 92 91 90**.

THAMES VALLEY *Berkshire, England* Eighteen grape varieties planted over 13ha (32 acres) from which 2 Aussies, viticulturist Jon Leighton and consultant winemaker John Worontschak, produce full-flavoured wines, many with antipodean-style use of oak. Fumé★ is a remarkable Graves-lookalike, and won the Gore-Brown Trophy in 1993. Worontschak is also mad keen on sweet wine★ and fizz★ (Heritage Brut won the Gore-Brown Trophy in 1996). Overall, my feeling about this entire vineyard is: we ain't seen nothing yet.

H THANISCH *Bernkastel, Mosel, Germany* This is the rump of the original Thanisch estate. The labels remain substantially the same, so look out for the VDP eagle, which will tell you that you have the wine which is still in family hands. The Thanisch heirs have kept a chunk of the famous DOCTOR vineyard too. Quality improved up to 1992 but has been erratic since. Best years: **1995 92 90 89 88 76**.

THELEMA MOUNTAIN VINEYARDS *Stellenbosch WO, South Africa* Improved vineyard and grape quality are prime focus points at this family-run winery, high in the Simonsberg mountains. The talents of CALIFORNIA's Phil Freese ensure there is no shortage of ideas, including unorthodox trellising methods. New leased vineyards should also help alleviate the stock shortage in this hugely popular range, which has won winemaker Gyles Webb local and international acclaim. Some of the best are a rich blackcurrant Cabernet Sauvignon★★, a ripe fleshy Merlot★★, a barrel-fermented Chardonnay★★, a poised Sauvignon Blanc★ and less-hyped Riesling★. Among many other pursuits, Webb is a partner with FAIRVIEW's Charles Back, John Platter and Jabulani Ntshangase in The Spice Route Wine Company, based on the west coast. Best years: (reds) **1995 94 93 92 91**; (whites) **1998 97 96 95 94 93 92 91**.

THERMENREGION *Niederösterreich, Austria* This region, south of Vienna, takes its name from the thermal spa towns of BADEN and Bad Vöslau. Near Vienna is the village of Gumpoldskirchen with its rich and often sweet white wines. The red wine area around Baden produces large amounts of Blauer Portugieser together with a couple of good examples of Pinot Noir and Cabernet. Best producer: Stadlmann★.

THREE CHOIRS *Gloucestershire, England* Martin Fowke makes the wine at this 28-ha (68-acre) vineyard. The impressive range includes zingy New Release, sold at the same time as BEAUJOLAIS NOUVEAU. Estate Premium Medium Dry★, from Seyval Blanc, Reichensteiner and Müller-Thurgau, is the main seller, and he has been making a sparkling wine★ since 1990.

TICINO *Switzerland* Italian-speaking, southerly canton of Switzerland. The most important wine of the region is Merlot del Ticino, usually soft and gluggable, but sometimes more serious with some oak barrel-aging. Best producers: Daniel Huber, Werner Stucky, Christian Zündel★.

TIGNANELLO, VINO DA TAVOLA★★ *Tuscany, Italy* The wine that broke the mould in Tuscany. Piero ANTINORI employed the previously unheard of practice of aging in small French oak barrels and used Cabernet Sauvignon (20%) in the blend with Sangiovese. Though labelled only as simple VINO DA TAVOLA, the quality was superb and Tignanello's success sparked off the SUPER-TUSCAN movement outside DOC regulations that has produced many of Italy's most exciting wines. Top vintages are truly great wines: lesser vintages are of decent CHIANTI CLASSICO quality. Best years: (1998) (97) (96) 95 94 **93 91 90 88 86 85**.

TINTA RORIZ See Tempranillo.

TOCAI FRIULANO Unrelated to Hungary's or Alsace's Tokay, Tocai Friulano is a north-east Italian grape producing dry, nutty, oily whites of great character in COLLIO and COLLI ORIENTALI and good wines in the Veneto's COLLI EUGANEI, as well as lots of neutral stuff in Piave. Best producers: Abbazia di Rosazzo★, Borgo del Tiglio★, Dorigo★, Livio Felluga★, JERMANN★, Edi Keber★, Pierpaolo Pecorari★, PUIATTI★, Ronco del Gelso★★, Russiz Superiore★, SCHIOPETTO★★, Specogna★, La Viarte★, Vie di Romans★, Villa Russiz★.

TOKAJI *Hungary and Slovakia* Strange, fascinating and unique, Tokaji wine has a sweet-sour-sweet, sherry-like tang. On the Hungarian-Slovak border, mists from the Bodrog river ensure that noble rot or botrytis on the Furmint, Hárslevelü and Muscotaly (Muscat Ottonel) grapes is a fairly common occurrence. Old single-vineyard Museum wines★★ from the Tokaji Wine Trust demonstrate the area's potential, and recent French and Spanish investments are currently exploiting it. After a long period of decline, quality is very much on the up, and the super 1993s (the first widely made post-communist vintage) have now been released; the best promise ★★★ quality when they've matured a bit. Tokaji should be sold ready to drink, though the oxidized nature of most old-style releases made you think you'd missed the boat a bit. Best producers: Disznókö, Megyer, Pajzos, Royal Tokaji Wine Company.

TOLLOT-BEAUT & FILS *Chorey-lès-Beaune, Burgundy, France* High-quality COTE DE BEAUNE reds with lots of fruit and a pronounced new oak character. The village-level CHOREY-LES-BEAUNE★, ALOXE-CORTON★★ and SAVIGNY-LES-BEAUNE★★ wines are all excellent, as is the top-notch BEAUNE Premier Cru Clos du Roi★★. Best years: 1997 96 95 93 **92 90**.

TORGIANO DOC & DOCG *Umbria, Italy* A zone near Perugia dominated by LUNGAROTTI. In the 1960s and 70s, while most central Italian red was harsh and fruitless, Lungarotti's Rubesco Torgiano was always ripe and plummy. While the basic Rubesco Torgiano is fairly simple, the Riserva Vigna Monticchio★★ is a fine black cherry-flavoured wine. Torgiano Riserva Rosso has been accorded DOCG.

TORO DO *Castilla y León, Spain* Toro makes mainly reds, which are strong, robust, full of colour and tannin, and pretty high in alcohol.

The main grape, Tinta de Toro, is a local deviant of Tempranillo, and there is some Garnacha. Whites from the Malvasía grape are generally heavy. Best producers: Fariña★ (reds), Vega Saúco.

TORRES *Penedès DO, Catalonia, Spain* Large family winery led by visionary Miguel Torres, making good wines with local grapes, Parellada and Tempranillo, but also renowned for French varieties. Viña Esmeralda★ (Muscat d'Alsace and Gewürztraminer) is grapy and spicy, Fransola★★ (Sauvignon Blanc with some Parellada) is richly grassy, and Milmanda★ is a delicate, expensive Chardonnay from a CONCA DE BARBERA vineyard, although it sports the PENEDES DO. Successful reds are Gran Coronas★, soft, oaky and blackcurranty (Tempranillo and Cabernet); fine, relatively rich Mas la Plana★★ (Cabernet Sauvignon); floral, perfumed Mas Borras★ (Pinot Noir); and raisiny Las Torres★ (Merlot). Best years: (Mas la Plana) 1993 90 89 88 87 83 81 76 75 73.

MARIMAR TORRES ESTATE *Sonoma, California, USA* The sister of Spanish winemaker Miguel Torres has established her own winery in the cool Green Valley region of SONOMA COUNTY, only a few miles from the Pacific Ocean. The first Chardonnays★ were big, intense wines, perhaps a shade heavy on the oak, best with 2–4 years' age. The full-bodied Pinot Noirs generally achieve ★★ quality. Best years: 1997 95 94 92.

MIGUEL TORRES *Curicó, Chile* After a long period of under-achievement from the man who re-awoke the Chilean wine industry, we are at last seeing good snappy Sauvignon Blanc★ once more, grassy, fruity Santa Digna rosé★ and a lean but blackcurranty Manso de Valasco Cabernet★. Best years: (Manso) 1996 95 94.

CH. LA TOUR BLANCHE★★ *Sauternes AC, 1er Cru Classé, Bordeaux, France* Owned by the French Ministry of Agriculture, La Tour Blanche regained top form in the 1980s with the introduction of new oak barrels for fermentation, lower yields and greater selection. Full-bodied, rich and aromatic it now ranks with the best of the Classed Growths. Best years: (1998) 97 96 95 90 89 88 86 85.

TOURAINE AC *Loire Valley, France* The general AC for Touraine wines in the central LOIRE. There are 6140ha (15,170 acres) of AC vineyards, divided half and half between red or rosé and white. Most of the Touraine reds are from the Gamay and in hot years these can be juicy, rough-fruited wines. There is a fair amount of red from Cabernets Sauvignon and Franc, too, and some good Côt (Malbec). The reds are best drunk young. Fairly decent whites come from the Chenin Blanc but the best wines are from Sauvignon Blanc. These can be a good SANCERRE substitute at half the price. Drink at one year old, though Chenin wines can last longer. As well as generic Touraine wine, there are 3 more ACs: Touraine-Amboise and Touraine-Mesland for reds, rosés and whites, and Touraine-Azay-le-Rideau for whites and rosés only. Best producers: (reds and rosés) Bergene★, Dom. de la Charmoise★, Ch. de Chenonceau★, Corbillières, J Delaunay★, Robert Denis★, Marcadet★, Octavie, OISLY-ET-THESEE co-op, Pavy★, Roche Blanche★; (whites) des Acacias★, Barbou, Baron Briare★, Dom. de la Charmoise★, Ch. de Chenonceau★, J Delaunay, Xavier Frissant, Marcadet★, Octavie★, OISLY-ET-THESEE co-op★, Pré Baron★, Roche Blanche★. Best years: (reds) (1998) 97 96 95 93 90 89; (whites) 1996 95 93 90 89.

TOURAINE MOUSSEUX AC *Loire Valley, France* A sparkling wine AC covering the entire Touraine region. The wines are rarely as good as the best VOUVRAY and CREMANT DE LOIRE. Best producers: Ch. de Chenonceau★, J Delaunay, Monmousseau.

TOURIGA NACIONAL High-quality red Portuguese grape which is rich in aroma and fruit. It is prized for port production as it contributes deep colour and tannin to the blend. Rapidly increasing in importance for table wines both in the DOURO and elsewhere in Portugal including the DAO, ESTREMADURA and even the ALENTEJO.

CH. LA TOUR-MARTILLAC *Pessac-Léognan AC, Cru Classé de Graves, Bordeaux, France* A GRAVES Classed Growth that for many years positively cultivated an old-fashioned image but which is now a property to watch. Organic practice is strictly followed in the vineyard, which has many ancient vines. In the past, the reds★ were deep, dark and well structured but they lacked charm. Things improved considerably in the 1980s. Since 1986 new-style vinification has also transformed the whites★★. Best years: (reds) (1998) 97 96 95 90 88 **86 85 83 82**; (whites) (1998) 97 96 **95 94 93 90 89 88**.

TRÁS-OS-MONTES *Portugal* Impoverished north-eastern province, traditionally a supplier of grapes for Mateus Rosé, but with 3 IPR regions, Valpaços, Chaves and Planalto-Mirandês, still producing pretty rustic stuff. However, the Vinho Regional Trás-os-Montes covers a handful of very good DOURO-sourced red wines. Best producers: RAMOS PINTO (reds Bons Ares★ and Reserva★★), Quinta do Sidro (Chardonnay★), Valle Pradinhos.

TREBBIANO The most widely planted white Italian grape variety – far too widely, in fact, for Italy's good. As the Trebbiano Toscano, it is used as the base for Galestro and any number of other neutral, dry whites, as well as in VIN SANTO. But there are also a number of grapes masquerading under the Trebbiano name that aren't anything like as neutral. The most notable are the Trebbiano from LUGANA and ABRUZZO – both grapes capable of full-bodied, fragrant wines. Called Ugni Blanc in France, and primarily used for distilling, as it should be.

TREFETHEN VINEYARDS *Napa Valley AVA, California, USA* An off-dry Riesling★ is one of the best wines from this NAPA estate, although the Chardonnay has won more renown. The Cabernet is haphazard, but the Reserve Cabernet★ and Merlot are solid examples. Good-value Eshcol Chardonnay and Eshcol Cabernet Sauvignon are frequently the most attractive wines made here. Best years: (reds) 1997 95 **94 92 91 90**.

TRENTINO *Italy* This northern region is officially linked with ALTO ADIGE, but they are completely different. The wines rarely have the verve or perfume of Alto Adige examples, but can make up for this with riper, softer flavours, where vineyard yields have been kept in check. The Trentino DOC covers 20 different styles of wine, including white Pinot Bianco and Grigio, Moscato Giallo, Müller-Thurgau and Nosiola, and red Schiava, Lagrein, Marzemino, Teroldego and Cabernet. Trento Classico is a special DOC for sparkling wines made by the Champagne method. Best producers: Nino Bolognani★, Bossi Fedrigotti, Castel Noarna★, Cavit co-op, De Tarczal★, Dorigati, FERRARI★★, Graziano Fontana★, Foradori★★, Letrari★, Conti Martini★, Maso Cantanghel★★, Maso Roveri★, Pojer & Sandri★, Pravis★, San Leonardo★★, Simoncelli★, Enrico Spagnolli★, Vallarom★★, La Vis co-op, A & R Zeni★. See also Teroldego Rotaliano.

DOM. DE TRÉVALLON *Provence, France* Iconoclastic Parisian Eloi Dürrbach makes brilliant reds★★★, mixing the wildness of Mediterranean herbs with a sweetness of blackberry, blackcurrant and black, black plums, and a tiny quantity of white★★★. Dürrbach's tradition-busting blend of Cabernet Sauvignon and Syrah, no longer accepted (since the 94 vintage) by the appellation les BAUX-DE-PROVENCE, is the finest wine to come out of Provence in the last decade. The wines age extremely well, but are surprisingly drinkable in their youth. Best years: (reds) 1999 97 96 95 **94 92 90 89 87 86 85 83 82**.

F E TRIMBACH *Alsace AC, Alsace, France* An excellent grower/ merchant whose trademark is beautifully structured, subtly perfumed elegance. Riesling and Gewurztraminer are the specialities, but the Pinot Gris and Pinot Blanc are first-rate too. Top wines are Gewurztraminer Cuvée des Seigneurs de Ribeaupierre★★, Riesling Cuvée Frédéric Émile★★ and Riesling Clos St-Hune★★★. Also very good ALSACE VENDANGE TARDIVE★★ and SELECTIONS DE GRAINS NOBLES★★. Best years: (1998) 97 96 95 **93 92 90 89 88 85**.

TRITTENHEIM *Mosel, Germany* An important MOSEL wine village with several excellent vineyard sites, most notably the Apotheke (pharmacy) and Leiterchen (or little ladder). The wines are sleek and with crisp acidity, balanced by plenty of fruit. Best producers: Ernst Clüsserath★, Clüsserath-Weiler, Grans-Fassian★, Milz-Laurentiushof★. Best years: (1998) 97 **95 93 90**.

TROCKEN German word for dry. In most parts of Germany and Austria Trocken means less than 9g per litre residual sugar. Trocken wines have become a fashion in Germany, but have not made great strides in other countries.

TROCKENBEERENAUSLESE German for 'dry berry selected', denoting grapes affected by noble rot (*Edelfäule* in German) – the wines will be lusciously sweet. Required Oechsle levels for Trockenbeerenauslese are 150 Oechsle for a MOSEL Riesling or 154 for a south BADEN Ruländer. An Austrian Trockenbeerenauslese must be 30 KMW or 156 Oechsle.

CH. TROPLONG-MONDOT★★ *St-Émilion Grand Cru AC, Bordeaux, France* Consistently one of the best of ST-EMILION's Grands Crus Classés and contentiously denied promotion to Premier Grand Cru Classé status in 1996. The wines are beautifully structured and mouthfillingly textured for long aging. Best years: (1998) 97 96 95 94 93 90 89 **88 86 85**.

CH. TROTANOY★★ *Pomerol AC, Bordeaux, France* Another POMEROL estate (along with PETRUS, LAFLEUR, LATOUR-A-POMEROL and others) which has benefited from the brilliant touch of the MOUEIX family. After a dip in the mid-1980s, recent vintages are getting back on form. Best years: (1998) 97 96 95 94 93 90 89 **88 82**.

TURSAN VDQS *South-West France* Wine of local interest only, made on the edge of les Landes, the sandy coastal area south of Bordeaux. The white is the most interesting: made from the Baroque grape it is clean, crisp and refreshing. Best producers: de Bachen★, Tursan co-op.

TUSCANY *Italy* Tuscany's rolling hills, clad with vines, olive trees and cypresses, have produced wine since at least Etruscan times, and today Tuscany leads the way in promoting the new image of Italian wines. Its 33 appellations are based on the red Sangiovese grape and are led by CHIANTI, BRUNELLO DI MONTALCINO and VINO NOBILE DI MONTEPULCIANO, as well as famous SUPER-TUSCANS like ORNELLAIA and TIGNANELLO. White wines, despite sweet VIN SANTO, and the occasional excellent Chardonnay and Sauvignon, do not figure highly. See also Bolgheri, Carmignano, Montecarlo, Parrina, Pomino, Rosso di Montalcino, Rosso di Montepulciano, Sassicaia, Super-Tuscans, Vernaccia di San Gimignano.

TYRRELL'S *Hunter Valley, New South Wales, Australia* Family-owned company with prime Lower HUNTER vineyards; the wines taste splendid on their home patch but only recently have achieved consistency on the export market. Makes superb Vat 1 Semillon★★★, generally excellent Vat 47 Chardonnay★★★, and Vat 5 and 9 Shiraz which can be fine. Vat 6 Pinot Noir is variable. Best years: (Semillon) 1998 97 96 95 94 **93 92** 90 89 87 86 79 76 74 72; (Chardonnay) 1997 96 **95 94 93 92 90** 89 87 86 84 79 76 73; (reds) 1995 **93 92** 89 87 85 84 83 81 75 65.

UGNI BLANC See Trebbiano.

UMBRIA *Italy* Wine production in this Italian region is dominated by ORVIETO, accounting for almost 70% of DOC production. However, some of the most characterful wines are reds from TORGIANO and MONTEFALCO. Latest interest centres on remarkable new reds made by outstanding enologist Riccardo Cotarella at estates such as Pieve del Vescovo (for Sangiovese-Merlot, Lucciaio★★) and La Palazzola (for Cabernet-Merlot, Rubino★★).

ÜRZIG *Mosel, Germany* Middle MOSEL village with a very famous vineyard site – the Würzgarten (spice garden) – that tumbles spectacularly down to the river banks and produces marvellously spicy Riesling wines from its red slate and sandstone soil. Drink with 5 years' age or more. Best producers: J J Christoffel★★, Dr LOOSEN★★★, Mönchhof★. Best years: (1998) **97 96 95 93**.

UTIEL-REQUENA DO *Valencia, Spain* Inland from Valencia, Utiel-Requena is renowned for its rosés, mostly made from the Bobal grape. A lot of Tempranillo has been planted recently, making better, longer-lasting reds. Best producers: Campo de Requena, Torre Oria, Vinival.

VACQUEYRAS AC *Rhône Valley, France* The most important and consistently successful of the COTES DU RHONE-VILLAGES communes was promoted to its own AC in 1989. The reds have a lovely dark colour, a round, warm, spicy bouquet and a rich deep flavour that seems infused with the herbs and pine dust of the south. They are lovely to drink at 2–3 years and good wines will age for 5 years or more. Best producers: Armouriers★, la Charbonnière★, Clos des Cazaux★, Roger Combe★, Couroulu★, la Fourmone★★, la Garrigue★, JABOULET★, Lambertins,

Montmirail★, Roques, Tardieu-Laurent★, Ch. des Tours★, Vacqueyras co-op★, Verquière★. Best years: (1998) 97 **95 94 93 91 90 89**.

VALAIS *Switzerland* Swiss canton flanking the Rhône above Lake Geneva. Between Martigny and Sierre the valley turns north-east creating an Alpine suntrap, and this short stretch of terraced vineyard land provides the majority of Switzerland's most individual wines from Fendant, Johannisberger (the local name for Silvaner), Pinot Noir and Gamay, and also including Syrah and Chardonnay, which are recent innovations. Best producers: Michel Clavien, J Germanier, Gilliard, Caves Imesch, Mathier, Dom. de Mont d'Or★, Raymond, Zufferey.

CH. DE VALANDRAUD★★ *St-Émilion Grand Cru AC, Bordeaux, France* ST-EMILION's recent high-priced sensation, the first vintage was in 1991. Big, rich, extracted wines produced from low yields from grapes mainly grown on the less favoured Dordogne plain. Time will tell. Best years: (1998) 97 96 95 94 93 92.

VALDEPEÑAS DO *Castilla-La Mancha, Spain* Valdepeñas offers some of Spain's best inexpensive oak-aged reds, but these are a small drop in a sea of less exciting stuff. In fact there are more whites than reds, at least some of them now modern, fresh and fruity. Drink young, although the best reds from Tempranillo will last 10 years. Best producers: LOS LLANOS★, Luís Megía, Real, Félix Solís, Casa de la Viña.

VALDESPINO *Jerez y Manzanilla DO, Andalucía, Spain* Old-fashioned, very high-quality family sherry business. Delicious wines include Inocente Fino★, Tio Diego Amontillado★★, the expensive but concentrated Palo Cortado Cardenal★★, dry amontillados Coliseo★★★ and Don Tomás★★, Don Gonzalo Old Dry Oloroso★★ and Pedro Ximénez Solera Superior★★.

VALDIVIESO *Curicó, Chile* Part of the Mitjans group and recipient of huge investment both in their Lontué winery and Curicó Valley vineyards. Best known for smooth Pinot Noir★, buttery Chardonnay★, slightly over-oaked Merlot★ and Cabernet Sauvignon★. Multi-varietal blend Caballo Loco★ is good but a long way from being a Chilean Grange (see PENFOLDS). Watch out for the new premium Stonelake series. Sparkling wines have been made here for 100 years, many by the tank method. However, recently there has been an overhaul of the vineyards and equipment, and a Frenchman, Raphael Brisbois, with experience in CHAMPAGNE, India and CALIFORNIA, is consultant for new traditional (Champagne) method sparklers made with Pinot Noir and Chardonnay.

VAL D'ORBIEU, LES VIGNERONS DU *Languedoc-Roussillon, France* A dynamic but erratic growers' association that sells in excess of 20 million cases of wine a year and is France's largest wine exporting company. It also owns LISTEL and now Cordier (BORDEAUX). Membership includes several of the MIDI's best co-ops (Cucugnan, Cuxac, Ribauté and Montredon) and individual producers (Dom. de Fontsainte, Ch. la Voulte-Gasparets). Also marketed by Val d'Orbieu are Chateau de Jau and the excellent BANYULS and COLLIOURE estate, Clos de Paulilles. Val d'Orbieu are now developing a range of blended wines (Cuvée Chouette★, Chorus★, Pas de Deux and la Cuvée Mythique★★), which are a judicious mix of traditional Mediterranean varieties and Cabernet or Merlot from Bordeaux. Best years: (1998) 96 **95 94 93 91 90 89 88**.

VALENCIA *Spain*   The best wines from Valencia DO in the south-east of Spain are the inexpensive, sweet, grapy Moscatels. Simple, fruity whites, reds and rosés are also good. Alicante DO to the south produces a little-known treasure, the Fondillón dry or semi-dry fortified wine, as well as a cluster of wines from native and foreign varieties made by a few quality-conscious modern wineries. Monastrell (Mourvèdre) is the main red grape variety. UTIEL-REQUENA DO specializes in rosés and light reds from the Bobal grape. Best producers: (Valencia DO) Vicente Gandía Pla, Schenk (Los Monteros), Cherubino Valsangiacomo (Marqués de Caro); (Alicante DO) Bocopa★, Gutiérrez de la Vega (Casta Diva Muscat★★), Enrique Mendoza★, Salvador Poveda★, Primitivo Quiles★.

VALLE D'AOSTA *Italy*   Tiny Alpine valley sandwiched between PIEDMONT and the French Alps in northern Italy. The regional DOC covers 17 wine styles, referring either to a specific grape variety (like Gamay or Pinot Nero) or to a delimited region like Donnaz, a northern extension of Piedmont's CAREMA, producing a light red from the Nebbiolo grape. Perhaps the finest wine from these steep slopes is the sweet Chambave Moscato. Best producers: Bonin, Charrère★, Les Crêtes★, La Crotta di Vegneron★, Institut Agricole Regional, Ezio Voyat.

VALLÉE DU PARADIS, VIN DE PAYS DE LA *Languedoc, France*   With a name like the valley of paradise, the wines from this area to the south-west of Narbonne ought to be heavenly. In fact, they're good, basic quaffers made principally from Carignan, Cinsaut and Grenache.

VALPOLICELLA DOC *Veneto, Italy*   This Veronese wine can range in style from a light, cherryish red to the rich, port-like RECIOTO and AMARONE Valpolicellas. Most Valpolicella from the plains is pale and insipid, and bears little comparison to Valpolicella Classico from the hills. Made from Corvina (the best grape), Rondinella and Molinara (eliminated from the blend when a more structured wine is required), Valpolicella Classico can be a light, cherryish red of great appeal, for drinking within 18 months of the vintage. A fuller wine of bitter-sweet complexity is made either from a particular vineyard (like ALLEGRINI's La Grola), or by refermenting the wine on the skins and lees of the Amarone, a style called Ripasso, which adds an exciting sweet-sour dimension to the wine. Some, such as the outstanding Romano DAL FORNO, actually ferment a portion of dried grapes in making Valpolicella. The wines are rich but more stable than Ripasso wines. Best producers: Accordini★, ALLEGRINI★★, Bertani★, Bolla★, Brigaldara★, Brunelli, Tommaso Bussola★, Castellani (La Bionda), Cecilia Beretta★, Corte Sant'Alda★, Degani, DAL FORNO★★, Aleardo Ferrari, Guerrieri-Rizzardi★, MASI★, Mazzi★, QUINTARELLI★★, Le Ragose★, Le Salette★, Serègo Alighieri★, Speri★, Tedeschi★, Tommasi, Villa Belini, Villa Spinosa★, Viviani, Fratelli Zeni★. Best years: (recent) (1998) **97 95 94 93 91 90 88**.

VALTELLINA DOC *Lombardy, Italy*   Red wine produced on the precipitous slopes of northern LOMBARDY. There is a basic, light red, made from at least 70% Nebbiolo (here called Chiavennasca), but the best wines are made under the Valtellina Superiore DOCG as Grumello, Inferno, Sassella and Valgella. From top vintages the wines are attractively perfumed and approachable. Sfursat or Sforzato is a dense, high-alcohol red (up to

14.5%) made from semi-dried grapes. Best producers: La Castellina★, Enologica Valtellinese★, Fay★, Nino Negri★, Rainoldi★, Conti Sertoli Salis★, Triacca★. Best years: 1998 97 96 **93 90 89 88 85**.

VASSE FELIX *Margaret River, Western Australia* One of the originals responsible for MARGARET RIVER rocketing to fame, with decadently rich, profound Cabernet Sauvignon★★ and rare but very special Shiraz★★. New flagship red is the delicious Heytesbury★★★. The whites are also very smart. Best years: (reds) 1996 **95 94** 93 91 90 88 **86 84 83 79**.

VAUD *Switzerland* With the exception of the canton of Geneva, the Vaud accounts for the vineyards bordering Lake Geneva, forming a seemingly unbroken line from Nyon to Montreux. There are 5 regions: la Côte, Lavaux, CHABLAIS, Côtes de l'Orbe-Bonvillars and Vully. Most of the production is Dorin (Chasselas) and it can be a delightful light white. Reds are from Gamay and Pinot Noir. Best producers: Badoux, Bovard, Conne, Delarze, Dubois Fils, Grognuz, Massy, Obrist, Pinget, J & P Testuz.

VAVASOUR *Marlborough, South Island, New Zealand* First winery in the Awatere Valley near MARLBOROUGH's main wine area, enjoying spectacular success. One of New Zealand's best Chardonnays★★, a superb but variable Cabernet Sauvignon-Franc Reserve★ and fabulous Sauvignon Blanc★★★. Best years: (1998) **97 96 94 91 90**.

VDP German organization recognizable on the label by a Prussian eagle bearing grapes. Membership is dependent on examination, and the quality of estates included is usually – but not always – high.

VDQS (VIN DÉLIMITÉ DE QUALITÉ SUPÉRIEURE) The second-highest classification for French wines, behind AC. Indications are that the authorities would like to phase it out.

VEENWOUDEN *Paarl WO, South Africa* This tiny cellar, one of the Cape's most exciting, is owned by international opera singer, Deon van der Walt, whose brother Marcel, an ex-golf pro, has become a dedicated and capable winemaker. Three reds only are made, each based on BORDEAUX varieties: Merlot★★ sumptuous and well-oaked, firm and silky-fruited Veenwouden Classic★★ blend and the 2nd label, Vivat Bacchus. The first 2 should mature for 9–11 years. Best years: **1996 95 94 93**.

VEGA SICILIA *Ribera del Duero DO, Castilla y León, Spain* Spain's most expensive red wines, rich, fragrant, complex and very slow to mature, and by no means always easy to appreciate. This estate was the first in Spain to introduce French varieties, and over a quarter of the vines are now Cabernet Sauvignon, two-thirds are Tempranillo and the rest Malbec and Merlot. Vega Sicilia Alión★★★ – the top wine – has traditionally been given about 10 years' wood aging, but this is now being reduced and volatility evident in some vintages should now no longer occur. Second wine: Valbuena★★. A subsidiary winery producing the more modern-style Alión★★, from different vineyards, was launched in 1995. Best years: (Unico) **1986** 82 81 80 79 76 75 74 70.

VELHAS, CAVES *Estremadura, Portugal* Caves Velhas buys, blends and sells wines from all over Portugal. Its non-DOC brands (Romeira, Caves Velhas Clarete and Caves Velhas Garrafeira) are largely made from wines bought in from the RIBATEJO or TERRAS DO SADO regions.

VELICH *Neuseidlersee, Burgenland, Austria* Casino croupier Roland Velich makes not only Austria's most minerally and sophisticated

Chardonnay from old vines in the Tiglat vineyard ★★, but since 1995 also spectacular dessert wines of ★★ and ★★★ quality. Best years: (dry white) 1997 95 **94 93 92**; (dessert) (1998) 96 95 **94 93 91**.

VENEGAZZÙ *Veneto, Italy* The Loredan Gasparini wine estate is known primarily for its red VINO DA TAVOLA, Venegazzù della Casa★. Both this and the more barrique-influenced Loredan Gorparini Capo di Stato★ are based on BORDEAUX varieties and can still pack a smoky, aggressive black-fruited punch. Best years: 1995 94 93 **90 89 88 85**.

VENETO *Italy* The Veneto region takes in the wine zones of SOAVE, VALPOLICELLA, BARDOLINO and Piave in north-east Italy. Its huge production makes it the source of a great deal of inexpensive wine, but the Soave and Valpolicella hills are also capable of producing small quantities of high-quality wine. Other hilly areas like Colli Berici and COLLI EUGANEI produce mainly large quantities of dull staple varietal wines, but can offer the odd flash of brilliance. PROSECCO DI CONEGLIANO-VALDOBBIADENE is Venice's preferred bubbly. The great dry red of this zone is AMARONE. See also Bianco di Custoza, Breganze, Recioto della Valpolicella, Recioto di Soave.

VERDICCHIO DEI CASTELLI DI JESI DOC *Marche, Italy* Verdicchio, grown in the hills near the Adriatic around Jesi and in the Apennine enclave of Matelica, has blossomed into central Italy's most promising white variety over the last decade. When fresh and fruity it is the ideal wine with fish, but some Verdicchio has the size and strength to age into a white of surprising depth of flavours. A few producers, notably Garofoli with Serra Fiorese★★, age it in oak, but even without wood it can develop an almost Burgundy-like complexity. Jesi is the classical zone, but the rarer Verdicchio di Matelica can be as impressive. A little is made sparkling. Best producers: (Jesi) Brunori★, Bucci★, Colonnara, Coroncino★, Fazi-Battaglia★, Garofoli★★, Mancinelli★, Moncaro★, Santa Barbara★, Sartarelli★★, Tavignano di Laconi★, Umani Ronchi★, Vallerosa-Bonci★, Fratelli Zaccagnini; (Matelica) Belisario★, Bisci-Castiglioni★, Mecella★, La Monacesca★★.

VERGELEGEN *Stellenbosch WO, South Africa* Andre van Rensburg has immediately made his mark as winemaker on this Anglo-American-owned historic farm, where vines were first planted in 1700. His first vintage, 1998, was a difficult white wine year, but he produced 2 enticing Sauvignon Blancs, a regular★ with New World tropical fruit, and a single-vineyard★★ which is flinty, dry and powerful. Also proving equal to the impressive octagonal cellar designed by a Paris architect is a cohesive, stylish Chardonnay Reserve★★. Early vintages of Merlot★★ and Cabernet★★ from new-clone vineyards showed great promise; these are currently on hold until they meet van Rensburg's exacting standards. Best years: (whites) **1998** 97 96 95; (reds) **1995** 94.

VERGET *Mâconnais, Burgundy, France* A négociant house specializing in white Burgundies, run by Jean-Marie Guffens-Heynen, an exuberant character with his own domaine. The Guffens-Heynen wines include excellent MACON-VILLAGES★ and POUILLY-FUISSE★★ but the Verget range extends to outstanding Premiers Crus and Grands Crus from the COTE D'OR, notably CORTON-CHARLEMAGNE★★ and BATARD-MONTRACHET★★.

VERMENTINO The best dry white wines of SARDINIA generally come from the Vermentino grape. Light, dry, perfumed and nutty, the best wines tend to be from the north of the island, where the more confined zone of Vermentino di Gallura is located. Occasionally it is made sweet or sparkling. Vermentino is also grown in LIGURIA and TUSCANY, though its character is quite different. **Best producers:** (Sardinia) Argiolas★★, Capichera★, Cherchi★, Piero Mancini★, Santadi co-op★, SELLA & MOSCA★, Vermentino co-op.

VERNACCIA DI ORISTANO DOC *Sardinia, Italy* Outstanding oxidized, almost sherry-like wines from the west of the island, which acquire complexity and colour through long aging in wood. Amber-coloured and dry, nutty and long on the finish. **Best producer:** Contini★.

VERNACCIA DI SAN GIMIGNANO DOCG *Tuscany, Italy* The dry white wine made from the Vernaccia grape grown in the hills around San Gimignano gained fame as Italy's first DOC in 1966. It has recently been promoted to DOCG, which hopefully will improve the quality of the wines, generally light quaffers. However, whether the allowance of up to 10% Chardonnay in the blend is a forward step is debatable. There is now a San Gimignano DOC for the zone's up-and-coming red wines. **Best producers:** Ambra delle Torri★, Baroncini, Casale-Falchini★, La Lastra (Riserva★), Melini (Le Grillaie★), Montenidoli★, Panizzi★, Pietrafitta★, Pietraserena★, San Donato★, San Quirico, Guicciardini Strozzi, Teruzzi & Puthod★★, Vagnoni★.

NOËL VERSET *Cornas AC, Rhône Valley, France* Massive, concentrated rustic reds★★ from some of the oldest and best-sited vines in CORNAS. Yields are tiny here and it shows in the depth and power that Verset achieves in his wine. Worth aging for 10 years or more. **Best years:** (1998) 97 96 95 94 **91 90 89 88 85**.

VESÚVIO, QUINTA DO *Port DOC, Douro, Portugal* Purchased by the Symington family in 1989 and already a consistently top performer. Differs from stablemates DOW, GRAHAM and WARRE – traditional shipper's labels – in that it appears whenever the high quality can be maintained (and not just in officially declared years). A brilliant medium to long-term port, best with at least 10 years' age. **Best years:** 1995 94 92 **91 90**.

VEUVE CLICQUOT *Champagne AC, Champagne, France* These Champagnes can still live up to the high standards set by the original Widow Clicquot at the beginning of the 19th century, although many are released too young. The non-vintage★ is full, toasty and satisfyingly weighty, or lean and raw, depending on your luck: the vintage★★ is fuller and the de luxe, called Grande Dame★★★ after the original widow, is hefty but impressive stuff. **Best years:** **1991 90 89 88 85 82 79**.

VICTORIA *Australia* Despite its small area, Victoria has arguably more land suited to quality grape-growing than any other state in Australia, with climates ranging from hot Sunraysia and RUTHERGLEN on the Murray River to cool MORNINGTON PENINSULA and GIPPSLAND in the south. The range of flavours is similarly wide and exciting. Victoria, with more than 170 wineries, leads the boutique winery boom today, particularly in Mornington Peninsula. See also Bendigo, Geelong, Goulburn Valley, Grampians, Pyrenees, Yarra Valley.

LA VIEILLE FERME★ *Côtes du Ventoux AC, Rhône Valley, France* A
brilliantly spicy, concentrated red produced in a lesser AC by the owners
of the world-famous Ch. de BEAUCASTEL in CHATEAUNEUF-DU-PAPE. If only all
COTES DU VENTOUX were as exciting. Best years: (1998) 97 **95 94 93 90**.

VIEILLES VIGNES French term for a wine made from vines at least 20
years old, if not twice that. Old vines give more concentrated wine.

VIEUX-CHÂTEAU-CERTAN★★ *Pomerol AC, Bordeaux, France* Slow-
developing and tannic red (because of the use of 45% Cabernet),
which after 15–20 years finally resembles more a fragrant refined
MEDOC than a gushing, hedonistic POMEROL. Best years: (1998) 96 95 94
93 90 89 **88 86 85 83 82 81 79 78 70 64**.

VIEUX TÉLÉGRAPHE *Châteauneuf-du-Pape AC, Rhône Valley, France*
One of the top names in the AC, less tannic than BEAUCASTEL perhaps
but with just as much aging potential. The vines are some of the
oldest in Châteauneuf and this Grenache-based red★★ is among the
best modern-style wines produced in the RHONE VALLEY. Recently
purchased les Pallières in GIGONDAS and will look for similar style and
quality there. There is also a small amount of white★, which is
heavenly to drink at the youngest possible stage. Best years: (1998) 97
96 95 **93 91 90 89 88 85 83**.

VILLA MARIA *Auckland, North Island, New Zealand* Founder and co-
owner George Fistonich also owns Vidal and Esk Valley. Vidal Cabernet-
Merlot★★★ and Villa Maria Reserve Cabernet★★★ are superb. Reserve
Chardonnay from Vidal★★ and Villa Maria★★ are power-packed
wines. Also produce 2 outstanding examples of MARLBOROUGH Sauvignon
Blanc; classic Wairau Valley Sauvignon Blanc★★ and even more
concentrated Awatere Valley Reserve Sauvignon Blanc★★. Riesling★★
is impressive, and, at the sweeter end, so is stunning Late Harvest
Riesling★★★, all from Marlborough. Best years: (1998) **96 95 94 91**.

VILLA SACHSEN *Bingen, Rheinhessen, Germany* Renowned estate
recently purchased by Prinz Salm of the Prinz zu SALM-DALBERG estate
in the NAHE. He needs to work harder, however, if the wines are to
match the high quality of the 1980s. Best years: **1996 90 89 88**.

VILLARD *Casablanca, Chile* Owner Thierry Villard (formerly of ORLANDO
in South Australia) produces his own range of wines at the Santa
Emiliana winery. A big, buttery Chardonnay Reserve★ and clean,
crisp Sauvignon Blanc★, both from CASABLANCA, have improved further
since the new winery opened in 1997. Also produces a good Merlot
from Cachapoal.

VILLIERA ESTATE *Paarl WO, South Africa* The down-to-earth Grier family
have a knack of achieving both quality and value for money in their
varied range. Their speciality is Cap Classique sparklers under the
Tradition label; the NV Carte d'Or Brut and vintage Première Cuvée★
are Pinot Noir/Chardonnay blends. Winemaker Jeff Grier is known for
Sauvignon Blancs (standard and Traditional Bush Vine★★); there's
also a consistent Riesling★ and a delicious, partly barrel-fermented
Chenin Blanc. Reds are equally good, especially minerally intense
Merlot and BORDEAUX-style blend Cru Monro★. Best years: (whites) **1998
97 96 95**; (reds) **1996 95 94 93 92 91 90**.

VIN DE PAILLE Sweet wine found mainly in the Jura region of eastern
France. Traditionally, the grapes are left for 2–3 months on straw (*paille*)

mats before fermentation to dehydrate, thus concentrating the sugars. The wines are a cross between SAUTERNES and amontillado sherry – sweet but slightly nutty. Vins de Paille can be found in COTES DU JURA, ARBOIS and l'ETOILE, and occasionally in the RHONE VALLEY and ALSACE. **Best producers:** CHAPOUTIER★★★, CHAVE★★★, Rolet★, A & M Tissot★, ZIND-HUMBRECHT★★★.

VIN DE PAYS *France* The phrase suggests a traditional wine from the country districts of France but the reality is a little different as many Vins de Pays are impressively modern and forward-looking and are now the source of some of France's best-value flavours. This category of wine was created in 1968 to give a geographical identity and quality yardstick to wines which had previously been sold off for blending. It is a particularly useful category for adventurous winemakers (such as SKALLI) who want to use good-quality grapes not allowed under the frequently restrictive AC regulations. Many Vin de Pays wines are labelled with the grape variety.

VIN DE TABLE French for table wine, the lowest quality level.

VIN DOUX NATUREL French for a fortified wine, where fermentation has been stopped by the addition of alcohol, leaving the wine 'naturally' sweet, although you could argue that stopping fermentation with a slug of powerful spirit is distinctly unnatural, but there you go.

VIN JAUNE *Jura, France* A Jura speciality made from the Savagnin grape. In CHATEAU-CHALON it is the only permitted wine style. Made in a similar way to fino sherry but not fortified. Vin Jaune usually ages well, too. **Best producers:** Ch. d'Arlay★, Bourdy★, Clavelin★, J-M Courbet★, Ch. de l'Etoile★, J Macle★★★, Perron★, Reverchon★.

VIN SANTO *Tuscany, Italy* The 'holy wine' of TUSCANY can be one of the world's great sweet wines – just occasionally, that is, for it is also one of the most wantonly abused wine terms in Italy (in particular avoid anything called Liquoroso). Made from grapes laid on mats after harvest to dry, the resulting wines, fermented and aged in barrels for up to 7–8 years, should be nutty, oxidized, full of the flavours of dried apricots and crystallized orange peel, concentrated and long. Also produced in UMBRIA and in TRENTINO as Vino Santo. **Best producers:** ALTESINO★★, Castello di AMA★, ANTINORI★, AVIGNONESI★★★, Badia a Coltibuono★, Brolio★, Cacchiano★, Capezzana★★, Carmignani★, Castell'in Villa★, FELSINA★, ISOLE E OLENA★★★, Pieve Santa Restituta★★★, POLIZIANO★★, Le Pupille★★, Rocca di Montegrossi★, San Felice★★, San Giusto a Rentennano★★★, SELVAPIANA★, Villa Pillo★, Villa Sant'Anna★★.

VIÑA CASABLANCA *Casablanca, Chile* King of the Valley Ignacio Recabarren successfully chases CLOUDY BAY dreams with tangy, intense Sauvignon Blanc★★. These are high-impact wines, particularly those using CASABLANCA-sourced fruit, while White Label wines use vineyards in Lontué, MAIPO and San Fernando. There is excellent quince-edged Santa Isabel Estate Chardonnay★★ and barrel-fermented Chardonnay★★ from the same estate, rose- and lychee-filled Gewürztraminer★★ and inky-black Cabernet Sauvignon★★. Successful experiments include a fabulous Chardonnay-Sauvignon blend★★ and low-yield Merlot★, together with the rich, juicy plums of the Merlot★ from the Santa Isabel Estate.

VINHO VERDE DOC *Minho and Douro Litoral, Portugal* 'Vinho Verde' is a region, a wine and a style of wine. 'Green' only in the sense of being young, it can be red *or* white, and in a restaurant the term often refers simply to the younger wines on the list. The demarcated Vinhos Verdes, however, come from north-west Portugal. Best producers: Quinta de Alderiz, Quinta da Aveleda★, Quinta da Baguinha★, Casa de Compostela, Quinta da Franqueira, Palácio de Brejoeira★, Ponte de Lima co-op, Casa de Sezim★, SOGRAPE (Gazela e Quinta de Azevedo★), Quinta do Tamariz (Loureiro★).

VINO DA TAVOLA *Italy* The term for 'table wine', officially Italy's lowest level of production, is a catch-all that until recently applied to more than 80% of the nation's wine with virtually no regulations controlling quality. Yet this category also provided the arena in the 1970s for the biggest revolution in quality that Italy has ever seen, with the creation of innovative, DOC-busting SUPER-TUSCANS. Every region of Italy has special wines that remain outside the control system, but recent legislation is now bringing most quality wines into the IGT or DOC categories, leaving Vino da Tavola to represent simple wines that carry no vintage or place of origin, if still a sizeable chunk of Italy's total production. See also Super-Tuscans.

VINO NOBILE DI MONTEPULCIANO DOCG *Tuscany, Italy* The 'noble wine' from the hills around the town of Montepulciano is made from the Sangiovese grape, known locally as the Prugnolo, with the help of a little Canaiolo and Mammolo. At its best, it combines the power and structure of BRUNELLO DI MONTALCINO with the finesse and complexity found in top CHIANTI. Unfortunately, the best was a rare beast until recently, though the rate of improvement has been impressive. The introduction of what is essentially a second wine, ROSSO DI MONTEPULCIANO, has certainly helped. Best producers: AVIGNONESI★★, Bindella★, BOSCARELLI★★, La Braccesca★ (ANTINORI), Le Casalte★★, La Casella★, Contucci★, Dei★★, Del Cerro★, Fassati★, Gracciano della Seta, Innocenti★, Il Macchione★, Nottola★, POLIZIANO★★, Redi★, Romeo★, Salcheto, Trerose★, Valdipiatta★, Villa Sant'Anna★. Best years: (1998) 97 **96 95 94 93 91 90 88 85**.

VIOGNIER A poor yielder, prone to disease and difficult to vinify. The wine can be delicious: peachy, apricoty with a soft, almost waxy texture, usually a fragrance of spring flowers and sometimes a taste like crème fraîche. Now found in LANGUEDOC-ROUSSILLON, Ardèche and the southern RHONE as well as in CALIFORNIA and Australia.

ROBERTO VOERZIO *Barolo DOCG, Piedmont, Italy* One of the best of the younger generation of BAROLO producers, emphasizing fruit and minimizing tannin. Dolcetto (Priavino★) is particularly successful, as is barrique-aged Nebbiolo with a little Cabernet, Vignaserra★★. He took time to adapt Barolo to his philosophy, but it is now very good even in a difficult year. There are 3 single-vineyard examples made in the best years: Brunate★★, Cerequio★★★ and La Serra★★. Best years: (Barolos) 1995 **93 91** 90 89 **88 85**.

COMTE GEORGES DE VOGÜÉ *Chambolle-Musigny AC, Côte de Nuits, Burgundy, France* De Vogüé owns substantial holdings in two Grands Crus, BONNES MARES★★★ and MUSIGNY★★★, as well as in Chambolle's top Premier Cru, Les Amoureuses. A succession of winemakers in the 1980s led to many disappointing vintages in that decade, but since 1990 the domaine has been back on magnificent form. It is the sole producer of minute quantities of MUSIGNY Blanc★★, but because of recent replanting the wine is now being sold as (very expensive) BOURGOGNE Blanc. Best years: (red) 1997 96 95 93 **92** 90.

VOLLMER *Pfalz, Germany* Large firm which produced Germany's first Cabernet Sauvignon wine. Mainly simple country wines, but from the Kirchenstück and Bubeneck sites come good Weisser Burgunder and Riesling. Very fine dry Auslese Gewürztraminer★★, a rich Gewürztraminer Trockenbeerenauslese★★ and sweet Ruländer★. Also a good Dornfelder★. Best years: (1998) 97 **96 93 92 91 90 89**.

VOLNAY AC *Côte de Beaune, Burgundy, France* Volnay is home to the finest red wines of the COTE DE BEAUNE in terms of elegance and class. The wines are attractive when young but the best examples can age as well as any Burgundy. The top vineyards, classified as Premier Cru, are Caillerets, Champans, Clos de la Bousse d'Or, Clos des Chênes and Santenots (which actually lies in MEURSAULT but is called Volnay by courtesy title). Best producers: R Ampeau★★, Angerville★★, R & P Bouley★★, COCHE-DURY★★, LAFARGE★★★, LAFON★★★, MONTILLE★★, Pousse d'Or★★, J Voillot★★. Best years: 1997 96 95 93 **91 90 89 88**.

VOLPAIA, CASTELLO DI *Chianti Classico DOCG, Tuscany, Italy* Produces light, perfumed but refined CHIANTI CLASSICO★★. Two stylish SUPER-TUSCANS, Balifico★★ and Coltassala★★, are both predominantly Sangiovese. Torniello★ is Sauvignon with a dash of Sémillon.

VOSNE-ROMANÉE AC *Côte de Nuits, Burgundy, France* The greatest village in the COTE DE NUITS with a clutch of 5 Grands Crus and 13 Premiers Crus (the best of these are les Malconsorts, aux Brûlées and les Suchots) which are often as good as other villages' Grands Crus. The quality of the village wine is also high. In good years the wines should have at least 6 years' aging and 10–15 would be better. Best producers: Robert Arnoux★, J Cacheux★, B Clavelier★, R Engel★★, GRIVOT★★, Anne Gros★★, JAYER★★★, F Lamarche★, MEO-CAMUZET★★, Mongeard-Mugneret★★, RION★★, Dom. de la ROMANÉE-CONTI★★★, Thomas-Moillard★. Best years: 1997 96 95 93 90 **89 88 85**.

VOUGEOT AC *Côte de Nuits, Burgundy, France* The 12.5ha (32 acres) of vines outside the walls of CLOS DE VOUGEOT only qualify for Vougeot AC. The wine, mainly red, is not bad and a lot cheaper than any Clos de Vougeot. Best producers: Bertagna★, Chopin-Groffier★, C Clerget★. Best years: 1997 96 95 93 **90 89 88 85**.

LA VOULTE-GASPARETS *Corbières AC, Languedoc, France* One of the MIDI's most exciting properties, producing 3 different styles of CORBIERES from old hillside vines. Unashamedly Mediterranean in style with flavours of thyme and baked earth. The Cuvée Réservée★ and Romain Pauc★★ are the most expensive wines, but the basic Voulte-Gasparets★ is almost as good. Drink young or up to 5 years from the vintage. Best years: (1996) **95 94** 93.

VOUVRAY AC *Loire Valley, France* Dry, medium-dry, sweet and sparkling wines from Chenin grapes east of Tours. The dry wines acquire beautifully rounded flavours after 10 years or so. Medium-dry wines, when properly made from a single domaine, are worth aging for 20 years or more. Spectacular noble-rot-affected sweet wines were produced in 1990 and 89 with an intense peach and honey soft sweetness but an ever-present acidity. The fizz is some of the LOIRE's best. Best producers: Allias★, Aubuisières★★★, Dom. Bourillon-Dorléans★★, Brédif★, Brisebarre, Champalou★★, P Delaleu★, P Foreau★★, B Fouquet★★, Ch. Gaudrelle★★, HUET★★, F Mabille, Orfeuilles, Pichot★. Best years: (1998) 97 96 95 93 **90 89 88 85 83 82 78 76 75 70**.

WACHAU *Niederösterreich, Austria* Stunning stretch of the Danube between Krems-Stein and the monastery of Melk and Austria's top region for dry whites. Riesling is the grape here, followed by Grüner Veltliner. Best producers: F HIRTZBERGER★★★, Högl★★, Emmerich Knoll★★★, NIKOLAIHOF★★, F X PICHLER★★★, F PRAGER★★★, Freie Weingartner WACHAU★.

WACHAU, FREIE WEINGÄRTNER *Wachau, Niederösterreich, Austria* Co-op long producing fine WACHAU white wines. Since directors Fritz Miesbauer and Willi Klinger took over in 1995, regular wines★ and vineyard-designated Grüner Veltliners and Rieslings★★ have reached new heights. Best years: (whites) (1998) 97 **96 95 93 92 91 90 88 86 83 79**.

WACHENHEIM *Pfalz, Germany* Wine village made famous by the BURKLIN-WOLF estate, its best vineyards are capable of producing rich, yet beautifully balanced Rieslings. Best producers: Josef BIFFAR★★, BURKLIN-WOLF★★, Karl Schaefer★, WOLF★★. Best years: (1998) **97** 96 **94 93 90**.

WAIHEKE ISLAND *North Island, New Zealand* GOLDWATER pioneered wine-making on this small island in Auckland harbour in the early 1980s. Hot, dry ripening conditions have made high-quality Cabernet-Sauvignon-based reds that sell for very high prices. A tiny, highly fashionable region that will soon be home to 24 winemakers. Best producers: Fenton★, GOLDWATER★★, Peninsula★, STONYRIDGE★★, Te Motu★.

WAIRARAPA *North Island, New Zealand* A cool, dry climate, free-draining soil and a passion for quality are this region's assets. Wairarapa is near the town of Martinborough in the large region at the southern end of North Island officially called Wellington. Makes some top Pinot and complex Chardonnay; intense Cabernet; full Sauvignon Blanc and honeyed Riesling. Best producers: ATA RANGI★★, DRY RIVER★★, MARTINBOROUGH VINEYARD★★, PALLISER ESTATE★, Te Kairanga★.

WARRE *Port DOC, Douro, Portugal* Top-quality vintage ports★★, and a good 'off-vintage' port from their Quinta da Cavadinha★. Sir William★, a 10-year-old tawny, is also delicious, and their Crusted★★ and LBV★ wines are both very welcome traditional, full-bodied ports. Warrior is a reliable ruby port. Keep vintage ports for 15–30 years before drinking. Best years: (vintage) 1994 91 85 83 **80 77 70 66 63**.

WARWICK ESTATE *Stellenbosch WO, South Africa* Set in the heart of the classic red wine belt, this farm concentrates on the traditional BORDEAUX varieties, in the complex Trilogy★★ blend, and as individual varieties, notably Norma Ratcliffe's favourite Cabernet Franc★. Traditional Bush Vine Pinotage★ reflects the area's heritage. Of late, Warwick reds have softened, but remain elegantly European in style. Best years: (reds) **1996 95 94 93 92 91 90**.

WASHINGTON STATE *USA* Second-largest premium wine-producing state in the US. The chief growing areas are in irrigated high desert, east of the Cascade Mountains. Although the heat is not as intense as in CALIFORNIA, long summer days with extra hours of sunshine due to the northern latitude seem to increase the intensity of fruit flavours and result in both red and white wines of great depth. Cabernet, Merlot, Chardonnay, Sauvignon Blanc and Semillon produce very good wines here. Some believe that the wines of Washington State could become the best in the US. Best producers: ANDREW WILL★★, Canoe Ridge, CHATEAU STE MICHELLE★, COLUMBIA CREST★, COLUMBIA WINERY, Covey Run★, Hedges Cellars★, HOGUE CELLARS★, KIONA★, L'ECOLE NO 41★★, LEONETTI CELLAR★★★, QUILCEDA CREEK★★, Salishan, Staton Hills★, WOODWARD CANYON★★.

GEOFF WEAVER *Adelaide Hills, South Australia* Geoff Weaver, who put many runs on the board as chief winemaker at HARDY, dedicates himself to crafting fine wines from grapes grown only at his Lenswood vineyard. He uses the PETALUMA winery to vinify his deliciously limy Riesling★, crisply gooseberryish Sauvignon★★ and increasingly stylish, fruit-driven Chardonnay★★. Cabernet-Merlot is only a mild success.

J WEGELER ERBEN *Bernkastel, Mosel; Oestrich-Winkel, Rheingau; Deidesheim, Pfalz, Germany* These 3 important estates used to be part of the huge Deinhard wine and Sekt empire until the Wegeler family sold off most of that business in late 1997 to concentrate on wines from their own vineyards. All 3 estates are dedicated primarily to Riesling, and today dry wines make up the bulk of production. At the beginning of the 90s, the use of vineyard designations was limited so that only wines from top sites such as Bernkasteler DOCTOR or the excellent but less well-known Winkeler Jesuitengarten are named on labels. Whether dry or naturally sweet Auslese, the best merit ★★ and will develop well with 5-plus years of aging. The MOSEL estate achieves the general standard of the 3 Wegeler estates; nearly all the wines are ★. Best years: (1998) 97 96 **95 93 90 89 88 83 76**.

WEHLEN *Mosel, Germany* Village whose steep Sonnenuhr vineyard produces some of the most powerful Rieslings in Germany. Best producers: Kerpen, Dr LOOSEN★★★, J J PRUM★★★, S A PRUM★, RICHTER★★, SELBACH-OSTER★★, J WEGELER ERBEN★, Dr Weins-Prüm.

ROBERT WEIL *Kiedrich, Rheingau, Germany* Previously known as Dr Weil, and now owned by Suntory, it is managed by Wilhelm Weil and makes majestic sweet Auslese, Beerenauslese and Trockenbeerenauslese Rieslings★★★ and also dry Rieslings★★. The wines are crisp and aristocratic in style. Best years: (1997) 96 **95 94 93 92 90 89**.

WEISSBURGUNDER See Pinot Blanc.

WEISSHERBST German rosé wine, a speciality of BADEN. The wine is usually dry. The label must state the grape variety.

WELSCHRIESLING See Riesling Italico.

WENDOUREE *Clare Valley, South Australia* Small winery using old-fashioned methods to make enormous, ageworthy reds★★★ from paltry yields off their own very old Shiraz, Cabernet, Malbec and Mataro (Mourvèdre) vines. There are tiny amounts of sweet Muscat★. Best years: 1996 95 94 92 91 90 **86 83 82 81 80 78 76 75**.

DOMDECHANT WERNER *Hochheim, Rheingau, Germany* Classy estate with well-sited bits of the Domdechaney, Hölle and Kirchenstück vineyards in HOCHHEIM that made especially good wines in 1990★ but had a disastrous 93 and a disappointing 95 and 97. Best years: 1994 **92 90 89 88**.

WESTERN AUSTRALIA Only the south-west corner of this vast state is suited to vines, the SWAN VALLEY and Perth environs being the oldest and hottest district, with present attention focused on Great Southern, MARGARET RIVER, Geographe and, most recently, PEMBERTON. Quality rivals the best of the eastern states.

WIEN *Austria* Region within the city limits of Wien or Vienna. The best vines come from the south-facing sites in Grinzing, Nussdorf and Weiden; and the Bisamberg hill east of the Danube. Best producers: Bernreiter, Kierlinger, Mayer, Schilling, Wieninger★.

WILLIAMS SELYEM *Russian River Valley AVA, California, USA* Pinot Noir★★ was the only wine made here until 1990 and much of the time it is very, very good; made in a traditional style, the wine is big, sometimes very fruity and sometimes just a bit off the wall. However, the winery was purchased in 1998 by John Dyson of New York, and it remains to be seen if the cult following for the Pinot Noirs, especially the J ROCHIOLI VINEYARDS, can be sustained. There is now some impressive Zinfandel★★ as well. Best years: (Pinot Noir) (1998) 97 96 **95 94 92 91**.

WINKEL *Rheingau, Germany* Rheingau village whose best vineyard is the large Hasensprung Einzellage but the most famous one is SCHLOSS VOLLRADS – an ancient estate that does not use the village name on its label. Best producers: August Eser, Johannishof★, J WEGELER ERBEN★. Best years: (1998) 96 **93 90**.

WIRRA WIRRA *McLaren Vale, South Australia* Owned by celebrated eccentric Greg Trott who consistently makes whites with more finesse than customary in the region. The arrival of ex-DOMAINE CHANDON chief Tony Jordan presages a doubling in output and a major planting programme. Well-balanced Sauvignon Blanc★, ageworthy Semillon blend★★, buttery Chardonnay★★ and soft reds led by delicious The Angelus Cabernet★★, chocolaty RSW Shiraz★★ and decadent Original Blend Grenache Shiraz★. Also a good-value 'WW' label. Best years: (reds) 1995 **94 93 92 91 90 86 82 80**.

WO (WINE OF ORIGIN) This South African certification system was first introduced in 1973. The laws are broadly based on those of France and Germany, but regrettably guarantee authenticity rather than quality and only 10% of the national harvest is certified. The three main quality influencing factors claimed by WO are grape variety, area of origin and vintage.

J L WOLF *Wachenheim, Pfalz, Germany* Ernst Loosen, of Dr LOOSEN in the MOSEL, heads the consortium which took over this underperforming estate in 1996. Its first 3 vintages have won it a place among the region's top producers. Best years: (1998) 97 96.

WOODWARD CANYON *Walla Walla AVA, Washington State, USA* Big barrel-fermented oaky Chardonnay★★ is the trademark wine, but there's also good Charbonneau Red (Cabernet Sauvignon-Merlot) and straight Cabernet Sauvignon labelled Old Vines. Best years: 1998 96 **95 94 91 89**.

WÜRTTEMBERG *Germany* Underperforming wine region centred on the river Neckar. More than half the wine made is red and the best comes from the Lemberger, Dornfelder or Spätburgunder grapes, the rest mostly from the awful Trollinger. These reds can be very light due to massive yields. Isolated steep sites sometimes produce fine Riesling.

WÜRZBURG *Franken, Germany* The centre of FRANKEN wines. Müller-Thurgau is the bread-and-butter grape, some Rieslings can be great, but the real star is Sylvaner. Best producers: Bürgerspital, JULIUSSPITAL★★, Staatlicher Hofkeller★. Best years: (1998) 97 **94 93 92 90**.

WYNDHAM ESTATE *Hunter Valley, New South Wales, Australia* This brand, ingeniously marketed in the 1980s by Brian McGuigan, is now part of Pernod-Ricard's ORLANDO group. It was the HUNTER's biggest winery, but production has been moved to the group's expanding Montrose winery at MUDGEE. An active exporter, the depressing quality decline of the past few years seems to be bottoming out at last.

WYNNS *Coonawarra, South Australia* The name is synonymous with COONAWARRA's oldest cellars and major vineyard holdings. After a low period in the 1970s, standard Cabernet★★ and Shiraz★ have improved steadily to the point where they are among the best value in the land. They also age well: better vintages from the 1950s and 60s are still alive and kicking. In peak years the cream of the Cabernet is released (since 1982) as John Riddoch★★★ and Shiraz (since 1990) as Michael★★, both powerful reds, the latter incredibly oaky. There is also Chardonnay★★ in an attractive, fruit-driven style plus oceans of cheap but nowadays excellent Riesling★★. Best years: (premium reds) 1996 94 93 **91 90 88 86 84 82 76 66 62 55**.

YALUMBA *Barossa Valley, South Australia* Distinguished old firm, owned by the Hill-Smith family, making a wide range of wines including estate wines Heggies★★ (restrained Riesling, nice plump Merlot, opulent Viognier and botrytis Riesling), Hill-Smith Estate★ (Sauvignon Blanc, fine Chardonnay and botrytis Semillon) and Pewsey Vale★ (fine Riesling and Cabernet Sauvignon). The Yalumba range is headed by 3 glorious reds: Signature Cabernet-Shiraz★★, Octavius Shiraz★★★ and Reserve Cabernet★★. Menzies Cabernet is ★ and rising fast, Old Vine Grenache★ is crunchy and satisfying. From these premium reds down to quaffer Galway Shiraz★, Yalumba reds across the board reflect major improvements. Oxford Landing Chardonnay, Sauvignon, Viognier★ and Cabernet-Shiraz are surprisingly successful RIVERLAND quaffers. Yalumba is also the pioneer of good 2-litre casks. Angas Brut is huge-selling, enjoyable fizz for the masses (me included); Yalumba Pinot-Chardonnay★ and Yalumba D★★ show a delicious toasty, creamy style and are now among Australia's best premium sparklers. The fortifieds are also excellent, notably Muscat★★. Best years: (Signature red) **1994** 92 90 88 87.

YARRA VALLEY *Victoria, Australia* With its cool climate, the fashionable Yarra is shaping up as Australia's best Pinot Noir region. Exciting also for Chardonnay and Cabernet-Merlot blends and as a supplier of base wine for sparklers. Best producers: COLDSTREAM HILLS★★, DE BORTOLI★★, GREEN POINT VINEYARDS★★, MOUNT MARY★★, Oakridge, ST HUBERTS★★, Seville Estate★, TARRAWARRA★★, Yarra Ridge, YARRA YERING★★★, Yeringberg★.

YARRA YERING *Yarra Valley, Victoria, Australia* Bailey Carrodus creates extraordinary wines from his exceptional vineyard. The reds, labelled Dry Red No. 1★★★ (Cabernet-based) and No. 2★★★ (Shiraz-based), are profound, concentrated, structured for aging, packed with unnervingly self-confident fruit and memorable perfume. The Pinot Noir★★★ is expensive but very fine, and getting finer and wilder by the vintage. Chardonnay★ is erratic, occasionally delicious. Best years: 1995 94 93 **92 91 90 86 82**.

YELLOWGLEN *Ballarat, Victoria, Australia* Big Champagne-method fizz producer owned by MILDARA. Basic, high-volume lines are Pinot Chardonnay NV, Brut Crémant and Brut Rosé. Cuvée Victoria is the finest. 'Y' premium and Vintage Brut are also well made, especially since 1994. Best years: (Cuvée Victoria) **1996 94 91 88**.

CH. D'YQUEM★★★ *Sauternes AC, 1er Cru Supérieur, Bordeaux, France* Often rated the most sublime sweet wine in the world, no one can question Yquem's total commitment to quality. Despite a large vineyard (100ha/250 acres), production is tiny. Only fully noble-rotted grapes are picked, often berry by berry, and low yield means each vine produces only a glass of wine! This precious liquid is then fermented in new oak barrels and left to mature for 3½ years before bottling. It is one of the world's most expensive wines, in constant demand because of its richness and exotic flavours; loony prices or not. A dry white, Ygrec, is made in some years. LVMH have recently won a 3-year battle to take over the château's vineyard from the Lur-Saluces family, owners for the past 406 years. Best years: 1991 90 89 88 86 83 **81 80 79 76 75 71 67 62**.

ZELL *Mosel, Germany* Most famous for the generic Schwarzer Katz (or black cat) wines which are rarely better than cheap and cheerful. Zell can produce good Rieslings which offer good value for money if you can find them. Best producer: Albert Kallfelz.

ZILLIKEN *Saarburg, Saar, Germany* Estate specializing in Rieslings★★ from the Saarburger Rausch vineyard. The Auslese and EISWEIN often achieve ★★★. Best years: 1997 95 94 93 91 90 **89 88 85 83 79 76 75 71**.

ZIND-HUMBRECHT *Alsace AC, Alsace, France* Olivier Humbrecht is one of France's outstanding young winemakers, producing a brilliant range. The family owns vines in 4 Grand Cru sites – Rangen, Goldert, Hengst and Brand – and these wines (Riesling★★, Pinot Gris★★, Gewurztraminer★★★ and Muscat★★) are excellent, as is a range of other wines from specific vineyards and lieux dits, which are regularly of ★★, often ★★★ quality, with the ALSACE VENDANGE TARDIVES and SELECTION DE GRAINS NOBLES ★★★. Sylvaners★ and Pinot Blancs★★ are fine. Best years: (1998) 97 96 95 **93 92 90 89 88 85 83**.

ZINFANDEL CALIFORNIA's versatile red grape can be used to make an insipid blush wine or a big, bruising, late-harvest-style dessert wine. In-between dry styles have fruit to the fore. Best producers: Cline Cellars★, FETZER, GRGICH HILLS★, KENWOOD★, NALLE★★★, QUIVIRA★★, Rafanelli★★★, RAVENSWOOD★★★, RIDGE★★★, Turley★★.

GLOSSARY OF WINE TERMS

ACID/ACIDITY
Naturally present in grapes and essential to wine, providing balance and stability and giving the refreshing tang in white wines and the appetizing grip in reds. Principal wine acids are acetic, carbonic, citric, lactic, malic and tartaric.

AGING An alternative term for maturation. Sometimes a term of criticism, as in aging prematurely.

ALCOHOL Ethyl alcohol, or Ethanol, is naturally formed during fermentation when yeasts act on the sugar content of grapes, producing nearly equal quantities of alcohol and carbon dioxide.

ALCOHOLIC CONTENT The alcoholic strength of wine, expressed as a percentage of the total volume of the wine. Typically in the range of 7–15%.

ALCOHOLIC FERMENTATION The process whereby yeasts, natural or added, convert the grape sugars into alcohol and carbon dioxide. Normally stops either when all the sugar has been converted or when the alcohol level reaches about 15%.

BARREL AGING Time spent maturing in wood, usually oak, during which the wines take on flavours from the wood.

BARRIQUE The *barrique bordelaise* is the traditional Bordeaux oak barrel of 225 litres (50 gallons) capacity.

BLENDING (Assemblage) The art of mixing together wines of different origin, styles or age, often to balance out acidity, weight etc.

CARBONIC MACERATION
Vinification method used to produce fresh fruity reds for drinking young. Bunches of grapes are fermented whole in closed containers – a process that extracts lots of fruit and colour, but little tannin.

CHAMPAGNE METHOD Traditional method used for all of the world's finest sparkling wines. A second fermentation takes place in the bottle, producing carbon dioxide which, kept in solution under pressure, gives the wine its fizz.

CHAPTALIZATION Legal addition of sugar during fermentation to raise a wine's alcoholic strength. More necessary in cool climates where lack of sun produces insufficient natural sugar in the grape.

CLARIFICATION Term covering any wine-making process (such as filtering or fining) that involves the removal of solid matter either from the must or the wine.

COLD FERMENTATION
Long, slow fermentation at low temperature to extract maximum freshness from the grapes. Crucial for whites in hot climates.

CORKED/CORKY
Wine fault derived from a cork which has become contaminated, usually with Trichloranisole or TCA, and nothing to do with pieces of cork in the wine. The mouldy, stale smell is unmistakeable once you've suffered it.

CUVE CLOSE A bulk process used to produce inexpensive sparkling wines. The second

fermentation, which produces the bubbles, takes place in tank rather than in the bottle.

DÉGORGEMENT
Process in the Champagne method of removing sediment from the bottle.

DOSAGE A sugar and wine mixture added to sparkling wine after *dégorgement* which affects how sweet or dry it will be.

FILTERING Removal of yeasts, solids and any impurities from a wine before bottling.

FINING Method of clarifying wine by adding a coagulant (for example egg whites, isinglass or bentonite) to remove soluble particles such as proteins and excessive tannins.

FLOR A film of yeast which forms on the top of fino sherries (and some other wines) preventing oxidation and imparting a unique dry flavour.

FLYING WINEMAKER
Term coined in the late 1980s to describe enologists, many Australian-trained, brought in to improve the quality, chiefly of bulk wines, in many of the world's under-performing wine regions.

FORTIFIED WINE
Wine which has high-alcohol grape spirit added, usually before the initial alcoholic fermentation is completed, thereby preserving sweetness.

LATE HARVEST
(Vendange Tardive) The harvesting of grapes after the ordinary harvest date to increase alcoholic strength or sweetness.

LEES A coarse sediment left in the bottom of the fermentation vessel consisting of dead yeast cells, grape pips (seeds), pulp and tartrates, referred to as the gross lees. A further finer sediment, the fine lees, may be left in contact with the wine in cask or removed by successive racking. See also 'Sur Lie'.

LAYING DOWN The storing of wine which will improve with age.

MALOLACTIC FERMENTATION Secondary fermentation whereby harsh malic acid is converted into mild lactic acid and carbon dioxide by lactic bacteria. Normal in reds but often prevented in whites to preserve a fresh taste.

MATURATION Positive term for the beneficial aging of wine.

MUST The mixture of grape juice, skins, pips and pulp produced after crushing (but prior to completion of fermentation), which will eventually become wine.

NÉGOCIANT French term for a merchant who buys and sells wine. In Burgundy and elsewhere a négociant-élèveur is a merchant who buys, makes, ages and sells wine.

NOBLE ROT *(Botrytis cinerea)* Fungus which attacks grapes under certain climatic conditions, shrivelling the bunches and intensifying their sugar through dehydration. A vital ingredient in the finest dessert wines, such as Sauternes and Trockenbeerenauslese.

OAK The wood used almost exclusively in the production of fine wines. There is an increasing mastery of the use of barrel maturation, bringing out the most apt qualities – be it flavour or structure – for the style of wine sought by the winemaker.

OECHSLE German scale measuring must-weight based on specific gravity.

OXIDATION Decay in a wine caused by over-exposure to air resulting in flat, vapid aromas. Slight oxidation, such as occurs through the wood of a barrel or during racking, is part of the aging process and, in wines of sufficient structure, enhances flavour and complexity.

PHYLLOXERA The vine aphid *Phylloxera vastatrix* attacks vine roots. It devastated European and consequently other vineyards around the world in the late 1800s soon after it arrived from America. Since then, the superior but vulnerable *Vitis vinifera* has generally been grafted on to resistant American rootstocks.

RACKING Gradual clarification of a quality wine as part of the maturation process. The wine is transferred from one barrel or container to another, leaving the lees behind. Racking also produces aeration necessary for the aging process, softens tannins and helps develop further flavours.

REMUAGE Process in Champagne-making whereby the bottles, stored on their sides and at a progressively steeper angle in *pupitres*, are twisted, or riddled, each day so that the sediment moves down the sides and collects in the neck of the bottle on the cap, ready for *dégorgement*.

'SECOND' WINES A second selection that helps in the maintenance of the integrity and quality of a property's top wine.

SEDIMENT Usually refers to residue thrown by a wine, particularly red, as it ages in bottle.

SOLERA Traditional Spanish system of blending fortified wines, especially sherry and Montilla-Moriles.

SUR LIE French for 'on the lees', meaning wine bottled direct from the cask/fermentation vat to gain extra flavour from the lees. Common with quality Muscadet, white Burgundy, similar barrel-aged whites and, increasingly, commerical bulk whites.

TANNIN Harsh, bitter, mouth-puckering element in red wine, derived from grape skins and stems, and from oak barrels. Tannins soften with age and are essential for long-term development in reds.

TERROIR A French term used to denote the combination of soil, climate and exposure to the sun – that is, the natural physical environment of the vine.

VARIETAL Wine made from, and named after, a single grape variety.

VINIFICATION The process of turning grapes into wine.

VINTAGE The year's grape harvest, also used to describe wines of a single year.

VITICULTURE Vine-growing and vineyard management.

VITIS VINIFERA Vine species, native to Europe and Central Asia, from which almost all the world's quality wine is made.

INDEX OF PRODUCERS

Numbers in **bold** refer to main entries.

305

310

316

317

ACKNOWLEDGEMENTS

Editor Anne Lawrance; **Wine Consultants** Phillip Williamson, David
Moore; **Editorial Assistant** Ingrid Karikari; **Indexer** Naomi Good;
DTP Consultant Jonathan Harley; **Production** Kâren Smith;
Publishing Director Claire Harcup; **Art Director** Nigel O'Gorman.

kGoJjbD4

fSNjuCtb

03120791010x6597